MODERN GERMAN
LITERATURE
1880-1950

STEFAN GEORGE

MODERN GERMAN LITERATURE
1880-1950

JETHRO BITHELL, M.A.

LONDON

METHUEN & CO LTD

11 NEW FETTER LANE · LONDON EC4

First published October 12, 1939
Second edition 1946
Third edition revised and reset 1959
Reprinted once
Reprinted 1968
Copyright © 1959 Jethro Bithell
Printed in Great Britain by
John Dickens & Co Ltd, Northampton
S.B.N. 416 35730

3·3

CONTENTS

ILLUSTRATIONS

* Reproduced by courtesy of Messrs Secker & Warburg Ltd

PREFACE

When, two years ago, I prepared the second edition of my *Germany: A Companion to German Studies*, I wrote an account of Nazi literature which turned out to be too bulky for inclusion in the volume unless my sketch of Nazi history was cut down to the barest outline; and the publishers agreed to my proposal that I should expand the essay on German literature after 1880 in the first edition to form a separate volume which should deal comprehensively and critically with the whole mass of the literature concerned. This literature of more than eighty millions – for I was bound to bring in the Swiss Germans as well as all the other *Auslandsdeutsche* – is so vast that even in the generous space allotted me by the publishers I have found it difficult to deal with all I considered worthy of treatment. The difficulties have been aggravated by the insistency of Nazi propaganda, which by its very nature keeps in the limelight those writers (*'die Künder des Dritten Reiches'*, *'die Dichter des heimlichen Deutschlands'*) who before 1933 had the foresight to be *volkhaft* or the prudence to be so after that date. Another difficulty was the suppression of biographical and bibliographical detail; e.g. such books of reference as *Wer ist's?* are maddening in their planned and regulated insufficiency. At all events, I have tried to do justice to all my authors, whether boomed or banned; and, since on this side of the water there could be no question of taking over Nazi valuations, the verdict is in every case my own.

I am very grateful for authorizations to quote poems – they include some of the very best of the period; and I must express my thanks to firms and individuals – to the Insel-Verlag, Leipzig, for Rilke; to Georg Bondi, Berlin, for Stefan George; to the Albert Langen/Georg Müller Verlag for Dauthendey; to the Deutsche Verlags-Anstalt, Stuttgart, for Liliencron; to the Otto

Müller Verlag, Salzburg, for Georg Trakl; to Frau Ida Dehmel, Frau Dr. Ricarda Huch, Frau Gertrud von Hofmannsthal, and Frau Margarete Morgenstern. (It is characteristic that my letters asking for permission to quote from works published by suppressed Jewish firms were not even returned by the German Post Office.) I am grateful, too, to those who have provided me with photographs; that of Stefan George is reproduced here for the first time; that of Rilke has been specially loaned by Dr. Stefan Zweig. For important details in the interpretation of Stefan George I have to thank two keen specialists – Frau Ida Dehmel and Dr. Helmut Küpper. It is an equal pleasure to acknowledge my debt to the research work of my own post-graduate students at Birkbeck College, whose dissertations find due place in the Bibliography, and to Dr. C. T. Carr of St. Andrews University and Dr. A. E. Eastlake for help in reading the proofs.

J. BITHELL

HEMEL HEMPSTEAD,
March 1939

PREFACE
TO THE SECOND EDITION

The normal procedure would have been, in the second edition, to add a chapter on whatever German literature of importance has appeared since the first edition was published. But the intervening years are those of the War, and books printed in Germany have been unobtainable. The supplementary chapter will be provided as soon as full information is available. In the meantime, corrections to the present text have been made.

J. BITHELL

PENZANCE,
July 1945

PREFACE
TO THE THIRD EDITION

The present edition fulfils the promise made in my last Preface. The text of the first edition has in the main been kept; but certain writers who in 1939 were in the forefront of interest have now passed to the rear and the space allotted to them has necessarily been shortened. Other writers on the contrary are now more accurately appreciated because of the indefinable musicality of their verse (Georg Trakl for instance) and because their mentality and moods gave scope for the deepened psychological probing of these later years. The writers of the Nazi period with their clamour and clangour have now only historical and symptomatic importance, except perhaps that their cult for racial reasons of *Heimatkunst* has kept the prestige it gained. After the advent of Hitler not a few of the most eminent writers, Jew or Gentile, found asylum abroad; some were naturalized in the country of their adoption; and those of them who were discussed in the first two editions and continued to produce in exile – some of them their best work – have had this later work fully treated. The glaring feature of the post-war *Blütezeit* is the vogue of Existentialism, and my supplementary chapters follow the genesis and the growth of this 'Magic Realism' or whatever we may care to call it, although the traditionalist opposition has been stressed and interpreted. One feature of the post-war period cannot be missed: from 1933 to the end of the war the Germans had been denied access to foreign literature, and inevitably, as soon as the gates were flung open, the new French and Anglo-American literature came as a revelation that instantly called forth work of sterling worth in the same style and spirit. The new literature may be remotely fanciful or it may strike out to the last limits of Neo-Realism, as for instance in the work of Heimito von Doderer;

the task of the critic is to interpret and appraise all tendencies, either as manifestations of the *Zeitgeist* or as lasting enrichment of international literature.

In conclusion I have to express my thanks for ready help to Dr. Rudolf Majut, Honorary Lecturer of Leicester University, and to another distinguished scholar who does not wish his name to be mentioned, for reading the proofs. In addition I am indebted to Frau Eva Kampmann-Carossa for permission to reproduce the portrait of her father, and to Frau Käthe Braun-Prager for the loan of her sketch of her brother.

J. BITHELL

PAIGNTON,
September 1957

I

NATURALISM

In a sense it is possible to say that the literature of the period 1880-1958 begins with the *bürgerliches Trauerspiel*, in which for the first time in literature middle-class characters are depicted as capable of tragic emotion. This development continues practically without interruption; for even the characters of the classical period belong for the most part to the middle classes: *Werther, Tasso, Wilhelm Meister*, and *Faust* illumine essentially the same problems of artistic mentality as those of Thomas Mann's fiction; the theme even of Schiller's *Don Carlos* is that political Liberalism which ferments in the writings of *Jung Deutschland*, moves the hectic tides of Spielhagen's novels, and is distorted in the communistically crazy preaching of universal brotherhood in the expressionism which followed the First Great War. In the main lines this literature of a century and a half is a gradual fading, culminating in the *reductio ad absurdum* of Thomas Mann's *Königliche Hoheit*, of the glamour in which monarchs and nobles lived a charmed life, and a corresponding intensification of the mental life of men belonging to all classes of society.

The drastic change of ideals at the beginning of our period had been gradually prepared; indeed, though the performance of Gerhart Hauptmann's *Vor Sonnenaufgang* in 1889 can be used as a landmark in the same way as the production of *Hernani* is used in dating the first crashing victory of the French Romantic movement, in reality it only marks the date when the existence of a new orientation in literature was forced on the consciousness of the nation at large. The origins of the new doctrine are to be found in Gutzkow, who preached 'the emancipation of the flesh'; in Spielhagen, who continued Gutzkow, particularly in his hostility to existing forms of government; and in the 'poetic realism' of such writers as Otto Ludwig and Gottfried Keller.

I

The state of literature in 1880 was respectable but stagnant. In lyric verse the scholarly poets of the Munich school had achieved a perfection of form which is apt to weary by its monotony and lack of rude masculinity; its themes were decent but hackneyed; and even the outer appearance of the volumes was used to typify it in the term of opprobrium, *Goldschnittlyrik*, cast at it by the new school. A flood-tide of verse tales in facile rhythms had followed Scheffel's *Trompeter von Säkkingen* (1854); Julius Wolff (1834-1910) continued to pour out his rhymed romances till near the end of the century. The exhaustion of the novel is seen in two genres, that of the sentimental tale which had its strongholds in the family journals (particularly *Die Gartenlaube*) and the historical novel, the so-called *Professorenroman* or *archäologischer Roman*. The vogue of the historical novel is to be explained by the hypertrophied race-consciousness which was the result of the victories of 1870[1]: from the glory of the present novelists like Gustav Freytag and Felix Dahn turned to the glories of the past; the conquest of Italy as related in Felix Dahn's *Ein Kampf um Rom* (1876) symbolized the superiority of the unspoilt Germanic tribes over the decadent, slothful, and shifty romance nations. The historical novel, in so far as it renewed the historical novel of Scott and Willibald Alexis by packing it with palatable erudition, had elements of novelty; the historical drama, on the other hand – it was christened *Ober-lehrerdrama* – is resurrected Schiller progressively debilitated. The theatre had existed mainly on the *Sitten- und Thesenstück*, which was, on the one hand, a continuation of the *Familiendrama* of Iffland and Kotzebue [ˈkɔtsəbuː], and, on the other hand, an imitation of the machine-made plays of Sardou and *hoc genus omne*; PAUL LINDAU (1830-1918) was one of the chief purveyors.[2]

Another consequence of the Franco-Prussian War was the sudden affluence of wealth, particularly in Berlin; in the Prussian capital there was an orgy of building and of speculation (*Gründer-tum*); it is depicted in Spielhagen's novel *Sturmflut* (1876). Berlin, mightily magnified, had become a European city conscious of its significance; it became a literary centre to which authors streamed

---

[1] Strangely enough, defeat in the First Great War had ultimately the same result.

[2] Two writers of flimsy farces of this generation scored successes in England: we know Gustav von Moser's (1825-1903) *Der Bibliothekar* as *The Private Secretary*, and Oskar Blumenthal's (1852-1918) *Im weissen Rössl* as *White Horse Inn*.

from the provinces; and the wealth of the upper and trading classes was matched by the grovelling poverty of the working population. But the workers were at the advent of their rise to power; Spielhagen's *In Reih und Glied* (1866) had already been a Socialistic novel, with a hero clearly modelled on the Socialist leader, Ferdinand Lassalle [laˡsal] (1825-64); labour and capital had faced each other as irreconcilable forces in the same author's *Hammer und Amboss* (1869); and henceforward Marxism[1] is to be reckoned with as a literary ferment. With Socialism goes a wave of pessimism, in stark contrast with the racial optimism of the historical novel. Goethe had overcome the *Weltschmerz* of *Werther*, though the teaching of *Faust* is still *Entsagung*; in the romantic period *Weltschmerz* had blended with Byronism; Schopenhauer (1788-1860) made pessimism a philosophic system the influence of which on literature was profound. It was not definitely displaced till Nietzsche's doctrine of the superman passed into the neo-romanticism of the impressionists; and even here it still acts as a secondary influence, for the neo-romanticists take over the moods of the French symbolists, who had themselves been deeply influenced by Schopenhauer. Into this stream of pessimism flowed a new current, deriving from Darwin's doctrines of the struggle for existence. Darwin's laws of heredity and environment (*milieu, Umgebung, Umwelt*) immediately provided catchwords for literature; even Gunther in Wilhelm Jordan's *Die Nibelunge* (1868-74) selects his *Bettgenossin* with an eye to *Zuchtwahl*. Darwin's theories, supplemented by the teaching of Ernst Haeckel (1834-1919),[2] were to revolutionize the conception of society, and, as a vision of irresistible cosmic forces, were already in 1880 shaking the crass utilitarianism which, as the accepted view of life, had accompanied the accession to wealth of the great cities. Wilhelm Scherer (1841-86), professor of German literature at the University of Berlin, was one of the first to proclaim the coming domination of science; he had declared that natural science was the '*signatura temporis: . . . sie drückt der Poesie ihren Stempel auf. Die Naturwissenschaft zieht als Triumphator auf dem Siegeswagen einher, an den wir alle gefesselt sind.*'

---

[1] The first volume of Karl Marx's (1818-83) *Das Kapital* had appeared in 1867.
[2] Haeckel's *Die Welträtsel* (1899) popularized his system of Darwinistic evolutionism; it is essentially the gospel of materialism, but in *Der Monismus* (1892) he had attempted to link science with religion by deriving moral goodness (i.e. ethics) and the cult of beauty (i.e. aesthetics) from the recognition of ultimate truth.

These changes of outlook would, no doubt, if they had been left to themselves, have worked their own way to a new expression. But Germany, always receptive to ideas, has at all stages of new development in her literature caught the vivifying fire from abroad. Now, while Marx and Darwin were working so to speak under the surface, ideas came in with a rush from three foreign sources: Russia, France, and Norway. Much as in the eighteenth century Rousseau had forced on literature a change of front with his paradox of 'back to nature', Tolstoy now, with his denunciation of the depravity of the cultured classes and his preaching of asceticism, raised a new ideal, and turned attention to the misery of the poor. His *Powers of Darkness* (1886) was a powerful influence. Dostoieffsky, with his minute and relentless psychology and his strange characters, pointed to new directions. Zola, following up Taine's theory of *milieu*, proclaimed that the meticulous methods of science should be applied to literature, that an author should give a slice of life seen through a temperament. Zola's procedure, deliberately photographical, seemed the denial of poetry and inspiration; in actual result, however, he achieves the effect of poetry by his gigantic symbolism. Ibsen, too, in the plays of his maturity, made a show of the abnegation of poetry in the shorn plainness of his dialogue; but he again in his latest plays wedded an illusory realism to a mystical and wistful symbolism. The stark ugliness of Tolstoy's picture of life reappears in the first period of naturalism. Zola is more than any one else the acclaimed model of the first naturalists, both in drama and the novel. Ibsen lends form and substance to the dramas of the iconoclasts; he himself, however, had continued the problem plays of Hebbel, and there is thus in the naturalistic plays which are modelled on those of Ibsen a chain of continuity with a link forged across the sea.[1]

Another strongly emphasized feature of the new naturalism is hostility to the doctrines of Christianity. This is, however, nothing new in German literature. There is anti-religious feeling in Gottfried Keller's *Der grüne Heinrich* (1854) and in Spielhagen's *Problematische Naturen* (1861); and the anti-clerical atmosphere of Paul Heyse's *Kinder der Welt* (1873) had been denounced as the glorification of Sodom and Gomorrha. Anti-clericalism goes together with the assertion of the rights of the senses (Gutzkow's

---

[1] Dramatists who continue Hebbel directly in our period belong to neoclassicism.

'emancipation of the flesh'); there had been much of this doctrine in Paul Heyse's long novel *Im Paradiese* (1876), and it is preached *ad nauseam* by the naturalists and, indeed, by the succeeding schools down to the present day; only in individual authors is there a questioning of this placing of morality beyond the pale of reason, as in Thomas Mann (e.g. *Fiorenza*). It is true that, although passion is hailed as sovereign, there is at the beginning of naturalism a kind of eugenic denunciation of individual vices, e.g. drunkenness in Hauptmann's *Vor Sonnenaufgang*; but even Hauptmann's drunkards, in his later plays, illustrate the general sentiment that: *tout comprendre c'est tout pardonner*. The argument runs that since mentality is shaped by *milieu* and hereditary tendencies, above all by the sexual impulse, man's will is not free; and, since the will is not free, morality is not absolute (i.e. a law for all) but relative (a law possible or impossible according to physical constitution, mentality, and environment). Action is due to nerves; and, since men are not responsible for their nerves, they are not responsible for their actions.

It is curious that this comparative contempt for 'morality' runs through the work of PAUL HEYSE (1830-1914), who was set up as a bogey-man to be shied at by the firebrands of the new realism. His attitude, however, was that of the old romantic poets, a mere over-emphasis of the beauty of passion; the objection to the Bohemian artists of his *Im Paradiese* is that, although they are sufficiently immoral, they are too unreal to be anything. Paul Heyse lived right through the period of naturalism, and he may be given his place in the period, alien to naturalism as he was, because he serves for contrast.

Closely associated with Paul Heyse was ADOLF WILBRANDT (1837-1911), and he too in his artist novel *Hermann Ifinger* (1892) blazed a partisan contrast between drab naturalists and eclectic classicists; there are pen-sketches too in this novel of the painters Makart and Lenbach and of the Munich school poet GRAF VON SCHACK (1815-94), another of the proud old school who has the attitude of an impressionist, the cloistered contempt for the reading public, and the cult of form for form's sake which was the pose of Stefan George. Wilbrandt's scholarly absorption in the personality of artists and writers and their style – his book on Heinrich von Kleist (1863) and his essays on Fritz Reuter (a fellow Mecklenburger) and Hölderlin are first-rate – led him to hammer out a

species of interpretative biographical novel (*Gedankenroman*) which
has some of the elements of the *vie romancée* of our own day: *Die
Osterinsel* (1895) is written round the gospel of Nietzsche, while
Hildegard Mahlmann (1897) has for central figure the peasant poetess
Johanna Ambrosius. As a dramatist Wilbrandt wrote comedies
(*Die Vermählten*, 1871; *Die Maler*, 1872) which were reckoned as
the best after Freytag's *Die Journalisten*, and 'Roman' tragedies
(*Gracchus*, 1870; *Arria und Messalina*, 1874) which edified by gorgeous pictures of ancient vice. In the history of the theatre he
counts, however, mainly by one play – *Der Meister von Palmyra*
(1889) – which answered the trumpet blast of the naturalists by
showing what might still be made of the old type of drama, however lifeless the lilt of the blank verse.

Two poets of the older generation belong more or less to the
new schools of naturalism and impressionism, Theodor Fontane
and Conrad Ferdinand Meyer; the former by virtue of his realism
and the relativity of his moral judgments, the latter by his use
of symbol and his handling of history and renaissance themes.
C. F. MEYER (1825-98), whose collected verse appeared in 1882,
used history to veil the intimate problem of his own personality,
and so cunningly that symbolism and psycho-analysis had to make
their impress on criticism before the hidden import of his verse
as of his tales could be unravelled. His physical development,
shocked by 'nervous breakdowns', was so imperfect that he did
not succeed in growing something in the nature of a moustache
till he was over fifty; he then married, and had a child. The salient
thing in his work[1] is his worship of strong men[2]; hence his love
of renaissance types.[3] In lyric verse he is the link between the

---

[1] *Huttens letzte Tage* (1872; the story in verse of the last days of Ulrich von
Hutten); *Jürg Jenatsch* (1876; his one novel, followed by short stories); *Der
Heilige* (1880; the story of Thomas à Becket shadows the German *Kultur-
kampf*); *Novellen* (1883: *Das Amulett, Der Schuss von der Kanzel, Plautus im
Nonnenkloster, Gustav Adolfs Page*); *Das Leiden eines Knaben* (1883; imaging the
writer's own tortured boyhood); *Die Hochzeit des Mönches* (1884; related by
Dante); *Die Richterin* (1885); *Die Versuchung des Pescara* (1887); *Angela Borgia*
(1890). He ranks with Theodor Fontane as a regenerator of the historical
ballad; *Die Rose von Newport, Der sterbende Cromwell* and *Miltons Rache* treat
English themes.

[2] '*Das Mittelmässige*', he wrote, '*macht mich deshalb so traurig, weil es in mir
selbst einen verwandten Stoff findet – darum suche ich so sehnsüchtig das Grosse.*'

[3] Widely read in historical literature, he was influenced by Jakob Burckhardt's (1818-97) *Die Kultur der Renaissance in Italien* (1860), one of the great
sources of inspiration for the impressionists.

flawless perfection of form and the priest-like pose of Platen and the consecration of self in symbol of Stefan George.

THEODOR FONTANE (1818-98) was – like his forerunner as a writer of tales of Brandenburg, Willibald Alexis (1798-1871) – of Huguenot descent (phoneticians give both French and German pronunciation for his name). He had lived a busy life as a journalist when, at the age of sixty, he began to write novels. His social novels deal mainly, and with complete freedom from prejudice, with three problems: *das Verhältnis* or liaison between gentleman and working-class girl, *mésalliances*, and adultery. *L'Adultera* (1882) is a tale in which a woman is seen gliding, not passionately but inevitably, into adultery with a baptized Jew; the husband has the good qualities of that husband from whom Dorothea Veit ran away to Friedrich Schlegel, but she feels the physical repugnance to him which Irene in *The Forsyte Saga* feels for Soames; she is made to feel – her own children recoil from her – that she has outraged society, but in the end she is forgiven even by the husband she has deserted; her action is questioned, but not judged; there is indeed symbolic reference to Tintoretto's picture of Christ and the woman taken in adultery. The central theme of *Irrungen, Wirrungen* (1888) is a love-affair between an officer and a working-class girl – '*das landesübliche Techtelmechtel*', as Otto Erich Hartleben in *Rosenmontag* calls such a *Verhältnis*; the girl is practical and far-sighted, gives up her lover, marries one of her own class, and lives – happily? In the girl's leave-taking there is a dramatic poignancy as of the old ballads Fontane loved – he wrote some of the best (modelled on our old border ballads) in German literature: 'And so,' she says, 'this is the last time I shall hold your hand in mine?' After *Irrungen, Wirrungen* the naturalists claimed Fontane for their own, and he with his wise old generosity acknowledged their right to a place in the sun. They were writing *Berliner Romane*, which are now forgotten; his remain. In *Effi Briest* (1895) a young girl marries an old lover of her own mother; he is a man of high position who is rather above her than with her; she falls to a lover rather from boredom than from passion, and returns to her paternal home to die; there is no pronouncement that she was guilty. Here again Fontane shows forces working, but does not judge those who are overcome by these forces. *Frau Jenny Treibel* (1892) shows Fontane at his best as a sly humorist: Frau Jenny is a parvenue with a mouth full of enthusiasm for higher things and an unerring sense of what is good and practical. Frau Jenny is ridiculous, but delightful; the irony lights up, but does not corrode. In Fontane's descriptions of the Prussian nobility, as in *Die Poggenpuhls* (1896), which shows the family of a dead officer struggling to keep up appearances, the irony touches very lightly. Fontane has a limited range of characters – junkers, officers, dear old aunts, gardeners, clergymen – but his types are sharply individualized by his masterly handling of dialogue; his technique depends largely on conversation or on self-expression in monologue and correspondence. R. M. Meyer calls Fontane 'the first consistent realist in German literature'; this is not quite correct: Fontane, it is true, is not a 'poetic realist' because he is without Romanticism (except in his ballads), but he differs from the 'consistent' naturalists because he is worlds removed from *Armeleutepoesie*; the working-classes only come into his work as foils to his gentry; his affinities with the new school are in tone rather than in texture – they show, not so much in his realism as in his large-hearted attitude to social problems, or, to repeat the catchword, in the relativity of his morality.

Two other forerunners of naturalism, Ludwig Anzengruber and Marie von Ebner-Eschenbach, are of very high rank in literature. The naturalistic drama really begins with LUDWIG ANZENGRUBER (1839-89), the dramatic effectiveness of whose plays is partly due to his training as an actor. He was a Viennese; i.e. a city man with a good knowledge of village life and a more or less artificially acquired knowledge of dialect – an advantage for stage purposes. He had learned something from Berthold Auerbach (1812-82); but, unlike Auerbach, he gets inside his peasants; and what he really continues is the old Viennese *Volksstück* (Mozart's *Magic Flute* is such a local play), which he modernizes by dropping the fabulous elements and some (but not all) of the irrelevant music, while still keeping the sensational machinery, thunder and lightning playing round the catastrophe, bullets whizzing in a gloomy gorge, etc. He made his reputation with *Der Pfarrer von Kirchfeld* (1870), which shows his qualities and his limitations. The hero Hell (a symbolic name), a perfect priest in a Tyrolese village, has reformed his parishioners, who idolize him, but his enlightenment is looked upon by the village lord (whose name, Graf von Finsterberg, symbolizes his obscurantism) as heterodoxy, and the play ends with Hell being summoned to appear before his ecclesiastical

superiors. He is shown to be dangerously in love with a picturesque maiden who helps his quaint old housekeeper with the
housework; but he is in complete control of himself, though his
kindly treatment of the girl is misconstrued. The play is a discussion of the moot topics of the day: marriages between Protestants
and Catholics are shown to be natural, and above all the action
drives home the moral that it is cruelty to priests to forbid them
to marry. *Der Pfarrer von Kirchfeld* is, therefore, at once a problem
play, pointed social criticism, and an attack on dogma. Where it
lags behind is in the naïve technique; this is frankly melodramatic,
but with its strange atmosphere as of a world of dream it is far
removed from vulgarity. The peasants speak an easily intelligible
dialect, and speak it naturally; here, too, Anzengruber is a pioneer.
The characters of *Der Pfarrer von Kirchfeld* are charming but childlike; the following plays show an advance in intensity of characterization. The hero of *Der Meineidbauer* (1871) is a kind of village
Richard III; there are sensational scenes, but the action grips; and
the belief of the Meineidbauer that he is safe in sin carries him
along in an inevitable course to destruction. *Das vierte Gebot* (1878)
comes nearest of Anzengruber's plays to the naturalistic formulas,
and was acknowledged by the naturalists as a masterpiece.[1] It is as
much an arraignment of existing morals as Sudermann's *Sodoms
Ende*: a turner and his bawdy wife bring up their daughter as a
whore, and their son ends as a murderer; another character sells
his daughter to a rascal; such is the world in which people are
bidden to obey the fifth[2] commandment.

There is the Shakespearian blending of comedy in Anzengruber's
tragedies; in the comedies proper fun runs riot, and the quaint
characters – they are like nothing on earth, but in their Tyrolese
setting they are as real as goitre – are a perpetual delight. *Die
Kreuzelschreiber* (1872) are villagers who have been persuaded to
affix their crosses – they cannot write – to a document which is in
intent an attack on Holy Church; the priest now orders the wives
to withhold marital rights, and peace is only restored by the mother-
wit of Steinklopferhanns, who tells the wives that their husbands
are to make a pilgrimage to Rome – with the unmarried women of

---

[1] It was far too modern for the Vienna of 1877 (the censor mangled it),
and only began its victorious career when produced by the *Freie Bühne* in
Berlin in 1890.

[2] The Lutheran Church has the Augustinian enumeration, with the first
and second commandment run together.

the village. Moral: priests should not interfere in family affairs. The hero of *Der G'wissenswurm* (1874) suffers from pangs of conscience because once on a time he had played loose with a girl; he recovers his peace of mind when he comes across her as a farmer's wife and happy mother – and she shows him the door; and when his old sin, in the shape of a merry girl, locks him in her arms and warms him like sunshine. Moral: morality should not be implacable, and conscience should not make cowards of us all. In *Doppelselbstmord* (1876) a pair of star-crossed lovers bury their parents' strife by making them believe they have committed suicide; they are discovered committing matrimony on the high mountains. *Jungferngift* (1878) glides gaily along the edge of obscenity: a rich lover is shied off by a story, only faintly offensive in a *fabliau* or a Viennese *Volksstück*, that the lady is strangely cursed – the first carnal touch of her brings death.

Anzengruber was equally a master of the *Dorfnovelle* or village tale. In *Der Schandfleck* (1876) he handles the theme of ungrateful children tormenting an old man, a village Lear, who finds refuge with a bastard child (the *Schandfleck*). The heroine of *Der Sternsteinhof* (1883-84), a masterly character study, sets her cap, poorest wench of the village though she is, at the richest farmer's son, and, a village Helen sticking at nothing, with her *'ehrfurchtgebietende Immoralität'* a Nietzschean unawares, achieves her end; she then shows herself to be a capable housekeeper, and rules her conquered realm with stern and implacable justice.

MARIE VON EBNER-ESCHENBACH (1830-1916), who is at her best where she describes the life of her native province of Moravia, is naturalistic in her rendering of *milieu*. The world of her tales (*Dorf- und Schlossgeschichten*, 1883 and 1886) is that of the Austrian nobility to which she belonged, but she also describes with innate sympathy the life of peasants and servants attached to the nobility; like another aristocrat, George Sand, she inclines with a sympathy akin to Socialism to the labouring poor; one of her main themes is the starvation of the mind by unfavourable environment and hereditary failings. She achieved fame with *Ein Spätgeborener* (1875), and her best novels were written in the two following decades. Although her marriage was childless, no one has ever described children better than she did. One of her best novels, *Das Gemeindekind* (1887), has for its hero a boy who is the son of a murderer, and whose mother is in prison; he has the whole village against him, but wins through by strength of character and by following the precept to requite evil with good. Marie von Ebner-Eschenbach shares the didactic tendency of the writers of village tales; her great lesson is that duty comes first and must be performed as much by a countess (*Unsühnbar*, 1890) as by a servant (*Božena*, 1876); not love, therefore, but renunciation is the chief thing in life. According to her, love is rare. What is essential for the wellbeing of the human race is not love of individuals but love of one's fellow-men. 'I look on love', she says, 'as the most cruel of all the means which an angry deity has invented for the punishment of his creatures.' Perhaps for this reason she often keeps her lovers apart.

A forerunner of a different sort was Duke Georg von Meiningen, who had set himself as the task of his life to reform the German stage. Not the least important step in this programme was his morganatic marriage to one of the actresses of his Court theatre; she with him superintended the rehearsals, drilled the company, and selected the plays, while the Duke himself did the scene-painting. Both launched into historical research work to ensure accuracy of *mise en scène* and costumes; and, as far as possible, furniture actually used at the time the plays represented was procured. This cult of realism on the stage went so far that in the production of ALBERT LINDNER's (1831-88) *Bluthochzeit* (1871; an *Epigonendrama*), which deals with the massacre of St. Bartholomew, the whole theatre was so full of real powder that the actors could scarcely speak for hoarseness and the spectators got sore eyes. The Meiningers were the forerunners of Max Reinhardt in this stage realism, as well as in their handling of crowds, which with them were an active part of the picture, not an inert mass. One of the great events in the history of the German stage was the visit, in 1874, of the Duke of Meiningen's company to Berlin, where they produced Shakespeare's *Julius Cæsar*. This was the beginning of the reform of the Berlin theatre.

A further stage in this reform was the establishment in 1883 of Das Deutsche Theater in Berlin. The director appointed was ADOLF L'ARRONGE (1838-1908). Adolf L'Arronge has some importance historically as a dramatist,[1] and he might be classified as a link between the *Sitten- und Thesenstück* and the naturalistic drama; his plays owed their vogue to their careful though not rigidly realistic painting of Berlin life, especially of the mushroom plutocracy

[1] *Mein Leopold* (1873); *Hasemanns Töchter* (1877); *Doktor Klaus* (1879).

which was to be more drastically pilloried in Sudermann's *Sodoms Ende* and Heinrich Mann's novel *Im Schlaraffenland*; and it was L'Arronge who first, though with a different moral, laid hold of the contrast between *Vorder- und Hinterhaus* and created a new type of play which culminated in Sudermann's *Die Ehre*. In the history of the German stage L'Arronge will always figure prominently. The great work of his life was his management of Das Deutsche Theater. L'Arronge gradually worked out his schemes of reform. He combined the scenic splendour of the Meiningers with the noble declamation, the cult of poetry in the spoken word, for which the Burg Theatre at Vienna had, under Heinrich Laube's management from 1850 onwards, become famous. He revived Shakespeare and Goethe and Schiller, and took down from the library shelves the noble dramatic poems of the later classics, Kleist and Grillparzer and Hebbel, and gave them at last a definite and enduring place in the life of the nation.

With the rejuvenation of the stage came better and before long great acting. L'Arronge discovered and trained talent. Joseph Kainz (1858-1910) and Agnes Sorma (1865-1927) found in him their first patron. How deeply the brilliant actors of the next decades influenced literature it would take too long to show, but a few words might be said of Joseph Kainz. He created a style of acting which was entirely his own; he owed absolutely nothing to tradition. Perhaps he followed a hint of Richard Wagner, who urged that the most essential reform of German acting was to double the speed of delivery. But though Kainz tore along at a furious pace, with absolutely no punctuation, his accentuation was so clear that never a word was lost. There was no rhetoric in his speaking, and if the dramatist had put it there he eliminated it. He worked in chiaroscuro; he spoke in dull tones to enhance the light of the passionate moments. In Ibsen's *Ghosts*, for instance, he was laconically conversational, and to spectators accustomed to the old school of acting seemed only to act in the last tragic moments; there he was overpowering. But though his speaking might be the grey language of everyday life, his gesture was always eloquent. Not that he threw himself about or made a windmill of his arms; gesture was to him the harmony of movement with the mind, the trailing rhythms of Oswald's diseased limbs in *Ghosts*, the tortured irresolution of Hauptmann's bell-founder, the lyric haste of Romeo. His flexible frame has been compared to a sword, and again to the body of one of Botticelli's Virgins. But people raved most about his hands. He acted as much with his hands – the thin wan hands of an aesthete – as with his voice. He best impersonated young men, neurasthenic boys, erotomaniacs, weaklings, lovers. 'His Hamlet', says Hermann Bahr, 'dies of youth – dies because youth remains when manhood should dawn.' He was naturally akin to his friend King Louis of Bavaria. And it is characteristic that he translated into verse and adapted for the stage Byron's *Sardanapalus* (1897).

Another event that was destined to be of the greatest importance in the history of the drama was the establishment in 1889 of the *Verein Freie Bühne*. The name was suggested by Antoine's *Théâtre libre*; whereas, however, the Parisian theatre was dependent for its existence on its box-office takings, the Freie Bühne aimed at producing plays with no popular appeal but new in inspiration. Among the founders of the club were MAXIMILIAN HARDEN,[1] later the editor of *Die Zukunft*, Heinrich and Julius Hart, and PAUL SCHLENTHER[2]; OTTO BRAHM[3] was the director. The first play produced by the Freie Bühne was Ibsen's *Ghosts*; it was soon followed by Hauptmann's *Vor Sonnenaufgang*. But the first dramatic successes of the period fell to tragedies that are really *Epigonendramen*, iambic verse plays in Schiller's manner. The first of ERNST VON WILDEN-BRUCH'S (1845-1909) successes had been *Die Karolinger* (1881), which centres round the quarrels of the grandsons of Charlemagne. Wildenbruch, a scion of the Hohenzollerns on the wrong side of the blanket (his father, the German consul at Beirut in Syria, where the poet was born, was the son of Prinz Louis Ferdinand), had served as a Prussian officer, and had abandoned the army for a career in the civil service. Of his 'Hohenzollern plays' the most interesting is *Die Quitzows* (1888); here he makes concessions to the naturalistic dogma by introducing the Berlin dialect – a chronological impossibility, since at the time of the action of the play

---

[1] 1861-1927; one of the most vitriolic of publicists. He showed acumen in the literary articles he wrote for *Die Zukunft*, which he founded in 1892. He 'discovered' Maeterlinck, boomed Ibsen, and wrote a notable essay on Maupassant. His style, with its flaring Jewish qualities, went to waste in conceited mannerisms. Political and literary essays in book form: *Apostata und neue Folge* (1892); *Köpfe* (1910).

[2] 1854-1912; from 1898 director of the Hofburgtheater in Vienna. His book *Gerhart Hauptmann* (1896) is well known.

[3] 1856-1912; see p. 29. Critical works: *Gottfried Keller* (1883); *Heinrich von Kleist* (1884); *Schiller* (1888).

(it describes the subjection of the unruly nobles of the March of Brandenburg by the newly imported Margrave Frederick of Nuremberg) *Plattdeutsch* was spoken in Berlin. There is an attempt to combine the grand historical style with up-to-date realism in the double drama *Heinrich und Heinrichs Geschlecht* (1896), in which the German Emperor's humiliation at Canossa provides a sensational scene. The action of Wildenbruch's plays[1] rushes along and culminates in such dazzling stage-effects; but they are poor as literature, owing to the naïve characterization; the characters are lyrically exuberant puppets, and the construction, instead of building up to a climax, reels from sensation to sensation. Wildenbruch, in his desire to be abreast of the times, joined company with the naturalists; in two of his plays, *Die Haubenlerche* (1890) and *Meister Balzer* (1892), he outwardly followed their formulas.[2]

The victory of the new realism which we have seen coming was being prepared by the beginnings of a new criticism. The early history of naturalism is that of two groups, one in Berlin and the other in Munich, each with a militant organ of its own. The Berlin naturalists gather round the brothers HEINRICH (1855-1906) and JULIUS HART (1859-1930), who launched the campaign in their review *Kritische Waffengänge*[3] (1882-84). Of this review only four numbers appeared; the campaign was fought out in *Die Freie Bühne*, the organ of the Free Stage Club, which long kept its vigour as *Die Neue Rundschau*.

The organ of the Munich group was *Die Gesellschaft* (1885-1902), founded and edited by MICHAEL GEORG CONRAD (1846-1927), who was one of the first devotees of the cult of Zola; he planned a series of novels of Munich life on the scale of the Rougon-Macquart cycle, but got no farther than diffuse sketches (*Was die Isar rauscht*, 1887). More interesting are two other novels, *In purpurner Finsternis* (1895) and *Majestät* (1902). *In purpurner Finsternis* is a Utopia; the period is A.D. 3000; and Teuta, a land where mechanical devices have eliminated nature, is contrasted to its disadvantage with

---

[1] *Harold* (1882) and *Christoph Marlow* (1884) mishandle English themes.

[2] Wildenbruch's short stories (*Der Meister von Tanagra*, 1880; *Das edle Blut*, 1892) are excellent of their kind.

[3] The second number contains an article by the Harts: *Für und gegen Zola*. The discussion was taken up again by Arno Holz in his essay *Zola als Theoretiker*, published 1890 in *Die Freie Bühne* and reprinted in *Die Kunst: ihr Wesen und ihre Gesetze*. Holz argues that Zola's conception of the *roman expérimental* and of *documents humains* is taken over from Taine, the Goncourts, and Claude Bernard.

Nordica, to which the hero escapes by aeroplane with the woman he loves and wishes to live with – a monstrous idea in this state of Nietzschean supermen, where the sexes are separated at puberty, though at fixed periods regulated by the chief physician males are admitted to the women's quarters. In Nordica nothing mechanical is allowed; for where machines rule there is neither craftsmanship nor leisure. (This had been the conclusion of William Morris's *News from Nowhere*.) *Majestät* is Nietzschean, in so far as it glorifies Ludwig II of Bavaria – '*eines Königs Majestät in tiefer Einsamkeit, einer jungfräulichen Künstlerseele in Purpur*', – and derides the masses. The change in outlook in these two novels is typical.

In lyric verse the revolt was heralded by an anthology published in 1884 in Berlin: *Moderne Dichtercharaktere*. It was edited by WILHELM ARENT (1864-?), a poet who prided himself on being crazy, and prefaced by two introductions intended as a manifesto, one by HERMANN CONRADI (1862-90) and the other by KARL HENCKELL (1864-1929) – brave words calling for new characters to write the new verse, but surprisingly empty. The poems of the anthology, as a matter of fact, present no innovation of form; what is new is the prominence given to 'modern' subjects, mainly in the direction of *Grossstadtpoesie*. Hermann Conradi had a certain originality; his note is that of half-disgust with the debauch into which his sensual nature hurled him down from the heights to which his intellect strove; this note lends a pathetic interest – for he died of pneumonia at the age of twenty-eight – to his book of verse *Lieder eines Sünders* (1887), with its sulphurous defiance as of Tannhäuser prisoned in the Venusberg, in the *mons veneris*. Conradi's half tragic, half-ridiculous fate, together with the partially realized intensely personal style of his novel *Adam Mensch* (1889), revived interest in him in the days of expressionism. He had previously published a collection of short stories, *Brutalitäten* (1886), and a novel, *Phrasen* (1887), which has historical importance as the first book to show the influence of Nietzsche. The two novels, moreover, are the first in the pathological manner of Dostoieffsky. Karl Henckell, as time went on, assumed the role of poet laureate of the Socialists (*Ausgewählte Gedichte*, 2 vols., 1903). Of the other poets of the anthology, few were destined to win lasting fame; but Otto Erich Hartleben, who distinguished himself later as a dramatist and humorist, was represented with odes in the ancient Greek style, and Arno Holz contributed poems which, though traditional in form, are excellent in their genre-painting.

ARNO HOLZ (1863-1929) it was who, in conjunction with his friend JOHANNES SCHLAF (1862-1941), put the match to the gunpowder. Arno Holz, an East Prussian, had begun as an imitator of Geibel, but in his volume of verse *Buch der Zeit* (1885), though the form is traditional, there is already *Armeleutepoesie*. Holz has described in his prolix treatise *Die Kunst: ihr Wesen und ihre Gesetze* (1890-92) how he discovered 'consistent realism'. On his return from Paris, where he had studied Zola's critical writings, he had taken rooms with his friend Schlaf in a Berlin suburb, and there he came across a boy's drawing of a soldier on a slate; to anybody else it might have been a camel, to the boy it was a soldier; the boy had failed in the first place because his tools were inadequate, and in the second place because he did not know how to handle the tools he had. From this Holz deduced his famous law: *Die Kunst hat die Tendenz, wieder die Natur zu sein. Sie wird sie nach Massgabe ihrer jeweiligen Reproduktionsbedingungen und deren Handhabung.* That is: art differs from nature only in the means of representation. There are as many forms of art as there are means of representing it. Since art strives to be nature, the stern aim of art must be to be 'consistent', or unswerving in the exact reproduction of nature. In illustration of this truth, Holz and Schlaf wrote three *Novellen*, which were published in 1889 as *Papa Hamlet* by Bjarne P. Holmsen. The name of the alleged author reflects the popularity at that time of Scandinavian writers. Papa Hamlet is an old actor who is always declaiming passages from *Hamlet*; when his baby Fortinbras cries he puts a pillow over its face; in the end he stifles the child. The characters of the three tales are grey ordinary beings; we get chunks of daily life narrated with photographic reality. Zola had defined art as life seen through the artist's temperament; Holz eliminates the artist's temperament and, in intention, photographs like a camera, with no apparent interest either in his characters or in their speech, which he gives in fragments and disjointed. The best of the tales is the third: *Ein Tod*, the description of a night passed by students at the death-bed of a comrade who has been wounded in a duel. Here the unfinished sentences and the three full stops to represent the unspoken words produce an atmosphere and admirably suggest the sleepy crawling of the night-hours. This style is known as *Sekundenstil* (the term was first used by Adalbert von Hanstein in his book *Das jüngste Deutschland*, 1900), i.e. a style

which laboriously produces the impression of every ticking second
of time; it is a minute notation of trains of thought and sensuous impressions which points forward to psycho-analysis and the 'stream
of consciousness' novel of recent years. *Papa Hamlet* owes its importance in the history of literature principally to the fact that
Gerhart Hauptmann in his first play, which was dedicated to Bjarne
P. Holmsen, *'dem konsequentesten Realisten'*, copied the externals of
its style, i.e. *Sekundenstil.*

In the first of these three tales, *Papa Hamlet*, there was so much
dialogue that it approached drama. Holz and Schlaf then provided
their model for a naturalistic style of drama in *Die Familie Selicke*
(1890), which was staged by the *Freie Bühne*, and of which Theodor
Fontane said: 'Here the roads part; here old and new separate.'
A father comes home drunk and goes to sleep on the sofa while
his family are watching by the bedside of a sick child. The child
dies; the daughter has to tell a theological student, the lodger,
that she cannot marry him, as she will be needed at home to keep
the peace between her drunken father and suffering mother. The
language is in the Berlin dialect and the strictest *Sekundenstil.*

After this the collaboration between Holz and Schlaf ceased.
Holz scored one popular success in a play which was not tied to a
theory – a drama of school life, *Traumulus* (1905), written in collaboration with Otto Jerschke. The action – a grammar-school
boy has an affair with an actress – was topical: the straining of the
educational machine in Germany had led to an epidemic of suicides
among schoolchildren, and the problem of educational methods,
both as regards teacher and taught, became so acute that there
was repeated discussion of it in literature.[1] Three other plays related in theme are Wedekind's *Frühlings Erwachen* (1891), Otto
Ernst's *Flachsmann als Erzieher* (1901), and Georg Kaiser's *Rektor
Kleist* (1905). Holz planned a *magnum opus*, a cycle of twelve plays;
of these he completed *Sozialaristokraten* (1896), a literary satire (the
characters transparently stand for notables of the literary Bohème
of Berlin, Bruno Wille, John Henry Mackay, Przybyszewski); *Son-
nenfinsternis* (1908), the tragedy of the artist; and *Ignorabimus* (1912),
the tragedy of the poet. In these later plays Holz sets himself the

---

[1] There are distressing pictures of school life in Thomas Mann's *Buddenbrooks*, Heinrich Mann's *Professor Unrat*, Friedrich Huch's *Peter Michel, Freund
Hein* (1902) by Emil Strauss, J. C. Heer's *Joggeli*, Hermann Hesse's *Unterm Rad*,
and Tovote's *Fräulein Grisebach* (1909, girls' school).

gigantic task of fixing the inner rhythm of everything that is spoken by every character: accentuation and gesture are not to be those of the author, nor those of the actor, but of the given character at a given moment controlled by a given emotion. These rhythmic studies run concurrently with the strange results arrived at in metrics by a very great authority, Eduard Sievers, who claimed that his system of analysing the sounds of a work (*Schallanalyse*) can fix whether a poet, ancient or modern, recited with his belly or his shoulders, and even his height and cubic measure. Holz, analysing the rhythm of Hauptmann's plays (even those in prose), finds that they scan with a monotonous rhythm in the author's brain: they are thus not naturalistic, or in other words Hauptmann is reproducing his own singsong, not the rhythms of characters flat in repose or varying with the varying strain of emotion.

In *Revolution der Lyrik* (1899) Holz declared war against established form in lyric verse, and the rhythmic theories here propounded shape the vast mass of the impressionistic verse collected in his *Phantasus* (1898-1916). All previous verse, says Holz, had been metrical; this metrical form he (like Victor Hugo pontifically dislocating the Alexandrine) 'smashes'[1]; and he replaces it by its diametrical opposite, rhythmical form. Rhyme and stanza vanish; the 'natural and necessary' rhythm constitutes the poem, which turns on an invisible central pivot (*Mittelachse*). Thus: *Der Mond steigt hinter Apfelbaumzweigen auf* is rank prose; but

> *Hinter blühenden Apfelbaumzweigen*
> *steigt der Mond auf*

is verse rotating round an invisible central pivot. Sceptically regarded this might seem to mean that any reciter may turn prose into verse by modulating his voice before and after a pause (traditionally: caesura); or that any compositor can arrange prose as verse by what Holz calls an 'acoustic picture'. Truth to tell, these poems in free rhythms (a term Holz rejects,[2] though critics insist

[1] '*Jede Wortkunst, von frühster Urzeit bis auf unsere Tage, war, als auf ihrem letzten, tiefuntersten Formprinzip, auf Metrik gegründet. Diese Metrik zerbrach ich und setzte dafür das genaue, diametrale Gegenteil. Nämlich Rhythmik.*' – '*Der Rhythmus allein ist unausschöpfbar. Dieser immanente Rhythmus wächst jedesmal neu aus dem Inhalt.*'

[2] '*Der freie Rhythmus geht aus einer musikalischen, der natürliche Rhythmus aus einer malerisch-plastischen Erfahrung hervor.*' (The 'plastic' visualization reminds one of the poems arranged typographically in the form of goblets, etc., by seventeenth-century German poets.) Historically Holz's '*Polymeter*' are,

on classifying the poems of *Phantasus* as such and ranging them with the attempts to reproduce something of Walt Whitman's 'barbarous yawp') depend for their effect on their inherent poetry, their grotesque humour, their vivid pictures.

Johannes Schlaf, after parting from Holz, continued to write plays (*Meister Oelze*, 1892; *Gertrud*, 1897; *Die Feindlichen*, 1899). The two latter dramas share with Schlaf's novels the quest of a new humanity; *Meister Oelze* is stark realism. In the loosely connected sketches of rural nature *In Dingsda* (1892) and *Frühling* (1894) we have nothing more than a nerve-racked city man's awakening to the healthiness of country life: much lauded as they were as poetry (though in prose) of the first water it is hard now to see in these feverish and peevish divagations more than a first reaction against the sordidness of the naturalistic *milieu*-painting. This doctrine of healing nature is transformed to a species of cosmic cult in Schlaf's later volumes of verse *Hell-Dunkel* (1899) and *Das Sommerlied* (1905) and in the prose poetry of his *Das Spiel der hohen Linien* (1927). Historically the most interesting thing in Schlaf's lyric prose is that it is a loose imitation of Whitman,[1] whose serious influence on German form begins here and in Holz's *Phantasus*. In his short stories *Sommertod* (1897), *Leonore* (1900), *Die Kuhmagd* (1900), and *Frühlingsblumen* (1901), and his two trilogies of novels *Das dritte Reich* (1900), *Die Suchenden* (1901), *Peter Bojes Freite* (1902), and *Der Kleine* (1904), *Der Prinz* (1908), *Am toten Punkt* (1909), Schlaf gets to grips with the multifarious problems of the present, from the decay of society to the absurdities of science and religion and the conflicts of love and marriage; for decadence he adumbrates a cure by religious exaltation of spirit and Whitmanesque care of body and mind. As the new man of his futuristic vision he points, in the three little monographs he has devoted to these writers, to Whitman,[2] Verhaeren, and Maeterlinck.

The two Hart brothers will live in the annals of literature for the part they played in the campaign for naturalism (*Stoffkunst*, *Herrschaft der Materie*, to use denominations of recent years). In memoirs and elsewhere – and indeed by reason of their solemn ideologies as much as by their personal characteristics – they are

though different, in the line of rhymeless Romantic verse and of Jean Paul's *Streckverse* in *Flegeljahre* (see Jakob Minor, *Neuhochdeutsche Metrik*, p. 333).

[1] Ferdinand Freiligrath (1810–76) had introduced Whitman in 1868 by an essay and translations.   [2] *Walt Whitman* (1904).

somewhat droll figures; as such they trod the stage, easily recognizable, in Ernst von Wolzogen's literary comedy *Lumpengesindel* (1892). Heinrich, the elder, began as a lyrical poet with *Weltpfingsten* (1872), failed as a dramatist with *Sedan* (1883), and followed up (though he denied it) Victor Hugo's *Légende des Siècles* and the *Nächte des Orients* (1874) of Adolf Graf von Schack, the Orientalist poet of the Munich school, in his *Lied der Menschheit* (1888-96), in intention a grandiose verse epic. Only three of the twenty-four cantos planned were completed: *Tul und Nahila* (1886), which takes some of its tropical colouring from Ernst Haeckel's *Indische Reisebriefe* (1882), shows the institution of monogamy (i.e. Darwin's *Zuchtwahl*) evolving from sexual promiscuousness in prehistoric Ceylon, while *Nimrod* (1888) and *Mose* (1896) take the nomad human race forward to fixed habitation, law, and religion. The interest of these fragments is that they are symptomatic: on the one hand they mirror the *Kulturphilosophie* of the Friedrichshagen naturalistic coterie – the Harts lived at the Berlin suburb of Friedrichshagen, and so did Bruno Wille and Bölsche – and on the other hand they are in the line of those typically German works which go back to Herder's *Ideen zur Philosophie der Geschichte der Menschheit* (1784-91). Julius Hart was at his best in the lyric[1]; and notably his descriptive poem *Auf der Fahrt nach Berlin* (1882) – it reproduces the poet's impressions on steaming into the railway station at Berlin when he first came from his native Münster – keeps its place in the anthologies; it takes rank as the starting-point of the *Grossstadtpoesie* which was to become so important a genre in the days of expressionism.[2] His naturalistic play *Der Sumpf*

---

[1] His poems were collected in *Sansara* (1879), *Homo sum* (1891), *Triumph des Lebens* (1899).

[2] The contributors to *Moderne Dichtercharaktere* claim to have inaugurated *Grossstadtpoesie* with Karl Henckell's *Berliner Abendbild* and Arno Holz's and Oskar Jerschke's pictures of Berlin and its suburbs. Hermann Bahr, quoting Arno Holz's poem *Zum Eingang (Buch der Zeit)*, says: '*Mit diesen Versen beginnt die Grossstadtlyrik.*' Each claim is open to question. In English poetry there is Alexander Smith's *Glasgow* (in *City Poems*, 1857) and Ferdinand Freiligrath's anthology of English poetry, *Rose, Thistle, and Shamrock* (1853), includes poems on cities. English influence is likely in Wilhelm Arent's *Aus dem Grossstadtbrodem* (1891); and John Davidson's London poems, Henley's *London Types* and Arthur Symons's *London Nights* seem to have left their mark on poems in Ludwig Jakobowski's (1868-1900) *Leuchtende Tage*. (Jabokowski was editor of *Die Gesellschaft*, and wrote two novels, *Werther der Jude*, 1892, and *Loki*, 1896, both in defence of Jews.) Academically a distinction may be made between the city poems of the naturalists – a continuation of descriptive

(1886) is also a picture of Berlin; the theme is much the same in outline as that of Sudermann's *Sodoms Ende*.

Like the Harts, two other popular philosophers of the group of naturalists progressed from Marxist materialism to animism: BRUNO WILLE (1860-1928) and WILHELM BÖLSCHE (1862-1939); both derived from the '*Psychophysik*' of Gustav Theodor Fechner (1801-87), the philosophy which teaches that there are reciprocal relations between psychic and physical processes.[1] Bruno Wille was a theologist turned Socialist freethinker; he kept up his preaching, though unauthorized, to the 'free religious' community he gathered round him. The title of one of his books, *Atheistische Sittlichkeit* (1892), is sufficiently informative. His poetry has passed into limbo. Wilhelm Bölsche strove, as a disciple of Zola, to link poetry and science: in his *Die naturwissenschaftlichen Grundlagen der Poesie* (1887) he argues that what mythology was for ancient poetry the Darwinian theory should be for the literature of today. The three volumes of his *Das Liebesleben in der Natur* (1898, 1900, 1902) are still read; with a kind of animal symbolism he shows that the functions of sex in man and animals are identical, and that the sexual significance of certain things (e.g. the hair under the armpits) has been obscured by culture: we must go to the beasts for elucidation, which he does. There is symbolism, too, in Bölsche's novel *Die Mittagsgöttin* (1891), as indeed there is (on a grandiose scale) in Zola's novels, which Bölsche too pedantically imitates.

Bölsche, Bruno Wille, the Harts, Holz and Schlaf were members of the literary club *Durch*, at which the programme of naturalism was discussed and defined. It was founded in 1886 by Conrad Küster, a doctor with literary tastes, Eugen Wolff (who coined the term *die Moderne* to distinguish the movement from *die Antike*), and Leo Berg (1862-1908), one of the best essayists of the period. Adalbert von Hanstein was another member; and Gerhart Hauptmann was to be the most famous. As far as political views go the

poetry – and those of the impressionists (following Verhaeren's *Les villes tentaculaires*), in which the use of symbol does create a new genre. But there are affinities of details: cf. for instance Julius Hart's '*engbrüst'ge Häuser*' with Rilke's '*und neue Häuser, die mit engen Brüsten | sich drängen aus den bangen Baugerüsten*'. Quite Verhaerenesque is *Die Grossstadt bei Nacht*, a poem by Max Haushofer, who was associated with the Munich School (*Gedichte*, 1864).

[1] Fechner, a laughing satirist (*Vergleichende Anatomie der Engel*, 1825), discusses the possibility of life after death in *Nanna oder das Seelenleben der Pflanzen* (1848), which explains R. M. Meyer's jesting remark that Bölsche progressed from Nana (*na, na!*) to Nanna. (Baldur's wife Nanna was goddess of plants.)

wildest was a young poet born at Greenock, JOHN HENRY MACKAY (1864-1933); in his prose writings and novels (*Die Anarchisten*, 1891, is a tale of London agitation) he was to popularize the doctrines of the classical work on anarchism, Max Stirner's (1806-56) *Der Einzige und sein Eigentum* (1844); his poetry (*Kinder des Hochlands*, 1885; *Dichtungen*, 1886; *Arma parata fero*, 1887; *Helene*, 1888) has the vigour of his Scots blood and the aggressiveness of his social creed.

One can hardly say that PETER HILLE (1854-1904) was an *habitué* of the Friedrichshagen circle. For Peter Hille – *'ewiger Waller und Wanderer'* – Berlin was a place of passage merely: literally he was a tramp who transported his belongings and manuscripts in a sack or stuffed into the greasy pockets of his billowing ulster, which covered his lack of coat and waistcoat. In London he lodged *'in einer der dunklen Höhlen Whitechapels'*, with niggers, Chinese, Socialists and Communists, such as are the characters of his novel *Die Sozialisten* (1887); the names of two, Beber and Triebknecht, are transparent. From an author who wrote as the spirit prompted, in the open air or in the vilest dens, orderly shaping of matter is not to be expected; but what we do get in this fragmentist – in *Die Sozialisten* as in Hille's other novel, *Die Hassenburg* (1905; an *Erziehungsroman* of a sort) – is a wealth of aphorisms, such as he would jot down on any scrap of paper – *'Papierschnitzel, Zigarrentüten, Briefumschläge'* – that the winds of Heaven blew upon him. These form the staple of the second volume of his *Ausgewählte Werke*, piously sorted from his sacks and edited by the Harts after his death. There is a curious interest too in his tragedy *Des Platonikers Sohn* (1897), which already handles the Father-Son motif with the pitiless impiety of the expressionists: Petrarch's son, a natural boy, rebels against the formative efforts of his scholastic father; what emerges is Hille's detestation of school scholarship. But the best of Hille is in his lyrics; here *was* the new poetry, though it was not written to Holz's recipe. Quaint and sly (like the little lilt of the schoolgirls gathering in the courtyard as a *Schulschlange* – that some day will crush the strong backs of men) – or verdurous and sonorous, like the roar of the wind in the forest, these poems live with the magic of Peter Hille's strange and wayward genius. The legend of Peter Hille – of 'St. Peter' – is to be read in *Das Peter Hille-Buch* which Else Lasker-Schüler, his great friend, devoted to his memory.

Two Berlin naturalists, Conrad Alberti and Karl Bleibtreu, wrote fierily for M. G. Conrad's *Die Gesellschaft*. What distinguished the Munich coterie from that of Berlin was that Conrad as long as he lived, and his lieutenants at least to begin with, saw the salvation of literature in Zola, while the Harts and later Arno Holz were – to quote the article in the second number of *Kritische Waffengänge* – for and against him. CONRAD ALBERTI (1862-1918) remains famous for one sentence of his in *Die Gesellschaft* – it serves to illustrate the *Heldenlosigkeit* of the naturalistic drama: '*Der Tod des grössten Helden steht hinsichtlich der künstlerischen Verwertbarkeit auf gleicher Stufe mit den Geburtswehen einer Kuh.*' KARL BLEIBTREU (1859-1928) forced himself into the polemical foreground with his pamphlet *Revolution der Literatur* (1886), a joke for historians of literature less for its wild judgments than for the outrageous picture on its jacket – an inkpot darting flashes of white lightning across a blood-red background. The conceited style of this treatise marks all Bleibtreu's critical work. His fiction *Kraftkuren* (1884), *Schlechte Gesellschaft* (1886; a collection of Novellen), and *Grössenwahn* (1888; a 'pathological novel') reek with the miasmas of the great cities; they expose the relations of artists and poets with prostitutes and barmaids. Of his dramas, *Schicksal* (1888) shows his worship of Napoleon; to the hero he fanatically loved and lauded are devoted his *Byron-Stücke* – *Lord Byrons letzte Liebe* (1881), *Seine Tochter* (1886), *Byrons Geheimnis* (1900). *Seine Tochter* is classed as the first Darwinian[1] drama: the poet's daughter, brought up in innocent ignorance of her father, finds his qualities in herself when she knows, and wards off a warning friend with the words: '*Die Vererbung ist unwiderstehlich und unüberwindlich.*' Bleibtreu claimed to have inaugurated a new genre, that of the *Schlachtennovelle*; his first one, *Dies irae* (1884), puts the tale of Sedan into the mouth of a French officer who is present at the battle; it is a curiosity of literature that the French translation was taken to be the original and translated back into German. Equally readable – and excellent in their unfolding of strategy – are *Deutsche Waffen in Spanien* (1885), *Friedrich der Grosse bei Collin* (1888), *Cromwell bei Marston Moor* (1889).

[1] The hero of *Grössenwahn*, despairing of Europe, retires to his Styrian estate to seek the doctrine of salvation in Darwin's works.

II

THE DRAMATISTS
OF NATURALISM

Arno Holz was all his life long a fanatical theorist experimenting out in the cold. The harvest of the new idea was reaped by GERHART HAUPTMANN (1862-1946) and his disciples. Gerhart Hauptmann was born in the Silesian health resort of Obersalzbrunn; his father was the landlord and owner of the hotel *Zur Preussischen Krone*. Silesian birth and upbringing and the events of his youth are of importance in the work of this poet, for his use of Silesian dialect belongs to the history of the development of literature, and his adolescence comes into the subject-matter of work after work. He was educated at Obersalzbrunn, and then at the *Realschule* of Breslau. He was so negligent or unreceptive at his studies that he was sent to his uncle's farm to learn practical farming. But he was too dreamy for this business, and was taken back and sent to be trained as a sculptor at the *Kunstschule* at Breslau, from which he was sent down for insubordination. At this period it was feared that he might be consumptive. Then he joined his brother Carl, who was studying at the University of Jena; here he attended lectures by Haeckel. Too restless for methodical study, he set out on a sea voyage from Hamburg to Spain and Italy; his impressions made up his first book of verse, *Promethidenlos* (1885), an imitation of *Childe Harold*; noteworthy is the marked sympathy in the book with the outcast. On his return, Gerhart married a well-to-do woman, whose means enabled him to live in Erkner, a Berlin suburb. Before settling down to domesticated reading he had, however, made a last attempt at being a sculptor in Italy. His studies at Erkner were mainly scientific or economic; he read Darwin and Marx. His social feeling was in the best sense religious: at the base of it was the goodness of his

24

mother, who had been brought up in the Moravian creed. He planned an epic on Jesus of Nazareth; it remained an idea, but his religious conception (in the main pity for suffering humanity) materialized years later in his novel *Der Narr in Christo Emanuel Quint*. In 1887 his short story *Bahnwärter Thiel* appeared in *Die Gesellschaft*; a man who tends a railway crossing is incapacitated by dependence on his virago of a wife. In these moods of social pity the theories of Holz unlocked Hauptmann's creative power: *Sekundenstil*, he thought, gave him the means of showing truth by depicting humanity in the raw; plan, development, selection, effect were not needed; what the artist had to do was to let situation follow situation; the situation would be vivid because actual, and pregnant with meaning because all life is full of tragic pity. He had been present at the historical performance in 1887 of Ibsen's *Ghosts* in Berlin, and had been deeply moved. He set to work and produced *Vor Sonnenaufgang* (1889). Alfred Loth, a Socialist agitator, comes to a Silesian mining village to do research in economic conditions. He is invited to stay in the home of a farmer enriched by the working of mines under his fields. The farmer is a dipsomaniac; his wife is unchaste; one of his two daughters, also alcoholic, does not appear on the stage, as she is expecting her confinement; the other, Helene, pure in spite of her environment, falls in love with Loth, the first clean man she has met. Loth, still unaware of the general degeneration of the family, makes a lovematch with Helene; but when he learns the state of things he breaks off the engagement and goes away – for he is a teetotaller and believes in heredity, – and Helene kills herself with a hunting knife.

Vor Sonnenaufgang was produced on the 20th of October, 1889, in the Lessing Theatre, under the auspices of the *Freie Bühne*. It was a battle like that of *Hernani*. The excitement culminated when a physician, at the moment when Helene's sister is near her confinement and there is a call for a midwife, threw a pair of forceps on the stage. The play was hissed and acclaimed and discussed for weeks after. Naturalism had arrived. The vogue of scientific determinism was established; i.e. the conception that the will is rendered powerless by heredity and *milieu*. Moreover, a new dramatic technique opened new vistas. Monologues and asides were declared antiquated. Stage directions were like a catalogue. The idea that a play should have a 'hero' gave way to the conception

(*Heldenlosigkeit*) that since the drama portrays men, and since men are weaklings, the purpose of the dramatist is not to weigh out a calculated sum of 'tragic guilt', but to arouse a tender pity for pathetic humanity; life is tragic because it is life, not because it is guilty.

But, since all the processes of art tend to become mechanical, the naturalistic drama, from the start, adopts an external machinery which makes it as stereotyped as the French classical drama. This rigid framework is as gaunt as anywhere in *Vor Sonnenaufgang*. It is an 'analytical drama' (*Drama des reifen Zustandes*): as in Ibsen's plays the characters are fixed (*fertige Charaktere*), i.e. they are not developed by the action of the drama, which is merely the unfolding of a catastrophe prepared by the course of events prior to the first act. The naturalistic drama is one, not of action, but of situation. Scenes or 'processes' from the lives of human beings are shown, not in shapely acts (in some naturalistic plays, e.g. *Das Friedensfest*, acts are called *Vorgänge*), but shapelessly fluid and cut off *in processu* by the fall of the curtain. There is neither beginning nor end, but just a 'chunk of life'.

Into the moral decrepitude of the Silesian mining village steps a 'saviour from afar' (*der Retter aus der Ferne*), another ingredient of the naturalistic drama as of Ibsen's plays. In Hauptmann's next play, *Das Friedensfest* (1890), a man who is on the verge of nervous collapse is to be saved by a healthy woman sweeping in from the outer world. A physician has married a woman inferior to him in intelligence, and friction ensues; this is a favourite theme of Hauptmann's, who (like Wedekind and Thomas Mann) constantly rehandles the same problem. The doctor had abandoned wife and children when one of his sons, Wilhelm, had slapped his face. Wilhelm is engaged to a healthy girl, but, conscious of his hereditary handicaps, he hesitates to marry her (as, to quote an instance familiar from literary history, Grillparzer for the same reasons had hesitated to marry his *ewige Braut*). However, there is a family gathering to celebrate the engagement, and during the rejoicings father Scholz unexpectedly returns. Wilhelm begs his father's pardon for having slapped his face; there is a general reconciliation; but the father dies of apoplexy. The final result is left in doubt: will Wilhelm marry Ida, and will the hereditary disease yield to her care; or is tragedy inevitable?

The third play, *Einsame Menschen* (1891), handled the triangular

GERHART HAUPTMANN

marriage (*Ehe zu Dritt*).[1] Johannes Vockerat is married to a woman intellectually beneath him (like the wife in *Das Friedensfest*); as a woman of means, she can give him creature comforts and the opportunity of living a student's life, but not intellectual comradeship. He is *l'homme incompris*; even his parents do not understand him, for they are pious and orthodox, and he is a disciple of Darwin and Haeckel. Into his quiet home comes a girl student from Zurich (*der Retter aus der Ferne*); *she* understands Johannes, and he falls in love with her; his wife despairs; Anna has to leave, and Johannes drowns himself. The outlines show a similarity with Ibsen's *Rosmersholm*, but (though it was a tenet of naturalism that personal interest should be eliminated) the inspiration was no doubt that which later found symbolic expression in *Die versunkene Glocke*. In any case, *Einsame Menschen* is a study of neurasthenia, just as *Das Friedensfest* had been a study of heredity and *Vor Sonnenaufgang* a study of alcoholism.

With *Die Weber* (1892) Hauptmann achieved European fame. The poverty-stricken condition of the Silesian weavers was at that time a topical question, and Hauptmann, himself the grandson of a Silesian weaver, studied the situation in his native mountains. There had been a revolt of the weavers in 1844[2]; and this past

---

[1] This is a prolific motif in German literature. It begins with the medieval legend of Graf von Gleichen; this crusader brought home a paynim maid who had freed him from captivity, and he is said to have obtained a dispensation from the Pope to cohabit with her conjointly with his legal wife. The legend has been dramatized by Wilhelm Schmidtbonn (*Der Graf von Gleichen*, 1906), Hermann Anders Krüger (*Der Graf von Gleichen*, 1908), and Ernst Hardt (*Schirin und Gertraude*, 1912, a '*Scherzspiel*'). In Goethe's *Stella* (first version) and Maeterlinck's *Aglavaine et Selysette* the two women agree to share the husband. In fiction Jakob Wassermann's *Das Gänsemännchen* adapts the life-story of the poet Bürger, who lived connubially with two sisters; Herbert Eulenberg in one of the Novellen of his *Casanovas letztes Abenteuer* shows Schiller considering the same solution of his problem; Max Kretzer in his novel *Drei Weiber* (1886) lets his hero live with a woman, her stepdaughter, and their servant; and Gerhart Hauptmann in *Buch der Leidenschaft* pleads passionately for the sweet reasonableness of the marriage to two. Fürst Hermann von Pückler-Muskau (1785-1871) bought an Abyssinian girl and lodged her in his castle, to the disgust of his wife. For Otto Erich Hartleben see p. 63.

[2] The sufferings of weavers are the theme of Ernst Willkomm's (1810-86) novels *Eisen, Gold und Geist* (1843) and *Weisse Sklaven* (1845; the rising of the Silesian weavers at Peterswaldau had just taken place and forms the basis of this novel). In his novel *Maschinen* (1895) Konrad Alberti shows the weavers attacking machinery, while Ernst Toller bases his play *Die Maschinenstürmer* (1922) on the rioting of the Nottingham weavers in 1811, and in his prologue translates Byron's maiden speech in the House of Lords in defence of the

revolt Hauptmann used to create the social drama of the present. There is no 'construction' in the accepted sense: the play consists of a series of pictures of abject misery. Naturalistic *Heldenlosigkeit* has here an interesting development: there is no individual hero, but the weavers collectively are the hero – each individually insignificant, but as a mass a sweeping force. *Die Weber* is the first play in which 'mass psychology' is successfully handled; here the mass does indeed express itself as a unity; all the individualities coalesce in an entity. How successfully Hauptmann has realized the conception can be seen by a comparison with Schiller's *Wilhelm Tell*: Schiller's idea was to make the Swiss people the hero of his play, but, since the Swiss people are expressed by William Tell (in the limelight), William Tell is the hero, not the Swiss people. The revolt is crushed; but morally the weavers are victorious. Whether *Die Weber* marks an actual advance in dramatic technique is a moot question; the opposite view is that the innovation is in the direction of making the drama epic (*Episierung des Dramas*), i.e. minute but haphazard and loosely billowing description of *milieu* takes the place of action selected and concentrated by a controlling mind.

The enslavement by sexual needs (the Samson motif) sketched in the short tale *Bahnwärter Thiel* finds deepened expression in *Fuhrmann Henschel* (1898). A Silesian carter has sworn to his dying wife that he will never marry their servant Hanne. But he cannot live without a wife, and he succumbs to Hanne's wiles. She is untrue to him, and he hangs himself. *Fuhrmann Henschel* and *Rose Bernd* (1904) are *bürgerliche Trauerspiele* which differ from Hauptmann's earlier plays in two important respects: the characters are developed by suffering, and their fate is not fixed by outside forces (heredity and *milieu*), but depends on volition; the characters are free to decide what their actions shall be; in other words, they are not puppets. Thirdly, there is a clean-cut ending (a catastrophe in the old sense) to both plays; we know that the gods have done their worst with Henschel and Rose Bernd. In *Rose Bernd* Hauptmann handles a favourite motif of the *Sturm und Drang*: Rose is the frenzied mother who murders her new-born baby; it is the eternal tragedy of woman sexually pursued and helplessly yielding.

German literature has only half a dozen or so of classical com-

rioters. The actuality of the theme dates from Heine's poem *Die Weber* (in *Zeitgedichte*, 1844).

edies; Hauptmann's *Der Biberpelz* (1893) is one of them. It has a cretain similarity to Kleist's *Der zerbrochene Krug*: in both comedies there is a culprit whose transgressions are investigated in court; but whereas in *Der zerbrochene Krug* the culprit is the investigating judge himself, whose cross-examination of innocent parties unravels his own guilt, in *Der Biberpelz* the judge is a pompous fool who is led by the nose by the culprit, the egregious washerwoman Frau Wolffen. This lady, unshakable in her brazen effrontery, gets the court bailiff to hold a lantern while she steals wood; to the judge she is the pattern of honesty. *Der rote Hahn* (1901), a sequel to *Der Biberpelz*, fell flat. *College Crampton* (1892), a study of alcoholism, is a kind of comedy, but the humour touches tragedy. The dipsomaniac is this time a professor of painting (obviously Breslau is intended); the weakness of the play is that whereas we are to believe that Crampton is a genius debased by alcohol, we see the effects of the alcohol but no evidence of the genius. Crampton has given way to drink because his wife did not understand him; he is another *homme incompris*, like Johannes Vockerat. There is again, as in *Das Friedensfest*, a contrast with a healthy family, who set the old man up in a sort of way in an atelier; there is, however, no solution of the problem, but (as in *Das Friedensfest*) the question is left undecided whether kindness and contact with normal beings can effect a cure; or, in other words, is disease a fault or is it fate? *College Crampton* is the carefully executed portrait of an artist; similar portraits of artists variously tormented and never understood by their (Strindbergian) wives are *Michael Kramer* (1900), *Gabriel Schillings Flucht* (1912), with its pictures of sea and dunes on Hiddensee, and *Peter Brauer* (1921). In *Michael Kramer* (as in *Das Friedensfest*) there is the conflict between son and father so dear to the expressionists.

An event of considerable importance in the history of the German theatre was the appointment in 1894 of Otto Brahm, one of the stalwarts of naturalistic propaganda, as director of the Deutsches Theater (later Lessing Theater) in Berlin as successor to Adolf L'Arronge; this theatre now became the temple of the Hauptmann cult. Here in 1896 Hauptmann's historical tragedy *Florian Geyer* was produced. It had been planned as a tragedy of the first magnitude: Hauptmann's intention was to apply the technique of the naturalistic drama on a large scale. In other words, it was in *Sekundenstil*, though (ostensibly at least) in the archaic language of the period depicted. It is the tragedy of the Peasants' Rebellion of 1525, unrolled in a series of loosely connected scenes; and the peasants as a mass are the hero, though the play takes its name from one of their leaders. To Hauptmann's immense sorrow the play was ill received; his grief is symbolically woven into the poetry of his next play, *The Sunken Bell* – '*Im Tale klingt sie, in den Bergen nicht*'; the bell of his art rang in the lowlands but not on the heights.

The reason for the immediate failure of *Florian Geyer* lay partly in a reaction of taste – neo-romanticism was beginning –, partly in the inherent weakness of the naturalistic conception of tragedy: in *Florian Geyer* we have a series of dissolving views which do not rivet the attention. But Hauptmann had already struck out into new paths: in *Hanneles Himmelfahrt*[1] (1893) he had combined naturalism with the time-old *Märchendrama*, the three essential ingredients of which – dream, allegory, supernatural beings – here harmoniously link and fuse. Hannele, the fourteen-year-old daughter of a drunkard in a Silesian village, runs away from her father's ill-treatment and tries to drown herself, as her mother had done before her, in the village pond. She is rescued, and is taken by her teacher to the workhouse; in the dreams of her fever, which pass over the stage, she sees Bible texts and fairy-tale story realized, with herself as the heroine in the magical white light of it. The awakenings of puberty lend a chill warmth to her visions: her teacher is the Saviour, whom she is to wed. The angel of death stands, black-robed and black-winged, in the room, sword in hand; a hunch-backed village tailor comes and robes her in a bridal dress of white silk, and puts glass slippers on her feet: the angel lifts his sword and vanishes: Hannele is dead. Angels lay her in her coffin; a stranger who resembles the village teacher bids her rise: she kneels at his feet: he takes all her lowliness from her, and angels take her to kingdom come.

Verse of great beauty had mingled with the naturalistic prose of *Hannele*: it is by the beauty of its verse that *Die versunkene Glocke* (1896) lives and will live. Only the old witch speaks in (Silesian) dialect, and even this is verse. All the naturalistic stock-in-trade (except the ethics of the rights of passion) is dropped: there are long resonant monologues, the only reality is folded in the spirals

[1] In later editions the title, owing to the indignation of Christians, was changed to *Hannele*.

of a defiant symbol, and the inspiration is intense personal experience and mental conflict. The heroine Rautendelein (Silesian for *rotes Ännlein*) is the first of the red-haired girls who – symbols of art, beauty, mystery, the lure of Bohemian genius – bewitch the heroes of Hauptmann's plays; it is well known that the model was Hauptmann's second wife, a gifted violin-player. The lesson of the play is that the artist must live in loneliness, out of society, but in communion with nature, here symbolized by sprites of woodland and water who have the quaintness of Böcklin's mythical figures – the *Nickelmann* rising, reeds in hair, from the well and snorting like a seal, the *Waldschrat*, a horned and goatfoot satyr. Heinrich the bellfounder has cast a wonderful bell which is to ring glad tidings down to humanity from the church on the mountains; on its way uphill the satyr upsets the cart and it tumbles into the mountain lake (the physical elements of nature – *Elementargeister* – are hostile to mental striving); Heinrich drags himself to the witch's hut, where he is tended by Rautendelein, with whom he is happy and inspired; the Philistine forces (parson, schoolmaster, barber) fetch him back to the village; but he cannot live there, and he finds his way back to the mountains to die on a last kiss of Rautendelein, who has joined the old watersprite at the bottom of his well (beauty, denied the struggling tormented artist, is the prey of primitive brute strength). Beauty at which all hands snatch, and which is crushed by the grasp of force, is the symbol, too, of the weird play *Und Pippa tanzt* (1906); Pippa (the name was taken from Browning) – frail as a Venetian goblet of cut glass – is rescued from those who pursue her by a consumptive apprentice on his way through the packed ice and snow of the Riesengebirge to the fairy world of Venice. She dies; Michel (i.e. *der deutsche Michel*, the dreamer, the poet) goes blind, but he sees Venice, and Pippa dances in his dreams: beauty, which shatters in the grasp of force, is only seen and possessed by the blind.

In three plays Hauptmann goes back to the old German period. *Der arme Heinrich* (1902) dramatizes the legend of the knight sick with leprosy who is told that only the blood of a maiden can save him; the daughter of the farmer at whose house he has found refuge offers the sacrifice (the stirrings of puberty move her as they did Hannele), but the knight, transformed morally by the miracle of love he beholds, stays the surgeon's knife, is cured by the grace of God, and weds the maid. In *Kaiser Karls Geisel* (1908) there is a contrast of senile eroticism[1] (in Charlemagne) with constitutional nymphomania in a girl of sixteen; the ethic problem is (as in Hebbel's *Agnes Bernauer*) whether one whose life is claimed for the public good has a right to personal indulgence.[2] In another medieval drama, *Griselda* (1909), Hauptmann turns the irritating old legend of wifely humility into a somewhat brutal study of uxoriousness and sadism; that is to say, we have here a husband whose pleasure it is to torture the woman he loves. Ulrich is, like so many of Hauptmann's characters, a pathological case; *'ich begreife es nicht,'* he says to Griselda, *'dass ich dich . . . mit aller erdenklichen Bosheit des Herzens martern muss.'* Marriage he defines as a relationship of hawk and dove, of horse and rider. Since he has the cats poisoned that she strokes it is not surprising that, as in the medieval legend, he is jealous of his own child and takes it away from the mother. Griselda, however, enjoys this cruelty; she has that passivity which is interpreted as masochism. It is in such medical details as this that Hauptmann adds a new – though it may be 'morbid' – phase to the dramatic rendering of psychology, as well as a new (and possible) reading to the apparent strangeness of ancient legends. Dramatically considered, the weakness of such plays is that they end with a query (as already *Das Friedensfest* had done); here Griselda tells her husband that he must love her less; this might indeed cure him, but his nature being what it is, will it?

The plays on legendary subjects (the heroine is usually a half-grown girl) have been classed as *Balladendramen*; one such play, *Winterballade* (1917), is actually called a ballad in the title; it is the dramatization of a tale by Selma Lagerlöf (as *Elga*, 1905, is a dramatization of Grillparzer's tale *Das Kloster bei Sendomir*); three weird Scots lairds, commanders of Scots mercenaries in the pay of the King of Sweden, murder an old clergyman; one of them, Lord Archie, stabs the clergyman's daughter to death; Elsalil, the foster sister of the murdered girl, witnesses the murder, but escapes.

---

[1] A pre-Freudian sketch to be compared with the cruelly elaborated studies of Georg Kaiser; see pp. 391ff.

[2] That is, it is a *Pflichtdrama*. The prototype of this peculiarly Prussian genre is Kleist's *Der Prinz von Homburg* (1821). Other notable *Pflichtdramen* are Paul Ernst's *Preussengeist*, Fritz von Unruh's *Offiziere* and *Louis Ferdinand, Prinz von Preussen*, Hermann Burte's *Katte* and *Herzog Utz*, and Wolfgang Goetz's *Der Ministerpräsident* (1936).

She goes mad. She resembles the murdered girl, and Lord Archie thinks she is the ghost of the girl he has stabbed: there are ghastly love-scenes between the crazy girl and the conscience-stricken laird; Elsalil drives her teeth into Lord Archie's wrist, and clings – it is the bite of a vampire from which he goes mad (occultism is in vogue at this period). The clergyman's son has challenged Lord Archie to a duel, but when he sees that the murderer is crazy he considers himself avenged by the hand of the Lord. With *Der weisse Heiland* (1920) the scene shifts to Mexico: Montezuma welcomes Cortés as the 'White Saviour' promised by old legend, but he himself is the Saviour, who is tortured and put to death by the Spaniards for greed of gold and in the name of religion. The undertone is poignant: in the almost sick denunciation of atrocities perpetrated in the name of fanatic patriotism and religion is to be heard Hauptmann's own disgust in the war years.[1] *Schluck und Jau* (1900) had transferred the main idea (life is a dream) of Christopher Sly's lordship to Silesia; *Indipohdi* (1920) is closely modelled on *The Tempest*: Prospero, dethroned by his son, has been wrecked on a Pacific island, where he is hailed by the Indians as the long-promised White Saviour. With him is his daughter (red-haired), who has grown up on the island; hunting an eagle on the mountains she meets a youth who turns out to be her own brother, wrecked in his turn; she falls in love with him, and proclaims her intention of living with him, even when she learns the relationship. (Incest[2] becomes a favourite theme at this period; it occurs, e.g., in Leonhard Frank's *Bruder und Schwester*, Hesse's *Demian*, Bierbaum's *Samalio Pardulus*, Thomas Mann's *Wälsungenblut*, Herbert Eulenberg's *Anna Walewska*, Fritz von Unruh's *Ein Geschlecht*, Max Brod's *Lord Byron kommt aus der Mode*, Kasimir Edschmid's *Lord Byron*.) The old magician, rather than sanction human sacrifices, which he has abolished, ascends a volcano, and (like Hölderlin's Empedocles) descends into the crater: his son and daughter are to rule united.

[1] The source is more or less Eduard Stucken's novel *Die weissen Götter* (pp. 273-4); Kotzebue's *Die Spanier in Peru* (1796; adapted by Sheridan as *Pizarro*) and Wolfgang Kirchbach's (1857-1906; one of Conrad's Munich circle) *Des Sonnenreiches Untergang* (1891) were also probably read.

[2] The motif had been handled before World War I, but the difference in treatment can be seen by comparing (e.g.) Anzengruber's *Schandfleck*, where sexual love fades when the relationship is discovered, with the consummation justified by the example of Byron.

Veland[1] (1925), in which the legend of Wayland the Smith is dramatized, is another study of sadism, and thus to some extent it repeats *Griselda*: here Veland enslaves Bödwild by twisting her hair round his fists and raping her, and the measure of her debasement by the (at first) forced exercise of the sex function is that of her passion for this man who 'bends her like a bow'. *Veland* can hardly be given dramatic value unless it is classed as a *Märchendrama*, but – though Veland is a god and though the finale symbolizes the self-liberation by rebellion of all oppressed workers – the general spirit is not that of the *Märchendrama*, nor could it well be so as a study of sadism. Veland can work magic, but he can only free himself from bondage by constructing wings to fly with. Hauptmann has de-humanized an old tale which has its own satisfying symbol of patient human endeavour. Masochism is again the theme of Hauptmann's next play, *Dorothea Angermann* (1926); the heroine is a parson's daughter who is seduced by a cook; he drags her through the mud, but does not destroy her devotion to him. The very title of *Spuk* (1929) hints at Hauptmann's progressive obsession by demonism; there are two plays in the volume, *Die schwarze Maske* and *Hexenritt*; in the former there is a gigantic nigger who blackmails his former mistress, now the wife of a burgomaster; the second is a Swedish scene with Satanism and a vampire. The title of *Vor Sonnenuntergang* (1932) seemed to hold forth a promise of cessation. It is one more study of senile eroticism, but this time an old man's right to the love and possession of a girl is defended as perfectly natural. The hero, a septuagenarian business man who has made his pile, infuriates his family by insisting on marrying a young Kindergarten teacher, and they attempt to foil his plan by suing for the application of legal restraint, which in Germany means immediate deprivation of rights of administration till the case is decided. His son-in-law is appointed curator, with tragic effects. That the play was galvanized into life by the distinguished actor Werner Krauss does not prove the thesis propounded by the drama that neither mind nor sex necessarily decay in advanced age.

It might be charitable not to mention three plays of Hauptmann

[1] Wagner's unfinished opera *Wieland der Schmied* was followed by Franz Held's *Weland der Schmied*, Eberhard König's *Wielant der Schmied* (1911), and Fritz Lienhard's *Wieland der Schmied* (1905). Karl Gustav Vollmöller's *Wieland* (1911) is a cynical travesty of the legend: Wieland is a German aviator, whose first flight is financed by Lord Northwick, proprietor of the *Evening Mail*.

which have always had a bad press. *Die Jungfern von Bischofsberg* (1907) is a comedy in which German humour is at its worst; there are four sisters in a household which copies that of the Thienemann family into which Hauptmann married in his green youth, and an incredibly credulous '*Monstrum in Oberlehrergestalt*'. *Die Ratten* (1911), defined as a '*Berliner Tragikomödie*', is said by Hauptmann to be his very first play; the characters represent the scum of Berlin – a childless woman gets her brother, a bully, to murder the Polish servant from whom she has bought a baby and who wants it back. The *Festspiel in deutschen Reimen* (1913), written to command in commemoration of the German War of Liberation, was hailed with derision when produced; Hauptmann was charged with glorifying Napoleon, whom he brings on to the stage together with the great men of the past – Frederick the Great, Fichte, Hegel, Heinrich von Kleist, Jahn – to interpret the German spirit. That there was a lukewarm acceptance of this play after 1933 decides nothing; it is a matter of literary history that it was carried by the actor Werner Krauss to Hitler, who accepted it as the *Festspiel* of the Third Empire, the justification being that it did in vision sweep the glorious future – which events were to prove near – when Germany should guide the world to Peace eternal. In form, it is an experiment which uses *Knittelverse* and, though intended for production before great audiences, frames the action as a *Puppenspiel*. Definitely anti-Nazi is the one-act play *Die Finsternisse*, which was written in 1937 but not published till 1947. The first title was *Requiem*, and it was written to honour a Jewish friend, whose family had been forced to bury him clandestinely. Though he was treated with suspicion Hauptmann remained in Germany, but reprinting of his works was forbidden and some of his plays were banned.

In his 'prentice days Hauptmann had written a short tale: *Der Apostel* (1890), at once a prose poem and a subtle presentment of religious mania. The kernel of the story is a dream of the *unio mystica*: the 'apostle' dreams that Jesus appears to him, and that the apparition cures him of the strange sensations of his brain. It is a coming of peace. This dream and the results of it are repeated in *Der Narr in Christo Emanuel Quint* (1910). In this novel Hauptmann has taken up the subject of his early short story, and, repeating some of the details, has worked out a more prosaic exposition of religious mania. Many Messiahs have appeared in the world, and Hauptmann lights up, sympathetically, the genesis and growth of their delusions, as well as the effect of their preaching on credulous minds. It is perhaps unfortunate that the career of his hero is so closely modelled on that of Jesus; for even to free-thinkers who take the book as it is meant, as an interpretation of the Gospels, the taking over of fact after fact – for instance, the hovering doves when Quint is baptized – will seem too obviously inartistic; while to some, of course, the story will be blasphemy. Again, the novelist has kept too close to science to keep the illusion of art; the events are so scientifically possible that they are improbable. The Moravian atmosphere of Silesian mountain villages, however, the atmosphere in which Hauptmann grew up, is wonderfully well reproduced; we are made to feel that religious revivals are just as inevitable among these weavers and tillers of the soil as they are in Wales. In *The Fool in Christ*, as in other books by Hauptmann, there is a struggle between the spirit and the flesh; but Emanuel Quint conquers the flesh by persuading himself that he is a spirit. This belief explains his teaching. He thinks that the Lord's Prayer is an address to the Ghost – that is, to the God-Spirit in man. It is with the spirit, therefore, that he baptizes. But he that is baptized of the spirit is born again of the spirit, and is therefore the Son of God. Quint merely wishes to save men from their dead selves – i.e. their bodies – by making them spirits, or God; but his hearers do not follow his admirably simple reasoning. To the learned among them it seems labyrinthine madness; to the starving peasants it seems to be the self-glorifica-tion of the Messiah, and as such they worship him, forming a community which wallows in mad orgies till he forbids them to read the Bible, the source of their delusions and selfish hopes. Quint is a prophet preaching in the wilderness; what his disciples want is not the kingdom of the spirit but better times. In the end he wanders about Germany, knocking at doors and saying he is Christ; and he is last seen in the mountains of Switzerland. When his corpse is found after the spring thaw there is a sheet of paper in his pocket, and on it, still legible, are the words: 'The mystery of the kingdom?' With this query the book ends.

Apart from the religious and psychopathic problems, there is much that is interesting in *The Fool in Christ*. There is an auto-biographical element: Kurt Simon is clearly a picture of Haupt-mann as an agricultural student; none the less self-portraiture is

Dominik, the Breslau student whose teachers will not allow him to come up for his examination 'on the ground of moral delinquency'. The period of Quint's appearance is set about 1890, a time when all Germany was in a ferment; and we have transparent portraits of celebrities of that time and after, e.g. Peter Hullenkamp is the hallucinated poet Peter Hille, the picturesque vagrom man among the naturalists.

There is an autobiographical substratum, too, in Hauptmann's second long novel. In 1884, while studying sculpture in Rome, he had been laid up with an attack of typhoid fever, and probably his life was saved by his *fiancée*, who came from Germany to nurse him. Ten years later he visited America. These are the two ex- periences which form the groundwork of *Atlantis* (1912). There is much else that is obviously autobiographical; probably the hero Friedrich von Kammacher, whose experiments in bacteriology have ended in a fiasco, is as much Hauptmann himself as Vockerat is in *Einsame Menschen* or Heinrich in *Die versunkene Glocke*. While Friedrich's scientific reputation was being torn to shreds his wife had gone mad; these two threads which the Parcae had woven into his life had snapped, but a third thread, his passion for a little vampire of a dancing girl, is still whole. He takes a berth on a steamer by which she is travelling to New York; and more than half of the book is taken up with the life on board the *Roland* till it is rammed by a derelict, with the escape of a boatful of passen- gers, including the doctor and his dancing girl, and with their rescue by a schooner. Minute as the description is, there is not a moment's languor; and accounts of actual shipwrecks by survivors seem illusory after the unerring balancing of psychological states which even Hauptmann could probably not have written if he had not been a pupil of Forel.[1] Moreover, the events as described are strangely prophetic of the disaster to the *Titanic*, which occurred shortly afterwards. In New York, Friedrich whistles his dancing girl down the wind, joins a circle of artists, and takes lessons in sculpture, at which he had tried his hands in his youth, from Eva Burns. But he cannot free his mind from the experiences of the shipwreck, and he would become a maniac if the 'poisons and putrid matter' in his body did not end his consciousness by an

---

[1] August Forel's *Die sexuelle Frage* (1904), Mantegazza's *Physiologie der Liebe*, and Krafft-Ebing's *Psychopathia sexualis* had considerable influence on this period.

4

attack of typhoid fever. He is nursed back to life by Eva Burns, and, his hysterical wife having in the meantime died to make way for the 'healthy woman' of so many of the novels of the period, he returns with her to Europe.

Greek paganism which literally amounts to phallus-worship gives a disquieting fascination to the novel *Der Ketzer von Soana* (1918). The hero is an Italian priest in Ticino, who, to unite himself with a beautiful girl, herself the child of incest, forsakes his creed and lives as a goatherd. The intention – Eve rules all, and there is no help for it – sounds ecstatic or hopeless according to attitude from the words in which the narrator, who as he descends the mountain meets the woman coming up, describes her: 'she rose up from the depths of the world – and she rises and rises, into eternity, as the one into whose merciless hands heaven and hell are delivered up.' That is, a man cannot escape love. That woman cannot deny herself to love is demonstrated with sly irony in *Die Insel der grossen Mutter* (1924). A ship is wrecked on the coast of a South Sea island: only the women escape, with one lovely boy. The women establish a matriarchy. In due course babies arrive: there is an Indian god on the island. The first child is looked upon as Messiah. As the boys grow up they are banished to Manland, whence in due course they return to conquer their willing mothers and sisters. *Phantom*, *Aufzeichnungen eines ehemaligen Sträflings* (1922) describes the inner life and transformation of a criminal. The hero of *Wanda* (1928) is yet another of Hauptmann's alcoholic artists: he pursues a vampire of a girl, who prefers to be attached to a circus.

The seizure of resistless bodies and souls by eroticism is again the theme of *Das Buch der Leidenschaft* (2 vols., 1929-30), in which the autobiographical element (the form is that of a diary) is patent – the whole book makes the impression of being a hysterical excuse for the neurotic implications of *Einsame Menschen* and *Die versunkene Glocke*. The *mot de Cambronne* with which Goebbels in 1933 hailed the burning by students of literary perversions might well have included this *Book of Passion*, for in set words it defends that *mariage à trois* which so many literary discussions (p. 27), as well as the tragedy of the poet Bürger, have shown to be immoral because destructive to at least one of the three. Interesting is the hero's account of the building of his castle in the Riesengebirge; here, at Agnetendorf, in 1899 Hauptmann built his own mansion.

The vampire in this *roman à clefs* is a Jewess from Odessa, 'white as milk and black as night' – '26 *Jahre höchstens war diese blutlos-wächserne Frau, die ihren Mann verlassen hat.*' The hero meets her while studying in Rome, where she is the mistress of an artist who says she is dead – and quotes Byron's *Bride of Corinth*. There is autobiographical interest too in the fantasy *Die Spitzhacke* (1930), in which Hauptmann pays a tribute of piety to the old inn he was born in, and where, too, the tragedy dramatized in *Fuhrmann Hen-schel* had taken place: he sleeps there before it is pulled down, and is visited (in dream) by the heraldic beasts which provide the familiar signs of inns. *Das Meerwunder* (1934) is another fantasy with a sailor's yarn and the South Seas and a mermaid. *Das Märchen* (1941), as Hauptmann acknowledges, directly follows the lines of Goethe's symbolic tale of the same title; how much in these closing years of his life the musings of *der alte Goethe* were in his mind is still further proved by his *Mignon* (1947), which was written in 1944. This, his last work to be completed (his long novel *Der neue Christophorus*, which was to be the final expression of his mysticism, remained a fragment), was written in 1944. It is again autobio-graphical in the sense that the gist of it is made up of the inner longing and the dreams of the writer. He who tells the story has fled from the humdrum life of duty to the magic of the Lago Maggiore, and here he meets a slip of a girl, a dancer who has run away from her father's itinerant circus and is on the tramp from inn to inn with an old beggar. They are Goethe's Mignon and Harper come to life again; and Goethe himself is recreated, as a kind of yokel. Mignon as a fairy being must fade out of the trammels of reality, and as she dies it is borne in on the teller of the tale why the incarnation of a poet's longing incorporates also the problem of life: whether what is demonic in our nature should prevail over what is factual.

Two of Hauptmann's works, the novel *Im Wirbel der Berufung* (1936) and the play *Hamlet in Wittenberg* (1935), complement each other, and, by making the problem of Hamlet serve as a symbol of life, in some sort continue Goethe's *Wilhelm Meister*. *Im Wirbel der Berufung* is in substance a re-hash of the old *homme incompris* matter – but this time there is a noble princess (of the very duo-decimo sort) as well as the inevitable intellectually independent little minx (this time not quite red-haired – '*sie hat einen Schwall goldbrauner Haare*'). Both ladies have the artistic temperament, but the Apollo-like princess yearns for the world of commoners as well; to her, as she inhales her endless chains of cigarettes, common clay has a reek which is not so rotten as that of any Court. Nevertheless, since the poet-hero takes advantage of an attack of haemorrhage (the end of the book finds him dubiously repentant at Davos) to avoid abducting her at her own special request, she has to put up with an English prince. One comforting feature of the book is that the hero gets a good dressing down from the doctor who attends his wife; this lady, true to Hauptmann's domestic type, is devoted, dull, and depressed by child-bearing. The scene of the action is a 'Residenz' on the coast of Rügen; since the island of Vilm is seen from the town it is obviously Putbus. The poet, whose arrival arouses interest even in the Castle, hobnobs with a company of ragtag and bobtail actors; and here comparison with *Wilhelm Meister*, inevitable in this novel, betrays Hauptmann's weakness in the creation of really human and lovable types. The strayed poet, Emanuel Gotter, is invited to direct a performance of *Hamlet* to celebrate the Prince's birthday; and the rehearsals provide Hauptmann with an opportunity of gradually unfolding his solution of certain problems of the play. The backbone of his argument is that Laertes as a rebel is impossible, that his role as such is due to an accidental transposition of names in the stage manuscript, and that, therefore, the rebel leader is not Laertes, but Hamlet. The whole drama may be interpreted as a *Leichenspiel*, a genre of drama connected with the cult of dead heroes in post-Homeric Greece, and in this light the ghost, for whose pacification all the blood is shed, is the most important character as he is the prime mover in the play. Hamlet's garb of black fits in with this interpretation, for the animals sacrificed in *Heroenkult* had to be black. The key to the theme both of *Hamlet* and of this novel is the vampire-motif: even the Princess has 'lips and nose like a bat'; and indeed Gotter comes to realize that as poet he has two series of vampires sucking his heart's blood: his calling ('*Berufung*') and women. To Hamlet his father's ghost is a vampire; and since Shakespeare is Hamlet and since Gotter (that is, Hauptmann, or the god-poet?) is Hamlet the theme stands clear. In the novel we are told that Hamlet – the first modern man, since blood-revenge was alien to his nature – would have saved himself if he had allowed his mother to persuade him not to return to Wittenberg – for heroic ghosts cannot do blood-sucking abroad. In *Hamlet in*

Wittenberg, however, Hamlet is ethically transformed (*gewandelt*) from a libertine of the Prince Hal sort because his father's ghost – like Undine he rises from a well in the courtyard – appears to him in a German castle and calls him home to sweep to his revenge. One of Karl Gutzkow's (1811-78) first dramatic attempts was a *Hamlet in Wittenberg*, but Gutzkow of course could never have conceived a Hamlet so pathological and nightmare-ridden as Hauptmann's 'Prinz Trauermantel', whose ambition it is to be a 'lecturer in poetics' (*Lektor für Poetik*). He practises *collegium logicum* in an interview with Magister Melanchthon, whom he assures that he is ripe for death; and to Melanchthon's charge that no puddle is too filthy for him to wallow in he replies that all precious things come from the muddied earth and that the ecclesiastical gentry, if they were consistent, should call the womb of woman filth and slime. What Hauptmann is touching here is the problem of royalty, or rather of the contact of royalty with commoners (as in the Hamlet novel; and Hauptmann's son married a duodecimo princess). Melanchthon drops logic for indignation when Hamlet asks him to marry him to the prostitute gipsy with whom he is living – to a succubus. Melanchthon protests! In the light of the theories exposed in *Im Wirbel der Berufung* this would seem to indicate the main theme of the twin book: Hamlet is the poet blessed by God with the power of idealizing dirt and with the double vampire sucking the blood of his brain. And so: *To be or not to be?* A play about the Inquisition, *Magnus Garbe*, though it was not published till 1942 (in *Das Gesammelte Werk*) was written in 1914-15; it is a scathing attack on religious fanaticism; stylistically it must be classed as *Surrealismus*.

In 1907 Hauptmann visited Greece, and described his experiences in *Griechischer Frühling* (1908). After this a species of Hellenism crops up in this work and that, but it took some time to ripen, and in his case it was not the ultra-refined Hellenism of Winckelmann and Goethe; so far as it was Greek at all it was Dionysian and Orphic. But in his first Greek play, *Der Bogen des Odysseus* (1914), it can be seen that the journey had deepened his conception of pagan myth and given a new sunniness and plasticity to his work. This drama of the return of Ulysses to Ithaca has something of the sunny mood of Homer; the action is mythical and impossible, but the interest never flags. Typically the opening scene is outside a farm with a swineherd rubbing his bow with tallow. These pleasantly contriving gods of Homer yield the stage in a tetralogy of Greek plays, written during the Second World War, to the chthonic deities of pre-Aeschylean Greece. Hauptmann on his visit to Delphi had come to the conclusion that 'the bloody root of tragedy lies in blood sacrifices'; and his Iphigenia, as the priestess of the moon-goddess Hecate, offers human sacrifices as part of the ritual to which she is dedicated. Following up the outlines in Goethe's *Italienische Reise* of a projected drama with the same title, Hauptmann had first written *Iphigenie in Delphi* (1941), which is chronologically the fourth of the tetralogy; he had then added *Iphigenie in Aulis* (1944); then followed the two centre pieces, *Agamemnons Tod* and *Elektra*, both in 1947. The *Atriden-Tetralogie* has clearly the psychopathic mood of the war years, and what is revealed is that in the cruelty and lust of destruction of our own day we have the survival, masked by illusory religions and spurious passions such as false patriotism, of primitive states of mind; Agamemnon has the brain-storms of a dictator who for self-aggrandisement sacrifices all that should be dear to him.

In the thirties Hauptmann produced a chain of what may be called romantic plays, somewhat light or even flimsy in texture, dream-like or fantastic: *Die goldene Harfe* (1932), *Das Hirtenlied* (1935) are of this type. Medieval legend and folklore provide the matter of *Die Tochter der Kathedrale* (1939) and (Hauptmann's last comedy to be completed) *Ulrich von Lichtenstein* (1939), in which an old Minnesinger roams the land dressed in women's clothes and parading as Frau Venus, as he does in the strange verse epic he wrote about himself and his antics.

As a lyric poet Gerhart Hauptmann hardly counts. As a member of the Friedrichshagen circle and of *Durch* he wrote lyrics in the style of the day; his *Nachtzug*, for instance, is clearly an echo of certain poems in Holz's *Buch der Zeit*. He collected this early verse in *Das bunte Buch* (1888), but printed only a limited edition. There is, however, song-like verse in *Die versunkene Glocke*; but even the songs of the elves in this lyric play would lose much of their magic if lifted from their organic unity with the dramatic atmosphere. With *Anna* (1921) Hauptmann attempted the rural idyll (*Dorfidylle*); but the hexameters are dreadful, much worse than the Spanish trochees of *Der weisse Heiland*. The poem is autobiographical in its outlines: the hero goes to a farm managed by his uncle, to learn the business of agriculture. There is a girl at the farm, Anna, with whom he falls in love; she denies herself to him because she is honest, and has already fallen to another uncle, a slimy drunkard employed on the farm. She is sacrificed in holy wedlock to a very greasy Moravian brother. In hexameters, too, is *Till Eulenspiegel* (1927), the 'adventures, tricks, pranks, visions and dreams of the great military aviator, tramp, and conjurer'. In the misery of the post-War years a famous aviator preaches truth in the form of mocking jest, finds allegorical answers to the problems of life, and passes from a trickster's buffoonery to the cosmic despair of Faust. His end is that of Emanuel Quint: in Switzerland the Saviour appears to him and in trying to find Him again he falls down an abyss. The epic poem *Der grosse Traum* was begun during the first World War and finished during the second; it was published on his eightieth birthday in 1942. It is again autobiographical and confessional. It is modelled on Dante's *Divina Commedia*: the poet is led by a spiritual guide – Dante himself for a time, but for the greater part of the way by Sataniel, in Gnostic concept the elder son of God – through the nether world. It begins with an invocation to the poet's mother, who as the embodiment of motherhood sits on the throne of God, and to her he returns at the end of his pilgrimage through the City of the Dead. At the end the poet ascends from the fiery centre to the peace of an Alpine landscape. The epic embodies the mysticism of Hauptmann's later years. Of his later volumes of verse *Die Ährenlese* (1939) is followed by *Neue Gedichte* (1946); the poems of the latter date from the 1890's to the 1940's, with nature poetry from the Riesengebirge and verses in the manner of Hafiz.

The autobiographical elements in the two volumes of *Das Buch der Leidenschaft* have been indicated; in the two volumes of *Das Abenteuer meiner Jugend* Hauptmann records the first twenty-five years of his life. He died, struck down by paralysis, shortly after an order of expulsion from his Silesian castle at Agnetendorf had reached him from the new Polish government. In the previous February he had by an unlucky chance witnessed the destruction of Dresden. He was buried at Hiddensee, that island with its long thin line of sand dunes that flanks Rügen in the Baltic; here he had spent his summers throughout the great part of his life.

The time is not yet ripe for an assured judgment on Gerhart Hauptmann's place in literature. He has written absolute rubbish;

one need only point to his prose versions of *Lohengrin* and *Parsival*[1] published in 1914 as a volume of the Ullstein-Jugendbücher; here there is absolute incomprehension of the beauty and meaning of the medieval tales; or there is a cynical distortion of them – 'for a handful of silver'. In Hauptmann's later years there is either pandering to the call of the public for sensational or erotic literature or there are obsessional themes. In any case his range is extremely limited; time and time again he portrays himself and makes capital of the same domestic conflict. There can be no doubt, however, that in the history of the drama he will always have a prominent place; his form of drama may not, according to Lessing's canons, be drama at all, since for 'hero' it substitutes the lurid illumination of a pathological state, but it bears the impress of an interesting personality; and his experiments and successes mark a new period in the history of the German stage. All his good work is on the side of progress and uncompromisingly bold; and for this reason he only just managed under the Nazi régime to save his face: he was branded as *volksfremd* because his work has no sense unless it defends the right of the individual – even to be immoral.

In every literary movement that pushes forward to extremes there is a group of cautious adherents who trail along with them something of the paraphernalia of the old school. They are followers, but not pioneers. In the period of naturalism they are classed, as far as the theatre is concerned, as *Kompromissdramatiker* (Sudermann, Fulda, Halbe, Otto Ernst), but they feuilletonize the novel just as much as they blend old and new in the drama. Both in drama and novel the typical pseudo-naturalist is HERMANN SUDERMANN (1857-1928). He has related the story of his hard youth in *Das Bilderbuch meiner Jugend* (1922). Born in East Prussia, he migrated to Berlin, and made a hit in 1887 with his novel *Frau Sorge*, an East Prussian variation of the Romeo and Juliet theme,[2] which already shows the salient features of Sudermann's novels: his characters are shown in grim contest with conditions imposed upon

---

[1] After Wagner's two operas and Wilhelm Hertz's (1835-1902) fine translation of *Parzival* (1898), the most notable poetic adaptation is that of Albrecht Schaeffer (p. 153). Vollmoeller's *Parzival: Die frühen Gärten* is a series of impressions in Stefan George's manner.

[2] A favourite motif of *Dorfnovelle* and *Bauerndrama*, e.g. Keller's *Romeo und Julie auf dem Dorfe*, Auerbach's *Erdmute*, Anzengruber's *Der Meineidbauer* and *Doppelselbstmord*.

them by the sins of others. *Frau Sorge* is the story of a poor boy
with a bad father; the dice of fate are loaded against him, but he
works his way to success. It is a *Bildungsroman* with a restricted
framework; whereas the *Bildungsromane* of the classical and romantic periods took their hero through phases of mental development
to a high stage of culture, the idea of *Frau Sorge* is success by work.
In this it follows Freytag's *Soll und Haben* and Julian Schmidt's
dictum blazoned thereon that the novel must seek the Germans
where they are at their best, at their work. It was to have a long
series of successful imitations, the best known of which is Gustav
Frenssen's *Jörn Uhl*. *Frau Sorge* is generally recognized as the progenitor of Frenssen's tale, but it does not seem to have been
noticed that there is a striking similarity between *Frau Sorge* and
Marie von Ebner-Eschenbach's *Das Gemeindekind*, which appeared
in the same year; in both tales the progress of the hero is shown
from childhood upward; he has to suffer for the sins of his father;
and in both tales there is symbolic use of a *'Lokomobile'*. How
loosely attached Sudermann is to consistent naturalism can be seen
by a comparison of the two novels: whereas Marie von Ebner-
Eschenbach is consistently scientific in her consideration of the
effects of heredity (the ending, as cautious as that of *Das Friedensfest*, leaves it questionable whether the boy will overcome his
hereditary tendencies or not – he relinquishes love because he is
conscious of homicidal passion), Sudermann, after letting his hero
overcome his adversaries by a show of physical courage (as Ebner-
Eschenbach does) ends with romantic happiness. The headlong
rush of action of Sudermann's narrations is seen at its best in *Der
Katzensteg* (1889); the period is that of the Napoleonic wars, but
the interest is psychological, not to say erotic (the hero loves his
dead father's sweetheart). Sudermann had begun with a collection
of short stories: *Im Zwielicht* (1886), trivial imitations of Maupassant; the short stories of *Geschwister* (1888) have that glowing
depiction of sensuality – hot blood and full flesh – which is the
note of his later fiction.

The success of *Vor Sonnenaufgang* was disputed; the first over-
whelming success of the new movement was that of Sudermann's
Die Ehre (1889). Looking backward now, one can see that the
success may have been due not to the identification of the drama
with the naturalistic movement, but to its skilful combination of
the old stage technique with the new social feeling. It was a

modernized *bürgerliches Trauerspiel* with the traditional contrast of classes, conflict between children and parents, augmented by a cynical valuation of sexual 'honour'. The scene is a house in Berlin; the front part is inhabited by a rich man, and the rear by the family of a man who is employed in the rich man's factory. The situation (*Vorderhaus und Hinterhaus*) became famous. There is a son and a daughter in each family; in the symmetry of the play (a dramatic chiasmus) the daughter of the rich man and the son of the poor man have risen above class prejudice, while the son of the rich man and the daughter of the poor man are moral degenerates; the good daughter and the good son are lovers; the poor man's daughter has been seduced by the rich man's son. The mouthpiece for the idea of the play (culture's elastic conception of 'honour') is Graf Trast, who has had to give up his career as an officer because of his inability to pay a gambling debt; he has since made a fortune in business. The end is that the naughty girl is paid off, while the son from the rear (a good match because he is Trast's heir) marries the girl at the front. As things are, the dishonoured girl will have a better chance of making a decent marriage (she has a dowry) than if she had been a virgin; Trast, who points this out, says that he is as raw as nature and as cruel as truth.

Die Ehre is, after all, constructed on the French model, and is in the line of Scribe and Sardou: Graf Trast is the *raisonneur* who voices the idea round which the characters turn. To this careful French technique Sudermann owed the success of the majority of his plays; when he deserted it, as in his comedy *Die Schmetterlings-schlacht* (1895), to attempt *milieu*-painting, he failed entirely. The production of his second play, *Sodoms Ende*, was at first forbidden by the police; when it was produced in 1890 it turned out to be a crass picture of just that stratum of Berlin society which bought theatre tickets and made or damned plays. Sodom is the Berlin society of the day; a young painter is seduced and debased by a rich dame; he comes home drunk in the dead of night and violates his foster-sister, a mere child; she rushes out and drowns herself, and he dies of haemorrhage. The next play, *Heimat* (1893), is well known in England as *Magda*: Sarah Bernhardt and Mrs Pat Campbell played the title-role. The characters are not really new: there is an old retired officer ('*der polternde Vater*'); his daughter, who had run away from home and now comes back as a famous singer ('the woman with a past'), and the man who seduced her when she was a girl, now a man of position. The latter is willing to marry a *prima donna*; and when the father hears the whole story he sees no other way out; the lady, however, has developed more than her chest; she despises the man who had abandoned her; her father levels a pistol at her, but has an apoplectic fit, and falls dead before he can pull the trigger. *Heimat* has again the traditional elements of the *bürgerliches Trauerspiel*: conflict between father and daughter, between passion and respectability, between social strata (here middle-class society and Bohemianism).

Das Glück im Winkel (1896) leaves the Sodomic city for the landed estates of the junkers, who by Sudermann's showing are as morally rotten as the Berlin plutocrats. In this play we get Sudermann's first type of the rural superman, to whom any woman is fair game; '*Ich will Weiber . . . ,*' he says, '*Ich brauche Weiber . . . Ich kann nicht leben ohne Weiber.*' The woman here concerned is a friend of his cold-blooded wife; she is poor, but, as von Röcknitz (with his experience) can see through her dress, she is full passionate woman. This contrast of cold dignified dame and hot lover is the theme both of Sudermann and Eduard von Keyserling, and by comparing these two writers of East Germany we can see where Sudermann fails: Sudermann gives us sheer brutality while Keyserling very delicately shows the inevitability, given the race and the *milieu*, of both the chaste lady on the one side and the sensual violence of junker and female inferior on the other. The heroine of *Das Glück im Winkel*, like Lessing's Emilia Galotti, fears her blood, and to escape the danger she marries the headmaster of a village elementary school, but von Röcknitz, finding her out, forces a confession that she loves him, and she is only saved from suicide by the generous intervention of her husband, who is warned by his blind daughter (by an earlier marriage). And so the woman's lot will be that happiness in a lost corner which, as the revelation of character in the play demonstrates, may be the irony of life. A volume of three one-act plays, *Morituri* (1897), contains what is generally agreed to be Sudermann's masterpiece – if he was capable of a masterpiece. This is *Fritzchen*. A lieutenant of dragoons, Fritzchen, comes home unexpectedly, to the delight of his invalid mother, his father (a fiery old officer of his son's regiment), and his cousin, whom in the natural course of things he should marry – but his father had told him to sow his wild oats first. He has to tell his father that he has come home because he has been turned out of his regiment – another officer had found him with his wife, and had horse-whipped him. Fritz to his father's angry question answers that he had been unable to use his sword, – because it was not handy. . . . Since he has been thrashed there is even the question whether he is entitled to fight a duel (*satisfaktionsfähig*). The tension is relieved when news comes that the regimental *Ehrenrat* permit the duel, and the play ends with a poignant farewell. It must be the last, for the injured officer is the crack shot of the regiment. Father and cousin bear up, like true Prussians; the mother does not know. Of the other two *Morituri* playlets *Teja* is a somewhat melodramatic but touching depiction of the last phase in the history of the East Goths in Italy (Teja, the last King of the race, marches out with the remnants of his army to meet a hero's death on the slopes of Vesuvius), while *Das Ewig-Männliche* – in verse which imitates the clever rhyming of Ludwig Fulda's versions of Molière – cynically shows that men, if real males (but there is a costume contrast of the doll-like dandies of Courts), are eternally fooled by the cat-like playing of glamorous woman. *Teja* had been a first slight essay in the historical drama; *Johannes* (1898) is a determined effort to capture a place by the side of Hebbel, whose dramatic manner is closely followed: the period is at a turning of history, and there is religious or social symbol as the essential theme of the action. The hero is John the Baptist, and he perishes because of the conflict between his fighting fervour and the news that reaches him that the Messiah, of whom he is the forerunner, is preaching love – which is an utter shock to his virility. And so he cannot cast the first stone at Herod and Herodias and Salome. The play, though its ethic pretension is well posed, is no more than a repetition of *Sodoms Ende*; in both plays the appeal to the audience must be in the dazzling picture of the rottenness of society. An equally ambitious attempt is *Die drei Reiherfedern* (1899), a verse *Märchenspiel*; Sudermann had a strange illusion that it was his best work. With *Johannisfeuer* (1900) he returned to the East Prussian scene and the right of any junker to any girl on his estate; the action glaringly but effectively uses symbol – leaping through fire in the night of the summer solstice (*Johannisnacht*) – to show how Christian morality is burnt up by heathen passion. *Es lebe das Leben* (1902) had an international vogue; it provided Eleonora Duse and Mrs Pat Campbell with an effective role. The heroine (much in the way of Pinero's Second Mrs Tanqueray) is the woman with a past; she has been the mistress of the best friend of her husband. With its poignant contrast of Ellen, the innocent young girl in the house, and the woman in whom no sin is suspected, the play is theatrically excellent. *Sturmgeselle Sokrates* (1903) is another venture in a new field, that of political comedy; a company of revolutionaries of the 1848 brand are shown up as, in the light of 1870, wildered Don Quixotes. In *Die Heimat* Sudermann had rehabilitated the woman with a past; in *Stein unter Steinen* (1905) he does for an ex-convict what Victor Hugo had done for Jean Valjean. Here again there is Sudermann's typical contrast of girlish innocence – this time the girl is deformed, but longs for children – with experienced brutes. The plays which followed hardly seem to be worth mention.

There will always be the question whether Sudermann is not better as a novelist than as a dramatist. *Iolanthes Hochzeit* (1892) is humorous but offensive to good taste. The characteristic novels of the later Sudermann are *Es war* (1894), with its peculiarly vile type of the East Prussian junker, and *Das hohe Lied* (1908), which, after the preliminary chapters, returns to Berlin. *Das hohe Lied* has all Sudermann's breathless rush and all his heaped sensationalism, and its ruthless veracity is relieved by his saturnine humour. Three spheres of Berlin life are photographed: the corrupt military circles form the background, and the life of plutocrats in the centre weaves into that of artists and authors in the foreground, while courtesans bind group to group. The heroine is the daughter of a musical genius who runs away from the odour of the kitchen and leaves behind him the score of an oratorio, 'The Song of Songs', which symbolizes the art of the future and echoes into the deeps of depravity in which it is carried about. In this novel woman is again dominated, in the Nietzschean sense, by the 'blond beast'. Lilly does not, like Magda, lead her sisters to battle, but yields and clings, only to be broken and cast away. She is initiated into degradation by General Baron von Mertzbach. This loathsome aristocrat is cunningly drawn. We first see him with the girl's eyes, when he comes like a glittering god to the musty circulating library where she dreams of love. Then, chapter by chapter, we hear of his dewlap, his rheumatism, his bow legs, his perversity, and of the hair in his ears, which Lilly first notices at a concert where she has dragged him to hear the Fifth Symphony. From the officers proper she passes to an officer of the reserves, and while his mistress she sees her fill of painters and poets, Secessionists and Symbolists. This is the outstanding part of the book. Sudermann does not paint the aesthetes as decadent; he is hostile, but he gives them their brilliance, their vitality, their rebellious courage. And the moral is that which – illusorily may be – gives its *raison d'être* to Sudermann's best work from *Frau Sorge* onwards: that there must be corruption where there is idleness, and that only in work is salvation – steady, even unremunerative work such as that of the historian of the Emotions, who is the only respectable character in the book. It was this more or less flaunted gospel of labour set in relief against decay which has in later years given Sudermann a kind of renascence in the German film. In the short tales of *Die indische Lilie* (1911) the thrills are again of the physical sort; there is once more the diapason of Sudermannian adjectives: *wonnig, schauernd, zuckend, reifgeküsst*. In *Litauische Geschichten* (1917), however, Sudermann weaves the intimity of his native district – the Memelland – into a series of tales which have the genuine humanity of *Frau Sorge*.

LUDWIG FULDA (1862-1939) has that mastery of form which goes to the making of a first-class translator; and possibly his translations of Molière and Rostand will live longer than his own plays, though *Der Talisman* (1895) and *Der Sohn des Kalifen* (1896) have importance in the revival of the verse *Märchendrama*. Fulda, though there was nothing in his composition (rather that of the cloistered scholar) of social pity, attempted a naturalistic drama in *Das verlorene Paradies* (1890), in which workmen strike and get what they want because their spokesman wins over the employer's daughter.

MAX HALBE (1865-1944) brought the landscapes and the mentality of Eastern Germany, with contrasts of German and Polish character, into the naturalistic play. His *Der Eisgang* (1892) symbolizes in the breaking of the ice on the Vistula the loosed flood-tide of Socialism sweeping away all rotten barriers. Halbe's *Jugend* (1893) was one of the great successes of the period. The scene is in Poland, in the home of an old Catholic priest; with him lives his niece, a girl of eighteen, the child of an unmarried mother. A cousin, who is just about to go to the university, comes on a visit. The two young people are left too much alone, and the girl goes the same way as her mother had done; her half-brother, a species of idiot, aims a bullet at the student; it misses him, but kills the girl. What was new in the play was the psychology of adolescence: these young people awakening to the facts of life expressed their feelings in language not unnatural but charged with poetry; and there was an air of reality and inevitability in the events, which in the girl's case might be explained by the laws of heredity. Other plays which reproduce the atmosphere of Polish West Prussia – Halbe's homeland – are *Mutter Erde* (1897), *Haus Rosenhagen* (1901), and *Der Strom* (1903). In *Der Strom* the climax is once again the breaking of the Vistula ice, this time as the symbol of a family catastrophe. Halbe's other plays have little significance, though his literary comedy *Die Insel der Seligen* (1908) has satirical portraits of Peter Hille and Wedekind. His *Jahrhundertwende: Geschichte meines Lebens 1893-1914* (1935) is important for the inner history of naturalism.

To Hauptmann's school belong the plays of his brother, CARL HAUPTMANN (1858-1921); he was prone to mould the matter and form of his plays (as indeed his brother was, but as he evolved) to the dramatic moods of the moment; thus he progresses from raw naturalism (*Marianne*, 1894; *Die Waldleute*, 1895; *Ephraims Breite*,[1] 1898 – in Silesian dialect) to neo-Romanticism (*Die Berg-schmiede*, 1902, a symbolist *Märchendrama*; *Des Königs Harfe*, 1903). In his trilogy *Die goldenen Strassen* (1916-18) he even moves close to Wedekind, while in stark contrast his *Der abtrünnige Zar* (1920) is a *Legendenspiel*. His novel *Mathilde* (1902), the heroine of which, a factory lass, arrives at a broad contentment in the humdrum existence of her class, is naturalistic; *Einhart der Lächler* (1907) follows the type of the *Bildungsroman*, but continues the development to the death of the hero, with details which fit in with the biography of Gerhart Hauptmann. Wolfram von Eschenbach's *Parzival* (often called the first of the *Bildungsromane*) has been described (adequately to friend or foe) as the story of a perfect fool; and the idea of a simple soul winding his devious and dubious way through the labyrinths of a mysterious world to the clear heights of contentment is the kernel of *Einhart der Lächler*, who never loses the smile of his simple nature. Einhart's father had married the adopted daughter of a rich middle-class family – really the daughter of a gipsy; and the boy feels an urge to follow the gipsies' caravans, but controls his impulses and by the pursuit of art becomes 'Einhart der Meister' and at last 'Einhart der Weise'. The Darwinian doctrine, too, goes to the making of another of

[1] =Brigitte. This *Bauernstück* is in the manner of Anzengruber.

Carl Hauptmann's novels: *Ismael Friedmann* (1912). Ismael Friedmann is the son of a Jew and the blond daughter of a clergyman;
and this racial mixture is responsible for his physical inhibitions,
which drive him to suicide. The discussion of the race question
gave this novel prominence, in spite of the fact that the racial
blend gives the hero an exceptional mind as well as a '*gespaltenes
Wesen*'.

Two dramatists, Georg Hirschfeld and Max Dreyer, scored
notable successes as disciples (to begin with at least) of Gerhart
Hauptmann. GEORG HIRSCHFELD (1873-1943) at the age of twenty-
three made a hit with *Die Mütter* (1896); his later work (*Agnes
Jordan*, 1898) did not fulfil the promise of his elegant youth. His
note is a delicate pencilling of character and wistful mood-painting.
MAX DREYER (1862-1946), a productive but glaringly imitative dramatist with a keen eye on the demands of the moment, began with
uncompromising naturalism; his *Drei* (1892) rehandles Ibsen's
problem of *The Doll's House* (a Nora-like wife leaves her Tesman-
like husband because he suspects the *Hausfreund* of being, like
Ibsen's Dr Rank, a cock in clover); the heroine of *Winterschlaf*
(1895) loves a Socialist, is deflowered by her *fiancé*, whom she does
not love, and strangles herself with her pigtails. The success of
his following plays Dreyer owed to manipulation of intrigue of
the compromise variety. Academically his interest today lies in his
symptomatic handling of motifs: thus *Der Probekandidat* (1900) is
the most definitely Darwinian play of the period, and another forerunner of the '*Lehrer- und Schülerstücke*'. The hero is on trial at a
Gymnasium as a teacher of biology, and lectures to the sixth form
on Darwinian lines. The headmaster and the ecclesiastical authorities are furious, and the iconoclast is forced, under threat of dismissal (which will mean losing the girl he is engaged to, the
daughter of one of the governors of the school), to lecture to his
class in the presence of his colleagues and of these authorities.
Instead of recanting, however, he sticks to his guns. There is
biographical interest in the play: Dreyer had himself been a theological student; and in this *Tendenzdrama* he has the merit of
claiming for the schoolmaster what Anzengruber in *Der Pfarrer
von Kirchfeld* had claimed for the clergyman – the liberation of the
individual from the shackles of officialdom. In another school-play
of Dreyer's, *Die Reifeprüfung* (1932), a schoolboy and a teacher
love the same girl. *Des Pfarrers Tochter von Streladorf* (1909) varies

the theme of Sudermann's *Heimat*: the daughter of a clergyman has given herself in the excitement of the *Johannisnacht* (like the heroine of Sudermann's *Johannisfeuer*) to the son of a wealthy man: after the seduction she weighs him up and decides that he is unfit to be her husband, though he is prepared to jeopardise his career by marrying her; and the old parson agrees that she is right. The title shapes itself on Bürger's famous ballad *Des Pfarrers Tochter von Taubenheim*. Of Dreyer's lighter plays the rococo comedy *Das Tal des Lebens* (1902) has that piquancy of theme for which he depended as a comedy writer: it is a jest on the impotence of reigning families. The village concerned is so called because of the fertility of its inhabitants. On the other hand, the ruling prince of the country has failed to produce an heir, and there is every prospect that Prussia will absorb another duodecimo state when he dies, especially as a rejuvenating elixir has no effect; however the Markgräfin approves of the sentinel who stands at her door, a boy from the Vale of Life; and in due course the elixir is understood to have acted.

III

HUMORISTS, SATIRISTS, SATANISTS AND VISIONARIES

FRANK WEDEKIND (1864-1918) disputed the right of the naturalists to portray their acquaintances in their plays, as, he thought, Hauptmann had done with him in *Das Friedensfest*; he brings this into his farce *Die junge Welt* (1898), in which he satirizes the mania for documentation: one of the characters, a poet, transfers to his note-book every quiver of his wife's soul. Wedekind cannot be called a naturalist because: (*a*) he has no pity; (*b*) the characters and action of his plays are not observed, but invented, i.e. they are caricatures of reality or quite fantastic; (*c*) the form of his plays is not analytic, but synthetic, a film-like sequence of scenes or pictures, as in the old *Sturm und Drang*, with an illusory division into acts. His characters have a habit of speaking as if they were alone on the stage, and what the next speaker says is not necessarily connected with this self-communing; this '*Aneinandervorbeireden*' is typical of Wedekind. The dialogue generally is jerky, as though marionettes were speaking; and Wedekind and his wife acted in his own plays with the stiff movements of wooden dolls. Wedekind is the creator of a new genre, the grotesque drama of manners, and in this respect, as in his rejection of the accepted canons of decency, he is the acknowledged prophet and forerunner of expressionism. To some extent his characters are, as in expressionist drama, types rather than individualized characters. The butt of his vitriolic attack is conventional morality, but he himself, in repeated self-interpretation through the mouth of his characters, claims to be a moralist, and, incredible as it seems to us, the claim has been upheld by the most serious academic critics of Germany. The explanation no doubt is that he came in on a flood-tide of popularity after his death as a critic of

pre-War society; but one asks whether the circus-proprietor who
offered Karl Hetman, the hero of *Hidalla*, obviously intended by
Wedekind as a portrait of himself, a post as clown, was radically
wrong in his estimation; the only objection is that his clowning is
too vile for laughter. His influence on literature, however, both
as regards form and substance, cannot be minimized. With Strindberg he provided a new eroticism; but whereas Strindberg represents woman as subjugating man by the patient exercise of low
cunning, to Wedekind she is a scintillating snake who fascinates
and poisons but can be tamed by brutality, which is the best thing
for her (in the famous prologue to *Erdgeist* man is the tamer with
the whip). To Wedekind as to Strindberg woman, '*das schöne, wilde
Tier*', is the source of all suffering, but while Strindberg hates her,
Wedekind sadistically adores her and paints her as irresistible,
even when she is (literally) smeared with the blood of her victims.
She is the 'earth-spirit' who draws down the mind of man to the
dust; but in the dust man is happy, for 'this bliss of the senses is
the beam of light that pierces the night of our existence'. It is the
cosmic urge, and it is holy, for it serves 'the morality of beauty';
regeneration of the race should come from this love – resistless
and therefore mystical – of the beautiful body of soulless woman.
Even a prostitute is divine, for she is flesh; copulation in a brothel
is, in the sulphurous light of Wedekind's hallucinations, a *unio
mystica*.

With this apostolic preaching of sex goes a corrosive criticism
of institutions and cherished ideals. *Frühlings Erwachen* (1891) initiates a long series of works by other writers in which parents and
teachers are accused of keeping children at the critical stage in
ignorance of the facts of life. During a storm a schoolgirl of fourteen takes refuge with a schoolboy in a barn; she is to have a baby
– to her great surprise –, but dies of means used to procure abortion – of anaemia according to her decent gravestone. It is the
fantastic atmosphere of the play which counts in literary history:
a schoolboy who fails in his examination commits suicide and,
with his head under his arm, meets, in the churchyard, the boy
who is responsible for the baby; the latter, instead of following
him into the grave, follows a *vermummter Herr* (= Wedekind), who
comes along to explain the idiocy of existence. *Erdgeist* (1895) is
the very shrine of Wedekind's eroticism; round the heroine Lulu,
a symbol of soulless woman, a mixture of vampire and vegetable,

dance lovers like moths round a flame. In the sequel, *Die Büchse der Pandora* (1904), long condemned by the censor, Lulu has degenerated into an object bought and sold; in the gruesome scene – very fine as Grand Guignol – at the end she is slit open in a London attic by Jack the Ripper. She shares this thrilling death with a countess who has clung to her with the devotion of a dog and the torments of unsatisfied Lesbian love. But to whatever depths of degradation she sinks she is, in Wedekind's intention, guiltless: within her is an elemental force which drives her, an unconscious victim, to destruction. *Hidalla* (1904) records the squabblings of a sect – 'The International Union for the Breeding of Beautiful Thoroughbreds' – who swear to give themselves in love at first asking to any fellow-member: a deed of public service in the interests of the race, since all are eugenically certified. Only the secretary, Karl Hetman, is deformed[1] and queer; since, however, he has an intellectual fascination the full-blooded females in sheer illogical perversity gravitate to him.

Whether Wedekind's presentation of reality by distortion merely reflects his serio-comic impression that life is a Hell of a joke (*ein höllischer Spass*) – with the joke delightful because it *is* Hell –, or whether, if one penetrates the surface, a more poignant solution is to be found in his personal tragedy of frustration, is problematic. Certainly the unmistakable self-portraiture cuts deeper in *Der Marquis von Keith* (1901) and *So ist das Leben* (1902). In any case, sheer nausea may turn serious students of drama away from experiments in drama that are at least as academically interesting as the equally lurid milestones in literature which we group as *Sturm und Drang*. The Marquis von Keith – title and name are stock-in-trade – is a scoundrel and impostor, but by calculation as well as by the urge of his blood; hereditarily stated, he is the bastard of a mathematician and a gipsy, or, as self-stated, a cross between a philosopher and a horse-thief. One cardinal point of his ethical and commercial creed is: '*Sünde ist eine mythologische Bezeichnung für schlechte Geschäfte*'; but the course of the action and the victory of society as constituted, backed up as it is by massed idiocy, forces him to confess that '*das glänzendste Geschäft in dieser Welt ist die Moral*'. He trains the woman he cohabits with to be such a *Lebenskünstler* as he is himself; but as events prove she too is commercialized; for when

---

[1] Wedekind had a lame foot. The attraction of contraries explains his admiration of strong men, particularly of the circus variety.

the crash comes and he is cornered she accepts the monetarily higher bidder who takes his place as the directing spirit of the gorgeous Palace of Pleasure (*Feenpalast*) which, by an ingenious flotation, he had planned to gild the life of the masses. That the horrible masses should be horrified by the discovery that their benefactor is a scamp is part of life's joke; but that the woman he loves should be as much a scamp as he is is tragically comic – '*Lachen Sie doch, meine Herren,*' he says in another play – and the injunction is revealing – '*dies ist ja alles sehr tragisch*'. He lifts his revolver to shoot himself, but lays it down with the remark that life is a slide ('*Das Leben ist eine Rutschbahn!*'): high and low, up and down, a scamp has always the chance of realizing his dreams and ideals.

The self-portraiture has less appeal in *Zensur* (1908); in *Oaha* (1908) it is repulsive – the titular hero is a formless monstrosity who is wheeled into the editorial rooms of the Munich comic journal *Simplicissimus*, which had printed much of Wedekind's work; the creature is deaf and dumb and the only sound he can make is Oaha! but, such as he is, his wit has made the reputation of the journal. That women flit round any notoriety as moths flit round a flame ('*Wir Künstler sind ein Luxusartikel der Bourgeoisie*') is the theme of *Der Kammersänger* (1897), a short sharp scene showing a tenor beset by nymphomaniac admirers; as he has to catch a train he dismisses the last comer somewhat rudely and comes across her dead body as he leaves the room. *Mit allen Hunden gehetzt*, the middle one-act play of *Schloss Wetterstein* (1910), would shock any psychiatrist by its refinement of the psychology of the lust murder: a man threatens a woman that he will give information about a crime committed by her husband unless she gives herself to him; she detects his diseased state of mind, and so tortures him by the way she offers him her naked body that he shoots himself. *Franziska* (1911) is Wedekind's version of the Faust theme: the heroine makes a pact with a theatrical agent that she will drain the cup of joy to the dregs, which she does, with the inclusion of a Lesbian marriage: nevertheless, like Shaw's Mrs Warren, she ends as a decent woman.

Wedekind's pathetic adoration of the female form gives some justification (if obsessional mania is allowed for – and those feelings which have always gone to the making of poetry) for his short story *Mine-Haha oder über die körperliche Erziehung junger Mäd-*

chen (1903). Typically, for the name of his Institution Wedekind takes a familiar name from Longfellow and turns the solemn sentiment it suggests into a screech. The thesis is that woman is born for the functions of sex. This being granted, girls should be taught to worship their own delightful bodies; they should, for instance, walk on their hands with bare legs poised rapturously aloft. This is true Wedekindian doctrine and the paganism of Greek statues as well: the rhythm in the movements of a woman depends on the structure of her limbs; and for this rhythm, as for dancing, and female pose, and fine ankles Wedekind throughout his work finds expression which goes somewhat to redeem his foulness. [Peter Hille has the same worship of woman's gait in two lines (*Nur ein Weib wandelt. Es ist, und Schönheit weilt von dannen*) of his poem *Schönheit: Sappho an Chloe*.] The Novellen collected in Wedekind's *Feuerwerk* (1905) have their quality in the audacity of their obscenity. The wickedness of such a tale as *Die Schutzimpfung* is incredible: a husband calls on a friend with whom his own wife is in bed; the friend has covered her up with the bedclothes – to take attention off the stockings, which might betray his guest – but rolls the sheets back to her neck – and the husband does not recognize his own wedded wife, but compliments his friend on his good taste. If there is philosophy in this it can only be that husbands, too, should go to school at Mine-Haha; what society needs is not decency but appreciation. The title *Feuerwerk* symbolizes the fire of sex that lights up the bunch of stories, in the first of which, *Der Brand von Egliswyl*, a farmer's boy who has been the village bull falls in love with a cold sort of girl, pines for her, and when at last he climbs through her window in the recognized South German fashion he is chilled to impotence by the very cold night and her cold response, but sets fire to the village to prove to her that he *can* burn. Being the sort she is she says he has hidden himself in her room, and he goes to jail. As a lyric poet (*Die vier Jahreszeiten*, 1905[1]) Wedekind only counts historically. The most typical of his poems were hits in the Überbrettl theatres; as, for instance, *Der Tantenmörder*:

> *Ich hab' meine Tante geschlachtet,*
> *Meine Tante war alt und schwach;*
> *Ich hatte bei ihr übernachtet*
> *Und grub in den Kisten-Kasten nach.*

[1] Reprinted with additions from *Die Fürstin Russalka* (1897).

Da fand ich goldene Haufen,
Fand auch an Papieren gar viel
Und hörte die alte Tante schnaufen
Ohn' Mitleid und Zartgefühl.

Was nutzt es, dass sie sich noch härme –
Nacht war es rings um mich her –
Ich stiess ihr den Dolch in die Därme,
Die Tante schnaufte nicht mehr.

Das Geld war schwer zu tragen,
Viel schwerer die Tante noch.
Ich fasste sie bebend am Kragen
Und stiess sie ins tiefe Kellerloch.

Ich hab' meine Tante geschlachtet,
Meine Tante war alt und schwach;
Ihr aber, ihr Richter, ihr trachtet
Meiner blühenden Jugend-Jugend nach.

'*Kisten-Kasten*' and '*Jugend-Jugend*' are just in the tone of the Über-brettl minstrelsy, which – ejaculatory and slyly or boisterously allusive – made a direct appeal to the risibility of an audience possibly for the most part soaked. The idea of the Überbrettl is set forth by that cracked genius Stilpe, the hero of Otto Julius Bierbaum's novel; actually it was nothing more than what Paris had long known as the literary café (*Le Chat Noir*, etc.); but in Germany the plan fastened on to the declamation by poets in the flesh of their own verse on a miniature stage. When Ernst von Wolzogen took up the idea practically in 1900 and founded *Das bunte Theater* in Berlin, while Otto Julius Bierbaum made an attempt to direct the Trianon Theatre, the movement fell through because of the inadaptability of poets; in Munich, however, a group of poets of whom Wedekind was one kept *Die elf Scharf-richter* going for a time by the mere attraction of their Bohemian intimity. Dehmel, on the other hand, protested against the degra-dation of his poems – some of which are among the most popular hits of the time – by minstrel recitation in what was after all a Philistine atmosphere. But, though the dream of physically linking music-hall and lyric poetry fresh from creation failed to materialize, the collection of verse selected as suitable for such recitation, or written specially for it, had huge sales – *Deutsche Chansons* (1900), with a persuasive preface by Bierbaum.

ERNST FREIHERR VON WOLZOGEN (1855-1934) – he was of that family which plays a part in the story of Schiller's life – had ample versatility but no depth. His humour or satire is that of bold strokes with no nuances; it is rather as a literary record that his comedy *Das Lumpengesindel* (1892), with its picture of the Harts and their friends, keeps its place on the critic's shelf, while his novel *Der Kraft-Mayr* (1897) is read for its portraiture of Liszt and Wagner and its recreation of old Weimar (without the family affection for the place of Helene Böhlau's *Ratsmädelgeschichten*). *Die Kinder der Excellenz*, a social satire, was popular both as a novel (1888) and a comedy, while his novel *Das dritte Geschlecht* (1899) continues that persiflage of the 'new woman' which we find already in Paul Heyse's poem *Frauenemanzipation* (1865).[1]

If popularity and sales were a safe criterion, OTTO JULIUS BIERBAUM (1865-1910) would rank as one of the first writers of the period. He is the type of the gifted University scholar – in Berlin he studied even Chinese – who takes to journalism or light literature much as a prostitute takes to her trade; and if there is poignancy in his work it is because through his extravagant mockery of his heroes there runs – as in the case of Wedekind – a consciousness of frustration (in Bierbaum's case, by too easy success, or by the low instincts of his reading public). His lyric verse[2] – that which he wrote from 1885 to 1900 is collected in *Irrgarten der Liebe* (1901) – is often delightful. It is palpably imitative; but the imitation brings out the charm of the model; as, for instance, in his collection *Nemt, Frouwe, disen Kranz* (1894), in which he recaptures the light lilt and the over-sweet sentiment of the Minnesingers:

> *Es ist ein Reihen geschlungen,*
> *Ein Reihen auf dem grünen Plan,*
> *Und ist ein Lied gesungen,*
> *Das hebt mit Sehnen an,*
> *Mit Sehnen, also süsse,*
> *Dass Weinen sich mit Lachen paart:*
> *Hebt, hebt im Tanz die Füsse,*
> *Auf lenzeliche Art.*

---

[1] Paul Heyse continues the theme in his short story *Abenteuer eines Blaustrümpfchens* (1896).   [2] *Erlebte Gedichte* (1892) was his first volume.

His songs of loose student life (*Gigerlette, Jeanette, Josephine*, etc.) are unforgettable; the immorality may be regrettable, but the insouciance is disarming. The very idiocy of his refrains has a charm; as in his song of the young witch, who rides out into the night air (*Rack, schack, schacke mein Pferdchen*) and all the while hears her baby's laughter (*Kling, ling, klingalalei*). His song *Der lustige Ehemann* was so popular that it more or less discredited the Überbrettl movement:

> *Ringelringelrosenkranz,*
> *Ich tanz mit meiner Frau,*
> *Wir tanzen um den Rosenbusch,*
> *Klingklanggloribusch,*
> *Ich dreh mich wie ein Pfau.*

The first of his satirical novels was *Die Freiersfahrten und Freiersmeinungen des weiberfeindlichen Pankrazius Graunzer* (1895), in which he tilts particularly at the foibles of art circles and parodies the Darwinian theory of natural selection. His great success was the long novel *Stilpe: Roman aus der Froschperspektive* (1897). The model is ostensibly Murger's *Scènes de la vie de Bohème*, but Bierbaum needed no prompting for his presentation of the student's and journalist's life he knew so well. The picture is sufficiently disgusting. Stilpe (like Bierbaum) is a *verbummeltes Genie*, who manages to make a splash in journalism and lays about him as a Berlin critic. The characters of this Berlin Bohème are portraits: *der Bärenführer* is Paul Scheerbart, *der Peripatetiker* is Peter Hille, Casimir is Przybyszewski, and *der Zungenschmalzer* is Julius Meier-Gräfe. There is internal evidence that the far-flung fame of Oscar Wilde – who at the time the novel was written had just been released from prison – shaped the characterization of Stilpe: the chosen colour of both is yellow. The influence of Wilde is patent in the novel *Prinz Kuckuck, Leben, Taten, Meinungen und Höllenfahrt eines Wollüstlings* (1907-8). The model of the hero is said to have been Alfred Walter Heymel, one of the Überbrettl poets; his name in the novel is Henry Felix Hauart, and he is called Prinz Kuckuck because he does not know who his father was and has always nested with other people. His mother is a Jewess, who sees him as rarely as the mother of Wilde's Star Child saw her son; and like the Star Child he denies his mother – for he is an anti-Semite. Like Carl Hauptmann's Ismael Friedmann he – '*eine Fratze zweier Rassen*'

– is cast out by the gentiles; when he sides with the Habsburg party he is hailed with the Shakespearean cry: '*Bravo Jud! Gut gebrüllt, Sarasohn!*' His cousin Berta has an incestuous love for her own brother, but marries Prinz Kuckuck for his money, only to sap his life-force, until he runs his car into the Arch of Triumph and so dies. The fascination of Oscar Wilde comes out in the orgies in which Karl and his cousin indulge, and Felix is offered a boy with the recommendation: '*Alle Engländer besuchen ihn.*' In England the couple (like Dorian Gray) dive into haunts of vice in Whitechapel; the 'Klub der Grünen Nelke' is mentioned, which suggests Robert Hichens's parody on Wilde, *The Green Carnation*. The influence of Huysmans is as patent as that of Wilde, as for instance in Felix's wavering between Catholic sensuality and the delights of the brothel, still more in incidents of the Black Mass. In *Samalio Pardulus*, the first Novelle of *Sonderbare Geschichten* (1908), this *fin de siècle* obsession for sexual perversity is heightened by the Renaissance atmosphere and by the doubling of the motif of incest: an old Italian count goes, dagger in hand, to slay his son and daughter whose sin he knows by the secret of his own blood; he finds them dead, the daughter naked, and in presence of her loveliness he stoically calls to mind what he himself has not dared to do. He has kept the law and lived; they have died young, for beauty's sake. The short stories of *Studentenbeichten* (1892 and 1897) and *Die Schlangendame* (1896) are vignettes of student life; those of *Kaktus* (1898) are mere fooling. The matter of his *Stilpe* was dramatized in *Stilpenkomödien*; an attempt at serious drama with historical colouring is *Stella und Antonie* (1902); the scene is Silesia, the time the beginning of the eighteenth century, and the action suggests the erotic illusions and instability of the poet Johann Christian Günther. One of Bierbaum's best titles to remembrance is that he, together with the art critic Julius Meier-Gräfe, founded the art journal *Pan* (1894-1900) and, in 1900, with Alfred Walter Heymel and Rudolf Alexander Schröder, the literary journal *Die Insel* (1899-1902), which published much of the best work of the succeeding years; at first the publishers were Schuster und Löffler in Berlin but in time these poets created their own publishing firm, the famous Insel-Verlag of Leipzig.

OTTO ERICH HARTLEBEN (1864-1905) comes near to Bierbaum as a *verbummeltes Genie* and as one who debased his great gifts. His humour is genuine and infectious, but it is *Bierhumor*; and, for all the delicacy of feeling that weaves a wistful music through the best of his elegiac verse (*Meine Verse*, 1895), with its flawless form (especially in rhymeless metres), he never did more than write for the moods of the moment, his own and the public's. In his life he lived defiantly through the scandal of the man with two wives; and in his case there was the unedifying spectacle after his death of the two women fighting, by the publication of his letters to them, for his body. His fun is delightfully naughty in his short stories *Die Geschichte vom abgerissenen Knopf* (1893), *Vom gastfreien Pastor* (1895), *Der römische Maler* (1898), and *Liebe kleine Mama* (1904). He is fond of placing the scenes of his fiction in his native district, the Harz Mountains. In his comedies he tilts at the absurdities of decent society (from which, an utter Bohemian, he excluded himself) and at morality, which, in common with many of the exponents of Consistent Naturalism, he regarded as unnatural. In *Angele* (1890) this contempt of morality bears the impress of Nietzsche; in *Hanna Jagert* (1893) the characters progress from Socialism to Nietzschean autocracy; in *Die Erziehung zur Ehe* (1893) and *Die sittliche Forderung* (1897; the theme parodies Sudermann's *Heimat*) the cult of immorality is yet more flagrant. He shared the admiration of his fellow poets for Ibsen, but parodied the master's later symbolist manner in *Der Frosch* (1891). His one-act play *Abschied vom Regiment*,[1] like Sudermann's *Fritzchen* and Schnitzler's *Leutnant Gustl*, plays with the time-honoured conception of military honour, while his very successful but theatrical *Rosenmontag* (1900) was one of those few plays of the pre-War period – Franz Adam Beyerlein's (1871-1949) *Zapfenstreich* (1903) was another – which attacked (and got away with it) the arrogance and profligacy of the Prussian military caste; the play has at least the merit – which it shares with certain of the *Sturm und Drang* dramas – of putting the superiority of caste feeling to the question.

Of the three Ottos who were the accredited humorists of naturalism OTTO ERNST (1862-1926) was the only one with any of the milk of human kindness. Neither Bierbaum nor Hartleben could have written, as Otto Ernst did (e.g. *Appelschnut*), delightful books for children. As a native of Hamburg (he was born in Ottensen) he has that rough Low German dialect colouring which – particularly by contrast with the cynical Munich wit of *Simplicissimus* – seems so boisterously healthy. Himself an elementary school-

[1] In *Die Befreiten. Ein Einakter-Zyklus* (1899).

master before he became an author, he satirized educational pedantries in his comedy *Flachsmann als Erzieher* (1902), in *Jugend von heute* (1900) the megalomania of would-be Nietzschean supermen in the literary world, and in *Gerechtigkeit* (1902) blustering journalists. As a dramatist he fails because he cannot get beyond the rough outlines of conventional types; thus his schoolmasters in *Flachsmann als Erzieher* have their qualities of lustful and tyrannical (the awful headmaster!), sporting, jocular, or born teacher (the awful hero!) stressed almost in the manner of pantomime. Otto Ernst gave an impetus to the revival of the *Bildungsroman* with his to a great extent autobiographical *Asmus Sempers Jugendland* (1905), *Semper der Jüngling* (1908), and *Semper der Mann* (1916), the hero of which rises from the working-classes to be an elementary teacher – a rank which in Germany (since Jean Paul wove the village schoolmaster's life into cloud-rapt idylls) has been associated with culture, influence, and (to quote Sudermann) *Glück im Winkel*.

Satire of the drastic and juicily outspoken Bavarian brand gives its tang to the comedies of JOSEF RUEDERER (1861-1915) and LUDWIG THOMA (1867-1921). Ruederer's *Die Fahnenweihe* (1894) was one of the most successful plays of the period; he was a born dramatist, with a sharply defined sense both of shapely construction and of vivid characterization with hard, cruel lines. *Fahnenweihe* is a pitiless satire of village life; and it has the mark of Ruederer's work generally – the delineation of the Catholic priests as self-serving rogues, and of their parishioners as keen on whatever profit they can get from their subjection to the priests; priest and scamps get off with everything, and decency is so dangerous that only an utter fool will risk it. Ruederer's satire is less bitter in his next comedy, *Die Morgenröte* (1904), which dramatizes the expulsion from Munich in 1848 of Lola Montez, the mistress of Ludwig I. *Wolkenkuckucksheim* (1908), an adaptation of the *Birds* of Aristophanes, was a failure, and Ruederer proved with *Der Schmied von Kochel* (1911) that historical drama was beyond his reach. His novel *Ein Verrückter* (1894) shows what happens to honest men: an assistant teacher actually dares to vote liberal and to say what he thinks; the result is that he is hounded to death by the village priest and the governors of his school. His short stories (*Tragikomödien*, 1896; *Wallfahrer-, Maler- und Mördergeschichten*, 1899) show Ruederer as a master of the grotesque as well as of the ridiculous. Ludwig Thoma, one of the mainstays of *Simplicissimus* (a journal which by the way owes its inception, in 1896, and growth to M. G. Conrad's Munich circle), is best known for his comedy *Moral* (1908), in some sort a rehandling with a crass Bavarian colouring of the Tartuffe theme. Thoma's *Lottchens Geburtstag* (1911) follows up the theme, tongue in cheek, of Wedekind's *Frühlings Erwachen*: a solemn professor insists that children should be taught the facts of life; and when Lottchen, the daughter of a colleague, has her twentieth birthday and is on the point of getting engaged he gets her father, by the exercise of moral pressure, to enlighten the couple. The father finds that the young man, being a zoologist by profession, is already informed of the process in question; while the sly minx of a daughter has actually, unbeknown to all, gone through a course in midwifery. Of Thoma's short stories *Lausbubengeschichten* (1905-7) belong to the most entertaining renderings of Bavarian life and habits; *Altaich* (1918) and *Tante Frieda* (1906) are in the same vein, while *Andreas Vöst* (1906) and *Der Wittiber* (1911) are realistic peasant novels.

Just as we expect British humorists to be on the staff of *Punch*, so German humour has been nourished by the *Witzblätter*, and for that reason hails mostly from Munich. This holds good too of WILHELM BUSCH (1832-1908), the humorist *par excellence* of the previous generation but *facile princeps* – at least so far as pure humour is concerned – to the end of his life. It was while contributing as an artist to *Fliegende Blätter* at Munich that he began to write his humorous verse; this has a double base – Schopenhauer's pessimism and a reaction, natural in Munich, to what must have seemed the pretty-pretty polish of Paul Heyse and the Munich School. The humour depends quite as much on Busch's quaint illustrations – a few black lines bring out the comicality of his figures – as on the drollery of the rhymes, and his caricature fastens on fixed types: the poet (*Dichter Bählamm*, 1883), the painter (*Maler Klecksel*, 1884), the hypocritical wench (*Die fromme Helene*, 1871). In *Die fromme Helene* as in *Der heilige Antonius* (1870) and *Pater Filucius* (1873) his antipathy to religion gives his satire a certain nastiness.

Parody such as Renaissance wits loved is the *Horatius travestitus* (1897) of CHRISTIAN MORGENSTERN (1871-1914), another Munich man (his father was a painter there). Morgenstern's humour owes nothing whatever to tradition or schools of any sort; it is *sui generis*, if ever anything was. His first book of humorous verse,

In Phantas Schloss (1895), shows the influence of Nietzsche, from whom he derived his questioning of the essentiality of words. The quaint and whimsical verse of *Galgenlieder* (1905), *Palmström* (1910), *Palma Kunkel* (1916) and *Der Gingganz* (1919) – collected as *Alle Galgenlieder*, 1933 – has to be labelled with a new term: *Sprachhumor*, a humour which flies like sparks from verbal quibbles. It is metaphysical humour: Gingganz, for instance, is Morgenstern's term for an ideologist. But Morgenstern was no ingenious punster: his wit is austerely intellectual, a diversion so to speak from his philosophical speculation on the relation of *nomen* and *res*, or *das Wort* and *das Ding an sich*. To flippant laymen *das Ding an sich* has always seemed mirthful; and Morgenstern, though strictly philosophical, strikes a mirthful philosophy from the very impossibility of name and thing being identical. In other words, while the thing is of the eternal essence the name for it is illusory, as the hopeless disagreement of thinkers on the nature of things shows. One has only to think of all the systems of scholasticism – each thought out and nailed down idea by idea with the incontrovertible logic of the best minds of the Middle Ages: *Nominalismus*, *Universalismus*, *Konzeptualismus*, *Terminismus*, and so forth – to appreciate what may have been Morgenstern's point of view that metaphysically it cannot be proved to the satisfaction of everybody that the idea (or name – *logos*, *Wort*) is the thing, or that the thing is the idea. His wit, therefore, plays – and with how clear a flame! – round the idiocy of our faith in words – which possibly convey no ideas at all, or, if they do, problematic ideas. And therefore he aims at an '*Umwortung aller Worte*'. Morality, the naturalists had proclaimed, is relative; Morgenstern, though less dogmatically, proclaims the relativity of knowledge. And miraculously into this spider's web of speculation the magic of poetry is caught: the mystical life that the *Volkslied* gives to birds and beasts and fishes, surprises of rhythm and diction, and sometimes in the very things that the poet questions he finds those tears that moved the soul of Virgil. He conveys mystery by the suggestion of double meanings: *Der Zwölf-Elf hebt die linke Hand:* | *Da schlägt die Mitternacht ins Land*. Interstices are removed from the laths of a fence (for if 'interstice' is a name for a thing what it represents is a thing; and a thing must be tangible; if not to the hands then to the mind that can work magic with it). A knee goes wandering round the world; the man it belonged to was shot away in the war, 'round and round' (a thing is part of a whole, but here is the question whether conceptually it is necessarily so). And sea-gulls all look as if their name was Emma: what do we mean if we say 'Emma'? What immemorial jesting, of poets and wits and tortured pupils, has gathered round the term 'gerund-grinder' or *Schulmeisterlein*, or *Pädagog*; and how pathetic and whimsical this is goes into *Der Werwolf*:

> *Ein Werwolf eines Nachts entwich*
> *von Weib und Kind und sich begab*
> *an eines Dorfschullehrers Grab*
> *und bat ihn: Bitte, beuge mich!*
>
> *Der Dorfschulmeister stieg hinauf*
> *auf seines Blechschilds Messingknauf*
> *und sprach zum Wolf, der seine Pfoten*
> *geduldig kreuzte vor dem Toten:*
>
> *'Der Werwolf' – sprach der gute Mann,*
> *'des Weswolfs, Genitiv sodann,*
> *dem Wemwolf, Dativ, wie man's nennt,*
> *den Wenwolf, – damit hat's ein End.'*
>
> *Dem Werwolf schmeichelten die Fälle,*
> *er rollte seine Augenbälle.*
> *Indessen, bat er, füge doch*
> *zur Einzahl auch die Mehrzahl noch!*
>
> *Der Dorfschulmeister aber musste*
> *gestehn, dass er von ihr nichts wusste.*
> *Zwar Wölfe gab's in grosser Schar,*
> *doch 'Wer' gab's nur im Singular.*
>
> *Der Wolf erhob sich tränenblind –*
> *er hatte ja doch Weib und Kind!!*
> *Doch da er kein Gelehrter eben,*
> *so schied er dankend und ergeben.*

It is a commonplace that the merriest jesters are sad men: how melancholy Christian Morgenstern can be is to be read in his non-humorous verse; the difference between the matter-of-factness of Wilhelm Busch and the cosmic vision of Morgenstern may be sensed, for instance, from *Vöglein Schwermut* (in *Ein Sommer*, 1899):

> *Ein schwarzes Vöglein fliegt über die Welt,*
> *das singt so todestraurig . . .*
> *Wer es hört, der hört nichts anderes mehr,*
> *wer es hört, der tut sich ein Leides an,*
> *der mag keine Sonne mehr schauen.*
>
> *Allmitternacht, Allmitternacht*
> *ruht es sich aus auf dem Finger des Tods.*
> *Der streichelt's leis und spricht ihm zu:*
> *'Flieg, mein Vögelein! Flieg, mein Vögelein!'*
> *Und wieder fliegt's flötend über die Welt.*

How skilfully Morgenstern weaves mood into rhythm is sufficiently clear from this little lyric alone: he produces an impression
of deep night by slow pace and heavy vowels at the sentence end,
with the dull flitting of the bird suggested by longer lines with
lighter vowels and three cunningly allocated dactyls; and there is
an impression of listless despair in the absence of rhyme. Morgenstern died of consumption, as his mother had done, at the age of
forty-three. In his last years he had turned mystic and immersed
himself in Rudolf Steiner's anthroposophism, which teaches that
transcendental, spiritual vision reveals the indestructible kernel of
our being. His nominological scepticism culminates in the pantheism of his later volumes (*Einkehr*, 1910; *Ich und Du*, 1911; *Wir
fanden einen Pfad*, 1914): 'Weder "ich" bin noch jener "Baum" ist,
sondern ein Drittes, nur u n s e r e V e r m ä h l u n g ist.' Break up
things, and the rest is silence – which is God. The world is the
marriage in God of 'I' and 'thou'. His ripest wisdom is gathered
into the aphorisms and notes of his posthumous *Stufen* (1918) and
Epigramme und Sprüche (1920), while *Mensch Wanderer* (1927) gathers
his serious poems from 1887 to 1914. There is a final gleaning of
his grotesques in *Die Schallmühle* (1928) – the title was changed to
Böhmischer Jahrmarkt in 1938 and to *Egon und Emilie* in 1950 – with
parodies of Whitman, d'Annunzio and others.

PAUL SCHEERBART (1863-1915) is classed as a '*Phantast*'; that is,
more or less an apocalyptic visionary, but of the scientific variety.
We might call him a cosmic humorist, for his novels – half scientific, half mystical – play about grotesquely with the cosmos: like
Shelley (to quote Francis Thompson) he runs wild over the fields

of ether and chases the rolling world. He is distinguished from his immediate circle of Berlin friends – Dehmel and Przybyszewski in particular – by his elimination of eroticism (*Antierotik*), which comes into his 'prentice novel only: *Tarub, Bagdads berühmte Köchin* (1897). In *Na, Prost!* (1898) he flies in an octagonal bottle into space. In *Die wilde Jagd* (1901) and *Kometentanz* (1903) the planets dance, while *Perpetuum mobile* (1910) discusses what the title indicates. And yet these tales bear no relation to those of Jules Verne[1]: Scheerbart's purpose is not primarily to foresee the advance of science, but to caricature the tendencies of his time: '*Aus Wut bin hic sogar Humorist geworden,*' he says, '*nicht aus Liebenswürdigkeit.*' He breaks ground for the cosmic impressionists because to the individualism of Nietzsche ('the God of journalists', he calls him) he opposes that cosmic feeling which foresees the future: '*Der Weltseele wollen wir näher sein,*' he says.

From the memoirs and diaries of the nineties we know of Scheerbart, Przybyszewski and Dehmel as three jolly boys in Berlin; entertaining Strindberg, for instance, in a night-club; and this companionship influenced literature profoundly in ideas of sex and Satanism which came from the strange brain of STANISLAUS PRZYBYSZEWSKI (1868-1927), who in these Berlin days of his wrote German but after his return to Poland was a leader of the Polish *Moderne*. Though his novels are now read by scholars only they have to be taken into account as the sources, partial at least, of the decadent Satanism of the period. Thus the wife of Bierbaum's *Prinz Kuckuck* deceives her husband with a Satanist whose creed is clear in the light of Przybyszewski's teaching; and, though the question of origins is complicated by the popularity of Barbey d'Aurevilly (*Les Diaboliques*, 1874; *Histoire sans noms*, 1882), Baudelaire, Huysmans, and Oscar Wilde, wherever there is decadent adoration of evil we are likely to have the influence, possibly indirect, of the demonic Pole. That Satanism as a theme should appeal to the naturalists is natural enough; for they describe life as it is, and life as they see it is diabolically wicked. If Satanism is taken to mean the negation of Christian principles – literally or

---

[1] The prototype of the scientific novel in Jules Verne's sense is *Auf zwei Planeten* (1897) by Kurd Lasswitz (1848-1910): a war between Mars and the earth is decided by the use of aeroplanes and submarines. Bernhard Kellermann's *Der Tunnel* (1913), the most popular novel of this sort, ranks rather with the anti-machinery literature: the hero just fails to construct a tunnel under the Atlantic, and the enterprise swallows up human lives like Moloch.

metaphorically the worship of evil instead of good – then it is as a matter of fact nothing new in German literature: it is defiantly expressed in the old ballad of Tannhäuser and in the Tannhäuser legend familiar to all from Wagner's opera; and even such a doggedly moral poet as Schiller wrote, in his effervescent youth, a Satanist poem (*Der Venuswagen*). Here already the devil and Venus are one. Satanism is in any case, as the reverse of the accepted standard of moral conduct, a modern version of medieval dualism. But the medieval parallel is illusory. What this modern Satanism springs from can be stated at least approximately: its literary origins are, firstly, Baudelaire's poetry; secondly, the anti-Christian individualism of Nietzsche; thirdly, that cult of refined physical sensations of which the gospel is Huysmans' *A rebours*; and fourthly, the sensation of Oscar Wilde's trial and the morbid thrill of his *Salome*, which, in Max Reinhardt's setting, was one of the most frequently produced plays of the period. So far as sexual cruelty is a part of Satanism (e.g. as handled by Gerhart Hauptmann, or by Eduard Stucken in *Die weissen Götter*, or in the numerous studies of incest) it derives from the earlier and crude pathology of the Marquis de Sade (1740-1814) and the Austrian novelist LEOPOLD VON SACHER-MASOCH[1] (1835-94). There is a ritual as well as a gospel of Satanism, and the culmination of this ritual is the Black Mass,[2] which for Huysmans' hero des Esseintes precedes his surrender to the (to him) sensual fascination of Catholicism. In German literature it occurs notably in Bierbaum's *Prinz Kuckuck*, Kurt Martens' *Roman aus der Décadence*, and (in barbaric splendour) in Eduard Stucken's *Die weissen Götter*; but primarily and as an inherent part of his sexual mysticism in the tales of Przybyszewski, '*der deutsche Sataniker*'. Przybyszewski's hero is always himself in his speculative capacity. *Totenmesse* (1893) shows this personal hero tortured by sexual atrophy due to cerebral hypertrophy (which we are to understand is the curse and abnormality of civilization); and he tries to lash this shrunk feeling into primitive plenitude by plunging into wild orgies. In vain, however; for such excitation of the senses cannot be more than the spurt of a dying flame. Physical deviation from the norm might be unobjectionable

---

[1] Sacher-Masoch's heroes show their love by using the riding-whip, often in a lurid Slav *milieu* (he was a native of Lemberg in Galicia). Typical novels of his are *Das Vermächtnis Kains*, *Venus im Pelz*, *Die Seelenfängerin*. *Masochism* is derived from his name (pp. 32, 34).

[2] There is a detailed description of a Black Mass in Huysmans' *Là-Bas* (1890).

if the brain could by its own vitality exert dominion and shape life to perfection; but the vital force of the brain cannot be sundered from that sexual vigour which makes full man: either there is vigour of sex or decay of the organism as a whole. The hero of *Totenmesse* is Przybyszewski as scientific thinker: the second tale, *Vigilien* (1894), presents him as the artist with sense and soul yearning for woman – as a 'balance' of his being, not, however to provide the contrary half to his masculinity, but to serve this forceful masculinity as a stimulus to artistic creation or as a narcotic. In the trilogy *Homo Sapiens* (1895-6) there is an examination of sex in all its possible manifestations and a more particular synthesis of the physical thrills of Catholic ritualism and Satanism (such as we get in Huysmans); and in this novel as in *Satans Kinder* (1897) Przybyszewski attempts, but in vain, to individualize his characters. Przybyszewski's importance in literary history lies in his preaching of sex as the ineluctable purpose of life and as the creative organ of art and literature. 'Art', he says, 'is nothing but a game that sex plays with brain.'[1] And, since life is made up of pain and disgust (Schopenhauer's doctrine), what life springs from – that is, sex – must be the same. It would be easy to show how Przybyszewski's doctrine is worked out by later writers: *Madenseligkeit*, for instance, by Thomas Mann (in *Der Zauberberg* particularly), and the vampire clutch of woman in Gerhart Hauptmann's work (particularly in *Im Wirbel der Berufung*). And, thus reasoning, Przybyszewski brands woman as '*dulce malum et vitiosa propago*', as the bait of Satan and temptation in the flesh. In this demonization of woman he agrees with the three *Frauenhasser* Schopenhauer, Nietzsche, and Strindberg; but Dehmel, while accepting sex as a demonic force, proclaims the power of the individual to transform this *summum malum* into the *summum bonum* by transfusing body with spirit.

Satanism in the stories of HANNS HEINZ EWERS (1871-1943) takes on the form of Prussian *Schrecklichkeit*, although he comes from the jolly Rhineland (he was born at Düsseldorf). The sub-title of his volume of short stories *Das Grauen* (1907) is '*Seltsame Geschichten*', and the strangeness of them is in direct line of descent from E. T. A. Hoffmann and Edgar Allen Poe (on whom he wrote an

---

[1] Wilhelm Bölsche in his *Die naturwissenschaftlichen Grundlagen der Poesie* (1887) puts the same view more scientifically. Remy de Gourmont put the view more succinctly: 'Poetry is produced by the genitals.'

essay): his own characteristic addition is orgiastic blood-lust, as in *Hahnenkampf*, the story of a cock-fight in *Die Besessenen* (1908), his most typical volume: the fighting cocks are stripped Spaniards with daggers in the gaunt mountains of Andalusia. Orgies of sex and blood fill the culminating scene, to which he leads up horror by horror, of his picture of hoodoo ceremonial in Haiti. In the cock-fight the obsession of blood is a matter of race and heroic *milieu*; in the hoodoo tale it is that frenzy of sex in the heat of tropical forests and sun-baked bodies which accounts for much of primitive religion.

This metaphysical fundament of Ewers serves him to probe a visionary truth behind the illusion of reality. As it happens, however, his own mind is of that variety which would look to real profit even in the exposition of irreality (he made his first reputation as a reciter for the Überbrettl, the history of which he wrote in *Das Cabaret*, 1905). What he gives us, therefore, is not so much metaphysical tales as sensational best-sellers. However, he forms the link between Poe's mathematical lucubration of mystery and the Romantic uncanniness of E. T. A. Hoffmann before him and a group of Prague Jews who do capture the mystic illusion of a supersensory reality, apparently because they have ethical conceptions for the suggestion of which they bring in the mystifications of the Jewish cabbala. Of these Prague Jews Gustav Meyrink and the painter Alfred Kubin (1877-) do not disdain sensationalism; in Franz Kafka, who combines the ethics of the expressionists with the raw realism of the naturalists, we have a pure mystic.

GUSTAV MEYRINK'S (1868-1932) novel *Der Golem* (1916) is by reason of its allusive handling of the robot-theme one of the most readable tales of the period. The Golem is an artificial man made according to a lost specification of the cabbala by a rabbi of Prague in the seventeenth century, to help him ring the bells of the synagogue. The creature lives only with a 'half-conscious vegetable life' by the virtue of a magic card (*Zettel*) inserted behind his teeth; this draws down the sidereal powers (the symbol is apparently that of the automatism of modern society; Heaven still moves us, though in our limp life of routine we are unconscious of it). When, one evening, the rabbi forgets to remove this card from the creature's mouth he runs amok through the streets, smashing whatever comes in his way, until the rabbi captures him and removes the card (symbolically: reduces the robot to brute matter –

there is not much difference; and also – if we lose priestly direction we are raging brutes). When the card is removed the Golem falls all of a heap, and nothing remains of him but the figure of a clay dwarf which is still shown in the Altneusynagoge at Prague. But the people in the ghetto of Prague believe the Golem still appears in the streets at intervals – '*ein vollkommen fremder Mensch, bartlos, von gelber Gesichtsfarbe und mongolischem Typus – in altmodische, verschossene Kleider gehüllt – mit schiefgestellten Augen und gespaltener Lippe*'. One person who has seen the Golem maintains that it can only have been her own soul which had stepped out of her body to face her; this, of course, is E. T. A. Hoffmann's *Doppelgänger-Motiv*, of which there is much in the book. A curiosity of Meyrink's tale *Das grüne Gesicht* (1916) is that the post-War topsyturviness is foreseen. In all his other tales (*Orchideen*, 1904; *Das Wachsfiguren-kabinett*, 1907; *Walpurgisnacht*, 1917; *Der weisse Dominikaner*, 1917) there is the same sensation-mongering in the guise of occultism or spiritism.

To English readers there is probably more appeal in his *Der Engel vom westlichen Fenster* (1927), for the scene of a great part of the tale is in England, and in the chain of magicians are St. Dunstan and Queen Elizabeth, while the hero is Sir John Dee, the descendant of a Welsh chieftain whose desire is to win Greenland for Gloriana. ('Greenland', as the tale unfolds, is the deep dead past, from which come ghosts and all mediumistic visions and succubi and the mirages of sexual desire.) The scene changes to Prague, where another *Teufelsbündner*, Kaiser Rudolf, wise and wily but in the toils of priests, directs the ever elusive quest for the philosopher's stone. The actual theme of the novel is the secret of existence, and this is revealed (darkly) by the complicated action as man's ceaseless battle with sex: a good man by his very nature strives frantically to achieve wisdom and selflessness, but this masculine ideal is thwarted by the demonic fascination of the female, in this tale sensationally embodied, obscene and divinely lovely, as the Pontine Isis (*die schwarze Isaïs*), with lithe limbs and panther's smell (*das Pantherweib*). Isis is eternal, for she is in the blood and is the blood of the male, whose only hope is to be mothered by some domestic woman, from whose shielding arms he is lured, however, by this vampire who is lust, not love. The demon may, when man's senses are cold, fill him with loathing of her functions, but her magic lies in the heating of his senses; and even if he would destroy her she seizes him in the very frenzy of his hate, for sexual desire is the adoration she craves. There is much play with elusive symbols: particularly with the dagger, or spear-head, of the hero's Welsh ancestor, which is at the same time an attribute of the cat-headed goddess (=phallus): the hero, in his successive incarnations, can only save his soul – and even then only when life is ending – by preserving this instrument from the greed of the evil powers. The mystic illumination of the problem of life comes from a weird rabbi who is versed in cabbalistic lore: and the lesson is (apparently) that man must choose between suppression after death or suppression in life of the brute element of sex – in other words between flesh and spirit, and that the true alchemistic *transmutatio* is achieved by the hermaphroditic marriage of the male with the female (element) within himself: thus Sir John Dee might win 'the Queen'[1]; not, as he deludes himself, Queen Elizabeth – who gives herself to him only as Isis in the shape of a succubus and lures his descendant in our own days as the medieval Dame World, fair in front and with hollow back wreathed with slimy snakes –, but the irradiation through strain and suffering of personality.

This cult of spooks, vampires, and demons has, of course, not been the monopoly of the Prague Jews: it occurs in the Novellen of Josef Ruederer (*Tragikomödien*), of Oscar A. H. Schmitz (*Haschisch*, 1892), in Gerhart Hauptmann's plays and fiction, in Wilhelm Walloth's[2] (1850-1932) *Im Banne der Hypnose* (1897), and in the later work of Wilhelm von Scholz. In the light of all this hair-raising matter Goethe's stage-directions following line 5298 of *Faust* II are amusing: '*Die Nacht- und Grabdichter lassen sich entschuldigen, weil sie soeben im interessantesten Gespräch mit einem frischerstandenen Vampyren begriffen seien, woraus eine neue Dichtart sich vielleicht entwickeln könnte.*' Goethe's contempt for 'hideous vampirism' comes out in his review of Mérimée's *La Guzla* (1827).

---

[1] See *Faust*, I, l. 1047. There is much use of this passage in the book; the 'red lion' appears variously, literally as the tamed pet of Kaiser Rudolf.

[2] One of M. G. Conrad's Munich group. He tried to better Georg Ebers by making the archaeological novel naturalistically real, but did worse (*Oktavia*, 1885; *Paris der Mime*, 1886; *Ovid*, 1890; *Eros*, 1906).

IV

THE NOVEL OF NATURALISM
AND DECADENCE

As far as the novel is concerned it is difficult to draw a clear line of demarcation between naturalism and decadence; the two movements merge. There are, however, distinguishing features of each. Naturalism implies sympathy for the working classes (*Armeleutepoesie*) and for outcasts of all sorts – prostitutes particularly, waitresses, factory workers, tramps, scamps; decadence is in the main the depiction of the artist as by his very nature misplaced in society and conventions, the hectic man of nerves, the seeker after sensations. Decadence is naturalistic in the sense that it claims to photograph real life; but it tends merely to photograph the inner life of exceptional beings, who as such are decadent, in a *milieu* either of drab reality or of Bohemian strangeness represented as real. Where, as in the 'artist novels', this strange lighting is focused on the strange hero, we have technically not naturalism but impressionism; but even here the *milieu* is likely to be more or less naturalistic. The swathing of a sensitively visioned inner picture by folds of raw reality indeed continues through the succeeding schools of impressionism, expressionism, *Neue Sachlichkeit*, and *Schollendichtung*; by this alone we can measure the importance of naturalism, once established, as a necessary part of certain phases of literature, particularly of the novel. A term which approximately comprises all novels of these schools which have at least a base of realism is *Milieuroman*. 'Experimental novel' (*Experimentalroman, experimenteller Roman*) on the other hand fits only those novels of the eighties and nineties which are built up, according to Zola's theory, by '*documents humains*'; that is, by the actual study or scientific observation, or (in Germany, at least) the pretence of such study or observation, of the characters and

75

strata of society concerned. Roughly stated, the difference between naturalism and decadence is that between Zola on the one hand and Maupassant, Huysmans in his second period, and Oscar Wilde on the other hand. There is, however, another line of growth: if to be a decadent is to be a man of delicate artistic perceptions – 'aesthete' (*Aesthet*), man of nerves (*Nervenmensch*) – but weak will, then its true home is Vienna.[1] But Conrad Ferdinand Meyer, a Swiss patrician of Zurich, had the same incapacity to face the noise and hardness of life[2]; and therefore, though Viennese writers through the ages tend to this shrinking softness, decadence is a matter (if it is real and not merely the fashion of the day) of individual mentality and physique: the problem of real decadence or of literary decadence meets us in the work of, say, Sudermann and Ompteda – both solid Germans with the stamina of cart-horses – contrasted with Heinz Tovote with his Parisian elegance and neurotic thrills.

Definitely a decadent was the Viennese writer FERDINAND VON SAAR (1833-1906); and we may say that he is the link between the involuntary decadence of Grillparzer and Conrad Ferdinand Meyer and the deliberate cult of decadence of the nineties. In one of his lyrics, *Die Entarteten*, Saar laments for those who are tainted before birth (*erblich belastet*, a favourite term which derives from the terminology of the alienists as much as from Darwin), battle vainly against secret sins, and die at last by their own hands or by those of the public executioner. This is the note, too, of many of Saar's short stories (*Novellen aus Österreich*, 1876 and 1897): his effeminate characters fail helplessly in whatever they undertake. (He himself died by his own hand.) His *Die Steinklopfer* (1873) is generally classed as '*die erste Arbeiternovelle*', while the heroine of his *Die Troglodytin* is an ex-convict woman tramp; and certainly the four short stories of his *Die Tragik des Lebens* (1894) rank him with the naturalists of the day.

This wave of sympathy in literature with the downtrodden and the outcast is of course a reflection of the social and political trend of the period; the law against Socialists (*Sozialistengesetz*) had to be abrogated in 1890; and Kaiser Wilhelm's known disgust at the performance in Berlin of *Die Weber* merely acted as an advertise-

---

[1] See p. 210.
[2] Cf. with his poem *Abendrot im Walde* Cowper's description of himself as a 'stricken deer'. *Sonntags* mirrors his morbid love of solitude.

ment. Not merely theologians like Bruno Wille turned Socialist: there was the glaring case of Moritz von Egidy, a lieutenant-colonel, who preached a kind of Saint-Simonian Christianity or Christian Socialism freed from all sectarian dogma; he stated his creed in *Ernste Gedanken* (1891). Such a socialization of Christianity was signalled at the Evangelisch-Sozialer Kongress in 1890.

One more distinguishing feature which should be pointed out is that, while naturalism proper is Socialistic, decadence tends to be Nietzschean. The question might at once arise: how can Nietz-scheanism, which is the cult of the strong, ruthless man, possibly be identified with decadentism? The answer is that Nietzsche's idea of the superman (*'Der Mensch ist etwas, das überwunden werden soll'*) implies contempt and loathing for man in his present state (see pp. 103-4). This self-loathing is not in contradiction with that admiration of the strong men of history which in the case of Jakob Burckhardt and Conrad Ferdinand Meyer took the form of worship of the *Renaissancemensch*; and generally speaking we may say that in the nineties literary Nietzscheanism in Germany splits into two phases: (1) the identification of the man of the Renaissance with the superman, principally in impressionism (e.g. the novels of Heinrich Mann); (2) decadent individualism; the latter, strengthened by the cult of Baudelaire (the French Satanist as Przybyszewski is the German Satanist), turns to Satanism, to Neronism (*Ich-Anbetung*), and to the glorification of the weakling with suicidal tendencies. Thus we get two main types of hero: *der Held der Tat* and *der Held der Kunst*.

The Zolaesque novel begins with Conrad Alberti (or Sittenfeld) and Max Kretzer. CONRAD ALBERTI (p. 23), the swashbuckler of naturalism, had the typical cynicism of Berlin Jews; his drama *Brot* (1888) is an attempt, before Gerhart Hauptmann's *Florian Geyer*, to dramatize the Peasant Rebellion; his novels (*Wer ist der Stärkere?* 1888; *Die Alten und die Jungen*, 1889; *Recht auf Liebe* 1890; *Maschinen*, 1894) died in their own dirt, and count only as experiments. In the short stories of his *Plebs* (1887) he sketches with a loose grip the life of Berlin metal workers and seamstresses; his imitation of Zola comes out more in the panoramic vision of Berlin which he tries to read into his novels; he fails because he sees merely a drab monotonous city, whereas Zola redeems his horrific picture by vivid and grandiose symbol. MAX KRETZER (1854-1941), an artisan who gradually shaped himself into a literary man but never mastered grammar and, despite his naturalistic doctrine, made his working people talk as they do in penny novelettes, did manage to animate his *Anklageliteratur* by something like poetic symbol: admirably almost in his best novel, *Meister Timpe* (1888), which has for theme the crushing of the small independent crafts-man by the mass production of factories; the crawling of the railway over old Berlin and past his little workshop has a night-mare effect. Fanatically as Kretzer imitates Zola's 'literature of accusation' a more congenial influence on him was that of Dickens; and indeed it is generally true of the novelists of naturalism that the influence of Zola is mainly on subject-matter. Like Dickens, he puts the matter of his own early experiences into his fiction: in *Der Fassadenraphael* (1911) he relates how he earned his living as a sign-writer, and the description of life in a lamp factory in *Der alte Andreas* (*Berliner Sittenbilder*, 1911) is also autobiographical, while in his memoirs, *Wilder Champagner, Berliner Erinnerungen und Studien*, he describes his apprenticeship to a china merchant. He has neither the humanity nor the variety of Dickens: his range is limited to the life of workers and outcasts, and to him this life is slavery; where the wealthier classes come into his picture he does not rise above caricature which betrays his complete ignorance of the ways and speech of better class society. Of his novels – all of them strictly *Berliner Romane* – *Die Betrogenen* (1882) has in outline of plot some resemblance to *David Copperfield*; it is the first full novel to describe the life of industrial workers in the capital, and its essential premise is that girls who work in factories must in-evitably augment their earnings by prostitution. *Die Verkommenen* (1883) suggests *Little Dorrit*, with the substitution of the Berlin block of flats (*Mietskaserne*) for the Marshalsea Prison. *Meister Timpe*, with its pathetic lament for the ever-growing mechaniza-tion of the world, derives apparently from both Zola's *Au Bonheur des Dames* and Dickens's *Hard Times*. Quite Zolaesque is *Drei Weiber* (1886), with its discussion of the man with more than one wife. There is satire of religion in *Die Bergpredigt* (1890); *Der Millionenbauer* (1891) reflects the moral ruination by sudden wealth of the farmer whose land has been swallowed up in the *Gründer-jahre* by the expansion of Berlin; in *Das Gesicht Christi* (1897) the Saviour moves as a symbol of pity among the poor of Berlin.

The *Berliner Roman* is of course a subdivision of the *Grossstadt-roman*, but practically speaking the metropolitan novel of early naturalism is confined to depictions of Munich in the loose sketches of M. G. Conrad's *Was die Isar rauscht* and to a very comprehensive series of Berlin novels. The latter, indeed, take in novels by writers of the previous generation: PAUL LINDAU's (1839-1917) trilogy *Der Zug nach dem Westen* (1886), *Arme Mädchen* (1887), and *Spitzen* (1888); FRITZ MAUTHNER's (1849-1923) *Berlin W.* (1886), HERMANN HEIBERG's (1840-1910) *Dunst aus der Tiefe*[1] (1890). Novels such as Karl Bleibtreu's *Schlechte Gesellschaft* fall under the heading of *Kellnerinnenromane*; these unroll unedifying pictures of the Bohemian life of the capital (Strindberg's *Röda Rummet* is the prototype of the genre) with mighty-bosomed waitresses or barmaids towering over quailing poets. Actually the *Berliner Roman* reaches its height in two nostalgic descriptions of the Jewish life in the capital in the days of crinolines: *Jettchen Gebert* (1906) and its sequel *Henriette Jacoby* (1908) by Georg Herrmann; but since these novels are *Charakterromane* rather than *Milieuromane* they belong to a later chapter.

The naturalistic *Künstlerroman* begins with Conrad Alberti's *Die Alten und die Jungen* – a gifted artist, submerged by mediocrity, dies by his own hand – and Bleibtreu's *Grössenwahn*. The latter novel, grotesquely formless, satirizes the members of the *Verein Durch*: the Hart brothers appear as *'die idealen Waffenbrüder'* (an obvious hit at their *Kritische Waffengänge*). These rambling novels were not, however, *Künstlerromane* in the more exclusive sense of the type created by WALTER SIEGFRIED (1858-1947), a Swiss merchant, with his *Tino Moralt* (1890), which is clearly influenced by Zola's *L'Œuvre*. It is a study of frustration: the hero, an artist, foiled in his relentless battle for perfection, loses his reason and commits suicide. *Tino Moralt*, like Hermann Bahr's *Die gute Schule*, reflects the author's experiences in the artistic world of Paris. Clearly autobiographical too is CÄSAR FLAISCHLEN's (1864-1920) *Jost Seyfried* (1905), a novel in epistolary and diary form; it relates the development (*Werdegang*) of a poet of the *Jüngstdeutsche Bewegung* (another name given to their movement by the naturalists to show their affinities to the revolutionary Jung Deutschland school of 1830-48). The spirit of the book is plaintively pessimistic: both naturalism and symbolism are represented as having degenerated from the soaring aims with which they began to a mechanical

---

[1] Heiberg's novel *Apotheker Heinrich* (1885) was praised by the naturalists, but his matter-of-fact style earned him the title of *'der Realist der Nüchternheit'*.

turning out of mass matter. The style, in a kind of Whitmanesque prose, runs parallel with that of Johannes Schlaf in the sketches of his rural divagations; and it is indeed as an experimenter in free rhythms that Cäsar Flaischlen has historical interest as a lyrical poet[1]: wistful moods he renders admirably in his seemingly artless verse. His dramas (*Toni Stürmer*, 1891, and *Martin Lehnhardt*, 1895) are in their reflection of the poet's own ripening of mood and character complementary to *Jost Seyfried*; *Martin Lehnhardt* counts also (say, with Max Dreyer's *Der Probekandidat* and Hermann Stehr's *Drei Nächte*) in the literature of religious anguish and revolt: a theological student, after a poignant argument with a clergyman, abjures the faith he was to have preached; here Flaischlen is trying to fashion (like Johannes Schlaf in his trilogies and like Kurt Martens) a kind of healed decadent (*gesundeter Dekadent*), one who has won his way to a moral Nietzscheanism.

The hero is levelled rather than raised in those novels of the period which stand for the social doctrines of the extreme political left. The typical Communistic novel, John Henry Mackay's *Die Anarchisten*, is less literature than programme; the typical Socialist novels are Hans Land's *Der neue Gott* and Felix Holländer's *Jesus und Judas*. The symptomatic feature of these tales, the abnegation of his 'higher' class and conventional faith by an aristocrat or theologian, who becomes one of the people, is of course common to the European life of the day; in Germany there were Socialist theologians such as Bruno Wille; and one clergyman, Paul Göhre, actually worked as a factory hand for three months and described his experiences in *Drei Monate Fabrikarbeiter* (1891) and *Denkwürdigkeiten und Erinnerungen eines Arbeiters*. An aristocrat had espoused the people's cause in fiction in George Sand's *Le Compagnon du Tour de France*; in German life an officer did so in the person of Moritz von Egidy, and in German fiction there is Fedor in Ompteda's *Deutscher Adel um 1900*, who refuses to be any longer 'noble by love of self' (*ein Adeliger des Egoismus*) and seeks to be 'noble by love of others' (*ein Adeliger des Altruismus*). The millionaire's son who gives up his wealth and turns Communist we get later in Jakob Wassermann's novel *Christian Wahnschaffe* and Georg Kaiser's dramas *Koralle* and *Gas*. The hero of HANS LAND's (1861-92) *Der neue Gott* is a count and lieutenant in the Hussars who lives in a garret and serves the Socialist party; he fails to adapt himself,

---

[1] *Von Alltag und Sonne* (1898), *Zwischenklänge* (1909).

however, and in the misery of poverty betrays the revolutionary aims of the party to the police. There is the same feeling for the masses in Hans Land's other novels (*Stiefkinder der Gesellschaft*, 1888; *Die am Wege sterben*, 1889; *Sünden*, 1892). There is more of the stuff of literature, despite the dismal flatness of the narration, in FELIX HOLLÄNDER'S (1867-1931) *Jesus und Judas* (1891): a student would fain be a Jesus to the workers but is forced by poverty to be a Judas – he betrays his party and jumps into the Spree. Holländer's most famous novel – one of the most notable of the whole period – is *Der Weg des Thomas Truck* (1902); the hero is the son of a provincial doctor who turns Socialist; in Berlin he has a disappointment with the wife of a millionaire who refuses to give up her life of luxury to share his ideals of social service; he marries a girl he meets at a Salvation Army meeting, a seamstress addicted to drink; she commits suicide, and he goes to the dogs in the Bohemian life of the capital, but is rehabilitated by his love for his cousin, and finds peace for his soul in Buddhism and the teaching of Tolstoy. WILHELM HEGELER (1870-1947) was a man of good family who literally for conscience' sake turned proletarian. In his first novel, *Mutter Bertha* (1893), an unmarried mother gives way to a doctor to save her child's life, and then makes good by hard work and self-sacrifice for the sake of the child. This theme of moral excellence latent in a 'fallen' woman and triumphing in the idea that the child is salvation occurs in a number of outstanding novels, from Helene Böhlau's *Das Recht der Mutter* to Vicki Baum's *Stud. Chem. Helene Willfüer*. Hegeler's best novels are *Ingenieur Horstmann* (1900) and *Pastor Klinghammer* (1903); in each the hero is a violent character whose blood gets the better of his culture.

Imitation of Zola in the sense of a heaping up from chapter to chapter of documented material is confined to early naturalism, although of course sporadically the process survives. What happened was that photographic naturalism was transformed by that surgical probing into states of nerves of which Maupassant (1850-93) was master. And as soon as the influence can be diagnosed as that of Maupassant we can no longer classify a work definitely as naturalism: studies of nerves belong to decadentism, and decadentism (since neurotic obsession and decay show in unreal impressions of the outer world) is more or less a part of impressionism. Sudermann from the first imitates Maupassant in his fiction, but he continues the poetic realism of his German predecessors, par-

ticularly in the sentimentalism of *Frau Sorge* and *Der Katzensteg*;
what he does (in his less reputable work at least) is to transfuse
the German pretence of moral goodness with French cynicism.
Maupassant's translator was Georg Freiherr von Ompteda, and
Ompteda strove doggedly to be the German Maupassant; the
German novelist who made the most of Maupassant's technique
and pose was, however, Heinz Tovote.

HEINZ TOVOTE (1864-1946) and GEORG VON OMPTEDA (1863-1931)
were both natives of Hanover. The glaring difference between
them is that while Ompteda takes over from Maupassant the cult
of piquancy and abnormality his sexuality is, comparatively speaking, sane and normal, while Tovote is genuinely decadent. Their
portraits alone proclaim this radical difference: Ompteda's solid
square face and clipped hair contrast with Tovote's elegant pointed
beard and shock of well-groomed hair. *Fallobst* (1890) is a collection of Novellen defined by Tovote himself as '*Novellen der Wurm-
stichigkeit*', and this 'wormeatenness' is equally high to the nostrils
in *Ich, nervöse Novellen* (1892); what Tovote gives us in these tales
is a series of hectic short studies of the fixed ideas or obsessions
of nervous people. For instance: two young people ripening to
the crisis of fruition have their blood chilled by the sight of a
horse's blood spilt in an accident (this is of course less telling than
Maupassant's story of a husband who ceased intercourse with his
wife because one day when she was ill he was sickened by the faint
odour of physical decay which met his nostrils as he bent over her).
Tovote made his reputation with his novel *Im Liebesrausch* (1890),
the hero of which is an aristocrat who marries a carter's daughter,
a girl with a past: as a waitress she was Lucie Nagel, as a sort of
lady she is Kitty Nail. Georg von Ompteda scores by his illumination of the life of officers; and in this respect his trilogy of novels
Deutscher Adel um 1900 (*Sylvester von Geyer*, 1897; *Eysen*, 1900;
Cäcilie von Sarryn, 1901) may prove to have permanent importance
as pictures of social conditions. In this trilogy the influence of the
Goncourts is pointed out by critics; but this influence too is less
discernible in Ompteda than in Tovote, in the sense that Tovote's
creatures are more literally (to quote Edmond de Goncourt's self-
definition) *machines à sensations* rendered with an *accent fiévreux*.
Sylvester von Geyer describes the life of a Saxon officer from the
cradle to the grave; his tragedy is that he is poor and that his
efforts to perfect his character are hampered by fits of nerves.

Eysen is the saga of a whole family, and *Cäcilie von Sarryn* unfolds the poignant tragedy of the old maid of noble family. The total theme of the cycle is the struggle for existence of an entire noble family; thus *Deutscher Adel um 1900* does for the nobility what Thomas Mann's *Buddenbrooks* does for a patrician family in a Hanse city; and in both it is the disintegration of the solid old stock by the nervous debility of modern life, with its problematic culture, which interprets the tragedy. The imitation of Maupassant is most glaring in Ompteda's early collection of short stories *Leidenschaften* (1896), with their ironical humour and piquant situations. The theme of Maupassant's *En Famille* – the frustration of artistic ambition by the fetters of marriage to a modern Delilah – occurs in *Philister über Dir!* (1899).

Two novelists, Wilhelm von Polenz and Kurt Martens, share with Johannes Schlaf the credit of aiming, for ethic and racial reasons, at the conquest of decadentism. WILHELM VON POLENZ (1861-1903), like Ompteda a retired officer, is today given rank as one of the forerunners of the *Blut- und Boden* novel; and it is true that in his agrarian novels he describes in patient detail the conditions of his native province of Upper Lusatia. Tales of his such as *Heinrich von Kleist* (1891) hardly count except for the subject[1]; and the sexual details of *Sühne* (1890), a novel of adultery, merely show dependence on Zola. Markedly Zolaesque too is *Wurzellocker* (1902), a study of industrial and artist life. *Der Pfarrer von Breitendorf* (1893) definitely places Polenz with the best novelists of his period. It is the first of a series of novels (e.g. Frenssen's *Hilligenlei*, Lulu von Strauss und Torney's *Lucifer*, Hermann Stehr's *Der Heiligenhof*) in which religious experience dominates the shaping forces of environment; in Polenz's tale the clergyman hero, like Cäsar Flaischlen's Martin Lehnhardt, wrestles with his faith and casts it aside, while another clergyman seeks release from doubt in death. *Der Büttnerbauer* (1895) is by common consent something of a masterpiece, not only because it vividly renders the landscape and rural atmosphere of Upper Lusatia and is therefore a new start, after the spate of metropolitan novels, in the peasant novel, but because of its powerful characterization of the Büttnerbauer, a farmer of the old school, obstinate and tireless in his labour to

---

[1] Georg Hirschfeld's short story *Dämon Kleist* probably suggested the title of Stefan Zweig's book of biographical essays (with a very frank interpretation of Kleist's mentality) *Der Kampf mit dem Dämon*.

save his heritage, but helpless in the grip of the Jew to whom he has mortgaged it; in his children there is no help, for they are degenerates; and when he can fight no more he hangs himself. The doctrine of the salvation of agriculture by self-dedication to it is enunciated in *Der Grabenhäger* (1897): a landed gentleman, a former officer with an officer's way with women and other things, is helped by his wife to restore his decayed farms to prosperity.[1] With *Thekla Lüdekind* (1900) Polenz returns to the metropolis and takes his part in the discussion of feminism by showing the qualities of emancipated women and of those who live to love.

In Polenz's novels the anti-decadent note is implicit in his return to country life and his unsympathetic handling of weak-willed creatures; in those of KURT MARTENS (1870-1945) it is expressly stressed. The masters Kurt Martens acknowledges are Stefan George and above all Hugo von Hofmannsthal; and with Hofmannsthal he has the common interest in the influence of decadence on personality. Whereas, however, Hofmannsthal portrays himself in his decadents Kurt Martens is quite objective. His titles alone indicate the stamp of his characters (*Sinkende Schwimmer*, 1892; *Die gehetzten Seelen*, 1897; *Roman aus der Décadence*, 1898): but he turns the tables on these pretentious petty Nietzscheans by branding their claim to licence by virtue of personality[2] ('*sich ausleben*' is a catchword of the school) as merely the lack of discipline of Philistines; he ranks an artist steeped in vice less than a plodding dullard. The hero of *Roman aus der Décadence* lives the life of the aesthetic snob: homosexuality, free love, boredom, conversion to Catholicism, *et toute la lyre*; but, unlike Hofmannsthal's Claudio, he frees himself from the cult of sensations and finds a refuge in study. The hero of *Die Vollendung* (1902) fails to save himself, but before he commits suicide he knows that his son will reach safety – by his love for a girl from America; and it is interesting that Martens points to English character as by national habit sane and sound.

There is an intellectual rather than a moral conquest of naturalistic depression in the later fiction of ANNA CROISSANT-RUST (1860-

---

[1] Adalbert Stifter's *Brigitta* (1843) romantically handles the same theme for a Hungarian estate.

[2] The typical decadent of this type is Hermann Conradi, in whose flaunting of vice there is at least the pretence of the desire to rise by the satisfaction of impulses (*Triebe*) above and beyond them. Dehmel, by his own showing, achieved salvation in this way.

1943); she remained 'consistent', but managed after the turn of the century to enliven her hard and relentless studies of working-class and peasant *milieu* with a peculiar humour, which served her, so she said, like a mackintosh in rain. She was the only woman among the primitive naturalists – as a member of M. G. Conrad's circle she wrote for *Die Gesellschaft* – who earned a niche in literary annals by the permanent merit of her work. She was rather a writer for the writing fraternity than for the mass of the reading public; the short stories with which she began (*Feierabend und andere Münchner Geschichten*, 1893; *Lebensstücke*, 1893) and her two plays (*Der standhafte Zinnsoldat*, 1896; *Der Bua*, 1897) were too true to the naturalistic type to appeal to light-minded readers. Her *Gedichte in Prosa* (1893), too, are interesting mainly as experiments in form; they belong to the imitations of Whitman which followed the lyric revolt of Holz and Schlaf. Her protective humour did, however, lend some popular appeal to her novel *Winkelquartett* (1908), and there is the regional attraction of *Heimatkunst* in the short stories of her *Pimpernellche* (1901) and *Aus unsers Herrgotts Tiergarten* (1906), which render the moods of her native Palatinate; she has strictly regional reality, too, in her novel *Die Nann* (1906), which unfolds the life of peasants in the Brenner Pass district.

7

V

FROM BAHR TO DEHMEL

Consistent naturalism did not very long hold the field as the movement of the day; before it had lost its strangeness it was challenged by a new movement, that of symbolism, neo-romanticism or impressionism (three names for much the same thing); and gradually naturalism merges with these new currents, some poets shifting as mood dictates from one style to the other. Impressionism is partly a reaction from naturalism, but to a great extent it derives from French symbolism, which was itself a reaction against two completely different styles, naturalism and Parnassianism; in Germany, however, the manner of the French Parnassians is imitated, e.g. by Richard von Schaukal, at the same time as that of the symbolists, i.e. the sculptured or pictorial Parnassian style blends with symbolist infolding of meaning.

Impressionism in painting loosely assembles light effects round blurred outlines. So, too, literary impressionism may produce (to quote Schiller's summing-up of Klopstock's nebulosity) a given state of mind without the help of a given subject. At all events, impressionism produces *Stimmung*, mood, atmosphere, *état d'âme*.

It is a law of physics that action and reaction are equal and in opposite directions. The direction which impressionism gives to art is away from nature. Hermann Bahr interpreted the phase somewhat whimsically: the poet or painter, he says, is the mirror in which nature is reflected; or, nature as we see it in the work of art is not seen directly but reflected in a temperament. If the temperament is abnormal, the reflection will be abnormal; but it will be art. Moreover, according to naturalistic theory nature must always appear the same in art, for art must be a photographic reproduction of nature; art would thus be infinitely monotonous; according to impressionistic theory, on the other hand, the re-

86

flection of nature in art differs as infinitely as artists differ in temperament. Only vision is true. A child watches its mother in a green shade and says to papa: 'Mama has a green nose!' Papa says it only seems so, but the child knows better, it says what it sees. Papa knows too much; his superior knowledge corrects his vision. In reality we never see anything as our intelligence tells us it is. But the appearance which intelligence says is untrue is beautiful; and art portrays the beautiful, which *is* the real, only the real is *underneath* it. '*Am farbigen Abglanz haben wir das Leben,*' wrote Goethe.

Impressionism first appears as programmatic in a novel which ran as a serial through the first volume of *Die Freie Bühne*, Hermann Bahr's *Die gute Schule* (1890). This is a typically decadent novel, with as much *Nervosität* as anything of Tovote's, and today its interest lies more than anywhere in the detection of the influences which go to its making; for it is an amalgam of imitations which are in themselves indicative of the fiction which follows. Critics insist on the crass use of Strindberg's misogyny, but certainly the chief influence is that of Huysmans' *A rebours*, which is, however, coupled with the psychogrammatic notation of Bourget's *Le Disciple*, then – it had appeared a year before – a literary sensation. Similarities have also been pointed out with George Moore's *A Modern Lover* (1883); both writers agree that 'the life of an artist should be a practical protest against the so-called decencies of life' (*Confessions of a Young Man*). HERMANN BAHR (1863-1934), an Austrian from Linz, had just arrived – elegant and scented, with pointed beard and Lavallière cravat – in Berlin after a stay in Paris (1889-90), where by this time the symbolist doctrines were the latest thing. The hero of the tale is a young painter who, after eating red salmon in green sauce, is pursued by these colours: he sees symphonies first of green, then of red ('*Es war der Lyrismus des Roten . . . ein kräftiges, männliches und tätiges Rot*' is a sample of the erotic symbolism of the book). The sub-title is *Seelische Zustände* (i.e. *états d'âme*), and this is symptomatic: the notation of states is here transferred from the outer to the inner world. 'The good school' is that of erotic experience: '*das Hamletische im Künstler verlangt eine Mätresse unbedingt*'; and the more perversity the greater the refinement of the nerves. Woman is, however, no more than an instrument in the refining process; she is and must be, as woman, a whore, '*ein liederliches Gemisch aus Kot und Honig*'. When the dross in his system is sufficiently burnt out[1] by his sexual paroxysms the painter hero, impotent in his art, has visions of a love without the female instrument: *'etwas ganz Nervöses, Raffiniertes, Kompliziertes müsste es werden'*, a dream-love, *'Glück der Enthaltsamkeit'*, *'die keusche Wollust'*; for fulfilment of desire destroys its mystic beauty. Here particularly – as in the rich colouring of the painter's nerve-whipped visions, in which the heavens open, wreathed in symphonies of purple perfumes and peopled by fire-red beings and blue vampires – we detect the influence of Huysmans. In *Die gute Schule* Bahr shows his uncanny flair for coming fashions; he (a *'Vorempfinder'*) is the herald of every new movement, and, if he did not actually turn the course of literature, he was at various stages the first to point out the change in direction. He had himself popularized the term *'die Moderne'*; in *Zur Kritik der Moderne* (1890) he shows what the movement is. In *Die Überwindung des Naturalismus* (1891) he exposes the ultimate absurdity of naturalism: *'Je dichter der Naturalismus der deutschen Dramatiker sich der Erfüllung seines eignen Prinzips nähert, desto weiter entfernt er sich von der Möglichkeit künstlerischer Wirkung. Je mehr er unpersönliche Wirkung wird, entgeisteter Stoff, desto mehr verliert er die letzte Gewalt über unser Gemüt. Er wirkt dann genau ebenso wie die Dinge selbst, die immer erst unserer Umarbeit brauchen, um für die Empfindung zubereitet und angerichtet zu werden.'* In *Expressionismus* (1914) he probes the new movement and interprets its theories. Bahr's criticism is from the first impressionistic; that is, while he lays down laws which he argues with a show of absolute logic and often with subtlety, he is for the most part expressing his own personality. Compared with academic criticism, in which close concatenation counts, such personal impressions in loose essay form may seem erratic; and Bahr, particularly in his later collections of essays,[2] may ramble on and intersperse irrelevant matter; giving himself, and whatever of his subject may shine through himself, his critical method is lightly selective and his aim is readability. His 'Protean personality' or 'fluid ego' (to use terms generally applied to him) fitted him admirably for his ceaseless outpouring of such easily gliding and soft if sinewy critical prose. His mind, for all its voracity of

---

[1] Like Des Esseintes, the hero of *A rebours*, *'sur le chemin, dégrisé, seul, abominablement lassé'*.

[2] *Wiener Theater* (1899), *Rezensionen* (1903), *Glossen* (1907), *Das Bilderbuch* (1921).

experience, was not strenuous: all that he wrote has the stamp of ease, and – taken *en masse* – a lack of depth; what gives it interest is the catholicity of his friendships and his capacity of appreciation of all styles and phases of literature and art. On his Russian travels he discovered Eleonora Duse, and is credited with having made her reputation. In *Renaissance* (1897) he proclaimed that the work of Hofmannsthal and Schnitzler heralded a new era in art, and he introduced to fame more than the close circle ('Jung Wien') who gathered round him to listen to his oracular discourse in the Café Griensteidl in Vienna, where he settled after his meteoric appearance in Berlin. His plays and novels are difficult to characterize: they would have to be classified in periods corresponding to his chameleon-like changes from Socialist and naturalist to impressionist and finally to a Roman Catholic and expressionist with the pose of a reformer of ethics. (He of all people! . . .) His naturalistic dramas have historical interest: *Die neuen Menschen* (1887) is modelled on Ibsen, and with its revolutionary hero between two women is in some sort a forerunner of Hauptmann's *Einsame Menschen*; his *Die Mutter* (1891), a pendant to Strindberg's *The Father*, shocked even the naturalists by its sexual craziness. In the traditional Viennese style of popular play (*Volksstücke*) are his *Aus der Vorstadt* (1893; in collaboration with Karlweis[1]), *Das Tschaperl* (1898), *Das Franzl* (1901). There is Viennese atmosphere, too, in his Napoleon drama, *Josephine* (1898), and *Der Krampus* (1901) conjures up the colourful grace of Maria Theresa's days, when Klopstock was the rage. Bahr's problem plays – *Der Apostel*, 1901; *Der Meister*, 1903; *Sanna*, 1905; *Der arme Narr*, 1905 (whose hero has Hugo Wolf for model) – are admittedly weak. Bahr is more in his element when he handles current problems in the comedy vein; thus *Die Kinder* (1910) touches the problem of incest and *Das Prinzip* (1912) disproves the theory of democratic equality by showing what follows when a Tolstoyan reformer agrees to the engagement of his son, a grammar-school boy, to a cook whose billowing bosom has revealed woman to him in a dance. Bahr's real successes were his comedies – or better farces. Two, which deal with conditions on the stage, are not without venom: *Der Star* (1899) makes game of actresses, and *Die gelbe Nachtigall* (1907), in which a malicious actor foists a Hungarian girl on a manager

---

[1] (=Karl Weiss, 1850-1901.) He wrote good *Volksstücke*: *Das grobe Hemd* (1897), *Der kleine Mann* (1896).

as a Japanese singer, was taken to be a hit at a famous producer. Musical virtuosi are the protagonists of *Die Andere* (1905), with its picture of the dual nature of Lida Lind the violinist, and of Bahr's most successful play, *Das Konzert* (1910), a rollicking farce in which a famous pianist is pestered by his pupils, whom he refers to as '*die Gänse*'. His wife is aware that according to the mood of the moment he selects one or the other for a night's recreation in his cottage in the forest; he is then, officially, called away to give a concert; she has the tolerance of a wise Viennese lady, and in the last act wins him back by going with the husband of the lady of the moment to the forest cottage and pretending that since her companion is her lover a double exchange is the obvious way out. There is too much of the fireworks of conversation in *Das Konzert*, but the characterization is effective; the pianist – said to be self-portraiture (Bahr boasted of his success with women) – is something of a stock figure (Wedekind's Kammersänger is the same type), but he has little ways which individualize him; the wife, with her pretence of indifference and her belief that an artist husband is a child and to be treated as such, is an effective stage rôle; and quite delightful is Eva, one of the pupils, tailormade in snake fashion ('*neunzehn Jahre; sehr schlank, phantastisch, auf Schlange stilisiert . . . versucht auf alle Weise nervös zu schillern . . .*'), who, just when the bad boy has promised to reform, arrives at the cottage in a state of erotic excitement. The curtain rings down with Eva in the hero's arms; she is telling the usual tale – '*Frau von Stein und Goethe*', '*Seeleneinsamkeit*', etc.; this philandering is second nature, part of the musician's business, and aids publicity (for if scandal ceases he is classed as worn out in body and music); and so, mechanically, he must go through the routine movements with Eva fainting in his arms to bliss. And with his wife in the next room! It would be interesting to compare Bahr's ironical depiction of erotic Viennese women in *Das Konzert* – as also in *Wienerinnen* (1900) – with that of Schnitzler; what one sees at a glance is that with Bahr the treatment is Don Juanesque and jovial, and with Schnitzler pathological and, under the cynical surface, sad. Bahr's novels and tales, after *Die gute Schule*, have little interest other than (where the originals of the characters were recognized) scandalous or as Austrain aspects. The short tales of *Caph* (1894) are in Maupassant's manner. After his return to the Roman Catholic fold, and under the influence of expressionistic ethics, Bahr planned a cycle of twelve novels which were to establish his new conviction that society must be transformed and that 'real life' must be created by 'real men'. In *Die Rahl* (1908) he shocked Vienna once again: a famous actress whose identity was guessed relieves a Jew grammar-school boy in one night of love of his virginity. Other novels of the series (*Drut*, 1909; *O Mensch!* 1910; *Die Rotte Korah*,[1] 1919) further reflect Bahr's irresponsible conception of 'real life'. Taken all in all, the man and his *milieu* are likely to be more interesting to posterity than his works; and in that respect his *Tagebücher* (1918), in which his expressionistic phase is recorded, *Das Hermann Bahr-Buch* (1913) and *Selbstbildnis* (1923) will serve for an epitome.

In the literary cafés of Vienna Bahr shared presidential authority with PETER ALTENBERG (1862-1918), the aphorist among the impressionists. His genius splits into fragments; and perhaps a comparison to diamond splinters, loosely collected, some brilliantly polished and too many with a muddied glitter, would be a fit description of his work (*Wie ich es sehe*, 1896; *Aschantee*, 1897; *Was der Tag mir zuträgt*, 1900). It is customary to classify him as a '*Momentphotograph*'; and his best pieces are indeed instantaneous photographs of something seen – Vienna with its suburbs, recollections of childhood, delicately pencilled portraits of women ('*verzwitterte Weibschattenwesen*') and girls (the Wiener Madl above all), cruelly clean sketches of predatory men; and all coloured by shifting moods. Grotesquely contradictory is the self-portrait of 'P.A.' which stands out from these fragments: the *habitué* of *Literatencafés*,[2] where he sits with his adoring and adored harlots, the poet of impromptus and *aperçus*, and with all this a pose of social reformer and preacher of the open-air life, controlled digestion, healthy bodies. Cynically colloquial, elegantly vulgar, pretentiously personal, ironically impaling the *clichés* of journalism, he is unique in his period, though historically in the line of the French *moralistes* (but what a moralist!) and of Lichtenberg. But, for all his keen observation and his sense of rhythm, he fails, because he has not the deadly earnestness of the true *moraliste*, whose very inspiration is pain of the spirit, while Altenberg's pain is that of the invalid poisoned by the perverse life of cities.

[1] Notable for its discussion of the problem of the Jews.
[2] Such a presidential poet with his halo of harlots in his Viennese *Stammcafé* is pictured by Werfel in *Barbara*.

Another Viennese aphorist was KARL KRAUS (1874-1936), a Jew, and today revered in Israel as one of the laureates of the race. In his day he was feared rather than loved, for he lashed about him with fine effect in his satirical journal *Die Fackel*, which he launched in 1899, and which for more than thirty years he wrote almost entirely himself. He is at his best in his aphorisms, which are collected in *Sprüche und Widersprüche* (1909) and *Nachts* (1919). He was a purist, a moralist, and an out-and-out conservative, and in this he ran counter to the trends of his time. His fierce fighting spirit rings out in his essays: *Sittlichkeit und Kriminalität* (1908), *Die chinesische Mauer* (1910), *Weltgericht* (1919). In *Der Untergang der Welt durch die schwarze Magie* (1922) he pours out the vials of his contempt on the liberal press. He was nowhere more a traditionalist than in his fight against the (as he saw it) progressive deformation of the language in the literature of the new schools; if the language is corrupted, he said, so is the people. This scrupulous care of pure form makes the vast body of his verse (*Worte in Versen*, 9 vols., 1916-30) run in a trodden track; there is more that sticks in the memory in *Epigramme* (1927) and in his satirical *Zeitstrophen* (1931). His *magnum opus* is the monumental drama *Die letzten Tage der Menschheit* (1919), which amounts to a corrosive catalogueing of all the evils of the time, with war in the forefront and the trend to war; World War II is seen brewing in the cauldrons of corruption fed by evil purpose. Other dramas are readable for their pungent wit: *Literatur oder man wird doch da sein* (1921), *Wolkenkuckucksheim* (1923; a colloquially Viennese modernisation, with its sting aimed at war, of the *Birds* of Aristophanes). *Traumtheater* (1924) and *Die Unüberwindlichen* (1928) hold up to ridicule what was to Kraus the new-fangled craze of psycho-analysis. His clarion warning reaches its culmination in *Die dritte Walpurgisnacht* (1952), in which he unfolds the perils of the totalitarian State.

Up to 1889 the trend of thought had been strongly 'social democratic', towards the masses. August Bebel[1] and Karl Liebknecht – both associated with the foundation of *Die freie Volksbühne* – were forces in the land. In 1889 the news was spread that Friedrich Nietzsche was mad, and his ideas began to be discussed in all quarters. A reaction set in towards individualism; 'the right of the strong', 'the will to power', 'the superman' became catchwords,

---

[1] His *Die Frau und der Sozialismus* (1883) is one of the most important handbooks of Socialism.

and were taken over as ingredients of impressionism. *Armeleute-poesie* and the chapter *Vom Gesindel* in Nietzsche's *Also sprach Zarathustra* were opposite poles. Nietzsche's '*Es gibt ein Leben, an dem kein Gesindel mittrinkt*' is what the new poets think (p. 98).

FRIEDRICH NIETZSCHE (1844-1900) was a Saxon like Lessing and Wagner, like Lessing a parson's son, and like Klopstock a pupil of Schulpforta. His father died at thirty-five of softening of the brain. At Bonn he was a pupil of Ritschl, whom he followed to Leipzig, together with the future Sanscrit scholar Deussen and Erwin Rohde, who was to write the famous history of Greek fiction (*Der griechische Roman*, 1876). At twenty-four, before he had taken his doctor's examination, he was called to Basel, on the recommendation of Ritschl, as professor of classical philology. From Basel, where he was the colleague of Jakob Burckhardt, he made visits to Tribschen on Lake Lucerne, where his great friend Wagner was living with Cosima. During the Franco-Prussian War he served as a hospital attendant, and fell ill with dysentery and diphtheria. Owing to continued illness he retired from his professorship in 1879, with a pension of 3,000 francs, from which he managed to save sufficient to pay for the publication of his books. These remained practically unnoticed ('*beim Verleger begraben, sie verfaulen förmlich*', he wrote), until in 1888 Georg Brandes lectured on him in Copenhagen. In the same year Nietzsche lost his reason. His medical sheet at Jena bore the words: '1866 *syphilitische Ansteckung*'.

His first book, *Die Geburt der Tragödie aus dem Geiste der Musik* (1872) – attacked immediately by Ulrich von Wilamowitz-Mollendorff[1] but defended by Erwin Rohde – reads strangely in the light of his later work: it is passionately reasoned propaganda for Wagner's 'music drama'. It is an interesting link in the chain of aesthetic theories; and while it buttresses Wagner's critical writings – *Das Kunstwerk der Zukunft* (1850), *Oper und Drama* (1851) – it supplements Schiller's classical division, in *Über naive und sentimentalische Dichtung*, of poetry into *naiv* (i.e. spontaneous) and *sentimentalisch* (i.e. reflective). Schiller had defined *das Naive* as the oneness of mind with nature, and *das Sentimentalische* as the conflict of mind with nature. Nietzsche derives art from the contest between Apollo and Dionysus; just as man and woman, though contrary and in constant strife, generate humanity by a periodic reconciliation, so

---

[1] One of the most famous of Greek scholars. He had been a fellow-pupil of Nietzsche at Schulpforta.

the union of *apollinisch* and *dionysisch* generates art. Apollo is form, plastic art, rationalism, subjective creation; Dionysus is formlessness, music, mysticism, intoxication creating in the forgetfulness of self (*Selbstvergessenheit im Rausche*). Art fluctuates between two extremes of perfect form and formlessness, between classical architecture and music, between fixed and unfixed. Between these two extremes – the two worlds of intoxication and dream (*Rausch und Traum*) – there is an ascending gradation in music, lyric verse, epic, plastic art, architecture towards fixity of image – each image (*Abbild*) being an Apolline dream-shape, or the will to existence as phenomenon of what is in the world beyond sense shapeless. Dream shapes that which is shapeless in chaos; the Greek gods themselves are dreamed visions of pure limbs in a vaporous void. This dream world of lovely illusion (*der schöne Schein*) is limited, and therefore calm; but intoxication is limitless, and therefore orgiastic. Judgment is calm, but ecstasy is drunken. All creation of life is in ecstasy; what is not created in ecstasy is without life; life can only come of life; calmness, even 'health', is barren, dead.[1] The calm shapers of vision – the Apolline or subjective poets – scorn Dionysiac orgies as morbid; little they know how livid and ghastly (*leichenfarbig und gespenstisch*) their 'health' looks when the glowing life of Dionysiac revellers reels past them. Apollo is raised above nature, not one with nature; but nature joins the mad rout of Dionysus: panther and tiger pace under his yoke; in Dionysiac frenzy man is one again with nature, he dances upwards into the air, he floats on enchanted clouds like the gods. Apollo is the artist with measuring mind and shaping hands – shaping an idolon; Dionysus drunk is more than artist, he is god, he is art itself; his frenzy of rapture creates the noblest work of art – man magnified and panting in passion. Now these two opposite ideals of *Traumkunst*, or shaping vision, and *Rauschkunst*,[2] or creation in ecstasy, are united in the ancient Greek tragedy, which springs from the chorus of satyrs; for in Greek tragedy Apollo shapes, in a symbolic vision, the oneness with nature of the drunken reveller. Music is the highest of the arts; for, though it shapes no visions, it expresses that ancient pain (*Urschmerz*) felt by man when by the

[1] Nietzsche has no inkling of Thomas Mann's insistent teaching (the biological fact) that creation kills the creator; that creation, while the highest manifestation of life, is also the beginning of the death of life.

[2] Ideas vital for the intelligence of literature after 1890.

process of becoming man he was wrenched from synthesis with the eternal. Music is the echo thrilled with pain of a lost divine harmony. And therefore the nearer to music, the more divine is verse. It follows that lyric verse is next in beauty to music; though by the very nature of lyric verse the lyric poet sings of self, he sings his intoxication with self, and is therefore Dionysiac. (In illustration one might say that Burns's poem *To Mary in Heaven* would be merely local gossip if it were not an echo in music of the *Urschmerz*.) The *Volkslied* clings in close imitation to music, and is thus the ideal of a poem, which merely expresses what in music is not expressed. The epic poet, on the other hand, is lost in contemplation of images or shapes. Music symbolizes the universe (*Musik ist Weltsymbolik*). As Wagner said, civilization is eclipsed by music as lamplight is by the sun's radiance. Art saves man from Buddha's denial of life; in utter disgust with life man is rescued from the horrible by the sublime and from the absurd by comic laughter. Greek art was saved by the chorus of satyrs. To the Greek the bearded satyr was nature; and whereas the flute-playing shepherd of modern pastorals was a pretence of nature, the Greek satyr was true man; not in Gessner's *Salonschäfer* but in Haupt-mann's *Waldschrat*, Nietzsche might have urged if he had read *Die versunkene Glocke*, is nature real and redolent. The regeneration of myth which was the inspiration of Greek tragedy was killed by Euripides, with his explanatory prologues, and by Socrates, that spinner of theories; stripped by logic (or rationalism) of music and mysticism, tragedy dies. But in German music (Wagner is meant) there is an awakening of the Dionysiac spirit, and a rebirth of (German) myth.

Nietzsche next, in 1873, launched an attack on David Friedrich Strauss[1] (1808-74) (*David Strauss, der Bekenner und der Schriftsteller*), whom he angrily dismisses as a '*Bildungsphilosoph*', that is, a scholar who does not seek truth, because he thinks truth has already been found by the mighty dead, a slave of barren learning, not a creator. His next work, *Vom Nutzen und Nachteil der Historie für das Leben* (1874), continues the attack on contemporary ideals of culture. The study of history, he proclaims, is useless unless it is a fertiliz-ing process creating the future: history studied on the principle '*fiat veritas, pereat vita*' makes man passive, retrospective, a living

---

[1] His *Der alte und der neue Glaube*, which has been called *Die Bibel des Bildungs-philisters*, had appeared in 1872.

lexicon, a eunuch. History reduced to knowledge has lost its germs like corn ground to flour. Thus contemporary culture is not culture, but a knowledge of culture; it produces scholars and philistines, but not men who, fighting history or the reality round them, make history. Thus, in these two books two new ideals are proclaimed: a new culture and new man. These two books were negative; the two next, *Schopenhauer als Erzieher* (1874) and *Richard Wagner in Bayreuth* (1876), are positive. New man can be imbued with the new culture in the school of Schopenhauer, and in Wagner's operas new man can be seen realized. The four works mentioned were collected under the title *Unzeitgemässe Betrachtungen* (1873-76): '*unzeitgemäss*' is what Schopenhauer and Wagner teach us to be, that is, hostile to circumambient reality, to the time we live in; they were men who, instead of bending their backs to the golden calf – pseudo-culture, a scarecrow hung with rags – wandered out into the wilderness and feared not to be alone. Real culture is a life-force surging from the heart and transforming the whole organism into a perfect unity.

The great crisis in Nietzsche's life was his loss of faith in Wagner, when the latter, as it seemed to Nietzsche, 'collapsed before the Christian cross'. He smashed his idol in *Der Fall Wagner* (1888). His *Menschliches, Allzumenschliches* (1878), published as his health broke for good, bears evidence of the mental storm and stress through which he had passed. It is, like all Nietzsche's books written after this crisis in his life, a collection of aphorisms.[1] Nietzsche here shows a violent reaction against current literature, both in its form and substance. The form was the natural outcome of the mode of composition. Nietzsche, doomed to death but with the will to live, lived in the open air and jotted down his ideas as they came. He never rounded his philosophy into a system: it remains in rudimentary form, aphorisms shot into shape, clear by force of repetition and hammering in, but not logically fitted in section by section. It has the freshness of mountain air and the poetry of surprise, as of sudden vistas opening out from a scaled height; it has a Biblical familiarity of style studded with Hebrew parallelisms and variation. In *Unzeitgemässe Betrachtungen* there had

---

[1] Both style and spirit owe something to La Rochefoucauld; e.g. *Das Christentum gab dem Eros Gift zu trinken: – er starb zwar nicht daran, aber entartete zum Laster*; or: *Der Mann soll zum Kriege erzogen werden und das Weib zur Erholung des Kriegers: alles andere ist Torheit.*

been drastic disillusionment; in *Menschliches, Allzumenschliches* even the illusions he had kept have gone. There are two kinds of poetry, we are told now: one (for mature men) is quiet and harmonious, the other (for women and children) is passionate and chaotic. The ideal poet is he who bodies forth types of the future: healthy, glad and beautiful men.[1] This poet's landscape is bathed in the light of a sun which lights up cobwebs in the mystic cave, rends the iridescent dreams of the romanticist, and shows up every metaphysical system that ever was as a mirage.

From *Menschliches, Allzumenschliches*, from *Morgenröte* (1881), *Die fröhliche Wissenschaft* (1882), and the following works Nietzsche's *Weltanschauung* has to be pieced together by the reader, who must disregard contradictions: seen from a scaled peak boulders flatten themselves out in the vast sweep of the slopes. Science, we are told, gives insight and calls for nobler natures than poetry and music – these are leaves falling in autumn, the swan-song of departing things. The highest state of the soul is a glad, roguish seriousness; and therefore Socrates was wiser than Christ. Men of old were glad; men of today merely shun pain; our descendants must be like our forefathers, and for this 'conscience' and the idea of 'evil' must be done away with. The prick of conscience is like a dog's bite in a stone; it is silly; the will is not free, and all is necessary. In nature there are no contradictions, only grades of difference. There is no basic difference between good and evil. Man must cultivate the animal he is; only so can he attain the highest development of his whole self. The hatred of our human, that is of our animal nature, came from the ascetic ideal of suffering, which is the will to annihilation (*Wille zum Nichts*), because suffering was ascribed to guilt, whereas suffering is but the corollary of joy.

Humanity has gone backwards since Christianity crossed the world's threshold. The rebellion of slaves against ancient philosophy was completed by Christianity, which enthroned the emotions love, fear, hope, and faith. Christianity by the trick of 'love' became lyric religion, by the trick of 'hell' it drew the timid into its fold. Its character was oriental and feminine; it identified misfortune and guilt, whereas antiquity was familiar with the idea of free and guiltless misfortune. Christianity brought pity, that can-

---

[1] '*Das Ziel ist der starke und schöne Mensch.*' Richard Wagner: *Die Kunst und die Revolution* (1849).

ker that has eaten into man's marrow. Christianity's altruistic morality – 'love thy neighbour' – is the morality of the helpless; it has ever been the foe of the strong, the lonely. No instinct is in itself moral, the same instinct can develop (e.g.) into cowardice or humility – and submission to morality is not moral. It may be called forth by slavishness or despair! The morality of the slave is not the morality of the strong man. Morality, in its quality of obedience to prevailing laws, is genetic nonsense; free man is genetically immoral. They were the strong, evil spirits that led man upwards. Morality is nothing more than the instinct of the herd. There must be a new adjustment of the table of values (*eine Umwertung aller Werte*). But for that a new man is needed who can stand like a giant among pygmies. The driving force in history is the will to power (*der Wille zur Macht, der Machtwille*; not, as in Schopenhauer's system, the will to live) in individuals as in nations.

Also sprach Zarathustra (1883-85) brings into relief the ideal figure of the great lonely man who breaks down all old values and replaces them by new, shows the steps that lead up to the super-man. In *Also sprach Zarathustra* we are told that men are not equal and never will be, and the ideal to strive for is that of the superman – the incarnation of the *Machtwille*, the man who stands beyond good and evil. *Also sprach Zarathustra* is the most popular of Nietzsche's books, probably because Zarathustra, the old man of the mountains, is a vivid idealization of Nietzsche himself, and at the same time a prose-poem with oracular utterances that sing themselves into the memory. The chanted texts have the pitiless fierceness and the violent images of the Hebrew prophets:

> *Das Leben ist ein Born der Lust; aber wo das Gesindel mittrinkt, da sind die Brunnen vergiftet.*
> *Allem Reinlichen bin ich hold; aber ich mag die grinsenden Mäuler nicht sehn und den Durst der Unreinen.*
> *Sie warfen ihr Auge hinab in den Brunnen: nun glänzt mir ihr widriges Lächeln herauf aus dem Brunnen.*
> *Das heilige Wasser haben sie vergiftet mit ihrer Lüsternheit; und als sie ihre schmutzigen Träume Lust nannten, vergifteten sie auch noch die Worte.*

Through all history, runs the main thread of Nietzsche's argument, there has been a bitter contrast between two contrary ideas of morality, between the morality of the rulers and the ruled, the

morality of masters and the morality of slaves,[1] the former characterized by the definition of values 'good – bad' (*gut – schlecht*), the
latter by that of 'good – evil' (*gut – böse*). Nietzsche explains the
origin and definition of values of these two moral principles in
Jenseits von Gut und Böse (1886), *Zur Genealogie der Moral* (1887), and
Der Antichrist (1888). The highly-placed, high-minded man looked
upon himself and his actions as 'good', that is, first-rate, in contradiction to the lowly-placed, low-minded man and *his* actions: by
means of this 'pathos of distance' he created values and the names
for them. This is the origin of the terms 'good – bad'. [Nietzsche
was guided by somewhat slippery etymologies, e.g. the fact that
schlicht (=plain) and *schlecht* (=bad) are originally the same word.]
Slave morality had a different origin. A chiasmus of equivalents
therefore arises:

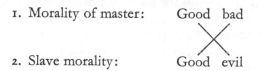

1. Morality of master: Good bad

2. Slave morality: Good evil

That is, what in the morality of masters was good was evil in
slave morality. To the slave the mighty lord is 'evil', i.e. 'evil' to
the slave is 'good' to the lord. The masters are optimists, the slaves
are pessimists. Slave morality was spiritualized and refined by
priests, for the caste of priests were weaklings, and it was in their
interest to turn the original statement of values upside down. The
rebellion began with the Jews, that hate-filled race of priests, and
the function of Jews in history was continued by Christianity:
Judaea conquered Rome. The ideal of antiquity came to life again
at the Renaissance, for the ideal of the Renaissance was '*virtù*' –
that is, plenitude of power exercised with no qualms of conscience; but the two great plebeian revolutions, the German and
the English Reformation first, and then the French Revolution,
tumbled the ruined temples of antiquity to the ground, and on them

---

[1] The idea may derive from Gobineau's *Essai sur l'inégalité des races humaines*
(1853-55), in which this French Wagner enthusiast proclaims the superiority
of the blond Germans over other races; he divides races into '*maîtres*' and
'*esclaves*'. The first flush of Gobineau's vogue in Germany was due to Wagner,
and Ludwig Schemann, the most insistent exponent of Gobineau's racial
theory, belonged to the Wagner Circle at Bayreuth. From here, and from
Houston Stewart Chamberlain's *Foundations of the Nineteenth Century*, derives
that racial doctrine which has meant so much in Germany.

the nineteenth century built its appalling barracks for workmen.

The ruling element in Christianity is altruism. It makes virtues of weaknesses and brands the strong, glad man as a criminal. It glorifies all those qualities by means of which it can maintain itself in the struggle for existence: charity, pity, self-sacrifice. An ascetic ideal which is hostile to life! 'Bad conscience' is merely the suppressed striving for freedom of an enslaved race; the instincts they exercised when free they must now, as slaves, resist and brand as evil. This race of 'conscience'-stricken slaves devised religious conceptions of sin against God; they conceive God as the extreme contrast of their suppressed but still stirring instincts; these instincts they interpret as sin against God, their sufferings they interpret as punishment for the sins with which they identify 'bad conscience'. It was religion's most eventful *tour de force*; it was the will *against* life, against the body, against the world, against beauty and happiness. And therefore away with 'bad conscience' and pity and ascetic ideas! We must be 'good Europeans', who have outgrown Christianity. Let us return to the clear-cut distinction of good (or strong) and bad (or weak). By the will to truth we shall find the way to the other side of good and evil, till the first-born of the new time come, the new Zarathustra, the blond beast[1] – like the dawn over the sea. Then, in the new Dionysiac age of gladness, with truth realized, the division into lords and slaves will be no more, for we shall all have crossed the bridges from ape to man and from man to superman. Equality will have been reached, not by depressing the strong and proud, but by elevating the weak and humble. Not to be happy in Heaven, to be happy on earth is the watchword of the new culture.

Götzendämmerung oder wie man mit dem Hammer philosophiert (printed 1888, published 1895) dates the decay of German culture from the foundation of the new Reich in 1871; of Socialists Nietzsche says here that, since the base of their creed is Christian feeling, their ideal of free men is illusory. The fevered megalomania of *Ecce homo* (written 1888, published 1908) is but a logical climax, heightened by disease and the lack of response, of what, after all, is Nietzsche's most vital idea: to leave all and magnify self ('*sich zu sich selbst verführen*').

The quintessence of Nietzsche's thinking is thus seen to be the permanent elevation of the type man. But this fiery optimism,

[1] '*die prachtvolle, nach Beute und Sieg lüstern schweifende, blonde Bestie.*'

with its acceptance of life, not in spite of suffering but because of it, is chilled by one philosophical shudder: the doctrine of eternal recurrence (*die ewige Wiederkehr, die Wiederkehr des Gleichen*), which Nietzsche substitutes for eternal life after death: the number of possibilities is limited, but time is unlimited; everything, therefore, must repeat itself, and therefore man must inevitably follow superman. Logically applied this doctrine neutralizes the doctrine of the superman: what will be, has been; the superman must come and go as one of the recurrent possibilities of existence. Nietzsche sought to make this conception endurable by teaching that we should live in such a way that we would gladly live again in the same way. Thus we *will* eternity. '*Vergiss nicht,*' he cries, '*dass du für die Ewigkeit handelst!*' (One might of course argue that voluptuaries, criminals, Christians, and happy fools may wish for a recurrence of *their* state.)

It has often been said of Nietzsche that he was more poet than thinker, and by his own confession ('*Man schreibt nur im Angesicht der Poesie gute Prosa*'[1]) he cadenced his prose to the rhythms of verse. Certain it is that the '*Dionysus-Dithyramben*' of *Zarathustra* have, as much or more than Walt Whitman's rolling line, gone to the making of the free rhythms of Arno Holz, Cäsar Flaischlen, Alfred Mombert, and others. His verse in traditional form (*Gedichte und Sprüche*, 1898) has been overmuch praised, but that of it which is unrhymed has the suggestiveness and haunting melody of impressionist poetry at its best; e.g.:

VENEDIG

An der Brücke stand
jüngst ich in brauner Nacht.
Fernher kam Gesang:
Goldener Tropfen quoll's
über die zitternde Fläche weg.
Gondeln, Lichter, Musik –
trunken schwamm's in die Dämmerung hinaus . . .

Meine Seele, ein Saitenspiel,
sang sich, unsichtbar berührt,
heimlich ein Gondellied dazu,
zitternd vor bunter Seligkeit.
– Hörte jemand ihr zu? –

[1] *Die fröhliche Wissenschaft.*

8

It is a rhymed poem, however, *Das trunkne Lied* from *Also sprach Zarathustra*, which is most quoted; and here the rhymes are necessary, for they echo the twelve strokes of midnight:

> *Oh Mensch! Gib acht!*
> *Was spricht die tiefe Mitternacht?*
> *'Ich schlief, ich schlief –,*
> *Aus tiefem Traum bin ich erwacht: –*
> *Die Welt ist tief,*
> *Und tiefer als der Tag gedacht.*
> *Tief ist ihr Weh –,*
> *Lust – tiefer noch als Herzeleid:*
> *Weh spricht: Vergeh!*
> *Doch alle Lust will Ewigkeit –,*
> *– will tiefe, tiefe Ewigkeit!'*

Out of its context the poem is cryptic. Midnight is symbolical; it stands for every moment which is between the past and the future – which is true of every moment. The 'deep dream' is the dark mysticism of religion. *'Weh'* is the pessimistic conception of life which seeks Nirwana; but joy knows that it is ever mate to suffering, and accepts suffering for the sake of eternity, *wills* the eternal recurrence.

Not the originality of Nietzsche's ideas but the lyric power with which he makes them his own and the fact that they constitute a doctrine directly opposite to the doctrines of Christianity and democracy explain their immense influence on literature after 1890. Indeed the literal originality of these ideas, which have passed as more or less commonplace into the common heritage of mankind, may well be questioned. *Übermensch* as a word has been traced back to 1527, was a favourite with Herder, and is used sarcastically by Goethe in line 490 of *Faust* and in the dedication to his poems; and its doctrinal significance was taught in ancient Greece by the sophists. *Die ewige Wiederkehr* is the palingenesis of the Pythagoreans, Heraclitus, and the Stoics, and is originally a religious tenet of the Babylonians. Nietzsche's ethical teaching itself finds a parallel in that of a contemporary philosopher whose writings have good literary qualities – EUGEN DÜHRING[1] (1833-1921), who bids man cast off the Jew-Christian conception of life as slavery and to

---

[1] *Der Wert des Lebens* (1865); *Sache, Leben und Feinde* (1882); *Wirklichkeitsphilosophie* (1895); *Waffen, Kapital und Arbeit* (1906); *Soziale Rettung* (1907).

be heroic and a law unto himself. Nietzsche's 'good European' is Dühring's 'modern European'.

One might sum up the effects of Nietzscheanism on literature somewhat as follows:

1. The cult of the superman appears principally in the glorification of Renaissance characters; that is, mostly in historical plays; and here there is continuity from Jakob Burckhardt and Gobineau to Conrad Ferdinand Meyer and Nietzsche and from these three Germans to impressionism. But the qualities of the *Renaissance-mensch* ('*Mensch der Tat*', '*Tatenmensch*') may be transferred to modern characters, with the main aspects of licentious egotism and ruthlessness, particularly in erotic experience; thus Heinrich Mann's banker Türkheimer (*Im Schlaraffenland*), a *Genie der Tat* who gathers artists and poets round him in materialistic Berlin, and Dehmel's superman, who immunizes himself from pessimism by the heroic gratification of his impulses, are Nietzschean derivatives. In this conception of the *Renaissancemensch* as *jenseits von Gut und Böse* and wilfully 'wicked'[1] the impressionists radically misunderstood Nietzsche's idea of *in die Tiefe steigen*. What matters to the literary critic, however, is that this false conception served as inspiration. Another source of impressionist immoralism was Stendhal, in whom Nietzsche had delighted; Heinrich Mann, for instance, lauds Stendhal as 'the prophet of energy'.

2. Decadent individualism leans on Nietzsche to justify its worship of the morbid ego. The text for this heroization of self-contempt may be found variously in Nietzsche: e.g. '*Was ist das Grösste, das ihr erleben könnt? Das ist die Stunde der grossen Verachtung. Die Stunde in der euch auch euer Glück zum Ekel wird und ebenso eure Vernunft und eure Tugend . . . Was liegt an meiner Tugend? Noch hat sie mich nicht rasen gemacht.*' (*Also sprach Zarathustra.*) This, of course, is a poor excuse for *das rasende Leben* of impressionists and expressionists; but it does provide a holy text. Stefan George's Algabal or any satanistic hero of Heinrich Mann is intelligible as a synthesis of Nietzsche and Baudelaire. The Neronism or Narcissism of Stefan George – worship of self as individual – is also such a synthesis. This Narcissism derives also from the works of Maurice

---

[1] Actually Nietzsche denied the moral values of his day as contrary to nature; his aim was to emancipate them by making 'nature' and 'morality' equivalent; the result would logically be 'natural immorality' or what he himself termed 'moral naturalism'.

Barrès (three of his novels have the collective title of *Le culte du moi*), who was himself influenced by Nietzsche. Barrès is definitely decadent in his doctrine that the full life is achieved by the stimulation of the senses[1] : love of self, he teaches, leads to the perfection of all our faculties of sensation, by which we comprehend and possess the universe; man is the sum of his sensations, and the more intense these are the more complete is the man.[2]

3. The theory of *Rauschkunst*, which is the base of expressionism.

The Renaissance dramas begin already in the naturalistic period, with Carl Bleibtreu's *Der Dämon* (1887), of which Caesar Borgia is the hero. Schnitzler's *Der Schleier der Beatrice* transfigures the hectic loving of the *cinquecento*; Rudolf Herzog's *Die Condottieri* (1905) was the greatest stage success among such plays. The *Tatenmensch* does his damnedest in a cycle of dramas, including a *Cäsar Borgia*, by WILHELM WEIGAND (1862-1949), who groups them under the title of *Renaissance* (1897-1909). Weigand is influenced by Gobineau's dialogues *La Renaissance* (1877) and by Stendhal. In his *Savonarola* he contrasts – as does Thomas Mann in *Fiorenza* – Christian and Renaissance ideals. [Lenau's long poem *Savonarola* (1837) remains the classical depiction, in spite of its Christian morality.] *Lorenzino* is too much of a copy of de Musset's *Lorenzaccio*. Weigand is too saturated with French culture to be a true impressionist; he strives for perfection of form, as in his verse (*Gedichte, Auswahl*, 1904) and for clarity, as in his *Essays* (1891) and *Das Elend der Kritik* (1895). His *Friedrich Nietzsche* (1893) was one of the first appreciations of the master. His best-known novel, *Die Frankentaler* (1889), reproduces with gentle irony the life of a small town in his native Franconia; in the humour of his short

[1] '*Je veux accueillir tous les frissons de l'univers*' [*Un homme libre* (1889), which Hermann Bahr hailed as '*das grösste Buch des Jahrhunderts*'].

[2] Nietzsche's idea of the superman may of course be interpreted, as may Conrad Ferdinand Meyer's cult of the *Renaissancemensch*, as the worship of contraries. Arthur Moeller-Bruck (*Die moderne Literatur*, p. 46), though he appreciates Nietzsche, ranks him as a decadent: '*Nietzsches ganzer Individualismus ist schliesslich nur die Kehrseite seiner persönlichen Hilflosigkeit dem Leben gegenüber.* . . . *Das Gefühl des Allein-Seins, der Vereinsamung steigerte sich mehr und mehr zu dem Bewusstsein, ein Ausgestossener zu sein* . . . *Immer war Nietzsche der Kranke, dem die eigene Schwäche die Befriedigung seiner Gelüste verbot; wie keine andere Persönlichkeit unserer Zeit illustriert er uns den Begriff: Dekadent.*' This is pretty much Thomas Mann's picture of the artist. Dehmel, on the other hand, who had the physical strength to do what C. F. Meyer and Nietzsche could not do – and who escaped syphilis – was *not* a decadent.

stories, *Michael Schönherrs Liebesfrühling* (1904) and *Der Messiaszüchter* (1906), there is entertaining literary satire and something of Gottfried Keller's spirit.

One striking feature of the naturalists' campaign for a regenerated literature was that they gave full acknowledgment to two poets of the older generation, both former officers – MARTIN GREIF (1839-1911) and HEINRICH VON REDER (1824-1909). Both contributed to *Die Gesellschaft*. In Heinrich von Reder's poems (*Federzeichnungen*, 1885; *Lyrisches Skizzenbuch*, 1893), particularly in the vignettes of hunting experiences, there is a realistic element, but what seemed to bring them close to the new ideals for verse was the hinted secondary meaning, the symbol of human sorrow in the aspect of nature presented, or in the fate of bird or beast; and it is just this flash of vision together with a gem-like perfection of form which still delights in the verse (*Gedichte*, 1868; final edition 1895; *Neue Lieder und Mären*, 1902) of Martin Greif, as in his *Der Geworbene*, a wistful epitome of what it means to be a soldier:

> *Sie gruben einen Soldaten ein,*
> *sie trommelten, präsentierten,*
> *sie schossen ihm ins Grab hinein,*
> *die Degen salutierten:*
> *'Leb wohl, Kamrad, leb wohl!'*

> *Und wie ihm nach die Trommel schlug,*
> *dem Kriegsmann in der Erden,*
> *da schwur der Knab, der's Kreuz ihm trug,*
> *auch ein Soldat zu werden:*
> *'Wohlan, O Knab, wohlan!'*

What touches the heart here is the contrast – not expressed but hovering in the air so to speak – of the chorister solemnly bearing his Cross, the ceremonial of church and army, the nation's need of the boy's desire and the pathos of it. And all this human feeling expressed with no pretence of poignancy – rather with an old soldier's weathered hardness – informs the lyrics of a book which shocked and delighted (much as Kipling's *Barrack-Room Ballads* did in their day in England) the few who read it (23 copies were sold in two years!) – the *Adjutantenritte* (1883) of Freiherr DETLEV VON LILIENCRON (1844-1909). Born (as a Danish subject) at Kiel, he belonged to an ancient stock of barons, whose rich estates had passed from them because the poet's grandfather had married a peasant girl. Detlev served as a Prussian officer, and was wounded in both the Austrian and the French wars; was discharged '*Wunden und Schulden halber*'; taught music and painted walls in America; returned and was employed by the government in administrative work by his native dikes (Hardesvogt on the lonely North Sea island of Pellworm, Kirchspielvogt at Kellinghusen); lived very penuriously on his literary earnings at Munich and then at or near Altona. The small pension the Kaiser was persuaded to give him as the century turned helped him no more than what he earned by reciting his poetry – and this particularly went against the grain: 'Don't come to my recitation,' he implores a friend, 'it nearly makes me sick . . . And then people stare at me! Ghastly!' This pride of race and training allied with genuine *bonhomie* and readiness to rub shoulders with the roughest people and his openly expressed disgust with literature as a profession give him a place apart from the class-proud poets he frequented. He was a Bohemian, but still an aristocrat. There is naturalism enough in his work, but it is rather the outrightness of a blunt soldier or the free-and-easy raciness of a hunting gentleman, not a programmatic choice. *Adjutantenritte* revealed him as one of the new characters which *Moderne Dichtercharaktere* were calling for to create the new verse; and the new leader was found far from all *cénacles*, absolutely unconscious of iconoclast theory, creating the new style out of the freshness of his originality. The date of *Adjutantenritte* is actually a year before that of *Moderne Dichtercharaktere*; and the strange thing is that these poems by virtue of their double sense of symbolism – Liliencron is fond of a quizzical glance at death or of a lighthearted but penetrating reference to man's mutability in the permanence of nature – point forward beyond the short fashion of naturalism to the succeeding school of impressionism. There are also in his work generally the elements of *Heimatkunst*. *Holsatia non cantat* was an old saying; but Detlev von Liliencron is yet another in the list (Hebbel, Klaus Groth, Theodor Storm) of poets of the first rank born and reared in Schleswig-Holstein; and he closely follows Theodor Storm (as Timm Kröger and Gustav Frenssen follow him) as a delineator of his native province; the virile martial note which the title of his first volume announces is doubled and relieved by the most vivid descriptions of *Marsch* and *Geest*, of the leagues of rolling heather by oozy mud-flats (*Watten*) bared

by the ebb of the tide on the coast of Holstein. His love of soldiering comes out in poem after poem; typical are *Kleine Ballade* or *Die
Musik kommt,* which quaintly pictures the passage through a village
street of a regiment of soldiers with the band going on before and
all the girls gazing at the haughty captain and the rosy-faced lieutenants. There is a deeper note in certain lyrics which show the
sadder side of soldiering (*Tod in Ähren* and above all *Wer weiss wo?*).
Improvisator and academically unschooled as he is, he is a master
of rhymecraft and of certain stanza forms, certainly of the *Siziliane*;
nothing indeed would represent him better here (for crass realism,
humour and irony, hinted meaning, and perfect construction)
than such a *Siziliane,* which has, moreover, the fascination of a
Dutch genre-painting:

DIE INSEL DER GLÜCKLICHEN

Das Hängelämpchen qualmt im warmen Stalle,
In dem behaglich sich zwei Kühe fühlen.
Der Hahn, die Hennen, um den Spross die Kralle,
Träumen vom wunderbaren Düngerwühlen.
Der Junge pfeift auf einer Hosenschnalle
Dem Brüderchen ein Lied mit Zartgefühlen.
Und Knaben, Kühe, Hühner lassen alle
Getrost den Strom der Welt vorüberspülen.

In the volumes of verse that followed[1] there is no development
except that the form grows both more supple and mannered.

In the historical panorama of German verse Liliencron stands
out as one of the most significant poets. Intellectually his range is
low; that is, he was no thinker. But he makes history by his style.
This marks an advance or a new direction in two main aspects.
Firstly, he flouts poetic diction. He accomplishes the reform – an
abandonment of traditional artificiality in favour of a language
new-coined to pass current in a new, less idealistic life – for which
Conradi and his merry men had been clamouring; but whereas
they had despite their theories carried on with the old style of
language Liliencron renews the language of verse without pre-
meditation by the mere trick of abolishing such devices as the
Dichter-e (*spielet* for *spielt*), and above all by admitting as poetically

---

[1] *Gedichte* (1889); *Der Haidegänger und andere Gedichte* (1890); *Neue Gedichte*
(1891). These collections are reprinted in *Kampf und Spiele* (1897), *Kämpfe und
Ziele* (1897), *Nebel und Sonne* (1900), *Bunte Beute* (1903).

effective words from everyday life (such as *Bureau, Zigaretten, Einglas*) previously regarded as too tawdry for the purpose. The second main element of his style is what is now interpreted as impressionism: Liliencron gives, not (like the naturalists) a drab section of a continuous state, but momentary, very vivid impressions of something unusual, or a series of such impressions with everything unnecessary eliminated. The difference is that between a photograph and a film; the naturalists freeze life, Liliencron shows it in flashes of movement. This verbal magic is enhanced by other qualities, above all by his delightful rough humour, which may come out in a juggling with words (*Tigert er auf dich heraus, | Tatz' ihn! wie die Katz die Maus*), or in a startling pretence of coarseness (*Das war der König Ragnar, | Der lebte fromm und frei. | Er trug gepichte Hosen, | Wie seine Leichtmatrosen, | Die rochen nicht nach Rosen, | Das war ihm einerlei*); he is a master, too, of sound-painting (*die Quelle klungklingklangt*) and of metaphor (*Ein Wasser schwatzt sich selig durchs Gelände; Es schleicht die Sommernacht auf Katzenpfoten*). His ballads,[1] mostly in the old pattern of rough quatrains, are best where they deal with historical episodes of his native province; savage frays and stark revenge is their theme. They may not pull at the heart-strings, as the best ballads do, but they have that fierce delight in fighting for its own sake which is the oldest element of German poetry. Liliencron's waywardness unshapes but lends a charm to his higgledy-piggledy epic (*'kunterbuntes Epos'*) *Poggfred* (1896-1908), in the style and stanza of Byron's *Don Juan* slowed down in the more serious parts by *terza rima*. The title is Low German for 'frog's peace', a pious fiction for the poet's country mansion (more likely his abode at the time of composition was in plain lodgings at Altona); the poem is a panorama of the memories and fancies of the poet's life shaped as humorous episodes or allegorical visions.

Of Liliencron's prose there is little to say, but more than of his dramas, which are unreadable. His novels[2] are written anyhow, and apart from his *Kriegsnovellen* (1894), which often have the literal truth of experience, even his short stories are negligible; the mass of them (*Aus Marsch und Geest, Könige und Bauern, Roggen und Weizen*; all 1900) have too much of the swagger of his famous poem *Bruder*

---

[1] Collected in *Balladenchronik* (1906).

[2] *Breide Hummelsbüttel* (1886); *Der Mäcen* (1890); *Mit dem linken Ellbogen* (1899); *Leben und Lüge* (1908; with biographical interest).

Liederlich: the bold bad baron comes and conquers some delightful female or other (peasant wench or princess is all the same) – and departs.

Liliencron and his immediate followers, such as Gustav Falke and Otto Julius Bierbaum, were entirely German in tradition; that is, in essentials their verse continues native styles – in particular the *Volkslied*, Heine, Theodor Storm, Conrad Ferdinand Meyer. Even their 'free rhythms' – e.g. Liliencron's famous rendering of the last stages of maudlin intoxication, *Betrunken* – are in the tradition of Heine's North Sea poems, and owe nothing to French *vers libres*. GUSTAV FALKE (1853-1916) was a music teacher, and the influence of popular songs and of strict musical rhythm count for much in his regular technique. He was born in Lübeck and settled in Hamburg, and was thus geographically close to the Schleswig-Holstein group of poets, but the local colouring in his verse[1] is scant; what does distinguish his poetry – after the elegiac playing with conceptions of death in his first volume and futile attempts to strike the bold erotic note in the fashion of his *entourage* – is gentle praise of the domestic idyll, as in *Aus dem Takt*. In this poem, as in others, poignant expression is given to Falke's physical inability – as a hopelessly decent man so to speak – to launch out into the lyric libertinage of Liliencron and Bierbaum and the sexual revolt of Dehmel; and there is always an undertone of disappointment in his acceptance of old-fashioned feeling and his idealization of hearth and home. *Resignationspoesie!* like that of Theodor Storm; but resignation brings peace, and after the defiant Nietzschean assertion of the rights of personality in the verse of his neighbours to read Falke satisfies some atavistic feeling and cleanses the mind. This spinner of quiet dreams finds the very stuff of poetry in evening slippers and flickering firelight (*Der Dichter*).

It was the reading of Liliencron's work which stimulated Falke to try his hand in verse. Liliencron encouraged him and, so to speak, launched him, and they remained close friends. Liliencron's friendship with another poet, RICHARD DEHMEL (1863-1920), was as close as that of Goethe with Schiller; and in later life, when Dehmel had left Berlin to settle in Blankenese, they were neighbours and allies in their war on literary and moral philistinism.

---

[1] *Mynheer der Tod* (1891); *Tanz und Andacht* (1893); *Zwischen zwei Nächten* (1894); *Neue Fahrt* (1897); *Mit dem Leben* (1899); *Hohe Sommertage* (1902); *Frohe Fracht* (1907).

In Liliencron and Dehmel the familiar contrast of Goethe and Schiller as naïve and sentimental is seen again. Liliencron's verse was spontaneous, Dehmel's was wedded to thought, sometimes tortured; his poems, he himself says, *'vollziehen sich aus Gefühlen,* | *Die den ganzen Menschen aufwühlen.'*[1] In another image Dehmel compared himself to an eagle rising heavily, but, once risen, floating freely; and the image adequately indicates the majestic sweep of his verse at its best. Liliencron's verse is sensuous, that is, it gives impressions of reality through the senses; Dehmel's verse is idealistic, that is, concerned with ideals or ideas – his poetry registers the processes of his thought probing his conception of the universe. It is nevertheless a question whether Dehmel's verse taken as a whole should be classed as *Gedankenpoesie*; his best lyrics – and when time has done its sifting one suspects that nothing will remain of him but a slender volume of lyrics which will be reckoned with the very best in the German language – are poems of experience (*Erlebnisgedichte*), whose rhythm and imagery are borne along on waves of intense emotion. His definition of rhythm (in *Licentia Poetica*, one of the disquisitions of *Betrachtungen*) as an undulation of vital energy, every stress being the crest of a wave of emotion and the rhythm pulsing with the tide of it, admirably fits his own lyric passion; on analysis it would be found that the rush of feeling – practically always sexual excitation – comes first, and that in the shaping of the feeling the idea is called in. The result is that the verse, though philosophical (and it is the startling nature of the philosophy throbbed into the passion of the lines which gives Dehmel his special place in the history of poetry), is not in the strict sense reflective or cerebral.

Like Falke, Dehmel was a Hamburg man by adoption, but his landscapes too are not those of Hamburg. Dehmel's landscape is that of the Spreewald where he was born: reed-rimmed or willow-fringed lakes or rivers, dark pine forests roaring in the wind, sandy heaths blue with heather, yellowing fields of lupin. He chose Blankenese because, on the pine-hung uplands by the Elbe, he thought the scenery came near to that of his homeland; but where his verse landscapes are most vivid (e.g. *Lied an meinen Sohn*) there is no doubt that they are the scenery his boyhood knew. He was born at Hermsdorf, in the heart of forests of which his father was ranger (*Revierförster*). When he was six years old his father moved

---

[1] *Denkzettel (Erlösungen).*

RICHARD DEHMEL

to Kremmen near by, and was ranger of the town forest there. It would be wrong to say that Dehmel's upbringing in these forests of the March of Brandenburg gives the individual note to his poetry; he is definitely an urban poet. But the Spreewald scenery serves again and again as background, or as contrast, or for imagery; it has even been seriously suggested that the belling of rutting stags rings out in the sexual fury of his most characteristic verse. Whether there is any justification in the familiar interpretation of his poetic manner as Prussian *Schrecklichkeit* controlling Slav hysteria is dubious; the cast of his features was admittedly Slav (in *Zwei Menschen* Lea speaks to Lux – that is Dehmel – of his 'Russian face'), and his birthplace lies in what was a Slav enclave; but (in *Kultur und Rasse*, one of the essays of *Betrachtungen*) he claims to be a *'waschechter Deutscher'*, though he admits that his stock was Silesian on the paternal side and that there is a Slav ring in the name Tschorsch which some of his ancestors bore. The hysteria is biographically authenticated: as a boy home from school he fell from a horizontal bar while practising gymnastics and had concussion of the brain, and as a result suffered from epileptic fits – because of which he was rejected for the army – till well on in life; in his essay *Naivität und Genie* (in *Betrachtungen*) he says that in time he overcame this tendency by self-observation and will power – except that he could always call up such *Klopfgeister* at will (he means that the demonic hallucinations he describes so vividly – particularly in the autobiographical sketches of *Lebensblätter* – were the gifts of this controlled morbid state).

His work also bears the mark of his rebellious nature as a boy. He was sent to Berlin and lodged with an uncle while he attended the Sophien-Gymnasium. One day he was called before his headmaster to answer for his activity as chairman of a scientific club (Darwin was then in the forefront of intellectual interest); and when he was asked if he wished to decorate a monkey-cage he refused to darken the school doors again. All his school years were marked by a violent conflict with his father, who was horrified at his wild ways; here we have in real life that *Sohn-Vater-Kampf* which was to provide so much matter for literature, and is reflected in Dehmel's own *Lied an meinen Sohn*. Finally Dehmel passed his leaving examination at the Gymnasium at Danzig and entered the University of Berlin (1882), where he studied science, philosophy, and history. As a *Couleurstudent* he was a fierce fencer, and the grim effect of his features in later life was partly due to duelling scars. Funds more than once gave out, as his father was apt to stop supplies; for one whole month of summer he slept on benches in the Tiergarten, till he was befriended by a Kellnerin, who took him home and kept him with her for a month. When he had no money for lodgings he often shared rooms with a Jewish medical student, Franz Oppenheimer, whose sister Paula awakened his poetic genius (was 'die erlösende Kraft', to quote his own words). He was engaged to her for three years. Her family objected to the match – for one thing he was a Christian, and for another he was without employment, though he had begun to earn money by journalistic efforts; they yielded, however, when he took his doctor's degree (his thesis was 'Eine Prüfung der Gründe für den ausschliesslich öffentlichen Betrieb der Feuerversicherung') and became an official with an insurance company; but he did not actually marry till 1889, after his appointment, with a salary of 250 marks a month, as secretary to the Verband Deutscher Privat-Feuerversicherungen. From 1880 to 1890 he was loosely associated with the Socialist movement in Berlin. He was never a member of the party; indeed after he read Also sprach Zarathustra in 1890 he was a Nietzschean, though with reserves. Nevertheless from his sympathies with the workers came poems which by common consent are among the best Socialist poems[1] in German literature: Bergpsalm, Zu eng, Vierter Klasse, Ein Märtyrer, Die Magd, Erntelied, Der Arbeitsmann.

Dehmel's first volume of verse, Erlösungen (1891), is feeble or tentative: the form of the poems is traditional, the sentiment may be maudlin and the modernity impudent rather than forceful. Perhaps the most interesting of the poems, in the light of Dehmel's lyric development, is Stromüber: here for the first time the projection of violent emotion into a visioned landscape succeeds in a new way which Dehmel in his next two volumes was to make his own. A man and a woman are crossing a river in the dark; there is a vague feeling of spring in the air, and the others in the boat are laughing. The second stanza trails heavily, with its dark vowels and hard consonants, to the fourth line; but this makes a rush into the first line of the third stanza, which then rises almost hysterically to the dramatic revelation of the last three words:

[1] In the Gesammelte Werke transferred from Erlösungen to Aber die Liebe. Dehmel spoilt the chronological position of his poems by such re-shuffling; in this essay the original editions are dealt with, so far as possible.

Der weite Strom lag stumm und fahl,
am Ufer floss ein schwankend Licht,
die Weiden standen starr und kahl.
Ich aber sah dir ins Gesicht

und fühlte deinen Atem flehn
und deine Augen nach mir schrein
und – eine Andre vor mir stehn
und heiss aufschluchzen: Ich bin dein!

The fourth stanza returns to the landscape (as the boat touches shore the black, trembling image of the rigid willows fades in the grey water), so that what we get is a moment's tense drama set in a mysterious and haunting glimpse of a dark landscape. The inspiration of the poem was what is on the face of it a sordid domestic event: while Frau Paula was away at the seaside Dehmel had an affair with the domestic help, Käte B. Two years later the girl died by her own hand, and a ring Dehmel had given her was returned to him by her direction; and this message from the grave inspired him with the poem *Drei Ringe* in *Weib und Welt*. It holds good of all Dehmel's best poems that one must know what woman they are concerned with and the exact moment of the relationship; then one realizes how real the feeling is. It may be disturbing to some that where Dehmel creates something startlingly beautiful it is when he is seized by this lust of possession. His '*Räubersinn*' is thrust forward throughout the mass of his lyric verse, and there is a letter from him (No. 32) in which he describes the wild hunger which grips him when a human being comes near him, '*der Eignes in sich hat. Als ob ein Raubtier die Nüstern bläht, fängt dann etwas in mir an zu fiebern: da ist Nahrung für dich, mein Blut.*' His attitude is here, as elsewhere, that he is the saviour (*Erlöser*) of the girls he deflowers; and the general sense of the title *Erlösungen* is, of course, erotic. This *is* Dehmel – for better or worse.[1]

The title of the next collection of verse, *Aber die Liebe* (1893), is assumed to question that of the first: marriage may be salvation, but what of love?[2] The *Leitwort* points to the themes: '*In allen Tiefen* | *musst du dich prüfen,* | *zu Deinen Zielen* | *dich klarzufühlen.* |

[1] For the facts of Dehmel's life Julius Bab's *Dehmel* has to be collated with the *Briefe* (1923) as edited by Frau Ida Dehmel; the latter are the main source of safe information.

[2] Mrs Dehmel says the title shows the influence of Strindberg.

Aber die Liebe | ist das Trübe.' What is best in the book reflects Dehmel's passionate wooing of Hedwig Lachmann. '*Wie aus dem Schilf die Wasserfee*', he hails her, '*tauchest du winkend aus der Schar | der andern um uns zu mir her | mit deinem langen schwarzen Haar | und deinem fernen Augenpaar.*' She was another Jewess. In *Betrachtungen* (*Kultur und Rasse*) he says of himself: '*Ich stamme aus durchweg blauäugigen und überwiegend blonden Familien und liebe die dunkeln jüdischen Frauen. Ich finde bei keiner andern Art Weib so viel hellen Geist mit seelischer Glut verbunden.*' HEDWIG LACHMAN (1870-1918) was a poetess of distinction; her original verse (*Im Bilde*, 1902) does not rise beyond formal perfection, but this very quality makes her translations of Rossetti, Swinburne, Poe, and Verlaine notable. Her poems *Begegnung* and *Spaziergang* reflect her feelings for Dehmel: he and she are like two birches at the rim of the forest; gossamer threads bind one to the other. She remained good, and in 1900 married Gustav Landauer, who wrote Socialist books, and was murdered in the street in Munich in 1919 at the time of the Communist troubles. Hedwig Lachmann's resistance stirred the poet to his very depths. It was the period when, according to his diary, he stood on a bridge and was near committing suicide. He was tortured by dreams and hallucinations; organ notes surged within him, and oracular words; or on the roof of his room he would see Christ's face with the crown of thorns burning with electricity. He could only rid himself of his hallucinations by projecting them into verse, and to this morbid state we owe the loveliest poems of *Aber die Liebe*. How individual his technique became under the stress may be seen from one of these Hedwig lyrics, *Ohnmacht*:

> *Doch als du dann gegangen,*
> *da hat sich mein Verlangen*
> *ganz aufgetan nach dir.*
> *Als sollt ich dich verlieren,*
> *schüttelte ich mit irren*
> *Fingern deine verschlossene Tür.*
>
> *Und durch die Nacht der Scheiben,*
> *ob du nicht würdest bleiben,*
> *bettelten meine Augen; und*
> *du gingst hinauf die Stufen*
> *und hast mich nicht gerufen,*
> *mich nicht zurück an deinen Mund.*

Vernahm nur noch mit stieren
Sinnen dein Schlüsselklirren
im schwarzen Flur, und dann
stürzten auf mich die Schatten,
die mir im Park schon nahten,
als wir den Mond versinken sahn.

Notice the consummate cunning of the imperfect rhymes and the harsh transitions from iambic to trochaic measure; they produce the effect of a mind driven frantic. And from now on evocations of such strange states of mind come to Dehmel, it would seem, effortlessly.

Such poems of passion are, as we have indicated, wedded to his sexual doctrine; but the source and origin of them is in his violent over-sexed nature. The sexual doctrine was, as we have shown, part of the decadent Nietzscheanism of the demonic Pole Przybyszewski, whose *Totenmesse,* dedicated to Dehmel, begins: '*Am Anfang war das Geschlecht*', and continues: '*So schuf sich das Geschlecht endlich das Gehirn.*' The biological aspects of sex Dehmel discussed with his University friend Carl Ludwig Schleich,[1] who was one of a circle (Bierbaum, Hartleben, Przybyszewski) who entertained Strindberg[2] at the *Schwarzes Ferkel* in the Dorotheenstrasse in Berlin; and Strindberg's pathological strangeness impressed Dehmel, though their attitude to women was radically different. Both regarded woman as the eternal peril, but Dehmel's teaching is that man must seek this peril and steel himself by it. Simply stated: man is only man by woman. But man is for the world as well as woman; he must grow heroic by woman, but for the world. Philosophically what matters is not so much *Weib* as *Welt,* and the root of Dehmel's conception of *Welt* or the cosmos is of course this defiantly proclaimed sexuality, which, however, he transfigures in the white heat of his ecstasy into a kind of religious mysticism ('*Wollust zur Welt*'). This sanctification of the sexual instinct as cosmic urge – Dehmel calls himself in an almost blasphemous image *triebselig* – might be interpreted as the logical outcome of Darwin's doctrines electrified by the Dionysiac call to joy of Nietzsche. According to Dehmel, man is ripest when he is

[1] He wrote *Von der Seele: Essays* (1918) and *Besonnte Vergangenheit: Lebenserinnerungen 1859-1919* (1922).
[2] There is a highly impressionistic portrait of Strindberg (with his '*scheue Frauenlippen*') in *Ein Ewiger (Aber die Liebe).*

nearest to nature, i.e. in the act of love[1]; love is a divine duty. Love is the elimination of the antagonism of 'I' and 'all'; it is both consciousness of self and forgetfulness of self, *'die Rundung des eignen Ich im All zum All'*. For Dehmel love is (to quote Gundolf) *'keine Askese, sondern eigenherrliche Glut, die sich ergiessen und kühlen will, und zugleich weihen was sie berührt'*. *Brunst* must be transformed to *Inbrunst*, and the dross (*'das Trübe'*) that must be purified in the process is the sexual act. It would be too raw a statement to say that this act must be transformed to a holy rite; to Dehmel the conflict between the spiritual nature of love and the animal act remains. Perhaps his efforts to wed the act to a conscious spiritual volition are too subtle, and it may be questionable whether he has proved anything more than the biological volition (*Weltwille*, 'cosmic urge') which such naturalists as Bölsche, in the wake of Darwin, had made it their business to demonstrate.

In the original edition of *Aber die Liebe* there was a series of poems entitled *Verwandlungen der Venus*. These raised a storm of indignation; *Venus sapiens* was erroneously read as a discussion of homosexual love in the persons of David and Jonathan; Dehmel's friends, however, say it symbolizes the triumph of spirit in the marital conflict. There was more justification in the horror aroused by *Venus perversa* – the poet watches a nun committing onanism: the *unio mystica*. Dehmel's plan – ruthlessly and brilliantly realized, in spite of some of the most loathsome pictures in literature – was to present the world with a kind of picture-gallery of *all* the manifestations of love, leading up to its spiritualization in *Venus heroica*. It may be consoling to squeamish people to read that when Dehmel was prosecuted for the indecency of these poems he was acquitted on the grounds that they were unintelligible! When, however, the *Verwandlungen der Venus* were published separately and expanded as Vol. IV of the Collected Works, they were denounced to the authorities by the poet Börries von Münchhausen, and by order of the Berlin *Landgericht* part of one of them, *Venus Consolatrix*, was expunged, so that the original poem can only be obtained in the very precious private edition printed by Dehmel for his friends. What was objected to was the blending in one person as 'consoling love' of Mary of Nazareth and Mary Mag-

---

[1] *Venus Natura* (in *Verwandlungen der Venus*) describes a peacock circling his hen with spread tail and ends with: *'O Mensch, wie herrlich ist das Tier, | wenn es sich ganz als Tier entfaltet!'*

dalene. The poem is a necessary part of the cycle, for it leads up to the interpretation of love as '*Ehrfurcht vor dem Übermächtigen*'.

Dehmel was a wonderful translator. His verse renderings of poems by Villon and Verlaine are gathered in *Aber die Liebe*, as are also his adaptations of Chinese poems. In his renderings of three poems of Li-Tai-Pe he was helped by Hans Heilmann, who later published a volume of prose translations of Chinese lyrics. Imitations of Oriental poetry thereafter belonged to the order of the day: Hans Bethge's *Die chinesische Flöte* (1907) and *Japanischer Frühling* (1911) may be mentioned. But the only poet who could lay claim to some knowledge of Chinese was Bierbaum, who began as an orientalist. Dehmel's *Lieder der Bilitis* were published in a separate volume; the original, Pierre Louys' *Chansons de Bilitis* (1894), played with the theme of Lesbian love, which we find in odd corners of impressionist literature.

Paula Dehmel was a gifted woman: she collaborated with her husband in writing the poems for children which form Vol. VI of the Collected Works (*Der Kindergarten*). But Dehmel, though he was devoted to his children, found domestic life with her hard to endure; she was a chronic sufferer from asthma, and aged rapidly. He seriously entertained the idea of adding Hedwig Lachmann to his household as second wife. But Hedwig was one of his wife's most helpful friends, and remained so. In 1893 Dehmel fled to Hamburg, without taking even a toothbrush; this time, however, Paula fetched him back to home – and duty at the insurance office; he was, however, granted leave of absence and spent a holiday in Italy. It is almost an ironical detail that Dehmel was at last, in 1894, able to resign his insurance post because Paula came into money. By this time Dehmel had met the third Jewish lady who swept him off his feet. An essay of his on the paramount performances in the art of the day had just appeared in the second number of *Pan*, which he had helped to found; and he received a letter from a lady in which she expressed her surprise that the essay did not mention Stefan George; accompanying the letter were one of George's volumes of verse and one year's issue of *Blätter für die Kunst*. The lady was Frau Konsul Auerbach of Berlin, and when Dehmel called on her he found she was twenty-five, recently married to a well-to-do Jewish merchant, and on the way to have a baby. Her maiden name was Ida Coblenz ('Idda' for short, but Dehmel called her Isi, and as Frau Isi she will live in literature).

9

She belonged to a patrician family long settled at Bingen on the Rhine; near the family mansion was the house where Stefan George grew up, and this poet was a frequent visitor to her home after she had proved to him that she could understand his poetry. When, therefore, Dehmel took leave of Frau Auerbach, after a visit which lasted two and a half hours, it is not surprising that he promised to read Stefan George's books. What he really thought of *l'art pour l'art* we know from his essay *Hörer und Dichter* in *Betrachtungen*. It was a dramatic coincidence that the only time he met Stefan George was on the doorstep of Frau Auerbach's house: he was coming, George was departing. And when, afterwards, Frau Ida wrote to George that she was interested in Dehmel, she received the withering reply: '*Wenn einer anfängt schön zu finden, was dem andern gemein ist, dann ist es Zeit zum Abschiednehmen.*' The months which followed were productive: this love for another man's wife inspired Dehmel with poems such as *Beschwichtigung*, *Enthüllung*, *Drama*, *Warnung*, *Drohung*, *Hans im Glück*, and the delightfully humorous *Schneeflocken* – it has just the magic of snowflakes falling. Paula and Frau Auerbach met, and tried to be friends. Then Consul Auerbach went bankrupt and his wife went to live in the house next to that of the Dehmels; Dehmel had prepared this new home for her. The *mariage à trois* was of short duration; Dehmel once again fled to Hamburg, and this time he was fetched back by two women. In the end Dehmel fled with Frau Isi, and when divorced married her (1901).[1]

The poems inspired by the wooing and winning of Frau Isi may easily be detected in *Weib und Welt* (1896). Such lyrics as *Mannesbangen* are electric with passion. There is a curious Oriental effect – torrid desert and on the far rim wafting palms – in *Ruf* and *Berückung*. *Wirrsal* and *Der gute Hirte* – in the latter the poet is Jacob calling to Leah and Rachel – defend the triangle arrangement with frankness and shameless humour. Some of the lyrics of the volume date from an earlier period. Of these the most significant is *Die Harfe*: the roaring wind strikes its wild music from the dark pine-wood, as the wind of primeval passion stirs the deeps of Dehmel's soul: '*Ich habe mit Inbrünsten jeder Art | mich zwischen Gott und Tier herumgeschlagen.*' In the present edition of *Weib und Welt*, too, those lovely lyrics find place which render moods of dusk and night (*Dämmer- und Nachtgedichte*) – *Helle Nacht*,

---

[1] His justification is frankly stated in No. 241 of *Ausgewählte Briefe*.

Manche Nacht, and *Die stille Stadt* are the most famous. *Aus banger Brust* is such a night-piece, but the thrill of this *Ehemannsgedicht* is in the unashamed image of copulation. Much quoted is the *Leitwort* of the original edition: '*Erst wenn der Geist von jedem Zweck genesen | und nichts mehr wissen will als seine Triebe, | dann offenbart sich ihm das weise Wesen | verliebter Torheit und der grossen Liebe*'; this agrees with Nietzsche's command that we should clasp our passions to our bosoms as our highest aim. All this sexualism of Dehmel hardly seems compatible with a gentleman's respect for ladies, which does exist in Germany, even when as in Eduard von Keyserling's Baltic novels there may be one woman for respect and another for passion.

The drama of Dehmel's second marriage provides the matter of the curious connubial epic *Zwei Menschen* (1903). Dehmel regarded it as a cycle of ballads, but ballads stripped of antique flummery, and modern because the experience transmutes the physical thrill of sex to spirituality; he wrote to Frau Isi in an early stage of their acquaintance: '*Ich habe die Form der neuen Ballade gefunden, die keines antiquarischen Mummenschanzes bedarf, und eine Form, die es erlaubt, in tausend Variationen ein ganzes Seelenleben und Menschenschicksal vorzuführen.*' The classification of the poem as a *Romanzenroman* is satisfying: it is a novel made up of linked lyric snatches – a *Romanzero* loosely in Heine's sense (not in the Spanish sense of a ballad collection). FERDINAND AVENARIUS[1] (1856-1920) had made much of his idea of a lyric epic, but his *Lebe* (1893) is not a novel; nearer to Dehmel's innovation is Coventry Patmore's *The Angel in the House*. But what a difference in spirit! The English poet does not shirk the physical implications of marriage, but the very idea of his poem is to glorify wedded love as spiritual communion and social decency. Dehmel's poem on the other hand is a defiant challenge to accepted notions of decency. The animality of love is stressed, and there are renderings of physical passion made quiveringly perceptible by the rise and fall of the rhythm. The violence is sometimes appalling. The story itself is admittedly ridiculous: the architect Lux at some duodecimo German court or other purloins papers and has a love-affair with Lea, the wife of the ruling prince. She kills her blind baby. The wife of Lux dies; Lea says:

---

[1] He founded (1887) and edited *Der Kunstwart*, one of the most important literary journals of the period. His volumes of verse are *Wandern und Werden* (1881) and *Stimmen und Bilder* (1898).

'*Ich war ihr Vampyr.*' They flee together, and in their union realize the new doctrine of the spiritualization of the flesh. Lea has symbolic variety: she is the goddess Isis; she is Frau Welt; but she is the physical image of Frau Isi. And Lux is in every physical detail Dehmel: '*seine offne Stirn, den kurz gehaltnen Bart,* | *den Mund von träumerisch verschlossener Art,* | *Hiebnarben neben den heftigen Nüstern . . .* ' It is the tense reality of the story beneath the tinsel that gives the poem its interest; and added to this there is the lyric splendour of certain passages.

Stern reproof and partial praise had combined to give Dehmel the notoriety which made the publication (1905-9) of his *Gesammelte Werke* in ten volumes possible. His last volume of verse, *Schöne wilde Welt* (1913), is pathetic; even a last extra-marital escapade had not prevented his poetic vein from calcifying. Even when he re-states his sex doctrine we get: '*Dass der Mensch am Weib sich freut,* | *dass die Freude Samen streut,* | *das ists, was die Welt erneut.*' *Die Musik des Mont Blanc* shows the poet as the keen Alpinist he was in his later years. That he was physically fit he proved by enlisting on the outbreak of war in 1914; he served in the trenches, won the Iron Cross, was promoted to lieutenant, was wounded, had an attack of thrombosis, was declared unfit for active service but kept in the army till the end of the War. He died in 1920 of thrombosis.

Dehmel will keep his place in the annals of literature if only by the sheer strangeness of his personality and by the fascination which emanated from his person as from his works. It would be quite possible to liken him to Mephistopheles: he had a sulphurous effulgence. He denied all that the parson calls good, and what he called good, the parson might very well say, was the lure of the devil. That he wrote devilishly fine poetry would not make an angel of him.

Dehmel had his school (Paul Zech, Winckler, etc.), but as disciples they were bound to follow his own Nietzschean injunction: *Sei Du!* OSKAR LOERKE (1884-1941) is a *Dehmelianer*, but rather in the sense of personal devotion to a master than in style and doctrine; his nearness is that of North German mentality, and actually he continues Annette von Droste-Hülshoff; he has Annette's close vision of the mystic earth and her rough-hewn rhythms covering vibrant feeling. He is a 'cosmo-centric' poet who strives to take the absolute into himself; he loves, as parts of the absolute, not only his fellow-men but inanimate nature: the mist that folds him on the heath – his 'dear brother'; the starveling pines in the heather-blue Prussian sand – his 'comrades'. He grieves for the decay of all he loves, grieves even for the decay of grief, and knows that he is one of a hard new race that makes a cool reckoning with existence. He is not an easy poet: the meaning of his verse[1] is often embedded under a crust of far-fetched imagery. He has regional consistency in his depiction of North German landscapes: skies ever grey brood over plains where the hard wind, a grey minstrel, strikes his grey music from bone-white beeches. This impressionistic rareness of imagery gives a mannered effect to his prose[2]; but he is one of those who have renewed the Novelle by the infusion of personality.

[1] *Wanderschaft* (1911); *Die heimliche Stadt* (1921); *Der längste Tag* (1926); *Pansmusik* (1929; second edition of *Gedichte*, 1916); *Atem der Erde* (1930); *Der Silberdistelwald* (1934); *Der Wald der Welt* (1936); *Die Abschiedshand* (1949).
[2] Short stories: *Vineta* (1907); *Das Goldbergwerk* (1919); *Der Chimärenreiter* (1919); *Der Prinz und der Tiger* (1920). Novels: *Der Turmbau* (1910); *Der Oger* (1921). Essays: *Zeitgenossen aus vielen Zeiten* (1929).

VI

STEFAN GEORGE
AND HIS CIRCLE

Dehmel assimilated French symbolism, but remained German to the core; his matter is Nietzschean touched up with decadent refulgence. In Stefan George (1868-1933) and his 'circle' Romance influence is predominant. Reminiscences of the German Romanticists, however, and above all of Hölderlin, deepen the French ultra-refinement of George; and two German poets with whom he has striking affinities are Platen, an artificer of verse equally patient though with tools less delicate, and Conrad Ferdinand Meyer, an aristocrat equally feminized by French culture, one who in an equal degree was pained by contact with crowds and who likewise veiled his personal experience in recondite symbols. Something, too, of the atmosphere and colouring of the English Pre-Raphaelites and aesthetes illumines the Mallarméan scroll of George, in whose work are renderings of Rossetti, Swinburne, and Ernest Dowson. This poetry of George and his circle is, literally, *l'art pour l'art* (*Artistenkunst*), and they are academically classed as *die Artisten*; they seek to displace *Stoffkunst* or naturalism by *Formkunst*. In this respect they still further refine the formal perfection of the Munich school (and for aristocratic aloofness Stefan George might well be compared to Graf von Schack); but there is the vital difference that whereas the poets of the Munich school regard clearness of meaning as a necessary quality of perfect form George writes only for those who have the mental keenness to pierce to the sense – to him *Formvollendung* means mathematical precision of rhythm and stanza and symmetrical construction with unity of idea of each volume of verse.

Stefan George was born at Büdesheim, near Bingen on the Rhine; his father was the landlord of the *Wirtschaft zur Traube* there. His pedigree has been carefully traced, and it is claimed that he was of pure German blood[1]: he had 'brownish golden' hair and pale blue eyes like turquoises. His early environment is assumed by his biographers to have influenced the spirit of his work in two directions: his sense of architectural construction, seen in the symmetrical shaping of his volumes of verse, and that unbending hardness and even cruelty which made him a literary dictator and eliminated all tenderness from his work are attributed to an atavistic imprint of the old Roman colonization of his homeland,[2] while to the Roman Catholic pomp and ceremonial of the Rhineland he instinctively owed his pose as poet-priest and the symbolistic ritual of his freethinking. These tendencies, we are told, were so deeply inherited in him that they surged up from his inner consciousness and were born anew, instead of being a cultured revival such as informs neo-hellenism and romanticism. Whereas the neo-hellenists have shown their literary affiliation by outward signs such as the use of Greek metres, George's every nerve tingles atavistically with the essential spirit of Hellas: the deification of the body and the embodiment of the deity (*die Vergottung des Leibes und die Verleibung des Gottes*). (*Dâ hœret ouch geloube zuo*, as Walther von der Vogelweide remarked; but faith is required for any appreciation of George.) At the Realschule at Bingen George did best in languages; Italian he learnt out of school. At the age of fourteen he entered the Ludwig-Georg Gymnasium at Darmstadt. Here in 1886 his *juvenilia*, some preserved in *Die Fibel*, begin; already the influence of Italian poets – Petrarch and Tasso – is giving austerity to his form. He learnt Norwegian to read Ibsen; and indeed when he left school in 1888 foreign languages had laid such a spell on him that his father agreed that he should fit his career to this main interest. He went to London, and what appealed to him in his stay there is indicated in his poem *Von einer Reise 1888-89* in *Die Fibel*, while *Die Glocken*, one suspects, imitates rhythmically the chimes of some London church. Thereafter he stayed for a time in Montreux, and thence went to Italy and Paris, where he made friends with one of the standard-bearers of the young symbolist movement, Albert Saint-Paul. This

---

[1] But Josef Nadler (*Literaturgeschichte der deutschen Stämme und Landschaften*) insists that George's father was a Walloon, and that his mother came from Lorraine. See also Frau Ida Dehmel, '*Der junge Stefan George*', *Berliner Tageblatt*, July 1st, 1935: '*Die Familie Georges ist französischen Ursprungs*'.
[2] See his poems *Porta Nigra* and *Ursprünge* (in *Der siebente Ring*).

friendship was decisive: soon the young poet was associating with the poets of the Pléiade; and at their instigation he read Baudelaire, Rimbaud, Edgar Allen Poe. He was a guest at the Tuesday evening gatherings in Mallarmé's *salon* in the rue de Rome, and here he met Verlaine. His acquaintance in the French capital with three young Mexicans induced him to learn Spanish; and when he visited Spain in 1889 he dreamed himself into the illusion that he had returned to a land of which long, long ago he had been ruler and tyrant – an illusion which he was to weave as poetic reality into his *Hymnen, Pilgerfahrten,* and *Die hängenden Gärten.* Spain, according to his own account, transformed his very soul: the hard, sharp lines of the landscapes round about Toledo and Madrid and the dark forbidding royal palaces filled him with that feeling of regal loneliness and unapproachable pride which he was to read into his first published book, and which was to be the mark of his life-long poetic pose.

In 1889 George went to Berlin to study languages at the University. Here he revelled in the melody and colour of the Spanish language as he spoke it with his three Mexican friends, whom he had found here once again; and here, too, his immersion in Romance studies alienated him more and more from German literature, which was then in its heyday of naturalism. Indeed, German seemed so harsh to him that in addition to attempting French verse he put together a language of his own which shaped Latin roots into the form and melody of Spanish; and in this *lingua romana* he first couched his *Zeichnungen in Grau* and the first of the *Legenden* which later he transposed into their present German form.[1] In this undergraduate's verse as we now read it in *Die Fibel* the poet to be is already adumbrated. The *Zeichnungen in Grau* are occupied with a boyish resistance to the peril of sensual enjoyment (*'tierische Zuckungen'*): the youth must watch lest the divine goal should vanish and a moment's flame transfigure a clay image. There are strange glimpses of a temptress – in *Gelbe Rose* she is swathed in yellow silk in the yellow refulgence of false daylight in warm air quivering with perfumes: a Hindoo goddess from the Ganges, she seems a figure of wax, and soulless save when her densely shaded eye, weary of rest, suddenly lifts its lid.

In George's first published trilogy of verse – *Hymnen*, 1890; *Pilgerfahrten*, 1891; *Algabal*, 1892; now in one volume – travel

[1] Specimens of the first version are printed in *Die Fibel* (1901).

impressions shape themselves discreetly to French models; but the collective theme continues that of the *juvenilia* – the self-isolation of the consecrated poet. *Hymnen* were first published in a *plaquette* intended for the poet's friends only. The first poem, *Weihe*, gives the note of the triple collection – the poet, awakening to the consciousness of his divine poet's mission, seeks, in the shade of evening by the reed-rimmed river, the consecration of the Muse. Already in this first poem those metrical devices and tonal qualities show which were to be his system: *audition colorée*, assonance (*Vokalharmonie*) throughout the line or stanza ('*Hinaus zum strom! wo stolz die hohen rohre | Im linden winde ihre fahnen schwingen*' – *o* and *st, i* for rapidity), clipped interior rhymes (*Im linden winde, Zum ufermoose kosend*). The second lyric shows the poet in the spring morning, in the pleasaunce of a great lonely park, but far sundered from men and their allurements, for . . . '*heut darf ihre weise nicht ihn rühren, | Weil er mit seinen geistern rede tauscht: | Er hat den griffel der sich sträubt zu führen*'. The French Parnassian manner – the concentration of the character and spirit of an epoch or of a country in one short poem – illustrates *Hochsommer* (a transposition of the soul of Watteau's pictures) and the two 'pictures' (*Bilder*), *Der Infant* and *Ein Angelico*. *Der Infant*, ostensibly the reproduction in verse of a painting in its oval frame of dark gilt, thrills with the tragic fate of Spanish royalty: this white-faced prince smiles on eternally, never regretting that he did not grow up to be a gloomy tyrant; the blessing vouchsafed to him is that when the moon slants through the pomegranate glass globes in the room a bright elfin maid comes for him, and they play with the silken ball that still gleams rose-red and olive-green on the oak pier-table. *Ein Angelico* is descriptive, but it is that description by successive details of action which Lessing, in *Laokoon*, approves in Homer's description of the shield of Achilles.[1] In this skilfully manipulated sonnet, in which the rhythm and the sense of each of the four parts rises to a pregnant closing line and the mood of the whole poem is gathered into the pensive last verse, we see the picture of the Virgin, '*die braut mit immerstillem kinderbusen*', come into being stroke by stroke:

> *Er nahm das gold von heiligen pokalen·*
> *Zu hellem haar das reife weizenstroh·*

[1] Compare also the poem *Komm in den totgesagten park und schau.*

Das rosa kindern die mit schiefer malen·
Der wäscherin am bach den indigo.

Both infante and painter are of course self-portraits of George –
as the royal child to whom only the elfin joys of the spirit are
vouchsafed, and as the master of gradual colouring and inlaid suggestion. In *Pilgerfahrten* the image of the poet takes fixed form as
one and the same expanded ego, the pilgrim whose experiences
are those of George; the charm of such poems as *Gesichte, Mah-
nung, Verjährte Fahrten,* says Gundolf, lies in their 'monumental
intimity'. The theme is once again the conflict between physical
passion and intellectual yearning; but this conflict brings the gift
of song. In *Dass er auf fernem felsenpfade* . . . the pilgrim is lured by
night to the reedy marsh, '*Dass er in sturmes trieb sich stähle*'; from
the reeds rises a lily on a swaying stalk, wings in the milk-white
chalice quiver – an evil angel (demonic temptation) is luring him
from the straight path that leads to the Muse; the reeds murmur
as he follows the shadowy row of elms. The magic of such poems
lies in the very dimness of an idea, an idea which is hardly necessary for enjoyment: what matters is that mystery is evoked, and
that this mystery hinted line by line is all gathered into the last
verse which leaves the music quivering in the air: '*Den langen schat-
tenzug der rüstern | Verfolgt er jeder heilung bar· | Sein auge flackert irr
im düstern· | Die winde wirren ihm das haar.*' Spanish impressions
and the magic of Venice lend colour and a sensuous thrill to poems
(*Gesichte, Verjährte Fahrten*) which contrast with memories of the
poet's Catholic boyhood and dim imaginings of a time ere history
was. A landscape magically evoked is the famous *Mühle lass die
arme still*: it begins with the vivid and simple personification of
the *Volkslied*, but (as often happens with George) is ruined by a
Euphuistic conceit:

> *Mühle lass die arme still*
> *Da die haide ruhen will.*
> *Teiche auf den tauwind harren·*
> *Ihrer pflegen lichte lanzen*
> *Und die kleinen bäume starren*
> *Wie getünchte ginsterpflanzen.*

Pilgerfahrten ends with the two marvellous stanzas of *Die Spange*,
a mystic transmutation of George's verse technique:

Ich wollte sie aus kühlem eisen
Und wie ein glatter fester streif·
Doch war im schacht auf allen gleisen
So kein metall zum gusse reif.

Nun aber soll sie also sein:
Wie eine grosse fremde dolde
Geformt aus feuerrotem golde
Und reichem blitzendem gestein.

Nothing could be more satisfying as a definition of George's verse than this one of his own: hard and metallic, but lit with diamantine radiance.

In 1892 George visited Liége, and there met Paul Gérardy, a bilingual Walloon from Malmédy in the province ceded to Belgium after World War I, and with him he discussed his plan of publishing a poetical review. He then went to Paris, where he finished *Algabal*. In history Heliogabalus is a byword for vice and cruelty, an effeminate boy (*Weibjüngling*); Stefan George uses him as the appropriate symbol for his Nietzschean contempt of Christian and middle-class morality. Algabal is the supra-personal presentment of Stefan George himself as poet-priest[1] and poet-king: or in other words, the soul or mind of Stefan George limned in regal or sacerdotal poses, the autocrat twice consecrated, the poet self-imaged as his own dream and desire. Heliogabalus is chosen to represent such a spiritual ideal because he is as far removed as could be from the vile present of vile poets whom the dreamer would annihilate, and because, if he would annihilate them, he must be a tyrant sublimely ruthless, and because late-Roman and *fin-de-siècle* are both synonymous with that luxury and display and decay and despair which only a tyrant could by a gesture sweep away. Moreover, while preparing this volume George had been translating Baudelaire, and the influence of *Flowers of Evil* and *Artificial Paradises* shapes both the flawless form of the poems and the unity of beauty and decadence in the themes. There is, however, a subtle difference between Baudelaire and Stefan George: while to the French poet (and to the decadents who acknowledged themselves as his disciples) the gratification of strange lusts is in itself art, to

[1] Platen's pose was similar; in *Morgenklage* he cries: '*Ich schwöre den schönen Schwur, getreu stets zu sein | Dem hohen Gesetz, und will, in Andacht vertieft, | Voll Priestergefühl verwalten | Dein gross Prophetenamt.*'

the German aesthete art takes into its scope the dream which this gratification may bring. And since all is dream and symbol there is no need for moral disgust if Algabal is even a murderer:

Sieh ich bin zart wie eine apfelblüte
Und friedenfroher denn ein neues lamm·
Doch liegen eisen stein und feuerschwamm
Gefährlich in erschüttertem gemüte.

Hernieder steig ich eine marmortreppe·
Ein leichnam ohne haupt inmitten ruht·
Dort sickert meines teuren bruders blut·
Ich raffe leise nur die purpurschleppe.

For this merely means that the poet-king will not suffer the shadow of an affront, even from a beloved brother (the *teuer* is deliberate, and in its implication effective), to the majesty of his state. Vaguely, too, Algabal is a spiritualized image of Ludwig II of Bavaria, that crowned decadent whose spendthrift's palaces George had recently visited, and the news of whose suicide had shocked him profoundly. To Ludwig II, the '*verhöhnter dulderkönig*', the volume is dedicated by his younger brother Algabal (that is, the poet). Technically, if Stefan George is to be classed as a decadent at all it can only be by reason of this Baudelairean book. As it closes, a way of escape opens: the poem *Graue rosse muss ich schirren* unfolds a vista of the virgin spaces under a vaulted cold sky whence the Germanic hordes are to sweep down on the rottenness of Rome.

For the first time in George's production – and the following volumes will show varying but equally symmetrical construction – *Algabal* is mathematically graded in a triple arrangement, and the subjects of the three zones interlock and form a unified whole: *Im Unterreich* gives landscape and atmosphere, *Tage* limns the *milieu*, *Die Andenken* reveals the inner soul of the subject.

Important was George's meeting at this stage of his career with Hugo von Hofmannsthal, then a boy of seventeen but already known by *Gestern* and what he had published under the pen-name of Loris; his hope that in the Viennese poet he had found the closest of his disciples was destined to be disappointed; for Hofmannsthal, in George's opinion, pandered to the mob. But Hofmannsthal did help Gérardy and Karl August Klein in the launching of George's new cultural review: *Blätter für die Kunst*, the first number of which appeared in 1892. The title suggests the French symbolist review *Écrits pour l'art*. The review ended in 1919 with the eleventh and twelfth series; it had lasted twenty-seven years, a long period for so esoteric a publication. It is of the greatest importance in the literary history of the period, and fortunately the best of what appeared in it is available in the three volumes of selections (*Auslese aus den Jahren 1892–1898; 1898–1904; 1904–1909*). For the journal wrote the band of disciples, '*der Kreis um Stefan George*', joined as the years passed by Karl Wolfskehl, Alfred Schuler, Friedrich Gundolf, and others who must be dealt with separately for their own work. Distinguished foreigners, too, came in and carried the doctrine to their own country: thus Willem Kloos and Albert Verwey initiated in Holland the new movement in verse which is known as *De Nieuwe Gids Beweging* (because the poets concerned wrote for the journal *De Nieuwe Gids*), while Poland was represented by Waclaw Lieder, for whose sake George learned Polish, and England by Cyril Scott, who as a handsome boy of seventeen studying music at Frankfurt was admitted to inner intimity with George, although the English lad's laughing cynicism (he could not even take the Master himself seriously) kept a dividing-line between the two. Cyril Scott afterwards published a selection of translations of George's poetry and described their relations in his *Years of Indiscretion* (1924). What George expected from the Circle emerges from a strange poem in *Der Stern des Bundes*:

> *So weit eröffne sich geheime kunde*
> *Dass vollzahl mehr gilt als der teile tucht*
> *Dass neues wesen vorbricht durch die runde*
> *Und steigert jeden einzelgliedes wucht:*
> *Aus diesem liebesring dem nichts entfalle*
> *Holt kraft sich jeder neue Tempeleis*
> *Und seine eigne – grössre – schiesst in alle*
> *Und flutet wieder rückwärts in den kreis.*

The first number of *Blätter für die Kunst* proclaims the intention of the group to begin with poems from which rules can be deduced: the aim is, we are told, *die geistige kunst auf grund einer neuen fühlweise und mache*. ('*Mache*', normally a sarcastic or mercantile word, is here, in accordance with Georgean theory, ennobled by its context.) In the first *Hefte*, as far as the actual poems are concerned, the main interest is in the contrast between the soft rhythm and fluidity of Hofmannsthal (whose *Der Tod des Tizian* enriched the first number) and the hard metallic ring[1] and plastic contours of Stefan George's contributions. In other numbers of the first 'sequence' (*Folge* is the term used for the volumes of the journal) George printed his translations of Verlaine, Mallarmé, Swinburne, d'Annunzio, Jens Peter Jacobsen, and others. Klein in one of the essays he contributed pointed out that, whereas in France Parnassianism was completed, in Germany it was not. George is actually a Mallarméan Parnassian, just as (to give another example) Richard von Schaukal combines the pictorial and cumulative methods of the Parnassians with the mystic melancholy of the symbolists. It was Klein's function to explain the new technique; the foremost demand is that the poet should take words dulled by everyday usage and rear them aloft in a belt of radiance. Here we have the very secret of the new verse. The idea is not new; we have seen that Liliencron owed much of his originality to it. But whereas with Liliencron this elevation of common words was spontaneous or even devil-may-care, and at all events one of the elements of his realism, with the aesthetes it is a conscious canon of the revised poetics. George himself allocates these abrased words so cunningly in his setting that they are coined anew; they are the old words and rhymes, but used as they have never been used before. Rilke[2] states the doctrine: 'Not a word in the poem (by this I mean "*und*" or "*der*", "*die*", "*das*") is identical with the same word as it is known to conventional usage; in verse or in poetic prose these words are like enskied constellations linked by the vast law of Creation, transformed in the very heart of their being, in such collocation snatched from the mere intercourse of speech, beyond corporeal touch and undying.' And Rilke put the doctrine into beautiful verse (*Mir zur Feier*):

> Die armen Worte, die im Alltag darben,
> die zagen blassen Worte lieb ich so,
> aus meinen Festen schenk ich ihnen Farben,
> da lächeln sie und werden langsam froh.

---

[1] Albert Saint-Paul characterizes George's first poems as 'dreams of a hero sunk in gloom, dreams lit by a cold blue clearness, like rays of light striking on steel'.

[2] *Rainer Maria Rilke. Aspects of his Mind and Poetry*, ed. William Rose and G. Craig Houston, p. 169.

Sie wärmen sich die weissen Winterwangen,
am Wunder, welches ihrem Weh geschieht;
sie sind noch niemals in Gesang gegangen,
und schaudernd schreiten sie in meinem Lied.

George's style, Klein says in his first essay, is austerely classic: rhymes are pure, rhythm is faultless; and since the impression is conveyed by a meticulous choice of consonants and vowels the meaning need not be stated. Sensations are felt, not phrased. Verses which seem to be in another language plunge us into a strange unrest. And all runs into the vast diapason by which we are moved as by strong wine. Perfect as the form is, however, the worth of the poem lies in its deep spirituality (*Seelentiefe*). Novels are to be rejected as reporter's stuff (*Berichterstatterei*); and the theatre is on the face of it hopeless because it has to be commercial. A later essay by George himself is often quoted: '*Wir wollen keine erfindung von geschichten sondern wiedergabe von stimmungen, keine betrachtung sondern darstellung, keine unterhaltung sondern eindruck. Die älteren dichter schufen der mehrzahl nach ihre werke oder wollten sie wenigstens angesehen haben als stütze einer meinung: einer weltanschauung – wir sehen in jedem ereignis, jedem zeitalter nur ein mittel künstlerischer erregung.*' He explains that in his poetry symbol is threefold: that of the individual words, that of the separate parts, and that of the whole which holds the deeper meaning. Ludwig Klages then in another essay (II. *Folge*, v) took the measure of a poet by his power of finding signs (=symbols) 'for the mysterious values of soul and universe'. Poetry would thus be a kind of cipher, and the cult of poetry would be a secret intelligence system. But George in his further interpretation of his technique in his book of prose essays *Tage und Taten* makes more of the mood than of the veiling of the meaning. In any case the peril of this attitude – or pose – is that form becomes paramount: 'the worth of a poem is fixed', says George, 'not by the meaning of it – for then it might be wisdom, learning – but by its form'; the poet's task is thus to produce by means of form, or in other words by sound and rhythm ('*jenes tief erregende an mass und klang*'), a mood (*Stimmung*) which is not bound to sense or substance; we thus get a process akin to that of music. George, therefore, paints with vowels, or plays on them just as a pianist plays on keys; he tangles his constructions; he swathes the inner meaning of the poem in a floating veil of symbol. As (to use the image of one of his poems[1]) the linked figures frozen in a dance under dead boughs in the complicated pattern of an Oriental carpet come to life, some evening or other, with the dead boughs stirring, chilling the spectator's sense with the mystery revealed, so the secret woven intricately into the poem comes with the gift of its beauty – but not at call, not at any hour accustomed; to the many it comes never, and rarely to the rare. Poetry is thus esoteric, a priestlike evocation, only for the adept in the ivory tower.

The pose of perfection which George assumed for his verse he cultivated too in his personal appearance and in his relations with the outer world. Above all he kept his distance. His attitude to poets not in his Circle was almost that of Algabal:

> *ICH bin als einer so wie SIE als viele.*
> *Ich tue was das leben mit mir tut*
> *Und träf ich sie mit ruten bis aufs blut:*
> *Sie haben korn und haben fechterspiele.*

Which means: they are best-sellers; but poetry is mine. His garb and appearance were a godsend to caricaturists: they made his monocle and his long stiff hair pushing out Liszt-like below his tall hat, his *'viermalgeschlungene Kultkrawatte'*, and his clean-shaven ascetic face familiar to the irreverent. There was a rumour that he was an illegitimate son of Liszt; but he himself prided himself mightily on the resemblance of his pale face with its sunken cheeks to the Hell-marked profile of Dante. (He recited his verse in darkened Berlin *salons* with Rembrandtesque candle-light illuminating this ascetic profile with its projecting chin.) When Maximilian Dauthendey first met him he was almost frightened by his tall hat and frock coat and cardinal's face.

In 1895 appeared *Die Bücher der Hirten- und Preisgedichte, der Sagen und Sänge und der hängenden Gärten.* George's intention in this book was to conjure up from the depths of his being, where they had slumbered as an inheritance from the past, and to sing into verse the primitive forms of culture – (to quote Gundolf) 'the soul of God in the three phases of history – pastoral, medieval, oriental – whose ideals are the composite substance of present-day literature'. But whereas Classicism, Romanticism, and Orientalism had hitherto worked themselves back in the laborious toil of scholar-

[1] *Der Teppich* in *Der Teppich des Lebens.*

ship to the respective periods and read themselves into what of these vanished ages they recalled to life, George (in intention) re-creates them out of his submerged consciousness and puts them before us in the actuality of their ideals, that is, *as they were*. If this were true we could not reckon George with Platen and Rückert as one of '*die forcierten Talente*'; there would be nothing forced in these rebirths. The arrangement is that of a triple cycle of poems; and the strophic form and metres of each part are intended to convey those of the three periods re-created. That they actually do so is not likely to be admitted by scholars: the pastoral poems resemble those of the French neo-hellenists (e.g. Henri de Régnier); while of the medieval poems only *Tagelied* has the shape and melody of a Minnelied – but not of a *Tagelied*. Characteristically Georgean in the *Hirten- und Preisgedichte* are two pen-pictures of Greek youths, *Der Ringer* and *Der Saitenspieler*. The wrestler passes in the pride of his naked body, and does not see even his parents in the cheering crowd; and of the curly-headed lute-player when he has sung the boys dream, silently suffering and sleepless under the stars. *Der Auszug der Erstlinge*, in iambic trimeters, indicates the ethic purpose of the book: to show in ancient Greece the unity of God, man, and world, with an implied contrast of the religious, political and moral disharmony of the poet's own day; Greek youths on whom the lot has fallen accept their fate and depart to seek a new home. In all the variety of Greek life which the poems unfold there is a unity ordained by the gods, controlled by the state, and accepted by the people; as one might say – and this Georgean interpretation of a model state (in two senses) as a totalitarian contentment with what has been commanded from above was seized on in the Hitler period. George's historization of self appears again in the stately blank verse of *Der Herr der Insel*: fishermen relate that upon an island rich in spice and oil a bird with wings 'dyed as with ichor of the Tyrian snail' would by day hide in the forests and by night stray to the shore, and there sing so sweetly that dolphins, those friends of song, would swim landwards. But when, by happy guidance, white-winged ships found this island the bird made his moan and died. It is the legend of the poet who sings only in solitude and only to the lovers of song – not to the Phoenicians. Gundolf asserts that in the central series of lyrics, *Sagen und Sänge*, George by sheer intuition has captured the mystic essence of the Middle Ages, whereas the medieval

10

poets themselves had merely rendered the social conventions of their age. This is a fanciful statement. Stefan George's knowledge of the medieval mind was too shallow for these poems to have any value as interpretations of medieval mentality; what he gives us is merely his own conception of the states of mind of knight, squire, poet and hermit; and this conception is just what he intended it not to be – romantic; romantic, because it is based on false intuition. The situation and pose may be medieval; the spirit is modern. The Parzival and Holy Grail poems (*Die Tat, Irrende Schar, Der Einsiedel*) have the mood of Wagner, not of Wolfram. George's Frauenlob is not the dull, didactic rhymester of decayed Minnesong, but the romantic minstrel of the myth: he sees his black coffin, draped in black cloths, borne to the Minster by maidens who – widows now of Beauty's priest – pour noble wines and flowers and precious stones down into his grave. This is not to say that the distinctive elements of the medieval and of the other two periods, as they serve for literature, are not magically evoked; e.g. the plastic beauty of Greek form, Catholic spirituality and the ideals of chivalry,[1] the glaring colours of the Orient; notably in the medieval central piece *Sporenwache*, one of the most intense renderings in all literature of the theme of the spiritual consecration of the chosen one to his ideal. If we would appreciate these careful poems we must remember that the idea is: *I (ICH)* was this squire dreaming the night out in the visionary chapel, *I* was this Frauenlob unkissed and ripe for death; for in me is the multifarious, mysterious past; and this poem is a recovery for myself of a past dim phase of my existence. The theme of *Die hängenden Gärten* has some affinity with *Algabal*: it limns in a voluptuous setting the tyrannic power of Oriental potentates. The visions are again essentially romantic: the conqueror striding in the taken city over corpses and raising (as might Holofernes) his smoking sword to his god; the child who is to be Sultan pictured in all the pomp of his future state (*Kindliches Königtum*: no doubt once more the poet calling up the splendour in his blood); white aras with saffron-yellow crowns, songless and with wings never unfolded behind their grating dreaming of distant palms; the anointing of the bride with oil and salves for the Caliph's bed[2]; strophes of

---

[1] E.g. *Mannentreue* in *Der Waffengefährte*, *Marienkult* in *Das Bild*.
[2] An obsession of Heinrich von Kleist: '*Von Salben triefend wie die Perserbraut*'.

sensuous longing – exceptional in the work of this anti-feminine
poet – with the cumulative imagery of the *Song of Songs* –

> *Saget mir auf welchem pfade*
> *Heute sie vorüberschreite –*
> *Dass ich aus der reichsten lade*
> *Zarte seidenweben hole·*
> *Rose pflücke und viole·*
> *Dass ich meine wange breite·*
> *Schemel unter ihrer sohle.*

One essential feature of George's creed is that his books should
be typographically beautiful. *Das Jahr der Seele* (1897) and the
following volumes were produced by the artist Melchior Lechter,
who had already been the apostle in Germany of the Kelmscott
Press. And so Stefan George's books have the collecting lure of
fine porcelain. In *Das Jahr der Seele* we have a perfectly symmetrical
construction of three parts in each of three sections, with the first
section (*After the Vintage, Pilgrims in Snow, Triumph of Summer*)
and the third section (*Traurige Tänze*) revolving round the central
section (*Überschriften und Widmungen*: poems intensely personal or
devoted to the poet's friends). In this book George's figure as an
introspective comes with ghostlike footfall, freed from pilgrim's
weeds and Emperor's purple and priest's vestments – comes with
ever-varied visions as the pure soul of a poet. The poems are
mostly in the *Du* form, but George's hint in his foreword is that
Ich and *Du* are identical; the poems are addressed to *meine düstre
schwester*, who comes at twilight, as we are told in *Zu meinen träumen
floh ich vor dem volke*; by this happy device   George's usual dicho
tomy into self and personified soul (*Doppelung* or *Gegensätzlichkeit*
as in the case of Goethe) – the theme of the poems is covered by
a veil of gauze and reverie is dramatized. Mystery is intensified by
reminiscences of far-off long-forgotten things, or recalls the soul-
inspired moods of previous volumes. After the poet's wooing of
his dark sister soul come the *Überschriften*, superscriptions which
in the first person reveal the very nature of the poet and of his
verse, and the *Widmungen* to his friends. Then all the tragic sadness
of the poet who has sacrificed the world for the Muse is gathered
into the self-revelations of *Traurige Tänze*. The lyrics of the first
section have something of the charm of landscape, but this is
delicately remote. Really there is no landscape, but only crystalliza-

tions of the mood of a soul. What we do get are Baudelairean 'correspondences' of the poet's inner state with the outer state of nature,[1] with the dying splendour of autumn ('*glanzerfüllte sterbe-wochen*'), fullness of fruits, the sick scent of yellowing leaves carpeting the gravelled garden paths, the flight of wild swans – in short, all the old sensations of sight and sense of romanticism, but lifted out of personality into a spirit world.

The general scene of *Nach der Lese* is a city park with a pond and fountains with basins of basalt; but the famous poem *Komm in den totgesagten park und schau* . . . is not this park in autumn but the impressions of this particular autumn, with its fullness of colours to weave into the verse of an autumnal soul; *Wir schreiten auf und ab im reichen flitter | Des buchenganges* . . . is just *this* moment when through the grating of the park gate an almond tree is seen miraculously blooming for the second time in the year and ripe fruits are heard falling (and may there not be a second blooming of verse and ripe fruits of song?). These illusory landscapes, too, typically begin with a prepared situation; that is, the reader must create the situation by feeling himself backwards in the mood. Thus

> *Gemahnt dich noch das schöne bildnis dessen*
> *Der nach den schluchten-rosen kühn gehascht·*
> *Der über seiner jagd den tag vergessen·*
> *Der von der dolden vollem seim genascht?*
>
> *Der nach dem parke sich zur ruhe wandte·*
> *Trieb ihn ein flügelschillern allzuweit·*
> *Der sinnend sass an jenes weihers kante*
> *Und lauschte in die tiefe heimlichkeit . . .*
>
> *Und von der insel moosgekrönter steine*[2]
> *Verliess der schwan das spiel des wasserfalls*
> *Und legte in die kinderhand die feine*
> *Die schmeichelnde den schlanken hals.*

is, as Hofmannsthal interprets the poem in his *Gespräch über Gedichte*, a reminiscence of the poet's childhood literally recorded; the landscape setting – quite simple – is a boy by a pond in a park;

---

[1] Gundolf might call it *Zweieinigkeit*, a unity of two.

[2] Note the tangled construction: the first two stanzas question, the third with an abrupt transition relates what followed in the picture evoked.

and the magic lies not in the description of the scene but in the association of ideas with the evocative melody of the individual words: 'swan', for instance, is not the ornithological specimen but the snow-white neck, gleaming over dark waters, of Hebbel's poem[1] or (we might add) fondling the thighs of Leda[2]; this swan, as the word awakens ripples of memory, floats double, swan and shadow.[3] The magic, then, is in the words, not in the symbol; which recalls Herder's too energetic definition of poetry: *die in den Worten innewohnende Kraft*. But the magic may lie, too, in a startling transposition of sense: *Der reinen wolken unverhofftes blau* for instance – the blue is really *between* the clouds; but these must be *'rein'*, since they are rimmed with bays of blue. The *Superscriptions* at the heart of the book are, as self-characterization, superb. The pose of the poet tragic because poet is apt to be slightly comic, and the self-portrait of the second *Spruch für die geladenen in T.* is that by which those who scoff at George's 'pose' know him – as one fate-stricken in marble halls, melancholy even in the fulfilment of his mission, toying with the flashing gem on his tapering finger, clad in the purple of kings and with visage bowed down upon the purple. There can be no hiding the fact that George's poetry is from start to finish cult of self; and if aesthetics is a science deduced from extant masterpieces a canon should now be added to the effect that adoration of the ideal self is as fruitful an inspiration for poetry as adoration of the ideal female. In George's case the obsession is not offensive, partly because the poems are so delicate and subtle and partly because the poet himself is not shown as a reality but as a shadowy form or rather all spirit.

Der Teppich des Lebens (1899) is generally considered to be George's most difficult work; the pattern of the book is that of the Oriental carpet he describes in the first poem of Part II and which we have quoted to characterize the form and tenor of his poetry. The theme is – life; but life in the sense of the philosophers as the primitive force which appears in terms of space and time and which is only made conceivable to the human mind by the dissolution of these terms in death. Death, however, since it reveals the limits of space and time, is the perfection or perfecting (*Vollendung*) of life; here Stefan George touches Rilke, but whereas

---

[1] *Von dunkelnden Wogen.*
[2] Friedrich Schlegel, Prologue to *Lucinde*; Rilke's and Felix Braun's *Leda*.
[3] Wordsworth: *Yarrow Unvisited.*

Rilke's conception of development to divine perfection is centrifugal or pure humanity, that of George is centripetal or deification of the ego. The meaning of *Der Teppich des Lebens* is, apparently, that the world consists of chaos and form, and that form is created by life from chaos; but the law is that what is formed by life must perish. However, in all this alternation of creation and decay one form of creation, and one only, resists the eternal process of dissolution – what the mind creates, particularly what the mind of the poet creates; and therefore art is the sublimation of life. And since the artist creates his own world he too is related to creation as God is to His universe; he is, therefore, God, and as such to be adored. Once again the volume is monumentally architectural and in triple form: whether because (as in the sonnet) two pillars are needed to support a roof, or because (as in the Trinity) the arch of the spirit (*der Geist*) must span the two pillars of creator and created, or because Dante's *Divine Comedy* (to George the supreme revelation of art) is tripartite, is a problem which may be posed and looked at. One commentator[1] even points out that the three sections are dominated respectively by Verb (movement in time), Noun (fixed position in space), and Adjective (hovering above time and space); or in other words by Sense, Measure, Sound. In the face of George's insistent symmetry one is tempted to ask: can inspiration be mathematical? If one were to say that ecstasy does not create in polygons Stefan George's Circle might answer that God, as the spirit contriving beauty, does so create; to which the answer should be that Stefan George is an intellectual deviser of symmetrical forms but that perfect symmetry does not prove him to be an inspired poet. In sum, it is the old antithesis of mind and imagination; and, though both are good, even in poetry, the result might be that George sometimes awakens *Geist* but not *Begeisterung*.

In *Das Vorspiel*, the first part of *Der Teppich des Lebens*, a naked angel appears to the poet and announces that Life Beautiful (*das schöne leben*) has sent him as envoy. This has an air of medieval allegory; but it is philosophy – Life is here conceived as, according to Gundolf, the triad of forces interpreted in *Das Jahr der Seele*: nature, fate, and soul; which, as a unity, are given the name of spirit (*der Geist*); and the spirit which is the law, the meaning, and the shape of this life appears to the poet in corporeal form as the angel. The

[1] *Wolters*, p. 199.

angel brings a message which is interpreted as indicating a recovery by George of his German heritage: he bids the poet be cured of that *Drang nach Süden* which, as we all know, means so much in German literature; bids him turn away from the dizzy precipices[1] and the charmed miasmas of southern landscapes to the bracing breath of the northern spring, the eternal mystery of Nordic runes, and to the treasure of his own people guarded by the Rhine, that river green like fresh young life:

> *Du findest das geheimnis ewiger runen*
> *In dieser halden strenger linienkunst*
> *Nicht nur in mauermeeres zauberdunst.*
> ‹*Schon lockt nicht mehr das Wunder der lagunen*
>
> *Das allumworbene trümmergrosse Rom*
> *Wie herber eichen duft und rebenblüten*
> *Wie sie die Deines volkes hort behüten –*
> *Wie Deine wogen – lebengrüner Strom!*›

This seems a definite return to ideals which today would be called *volkhaft*; but poem VII still gives tender expression to George's neo-hellenism, with its contrast of crowds following the Cross that will for long be the light of the world with the little group on quiet paths on whose banners is inscribed: '*Hellas ewig unsre liebe.*'

Stefan George's prose is collected in *Tage und Taten* (1902). His prose style is clear and hard-toned; it has the aesthete's rarity of diction. Instead of the gliding undulation of Hofmannsthal's prose or the incapsulated complexity of Gundolf's, it has the conciseness of short periods weighted with authority, every individual word sharply marked and self-poised; the tone is supercilious and may be scornful, but is never witty. In the *Lobreden* the appreciations – of Mallarmé, Verlaine, Jean Paul, Hölderlin – are both generous and subtle. The *Betrachtungen* state in the shortest possible compass George's poetic creed. The second edition (1925) is expanded and revised.

George's verse translations take rank with the best in the language. Of his Baudelaire (*Die Blumen des Bösen*), and his translations from Verlaine, Mallarmé, Stuart Merrill, Henri de Régnier, d'Annunzio, Albert Verwey, Swinburne, Ernest Dowson, Waclaw Lieder, and others (*Zeitgenössische Dichter*, 2 vols.) one would

---

[1] Italy is imaged as in Goethe's *Kennst du das Land* . . .

hardly say that they fulfil Goethe's summary direction to translators: *Schöner!*, but they have the distinction and dignity of his own verse. French critics charge him with a wilful shaping to his own image of the poets he translates; thus Baudelaire was to him first and foremost the hieratic poet sundered by virgin austerity from the barbarians, and therefore he tones down by skilful manipulations the perversities and cynical pessimism of the *Flowers of Evil*. There is more to be said against his later translations of Dante (1912; Vols. X/XI of Collected Works), because he translated those parts of the *Divine Comedy* which he could identify with his own visions of the Realm of the Blest, and of Shakespeare's sonnets (1909; Vol. XII of *Gesamt-Ausgabe*), because what he brings out is the Georgean cult of male beauty (to quote his Introduction: '*die weltschaffende kraft der übergeschlechtlichen liebe*').

Few would deny that among George's most beautiful poems are those which give an angel-like semblance to some boy or other: *Der Infant, Der Ringer, Der Saitenspieler, Der Tag des Hirten, Sporenwache*. It is hard to see the angel in the figure of Algabal; but Algabal is, like all the other boys, the projection into an image of Stefan George himself as *ephebos*. Rilke projects his soul differently: his maidens image his soul in its virgin purity quivering for conception and creation; but both Rilke and George finish by fashioning their double rather than their image (though a double is of course identical) in the shape of a divine form. Rilke says 'angel', George 'God'; and it is almost incredible that George presents his 'God' in the person of a beautiful boy he discovers in Munich – Maximin. Of Maximin in the flesh all we know is that in addition to his physical beauty he was unspotted from the world ('*rein von allen Anwürfen der Zeit*'), heroic, that he had in his eyes the mystic glimmer of the far-away, and that he died young, leaving George inconsolable.[1] . . . The discovery of the God came at a time of mental stress: three of his disciples, Wolfskehl, Schuler, and Klages, had staged an incipient revolt: as a result of their antiquarian studies they had discovered that man at the dawn of history, and still more when he was a dweller in swamps, was the

[1] '*Wir wanden uns in sinnlosem schmerz dass wir niemals wieder diese hände berühren, dass wir niemals wieder diese lippen küssen dürften.*' George told the story of Maximin (a kind of *vita nuova* – and he stresses the fact that he met the *ephebos* 'in the midway of this my mortal life') in his *Maximin-Gedenkbuch*, printed 1909 and then reprinted separately from the third *Auslese aus den Blättern für die Kunst*.

slave of woman. Their gospel was the *Mutterrecht* (1861) of Johann Jakob Bachofen, who sees in the 'raging rapture and ordering motherly care' of woman the principle of the organic; and from this gynæcocracy they evolved a new cosmic philosophy (whence they are called, in the relevant literature, '*die Kosmiker*') in which Eros is female. It seemed possible that George might be deposed from leadership of the Circle because of his '*Personenkult*', that is, his cultus of male friends; and in any case this cult of the female in all her primeval superiority was bound to be anathema to a declared gynophobe like George. His lambs (including Gundolf) returned to the fold when he asserted his authority; and it is possible that the production of his God was not precipitated by this crisis; what is certain, however, is that Maximin restored his peace of mind. In Maximin he found the realization of his dream and the fulfilment of his religion: body made God and God made body. Having the spiritual idea of the God he demanded its visual perception. (As some of the schoolmen reasoned: the idea of a thing can only exist if the thing itself exists.) Thus he created God. Gundolf interpreting says that male beauty (Eros) excites the spiritual desire of procreation just as the beautiful female (Aphrodite) excites the physical desire of procreation. Only the Greeks[1] and the Germans, he adds, have deified beautiful youths, because these inspire to heroic deeds and spiritual creativeness.

Maximin as the new God appears in *Der siebente Ring* (1907-11). The book falls into seven parts, each with poems to a multiple of seven – a holy number. The central part is *Maximin*; and round the revelation of divinity in this central part revolve the poems of the other three parts on each side, the central idea being to show the existence of divine beauty in a world which had seemed deserted by God. Since God is revealed in the beautiful body of man, man is divine; and divine too is the world in which man appears as God; therefore we must animate all things with the divine essence which is thus proved to be on earth, and thus we shall prepare the 'new life'.

---

[1] Ernst Morwitz – whose book on George is the clearest and most sensible there is – points out '*dass die Griechen an einem wiederkehrenden Fest die Gestalt des Apoll in einem Knaben verkörpert sahen, ihn durch das Land sandten und das Geheimnis der noch alle lebendigen Keime umschliessenden Jugendform dadurch feierten, dass sie ihn während seines Umzuges als den Gott selbst anbeteten. Den Sinn dieses Erlebnisses sucht der Dichter in den Versen 'Auf das Leben und den Tod Maximins' von verschiedenen Sichtwinkeln aus zu fassen.*'

This quest of a new God ('*Gottsuchertum*') had been an obsession in Germany from the beginning of the century, and is traceable to the destruction of the Christian God by Nietzsche ('*der Mörder Gottes*') in order to create 'a living God'. Nietzsche's new God was an idea that different writers shaped to their own fashion. The '*Kosmiker*', George's own runaways, had aimed at making a new religion of the supremacy of woman, that is, of sex; Dehmel deified the sexual impulse; in Gerhart Hauptmann the speculation had taken the form of the interpretation of religious mania; Hermann Stehr probed the mystics; H. F. Blunck was later to quest a new Saxon God; and Thomas Mann in his novels of Jacob was to show that all religion can be reduced to a simple sex symbolism. The form this God-seeking took in *Der siebente Ring* horrified even some of the initiates of the Circle. The utter rejection of woman as divinity was rooted in George's masculine nature, but the expression of it was no doubt heightened by the divagations of the *Kosmiker*. The problem was whether or not Maximin was spirit. Albert Verwey pointed out that whereas hitherto for George the divine had been spirit, of which he was the priest, now he claimed leadership, in a concrete German state, of a defined sect of worshippers. And the God his community was commanded to worship, Verwey hinted, was a Greek Christ (that is, a beautiful youth hailed as divine), worshipped – as Christ had been by His disciples – in the recollection of his presence on earth. To Verwey, Dutch Protestant as he was (and Englishmen will generally agree with him), there was something Popish in this setting up of an idol; and to George's elevation of a mortal above his fellows Verwey opposed the Dutch doctrine of the equality of all as the very essence of religion. On the other hand, the worship of the dead God was accepted by the Circle generally as the logical culmination of George's God-seeking: in Maximin, they argue, he – like Nietzsche an enemy of Christianity – creates his own Christ, as a symbol that any one whose life is consecrated to divine aspiration may create God in himself. This is accepted mystical doctrine: 'God' is the image of ultimate spiritual goodness created by every religious individual, and as an image must bear the features of His creator's individual ideal: hence the Nordic featuring of Christ as a golden-bearded soft-eyed Vandyke gentleman. But George as a mystic proper is unthinkable – for he has not stripped his being of *I* – indeed he is all *I*. His God is thus merely his *I* projected from his Dantesque frame into the body of a beautiful boy. Gundolf, with a brilliant display of scholastic argument, identifies George's boy-God with the Greek Eros. To the Greeks, he says, Eros was not a God of sex but a God of pure spirit (*Seelengott*); and as such he appears as Beauty in Greek sculpture. God is made body by the ritual of Consecration, which the Roman Catholic Church has taken over in a transmuted form. But Christianity differs radically from this Greek religion in that for Eros it substitutes Caritas; and while Eros is the consecration and taking over into oneself of *Thou*, Caritas is the sacrifice of *I*, which passes into *Thou*. [This Christian process, moreover, is extended to man's love of woman, while the (Platonic) love of man for man enhances itself by absorbing the worshipped male.] And again: in Christianity the body (of Thou as of I) is cast aside and denied, while in the worship of Eros the (beautiful) body is the very substance of the cult. Nor does Christianity keep the primitive ideality of its doctrine: Caritas becomes Voluptas or sensual desire, and morality takes the place of holiness. Thus the Christian world is 'de-godded' (*entgottet*); except only that pantheism and mysticism use the term 'God' to denote something supranatural hid in the mists of distance. The very essence of Greek religion, however, was the actual *presence* of the god, that is (in all its implications) *Diesseitigkeit*, the doctrine that Heaven is here below, whereas Christianity is the religion of the Beyond (*Jenseitigkeit*), that is, the negation of the divine on earth as of the blessedness which comes from the adoration of the Beauty of this tangible *Presence*. When, therefore, Christians speak of paganism as the cult of lusts, as hedonism, they are blinded by the Christian lies which Nietzsche nailed to the Cross; deification of the body (*Vergottung des Leibes*) is not the same as the worship as divine (*Vergötterung*) of the functions of the body. Literally, what George does is to restore the non-sensual worship, in the primitive Greek and Platonic sense, of Eros, Kairos, Consecration, and Beauty. And to George Eros is love which creates man and world; Kairos is the fruit which grows from their wisdom; Beauty can be seen by those only who are transformed (*durchbildet*) by the purification of their sensorial life (*sinnliches Da-Sein*); and these by their very nobility (not by mystic ecstasy or asceticism) achieve the appearance of God in the body. That is (one assumes): the elect, and they only, recognize physical beauty and its divine attributes when they see it. If one asks why this

George-created Christ must needs be a beautiful boy the answer is of course that the Greek ideal of beauty is to give physical transfiguration to the pure spiritual conception of the divine. For Stefan George as for Nietzsche it is the Greek ideal, not the diseased Jewish denial of physical beauty, which is to rejuvenate the decayed world; and perhaps the worshipping of Maximin is nothing more than a cry to the incredulous: *Ecce homo*, Lo! this is Man. Or: new man by his new faith in beauty will himself be beauty transfigured by spirit.

Actually those who should know best (now that the individualistic subtleties and the self-assertion of the more intimate Circle members are fading into a semblance of myth) claim that the key to the Maximin problem is *mein urbild* (with *mein* stressed), the 'essential image of myself', in this poem of *Der Stern des Bundes*:

> *Wer ist dein Gott? All meines traums begehr·*
> *Der nächste meinem urbild· schön und hehr.*
> *Was die gewalt gab unsrer dunklen schösse*
> *Was uns von jeher wert erwarb und grösse –*
> *Geheimste quelle innerlichster brand:*
> *Dort ist Er wo mein blick zu reinst es fand.*
> *Der erst dem einen Löser war und Lader*
> *Dann neue wallung giesst durch jede ader*
> *Mit frischem saft die frühen götter schwellt*
> *Und alles abgestorbene wort der welt.*
> *Der gott ist das geheimnis höchster weihe*
> *Mit strahlen rings erweist er seine reihe:*
> *Der sohn aus sternenzeugung stellt ihn dar*
> *Den neue mitte aus dem geist gebar.*

And this self-revelation in vision is the secret of that *renewal* of style and conception, that new and divine consecration, which is throughout the very essence of George. There is no beauty like that of Greek poetry; and George has the intense conviction that he has found the secret of that ancient irradiation: the poetry that never was since the days of Hellas he has brought back because he has given it bodily shape, which is to be worshipped (in symbol) as Apollo was (in symbol) in Greece.

The opening poems of *Der siebente Ring*, in sonorous blank verse, amount to poignant self-revelation, often with an indignant rush of invective which sometimes breaks up the rigidity of George's icy lines in normal enjambments. In *Das Zeitgedicht* he pours scorn on those who would praise him now his rank is assured; in *Dante und das Zeitgedicht*, *Goethe-Tag* and *Nietzsche* he shows the affinity of his fate to those great creative geniuses who were isolated by the supremacy of their intellect. In *Gezeiten* we have George's one erotic burst. But there is nothing whatever to indicate that a female is the subject of these love lyrics; and they have morbid thrills: e.g. *Als glitten erkaltete finger | Auf wangen von sonnigem flaum*. But the absorbing interest is gathered into the middle part, *Maximin*. One poem, *Auf das Leben und den Tod Maximins*, is in six parts: the first apostrophizes the Munich friends: ' . . . *mit schimmer um die haare | Erschien ein gott und trat zu euch ins haus . . . | Preist eure stadt die einen gott geboren! | Preist eure zeit in der ein gott gelebt!*' The second describes a pious visit to the place where the God was born. *Einverleibung* is ecstatic mysticism: George worshipping Maximin calls himself the creation of his own son *(Ich geschöpf nun eignen sohnes)*.

Der Stern des Bundes (1914), again tripartite, continues the doctrine embodied by Maximin: physical beauty is not only the guerdon of love, it is the law of life and the very sense of the universe. Since Maximin was the perfect youth *('schön wie kein bild und greifbar wie kein traum')* George's doctrine is also worship of youth – and, since from the time of the appearance of *Der Stern des Bundes* the youth movement grew apace in Germany, it had its share in furthering the cult (so important as it has proved for military policy) of the beautiful and healthy body. It was one of the books – *Also sprach Zarathustra* and Rilke's *Die Weise von Liebe und Tod des Cornets Christoph Rilke* were two others – which soldiers carried in their knapsacks during the War. In George's 'third humanism',[1] which in this book he interprets, the principles of the Third Empire are foreshadowed: thus the children of God must keep apart from 'women of alien nature' *('Mit den frauen fremder ordnung | Sollt ihr nicht den leib beflecken | Harret! lasset pfau bei affe!')*.[2] Sundering dubious divinity from divine poetry one must give first place to the poems in this book in which what should be the monotonous

---

[1] The term *'dritter Humanismus'* derives, not from George himself, but from Lothar Helbing's essay *Der dritte Humanismus*.

[2] *fremde Ordnung=gemeines Wesen*. Racial application to 'blood-pollution' was inevitable.

theme of George – but it is not, because it is so intense and so varied –, his self-interpretation and proud assertion of self, are unfolded. In *Nennt es den blitz der traf den wink der lenkte* a poet once again gives inspired (though here difficult) expression to the nature of inspiration, and in this case its religious purpose. His rejection of his contemporaries, angry in *Der siebente Ring*, is hieratic in such poems as *Aus purpurgluten sprach des himmels zorn* and *Alles haben alles seufzen sie*. He speaks of One (Nietzsche is meant) whose warning was unheeded; now it is too late:

> *Einer stand auf der scharf wie blitz und stahl*
> *Die klüfte aufriss und die lager schied*
> *Ein Drüben schuf durch umkehr eures Hier . .*
> *Der euren wahnsinn so lang in euch schrie*
> *Mit solcher wucht dass ihm die kehle barst.*
> *Und ihr? ob dumpf ob klug ob falsch ob echt*
> *Vernahmt und saht als wäre nichts geschehn . .*
> *Ihr handelt weiter sprecht und lacht und heckt.*
> *Der warner ging . . dem rad das niederrollt*
> *Zur leere greift kein arm mehr in die speiche.*

And so (in 1914, and before the War!) George prophesies that they who heeded not the warning voice will be swept away in their tens of thousands by 'the holy war':

> *Ihr baut verbrechende an maass und grenze:*
> *‹Was hoch ist kann noch höher!› doch kein Fund*
> *Kein stütz und flick mehr dient . . es wankt der bau.*
> *Und an der weisheit end ruft ihr zum himmel:*
> *‹Was tun eh wir im eignen schutt ersticken*
> *Eh eignes spukgebild das hirn uns zehrt?›*
> *Der lacht: zu spät für stillstand und arznei!*
> *Zehntausend muss der heilige[1] wahnsinn schlagen*
> *Zehntausend muss die heilige seuche raffen*
> *Zehntausende der heilige krieg.*

Das neue Reich (1929) has again the hieratic Trinitarian arrangement. Here George, who appears as the Lord of the Present, has finished his pilgrimage from the underworld of Algabal to the 'New Empire', which is the spiritual Germany visioned by Goethe, promised by Hölderlin, and now realized between North Sea and

[1] *'heilig'* because the punishment of God.

Mediterranean, its horizon bounded by Hellas. *Goethes letzte Nacht in Italien* is an illumination of Goethe's mission to the German race: purified by his suffering he brings them his own transformation from Gothic to Classic. *Der Krieg* (published separately in 1917) is a poignant personal statement of his own warning to the nation before the War began:

> *Was euch erschüttert ist mir lang vertraut·*
> *Lang hab ich roten schweiss der angst geschwitzt*
> *Als man mit feuer spielte . . meine tränen*
> *Vorweg geweint . . heut find ich keine mehr.*

But after this lashing of his people George ends, in iambic lines of great dignity, on a note of confident hope – the land cannot perish, for youth is hailing the gods, and –

> *. . . Sieger*
> *Bleibt wer das schutzbild birgt in seinen marken*
> *Und Herr der zukunft wer sich wandeln kann.*

The credit for this *Wandlung* of the nation is given in *Der Dichter in Zeiten der Wirren* (1921) to the poet; and here by a miracle of history such as the prophecy of the coming of Christ by Virgil a passionate crescendo of prophecy would seem to have foretold the task and victory of quite another Führer than the poet: he acclaims:

> *Ein jung geschlecht das wieder mensch und ding*
> *Mit echten maassen misst· das schön und ernst*
> *Froh seiner einzigkeit· vor Fremden stolz·*
> *Sich gleich entfernt von klippen dreisten dünkels*
> *Wie seichtem sumpf erlogner brüderei*
> *Das von sich spie was mürb und feig und lau*
> *Das aus geweihtem träumen tun und dulden*
> *Den einzigen der hilft den Mann gebiert . .*
> *Der sprengt die ketten fegt auf trümmerstätten*
> *Die ordnung· geisselt die verlaufnen heim*
> *Ins ewige recht wo grosses wiederum gross ist*
> *Herr wiederum herr zucht wiederum zucht· er heftet*
> *Das wahre sinnbild auf das völkische banner*
> *Er führt durch sturm und grausige signale*
> *Des frührots seiner treuen schar zum werk*
> *Des wachen tags und pflanzt das Neue Reich . . .*

No wonder that Goebbels sent George a telegram of congratulation on his birthday – which, one hears, George never acknowledged. The Führer may have been taking the poet-dictator's birthright.[1] In any case it is not quite clear whether George's Third Reich can be identified with that which was now established. George's Reich, like that of Rilke, should be of the spirit. Surely George's own message is that they who would enter the spiritual realm must cast off race and homeland and family:

> Dies ist reich des geistes: abglanz
> Meines reiches . . Neugestaltet, neugeboren
> Wird hier jeder: ort der wiege
> Heimat bleibt ein märchenklang.
> Durch die sendung durch den segen
> Tauscht ihr sippe stand und namen
> Väter mütter sind nicht mehr.

Stefan George died on December 4th, 1933, and was buried at Minusio. He had lived through nearly a year of Nazi rule. The rumour that in his will he asked that he should not be buried in Germany is false but significant.

A first glance at Stefan George's verse is likely to repel a newcomer. It is intended to; the orthographical peculiarities have been described as barbed wire to scare intruders ('Stacheldraht wider Unberufene'). The new reader can only prove that he does not belong to the profanum vulgus by reading desperately on; and if he does so it is quite likely that familiarity will breed comprehension. The salient innovation is that capitals for nouns are discarded. Historically these date only from the seventeenth century as a device of ornamental Baroque; Jakob Grimm rejected them, and since his days small letters for nouns have been a feature of Gelehrtendeutsch. George uses capitals for strong emphasis. Where he has his own spelling he is strictly logical, as in lezt for letzt. His punctuation, after all, is just that of lawyers drawing up wills, and for the same reason: the pith of the meaning, because it is so vitally important, is guarded by being run on without stops or with very few.

---

[1] Hans Naumann dedicates the 6th edition of his Deutsche Dichtung der Gegenwart (1933) to 'Unsere Führer', that is, George and Hitler, and draws a parallel between the two; both spring from the holy lap of sound peasant stock, both are unfettered by kith and kin and wife (unbesippt und unbeweibt), both cherish the same ideals of race and leadership, both have grown tree-like speech by speech and Ring by Ring, and both live only for followers and Cause.

George is credited with having formulated the rule: *Kommas sind für Kommis*. In his treatment of separable prefixes he goes with the philosophers, who may require the literal meaning of each part of the word; thus *da-sein* has its literal meaning and not the paled significance of *Dasein*. George's grammar is only occasionally wilful. He makes a phrase more opaque by using the Saxon genitive after a preposition: *In all der sommerstunden glühender dürre* . . . *Mit deiner steilen gebüsche verschwiegnem verlies | Sonnig gebreiteter gänge nie furchendem kies*. He copies the delightful practice of children who make weak verbs strong; but he would not intend his *zugewunken* to have the same effect as little Alice's 'he wunk at me', and equally entertaining is *Bis euch der sturm in weite öden jug. Warden uns erdachte seligkeiten* must make any philologist wince. His invention of verbal nouns (*welke* for *Welken*, *leite* for *Leitung*) is otiose, and in his parading of Middle High German words (*tucht* for *Zucht*, *selde* for *Glück*, etc.) he misses the magic effect of Rilke in *Die heiligen drei Könige*. His obsession for foreign words may sometimes prove a pitfall for the unwary: thus *denkbild* in his verse does not mean 'monument' but *gedachtes Bild*; it is the Dutch *denkbeeld* taken over to mean the Apollonian vision of a shape. *Ewe*, too, has the meaning of Dutch *eeuw* (=century). He may clip a senseless syllable (*dächtnis* for *Gedächtnis*), but he permits himself an occasional *Dichter-e* and archaic forms such as *fleucht* for *fliegt*. He uses *die* for *die(jenigen)*, *die*; i.e. he omits the demonstrative. He will make a preposition serve for adverb (*und väter die ich seit zur gruft geleitet*) or for conjunction (*Der kelch einer zeitlose duftete vor er sich schloss*). His syntax is fairly normal, but he plays with Romance constructions and anacolutha.

The subtlety of George's technique does not lie in such curiosities; it lies in his modulation of vowels (*ü=Süsse; ei=Eisigkeit;* etc.) to evoke differing moods, his manipulation of alliteration, and his tireless variation of these tonal qualities. These devices give him a gorgeous (or shall we say Georgeous?) style which can at once be detected as his if any scrap of it is put before one who has once read his way into it.

George's metrical qualities will inevitably be compared with those of Rilke, and here there are two features which no one can miss: firstly George's preference for monosyllables, and secondly his avoidance of or peculiar use of enjambment. George's enjambment is often illusory. In other words he has a sharply defined

11

Endstil, and thus has not that marvellous fluidity which Rilke gets by his masterly *Hakenstil.* In Rilke's verse the flawless flowing into each other of line and line is a result of the ecstatic rapidity of his thought, while the steady halts of George's verse are due to his measured and vigorous tread. Rilke's verse flows as a molten mass; George's verse has passed the state of molten flux and is given us in shaped rigidity. The molten flux is Dionysian *Rausch,* and Rilke gives it as such; George transforms *Rausch* to Apollonian *Gebilde.* Another feature is the steady regularity of George's lines; they are intended to be scanned – and generally *must* be scanned – in Herr Opitz's way. But it is just this steady beat of scansion which marks George's verse, in its period, with strangeness. The most perfunctory analysis of German verse will show that even where Herr Opitz's rules are most rigorously applied scansion by the old German rule of so many lifts to the line and with the number of dips free is not only possible but may even show where the melody of the verse lies. Scansion by classical feet takes no account of subsidiary stress; or at least a subsidiary stress must be reckoned, very artificially, as a main stress; whereas in Germanic scansion the main stresses bring the chief words into prominence while the subsidiary stresses recede. George's scansion is governed by the slow pace the reading requires to get the effect – and the use of monosyllables slows down the line; so that in such lines as *Nennt es den blitz der traf den wink der lenkte:* | *Das ding das in mich kam zu meiner stunde* there is a kind of level stress throughout, not with trochee for iambus at the beginning of the first line, not with the natural three stresses (*ding, kam, stunde*) in the second. But George's short-lined lyrics – and they are his most musical – *may* be read with Germanic scansion:

> Keins wie dein feines ohr
> Merkt was tief innen singt
> Was noch so schüchtern schwingt
> Was halb sich schon verlor.

There is of course no suggestion that George's verse has the wooden regularity of Opitzian verse. It has George's personal rhythm: he strides on with his relentless firm tread (*weiterschreiten* is a favourite word of his). Some one has said that his metrical feet pass like a regiment of grenadiers doing the goose-step. Marvellous, too, is the way the cold breath of his pride or the withering hiss of his scorn chills his lines, particularly his blank verse: it is a commonplace to refer to his *eisige Blankverse*. His stanzas have generally the insulation of his individual lines, though overflow of stanza into stanza (*Strophenverschlingung*) does occur (e.g. in the first poem of *Der Teppich des Lebens*). Every stanza is as a rule a separate entity; if for instance we examine *Wir schreiten auf und ab im reichen flitter* we can, as Schaeffer shows, transpose the first and last stanzas without changing the effect of the poem.

Of the Georgeans (*die Georgeaner*) it might be said that, with the exception of Gundolf perhaps, only those who moved away from the Circle achieved a permanent place in literature. KARL WOLFSKEHL (1869-1948), a Jew, hailed from George's Gymnasium at Darmstadt; he devoted himself at the University to Germanic philology; his *Älteste deutsche Dichtung* (edited in conjunction with Friedrich von der Leyen), and his epics (*Wolfdietrich, Thors Hammer*) are evidence of these studies.[1] LUDWIG KLAGES (1872-1956) philosophized and (like Ernst Bertram) went Nordic; his *Die psychologischen Errungenschaften Nietzsches* is important. FRIEDRICH WOLTERS (1876-1930) specialized as an adapter of old hymns, psalms, and sequences, but counts most for his monumental work on George and the Circle. ERNST BERTRAM (1884-1957), Professor of German literature at Cologne, is the only one of the Circle who found favour with Nazi critics; and this because of his racial correctness. George's own racial attitude was, as we have seen, suspected: he had said that he had fled from the claws of the damp dragons of the North to drink in the sun of the South (*Dort sog ich sonne | Nach einer flucht aus feuchter drachen krallen*) and in *Rheintafeln* he had bidden his Germans talk of the New Empire only when his own fiery blood, his Roman breath (*'mein römischer hauch'*) coursed through their obtuse and obstinate souls; it is pretty clear that he himself as a Rhinelander dreamed of bringing the mellow culture of the Romance races to his benighted brethren. Ernst Bertram defected from this sunny doctrine and discovered the stars of hope in Nordic night and mist: in the poetry of his *Das Nornenbuch* (1925) he bodies forth the qualities of Teutonic culture, and seeks to renew Nordic myth. In his book of essays *Deutsche Gestalten* (1934) he brilliantly interprets Stifter, Nietzsche, and Kleist. But

[1] *Gesammelte Dichtungen* (1903).

the great literary critic of the Circle was FRIEDRICH GUNDOLF (1880-1931), a Darmstadt man, and like Wolfskehl a Jew (his real name was Gundelfinger). He joined the Circle in 1899 as a nineteen-year-old very handsome boy with a mop of blue-black hair and a nose only imperceptibly vaulted, and beneath a broad brow brilliant bright blue eyes with the flat pupils of eagles (to quote the Georgeous description of Wolters). His criticism is perhaps too dazzlingly subtle and intricate to stand the test of time; and he is apt, as in his *George* (1920), to prove in philosophically technical language, in which only a Hegelian could find flaws, his monumental conception of the idol in the worship of whom he erects his own monument. He is a schoolman (*Scholastiker*), armoured with authority, but with a poet's verbal magic: and the term 'heroic criticism'[1] is fitting because of Gundolf's relinquishment of creative poetry to create an interpretation of it which is, or is intended to be, of equal artistic value. His Georgean translation of Shakespeare (*Shakespeare in deutscher Sprache*, 10 vols., 1908-14) fails because it is Georgean.

RUDOLF BORCHARDT (1877-1945) was rather a meticulous stylist of the Georgean pattern than one of the Georgeans proper, with whom indeed he carried on an embittered feud. As such formalists are apt to do, he pondered his work till ripe maturity; it was not till after the War that he released his *tours de force*: his epic of chivalry *Der Durant* (1921), in which a knight sinks from the over-refined subtleties of courtly love to the low level of *nideriu minne*; his translation of Dante's *Vita nuova* into a kind of Middle High German was followed by his rendering in the same lingo of the *Divina Commedia*, which was published in 1930 as *Dante Deutsch*; *Verkündigung* (1920), his dramatic challenge to Paul Claudel's *L'annonce faite à Marie*; his pastoral play in alexandrines, *Die geliebte Kleinigkeit* (1923). But he had already expounded his new conception of classical style in *Gespräch über Formen* (1905; attached to his translation of Plato's *Lysis*) and in his *Rede über Hofmannsthal* (1918), while in his Biblical experiment *Das Buch Joram* (1907) he had exemplified his programme of classical form achieved by a mastery of archaic language. His essays (*Handlungen und Abhandlungen*, 1928) have laboured brilliance. His interpreta-

---

[1] *Shakespeare und der deutsche Geist* (1911); *Hölderlins Archipelagus* (1911); *Goethe* (1916); *Kleist* (1922); *Cäsar* (1924); *Paracelsus* (1927); *Shakespeare. Sein Wesen und sein Werk* (1928); *Romantiker* (1930).

tions of Hofmannsthal's *Alkestis* and Stefan George's *Der siebente Ring* are quite wonderful in their way. He, too, translated Swinburne.

ALBRECHT SCHAEFFER (1885-1950), like Rudolf Borchardt, rejects George's circle as sterile imitators. He is, however, a confessed Georgean, though he swerved to drama (*Demetrius*, 1922) and to the novel. He counts mostly for the ultra-refinement and rich colouring of his prose, which make the three volumes of his aesthetic novel *Helianth* (1920) one of the notable works of the period; it has been likened, with its infolded pictures, to a majestic gobelin. His work in verse and prose is so voluminous and varied that for a clear idea it would have to be sectioned off according to periods, theme, and style. To his Hellenistic phase belong *Attische Dämmerung* (1914), *Heroische Fahrt* (1914), and the two volumes of *Griechische Heldensagen* (1929-30). His poem *Der göttliche Dulder* (1920) forms a group with his translations of the *Odyssee* (1927) and the *Ilias* (1929). In his 'Attic myth' *Der Raub der Persephone* (1920) the interest lies in the metrical manipulation to fit the shifting moods and in the delicate coloration. The myth is spun out to thin threads; the throb of interest is anaemic, the aim being to achieve verbal effects. The poem is therefore a typical product of Georgean *Artistenkunst*, though there is a loosening here, as elsewhere, of George's strict prosodic pattern. Schaeffer's Novellen (collected in *Das Prisma*, 1924; *Mitternacht*, 1928; *Das Opfertier*, 1931; *Knechte und Mägde*, 1931) belong to expressionism in so far as they have for theme the regeneration of the protagonist from a degraded phase of humanity to a high conception of duty and of fellowship with other mortals (*Wandlung*). This is a far fling from the classical definition of the Novelle as the unfolding of a strange event (*eine unerhörte Begebenheit*) and its impact on characters already formed and finished (*fertige Charaktere*). Thus the protagonist in two of Schaeffer's typical Novellen, *Christacker* and *Fidelio* are morally re-created by what happens. *Christacker* is the Scrooge theme of redemption by pity: the dreams of a night bring an ice-cold curmudgeon closer to his fellow men. The lines are still grotesque, but there is not the loud humour affected by Dickens, and there is a complicated psychological basis with a refined symbolism. The surname itself is symbolic: it has been changed from a coarse-sounding name (apparently Mistacker); the character is faintly imaged as a field in which is sown the seed of Christian charity. The agent of conversion is a demonic cat, which turns out to be the hero's own faint life lying like a dead weight on his chest. *Fidelio* is the story of a bovine bass opera singer (*Bassbuffo*) – formerly a locksmith – who murders his mistress in a fit of jealousy and afterwards hardly remembers the deed. He is schizophrenetic, and it is only when, after release from prison, he is nobly treated that he realizes what he is and what he has done, and sets out with his forgiving wife and children to begin a new life in America. His father was a Slav, and there is the implication that the criminal half of his psychology comes from the paternal side. There is the same generous interpretation of moral disgrace and degradation in *Das Gitter* (1923), a study of incest on the part of brother and sister. *Josef Montfort* (1918) has elements of the macabre novel, while *Elli oder sieben Treppen* (1920) records a girl student's descent to prostitution. To begin with she acts as secretary to a learned writer, who is taken to be Karl Wolfskehl. The book is notable for its presentation with malice prepense of the overwrought Georgean atmosphere. In 1938 he found asylum in New York and did not return till 1950; in New York he wrote his last novels *Rudolf Erzerum oder des Lebens Einfachheit* (1945), *Janna du Coeur* (1949), and *Der Geisterlehrling und seine Frauen* (1949). The scene of *Janna du Coeur* shifts from England in the time of Cromwell to Germany after the Peace of Westphalia; the novel has the atmosphere and colouring of *Barock*, but the heroine matures in the chaos of a post-war period in which our own period is adumbrated.

The next school of lyrists, 'die Charontiker', definitely opposed George's antique and Romance culture and demanded a German style and a simplicity which should without strain and without scanning by feet express the 'immanent rhythm' Holz demanded. The monthly journal of the group, *Der Charon*, was founded in 1904 by OTTO ZUR LINDE (1873-1938) and Rudolf Pannwitz. Charon is conceived as the ferryman plying between the reality of today and the realm of dream and spirit beyond. It was in *Charon* that the term 'expressionism' was used for the first time by Otto zur Linde in 1911. Historically considered the importance of the Charontiker lies in the influence they have had on the development of poetic form. As to the rejection of scansion the problem is: how much of this derives from the Dionysian rhythms of Nietzsche's *Zarathustra* or from Walt Whitman's 'barbarous yawp'?

As regards this we have zur Linde's statement in his *Arno Holz und der Charon*, which he wrote to counter Holz's system: '*Ich kenne Walt Whitmann*' (*sic*) '*nicht, habe wohl nie einen englischen Vers von ihm gelesen, und an Übersetzungen nur etwa hundert zitierte Verse*'. What he admits he had seen might of course have been sufficient; and Freiligrath's translation, as well as the more recent one of Karl Knortz and T. W. Rolleston, was available, as well as Johannes Schlaf's first essays on Whitman (1898). It is probably accidental that zur Linde's 'phonetic rhythm' is (in practice) identical with that of Stefan George: reiteration in a line of the same consonant or vowel, inner rhymes, assonance, alliteration. But distinct from George's technique is zur Linde's use of impure rhymes, and frequent rhyming of short and long vowels: *flog—noch, Kluft—ruft, Tod—Gott*. The chief factor in the revolutionary structure (if it *is* revolutionary) is accentuation. The free distribution of stresses is sometimes drastic, and zur Linde is particularly fond of contriving lines with, say, three unstressed to seven stressed syllables. But the apparent clash of stresses in such a line as '*Dann wird die Wélt gráu bis zum Abendrot*' is as old as the hills (Luther's *Der altböse Feind*!); phonetically there is no clash, for there is (there must be) a pause between the two consonants. There is greater daring in such a line as '*Auf endloser, weisser heisser Heide ging ich hin*'; this is not cacophonous; the rhythm drags from stress to stress to give the dragging of weary feet over white sand. Systematic is zur Linde's lengthening or shortening of lines; often there is a long loose preparatory roll with, at stanza ends, a short or shorter line perhaps with heaped stresses like the last hammer-blows – a driving home by intense concentration. Quite recently the loosely billowing line, not of Whitman but of Klopstock (phonetically spurious hexameters!) has been put forward as a vital influence in contemporary verse structure. One of the poets of today, Hans Egon Holthusen, agrees: 'we have Klopstock in our bones', he writes to me; but he adds that his own linear rhythm may go back to '*der freigefüllte Vers der althochdeutschen Heldenlieder* (*Hildebrandslied!*)'; and in any case he and the other German poets of today, however much they may crack up *Eliotismus*, are (as Holthusen says) '*im Strahlungsbereich der späten Lyrik Rilkes*'. Research might show that there is the hardening of the *Duineser Elegien*, to ring in harmony with the hardened mentality of today, in the new Anglo-American verse. Simply stated zur Linde's sys-

tem is (and it does correspond to the German *Eliotismus* of today):
put the stress where the sense needs it, and that will give '*Eigen-
bewegung*'; every poem will then have its own rhythmic movement,
just as every separate thing – a train, a clock, a wave – has its own
rhythm, and division into lines is then illusory, for there is one
continuous wave of rhythm. The individual poem reproduces
undulations of feeling in the poet, and these undulations of feeling
constitute the rhythms – not the rhythm – of the poem; no rhythm,
therefore, is fixed, but follows this flux of feeling; rhythm, therefore, being unfixed, is infinite, and verse is to be measured by the
intensity of the poet's feeling, which may swerve and vary and
rise and fall in any individual poem. But the conceptions, and the
ideas, which inspire the poem, also float and flash and vary: in an
individual poem we have a flux of things seen and visioned; and
the vision is intimately wedded to the dynamic rhythmical flux.
Rhythm is phonetic in the sense that it reproduces the actual
voice of the individual poet, with the rising and falling stress and
the melodic colouring fashioned physiologically. But the words of
the poem themselves change their sense and import as the vision
and the rhythm change; there is no fixity of meaning in words
and no fixity of meaning in a concept; for inspiration is instantly
creative. Here zur Linde's technique, his '*Wort-Magie*', is the very
secret of Dylan Thomas's word-worship – '*die Magie des Etymolo-
gischen*', such as we find it here and there in Klopstock; zur Linde
has an urge, as Rudolf Pannwitz puts it, 'to extract words with
their roots'; that is, he pierces to the mystic meaning in the very
sound. It is really the *assoziatives Denken* of a later period (p. 471).
Zur Linde's principles of verse structure – and at the same time
his philosophy of life – are laid down in *Die Kugel. Eine Philosophie
in Versen* (1906, 2nd ed. 1923) as well as in *Arno Holz und der
Charon* (1911). His *Gesammelte Werke*, which had begun with *Thule
Traumland* (1910), followed in eight volumes till 1925. Very helpful
is: Otto zur Linde: *Charon. Auswahl aus seinen Gedichten*. Einführung
von Hans Hennecke, 1952. As to the matter of his verse zur Linde
is the first of the cosmic *Mythiker* – Pannwitz, Mombert, Däubler
follow – who concentrate aeons into a moment of time; and what
these aeons have created is re-created in a flash in their mood of a
moment; what rolled around them as chaos takes close-seen televisionary form in the moving mirror before them and is fashioned
in phases with its inner meaning sung into words. Chaos is cos-

mos; for it is close-visioned as shape and heard as the harmony of the divine purpose. The poet's mind thus fixed and functioning is itself the universe as it was, as it is and ever shall be, and the sense of existence sings itself into floating rhythms that shape themselves to the very feeling of the ideas they convey and wed themselves to the inner melody of the ever-moving cosmos.

RUDOLF PANNWITZ (1881-) described his development in his *Grundriss einer Geschichte meiner Kultur* (1921) and explained the aims of the *Charontiker* in his *Kultur, Kraft, Kunst* (1906). He parted from zur Linde because he had come to the conclusion that in the Charontic style there was formlessness due to the rejection of the culture of Greece and Rome (*die Antike*). He then returned to his previous allegiance to Stefan George and adopted the Georgean orthography with small letters for nouns and scant punctuation. His work, which covers a vast range, is at first densely obscure but clears gradually, and there is still a following for his abstruse metaphysical and mythical poems, in which, in the wake of Nietzsche, Otto zur Linde, and Stefan George, he probes a way to a new cosmic *Mythos*, as in his epics *Das Kind Aion* (1919), *Mythen* (in ten parts, 1919-22), *Episches Zeitgedicht* (1919), *Das Geheimnis* (1922) and *Die Trilogie des Lebens* (1929). Pannwitz is himself with his remote personality a mythical figure; from 1921 to 1948 he lived the life of a recluse on a Dalmatian island, and here his mature works were completed. In the drama he is represented by *Dionysische Tragödien* (1913), *Baldurs Tod* (1919), and then *Philolethes* and *Orpheus* (1922). His lyric verse is best studied in *Urblick* (1926) and his selection *Landschaft-Gedichte* (1954), to which he has attached an interpretative *Nachwort*. The best known of his narrative prose works are *Orplid* (1923) and his 'Bildungs- und Erziehungsroman' *Das neue Leben*, which attempts the scope of Goethe's *Wilhelm Meister*. Of his paedagogical and philosophical works the most important is *Die Krisis der europäischen Kultur* (1917), in which he interprets Greek tragedy, French classicism, Shakespeare and Byron and adumbrates the possibility of a culturally united Europe, a 'new European cultural humanity', an idea which is also the base of his *Deutschland und Europa* (1918) and *Die deutsche Idee Europa* (1931). His dithyrambic *Die deutsche Lehre* (1919), Nietzschean with Stefan George's devices, might be taken to be spreading Nazi ideology at a time when Hitler was still a brooding ex-Feldwebel.

Of the other members of the Charontik group KARL RÖTTGER (1877-1942) wrote, as well as verse, dramas (*Simson*, 1921) and novels (*Die Berufung des Johann Sebastian Bach*, 1933; *Wolfgang Amadeus Mozart*, 1941), while RUDOLF PAULSEN (1883-), a son of the Berlin philosopher Friedrich Paulsen, gave a philosophic tinge to his poetry and, in days which crowned the Nordic ideals of his group, qualified as a Nazi hymnist.

VII

RILKE

If the judgment of the most reputed critics is to be accepted the greatest lyric poet of modern times in Germany, and one of the very greatest writers in the whole history of German literature, is RAINER MARIA RILKE (1875-1926). Rilke met Stefan George in 1897 in Berlin, but was never actually a member of the circle; and though his technique is related to that of Stefan George this is probably to be explained as common adhesion to a contemporary reaction against naturalism and to imitation – which was in the air – of the tonal devices of the French symbolists. Rilke himself acknowledged primary discipleship to the Danish writer Jens Peter Jacobsen and to Maeterlinck. Jacobsen's *Niels Lyhne*, Rilke thought, might have been his own biography; and it taught him to seek in nature sensuous equivalents of what was most delicate and incomprehensible in himself. To Jacobsen, too, Rilke owed his perception of the matter of poetry in whatever lay before his eyes ('*Bereitschaft zu unwählerischem Schauen*'[1]); while Maeterlinck's early work (*Le Trésor des Humbles*) taught him that there is deeper tragedy in the reality of everyday life than in the figments of adventurous romance. These influences remained as the base of his development, but there is no tangible evidence that George added anything to the towering superstructure. Rilke was a mystic, but with a mere inkling of what is mysticism to the philosophers; he told Hermann Pongs that except for a few pages of Schopenhauer he was unread in mysticism and philosophy. For his meetings (1898-1900) with the Berlin philosopher Georg Simmel see page 180. Later he read Plato and Bergson, and towards the end of his life Juan de la Cruz. The great influences of his maturity were impressions of travel, and above all the shaping of his conception of God by his two visits to Russia and his Russian studies.

[1] = *Alle Dinge sind poesiereif.*

In his closing years his study of Paul Valéry may have sustained him in the last distortions of his style. But to a mind so original influences count for comparatively little; Rilke made himself, in utter loneliness of spirit and in restless mental torment.

Rainer Maria Rilke was born at Prague on December 3rd to 4th, 1875, at midnight, that hour in which the Saviour was born, for which reason he was christened Maria as well as René. This second name he himself changed, in 1899, to Rainer, because this name was 'beautiful, simple, and German'. His birth was premature; this may explain something of his shrinking delicacy throughout his life. It has been shown that there is no foundation for the romantic fancy he himself nursed so pathetically that he was the last scion of a noble family of Carinthia, a long line of officers; on the father's side his ancestors were peasant proprietors in Bohemia, on the mother's burghers of Prague. There is no need to regret the illusion, for in the ripeness of time it was the inspiration of one lovely poem in honour of an imaginary ancestor (*Die Weise von Liebe und Tod des Cornets Rilke*), and, in 1906, of his *Selbstbildnis*, much more attractive than the best portraits the photographers could manage:

> *Des alten lange adligen Geschlechtes*
> *Feststehendes im Augenbogenbau.*
> *Im Blicke noch der Kindheit Angst und Blau*
> *und Demut da und dort, nicht eines Knechtes,*
> *doch eines Dienenden und einer Frau.*
> *Der Mund als Mund gemacht, gross und genau,*
> *nicht überredend, aber ein Gerechtes*
> *Aussagendes. Die Stirne ohne Schlechtes*
> *und gern im Schatten stiller Niederschau . . .*

It may, too, have been an illusion that his mother was cruel to him in his childhood; as the daughter of an Imperial Councillor she was of somewhat better class than her husband, a railway official, from whom she separated in 1884. It is known that till he was five she brought him up as a girl, with a girl's long hair and clothes, and gave him dolls to play with. The boy was educated at the Cadets' Schools of St. Pölten and Weisskirchen in Moravia. At Weisskirchen he was bullied by the more robust boys, and his spiritual suffering marked him for life; at first he humbled himself

to suffer like Christ,[1] and then – a strange experience for a mystic –
he turned away from Jesus because, he thought, He barred the way
to God. This hatred of Jesus[2] shows violently in his early work,
e.g. in his short story *Der Apostel* (1896), though here the main
ferment may have been Nietzsche's denunciation of Christianity.
In 1891 he was taken away from the cadet school on the grounds
of persistent ill health, and studied for a year at the Handelsschule
at Linz. In 1894 he passed his leaving examination. On his return
to Prague he began to write. His *Leben und Lieder* (1894), of which
only five copies remain in existence, represent his *juvenilia*; in
Larenopfer (1896) his cult of death begins to appear; in the lyrics
of *Wegwarten* (1896), of which three hundred copies were printed
to be given away to the sick in hospitals and to the poor, we find
the poet's first experimental touches in alliteration, pictorial com-
pounds, and verbs for adjectives: *Die Luft lechzt lerchenlüstern . . .,
blütenbezwungene Zweige, blauender Waldsee.*

In 1896 Rilke went to Munich and in 1897 to Berlin. Between
1898 and 1900 he stayed a few months in Italy and twice visited
Russia. The Russian experience was vital. His guide was Lou
Andreas-Salomé (p. 333). In 1899 Rilke stayed a week at Moscow
and six weeks at St. Petersburg, and on his return to Germany he
plunged fiercely into the study of the Russian language and of
Russian history. On his second visit in 1900 he travelled in South
Russia and the Ukraine, spent a few hours with Tolstoy at Jasnaya-
Poliana, and went up the Volga to Saratov. He had thought that
he had found his spiritual homeland in Italy; now he was sure he
had found it in Russia. Florence, with its beggars ever creating
God in the frescoes of Fra Angelico, had merely prepared him for
Moscow. The level Russian plain stretching away to infinity, the
simple religion of the peasants, to whom God was near as a
neighbour, made a deep impression on his mind. A few years
later he was to write to his friend, the Swedish writer Ellen Key:
'*Russland wurde für mich die Wirklichkeit und zugleich die tiefe, tägliche
Einsicht: dass die Wirklichkeit etwas Fernes ist, etwas, was unendlich
langsam zu jenen kommt, die Geduld haben. Russland – das ist ein Land,
wo die Menschen einsame Menschen sind, jeder mit einer Welt in sich, jeder
voll Dunkelheit, wie ein Berg; jeder tief in seiner Demut, ohne Furcht,
sich zu erniedrigen und deshalb fromm. Menschen voll Ferne, Ungewissheit*

---

[1] '*Ich leide es, weil Christus es gelitten hat, still und ohne Klage.*'
[2] Equally marked but less strange in the verse of the Jew Albert Ehrenstein.

und Hoffnungen – Werdende.' And over all a God who has never been defined, who eternally transforms Himself and grows. A God who ripens stage by stage with the ripening of those who seek Him. And Rilke believes that he must now ripen himself by ripening the God within him: his God will only be great if he himself is great.

At Florence Rilke had met the painter Heinrich Vogeler, and at his invitation he visited Worpswede, a village in the flat heathland (*Moordorf*) near Bremen; here a colony of artists had gathered whose ideals touch those of the impressionists: influenced by Julius Langbehn's *Rembrandt als Erzieher* (pp. 444-5), they regarded themselves as the heralds of a new spirit which should regenerate the intellectual life of Germany by freeing it from the miasmas of city life. Vogeler contributed to impressionism by his book illustrations, and the Worpswede artists point forward to *Heimatkunst*: one of them, Fritz Mackensen, proclaimed: '*der rechte Künstler kann gar nicht lokal genug sein*'. They specialized in heaths and silver birches, and the far vistas of the North German plain, in which Rilke thought he might recapture his Russian sensations of distance and infinity. At Worpswede Rilke met a young sculptress, Clara Westhoff, whom he married in the spring of 1901. A daughter was born in December, but in the following May they separated; there were financial difficulties (publishers refused to lend on prospects); and in any case Rilke's incapacity for wedded life stands out stark and clear from his correspondence. But the two remained friends, and met occasionally; the daughter married Carl Sieber, the editor of the poet's letters. Rilke was doomed by his restless nature to be a homeless wanderer over the face of the earth; but from his homelessness he drew the mood of some of his most poignant writing. Life in common with the artists of Worpswede had turned his mind to consideration of the nature of art, particularly of sculpture; his wife had been a pupil of Rodin in Paris, and Rilke began to surmise that in Rodin he had discovered his pattern. He stayed in Paris from August, 1902, to March, 1903, returned repeatedly, and in due course lived in Rodin's house at Meudon as the sculptor's secretary. In his first stay in Paris Rilke suffered acutely from the noise of the city; he had the sensation of being run over by vehicles. To his wife he wrote: '*Mich ängstigen die vielen Hospitäler, die hier überall sind. Ich verstehe, warum sie bei Verlaine, bei Baudelaire und Mallarmé immerfort vorkommen. Man sieht*

Kranke, die hingehen oder hinfahren, in allen Strassen . . . Man fühlt auf einmal, dass es in dieser weiten Stadt Heere von Kranken gibt, Armeen von Sterbenden, Völker von Toten.' He had not been conscious of the misery of the other great cities he knew. He did not run away: like Verhaeren nerve-wracked in his tentacular city he hardened himself, *'eben weil es schwer ist'*. (Carlyle: 'Do that which thou fearest to do.') He shut himself off from company, but spent days in the *Bibliothèque Nationale*. In 1903 he escaped, a sick man for all his defiance of his *malaise* (as he calls it), to Viareggio near Pisa. The last half of 1904 he spent at Borgeby Gård in Sweden and at Charlottenlund near Copenhagen. From May, 1908, to February, 1910, he was again in Paris, where he wove his Scandinavian memories into the nostalgic prose of *Die Aufzeichnungen des Malte Laurids Brigge*. In 1912 he spent four months in Spain; he was fascinated by Toledo and Ronda, and from Cordova he wrote to the Princess of Thurn and Taxis – who from now onwards is in the position to him of one of the *grandes dames* of previous centuries to their impecunious poets – that since he had seen this city he felt furiously anti-Christian: Christianity, he declared, was an empty fruit whose skin should be thrown away. Mahomet, he adds, spoke to God directly, whereas Jesus was a telephone to God. 1911-12 he stayed at the castle at Duino on the Golfo di Penzano on the Adriatic coast; it had been placed at his disposal by the Princess of Thurn and Taxis. Here he found the mood to write the first two of the elegies which bear the name of Duino. The years of the War paralysed his genius. In 1916 he was declared fit for service, but broke down under the weight of his knapsack, and was mercifully given sanctuary in the Press censorship at the War Office in Vienna; here he had friends for company – Stefan Zweig, Franz Karl Ginzkey; and the colonel in charge asked him just to put in an appearance in the mornings and busy himself with his own work. This kindness he rejected, for conscience' sake; but friends procured his release. 1917-19 he spent at Munich; he was expelled because he was now a Czech and as such could not claim Austrian protection. His contribution to the literature of the War are the *Fünf Gesänge*, now in *Letzte Gedichte*; he began with praise of the God who carries a whole nation with Him; but from the third song onwards to this God war is horrible, and the fifth song begins: *'Auf, und schreckt den schrecklichen Gott! Bestürzt ihn. | Kampf-Lust hat ihn vorzeiten verwöhnt . . .'* Rilke's attitude to

post-War Germany is pathetically expressed in a letter of 1923[1];
in 1918, he says, Germany might have shamed the world by accepting humiliation and changing its pre-War policy. After wandering
about in Switzerland, Italy, and France he stationed himself – one
cannot say that he settled – in the Rhone valley, and passed his
last years in an old tower dating from the thirteenth century near
Sierre in Valais, his Château de Muzot sur Sierre, placed at his
disposal by the Swiss patron of literature Werner Reinhart of
Winterthur, whom Rilke ever afterwards referred to as his *Lehns-
herr*. Here in the little garden he had a hundred roses planted;
and he died in 1926 from blood poisoning caused by pricking
himself with the thorn of one of his roses he gathered one day for
a lady visitor. He is buried in the cemetery at Rarogne.

Outwardly Rilke's life was eventless; and yet it is the intensity
of his experiences which we follow up in his work from stage to
stage. In his early verse there is naturally more imitation than experience, certainly in *Larenopfer*, the only strictly juvenile poems
admitted to *Erste Gedichte* (1913), where they take place with
the three verse collections which chronologically followed them:
Traumgekrönt (1897), *Advent* (1898) and *Mir zur Feier* (1899). *Larenopfer* is – if one may be allowed a paradox – urban *Heimatkunst*: the
poems reproduce the architecture and the medieval and Baroque
aspects of Rilke's native city of Prague. Metrically the stamp is
that of Heine:

> *Alte Häuser, steilgegiebelt,*
> *hohe Türme voll Gebimmel, –*
> *in die engen Höfe liebelt*
> *nur ein winzig Stückchen Himmel.*
>
> *Und auf jedem Treppenpflocke*
> *müde lächelnd – Amoretten;*
> *hoch am Dache um barocke*
> *Vasen rieseln Rosenketten.*

Heine-esque ballads rub shoulders with crass *Armeleutepoesie*. But
there is already Rilke's verbal invention and glaring imagery:

> *Die Stadt verschwimmt wie hinter Glas.*
> *Nur hoch, wie ein behelmter Hüne,*
> *ragt klar vor mir die grünspangrüne*
> *Turmkuppel von Sankt Nikolas.*

[1] *Briefe an eine junge Frau*, pp. 43-4.

The architectural mood is of course German rather than Czech; and only a few scraps of Czech indicate Rilke's nodding acquaintance with the language of the Czech poets whom he was at this time meeting in the literary cafés of the city; but his sensitiveness to the melodies of Czech folksongs comes out in *Volksweise*:

> *Mich rührt so sehr*
> *böhmischen Volkes Weise,*
> *schleicht sie ins Herz sich leise,*
> *macht sie es schwer.*
>
> *Wenn ein Kind sacht*
> *singt beim Kartoffeljäten,*
> *klingt dir sein Lied im späten*
> *Traum noch der Nacht.*
>
> *Magst du auch sein*
> *weit über Land gefahren,*
> *fällt es dir doch nach Jahren*
> *stets wieder ein.*

In *Traumgekrönt* the Heine-esque note continues, but there is an inner radiance (as well as the crystal coruscation of Christmas cards) in such a poem as:

> *Es gibt so wunderweisse Nächte,*
> *drin alle Dinge Silber sind.*
> *Da schimmert mancher Stern so lind,*
> *als ob er fromme Hirten brächte*
> *zu einem neuen Jesuskind.*
>
> *Weit wie mit dichtem Demantstaube*
> *bestreut, erscheinen Flur und Flut,*
> *und in die Herzen, traumgemut,*
> *steigt ein kapellenloser Glaube,*
> *der leise seine Wunder tut.*

Here the ecstatic rise of the rhythm in the antepenultimate line and the folding appeasement of the last are typically Rilkean. In other poems there is a gliding softness and rhythmical regularity (admirably fitted to the mood) which we do not find in Rilke's mature verse:

12

Das war der Tag der weissen Chrysanthemen, –
mir bangte fast vor seiner schweren Pracht . . .
Und dann, dann kamst du mir die Seele nehmen
tief in der Nacht.

Mir war so bang, und du kamst lieb und leise, –
ich hatte grad im Traum an dich gedacht.
Du kamst, und leis wie eine Märchenweise
erklang die Nacht . . .

This lyric – which has been taken into the anthologies – shows
exactly how imitative Rilke is in this early verse: he is literally
fitting words to one of the best known of German tunes, that of
Hermann Gilm's *Stell' auf den Tisch die duftenden Reseden,* | *Die letzten
roten Astern bring herbei,* | *Und lass uns von der Liebe reden,* | *Wie einst
im Mai*; all he does is to lengthen the third line by one foot. The
poems of *Traumgekrönt* are decadent in tone. It is as though Rilke
had been reading Maeterlinck's *Serres chaudes*. Not that there is
painting of disease; indeed the attitude to death is already that
idealization of ripened readiness which Rilke was to make his
gospel; the *fin-de-siècle* tints are rather in the adjectival and nominal
evocations (*weisse Wünsche, verblühte Sterne, nächteblasse Sehnsucht,*
etc.), and in the prevailing landscapes of snowed-up winters and
faint springs in which the symbolist paraphernalia (gaudy pea-
cocks, shimmering swans, dark pools, etc.) serve for splashes
of colour. Into these lorn landscapes are projected the personal
moods of the poet – his thwarted childhood (*Warst du ein Kind in
froher Schar . . .*), his loneliness (*Der Tag entschlummert leise*) and his
(later so wistful) association of his unfulfilled longing with the
erotic expectation of maidens. *Advent*, too, ranges itself with the
literature of the late nineties by its decadent tints and morbid
images (*blütenblasse Maiennächte, silberstille Teiche, liebeleise Arme*).
But the real Rilke – his rapid, fluent rhythm – begins in such
poems as *Der Abend kommt von weit gegangen*. Notable is the adum-
bration of the poet's spiritual growth in the introductory poem:

Das ist mein Streit:
sehnsuchtgeweiht
durch alle Tage schweifen,
dann, stark und breit,
mit tausend Wurzelstreifen

tief in das Leben greifen –
und durch das Leid
weit aus dem Leben reifen,
weit aus der Zeit!

This programme was the very opposite of what was to shape the
poetic personality of Stefan George, with whom all striving is
ego-centric: George's mission is to ripen life to his own ideal,
that of Rilke to ripen personality beyond the range of life – but
by sinking into it and rising out of it to the skies like a tree widely
rooted in the earth of reality. And there is already in *Advent* the
theme of pilgrimage to God, already the first hints of Rilke's later
definition of God as a direction given to love, and of death as a
portion of personality; and thus the book is in some sort a prelude
to *Das Stundenbuch*. The dreamy wistfulness of the *Mädchen* poems,
too, is sketched in *Alle Mädchen erwarten wen, | wenn die Bäume in
Blüten stehn*, and in the very lovely:

> *Lehnen im Abendgarten beide,*
> *lauschen lange nach irgendwo.*
> *'Du hast Hände wie weisse Seide . . . '*
> *Und da staunt sie: 'Du sagst das so . . . '*
> *Etwas ist in den Garten getreten,*
> *und das Gitter hat nicht geknarrt,*
> *und die Rosen in allen Beeten*
> *beben vor seiner Gegenwart.*

Here again there is imitation probably – of Maeterlinck's *L'Intruse*.

Rilke's mystical losing of himself in individual phenomena
('*Dinge*')[1] takes definite shape in the poems of *Mir zur Feier*[2] (1899),
the first book to be signed with the new name of Rainer Maria
Rilke. Later he proclaimed it to be his first book. Now he is conscious that he is a dreamer ('*zu Hause zwischen Tag und Traum*') who
would fain proffer yearning in his rhymes (*eine Sehnsucht reichen in den
Reimen*); henceforth his soul shall be like a festal garment covering
thinking things ('*breite dich wie ein Feierkleid | über die sinnenden
Dinge*'). His 'gospel of things' takes concrete shape in this volume
in a group of poems which deal with the relativity of the names of
things to the essence of these things: words, says Rilke quizzically

---

[1] '*Auflösung des Ich-Seins hinein in das Sein der Dinge.*'
[2] The second revised edition (1907) changes the title to *Die frühen Gedichte*.

(another mystic, Christian Morgenstern, turned the idea into jesting rhymes), express so clearly – 'dog' and 'house' show a beginning and an end. But has *the thing* the sense and limits of *the name*? The schoolmen of the Middle Ages – nominalists, terminists, conceptualists – had disputed for generations on this problem. But the schoolmen did not dream of the task Rilke sets himself: '*dienend durch die Dinge zu gehen*', to listen to the stirring of their hidden spirit, and to weave this inner life of things with their own rhythm (which expresses God) into his verse. '*Alle Dinge, an die ich mich gebe*,' runs a later poem, '*werden reich und geben mich aus.*' And in *Mir zur Feier* Rilke gives his warning: you are killing these things you define by name, these things that *I* love to hear singing. In *my* arms forests sleep, and I am the music over their tops, and all the darkness of my nature is the darkness that is in violins. Things are the mystery – the bleeding goblet – revealed to the pilgrim when the last curtain falls from the altar; and then he cannot turn back from salvation: the mystic arrow has hit the Player's aim. And (since the Divine is in me and in all these things) is not my life the life of things? He asks:

> *Kann mir einer sagen, wohin*
> *ich mit meinem Leben reiche?*
> *Ob ich nicht auch im Sturme streiche*
> *und als Welle wohne im Teiche,*
> *und ob ich nicht selbst die blasse, bleiche*
> *frühlingsfrierende Birke bin?*

The final poem links *Mir zur Feier* with *Das Stundenbuch*:

> *Du darfst nicht warten, bis Gott zu dir geht*
> *und sagt: Ich bin.*
> *Ein Gott, der seine Stärke eingesteht,*
> *hat keinen Sinn.*
> *Da musst du wissen, dass dich Gott durchweht*
> *seit Anbeginn,*
> *und wenn dein Herz dir glüht und nichts verrät,*
> *dann schafft er drin.*

Where God is not, where even His seasons are anaemic or feverish, is in the tentacular city:

> *Das ist dort, wo die letzten Hütten sind*
> *und neue Häuser, die mit engen Brüsten*

sich drängen aus den bangen Baugerüsten
und wissen wollen, wo das Feld beginnt.

Dort bleibt der Frühling immer halb und blass,
der Sommer fiebert hinter diesen Planken;
die Kirschenbäume und die Kinder kranken,
und nur der Herbst hat dorten irgendwas

Versöhnliches und Fernes; manchesmal
sind seine Abende von sanftem Schmelze:
die Schafe schummern, und der Hirt im Pelze
lehnt dunkel an dem letzten Lampenpfahl.

This nostalgic lyric – a dirge of the pastoral fields dying as the tentacles of the creeping town reach them – belongs to *Grossstadtpoesie*, a genre which (influenced by Verhaeren) is to picture the city as a nightmare – as to Rilke, as we shall see, it literally was. Symbol and personal feeling blend to make the tripartite cycle *Mädchengestalten, Lieder der Mädchen, Gebete der Mädchen zu Marie*, the most fascinating part of *Mir zur Feier*. Certainly these poems have full value as exquisite poetry apart from their mystical meaning: with the quaint imagery set in their simple phrases they do sensitively evoke the stirrings of first maiden puberty, the fear, and the expectation. No poem in the world proves the purity of sexual union as does this prayer of the maidens to Mary:

Schau, unsre Tage sind so eng
und bang das Nachtgemach;
wir langen alle ungelenk
den roten Rosen[1] nach.

Du musst uns milde sein, Marie,
wir blühn aus deinem Blut,
und du allein kannst wissen, wie
so weh die Sehnsucht tut;

du hast ja dieses Mädchenweh
der Seele selbst erkannt:
sie fühlt sich an wie Weihnachtsschnee,
und steht doch ganz in Brand.

[1] In the *Volkslied* (as in Goethe's *Röslein rot*) red roses signify the loss of virginity.

The rendering of sensuous impressions is throughout *Mir zur Feier* equally gentle and equally poignant, and is in itself sufficient for the stamp of exquisite poetry. But to Rilke what to us is the very soul of poetry is merely the veil of the meaning: '*Die Worte sind nur die Mauern.* | *Dahinter in immer blauern* | *Bergen schimmert ihr Sinn*'; and the wistful maiden of these poems is interpreted as Rilke's image at this stage of his mysticism for his own maiden soul – maiden because of its union, in purity, of physical and spiritual life, of inner urge and dream projected into outer phenomena.

Between 1895 and 1902 Rilke attempted plays, in which he advances from the crass realism of the naturalists to a symbolism influenced by Maeterlinck, as in *Die weisse Fürstin*, which appeared in 1899 in *Pan*, and was reprinted in *Mir zur Feier*. It is the only one of his plays which he included in his collected works. *Die weisse Fürstin* is in the nature of a curiosity among those playlets of the period which take rank, in spite of their thinness of action, by reason of their new lyrical suppleness. All there is in the play – but it has the fascination of some strange hot-house flower – is the unfolding by the White Princess and her young sister, Monna Lara, of their sexual state. Whether the White Princess is (like Hebbel's or Georg Kaiser's Judith) physically a virgin – she has long been married to a man who does not heed her – or merely virgin in soul (she has been in bed with the ebony Cross of Christ) and waiting for her lover is not clear. Her sister has the fire and snow of Rilke's maidens who pray to Mary. What one does not forget is the Pre-Raphaelite picturing in the sultry atmosphere of the night, particularly in the stage directions: '*Monna Lara hat sich knieend zurückgeworfen und hält mit beiden Händen ihre Brüste hin, als warte sie, dass sie sich füllen sollten.*' The erotic problem is in any case that of Hofmannsthal's *Elektra*, and there is nearness to the hysteria of *Elektra*, as in Monna Lara's plaint:

> *Wenn ich mir denke, dass ich noch ein Jahr*
> *herumgehn soll mit unerklärtem Blut,*
> *unausgeruht, – von meinem eignen Haar*
> *hochmütig übersehen wie ein Kind,*
> *allein und blind immitten meiner Brände,*
> *sogar den Hunden neu und wie versagt,*
> *mir selbst so fremd, dass mich die eignen Hände*

anrühren wie die Hände einer Magd . . . :
wenn ich ein Jahr noch also leben soll,
so werf ich mich nach diesem einen Jahre
einem Bedienten in den Weg wie toll
und fleh ihn an, dass er mir das erspare.

The influence of Maeterlinck appears too in several of the short tales (collected in 1928 as *Erzählungen aus der Frühzeit*). Rilke as a German Czech gives us in *Zwei Prager Geschichten* (1899) the atmosphere of Prague, sketches the life of its literary cafés, and links the discussions of acting and literature to a student conspiracy against the Austrian Government. The neo-romanticism of the day lends a thrill to Luisa, a hysterical erotic creature who has visions of Julius Caesar, the illegitimate son of Kaiser Rudolf II, hunting women as a ghost in a castle: one of her hallucinations is very fine as a prose passage. The eleven stories collected in *Am Leben hin* (1898) mark Rilke's desertion of naturalism for symbolism. The characters pass along 'on the rim of life'; like Hofmannsthal's Claudio they miss life because of their lack of ideal love: only those live the life of the spirit who have been cured of reality by illness or some infirmity. The formative influence is that of J. P. Jacobsen: from him Rilke has learned to build up a total psychological interpretation from a cumulation of impressions or rather *aperçus* – of life as it presents itself to the dispassionate observer, with physical and mental decay and death in the forefront. One is reminded of the Spanish vignettes of Azorin; the difference is that while Azorin in his quite ordinary moods and happenings shows the poetry of landscape and environment and the haunting tragedy of decay Rilke limns his types with a surprising analytical cruelty and probes with a grim curiosity. There might have been great possibilities of a new fiction in this style if he had continued it; or it might have shaped him to a kind of intellectualized Dickens; and it is only by holding this tentative work against that of his maturity that we can realize the growth of his mind. At the same time the comparison shows that he was by nature lacking in warm humanity; the apparent pity for poverty in his later work was obviously of the aesthetic type. In this early work he is outside the life he observes but on a level with it, while later he sees it from above and transfigured by the 'distance' which for him became the necessary condition of poetry. There is both literary and autobiographical interest in the individual stories of *Am Leben hin*. *Das Christkind* was written in 1893, the date of the appearance of Hauptmann's *Hannele*; it is the tale of a little girl ill-treated by her stepmother; she dies in hospital after being found in the snow in the forest, where she has taken a couple of candles and other trifles to offer to the stone image of the Virgin. Here we have, as in *Hannele*, a blending of raw *Armeleutepoesie* with the mystic lights of a child's dreaming as she dies. *Einig* (1897) is a handling of the son-mother motif which is so poignant in Rilke's own life. The mother's name in the tale is Sophie – the name ('Phia' for short) of Rilke's own mother. When she asks her son if he does not love the recollection of his childhood he replies: *'O ja. Ich liebe sie, wie man eine Lüge liebt, durch die man glücklich wird . . . Ich liebe alle Wege, welche du mich geführt hast, diese leisen, lautlosen Wege ums Leben herum zu deinem Gott.'* Like Ibsen's Oswald this young man is dying with an illness he owes to his father. Interesting in the style of *Am Leben hin* is the appearance of Rilkean onomatopoeia: thus (in *Das Christkind*) a symphony in *i*: *'Die Stimmen aus Bach und Kraut versickern in dem Dunstmeer, und nur das Wimmern windgequälter Wipfel zittert durch den einsamen Tann'*; and on the same page a play on *ä* with interior rhyme: *'Das mondscheinfarbene Licht flutete weich wie eine an flachem Sande landende Welle durch den Raum.'*

The son-mother motif recurs in the short story *Die Letzten* (1902), the last of the tales collected under this title. The hero, a lad engaged to a robust girl of peasant stock, dies of consumption: his long line of ancestors – generals, bishops, etc. – have taken the vigour from his blood. His mother has kept him from life. Like Hofmannsthal's Claudio he has not lived; he complains that his mother would have kept him from *'das Fremde, Neue, Unruhige, das ich nicht begreife'*. 'O these books!' she moans. In Rilke's eyes a man unformed by woman is left in the raw, and the natural thing is that the mother should do the first shaping; but it is clear that in his argument the mother tends to keep her son away from the shock of life – and the other woman or women – that alone would harden him for experience.

Rilke's mysticism finds its first mature expression in a volume of short stories, *Geschichten vom lieben Gott* (1904) and in the verse of *Das Stundenbuch* (1905). The difference between the mysticism of the two books is, roughly, that while in the first God, abandoned and feeble, hiding modestly behind the cover of things, is seeking

RAINER MARIA RILKE

man, or rather seeking Himself in man, in the second man is desperately seeking a God of strength who is only to be won by wrestling and tribulation; the first is the God of everyday life, the second the God man is to create. *Das Stundenbuch*, by which Rilke achieved fame, is composed of three books: *Das Buch vom mönchischen Leben, von der Pilgerschaft, von der Armut und vom Tode*. The *Book of the Monastic Life* had been written in 1899 after Rilke's visit to Italy, but before he had seen Russia; the inspiration must, therefore, be Italian. The *Book of Pilgrimage* (written 1901) is based on impressions of Russia. The *Book of Poverty and Death* (1903) reproduces the terrible suffering of the poet's first stay in Paris. The three books together develop Rilke's persistent idea that man is both creature and creator. Man's primitive conception of God was that He is perfect (in the sense of 'completed', '*vollendet*'), so that evolution and God were terms which excluded each other. This conception, Rilke believed, was only possible with primitive beings who were not conscious that man evolves; and Rilke's reasoning is that God must evolve as man evolves. Such a doctrine is of course only possible to one who believes that God is an idea and as an idea (or ideal) sprung from the yearning brain of man. '*Mit meinem Reifen | reift | dein Reich*,' he calls out to God in *Das Stundenbuch*. The conception of God as created by His own creature comes out in the famous passage of *The Book of the Monkish Life*:

Was wirst du tun, Gott, wenn ich sterbe?
Ich bin dein Krug (wenn ich zerscherbe?)
Ich bin dein Trank (wenn ich verderbe?)
Bin dein Gewand und dein Gewerbe,
mit mir verlierst du deinen Sinn.

Nach mir hast du kein Haus, darin
dich Worte, nah und warm, begrüssen.
Es fällt von deinen müden Füssen
die Samtsandale, die ich bin.
Dein grosser Mantel lässt dich los.
Dein Blick, den ich mit meiner Wange
warm, wie mit einem Pfühl, empfange,
wird kommen, wird mich suchen, lange –
und legt beim Sonnenuntergange
sich fremden Steinen in den Schoss.

Was wirst du tun, Gott? Ich bin bange.

That the main idea of these lines is good mystical doctrine (it could not be orthodox Catholic doctrine) is shown by a comparison with certain lines of the seventeenth-century mystical poet Angelus Silesius in *Der Cherubinische Wandersmann: 'Gott ist so viel an mir, als mir an ihm gelegen, | Sein Wesen helf ich ihm, wie er das meine, hegen. | . . . Ich weiss, dass ohne mich Gott nicht ein Nu kann leben, | Werd ich zu nicht, er muss von Not den Geist aufgeben.'* But it is a long cry from Catholic or metaphysical mysticism to Rilke's poetic mysticism. Rilke does not evolve his God by logical processes (as the true mystics do), but attains Him by a species of hallucinated illusion of physical contact. In the true mystics all the images of sensuous love merely make ideas visible; in Rilke's mysticism the sensuous love creates a succession of vivid images which cannot be resolved in strictly connected ideas. How very realistic – even grotesquely realistic, but with a grotesqueness that continues that of the old German folksongs which give rough woodcut shape to the Holy Family – are the familiar images of God in *Das Stundenbuch*: *'Du hältst mich seltsam zart | und horchst, wie meine Hände gehn | durch deinen alten Bart'; 'Nachbar Gott'; 'Du bist der raunende Verruste, | auf allen Öfen schläfst du breit'*, etc.; and how poetically real is the poet's identification of his soul (in *The Book of Pilgrimage*) with Ruth. But, in poetry which strikes right into the heart like this, what grovelling mind would bother about whatever meaning there may be? What matters is the feeling, not the meaning. If we must nail down whatever ideas are tangible (and to any one with an inkling of philosophy they must be commonplaces), then all we need say is that Rilke's mysticism is pantheism: for to him God is not en-skied, but en-earthed – in things. Or: it is a poetical version of the philosopher's doctrine of 'immanence': God is *in* things.

The sensuous bed of Rilke's thought gives a tender warmth to many of the cumulative images:

Ich finde dich in allen diesen Dingen,
denen ich gut und wie ein Bruder bin;
als Samen sonnst du dich in den geringen
und in den grossen gibst du gross dich hin.

Das ist das wundersame Spiel der Kräfte,
dass sie so dienend durch die Dinge gehn:
in Wurzeln wachsend, schwindend in die Schäfte
und in den Wipfeln wie ein Auferstehn.

Love is finding; and therefore the divine in things is a magnet to love. With this pantheistic doctrine of immanence Rilke blends a sublimated 'animism' or belief in the soul of things (*Ding-Seele*): every *thing* is animated by soul, which is God. But what is 'life' but 'things'? For Rilke God and life (rather than God and nature) are identical; for God is immanent in all the manifestations of life. His aim is, therefore, to attain a consciousness or a realization of God in life; and this means that life for him is an intense and unremitting quest, a desperate wrestling with all in life which may reveal God to him. This explains the intensity of his mystic poetry; and, since he is always finding God, its ecstasy. Life to Rilke is the marriage of the consciousness of things (=soul) with the God who is in these things; or, to put it differently, the consciousness of experience (=ecstasy) unites with the cause of experience (= God), in Spinoza's sense that God is the immanent cause of all things and therefore exists only in effects, that is things. For the interpretation of Rilke Kant's extension of the doctrine of immanence is needed too. To Kant immanent means 'remaining in experience' (*innerhalb der Erfahrung bleibend*); Rilke said (*Briefe an einen jungen Dichter*): '*Jedes Gedicht ist eine Erfahrung*'; if then God is immanent in every experience, and if every poem is an experience, then every poem is God; thus the criterion of a poem must be that it is *gottvoll*; and applied to Rilke's poems this means that (like all mysticism) they are ecstatic. There could be no clearer statement of the poet's religious conception than his own in a letter to Ellen Key: '*Das Ziel der ganzen menschlichen Entwicklung ist, Gott und die Erde in demselben Gedanken denken zu können. Die Liebe zum Leben und die Liebe zu Gott muss zusammenfallen, anstatt, wie jetzt, verschiedene Tempel auf verschiedenen Anhöhen zu haben; man kann Gott nur anbeten, indem man das Leben zur Vollkommenheit lebt. Ihm immer höhere Formen zu geben, einen immer reicheren Zusammenhang zwischen ihm und dem scheinbar Unbelebten herbeizuführen, das heisst Gott schaffen. Mit anderen Worten, Gott ins Leben hinabsenken oder das Leben zu Gott emporblühen zu lassen.*'

And since God is life Rilke gives Him all the manifold shapes of life. '*Du bist der Wald der Widersprüche*', he hails Him; since all is God, He must be all contraries. God is '*der uralte Turm*' round which the dove of yearning circles through the ages; He is the '*Rätselhafte, um den die Zeit im Zögern stand*'; He is '*das grosse Heimweh, das wir nicht bezwangen*'; he is part of the poet's loneliness ('*du *bist der Zweite meiner Einsamkeit'*); He is 'neighbour God', and there is only a narrow wall between them which the poet's cry may suddenly cast down. He is the cathedral we build atom by atom:

> *Wir bauen an dir mit zitternden Händen*
> *und wir türmen Atom auf Atom.*
> *Aber wer kann dich vollenden,*
> *du Dom?*

And this image is magnified in a gorgeous passage which may at the same time stand for a rushed, quivering statement of the process of all inspiration:

> *Werkleute sind wir: Knappen, Jünger, Meister,*
> *und bauen dich, du hohes Mittelschiff.*
> *Und manchmal kommt ein ernster Hergereister,*
> *geht wie ein Glanz durch unsre hundert Geister*
> *und zeigt uns zitternd einen neuen Griff.*
>
> *Wir steigen in die wiegenden Gerüste,*
> *in unsern Händen hängt der Hammer schwer,*
> *bis eine Stunde uns die Stirnen küsste,*
> *die strahlend und als ob sie alles wüsste*
> *von dir[1] kommt, wie der Wind vom Meer.*
>
> *Dann ist ein Hallen von dem vielen Hämmern*
> *und durch die Dinge geht es Stoss um Stoss.*
> *Erst wenn es dunkelt lassen wir dich los:*
> *Und deine kommenden Konturen dämmern.*
>
> *Gott, du bist gross.*

God is not defined by this swift succession of images of his multiformity (*Allgestalt*), for of course God is indefinable; all we can hope to feel is that they bring us close to the essence of God by bodying Him forth in familiar human terms. Lovely is this velvety perception of His omnipresence:

> *Du kommst und gehst. Die Türen fallen*
> *viel sanfter zu, fast ohne Wehn.*

---

[1] Note the metrical effect of the stress on this word, the thrilled tenderness of the level stress *dír kómmt*, and then the wind-like rush to the end of the line.

Du bist der Leiseste von allen,
die durch die leisen Häuser gehn.

Oft wenn ich dich in Sinnen sehe,
verteilt sich deine Allgestalt:
du gehst wie lauter lichte Rehe,
und ich bin dunkel und bin Wald.

'*Allgestalt*' implies great and small; and if God as Creator is magnified, as the Created One He is diminished:

Und du: du bist aus dem Nest gefallen,
bist ein junger Vogel mit gelben Krallen
und grossen Augen und tust mir leid.
(Meine Hand ist dir viel zu breit.)

The most devout Christian need not be pained at such relentless playing with every possible idea of God: since He takes all forms He fills us not only with worship of His magnificence but also with tenderness for what is helpless.

The influence of the Italian journey appears in a strange passage in which Christ and the Virgin as symbols in the paintings of the Renaissance are mystically interpreted. Typical of Rilke's *Wortkunst* is the new or double meaning to *heimgesucht* in this passage:

Da ward auch die zur Frucht Erweckte,
die schüchterne und schönerschreckte,
die heimgesuchte Magd geliebt.
Die Blühende, die Unentdeckte,
in der es hundert Wege gibt.

Renaissance religious painting was the 'Tree of God' whose branches in those days spread blossoming over Italy. Rilke comes nearest to the fourteenth-century mystics in his conception of God as the Tree of Life; but whereas the medieval mystics allegorized the Tree as rising from the roots of repentance, confession, and penance to the joys of Paradise, to Rilke Tree and God are one – '*ein Gewebe von hundert Wurzeln, welche schweigsam trinken*'; and the divine essence which permeates the world is the sap of the Tree. In this Renaissance passage the Virgin is figured as the Fruit of the Tree; but all the gorgeous Mariolatry of the great painters was vain; for She (the confusion of images is to be expected in poetic mysticism), alas! bare, not the Greatest One, 'but only the Spring of God, the Son, the Word'. And so God is still waiting for His tree to ripen, in a land where lonely men – men as lonely as the monk of the poem – listen; and they will all behold a different God, for God is like a wave that flows through beings. What is clear in these lines is Rilke's peculiar rejection of Christ, for which his mother is blamed: she made him, as a boy, kiss the marks of the nails in images of the Crucified Saviour. Very curious is the poet's description of God as his own son (just as Stefan George imaged himself as both father and son of Maximin). Rilke even figures God as his prodigal son, who left him to win a kingdom (the God I create, being an idea, wanders away from me and grows). A passage follows which seems hard on fathers, and may be coloured by the son-father conflict of the time:

> Liebt man denn einen Vater? Geht man nicht,
> wie du von mir gingst, Härte im Gesicht,
> von seinen hülflos leeren Händen fort? . . .
> Ist uns der Vater denn nicht das, was war;
> vergangne Jahre, welche fremd gedacht,
> veraltete Gebärde, tote Tracht,
> verblühte Hände und verblichnes Haar?

Then suddenly the image changes, and in a passage of feminine tenderness there is the old mystic conception of God as the soul's lover; and of the soul as Ruth amid the alien corn:

> Und meine Seele ist ein Weib vor dir.
> Und ist wie der Naëmi Schnur, wie Ruth.
> Sie geht bei Tag um deiner Garben Hauf
> wie eine Magd, die tiefe Dienste tut.
> Aber am Abend steigt sie in die Flut
> und badet sich und kleidet sich sehr gut
> und kommt zu dir, wenn alles um dich ruht,
> und kommt und deckt zu deinen Füssen auf.
> Und fragst du sie um Mitternacht, sie sagt
> mit tiefer Einfalt: Ich bin Ruth, die Magd.
> Spann deine Flügel über deine Magd . . .

In *The Book of Poverty and Death* the salient feature is that the great leprous city rises between Rilke and the God he seeks. Very little in *Grossstadtpoesie* transfigures drab reality as does the following passage:

> *Denn Herr, die grossen Städte sind*
> *Verlorene und Aufgelöste;*
> *wie Flucht vor Flammen ist die grösste, –*
> *und ist kein Trost, dass er sie tröste,*
> *und ihre kleine Zeit verrinnt.*
> *Da leben Menschen, leben schlecht und schwer,*
> *in tiefen Zimmern, bange von Gebärde,*
> *geängsteter denn eine Erstlingsherde;*
> *und draussen wacht und atmet Deine Erde,*
> *sie aber sind und wissen es nicht mehr.*
> *Da wachsen Kinder auf an Fensterstufen,*
> *die immer in demselben Schatten sind,*
> *und wissen nicht, dass draussen Blumen rufen*
> *zu einem Tag voll Weite, Glück und Wind, –*
> *und müssen Kind sein und sind traurig Kind.*
>
> *Da blühen Jungfraun auf zum Unbekannten*
> *und sehnen sich nach ihrer Kindheit Ruh;*
> *das aber ist nicht da, wofür sie brannten,*
> *und zitternd schliessen sie sich wieder zu.*
> *Und haben in verhüllten Hinterzimmern*
> *die Tage der enttäuschten Mutterschaft,*
> *der langen Nächte willenloses Wimmern*
> *und kalte Jahre ohne Kampf und Kraft.*
> *Und ganz im Dunkel stehn die Sterbebetten*
> *und langsam sehnen sie sich dazu hin;*
> *und sterben lange, sterben wie in Ketten*
> *und gehen aus wie eine Bettlerin.*

The problem for Rilke in this book is – since poverty is inevitable – to find the relation (*Bezug*,[1] in his own language) of poverty (particularly as he sees it in its worst form, in the teeming cities) to God; and this he does by showing that they whose life is all a preparation for the 'great death' are necessarily poor. With the rejection of the great city goes the acceptance of death as itself a form of life. In shaping his conception of death Rilke may have

---

[1] Rilke's own term for the equivalence of the interior life of the poet with the exterior phenomena of nature is '*die Welt der Bezüge*'. Cf. p. 466.

been influenced by the philosophy of Georg Simmel, whose friend and pupil he had been at Berlin, though on the other hand Simmel may have been influenced by Rilke. Simmel rejects the dualism of good and evil, life and death as too simple a procedure; he groups these apparent contraries at the centre of life in the absolute sense. In his book on *Rembrandt*[1] Simmel rejects the current conception of death as the sudden snapping of life – as the intrusion of the Parcae ('Comes the blind Fury with th' abhorrèd shears | And slits the thin-spun life'): Simmel argues rather that death is spun into the web of life; death, he says, is not some future problematic happening but *'eine innere Immer-Wirklichkeit jeder Gegenwart, ist Färbung und Formung des Lebens, ohne die das Leben, das wir haben, unausdenkbar verwandelt wäre. Der Tod ist eine Beschaffenheit des organischen Daseins, wie es eine von je mitgebrachte Beschaffenheit, eine Funktion des Samens ist, die wir so ausdrücken, dass er einst Frucht bringen wird.'* As a confirmation of his own views Simmel quotes Rilke's lines –

> *O Herr, gib jedem seinen eigenen Tod,*
> *das Sterben, das aus jenem Leben geht,*
> *darin er Liebe hatte, Sinn und Not.*
>
> *Denn wir sind nur die Schale und das Blatt.*
> *Der grosse Tod, den jeder in sich hat,*
> *das ist die Frucht, um die sich alles dreht.*

We bear this death within us, Rilke declares, as a germ from birth; in the great cities, in the shadow of hospitals as a green bitter fruit that will not ripen; or we are like women who, when their hour of deliverance comes, give birth to an abortion: *'und wenn das Kreissbett da ist, so gebären | wir unseres Todes tote Fehlgeburt'*. There are two kinds of death: *der kleine* or *der fremde* (=alien) *Tod* and *der grosse* or *eigne Tod*. The 'small death' is died by those who lie down and die like beasts; the great death by those who consciously ripen their life to this its fruit and culmination, the final unfolding of *'das Stück Ewigkeit in der Brust'*. But Rilke did not intend the consciousness of death to be depressing; on the contrary he says it is an intensification of life: *'das erste grosse Ergriffensein vom Bewusstsein des Todes, welches zugleich der erste Moment gesteigerten, allseitigen per-*

---

[1] *Rembrandt. Ein kunstphilosophischer Versuch*, 2nd ed., Leipzig, 1919. Simmel maintains that the conception of death he here interprets can be seen in Rembrandt's best portraits.

sönlichen Lebens ist'. Life has a purpose: death; and the ripening
unto death should be like the ripening of fruit, in sunshine and
sweetness: *'Wir stehn in deinem Garten Jahr für Jahr | und sind die
Bäume, süssen Tod zu tragen.'* Salvation from unnatural wilting to a
mean death in great cities can only come from a Saviour; *'der
Grösste'*, whom the Virgin did not bear; and in a terrific sexual
image the poet calls for the creation of this One who, figured as
female (*'bau seinem Leben einen schönen Schoss, | und seine Scham errichte
wie ein Tor[1] | in einem blonden Wald von jungen Haaren'*) because recep-
tive of a thousand germs, shall in a great night conceive the future
from the *membrum virile* of *der Unsagbare*. This Greatest One is the
Messiah come at last: not Christ, but the Progenitor of Death (*der
Tod-Gebärer*), the bringer to all of the great individual death, with,
in his wake, the white-mounted legions (of self-perfection). 'And
let me', the poet continues, 'be mouth of this new Messiad.' Here
of course we have something analogous to Stefan George's 'third
humanism', his poet's vision (in *Das neue Reich*) of the poet-creator
of the New Realm; where the two seers differ is in the value they
attach to life here below – George, with his call to vitalize the
present, stands for *Diesseitigkeit*, Rilke, with his old Catholic doctrine that life is noble only in so far as it prepares for a noble
death, stands for *Jenseitigkeit*; and thus in the two greatest of
modern poets we find the typically German accentuation of dualism. And yet there is *Weltfreude* in neither, and *Weltflucht* in both;
both are austere; and there is actually less austerity in the praiser
of death than in the praiser of life; where both agree is in their
rejection of common aims.

In his interpretation of 'rich and poor' Rilke calls to mind (like
George in *Die hängenden Gärten*) the glories of ancient culture – of
the rich who forced life to be infinitely wide and warm. But the
days of the rich (in this sense of the harmony of wealth and poetic
life) have passed away, and we will not pray to God for their
return – but we will pray that the poor shall again be poor. They
whom we call the poor are merely the not-rich, they who are
without will and world, marked with the stigmas of utter misery,
wilted and withered in the dust of cities. And yet all they need to
be a ring of roses on God's earth is to be permitted to be as poor
as they really are (*'so arm sein dürfen, wie sie wirklich sind'*); and Rilke
now gives his interpretation of poverty as a glory radiated from

---

[1] There is the same gross physical image in the poem *Verkündigung* (p. 189).

13

within ('*Denn Armut ist ein grosser Glanz von innen*'). God Himself
is the poor man, the leper cast forth and passing through the city
with his rattle:

> *Du bist so arm wie eines Keimes Kraft*
> *in einem Mädchen, das es gern verbürge*
> *und sich die Lenden presst, dass sie erwürge*
> *das erste Atmen ihrer Schwangerschaft.*
>
> *Und du bist arm: so wie der Frühlingsregen,*
> *der selig auf der Städte Dächer fällt,*
> *und wie ein Wunsch, wenn Sträflinge ihn hegen*
> *in einer Zelle, ewig ohne Welt.*

And – in his baroque cumulative manner, or as in the chained
incongruous images of the Litanies to the Virgin – Rilke hymns
the agonies of men, which are less than those of God, who is
poorer than all the poor. The poor are like things almost ('*fast
gleichen sie den Dingen*'); they are dark as an idle tool. They are
guardians of treasures they themselves see not. From the poor are
to be born the regenerating race who ripen for the great death;
and therefore the sexual image is repeated:

> *Und sieh: ihr Leib ist wie ein Bräutigam . . .*
> *In seiner Schlankheit sammelt sich das Schwache,*
> *das Bange, das aus vielen Frauen kam;*
> *doch sein Geschlecht ist stark und wie ein Drache*
> *und wartet schlafend in dem Tal der Scham.*

And where is he who grew strong even unto poverty, and on the
market-place put off his raiment and went forth naked before the
bishop in his robe? In the smile of whose countenance was childhood ripening as maidens do. And when he sang hearts cried in
the sisters whom he touched as a bridegroom. And then the pollen
of his song wafted dreaming from his red mouth unto the love-
laden and fell into open corollas . . . And the Unpolluted received
him in their body which was their soul, and their eyes closed like
roses, and full of love-lights was their hair . . . And when he died
he was already scattered abroad: his seed ran in brooks and sang
in trees and quietly watched from flowers. O whither is he faded
into melody? – the great evening star of poverty.

Thus ends the sheer inexhaustible poetry of *Das Stundenbuch*. To many it will be – like Blake for instance – a mass of crazy images; to others it will be a gospel, perhaps the old gospel interpreted anew, but certainly an inspired gospel.

For a full intelligence of Rilke's conception of death and of his attitude to the great cities study of *Die Aufzeichnungen des Malte Laurids Brigge* (1909) is essential. If it is a novel it is one with practically no story; one might group it with the waves-of-consciousness novels. It is the retrospect, in Paris, of a very nebulous youth, very poor and very ill, and very near to mental derangement. He is the last scion of an ancient Danish family – on his mother's side he is a Brahe; but the essential thing is that he is a *fin-de-siècle* poet in Paris differing only by greater morbidity and more poignant mental complications from the German artists in Paris of the earlier *Künstlernovelle* (the heroes of *Die gute Schule* and *Tino Moralt*). The city is shown as it reflects itself in his diseased imagination, a nightmare city, leprous and lecherous. He is isolated, brooding, baffled. He has the feeling that the electric trams crash through his attic and that motor cars run over him. Still more awful is the silence of the city. ('*Das sind die Geräusche. Aber es gibt hier etwas, was furchtbarer ist: die Stille.*') The city stinks; as all cities do in summer. He is hallucinated by the stains of a w.c. pipe where a house has been demolished. If he goes out what he sees is hospital after hospital. The Hôtel-Dieu looms over him. '*Dieses ausgezeichnete Hôtel ist sehr alt, schon zu König Chlodwigs Zeiten starb man darin in einigen Betten. Jetzt wird in 559 Betten gestorben. Natürlich fabrikmassig ... Man stirbt, wie es gerade kommt; man stirbt den Tod, der zu der Krankheit gehört, die man hat.*' In all these feverish divagations there is no pretence of cohesion: the dream-like procession of the years of childhood flit between the crass pictures of Paris streets and hospitals and the visions of old France. Malte is of course Rilke (though the poet denied it), Rilke calling back and idealizing his own childhood and years of growth. But the Danish fiction of the memories is well rendered, from the experience of the 1904 visit to Denmark and the moods and colouring of J. P. Jacobsen's tales. The lesson of Malte is that which Rilke learned for himself: that the artist must not escape from life into dream, but accept it integrally, with all its disease and putrition; accept even the great cities, for the great city is reality, which it is the poet's task to re-create in art, not because he loves the things that compose it but because – as Rilke learned from Van Gogh and Cézanne – his mission only begins when he has risen above the need of love. The book is simply Rilke in search of himself. But also in search of God. And the two quests are really the same, for Rilke's God is only his own perfected personality. This constitutes a sort of realism, in spite of all the nebulousness: the mysticism is realistic because it is the inner illumination of a 'thing', a pathetic human being. But this light that burns inwards burns outwards too: there is throughout the book an irradiation of five main themes – the great city, poverty, childhood, love, and death

Critically regarded, *Die Aufzeichnungen des Malte Laurids Brigge* is probably over-estimated in the present craze for Rilke: it is actually to be classified as yet another misbirth of that cult of disease which gave us Maeterlinck's *Serres Chaudes* and Verhaeren's trilogy of disease (from which *Les Villes tentaculaires* is an escape) *Les Soirs*, *Les Débâcles*, *Les Flambeaux noirs*. In this book Rilke is rather a decadent than an expressionist. What there is of expressionist doctrine lies in the slow building up of the theory that death is the consummation of life, not in the sense of dissolution, but of perfection. Life ripens (or should ripen) round the fruit which grows from the inborn germ of death. The doctrine is perhaps no more than a mystic deepening of the doctrine of perfecting in the *Bildungsroman*, quickened with something of a Christian leaven – life is a preparation for the beyond; the difference is that Rilke projects the vision of fitness for death, not life – the aim and desire of man should be to ripen, to be mellow, and then to fall, richly coloured and rounded, like the apple to the grass: here is at least sweetness before putrition.

Very subtle in this book is Rilke's handling of the theme of love. With the interpretation of Sappho as the great exemplar is interwoven an interpretation of Lesbian love as an interruption of the temporal purpose of sex by its eternal intention: that the lover borne to the couch by the weaker belovèd should be the inner glow of selfless love transformed from belovèd to lover. Some of Rilke's most penetrating interpretations are those of women who have loved deeply and in vain, the figures of the *Heroides*, and added to them his own particular discoveries – among them the Portuguese nun whose letters he was to translate (p. 205); women whose determined hearts were willing 'to fulfil love to the uttermost'. And the fruit of death as the perfection of life is attained by

complete self-surrender in love; for which reason (a very mystical
and favourite idea of Rilke's) while to be loved is merely to be
consumed – in other words a neutral process, feeding merely selfishness and stunting the soul – to love for love's sake is illumination. Think of the troubadours who feared nothing so much as
to be granted their desire! This apparent excess of love and self-
surrender is, in Rilke's doctrine, the new measure of love and
sorrow: sorrow must fade into love and be one with it. Rilke
gives, as one of his quaint marginal glosses to what is assumed to
be an unshaped autobiographical fragment, his famous definition
of love: – To be loved is to be consumed. To love is to shine with
oil that cannot be exhausted. To be loved is to perish, to love is
to endure. Only by the power of this enduring love can the heart
attain direct contact with God. The story of the Prodigal Son is
the legend of one who fled from being loved; and in this interpretation of the Bible story no doubt we have again an explanation
of Rilke's separation from his wife and his eternal homelessness:
he would be alone and love, even the filth of life; but he would
not have the richness of his loneliness diminished by even the love
of a dog. Slowly he learns to illumine what he loves with the rays
of his feeling so that it be not consumed with it, until through the
ever more transparent shape of what is loved the vast Beyond
opens out in the rapture of possession. To be alone is to be a
buccaneer or a condottiere or Saint George slaying the dragon.
And this is the consecration of what to the outside view was
Rilke's life of utter poverty and misery: he chose to be a prodigal
son that he might live the heroic life. But the new meaning he
gives to the parable of the prodigal son is more than personal.
Applied to the divine, the doctrine that to love is all and that
there is no enhancement in being loved results in Rilke's famous
definition: 'God is a direction given to love, not its object'; that
God will return this love is not to be feared, and God denies us
His love in order that our heart may fulfil itself to the last limit.

There is nothing mystical in the love experience of *Die Weise
von Liebe und Tod des Cornets Christoph Rilke*; but, though it was not
published till 1906, it was written in 1899, in Rilke's period of full
mysticism. The ultimate theme might be briefly defined in film
language as 'one night of love'. But no one who has read the poem
– an expanded and lyricized ballad – will wonder that young officers had it with them to read in the trenches. The source is an old

chronicle which relates that Christoph von Rilke fell fighting the
Turks in Hungary in 1663. The poet, dreaming his yearning youth
into an imaginary and heroic relative in the days of old, gives us
his rapid sketch in a series of vivid snapshots. Noble boys riding
together, with dust on their fine clothes, dreaming of home and
beauty, tell of their mothers. Christoph, eighteen years old, brings
a message to a general, who appoints him cornet. He writes to his
mother: – a slow letter in great erect characters: *'Meine gute Mutter,
seid stolz: ich trage die Fahne.'* The regiment comes to a castle; comfort again . . . *'in seidenen Sesseln sitzen und bis in die Fingerspitzen so:
nach dem Bad sein. Und wieder erst lernen, was Frauen sind'.* The short
sentences of the picturing prose burst into lovely verse with
strangely scattered rhymes when the cornet comes to his love
story. *'Die Gräfin lächelt.'* He is her page . . . Childhood, that dark,
soft robe, falls from his shoulders. *'Die Turmstube ist dunkel. Aber
sie leuchten sich ins Gesicht mit ihrem Lächeln. Sie tasten vor sich her wie
Blinde und finden den andern wie eine Tür. Fast wie Kinder, die sich vor der
Nacht ängstigen, drängen sie sich ineinander ein. Und doch fürchten sie sich
nicht. Da ist nichts, was gegen sie wäre: kein Gestern, kein Morgen; denn
die Zeit ist eingestürzt. Und sie blühen aus ihren Trümmern.'* The Turks
arrive – drums beat – clarions call – but the banner is not there.
The Turks set fire to the castle. Cornet Rilke rushes out. *'Auf
seinen Armen trägt er die Fahne wie eine weisse, bewusstlose Frau. Und er
findet ein Pferd, und es ist wie ein Schrei . . . Und da kommt auch die
Fahne wieder zu sich, und niemals war sie so königlich; und jetzt sehn sie
sie alle, fern voran, und erkennen den hellen, helmlosen Mann und erkennen
die Fahne.'* And sixteen scimitars swirling round the cornet's head
end his saga. *'Der Waffenrock ist im Schlosse verbrannt.'* The fascination of the story is heightened by its very lack of description:
details are thrown out which must be pieced together; as for
instance the last sentence, which reveals that the boy had rushed
out from the alcove without his *Waffenrock*.

Das Buch der Bilder (1902) marks a transition from the mysticism
of *Das Stundenbuch* to *Neue Gedichte*, in which picture and mysticism
blend. The title and the poems of *Das Buch der Bilder* show the
influence of Rilke's residence among the painters of Worpswede,
where the business of the day was the making of pictures – and
pictures of a real world. The volume is made up of a series of
impressions and sensations (*'Erlebnisse'*), each of which is shaped
to a picture. Notable is the metrical skill with which the intensi-

fication or appeasement of the sensation is conveyed by changes
of rhythm (*Taktwechsel*) or variation of line length. Of the themes
handled death is the most insistent. In *Ritter* death is a prisoner
in the knight's body, waiting for the inevitable sword-thrust to
release him:

> *Reitet der Ritter in schwarzem Stahl*
> *hinaus in die rauschende Welt.*
> *Und draussen ist alles: der Tag und das Tal*
> *und der Freund und der Feind und das Mahl im Saal*
> *und der Mai und die Maid und der Wald und der Gral,*
> *und Gott ist selber vieltausendmal*
> *an alle Strassen gestellt.*
>
> *Doch in dem Panzer des Ritters drinnen,*
> *hinter den finstersten Ringen,*
> *hockt der Tod und muss sinnen und sinnen:*
> *Wann wird die Klinge springen*
> *über die Eisenhecke,*
> *die fremde befreiende Klinge,*
> *die mich aus meinem Verstecke*
> *holt, drin ich so viele*
> *gebückte Tage verbringe, –*
> *dass ich mich endlich strecke*
> *und spiele*
> *und singe.*

Rilke's psychological (and therefore unromantic) note comes out
clearly in this poem, in which we have romantic paraphernalia
enumerated to evoke a medieval atmosphere, but only because
the idea of death encased in chain-mail enhances the doctrine of
man's body as death's prison-house. There is the same medieval
note in *Strophen*, where death is an artificer of cathedral beauty:

> *Ist einer, der nimmt alle in die Hand,*
> *dass sie wie Sand durch seine Finger rinnen.*
> *Er wählt die schönsten aus den Königinnen*
> *und lässt sie sich in weissen Marmor hauen,*
> *still liegend in des Mantels Melodie;*
> *und legt die Könige zu ihren Frauen,*
> *gebildet aus demselben Stein wie sie.*

Ist einer, der nimmt alle in die Hand,
dass sie wie schlechte Klingen sind und brechen.

The poem at once recalls the medieval folksong '*Es ist ein Schnitter heisst der Tod*', of which perhaps the opening inversion is a reminiscence; and in both poems it is the *picture* which brings the message home: there the skeleton reaper mowing all the familiar flowers of the field, here the refulgence of the marble in the dim cathedral aisles. How effective is the synaesthesia of *des Mantels Melodie*: we pass by the sarcophagi of lovely queens and mighty kings and the association of picture and idea is a faint music in our minds. Other lyrics deal with childhood (*Kindheit, Aus einer Kindheit*). The sexual expectancy of boys and maidens occurs again; in *Die Heilige* the theme shapes itself definitely to *Pubertätspoesie*, while in *Von den Mädchen* there is the mystical presentation of the soul of 'dark poets' as inviolably virgin: '*Keine darf sich je dem Dichter schenken, | wenn sein Auge auch um Frauen bat; | denn er kann euch nur als Mädchen denken ...* ' The nature and functions of angels inspire another group of poems. *Der Engel* daringly begins: '*Sie haben alle müde Münde | und helle Seelen ohne Saum. | Und eine Sehnsucht (wie nach Sünde) | geht ihnen manchmal durch den Traum ...* ' Angels are the divine essence sent by God to shape the chaos of what is still a beginning:

> *Nur wenn sie ihre Flügel breiten,*
> *sind sie die Wecker eines Winds:*
> *als ginge Gott mit seinen weiten*
> *Bildhauerhänden durch die Seiten*
> *im dunklen Buch des Anbeginns.*

In *Der Schutzengel* the guardian angel is the bird that comes to the poet when he awakens in the night and calls – with arms, not with a name, for that is an abyss a thousand nights deep; and thus the angel is the shadow in whom he went to sleep, the picture of which he is the frame; he hails the angel:

> *Du hast mich oft aus dunklem Ruhn gerissen,*
> *wenn mir das Schlafen wie ein Grab erschien*
> *und wie Verlorengehen und Entfliehn, –*
> *da hobst du mich aus Herzensfinsternissen*
> *und wolltest mich auf allen Türmen hissen*
> *wie Scharlachfahnen und wie Draperien.*

The angel is the revelation of the unspeakable God: and may the
poet question the angel concerning God? –

> *Du Seliger, wann nennst du einmal Ihn,*
> *aus dessen siebentem und letztem Tage*
> *noch immer Glanz auf deinem Flügelschlage*
> *verloren liegt.*
> *Befiehlst du, dass ich frage?*

In these varying pictures of the angel the base is of course the
imagery of the Christian church; but how vivid – and childlike! –
is the idea of the enamel on the angel's wings, *forgotten* but still as
bright as it was on the seventh day of Creation. The most mysterious of the angel poems is *Verkündigung*. The angel, coming
with his Annunciation to Mary, says:

> *Du bist nicht näher an Gott als wir;*
> *wir sind ihm alle weit.*
> *Aber wunderbar sind dir*
> *die Hände benedeit.*
> *So reifen sie bei keiner Frau,*
> *so schimmernd aus dem Saum:*
> *Ich bin der Tag, ich bin der Tau,*
> *du aber bist der Baum.*
>
> *Ich bin jetzt matt, mein Weg war weit,*
> *vergib mir, ich vergass,*
> *was Er, der gross in Goldgeschmeid*
> *wie in der Sonne sass,*
> *dir künden liess, du Sinnende,*
> *(verwirrt hat mich der Raum).*
> *Sieh: ich bin das Beginnende,*
> *du aber bist der Baum.*
>
> *Ich spannte meine Schwingen aus*
> *und wurde seltsam weit;*
> *jetzt überfliesst dein kleines Haus*
> *von meinem grossen Kleid.*
> *Und dennoch bist du so allein*
> *wie nie und schaust mich kaum;*
> *das macht: ich bin ein Hauch im Hain,*
> *du aber bist der Baum.*

Die Engel alle bangen so,
lassen einander los:
noch nie war das Verlangen so,
so ungewiss und gross.
Vielleicht, dass Etwas bald geschieht,
das du im Traum begreifst.
Gegrüsst sei, meine Seele sieht:
du bist bereit und reifst.
Du bist ein grosses, hohes Tor,
und aufgehn wirst du bald.
Du, meines Liedes liebstes Ohr,
jetzt fühle ich: Mein Wort verlor
sich in dir wie im Wald.

So kam ich und vollendete
dir tausendeinen Traum.
Gott sah mich an; er blendete . . .
Du aber bist der Baum.

The key to the meaning – it does not leap to the eyes – is Rilke's doctrine of the patient maturing of personality. '*Du bist bereit und reifst*' may be said to any human being in the growing stage, and any virgin is the most fit symbol for what may pass into the great gate of growth (the sexual image should not be taken as offensive). The striking thing is the bold contrast between angel and Virgin. The angel, too, is a beginning[1] – of the new conception of the nature of angels, but in that sense his growth is not within himself but in the shaping mind of contemplative man, whereas the Virgin is in herself organic growth. And she may bear the Messiah announced in *Das Stundenbuch*; she is the Tree of fruit to be. Rilke is very fond of 'tree' as an image for organic life springing from roots deep in the soil into the kiss of air and wind and spreading a majestic crown of leaves. And for Rilke '*Bereitschaft*' is synonymous with '*Empfängnis*'. The Virgin then (any virgin) is the symbol of maturity to bear, of fertility, while the angel is only the beginning of the radiance which in the fullness of days will flow between the teeming dark deeps of earth which feed existence and the dazzling golden glitter of Heaven.

Rilke's own full maturity is in the two volumes of *Neue Gedichte*

[1] Cf. *Der Engel* in *Neue Gedichte*.

(1907, 1908). The interest of the poems here gathered in is so ramified that in the scope of such an essay as this only a hint of their significance can be given. They have, as is the case with Hebbel's plays, threefold sense: that of object, type, and symbol. Rilke also aimed at achieving congruence of object, rhythm, and atmosphere. The *New Poems* are yet another attempt at a *Légende des siècles*, for they give a picture of all the phases of culture – Biblical, Greek, Roman, medieval, Baroque, Oriental, modern. A chronological division is, however, quite illusory; for all these periods merely serve to provide subjects which illuminate present-day states of mind. The terrible despair of Christ in *Der Ölbaumgarten*, for instance, is worlds removed from the spirit of the New Testament: Christ in His agony (the agony of any man whose ideals crumble into dust) denies God and all divinity.

The predominating influence is that of Rodin. Rilke himself stated what Rodin had taught him: to labour patiently. *'Travailler toujours!'* was Rodin's advice. Hitherto Rilke had thought that inspiration was sufficient; from Rodin's example he learned that inspiration must be laboured into the flawless work of art. Now the poet's aim is to create *'Kunstdinge'*, which, he says in a letter to Lou Andreas-Salomé, have the need of existence of the created thing they represent. The aesthetic doctrine of 'things' which Rilke applied in *New Poems* he interpreted in the second part of his lecture *Auguste Rodin* (1907). 'Thing', he says, implies fixed contours in space; a shape in which all movement has ceased and which is something permanent in the shape in which it is seen. A thing endures, a human being does not endure. If the beauty we see anywhere is by imitation transferred to a thing, then this thing lasts longer than that from which it was imitated. Not only does it last, it *lives* – as eternal beauty; it lives, because it stirs emotion. Rilke thereupon shows that Rodin by the distribution of light on his surfaces accomplishes the miracle of expressing movement and of expressing by this suggestion of movement what is going on *within* the object imitated; that is, he gets soul as well as body into his sculpture. And this is what Rilke attempts in his *New Poems*. Movement of course must be progressive; and progressive movement (*fortschreitende Handlung*) is according to Lessing (the great authority on the relations to each other of the arts) the very essence of poetry: while poetry reproduces action consecutive in *time*, plastic art can only fix in space an action taken at its 'most pregnant moment', that is, at the moment when all the meaning of the action has most significance for the purpose of art. If, therefore, Rilke was right in thinking that Rodin manages to suggest progression in his fixed pregnant moment, then Rodin's sculpture gives the lie to Lessing's sharp division between plastic art and poetry, and Rilke continued the disproval by looking at the object of his poem with a sculptor's eye and suggesting progression to and from the pregnant moment or crisis, or fixed object in space into which he reads the stirrings of a soul, by projecting such a moment into a magic light. But he does more than that: to the magic light in which he bathes the picture he adds the suggestiveness of his subtle music. Theoretically then – and Rilke was no doubt aware of the possibilities of his *mélange des genres* – the poems he aims at creating are, literally, a synthesis of philosophy, plastic art, music, and poetry. Whether the intention is or is not realized is another matter – if not, then Lessing's relentless mathematical reasoning still holds; but certainly the fascination of Rilke in his maturity does lie in a glimpsing, however baffling, of manifold meaning.

These poems of Rilke in which he applies his new aesthetics are today classed as '*Dinggedichte*'. The term was coined by Hermann Pongs in *Euphorion*, Vol. 32, 1931; he says: '*Sein eigentümliches, plastisches Formideal drängt dahin, "Dinge zu machen", "Wirklichkeiten, die aus dem Handwerk hervorgehen" (Briefe III, 119) ... Kein Sichwerfen in die Ichgefühle mehr wie in der Frühlyrik, vielmehr ein Absehen vom Ich, das sich steigert bis zum Absehen vom Menschlichen überhaupt, um die Atmosphäre der Dinge ganz echt zu geben, "Dinggedichte" sozusagen. Nicht am wechselnden Eindruck haftet er wie der Impressionist, er sucht das Wesen mit allen Seinsbezügen, die jedes Ding erst zum Phänomen erheben.*'

Pongs with his '*Absehen vom Ich*' refers to another salient feature of *New Poems*. Rilke has here completed his progression from personal lyricism to the depersonalized realization of things. (Oskar Walzel[1] sees in what he calls '*Entichung der Lyrik*' a characteristic of recent lyric verse, e.g. in that of Däubler, Werfel, and Trakl.) The elimination of personal feeling had of course been one of the imperative demands of the French Parnassians; but one has only to compare *Neue Gedichte* with Richard von Schaukal's more or less Parnassian poems to realize that Rilke's depersonalized reality

[1] *Deutsche Literatur seit Goethes Tode.*

is vitalized by personality. If, for instance, in Rilke's *Panther* there is Rilke himself, then the poem is intensely personal; that is, it is a true lyric, and not a careful Parnassian elaboration; what matters is the feeling, not the picture or the cosmic sense of the picture. It is true that though the symbolism is highly personal the person of the poet symbolizes the higher intelligence of man; and thus we get what we might call an intellectualized cosmic symbolism. Rilke projects himself, if only as depersonalized intelligence, into his object; and it may be wrong to say that in *Der Panther* – which may serve as a type – he reflects the inner nature of his object. He is perhaps only impersonal in so far as he says 'panther' instead of 'I'. We know how this particular poem came into being. Rodin in his bluff way had said to the poet: 'You can't see, go to the Jardin des Plantes'; and Rilke had obeyed, had watched, and tried to pierce into the inner life of the animals behind the bars. The result was a poem as poignant, from the animal point of view, as Ralph Hodgson's famous poem; but cruelty to animals is not Rilke's subject. The picture of the caged animal is the object of the poem, the panther is the type, and the symbol is man cribbed, cabined, and confined in the torment of irrealizable creative desire:

> *Sein Blick ist vom Vorübergehn der Stäbe*
> *so müd geworden, dass er nichts mehr hält.*
> *Ihm ist, als ob es tausend Stäbe gäbe*
> *und hinter tausend Stäben keine Welt.*
>
> *Der weiche Gang geschmeidig starker Schritte,*
> *der sich im allerkleinsten Kreise dreht,*
> *ist wie ein Tanz von Kraft um eine Mitte,*
> *in der betäubt ein grosser Wille steht.*
>
> *Nur einmal schiebt der Vorhang der Pupille*
> *sich lautlos auf – . Dann geht ein Bild hinein,*
> *geht durch der Glieder angespannte Stille –*
> *und hört im Herzen auf zu sein.*

The '*Kongruenz von Objekt, Rhythmus und Atmosphäre*' is obtained by the regularity of the rhythm, as regular as the pacing of the animal in his confined space; and the fatigue and despair is indicated by the slow monosyllables and the truncation of the last line, while the passing of bar by bar before the panther's eyes is suggested by

Stäbe gäbe. The tonal qualities of *Der weiche Gang geschmeidig starker Schritte* (velvety softness wedded to striding strength) will be missed by no one.

What new meaning Rilke can get into a *Dinggedicht* may be seen by comparing Conrad Ferdinand Meyer's *Der römische Brunnen* with *Römische Fontäne*: the Swiss poet's poem is just a fine picture of a *chose vue*, while in Rilke's poem, though all seems to be just a picture, he himself is the tiered fountain gathering impressions and calming them to the perfection of dream. The isolation of majesty (probably in Stefan George's sense) is conveyed by *Die Treppe der Orangerie: Versailles*:

> *Wie Könige die schliesslich nur noch schreiten*
> *fast ohne Ziel, nur um von Zeit zu Zeit*
> *sich den Verneigenden auf beiden Seiten*
> *zu zeigen in des Mantels Einsamkeit – :*
>
> *so steigt, allein zwischen den Balustraden,*
> *die sich verneigen schon seit Anbeginn,*
> *die Treppe: langsam und von Gottes Gnaden*
> *und auf den Himmel zu und nirgends hin;*
>
> *als ob sie allen Folgenden befahl*
> *zurückzubleiben, – so dass sie nicht wagen*
> *von ferne nachzugehen; nicht einmal*
> *die schwere Schleppe durfte einer tragen.*

Here the central object is the staircase – marble is not mentioned, but marble is what we see – filling the picture, but in a fantastic light, magnified by the symbol of lonely kings (and by the swift association of ideas of all those who are isolated from their fellows by the grace of God) trailing all their magnificence, even their heavy train.

In the *New Poems* Rilke often paints by adding detail to detail, but with the inner sense in equal progression, so that revelation of the total idea synchronizes with the finishing of the picture. This process is quite wonderful in *Corrida*, in which we see first the black bull and his bull's feelings for the picador, then the picador in gold and pink silk, and at the end heaped adjectives picturing the masterly and nonchalant death-thrust. Very striking in *Jugend-Bildnis meines Vaters* are the closing lines which give meaning to this splendidly touched up family portrait (the poet's father in the officer's uniform he wore in his pre-railway days): *Du schnell vergehendes Daguerrotyp | in meinen langsamer vergehenden Händen*: faded old portrait from the days when photography began, in my hands that fade too, though less quickly (but this, the *Kunstding* I have made of it – if it is such – will not fade). *Geburt der Venus* would be no picture at all if Lessing's dictum were true that description *seriatim* is futile because we see only one detail at a time. Rilke paints a picture of Venus from top to toe, with shifting light and shade. The poem thrills, however, not by the elaboration of a picture but by the consistent visualization of the process of birth (Venus does not rise from the sea, but is literally born from the broad vulva of waves rimmed with pubic hair of foam) and the surprises of the imagery which fondle the divine limbs, not, however, as in certain full-length erotic portraits,[1] merely as a prurient pretext to throw the sexual parts into relief, but with a cool detachment which fastens on the symbolic newness of the suggestions:

> *Und in dem Kelch des Beckens lag der Leib*
> *wie eine junge Frucht in eines Kindes Hand.*
> *In seines Nabels engem Becher war*
> *das ganze Dunkel dieses hellen Lebens.*
> *Darunter hob sich licht die kleine Welle*
> *und floss beständig über nach den Lenden,*
> *wo dann und wann ein stilles Rieseln war.*
> *Durchschienen aber und noch ohne Schatten,*
> *wie ein Bestand von Birken im April,*
> *warm, leer und unverborgen, lag die Scham.*

The wind freshens and fills the new breasts so that like sails full of distance they float the diaphanous maiden to the shore. And at noon, in the heaviest hour, the sea once more rises and casts a dolphin on to the self-same stretch of sand – '*Tot, rot und offen*'. Life is born of death . . .

The full sense of some of the poems can only be gathered from knowledge of Rilke's previous books or of his correspondence; thus *Der Auszug des verlorenen Sohnes* is clarified by the light of the passage in *Malte*: '*Man wird mich schwer davon überzeugen, dass die*

[1] Shakespeare's *Venus and Adonis*, J. C. Günther's *Bridal Night* poem.

Geschichte des verlorenen Sohnes nicht die Legende dessen ist, der nicht geliebt werden wollte.' This, as we have shown, is literally true of Rilke's own life; and he handles his determined homelessness in other poems (*Der Dichter, Der Fremde*). Sex problems form the theme of many of the *New Poems*, and all phases of sex life are touched, from the rejection of the male to sexual exhaustion; the latter theme is in *Abisag* linked to a picture of maiden pre-puberty. Woman in all her phases, from the pre-puberty of Abishag to the gorgeous cruelty of *Die Kurtisane*, in whose hair is the gold of her native Venice (and thus the picture is a Titian), whose eyebrows are like the bridges leading over the canals to the throb and peril of the sea:

> . . . *Wer*
> *mich einmal sah, beneidet meinen Hund,*
> *weil sich auf ihm oft in zerstreuter Pause*
> *die Hand, die nie an keiner Glut verkohlt,*
>
> *die unverwundbare, geschmückt, erholt –.*
> *Und Knaben, Hoffnungen aus altem Hause,*
> *gehn wie an Gift an meinem Mund zugrund.*

Very penetrating are the poems which illuminate the state of mind of prophets, medieval saints, béguines. In these religion is psychologically interpreted; *Vor-Ostern: Neapel* forms a gross contrast to these, and will by most be read as an obscene mockery of the Catholic religion. *Dinggedichte* in the most literal sense are poems which show the inner life of dead matter: poems on churches, *Die Laute, Die Sonnenuhr*. Those poems which come under the heading of flower-symbolism and animal-symbolism sometimes play with recondite but luring significance (*Das Roseninnere, Blaue Hortensie*). The transpositions of pictures may betray the influence of Cézanne and Van Gogh, as for instance *Auswanderer-Schiff: Neapel*. In this picture of an emigrant ship in the Bay of Naples taking in oranges, fish, and bread no colour is mentioned except '*das grosse graue Schiff*'; nevertheless one sees over the deep blue of the sea the terraced shore and, in splashes, the yellow of the oranges, the warm brown of the bread, the silver scales of the fishes, and, in grim contrast (life and death) the womb of the ship gaping open to take coal in. A painting might have created the same impression, but more dubiously, for the poem is staged skilfully to the grotesque of the ending words '*offen wie der Tod*'. The transpositions of statues (*Früher Apollo, Archäischer Torso Apollos, Kretische Artemis*) provide perhaps the best object-lessons for testing Rilke's sculptural theories. The conception of permanence in a *Kunstding* is brought out in *Tanagra*. The very soul of dancing flashes and flames in *Spanische Tänzerin*. *Die Insel: Nordsee* is one of the comparatively rare poems with German themes: the taciturn character of Holstein men is interpreted by that turning inwards of the spirit which means so much to Rilke; we get it even in *Morgue*, attributed to corpses washed out of the Seine – '*Die Augen haben hinter ihren Lidern | sich umgewandt und schauen jetzt hinein*'. *Morgue* is not intended to be grotesque; the grotesque poems proper are *Legende von den drei Lebendigen und den drei Toten, Der König von Münster, Totentanz, Das jüngste Gericht, Die Versuchung, Papageienpark. Kreuzigung* (and this will shock many) is also in the nature of a grotesque. For humour veiling pathos *Der König* should be read – and compared (as a portrait of a Spanish prince) with Stefan George's *Der Infant*.

On May 19th, 1922, Rilke wrote from his tower at Muzot to a lady[1] that zest in creation had returned to him: '*Die mir über alles lieben (1912 in grossartiger Einsamkeit begonnenen und seit 1914 fast ganz unterbrochenen) Arbeiten konnten wieder aufgenommen –, konnten unter unendlicher Fähigkeit, zu Ende gebracht werden. – Daneben ging eine kleine Arbeit her, fast ungewollt, ein Nebenstrom, über 50 Sonette, die Sonette an Orpheus genannt, und geschrieben als ein Grabmal für ein jungverstorbenes Mädchen.*' He is referring to the *Duineser Elegien* (1923). The first of them had been written in 1912 at Duino (p. 163); hence their title. Rilke not only loved the *Duineser Elegien* 'more than all else', but he actually rated them as his best work; and this is one reason why critics and academic teachers burrow into them to earn the *cachet* of superior intelligence. The form alone should make one sceptical. Rilke called these poems 'elegies' because they are approximately in elegiac metre. Technically this implies distiches of rising hexameter and falling pentameter to give the sob and sigh of plaintive feeling, but the *Duineser Elegien* are far from conforming to this traditional type – the lines are merely hexameter-like, but not so like as those at which Tennyson turned up his classic nose – 'barbarous experiment, barbarous hexameters'. It is of course quite consistent with Rilke's general system of effect

[1] *Briefe an eine junge Frau* (1930).

14

by irregularity that he should vary this pattern of six-foot lines by shortening to five: '*Wer, wenn ich schriee, hörte mich denn aus der Engel | Ordnungen?*' The rhythm is rarely fluent; and it is hard to escape the conviction – confirmed by Rilke's letters from the period of composition (the passage quoted hints at impotence which cannot all have been due to the nightmare of the War) – that they are the product of an exhausted mind. If the verse flows like a clogged river, the sense too has to be recovered by diving beneath the surface. It is only by battling hard with the *Duino Elegies* and their 'tributary stream', the *Sonnets to Orpheus*, that we realize where the irresistible magic of the *New Poems* lies – in the sheer music of the verse. On the other hand it must be admitted that there is a vital ripening of the poet's nursed ideas; and it may be true that rhythm and language are with desperate ingenuity devised to fit the other-worldliness of the themes – for the spirit message a new spirit language and melody.

In the 1st and the 2nd Elegies man and angel are contrasted. If an angel took the poet to his heart the poet would perish. For the beautiful is the beginning of the terrible, and every angel is terrible. Where are the days of Tobias when an angel stood at a simple threshold (*Zur Reise ein wenig verkleidet und schon nicht mehr furchtbar*)? The angels feel beauty and do not perish; we mortals are consumed by beauty; it slackens us fire by fire. And they who are beautiful perish: the divine flashes in their face and fades. If we attain ourselves (that which in us is divine) it passes like the morning dew on grass. We perfect ourselves, and die into matter; but matter retains nothing of the perfume of our perfection. May it be that this perfection we have striven for passes into the angels? If that were so, what we achieve of beauty is immortal (it exists in the *idea*). Rilke's worship of angels is a reaction from his contempt of the human body. Really it all comes to saying that the human body is a horrible hindrance. But Rilke was a very sick man when he wrote the *Elegies* – diseased physically, and obviously (with his *Angstneurose*) at the limits of sanity. His fear of pain deprived him of a normal man's attitude to his body. To him the body was the wretched mid-way thing in which world and soul fought their pitiless battle – 'a magic circle', he says, 'which shuts me in as in an Inferno by Breughel'. The body is Hell because, being possessed by the world (which to Rilke at this stage meant physical suffering and the fear of it), it is beyond the reach of angels. But by the law of contraries – and by his very nature Rilke has the pictorial logic of the old mystics – if the body is the devil then there must be, however far remote, that divine something which the devil's very close presence proves; and Rilke chooses to call this divine and luminous something, this contrary of the body fixed helplessly in disease and darkness, 'angel'. The terrible thing is that man, for all his yearning to transform what within him is earthly to the divine – by that eternal transformation which is the will of the universe – cannot project himself into the angels as (by the law of heredity) he can project himself into his descendants: there are mechanical Darwinian laws for the brute body but not for the soul.

The 1st Elegy, then, is negative. But Rilke in a letter written a year before his death interprets the general sense of the Elegies as affirmative of life: '*In den Elegien wird . . . das Leben wieder möglich, ja es erfährt hier diejenige endgültige Bejahung, zu der es der junge Malte . . noch nicht führen konnte. Lebens- und Todesbejahung erweist sich als Eines in den Elegien. Das eine zuzugeben ohne das andere, sei, so wird hier erfahren und gefeiert, eine schliesslich alles Unendliche ausschliessende Einschränkung. Der Tod ist die uns abgekehrte, von uns unbeschienene Seite des Lebens: wir müssen versuchen, das grösseste Bewusstsein unseres Daseins zu leisten, das in beiden unabgegrenzen Bereichen zu Hause ist, aus beiden unerschöpflich genährt. . . . Die wahre Lebensgestalt reicht durch beide Gebiete, das Blut des grössesten Kreislaufs treibt durch beide: es gibt weder ein Diesseits noch Jenseits, sondern die grosse Einheit.*'

The 1st and 2nd Elegies continue the interpretation of love and lovers which in *Malte* is so subtle; here again the love of man is depicted as a biological impulse, while that of women such as Gaspara Stampa and Maria Alcoforado (see p. 205) is pure and essential because it is not merely in the blood. This 'hidden and guilty river-god of the blood' is in the 3rd Elegy used to shadow forth Rilke's gospel of sex, which is anything but romantic. After the War Rilke's religion had developed into a species of worship of sexuality: this was heightened by his acquaintance with Freud, and was expressed in two letters published in 1933 under the title of *Über Gott*. There had been idealization of sex too in the Rodin lecture: '*Hier hungert die Menschheit über sich hinaus. Hier strecken sich Hände aus nach der Ewigkeit. Hier öffnen sich Augen, schauen den Tod und fürchten ihn nicht . . .* ' What in the 3rd Elegy is dimly celebrated is the cosmic force which impels man and maid to their embraces, which for purpose have not the unborn child but the fathers lying like crumbled hills in our deeps and the dry river-bed of mothers to be . . . Man's love does not pulse at the call of mother or gentle maiden, but is the heart-beat of countless generations.

In *The Book of Poverty and Death* and in *Malte* Rilke had shown death to be an integral part of life. In the Elegies death is a means of transcending life, a transformation such as that of the child from womb to world.

In the 1st Elegy Rilke deals with an apparent difficulty: if what we mature by a rich life passes over into death, then those who die young take over an unripened fruit, and to them death is strange. But since life and death form a unity then the living can help these unripened dead until they grow conscious of eternity. The 4th Elegy – which is in decasyllabic iambic blank verse – deals with the drama of life which is played in the consciousness of death's presence, mourns the disharmony in the adult of mask and being, and points back to the undisturbed unity of childhood in which, since there is no consciousness, there is no mask. The implication is that if man could strip off appearance and attain the reality of his inner being he would lose all consciousness of seeming and act, as puppets do in a play, without seeking something by the acting. In the 5th Elegy – one of the most difficult – acrobats are celebrated as being more fugacious than other men '(*Wer aber sind sie, sag mir, die Fahrenden, diese ein wenig | Flüchtigern noch als wir selbst?*'). The idea – conveyed by a series of shifting associations which pass and fade as in a half-remembered dream – is that acrobats are a model for us, because they act to the will of the spectators – that is, as puppets; as we might act – instruments responding to a divine touch – to the will of the angel, if our actions were controlled by what the devising force above us desires. This image of acrobats, possibly suggested by Picasso's picture *Les Saltimbanques*,[1] is a link in Rilke's final argument that suffering is a necessary part of our functions under divine guidance. The 6th Elegy, the shortest, unfolds from contemplation of a fig-tree which fruits without blossoming the conception of the

---

[1] But see *The Fifth Duino Elegy* (in *The Welsh Review*, Vol. III, No. 2, June 1944) by B. J. Morse, who quotes a letter describing a performance by a troupe of acrobats in Paris in 1906; the persons mentioned correspond closely to those of the Elegy.

hero who, in his fullness of being and deed, does not stay to ripen
his fruit, but, like those who have passed away in youth, rushes
to death. (The idea is mooted in the 1st Elegy: '*Denk: es erhält sich
der Held, selbst der Untergang war ihm | nur ein Vorwand, zu sein: seine
letzte Geburt.*') But if the hero is praised for his disregard of life
the implication might be that life is without value. The 7th Elegy
disproves this by glorifying existence. '*Hiersein ist herrlich.*' And
therefore the poet, addressing the angel, whom he fears no more,
lauds what life has created – cathedrals, music, love. The essential
thing is that now in the 7th Elegy the human race is magnified –
for its achievements – whereas hitherto only individual representatives of humanity – lovers who love for love's sake, those who
died young, the acrobat, the hero – had been praised. – The 8th
Elegy is a variant of the 4th in which children are shown to have
unity of being; in the 8th animals have it, for they too live an
'open' life unburdened by consciousness; that is, in a state of pure
existence, which man can attain by death only. The 9th Elegy, a
hymn to life, answers the question asked in the 1st Elegy: What
is the purpose of human existence? The answer is that we do not
live to gain experience, knowledge, happiness, but for the sake of
existence itself. We must, therefore, praise existence, praise the
simple *things* of life, and give them permanence by making visible
in them that which is invisible in ourselves. Here we have again
Rilke's doctrine of things to which we, the most transitory of
beings, give permanence by shaping them in art. There is another
late elaboration of the theme in the poem *Der Goldschmied*,[1] the
seizure of the artist by the thing and the projection into the thing
of the artist's soul:

> *Raum greift aus uns und übersetzt die Dinge:*
> *dass dir das Dasein eines Baums gelinge,*
> *wirf Innenraum um ihn, aus jenem Raum,*
> *das in dir west.*

Having thus, in the 9th Elegy, justified life, in the 10th the poet
accepts pain and sorrow, which will pass with us into the next
world. Life is the city of pain (*Leid-Stadt*), death is the land of pain
(*Leidland*). 'If I were to cry out,' the 1st Elegy begins, 'who would
hear me in the cohorts of the angels?' In the 10th Elegy the angel
has heard and has approved all; approved, too, the 'grim insight'

---

[1] *Letzte Gedichte und Fragmentarisches.*

with which the mysteries have been probed. The path has been through Hell (the Hell of *Malte*) upwards to the Angel – not *with* the Angel, as was the case with Dante and Stefan George. Now the Angel is near, and, though still terrible, the terror and the mystery of his super-humanity are known to the mortal, and therefore the mortal can adore in jubilation. Here the aim which had throughout his poetic striving lured Rilke, to *interpret* life, is (in his own belief) realized at last, and to the full. Realizing that the 'God' he had created in *Das Stundenbuch* had been himself, above all a projection of his own loneliness, and that Malte too had been a poignant re-creation of himself, he had turned to the creation of things without himself in the *Dinggedichte*, but even in these, as we have seen – and as the 9th Elegy confirms – the reality is transferred personality. The *Duino Elegies* represent a third stage in his development, complete objectivity or utter elimination of himself, solution of the mysteries achieved by love of life which asks for nothing except life to suffer in. Rilke indicates the nature of his *volte-face* in his poem *Wendung*[1]: what he had hitherto achieved had been first by a mystic worship and then by a visual process. Into his vision he had taken beasts and birds and flowers, and he had been they. But in alien rooms of strange inns and in his torturing bed it had been borne in upon him that in all this there was naught of love, and that to what he might still do of this nature consecration would be denied. For to vision, he says, there is a limit, and what vision has by the infusion of soul made more than a thing seen should grow and thrive in the folds of love. When the eyes' task is completed the heart should cherish the prisoned pictures. For the poet, though he overpowers and possesses these things, does not *know* them. Knowledge, as the *Duino Elegies* climb stage by stage to their culmination, is achieved by the justification of suffering, that dark evergreen of life in which we abide. A youth may for a short space follow, as he would a luring female, Lament when he finds her haunting the noisy fair-booth of life. But Lament is friend and solace only to those who have died young, and to maidens: to them she reveals the treasures she wears, pearls of pain and delicate veils of suffering. In the Valley of Pain one such youth who has died young questions a Lament, an ancient of days, and answering she tells him how mighty the race of Lament has ever been:

[1] *Letzte Gedichte und Fragmentarisches.*

Und sie leitet ihn leicht durch die weite Landschaft der Klagen,
zeigt ihm die Säulen der Tempel oder die Trümmer
jener Burgen, von wo Klage-Fürsten das Land
einstens weise beherrscht. Zeigt ihm die hohen
Tränenbäume und Felder blühender Wehmut,
(Lebendige kennen sie nur als sanftes Blattwerk);
zeigt ihm die Tiere der Trauer, weidend, – und manchmal
schreckt ein Vogel und zieht, flach ihnen fliegend durchs Aufschaun,
weithin das schriftliche Bild seines vereinsamten Schreis.

(The extract is sufficient to provide hostile critics with a cry that this is an anaemic allegory of the medieval sort; nor will such a critic be impressed by the picture of the ominous bird flying through the spectator's upturned vision and writing the image of its lonely wail – really a fair example of Rilke's characteristic way of *seeing* his images complete as pictures or sculpture.) This age-old Klage points to the monument that, like the sphinx by the Nile, has a human face whose ripe rounding is marked in the dead boy's hearing as he gazes by the slow flitting of an owl past its cheek. (Again a *picture* which might be cryptic if we did not know from Rilke's correspondence that it is a reminiscence of his Egyptian travel.) Thence she leads him to the moonlit gorge whence flows the river of Joy into the land of men.

It would be idle to claim that there is variety of theme or speculation in the *Duino Elegies*, or indeed – since in these *Elegies* the ideas which have haunted Rilke from his earlier years shape themselves as a finished flower round his central conception of the divine – in his work as a whole. Irreverent medical men have written tractates to prove that the poet was a sufferer from obsessional mania. But even if this is admitted it might be shown that there is escape from the obsession of Death (to Rilke the goal to which childhood, poverty, and love converge) in the praise of life because of – not in spite of – the suffering it brings. At a cursory glance, too, it might seem that the *Elegies* show an escape from the obsession of God. Actually even in *Das Stundenbuch* God fades into the background after *The Book of Monkish Life*: God is then the Messiah who is to be born of perfected man.[1] In the *Elegies* God is mentioned only once – and casually – in the 1st Elegy, which was written in 1912. Rilke in one of his letters explained

[1] *'der Kommende . . . , der von Ewigkeit her bevorsteht, der Zukünftige, die endliche Frucht eines Baumes, dessen Blätter wir sind.'* – *Briefe an einen jungen Dichter*, p. 34.

this 'discretion' in his use of the name of God. He had used it, he says, when Russia revealed to him the darkness and the brotherliness of God. In the Russian ecstasy the 'properties' of God had rushed into a multitude of images: now there is no image which will speak Him: God rises from the breathing heart and covers the skies and falls down as rain. Christianity has familiarized us with God; but as Christianity fades what looms in our consciousness is the primitive God (*der uralte Gott*) of the Old Testament.

If the *Duino Elegies* mark a progression from spiritual fear to reasoned appeasement the *Sonette an Orpheus* (1922), which have the baffling obscurity of the *Elegies* but not always their flight from musicality, show this appeasement transfigured. There is at least the illusion of a new theme: the reduction of all existence to the plain principle of rhythm: all that is – the face of the earth with mountains and valleys, man and woman with the phases of sex, rise and fall of all movement, arsis and thesis, *Hebung und Senkung*, thrust and recoil, joy and sorrow – all that is, physical and spiritual, arises from the juxtaposition and alternation of these mathematical contraries. Life and death themselves form a dual realm (*Doppelbereich*), just as do the shadowing wooded hill and its reflection in the lake (I, IX). Music then, or rhythm, is the secret of existence; and behind music and rhythm is the Musician or Poet – the Divine Will. The general sense is tangible in the 18th sonnet of Part II: *Tänzerin: o du Verlegung | alles Vergehens in Gang* . . . The dancer is used as a symbol of motion; and motion in the shaper's hand becomes pitcher or vase (*moment figé*=plastic art, and in Rilke's conception poem too). And rhythm is the principle, not merely of all creation, whether of life or art, but also of death: for motion must fade into rest. The intrusion of music as a symbol into Rilke's limited fund of tense ideas is explained by the awakening of his musical sense during his residence at Duino by his association with the concert pianist Magda von Hattingberg-Riechling; hitherto he had shunned and rejected music; now the greatness of Beethoven dawned upon him. Apart from the *Sonnets to Orpheus*, however – and even here the laboured exploitation of music as a symbol proves no real sense of music – Rilke is yet another poet whose verbal music is superb and who is dead to music.

The rest of Rilke's work, full of interest as it is, is subsidiary. *Das Marienleben* (1913) takes its title from those medieval series of pictures which represent the life of the Virgin. Joseph's question-

ing of the Virgin's virginity is more or less in consonance with
the comic role Joseph plays in Germanic folksongs. *Letzte Gedichte
und Fragmentarisches* (Vol. III of *Collected Works*, 1927) are for the
most part complementary to the *Duino Elegies*. Rilke's translations
(Vol. VI of *Collected Works*) are mostly interesting for the light
they throw on the bent of the poet's mind and for help in the
interpretation of his themes: thus his versions of Elizabeth Barrett
Browning's *Sonnets from the Portuguese* (1919); *Portugiesische Briefe*
(1913), his translation of the letters of the Portuguese nun Mari-
anna Alcoforado; and his *Die vierundzwanzig Sonette der Louize Labe
Lyoneserin* (1918) elucidate his conception of the selfless nature of
true love. These translations were made at Capri in 1907; Rilke
was helped by his hostess and by Dora Heidrich, who was by
birth an Englishwoman. The *Portugiesische Briefe* were made from
the French translation. Rilke's translations at Muzot of certain of
Paul Valéry's poems and his own French poetry (*Poèmes français*,
Paris, 1935) represent his last phase.

There is no need to distil Rilke's poetic creed, for he states it in
his *Briefe an einen jungen Dichter*[1] (1929) and above all in a famous
passage of *Malte*:

'*Ach, mit Versen ist so wenig getan, wenn man sie früh schreibt.
Man sollte warten damit und Sinn und Süssigkeit sammeln ein ganzes
Leben lang, und ein langes womöglich, und dann, ganz zum Schluss,
vielleicht könnte man dann zehn Zeilen schreiben, die gut sind. Denn
Verse sind nicht, wie die Leute meinen, Gefühle (die hat man früh genug)
– es sind Erfahrungen. Um eines Verses willen muss man viele Städte
sehen, Menschen und Dinge.*' (Take with this his poems which have
Heimatlosigkeit for theme, above all *Der Fremde*.[2]) '*Und es genügt
auch nicht*', we read further, '*dass man Erinnerungen hat. Man muss
sie vergessen können, wenn es viele sind, und man muss die grosse Geduld
haben, zu warten, bis sie wiederkommen.*' ('Emotion remembered in
tranquillity'!) '*Denn die Erinnerungen sind es noch nicht. Erst wenn
sie Blut werden in uns, Blick und Gebärde, namenlos und nicht mehr zu
unterscheiden von uns selbst, erst dann kann es geschehen, dass in einer
sehr seltenen Stunde das erste Wort eines Verses aufsteht in ihrer Mitte
und aus ihnen ausgeht.*'

[1] The young poet was Franz Xaver Kappus (1883-), who made a reputation later by his sensational novel of the post-War period, *Die lebenden
Vierzehn* (1918).   [2] *Neue Gedichte*, II.

In *Briefe an einen jungen Dichter* Rilke insists on loneliness as a necessary condition of poetic production, and this loneliness he couples with distance (*Weite*) from those who are near; which means that the true poet must relentlessly alienate himself from friends and relatives. This is the utter isolation to which he subjected himself after his Worpswede days; elsewhere he refers to his own *Einsamkeitsfanatismus*. '*Was not tut*', he urges his young poet, '*ist doch nur dieses: Einsamkeit, grosse innere Einsamkeit. In-sich-Gehen und stundenlang niemandem begegnen, – das muss man erreichen können. Einsamsein, wie man als Kind einsam war, als die Erwachsenen umhergingen, mit Dingen verflochten, die wichtig und gross schienen, weil die Grossen so geschäftig aussahen und weil man von ihrem Tun nichts begriff.*' This *Verinnerlichung* is of course much more determined than the *Sammlung* (German words alone express the conceptions) which poets of previous generations had called for.

Somewhat surprising in Rilke – though we have seen that at one period of his life he identified sex with religion – is the attribution in these *Letters to a Young Poet* of the creative impulse of genius to the stirrings of sex. '*Und tatsächlich*', he argues while discussing Dehmel's sexualism, '*liegt ja künstlerisches Erleben so unglaublich nahe am geschlechtlichen, an seinem Weh und seiner Lust, dass die beiden Erscheinungen eigentlich nur verschiedene Formen einer und derselben Sehnsucht und Seligkeit sind.*' In another letter to this young poet he discusses the grievous burden of sex, but nevertheless describes sexual pleasure (*die körperliche Wollust*) as '*eine grosse unendliche Erfahrung, die uns gegeben wird, ein Wissen von der Welt, die Fülle und der Glanz alles Wissens*' and as '*Sammlung zu Höhepunkten*'. And he continues: '*denn auch das geistige Schaffen stammt von dem physischen her, ist eines Wesens mit ihm und nur wie eine leisere, entzücktere und ewigere Wiederholung leiblicher Wollust*'. See p. 71.

In the outward aspects of his work Rilke is what the French call '*un visuel*'; that is, he reproduces *visual* impressions. He *sees* like a painter or sculptor; and therefore the effect of his most characteristic poetry lies perhaps more in painting or grouping than in magic of rhythm, though in this he is unsurpassed. If the devices of his technique were grouped they would coincide with those of Stefan George – vowel harmony, alliteration, assonance, interior rhymes. There is similarity, too, in the way both poets reveal the theme of a poem *gradatim*; there is, however, the difference that Rilke's title may give an indication. But in spite of such external correspondences of technique Rilke is far removed from Stefan George in the essential qualities of his poetry, above all in the tempo and the inner rhythm of his verse. Thus, while George has the monotonous regularity and (except when whipped by indignation) the majestic tread of the great classics, Rilke strikes metrical magic from a complicated irregularity: he fits the rhythm of emotion or the shocks in the sense to truncated or elongated lines, or marks the flow of feeling by sudden changes of metre (*Taktwechsel*). He is unsurpassed in the intricate linking of sentences and in the folding over of verse lines to give snake-like suppleness to the pattern of the stanza or poem. He is capable of such *tours de force* as the building up of a longish poem of one sentence (*Der Apfelgarten, Römische Fontäne*). His rhymecraft is marvellous; and here his skill does not lie so much in the rareness of the rhyme (e.g. *Nähe – Skarabäe; müde – Etüde*) as in his juggling with unstressed vocables (*wie – die; und – Mund*), by which he may depress one rhyme and lift the other into high relief. Where foreign words fit the mood of the poem he heightens this mood by using them ingeniously as rhymes (e.g. *Die Parke*[1]). Not infrequently the pith of the poem rings resonantly or echoes sadly in a last carefully spared rhyme. His vowel-colouring is as rich and sensuous as he hints it to be in *Persisches Heliotrop*[2]:

> *Denn sieh: wie süsse Worte nachts in Sätzen*
> *beisammenstehn ganz dicht, durch nichts getrennt,*
> *aus der Vokale wachem Violett*
> *hinduftend durch das stille Himmelbett.*

His handling of words is just as masterly, and ranges from apparent simplicity of diction (*Die Erblindende*[1]: *Die Liebende*[2]) to daring neologisms and scientific or erudite terms, which surprise and yet seem inevitable in the place accorded them. Like Stefan George he may venture into medieval German (with a quaint charm as in *Die heiligen drei Könige* – '*Magenkraft*'!) or use dialect forms – e.g. *geel* (M.H.G. *gel*) for *gelb*.[3] He forms arbitrary plurals to create the impression he desires: *Smaragda und Rubinien*[4] for an Oriental effect; or he may vary his plural – thus quite close as the pages turn we

---

[1] *Neue Gedichte*, II.   [2] Ibid., I.
[3] *Schwarze Katze, Neue Gedichte*, II.
[4] *Die heiligen drei Könige* in *Das Buch der Bilder.*

find *Münde* and *Munde* as the plural of *Mund*. His love of substantive +adjective or verb he caught, probably, from J. P. Jacobsen: *angstwarm, kinderkühl, waldeigen, märchenallein, blutdurchglüht, du Kindgewesene*. Typical of his early work is the use he makes of present participles to indicate hidden movement or growth: *wachsende Nacht, weckender Regen, bleichendes Blühn, zögerndes Erleben*. In the *New Poems* his substantivation of past participles amounts to mannerism: *die Aufgetane, der mit Umriss Angetane*. He shares George's omission of the antecedent pronoun: *Und auch, die lieben, sammeln für dich ein*. He skilfully substitutes *wer* for *jemand* and *wo* for *irgendwo*: *Alle Mädchen erwarten wen, | wenn die Bäume in Blüten stehn; weil eine Kirche wo im Osten steht*. His syntactical tricks serve him to veil the meaning in his last Duino and Muzot phase: phrases such as *nicht dass du Gottes entrügest die Stimme* and *Manche, des Todes, entstand ruhig geordnete Regel* read like transliterated Latin.

The Viennese poet RICHARD VON SCHAUKAL (1874-1942) is, to begin with, in the line of Stefan George: he has no finesses of rhythm or diction and his meaning and intention are clear; but he does adopt George's pose of hostility to the decayed style of his day. He sketches his own personality and opinions in his aphoristically shaped disquisitional 'novel' *Leben und Meinungen des Herrn Andreas von Balthesser, eines Dandys und Dilettanten* (1907), recalls the mellow culture of a past period in his nostalgic *Grossmutter* (1906), hallows style in another imaginary portrait, *Kapellmeister Kreisler* (1906), and supplements these confessions of artistic faith in the witty dialogues of *Literatur* (1907) and *Giorgione* (1907), and in the essays of *Vom Geschmack* (1910). This cult of culture marks the finely phrased style of his short stories: *Eros-Thanatos* (1906), *Schlemihle* (1907), *Die Märchen von Hans Bürgers Kindheit* (1913). It is as a lyric poet, however, that he has created a little genre of his own: like Rilke in the *New Poems* he blends impressionism with Parnassian precision in his '*malerische Moment-Gedichte*', the best of which (collected in *Bilder: Der ausgewählten Gedichte zweiter erweiterter Teil*, 1909) are transpositions of real or imaginary pictures or delightfully wicked sharply outlined portraits which, in the Parnassian way, characterize at a glance a period or a class (*Empire, Salome, Porträt eines spanischen Infanten von Diego Velasquez, La Duchesse de . . . , Huldigung des Chevalier de . . . an die Duchesse de . . . , Goya, Musset*). A good example is *Porträt des Marquis de . . .* :

Halte mir einer von euch Laffen mein Pferd,
hole mir einer von euch Lumpen mein Schwert:
ich liess es bei einer Dame liegen.
Lass einer von euch Schurken einen Falken fliegen:
ich will ihm nachsehn und mich ins Blau verlieren.
Störe mich keiner von euch Tieren!

Another Austrian poet, FRANZ KARL GINZKEY (1871-) weaves his symbolism into folksong style (*Das heimliche Läuten*, 1906; *Befreite Stunde*, 1916); his novels (*Jacobus und die Frauen*, 1908, has autobiographical elements) have the soft sadness of the blue Danube. Of the Prague group of poets FRIEDRICH ADLER (1857-1938; *Gedichte*, 1898; *Neue Gedichte*, 1899) adapted Spanish dramas, while HUGO SALUS (1866-1929) in *Ehefrühling* (1899) lyricized the intimities of wedlock, proved his mastery of form in a succession of verse volumes (*Ausgewählte Gedichte*, 1901) and dreamed a lyric formlessness into *Novellen des Lyrikers* (1903).

VIII

HUGO VON HOFMANNSTHAL

rtistenkunst is of the Rhineland and the French border:
George's esoteric art centres in the Rhine province, Darmstadt, Frankfurt-am-Main. And yet the victories of symbolism were won, as far as the world at large is concerned, not
along the Rhine, but in Vienna. Not for the first time in the history
of German literature, Austria now leads: in criticism (Hermann
Bahr), in aphorism (Peter Altenberg), in the lyric (Schaukal, Rilke),
in the epic (Däubler), but above all in the lyric drama. Voluptuous
Vienna, between the nations, takes into its literature moods from
all its neighbours and becomes international, the more easily as
its greatest writers are Jews or half-Jews who have the typical
Viennese mentality (soft and cynical and half-despairing – Vienna
is the city of suicides), and are yet, with their limitless receptivity,
half-Italian, or half-French, or half-Slav.

Viennese decadence exposes its most corpse-like glints in the
verse of FELIX DÖRMANN (1870-1928), a Jew complete: *Neurotica*
(1891), *Sensationen* (1892). The women he loves and describes lie,
with '*wurzelwelke Nerven*', expectant or exhausted:

> *Ich liebe die hektischen, schlanken*
> *Narzissen mit blutrotem Mund;*
> *ich liebe die Qualengedanken,*
> *die Herzen, zerstochen und wund.*

> *Ich liebe die Fahlen und Bleichen,*
> *die Frauen mit müdem Gesicht,*
> *aus welchen in flammenden Zeichen*
> *verzehrende Sinnenglut spricht.*

> *Ich liebe die schillernden Schlangen,*
> *so schmiegsam und biegsam und kühl;*

ich liebe die klagenden, bangen,
die Lieder voll Todesgefühl . . .

This neurotic brand of verse is of course not confined to Vienna, but it is such morbidity which is the base of very great Viennese poets; in their work, however – because they are great poets and personally decent –, the dissection of diseased feelings and experiences is transmuted to literature of the first quality.

The relation of this literary morbidity to the Georgean school might be an interesting problem. One aspect is clear: while the Rhenish Georgeans are masculine the Viennese neo-romantics are feminine (even Schnitzler has this soft womanish passivity, and Hofmannsthal and Beer-Hofmann have the illusion of manliness only when they take into themselves the male spirit of Greek or Elizabethan poets). In any case the two schools yawn apart, in spite of coincidences of verse technique, in their attitude to the reading public: only poets are expected to read George, but the very morbidity – often sensational – of Hofmannsthal and the Viennese group make them interesting to the many. Moreover, to the general reader, they have the philosophical obviousness of Maeterlinck, from whom they take so much. Two poets in particular who, to begin with, were attached to George broke loose and alienated the Master because they wrote plays and stories and became best-sellers, Hofmannsthal and Max Dauthendey, the latter not a Viennese but, as a native of Würzburg, a South German.

HUGO VON HOFMANNSTHAL (1874-1929), of Jewish and Italian descent, returned to the Catholic Church in his maturity, and died shortly after the suicide of his son. He might be effortlessly characterized by a mere enumeration of the pet terms of appreciative or depreciative critics: *Überreife; frühreife Müdigkeit; schwermutvolle, kulturgesättigte Müdigkeit; gedämpfte Angst; nervenzarte Weltangst; seelisches Greisentum; senile Jugend; raffinierte Sehnsucht; ein parasitisches Edelgewächs; Verschmelzung von Rokoko und Renaissance; Traum-Mystizismus; 'ein Traum, der sich selbst bezweifelt'* (a famous term applied to Hebbel). The summing up by Thomas Roffler is as good as any: *'sie' (seine Kunst) 'hat jene blasse und auf die Dauer entnervende Zartheit, welche klingt wie das abgedämpfte Spiel einer Geige, fein und fern, narkotisch süss und unendlich müde'.* But the most telling description of Hofmannsthal's nature and that of the Viennese

neo-romantics is that which he himself weaves into his prologue
to Schnitzler's *Anatol*:

> *Also spielen wir Theater,*
> *Spielen unsre eignen Stücke,*
> *Frühgereift und zart und traurig,*
> *Die Komödie unsrer Seele,*
> *Unsres Fühlens heut und gestern,*
> *Böser Dinge hübsche Formel,*
> *Glatte Worte, bunte Bilder,*
> *Halbes, heimliches Empfinden,*
> *Agonieen, Episoden. . . .*

(The greatest of Viennese poets, Grillparzer, also *lebensmatt*, had
in his *Abschied von Wien* stressed the *Halbheit* of Viennese poets
enervated by the 'summer breath' of that *'Capua der Geister'*: *'Man
spricht nicht, denkt wohl etwa kaum | Und fühlt das Halb-Gedachte'* . . .
'Man lebt in halber Poesie, | Gefährlich für die ganze . . .')

What the spirit of poetry should be Hofmannsthal defines in his
*Gespräch über Gedichte; 'eine Ahnung des Blühens, ein Schauder des Ver-
wesens, ein Jetzt, ein Hier und zugleich ein Jenseits, ein ungeheures Jenseits'*.
And indeed what we do get in his work – particularly in his lyrics –
is such a linking of bloom and decay, a questioning of the present
life and fear of what may follow, 'blank misgivings of a creature
moving about in worlds unrealized', expressed often enough with
the naïve wistful wonderment of Maeterlinck.

Hofmannsthal, world-famous as a dramatist, is essentially a lyric
poet, even in his dramas. And yet his collected poems (*Gesammelte
Gedichte*, 1907; *Nachlese der Gedichte*, 1934) make slender volumes.
The craftsmanship is masterly: the blank verse has a gentle, low-
toned dignity, the Spanish trochees softly glide and glitter, and
above all the interlacing *terze rime* solemnly weave a web of question or description bound together by a majestic final line. As in
Ballade des äusseren Lebens:

> *Und Kinder wachsen auf mit tiefen Augen,*
> *Die von nichts wissen, wachsen auf und sterben,*
> *Und alle Menschen gehen ihrer Wege.*
>
> *Und süsse Früchte werden aus den herben*
> *Und fallen nachts wie tote Vögel nieder*
> *Und liegen wenig Tage und verderben.*

Und immer weht der Wind, und immer wieder
Vernehmen wir und reden viele Worte
Und spüren Lust und Müdigkeit der Glieder.

Und Strassen laufen durch das Gras, und Orte
Sind da und dort, voll Fackeln, Bäumen, Teichen,
Und drohende, und totenhaft verdorrte . . .

Wozu sind diese aufgebaut und gleichen
Einander nie? und sind unzählig viele?
Was wechselt Lachen, Weinen und Erbleichen?

Was frommt das alles uns und diese Spiele,
Die wir doch gross und ewig einsam sind
Und wandernd nimmer suchen irgend Ziele?

Was frommt's, dergleichen viel gesehen haben?
Und dennoch sagt der viel, der 'Abend' sagt,
Ein Wort, daraus Tiefsinn und Trauer rinnt

Wie schwerer Honig aus den hohlen Waben.

The *Terzinen über Vergänglichkeit* adumbrate one of Hofmannsthal's obsessions – the unity and continuity of creation; the idea: I am my ancestors ('. . . *dass ich auch vor hundert Jahren war | Und meine Ahnen, die im Totenhemd, | Mit mir verwandt sind wie mein eignes Haar, | So eins mit mir als wie mein eignes Haar*'). This conception of continuity, of course, implies that I am the future as well as the past: I am my descendants too, an idea stressed particularly in the Maeterlinckian story *Die Frau ohne Schatten*. The third *Terzine* has the lovely image of children under cherry-trees, gazing upward in the light of the full moon:

Wir sind aus solchem Zeug, wie das zu Träumen,
Und Träume schlagen so die Augen auf
Wie kleine Kinder unter Kirschenbäumen,

Aus deren Krone den blassgoldnen Lauf
Der Vollmond anhebt durch die grosse Nacht . . .

Die Beiden is just an outlined situation: the rider with his firm hand takes the brimmed goblet from the light-foot maid by the fiery charger he stays with a negligent gesture: but as hand moves to

15

hand the goblet is heavy, and dark wine rolls on the earth. Hofmannsthal's mournful imaging of death begins in *Erlebnis* – death is music: '*Gewaltig sehnend, süss und dunkelglühend, | Verwandt der tiefsten Schwermut.*' In *Verse auf ein kleines Kind*, and elsewhere in the poet's work, there is a mystic idealization of children which does not derive from Victor Hugo (on whom Hofmannsthal wrote his doctor's thesis) but from Maeterlinck ('*l'enfant qui se tait est mille fois plus sage que Marc-Aurèle qui parle*'), and is indeed one of the tenets of his creed; in his essay on Peter Altenberg he says that the neo-romantic poets are all striving to be children again, '*und es ist auch niemand vornehmer, niemand anmutiger als die, die noch kein Gedächtnis haben, und ganz von der Wahrheit bewegt werden*'. This more or less agrees with Rilke's wish that the man might be the child; but of course the idea has a long Neo-Platonic pedigree. The idea that life is a dream is more than any other neo-romantic conception Viennese: Grillparzer had transposed Calderon's *La vida es sueño*, and Schnitzler weaves the fancy through the mass of his work. For the poems grouped as *Gestalten* the influence of Browning's dramatic monologues has been claimed; but, though Hofmannsthal studied Browning, it is hard to find similarities in these lissom musings; indeed, only three of the poems are monologues, and these are hardly dramatic. *Idylle*, included in the *Poems*, is really the first of Hofmannsthal's 'revenge dramas'. It was probably suggested by Böcklin's picture *Der Kentaur in der Dorfschmiede*, and thus groups itself with the poem *Zu einer Totenfeier für Arnold Böcklin* and with *Der Tod des Tizian*, which, begun in 1892, was completed when Böcklin died in 1901. A centaur comes to a smithy to have his spear sharpened, and while this is being done he fascinates the smith's wife with tales of the free open spaces and the roving life. She is the very modern *femme incomprise*, home-bound but dreaming ever of beauty. Her father was a potter, and she transposes into supple trimeters the pictures on the urns he had made, to which and to the centaur's flights of fancy the burly smith hammers out Philistine maxims of home and duty and happiness in a hole and corner. He goes within to give the last filing to the spear-head, and now the wife leaps on to the centaur's back and he gallops away to the river; but the husband, returning, transpierces her with the centaur's spear. The revenge theme points forward; but *Idylle* is poem rather than drama because of its vivid fleeting pictures: the 'idyll' dreams a story into the scene on a

HUGO VON
   HOFMANNSTHAL

FRANZ KAFKA

Grecian urn – centaur with wounded woman by a river's rim; and it would be interesting to compare Hofmannsthal's highly coloured Greek vignettes in this poem with those of Stefan George in *Das Buch der Hirten- und Preisgedichte*: while George reads into his translucent moment of Greek life the spirit of the period Hofmannsthal sensuously gives merely plastic picture and erotic undertone:

Er schuf, gestreckt auf königliche Ruhebank,
Der Phädra wundervollen Leib, von Sehnsucht matt,
Und drüber flatternd Eros, der mit süsser Qual die Glieder füllt . . .

or the vivid play of colours: '*Eben stürzt sich der Centaur in das aufrauschende Wasser des Flusses. Sein bronzener Oberkörper und die Gestalt der Frau zeichnen sich scharf auf der abendlich vergoldeten Wasserfläche ab.*'

The lyric dramas proper begin with *Gestern* (1892), written when the poet was a boy of eighteen. It is a playlet of one act, in rhymed verse; the scene is Italy in Renaissance days. The hero Andrea, the first of Hofmannsthal's typically decadent heroes, is a sick artist whose life has been an eternal quest of new thrills and sensations that might enhance his own sensitive personality. He shuns the shallow levels of livid morality and finds infinite variety in perversion ('*Eintönig ist das Gute, schal und bleich,* | *Allein die Sünde ist unendlich reich*'); and even when his delicate nerves are jaded to exhaustion it is not in repentance that he turns ascetic and flagellant, but still in search of a sadistic new thrill – '*Es gibt noch Stürme, die mich nie durchbebt,* | *Noch Ungefühltes kann das Leben schenken*'. Such a life, he feels, is sterile; and yet he refuses to recognize 'yesterday' – except as the 'cold ashes' of sensation. What at last forces him to a realization of the truth – the supreme sensation of his life – is the faithlessness of Arlette. *Der Tod des Tizian* (1892) presents quite another sort of hero: Titian, strong-willed and toiling with indomitable energy to the moment of his death. Two only of Hofmannsthal's characters dominate life by sheer strength of will: Titian and the grandmother in *Der weisse Fächer*, while the Baron (=Casanova) in *Der Abenteurer und die Sängerin* is unbowed by life because he is too animal to do more than spend himself from enjoyment to enjoyment. *Der Tod des Tizian*, a panegyric of beauty on the lips of Titian's pupils as he dies painting his last picture, is the very manifesto of German symbolism –

Venice, seen far below the terrace where youth gathers in picturesque poses, merged in the deep night tints of the Italian landscape, is transfigured to beauty by distance, though ugliness and
beauty dwell there, and mad folks with bestial:

> *Und was die Ferne weise dir verhüllt,*
> *Ist ekelhaft und trüb und schal erfüllt*
> *Von Wesen, die die Schönheit nicht erkennen*
> *Und ihre Welt mit unsern Worten nennen . . .*
> *Denn unsre Wonne oder unsre Pein*
> *Hat mit der ihren nur das Wort gemein . . .*

Critics have made too much of the depiction of Titian as a *Tatenmensch*. Even this picture of life-force is swathed in soft undulating
rhythms and in a feminized mood: Tizianello, Titian's son, sobs
and weeps and sleeps with Gianino, a lovely lad of sixteen, as
girl-like as Lisa, with the yellow rose-bud in her raven hair, is
boy-like. The problem is one which falls naturally into Hofmannsthal's limited range: what passes through the mind in the hour of
death, the mysterious return of things long merged in forgetfulness, and, it may be, a last clearness of will and purpose and a
poignant realization of lost chances. This is the sum and substance
of *Der Tor und der Tod* (1892). The hero, Claudio, is yet another
sterile dilettante; and it is only when death appears that he realizes
the inanity of his sensual and selfish life, in which nobody was
anything to him and he was nothing to anybody. He has been one
of those who, in Dante's words, seek 'to make themselves perfect
by the worship of beauty'; but the aesthete's enjoyment of life,
the lesson runs, is not *life*, and Claudio makes the terrible discovery that he has never lived; his agonized cry to Death, who
comes, not as a skeleton but as a handsome fiddler elegantly clad,
is: '*Ich habe nicht gelebt!*' It is hardly accidental that Claudio is a
namesake of the hero of *Measure for Measure*; both are 'not prepared for death'. There is no doubt that *Der Tor und der Tod* is a
modern version of the medieval Dance of Death: the play ends
with the shades of Claudio's mother and his discarded love following Death as he departs playing his violin, with a shape that
resembles Claudio bringing up the rear. It is perhaps accidental
that Shelley in his preface to *Alastor* and Keats in *The Fall of
Hyperion* inculcate the same moral. Shelley delivers stern judgment

on the poet's self-centred seclusion – such a man, he says, is morally dead; and Keats argues that the life of the dreamer who lives in a factitious world of art is selfish. But self-centred seclusion is the very condition (according to Stefan George and Rilke) of poetry for poetry's sake! It would be rash, however, to conclude that Hofmannsthal is contradicting the Georgean creed. What interests him is the mystery of the death hour and the presentation of the decadent type; and indeed nearly all his male characters live remote from the realities and poignancy of life in a dream world of their own creating. Contrasted with these men of finely strung nerves are Hofmannsthal's women (from the smith's wife in *Idylle* onwards), whom the men cannot understand.

The plays which follow *Der Tor und der Tod* often betray, as the lyrics do, the influence of Maeterlinck: the characters are marionettes:

> *Es wär' mir lieber, wenn nicht Menschen*
> *Dies spielen würden, sondern grosse Puppen,*
> *Von einem, der's versteht, gelenkt an Drähten.*
> *Sie haben eine grenzenlose Anmut*
> *In ihren aufgelösten leichten Gliedern –*
> *Und mehr als Menschen dürfen sie der Lust*
> *Und der Verzweiflung sich hingeben*
> *Und bleiben schön dabei . . .*

Das Bergwerk zu Falun (1899) is a dramatization of E. T. A. Hoffmann's tale; the hero feels lonely in the company of men; alone he feels the companionship of spirits. The theme is that sojourn on earth should be a preparation for the spirit world. The ascetic hero of *Der Kaiser und die Hexe* (1897) sets himself the task of liberating himself from the toils of a woman, who has enslaved him for seven years, by keeping away from her seven days and nights; she appears to him in visions, as a dove, an empress, etc. The grandmother in *Der weisse Fächer* (1897) is, like Titian, an exponent of the life-force; *nihil a se alienum putat*; she loves life. The hero and heroine conquer by renunciation – as do Vittoria in *Der Abenteurer und die Sängerin*, the old merchant in *Die Hochzeit der Sobeide*, and the poet in *Das kleine Welttheater* (1897), who, cheated by life, finds in his poetry consolation and the will to live. *Theater in Versen* (1899) collects the three following recently pro-

duced one-act plays. *Die Frau im Fenster*, a dramatization of d'Annunzio's *Sogno d'un mattino di primavera*, is the prototype of a series of 'revenge dramas' which belong to the most characteristic things in the neo-romantic movement. They definitely belong to the Renaissance fashion; and since the avenging husband is a *Kraftmensch* Dante's story of Paolo and Francesca is in the background. We expect in these plays a balcony and a rope ladder; and the lady will unbind her hair or let it hang down into the high-walled garden. The lady with the hair down-hanging comes primarily, one assumes, from Maeterlinck's *Pelléas et Mélisande*; but one remembers too Gottfried Keller's *Hadlaub*, Rossetti's *The Blessed Damozel*, William Morris's *Rapunzel*. To Venice Hofmannsthal gravitates again and again: to him the city on the lagoons is the symbol of mystery and romance. In *Der Abenteurer und die Sängerin* Baron Weidenstamm ('from Amsterdam') returns to Venice after an absence of seventeen years. It is clear from the story that the Baron is Casanova; and Hofmannsthal draws the most fascinating picture in literature of this irresistible man of pleasure. As he sits in the theatre he is recognized from the stage by Vittoria, a *prima donna*, one of all those women ('like waves, like the sands of the sea, the notes of music') he has loved and left. She is now married, and has a 'brother', Cesarino, a lovely boy, the very image of the Baron seventeen years before. The old lovers meet, and Casanova would snatch back a faded memory, but for her there can be no question of a return. Her husband suspects, and is told that Cesarino is indeed the Baron's son, but that the sin is her mother's. At the corner of the stage in a crowded company the Baron tells the wide-eyed boy of all the magic of foreign lands, of gay festivals – of women
. . . he lesson of the play is that Vittoria, though she has been a mere episode in the Baron's life (he does not even remember clearly in which city he loved her!) owes herself, and her art, and her son to him. Love has brought no fruition to him: he has been merely *taurus ruens in venerem*. He is like the composer who passes as a symbol at the background of the action, dead in his dotage to his own divine music. And the play ends with Vittoria singing the *aria* from *Ariadne* – as she has never sung it before. . . . Vittoria, perfect woman and great artist, is Hofmannsthal's most beautiful realization of one of his salient themes: that renunciation of life gives strength for the perfection of that which is most precious in oneself. *Die Hochzeit der Sobeide* is based on an Indian story. The

scene is an old town in Persia; the time evening and night after the marriage of a rich old merchant to Sobeide. She tells him, when left alone with him, that she loves Ganem, the carpet-dealer's son. She has married the old merchant because her father in his impoverished state is in debt to him. The merchant, a wise old man, tells her she is free to go, wherever she wishes. She goes to the house of Ganem's father, and there finds that Ganem loves a loose woman, his father's mistress; after witnessing revolting scenes she throws herself down from a tower in her husband's garden. Sobeide has seen love in its loathliest aspects, and she dies a virgin, to cleanse her body of the contamination. But the action is not convincing; for if these filthy creatures, who take the bloom from Sobeide's virgin fancies, are loathsome, true lovers are not. The dramatic effect of the play is in the shudder at the spectacle of wild vice. There is in this play – and in this respect it is true to the type of the neo-romantic play – something of the fantastically evolved sensationalism of the more theatrical Elizabethans; but the horrors are not, as with the Elizabethans as a rule they are, organic: the tints of rottenness are so to speak painted on to a flimsy canvas, not woven into a fabric that will bear the critic's rending hands.

This livid sensationalism is sicklied o'er with Hofmannsthal's fatigue of spirit, from which he tried to escape by modernizing the plays of vigorous dramatists of old time. There is some evidence that these revivals of old plays are influenced (distantly perhaps) by the poet's admiration for Swinburne's *Atalanta in Calydon*: in his essay on Swinburne he refers to its '*wunderbare Verlebendigung des erstarrten Mythos*' and adds: '*nicht das zur beherrschten Klarheit und tanzenden Grazie emporgezogene Griechentum atmete darin, sondern das orphisch ursprüngliche, leidenschaftlich umwölkte*'. Hofmannsthal's recipe for such modernizations (cf. Gerhart Hauptmann's Greek Plays, pp. 41-2) would thus seem to be that the poet should plunge back beyond the (to him too humanized) classical Greek tragedy or the romanticized humanity of the Elizabethans to reveal the ultimate springs of the passion by piercing through the cloud which hid, even to the old dramatists with their keen insight into psychology, what set the action going. More or less this will mean that psychology yields to the exposure of physical states, and that the dramatist of today dissects complexes which, though apparently abnormal, he proves to be normal because they show forth that primitive animal nature which the decency of custom merely covers. What this in practice amounts to is that some strange sexual act or frenzy is interpreted as human; and tragedy, instead of being, in the Aristotelian sense, a purification of passion in the spectator, is an exposure of the roots of passion and mental disease in the protagonist. Thus tragedy is turned to a discussion of sex pathology, the result being that the canon of 'tragic guilt' fades out of the picture, for guilt is explained as the product of introversions and repressions. The vogue of these pathological studies probably owes something to the writings and example of Arthur Schnitzler, who as editor of the *Internationale klinische Rundschau* discussed the theories of Krafft-Ebing,[1] Freud,[2] and Lombroso.[3]

Alkestis (1894) was written immediately after the essay on Swinburne. It reads the poet's preoccupation with death and the fear of it into the tragedy of Euripides. The Fates have promised Admetus that he shall be spared death, provided always that, when the time comes, someone will offer to pass to the shades in his place. The call comes; and none will make the sacrifice of life except his beautiful young wife. His father, a walking shadow, clings to the shred of life that remains to him. The handling of the problem – why should death take those whose life is precious to themselves and to others – seems amateurish if compared at a glance with the rigid logic of the pre-Renaissance discussion of the theme, *Der Ackermann aus Böhmen*: actually in Hofmannsthal's version the effect is apt to be comical; for not logic but pathos is the means of appeal. In *Elektra* (1904) there is perhaps more of Oscar Wilde's *Salome* than of Sophocles: the imitations are indeed as glaring as they are in Vollmoeller's *Katharina, Gräfin von Armagnac*. There were several translations of *Salome*, one by Hedwig Lachmann; and as one of Max Reinhardt's gorgeously pictorial productions it held the stage for years.[4] The influence of the English play is shown in the concentration of the interest on the ragged figure of Electra – she never leaves the stage – while Orestes is reduced to a minor figure. The theme of both *Salome* and *Elektra* is the sexual repression of the heroine. In the drama of Sophocles there is merely a hint of such a conception: the name

---

[1] See p. 37.   [2] *Studien über Hysterie* (1895), *Traumdeutung* (1900).
[3] *La Donna delinquente, la Prostituta e la Donna normale* (1893).
[4] The German picture of Salome may owe much to the description of Gustave Moreau's painting in Huysmans' *A rebours* (1884).

Electra means 'the unmated', and she does bemoan her fate as an unmated woman. To provide a foil for the abnormality and sexual hysteria of Electra Hofmannsthal brings out the sane character of Chrysothemis, sexually ripe and therefore stung with desire but normally so: she urges Electra to accept things as they are so that she may mount the bridal bed. This contrasting ripeness of body in her sister Electra caresses:

> ... *Du bist voller Kraft* ...
> *Ich spüre durch die Kühle deiner Haut*
> *das warme Blut hindurch, mit meiner Wange*
> *spür' ich den Flaum auf deinen jungen Armen:*
> *Du bist wie eine Frucht am Tag der Reife* ...

But Electra is withered and stunted by the frenzy of her hate. She is physically incomplete: ... '*hab' langes Haar und fühle | doch nichts von dem, was Weiber, heisst es, fühlen*'. The conflict between her thwarted sex instincts and the domination of her mind by the lust of vengeance on those who have murdered her father has deflowered her: '*ohne Brautnacht | bin ich nicht, wie die Jungfraun sind*'. She has lost her virgin state because she has had hate for a bridegroom; to Orestes, when at last he comes to do the deed she herself was about to attempt, she says:

> *Verstehst du's, Bruder! diese süssen Schauder*
> *hab' ich dem Vater opfern müssen. Meinst du,*
> *wenn ich an meinem Leib mich freute, drangen*
> *nicht seine Seufzer, drang sein Stöhnen nicht*
> *bis an mein Bette? Eifersüchtig sind*
> *die Toten: und er schickte mir den Hass,*
> *den hohläugigen Hass als Bräutigam.*
> *Da musste ich den Grässlichen, der atmet*
> *wie eine Viper, über mich in mein*
> *schlafloses Bette lassen, der mich zwang,*
> *alles zu wissen, wie es zwischen Mann*
> *und Weib zugeht.*

In a sense, then, she has been deflowered by the ghost of her father as a vampire (an idea which occurs again in Hauptmann's conception of the ghost of Hamlet's father as a vampire). And Electra herself has turned into a vampire lusting for the blood of

the slayers of her father, on whom her mind and senses dwell with
the pitilessness of a Freudian complex. Thus, too, Wilde's Salome
turns vampire lusting for the blood of John the Baptist, who is
ice to her sexual flame. In *Elektra* as in *Salome* the paramour is
depraved and degenerate, man turned brute, while Herodias and
Clytemnestra, both animal women (Herodias with her love of big
men and Clytemnestra with her diseased liver and livid face with
the swollen eyelids over her scarlet gown), are haunted by the
fear of vengeance; and as in Wilde's play the moon turns red when
Salome dances so in *Elektra* the rays of the moon fall aslant on the
courtyard through the boughs of a fig-tree and cling like blood-
stains round the feet of Electra. Interesting are certain analogies
with the discredited fate-play: thus, though Aegisthus is not slain
with the axe that slew Agamemnon, Electra has hidden it for that
purpose in the ground, and Orestes, when he comes, finds her
digging out the 'fatal requisite' with her nails. *Ödipus und die Sphinx*
(1906) is by tradition the model of the fate-tragedy in the reputed
sense, but Hofmannsthal varies the Greek conception by giving
Ödipus foreknowledge of what is to happen. It *will* happen because
it is in the stream of his blood. His ancestors roll through his blood.
The oracle has said that he shall marry his mother – and he loves
the mother he knows; and therefore he will not return home. He
is haunted by the mother-complex as Electra is haunted by the
father-complex. The thrill with which the play ends is typically
decadent: Ödipus has overcome the sphinx, and descends the
mountain amid acclaims with Jokasta holding his hand in hers;
and the spectators know that they are passing on to incest. In *Das
gerettete Venedig* (1905), his modernization of Otway's *Venice Preserved* (a theme which tempted Schiller), Hofmannsthal improves
the motivation of his original by providing a more apparent justification for the treachery of the hero – who nevertheless remains
a spineless decadent – in the utter rottenness of Venice at the time
of the action, brought out by the introduction of such corrupt
characters as the old roué Senator Dolfin, as a type of the Venetian
signoria, and by bringing the secondary characters into prominence.
The motivation depends, however, on the surrender by Jaffeir of
his wife, as a pledge of his reliability, to the cut-throat conspirators,
and when one of them attempts to violate her he betrays the plot.
He has good reason to abandon his confederates – if he can; but
the very fact that he joins them proves his lack of judgment; while

the surrender of his wife, and his wife's acquiescence in the surrender, are incredible dramatic faults. There are, however, fine descriptive passages, coloured and sensuous, and even good dramatic moments. Moreover, Otway's blank verse is rendered into a loosely running metre which often gathers the tirades into long loops with the vital words flung where the breath pauses – a notable contrast to the controlled undulating flow of Hofmannsthal's usual dramatic measure.

With *Jedermann* (1912) Hofmannsthal began a revival of the medieval morality or mystery play. He had been preceded by another Viennese poet and scholar, Richard von Kralik (1852-1934; *Weihnachtsspiel*, 1893; *Osterspiel*, 1894-5), and he was followed by Max Mell, another Austrian. The success of these rejuvenations of an apparently extinct species was astonishing: Max Reinhardt's production of *Jedermann* before the portals of Salzburg Cathedral was a theatrical sensation, Vollmoeller's *Mirakel* (1911) was produced all over the world, Wilhelm von Scholz's *Das Herzwunder* (1918) was a great success, and one of Max Mell's religious playlets has been broadcast from London. The imitation in *Jedermann* of the metrical, syntactical, and glossarial form of Hans Sachs is an experiment which, though technically skilful, lacks the sap and freshness of Goethe's assimilation of the cobbler poet's style; in *Jedermann* the metrist's shaping fingers are always perceptible. The rendering of *Everyman* is pretty close, but certain elements of Hans Sachs's Protestant adaptation (*Komödie vom sterbenden reichen Manne*) are taken over. Thematically the handling is not happy: what the play unintentionally demonstrates is the comic idiocy of redemption by repentance. Catholic elements are specifically eliminated because the poet was eager to make the old play once more the 'living possession' of the German people: thus Confession fades out, and with her the doctrine of penance. But *Jedermann* is not anti-Catholic: indeed, the hero follows the silent figure of the monk who has been shadowing the background; the play rather represents the transition from the epicurean paganism of *Der Tor und der Tod* to the conventional Catholicism of *Das Salzburger Grosse Welttheater* (1922). Hofmannsthal's own drift to conversion is indicated in these three variations of the medieval Dance of Death: Claudio has no use for the crucifix which should bring down flame to the supplicant but remains icily cold to the tips of its bleeding ivory feet, and he follows Death with no hint of salvation, despite his repentance; Jedermann *is* saved by repentance; in *Das Salzburger Grosse Welttheater* the Beggar is called to glory while the Rich Man remains in utter darkness. *Das Salzburger Grosse Welttheater* is an adaptation of one of Calderon's *autos* – the Spanish development in the *siglo de oro* of the mystery play – which shows that all the world's a stage on which the characters play the parts allotted them by God: in Maeterlinckian terms they are puppets pulled by strings from the sky. Actually in the *auto* the parts are distributed to the actors by the author himself, clad in a star-spangled mantle and with his brow lit by triple rays: Hofmannsthal substitutes an angel. Both *auto* and adaptation rise from spectacle to drama when the Beggar protests against the part he is expected to play, but the divine argument – it might be argued that it transfigures Communism – prevails. There is a difference that whereas in the *auto* the actors are mimes in Hofmannsthal's play they are unborn souls (Maeterlinckian mysticism perhaps), with no sign of sex or age. Hofmannsthal had already turned to Calderon for his *Dame Kobold* (1919), an adaptation of one of his comedies (*La dama duende*). Much more important is *Der Turm* (1925), in which there is something of Calderon's mood – or rather of the neo-romantic conception of Calderon's mystic manner: the heir to the throne of Poland bears the name of Sigismund, the reigning king that of Basilius, and these names, with elements of situation and plot, are lifted from *La vida es sueño*, that famous play of Calderon's which has meant so much to German literature (the prince imprisoned from birth by a father who fears that disaster will come from him and escaping at maturity occurs again in Jakob Wassermann's *Caspar Hauser*). Sigismund has been put away because of a prophecy that he would set his foot on his father's neck; this prophecy is realized in the play, but what is dreamily conveyed is that Sigismund, reared in seclusion, is pure spirit, while the reigning king stands for those Jesuit practices and that hocus-pocus of church-ridden epileptic monarchy which the proletariat, led by a bull-necked adventurer with the eyes of a dog, demolish in the course of the vaporous action. The conclusion is that the state should be based on authority, but that this authority should be of the spirit; and thus Hofmannsthal's final political philosophy (matured by the chaos in Austria after the War) agrees approximately with that of the hierarchic state postulated by Stefan George. Sigismund, though the son of the king, has suffered the direst poverty and humiliation, and thus he is doubly entitled to be the leader of a proletarian revolution whose aim is the establishment of that order in the state which shall give the subjects of the state freedom to live their lives to the full. Olivier, the upstart leader, following his brute instincts, would have replaced tyranny by tyranny, while Sigismund's policy is to re-establish authority on the basis of spiritual values. Whether, of course, a Habsburg prince transfigured by adversity or a spiritualized Hohenzollern might, rather than some dog-eyed proletarian with the problematic education of Olivier, have given German poets and scholars peace and order to fulfil themselves in is pure speculation. But even as a vision of post-War conditions the play does not grip: what interest there is lies in the weary throw-back to the pseudo-Spanish manner – in creeping prose, however, not in singing trochees.

Hofmannsthal as a librettist is not quite so submerged by music as that other Viennese poet, Schikaneder, was by Mozart; but to the generality he is known only as purveyor to Richard Strauss. *Der Rosenkavalier* (1911) has the moral unwholesomeness of rococo libertinage; the other libretti – *Ariadne auf Naxos* (1912), *Die Frau ohne Schatten* (1920; a dramatization of the novel by the author); *Die ägyptische Helene* (1928); *Josephslegende* (1914; in collaboration with Graf Harry Kessler) – fulfil their purpose.

Hofmannsthal's comedies are experiments which fail because of their lack of clear-cut character-drawing. *Cristinas Heimreise* (1908) and its variant *Florindo* (1923) dramatize an early episode of Casanova's memoirs; what holds the reader is the Venetian mood. *Der Schwierige* (1921) almost belies this poet, who in his person and his moods is the very embodiment of Vienna, by having its scene in his native city. But it is post-war Vienna; and in this period of depression and frustration his moods were changing and his weary mind was turning churchwards. The critical hero is said to be critical self-portraiture. *Arabella* (1933) was his last attempt in this field.

As a prose writer Hofmannsthal has great distinction, but more as a suggestive and stimulating if not always convincing critic than as a writer of stories, into which he spins too much metaphysical speculation. *Die Frau ohne Schatten* (1919), in very fluid *Märchenstil* (sentences joined by comma after comma), has for its main theme the brutality of sex relations in childless marriages.

The *milieu* is mystically oriental, and the concatenation of opaque symbols and the ideology have a faint impress of Maeterlinck's *Blue Bird*: unborn children (here '*die Ungewünschten*') live in the cave of perfect beauty and morals, and to them alone is granted the vision of the divine. In true marriage the wife is not a tethered goat, nor the husband (in the act) 'something of panther and snake'. Sexual desire is symbolized as a demon with hypnotic power over the female. But woman has a spiritual virginity, and this is only well lost when spirit enters spirit; and thus the wife in the story who submits to her husband's contact is made woman by desire for a spirit being.[1] What the 'shadow' is is not very clear; it is, however, clear that the woman's shadow floats away when for the first time she is united in spiritually passionate love with her great hulk of a husband; and, therefore, to cast a shadow means to have a baby. In *Das Märchen der 672. Nacht* (1904) – the style of which points forward to Franz Kafka – we have again the theme of *Der Tor und der Tod* – the rich young aesthete who by his very riches is removed from the poignancy of life.

Hofmannsthal's *Erfundene Gespräche und Briefe* contain some of the most fascinating criticism of recent years. The essay *Über Charaktere im Roman und im Drama*, an imaginary conversation between Balzac and the German orientalist Hammer-Purgstall, puts in the mouth of the French novelist what is really a terrible description – notable in contrast with Thomas Mann's doctrine – of the artist as the stoker who, half-naked, grimed, and with blood-shot eyes, in the South Seas creeps for a short space on to the deck of the luxurious steamer, throws himself on a bundle of tow, casts a surreptitious glance at the first-class passengers, and plunges down into the hold again without having seen the lovely islands in the haze. And yet he is not wretched – his fate is in his work, which gives him everything down below. *Farben* is an interpretation in epistolary form of impressionism, with Van Gogh as pattern: the secret of impressionistic technique is to take *anything* (Rilke's '*unwählerisches Schauen*'), show its innermost life, its very nature, and to set this in high colours and in prominent grouping against a meaningless background; and such impressions of existence prove existence simply because by the very vividness of their colouring and contours they shock the spectator out of his dulled conscious-

---

[1] '*Er hat mich zur Frau gemacht, ohne mich zu berühren*' – the motif which occurs in *Elektra*.

ness of the existence of existence. These shreds of nature sweep us off our feet because they are the fixed expression of an intense emotional experience: just as, for instance, grotesquely poised boulders reveal the force of the tempest that flung them into the picture they are. And therefore we cannot appreciate art unless we realize the miracle of the feeling that produced it. *Unterhaltung über die Schriften von Gottfried Keller* reveals the Rembrandtesque chiaroscuro of the Swiss writer, and illuminates his abrupt transitions from the ridiculous to the pathetic. *Das Gespräch der Tänzerinnen*, in which a Greek dancer is fascinated by a sailor's yarn of life on a barbaric island, once more interprets a favourite theme of Hofmannsthal's: the intolerable limpness (*Dumpfheit*) of life: life *is* not save as vibrant emotion of the inner spirit, as on this sailor's uncharted island, where there is a religious purity even in passion. Life is not life unless it quivers with feeling, unless all animal functions have that spiritualization which is pure nature and is thus the expression of the divine. And this spiritualization of life is Hofmannsthal's mysticism. *Gespräch über Gedichte* interprets poems of Stefan George in *Das Jahr der Seele*, and from this starting-point proceeds to a subtle discourse on the nature of poetry.

Hofmannsthal's posthumous works are *Nachlese der Gedichte* (1934); *Dramatische Entwürfe aus dem Nachlass* (1936); *Loris. Die Prosa des jungen Hugo von Hofmannsthal* (1930; his first writings had been signed 'Loris'); *Die Berührung der Sphären. Reden und Aufsätze* (1931); and *Andreas oder die Vereinigten* (1932). *Andreas* is the fragment of a novel which was planned at the latest in 1911 and partly written 1912-13. Notes from 1917 and 1918 are added. The poet's reaction to post-War conditions prevented completion. It was to have been a sort of Austrian *Wilhelm Meister*, the record of a spiritual journey and the ripening of a soul. It depicts Venetian types in whose wickedness there is always something redeeming. Venetians are always masked, and thus are compact of dualism; whereas the Northerner is simple, and what he seems. Under the influence of this Venetian dualism Andreas finds his nature splitting into two halves, and he can only restore his double self to integration by fleeing from Venice – that is, from beauty and romance, which is the lure of life – to morality, to simplicity – which (perhaps) is happiness. (Flight from Venice – and beauty – we have again in Thomas Mann's *Tod in Venedig*.)

IX

THE NEO-ROMANTIC AND
AUSTRIAN DRAMATISTS

The Viennese poet RICHARD BEER-HOFMANN (1866-1945) stands with Hofmannsthal as the exponent of the decadent neo-romantic verse drama. He has the same soft lyric flow, and the same conception of drama as a registering of impressions on the passive sensitiveness of a bewildered dreamer. Schnitzler in his burlesque marionette play *Zum grossen Wurstl* made game of such dramas (including his own):

> *So viel will ich von mir verraten:*
> *Zu Stimmungen neig' ich, nicht zu Taten,*
> *Und sage statt weitern langen Berichts:*
> *Ich bin der Held des Stücks, sonst nichts.*

Moreover Beer-Hofmann, like Hofmannsthal, uncovers the springs of what action there is behind the richly figured language in primitive erotic urges, and he too has the naïve Maeterlinckian questioning of the nature and purpose of life. He won fame with *Der Graf von Charolais* (1904), adapted and lyricized from Massinger and Ford's *The Fatal Dowry*. [The Elizabethan imitations begin with Maeterlinck's *Annabella* (1895), an adaptation of Ford's *'Tis Pity She's a Whore*.] Graf von Charolais insists on going to prison to redeem the body of his father, which has been seized for debt (one of the creditors, the Jew Itzig, is a creditable imitation of Shylock); but the judge whose task it is to send him to prison saves him by giving him his own daughter with a rich dowry. Beer-Hofmann radically changes the character of this daughter: in the English play she is a lustful creature who inevitably drifts to adultery; in the Viennese play she is a decent and dainty little lady who is overcome, momentarily but fatally, by a sudden stir

228

in her blood when the tempter – whom she sees through and despises – presses his urge for her body with all the skill of practice. Beer-Hofmann's theme is obviously – and this it was which made the play a draw on the stage – that the most refined and decent woman is at given moments a bitch in heat. This revolting idea is over-stressed; and indeed there is no dramatic possibility of the delicate girl we have seen in Act III allowing herself to be taken, in Act IV, to the filthy inn which in Act I we have seen as the haunt of profligates and of old men with boys. What is good is the revelation of the distinguished old judge's state of mind (senile eroticism in a perverted form): he has married in old age, without love and to have a child who should cherish his declining years (hence, perhaps, the medical motivation of his daughter's weak character – like Baudelaire she is the child of senility); and he recoils in horror when his secretary suggests to him that even his daughter may need a husband, for she is (ghastly word!) a *'Weib'*. And therefore he finds her a husband who – since he would go to prison for a corpse – must be noble. In the hectic 5th Act, which has strong dramatic (if sensational) effects, Charolais forces the father to judge his own daughter, and she stabs herself. What drives her to death is not tragic guilt, but the cruel force behind existence: ' *"Es" trieb uns – treibt uns! "Es!" Nicht ich – nicht du!'* – Beer-Hofmann's second drama, *Jaákobs Traum* (1918), belongs to the not inconsiderable biblical literature[1] of the period; it was intended to be the *Vorspiel* of a monumental trilogy, *Die Historie von König David*, but the depressing conditions of the post-War period stayed the poet's always hesitant pen. His poem *Schlaflied für Mirjam* has been famous and anthologized since it first appeared in the 4th year of *Pan*; one fails to see, however, that there is anything in it except the wistful questioning of 'whence?' and 'whither?' and the heritage within us of our ancestors so familiar from Maeterlinck and Hofmannsthal.

ARTHUR SCHNITZLER (1862-1931) was born in Vienna, and lived there, as a practising physician and famous author, all his life. One

---

[1] The Christ-novels have a chronological scale of effectiveness: Peter Rosegger's *I.N.R.I.* (1905), Gustav Frenssen's *Hilligenlei* (1906), Gerhart Hauptmann's *Der Narr in Christo Emanuel Quint* (1910). When in Johannes Schlaf's tale *Jesus und Miriam* (1901) Mary Magdalene, dancing in a tavern, sees Jesus and falls in love with Him, the consciousness of His Messianic calling stirs in Him. Then there are notable poems of Rilke, Sudermann, Stefan Zweig's *Jeremias*, Thomas Mann's *Tales of Jacob*, Anton Wildgans' drama *Kain* (1920), Karl Wolfkehl's drama *Saul*. See also p. 256, *Der Heiland*.

might say of him at once that he would have been an adept in psycho-analysis if this had not been elaborated as a system by that other Viennese Jew, Sigmund Freud. Schnitzler attempted the naturalistic play with *Freiwild* (1896), which discusses the ethics and idiocy of duelling, and *Das Vermächtnis* (1898), on the theme of the unmarried mother; but for his other plays he turned his back on the proletariat, keeping only the working-class girl – *das süsse Madl* – as a toy for his men about town. He had already, with *Anatol* (1893), a cycle of seven one-act plays, found his natural manner. These psycho-grammatic playlets are something quite new. They tend to be novelettes in dialogue form – more or less the French *causerie* as cultivated by (e.g.) Paul Hervieu. But there is nothing French in the substance or mood of the plays: Schnitzler does, it is true, handle his characters with malice afore-thought as puppets – one cycle of playlets (*Marionetten*, 1906) indi-cates this by the title; but probably he owed nothing more than suggestion to Maeterlinck's *drames pour marionettes*. Schnitzler's characters are only marionettes in the sense that they are creatures of nerves and impulse ('*Stimmungen unterworfen*', like the novelist in *Literatur*); they have no will, the will that moves them is in the purpose of the universe, not in them. *Anatol* fixed Schnitzler's reputation from the start as a cynic of 'melancholy cheerfulness'. Anatol is the *viveur* of so many of Schnitzler's plays and tales, not (to misquote Dryden) cursedly confined to one, but lighting the extinguished torch (or rather spluttering candle) of one love in-stanter at the bosom of the next. Two men are constant to the seven playlets, Anatol and Max; the women change from play to play. Anatol dreamily sentimentalizes his lady of the moment: his *süsses Madl* will have '*die weiche Anmut eines Frühlingsabends*', '*den Geist, . . . der zu lieben weiss*', '*lächelnde, schalkhafte Wehmut*', the lifting grace of the Blue Danube waltz. Max faces his boon com-panion as the cynical *raisonneur* who disperses with a cold breath the cobwebs of love-borne fancy. Anatol is conscious of his elegant decadence: '*Ich fühle*,' he says, '*wie viel mir verloren ginge, wenn ich mich eines schönen Tages "stark" fände . . . Es gibt so viele Krankheiten und nur eine Gesundheit – – . Man muss immer genau so gesund sein wie die anderen – man kann aber ganz anders krank sein wie jeder andere.*' In other words, the interesting thing is the infinite variety, to a dissect-ing dramatist, of disease; and what we must expect in Schnitzler's work is dissection and illumination of phases of disease, of decay, physical and moral. Life is thus a fermenting swamp, and the haze above is the illusion of happiness or beauty, the dream over the hopeless reality. Another Viennese dramatist, Grillparzer, had represented life as a dream and dream as life; and so does Schnitzler. His leit-motif is that life is an actor's make-believe. That make-believe and life flow into each other is the idea of one of the most effective of his playlets, *Der grüne Kakadu* (1899): French aristocrats meet nightly in a low tavern to watch actors (a new sensation) making believe that they have committed atrocious crimes; on the night the Bastille is taken they still, with death at their throats, think the frightfulness is play-acting; here indeed the dream is life. There is the same interlacing of life and dream in *Paracelsus* (1897). The first of modern doctors returns to Basel and is brought home by the armourer Cyprian, who, being the more solid man, had years before been given the hand of Justina, whom they both loved. A noble youth, Anselm, has been making love to the buxom wife, but she has laughed at him. Paracelsus with his hypnotic power puts her in a trance, in which she dreams that she has given herself to Anselm. Anatol, promised that the secret life of his mistress should be revealed to him in a hypnotic trance, had declined the experience: he is content with illusion . . . Cyprian too has been living in illusion: it was when he was at the tavern, the dream says, that Justina had fallen; that is, he had neglected her in his belief that all her nature needed was home and (now and then) husband. She has not sinned; except in the dream . . . But is the life her husband, perfect *Bürger* as he is, asks her to live, the life of her soul? This sanative scrutiny of connubial neglect recurs throughout Schnitzler's work as an equal source of tragedy with that custom of the country the *Verhältnis*. *Paracelsus* ends with a kind of epilogue by the doctor who has, as the directing force above them, made these marionettes act:

> *Es war ein Spiel! Was sollt' es anders sein?*
> *Was ist nicht Spiel, das wir auf Erden treiben,*
> *Und schien es noch so gross und tief zu sein? . . .*
> *Mit Menschenseelen spiele ich. Ein Sinn*
> *Wird nur von dem gefunden, der ihn sucht.*
> *Es fliessen ineinander Traum und Wachen,*
> *Wahrheit und Lüge. Sicherheit ist nirgend.*
> *Wir wissen nichts von andern, nichts von uns;*
> *Wir spielen immer, wer es weiss, ist klug.*

Here, obviously, Paracelsus is speaking for the physician-dramatist. Life had been wistfully imaged in the prologue written by Hofmannsthal for *Anatol* (p. 212) as a weary play-acting with *halbes Empfinden*. Such low pressure of emotion implies *Heldenlosigkeit*; and indeed even the heroes of Schnitzler's Renaissance tragedies are creatures of mood. Only once, perhaps, in Schnitzler's work is this *halbes Empfinden* intensified to full tragic feeling: in *Liebelei* (1895); a youth has had a dangerous liaison with a married woman, has freed himself and attached himself to the usual *süsses Madl*, but is killed in a duel by the husband of his former mistress; the girl cannot at first realize that what she thought was love was *Liebelei*, and when she does she commits suicide. The ten dialogues of *Reigen* (1900) are necessarily indecent, because they are the demonstration of facile coition, such as any physician or court missionary could piece together from experience of human nature – which is literally, at its erotic rawest, as here presented. We go round a lively circle of clasped playlets: in the first street-girl and common soldier have their sordid moment, in the second this soldier and the housemaid, then housemaid and son of the house, and so on till in the tenth dialogue the circle meets with the street girl coupling with a count. Thus all classes and ages are linked by one common need. In *Literatur*, one of the three one-act plays of *Lebendige Stunden* (1902), Schnitzler comes nearest to the accepted idea of comedy: there is real fun in the gradual discovery by two lovers who have separated that each has embodied the love-letters of the other (copies having been kept of what each wrote as well as the replies) in novels actually in the press.

Schnitzler's full-size plays lack the formal perfection of his curtain-raisers, and rely mostly for their effect on the discussion of some social problem – that is, they are tendentious. *Der Schleier der Beatrice* (1899) is a full-fledged Renaissance tragedy: the crowded, complicated, and kaleidoscopic action passes in one short night, which is sufficient to fashion forth the rushed fierce joy of living of the *cinquecento* – '*das Leben ist die Fülle, nicht die Zeit*', runs the last line. In style and construction the play comes near to de Musset's *Lorenzaccio*; both plays have fullness without form. Cesare Borgia – a red demon lighting up the livid background – is expected to storm Bologna on the morning following the events, and the Duke has the idea of ending life with a splash by marrying a beautiful girl of the lowest class whom he has seen by chance in the street. A formal marriage might seem a waste of ceremony, but the girl makes this condition – she has dreamed that she was Duchess of Bologna, and she has related the course of this *Wunschtraum* to her lover, Filippo Loschi, a poet so lost in musings that he does not even remember his own poetry. He interprets the dream as a revelation of inner lubricity, calls her the soiled '*Dirne ihres Traums*', and sends her packing. She glides away from the marriage festival, in her long white veil, and goes to Filippo, who asks her to die with him. But she is afraid of death, and when he quaffs his cup of poison she goes back to the Duke, in her confusion leaving her veil behind her. The Duke will forgive her absence on one condition: that she takes him to the spot where she has left the veil. She does so, and is stabbed by her brother by the corpse of her lover. The play tells on the stage by its picture of Renaissance licentiousness; the orgy in the dark of night in the Duke's garden is like an exhibition, from a doctor's point of vision, of all erotic frenzy and perversion. The psychological problem is in the girl's attraction to and fear of death. In *Der einsame Weg* (1903) there is something of Ibsen's probing technique. The action which matters is unrolled in the past of twenty years before, when Fichtner had a liaison with the mother of Felix, who – a good boy – is shocked by the revelation that his real father is not the husband of his mother – who dies at the start of the play –, but this extinct painter, who claims possession of his son because he is pathetically old and lonely. But Felix denies his right to possession – he has procreated him, but not reared him; and to Felix the tragedy is in the cheating, by his mother and Fichtner, of his good if humdrum father. The theme runs parallel with that of Schnitzler's long novel *Der Weg ins Freie*: in both works the artist abandons the girl he loves for the sake of freedom in his art, and in both the freedom is illusory – the painter loses his productivity, while the composer in the novel is doomed to be an eternal dilettante. In play and novel Schnitzler exposes the biological and social effects of the *Verhältnis*. The most subtle of Schnitzler's plays, perhaps, is *Zwischenspiel* (1904). Amadeus, a musical conductor, has always been faithful to his wife Cäcilie, an opera singer, and she has been true to him through the boredom of family life; but now they feel that their marriage is loveless, and they agree to each other's freedom. The conductor goes away with a countess who has thrust herself upon him, and Cäcilie fulfils an engagement in Berlin with Sigismund, a former pupil of her husband, in attendance. Amadeus is soon finished with the Gräfin; his heart is in his work. But Cäcilie comes back one evening from Berlin, changed by her experience with Sigismund: she now wants 'adventures' and thrilling experience from life. Amadeus is horrified! She is not the woman he has lived with for seven years. She makes no confession; and he does not realize that although, as she cries out desperately, she is aching for love, her relations with Sigismund – who, though in love with her, is a gentleman – have been correct. In any case she has come back, lovely and excited and disputatious – at bedtime; and, though she resists, Amadeus seizes his marital rights. The morning after she is, as she tells her husband, really a changed woman. She has yielded to him, but only in the shock of the psychological moment: any other man might have taken her just then. In her own eyes she has been untrue to herself: after months of resistance to her lover she has been seized by her own husband; and she has been untrue to her husband because their contract of freedom has been overthrown by the surprise of passion. This reasoning is beyond the man's conception. He wishes to return to connubial possession; but Cäcilie *'ist eine andere geworden'*. He packs his things and goes away, taking his manuscripts with him; Cäcilie bows her head on her hands, and weeps gently. There is in this play – it probes deeper than *Paracelsus* – a penetrating contrast of the man's attitude to freedom from the marital bond and that of an emancipated and sensual but decent woman. If Amadeus' conception of love had been higher – and more sensual, certainly more Casanova-like – Cäcilie would have been true to him in the sense in which she conceives the word. Amadeus is not quite a Tesman – he is brilliant and a true artist –, but he has the Viennese conception of the casualness of love added to the German idea of connubial routine. Cäcilie on the contrary has all the physical and mental qualities of the passionate woman artist, but at the same time absolute respect for herself. And this clash of character produces the marital conflict. The ladies of Schnitzler's plays drew the solemn reminder from Vogt and Koch (in their *Literaturgeschichte*) that ancient German women had something holy and that even Goethe had some idea of non-animal decency in women; Cäcilie, one hopes, *has* something holy – but as a contemporary of Schnitzler, not of Tacitus. *Der junge Medardus* (1910), an historical drama of Vienna in 1809, has the crowded action of

Der Schleier der Beatrice. Professor Bernhardi (1912) has poignant interest today because of its discussion of the problem of the Jews in Vienna. A girl is dying of abortion in the clinic of which Bernhardi, a Jew, is the director. The girl is in a state of euphoria; she is having perhaps the happiest moments of her life, dreaming that she is getting better and that the lover who is responsible will soon be coming for her. A pious nurse, without instructions to do so, sends for a priest to administer the Last Sacrament, but Bernhardi, knowing that as soon as the patient sees the priest she will know she is dying, refuses to let him pass. This Jewish procedure (actually a Christian doctor might have done the same) gives rise to a great scandal in clerical Vienna, and Bernhardi is sent to prison for contempt of the State and religion. The play is as tendentious as a play can well be; and the interest lies in the clash of argument, the caricature of politicians, and in the depressing picture of Austrian obscurantism and anti-Semitism. *Die Schwestern oder Casanova in Spa* (1919) is a good example of Schnitzler's lighter manner. Casanova slips away from the card-table to climb to the bedchamber of a young wife who has given him the glad eye: in the dark he jumps through the wrong window, but the wife who happens to be there yields to the moment and to him. The problem – ironically treated – now is: which female is wronged, the one who was waiting, or the one who was not? The two women, meeting the morning after, fly at each other; but all ends well, for Casanova hath charms . . . Seriously treated for the space of a scene is the problem which provides the action for Beer-Hofmann's *Der Graf von Charolais*: the wife who yielded to the urge of the moment argues with her husband, the morning after, that nothing has happened: she woke up, she says, feeling just the same as she did the morning before. She assures her husband that she is still his, because the man who took her is a casual stranger favoured by the moment; this moment, she swears, will never return; to which the husband replies that she will always bear the smell of it in her hair. The conflict is between medical fact – which in this respect sees no difference between a woman and a rabbit – and the husband's natural obsession that any other man contaminates the object.

In Schnitzler's tales and novels there is the same sparkle of wit, the same delicate rendering of nuance, that we find in the plays; but the filling in of the narration makes them less perfect and

life-like. His most poignant Novelle is *Sterben* (1895): a young
man hears from his doctor that within a year he will be dead of
consumption; his mistress refuses to leave him, and she nurses
him through the dreadful illness in a lovely region of a southern
coast. As death approaches the young man is tortured by the idea
of leaving her behind, and tries to take her with him by murdering
her, but the attempt brings on an attack of haemorrhage, which
causes his death. The girl has been faithful to the end, but the
death of her love has kept pace with the dying of her lover. There
is a haunting melancholy in the tale: how sweet life is, with love;
how terrible is death when love must be left; and how weary is
life when love dies. One of the short tales, *Leutnant Gustl* (1901),
is the long monologue of an officer who is about to commit
suicide because he has been insulted by a vulgar civilian who is
not *satisfaktionsfähig*; it is very much like the 'waves-of-consciousness tales' of these later days. The genre is not quite new: there is
the idea of it in Richard von Meerheimb's (1825-96) '*Psycho-
dramen*' (*Psychodramenwelt*, 1887). *Fräulein Else* (1925) is another such
monologue; it is spoken by a Viennese girl of nineteen, in a holiday
resort where she is staying. News comes from home that her father
is on the verge of fraudulent bankruptcy. There is a chance of
saving him – if she agrees to the conditions of a financial magnate
at the hotel to whom she appeals for help: he must see her naked
in the star-lit forest. 'If one man sees me,' she says, 'others shall
see me.' Naked under her mantle she comes down into the hall,
shows herself, faints, is taken to her room, takes veronal, dies.
The resemblance to Maeterlinck's *Monna Vanna* cannot be missed.
The Novelle *Casanovas Heimfahrt* (1918) is a picture of the legendary lover in the decay of old age, still lustful but on the verge of
impotence. As in *Die Schwestern* Casanova finds his way into a
lady's room and pretends to be her lover; but when she looks at
him in the morning he shows that night's efforts furrowed deep
into his yellow face; and what he reads in her eyes is not, as it
used to be, 'rascal!', but 'old man!' If to women he is an old man,
to himself he is dead. The short novel *Frau Berta Garlan* (1901)
has the shuttle-like to-and-fro of fevered thinking of the two
monologues. It is the story of a handsome woman with the artistic
temperament who, after three years of widowhood, in the vigour
of her thirties, dreams herself into an infatuation for a musician,
now famous, with whom she had innocently flirted when they

were students together at the *conservatoire*, and she is hunted by
the titillation of her senses into his arms; but to him she is just a
woman who calls and is done with. '*Verlangende Weiblichkeit*', she
discovers, is an illusion. *Der Weg ins Freie* (1908), Schnitzler's
longest novel, is his weakest work. Apart from the reasoned rejection of the *Verhältnis* there is endless discussion of the Viennese
Jew problem, and a crowded canvas of not very edifying Jews.
Therese (1928), the 'chronicle of a woman's life', is a sordid and
dreary novel. Therese, the daughter of an insane officer in Salzburg, is cast off by a doctor and a lieutenant, and has to earn her
living in Vienna as a servant. She has a series of love affairs, and
she dies when her illegitimate son, for whom she has worn herself
to the bone – he is a thief and *Zuhälter* by trade – gags her while
he breaks her box open.

To the school of Schnitzler belong FELIX SALTEN (1869-1945)
and RAOUL AUERNHEIMER (1876-1947). Salten, born in Budapest
but resident in Vienna, wrote one-act plays in Schnitzler's manner
(*Vom anderen Ufer*, 1907); Auernheimer, in addition to comedies
(*Die grosse Leidenschaft*, 1904), wrote such short stories as *Casanova
in Wien*, in which the hero, staying with his Philistine brother in
Vienna, at a time when Maria Theresa was forcing the Viennese
to be good, is tempted to be good too, but is saved from this fate
by an order of expulsion.

The once almost hectic reputation of two of the neo-romantic
poets, Gustav Vollmoeller and Ernst Hardt, has faded rapidly.
Time was when Vollmoeller dazzled London and Ernst Hardt
was devoured like chocolates. VOLLMOELLER (1878-1948) began
with Georgean verse (*Parcival: Die frühen Gärten*, 1903) and made his
reputation with the revenge drama *Catharina, Gräfin von Armagnac*
(1903). This play, in highly decorative verse with prose passages,
provided a macabre thrill: the lady's husband comes into the room
with the head of her poet lover and stands it on the mantelpiece.
He leaves it there, and Catharina addresses it in melting verse,
kisses the bloody chops, recalls their hours of dalliance, and then
jumps out of the window with it into the river. For Max Reinhardt
Vollmoeller wrote wordless plays: *Mirakel* (1911), and *Venezia-
nische Abenteuer* (1912), the former a symbolic handling of the
legend (familiar from Gottfried Keller's tale, John Davidson's
ballad, and Maeterlinck's play *Sœur Béatrice*) of the runaway nun
whose place as doorkeeper of the convent is taken by the Virgin

till she returns, a penitent. Vollmoeller's flippant adaptation of Gozzi's *Turandot* (1911), with the three riddles obscenely transmuted, was produced, in Max Reinhardt's gorgeous Berlin setting, by Sir George Alexander in London. – ERNST HARDT (1876-1947), after World War I director of the National Theatre in Weimar, also began with Georgean verse (*Aus den Tagen des Knaben*, 1904), but went over to drama. His *Tantris der Narr* (1908) owed its success to the macabre thrill taken over from the more primitive form of the legend: King Mark delivers Isolde naked to the lepers. *Gudrun* (1911) also provided a shock: the heroine loves, not the betrothed from whom she is snatched, but the more dashing warrior who abducts her; this reading of her mind can as a matter of fact be read between the lines of the old epic. *Schirin und Gertraude* (1913) is a travesty of the medieval legend of *der Graf von Gleichen*, the crusader who is permitted by the Pope to have two wives, the Saracen woman who freed him from captivity and the one he had left at home (see pp. 27, 270).

The robustiousness and reek of mother earth that are lacking in the work of the Viennese aesthetic dramatists give a racy flavour to the dramas of KARL SCHÖNHERR (1869-1943), the full-blooded continuator of Anzengruber. Whereas Anzengruber was a man from Vienna who recorded the ways of Tyrolese peasants as an outsider, Schönherr was born and reared out at Axams in the Tyrol, though he settled as a practising doctor in Vienna. He finds his dialect-speaking characters in the same mountain villages that are Anzengruber's world, and he, too, mixes old-world sentimentality and ruthless reality. In his first plays there is more of sentiment; in *Sonnwendtag* (1902), as in Sudermann's *Johannisfeuer*, an old pagan festival with its pagan spirit clashes with religious narrowness of faith; there is an anti-Catholic ending, with the image of the Virgin, whom the action proves to be impotent to save, symbolically abandoned in the home that must be left behind. *Familie* (1905) attempts strict psychological depiction, and *Das Königreich* (1908) is another experiment, this time in the romantic *Märchendrama*, with a contrast of the two worlds of aristocratic luxury and innocence in poverty: the devil disguised as a courtier tempts and destroys the children of the court fool. With *Erde* (1908) Schönherr revealed his full powers; the comedy is grim indeed in its black lines as of an old woodcut. The tenseness of the action and (for a German audience) the involved humour depend on the

peasant custom that the father is lord of the house till the eldest
son marries; to him the father must then relinquish his rights. In
Erde the son cannot marry till the father dies; at the beginning
of the play hope dawns that he may soon be gathered unto his
fathers, for he is kicked by a horse, orders his grave, has his coffin
made; and while he is bed-ridden the son makes a cradle and (the
housekeeper anticipating the joys of possession) the baby for it;
but the old peasant is indestructible: he rises from bed and hacks
the coffin to pieces. He has touched the earth he loves and is renewed. In *Glaube und Heimat* (1910) there is warm feeling; the
period is that of the Counter-Reformation; the order has come
that Protestants are to be driven out of the country, and Tyrolese
peasants die clinging to Luther's Bible. The idea which animates
the play is that of reconciliation between the two creeds – that
tolerance the sweet reasonableness of which Anzengruber had
shown in *Der Pfarrer von Kirchfeld* and which Schönherr found –
whether or no there was anything in the charge of plagiarism –
in Enrica von Handel-Mazzetti's Styrian novel *Jesse und Maria*. In
Der Weibsteufel (1914) there is insight into the inner nature of
woman as penetrating as that of Schnitzler, but with the Strindbergian valuation of female domination by means of sex. There
are only three characters, labelled in the way the expressionists
were to adopt, *Der Mann – sein Weib – Ein junger Grenzjäger*. The
husband is a physical wreck, unable to work, but with the cunning
to enrich himself by acting as receiver to smugglers. His young
wife, vigorous but with her senses dormant, mothers her invalid,
until he sets her to beguile the young customs officer who is on
the point of discovering where the contraband goes to. But she
plays with fire; and the flames burn high, both in her and the
Grenzwächter. She sees her chance of getting rid of both men;
she goads the customs man into murdering her husband, and over
the dead body, she cries exultingly: '*Ihr Mannsteufel, euch ist man
noch über.*' She knows she will inherit her husband's ill-gotten
wealth; and with that she can have any man she wants. A woman-
devil can beat a man devil. Schönherr's medical experience is turned
to account in *Es* (1923), of which the only characters are '*der Arzt*'
and '*die Frau*', and in *Der Armendoktor* (1925) and *Chirurgenspiel*
which show up the farce life is.

Hofmannsthal's revival of the medieval mystery play proved
the making of another Austrian poet, MAX MELL (1882-). Born

at Marburg an der Drau in Styria he grew up in Vienna. He began with Novellen: *Lateinische Erzählungen* (1904), *Die Grazien des Traums* (1906), *Jägersage und andere Novellen* (1910). His best short stories he selected for the collections *Das Donauweibchen* (1938) and *Verheissungen* (1954). The most famous of these *Bauernnovellen* is *Barbara Naderers Viehstand* (1914), the tale of a robust wench who is a spinster because she had turned up her nose at those who would have had her; now she runs her own little farm in the Styrian uplands and steals a calf which belongs to a Protestant gentleman. She rears it till it is itself ready to breed, and there are drastically realistic stories of its affairs with two different bulls. In a time of great shortage of fodder she returns from a foraging expedition to find all her cattle dead. This tragic end was inevitable, we are told as the story closes: '*Beicht ablegen hätt ich gehn sollen*', she tells herself, '*dann lebeten s' noch*'. Mell's Catholicism, as here, is orthodox to the last degree, and thus he differs from Rosegger, who remains the unsurpassed laureate of Styrian peasant tales; indeed the whole purpose of Mell's story-writing seems to aim at showing that salvation for the individual and country is unquestioning belief in what the priest says. This is expressly stated in *Waldheimat*, one of the tales in *Steirischer Lobgesang* (1939). The tone and temper of Mell's mystery plays is foreshadowed in his verse tale (in four-feet rhymed trochees) *Die Osterfeier* (1921) and take shape in *Das Wiener Kripperl von 1919* (1921), which is inspired by the post-war return to religion. Crude realism runs through *Die Osterfeier*; but what counts is – as Hofmannsthal pointed out in words of high praise – the ingenious invention of the interlocking action, the presentation of Catholic symbol as poetry that acts magically on simple minds, and the delicate delineation of mental states. His masterpiece is *Das Apostelspiel* (1922), at once a mystery play and a peasant drama (*Bauernspiel*); that is, one with primitive peasants for players in a rough village location. The scene is a lonely hut in the mountains in the depth of winter; no one is there but a young girl; two robbers break in; she takes them to be the apostles John and Peter, questions them about obscure passages in the gospels, and so confuses them that they slip out into the dark night with a ray of light in their awakened souls. *Das Schutzengelspiel* (1923) is more fanciful: a girl is so proud of her piety that her guardian angel orders her to stand at the church door saying *Heirate mich!* to those that pass; this trial withstood she is forgiven and admitted to the 'life-order of women' – they who bear any fate when the eyes of a child fall upon them – by a sister she had before despised as the mother of illegitimate children. In *Das Nachfolge-Christi-Spiel* (1927) a Styrian nobleman, in the days of the Turkish wars, is nailed to a cross by a band of marauders and is so moved by his 'imitation of Christ' that he prays for his tormentors, and thus converts them. With *Die Sieben gegen Theben* (1932) Mell turns to blank verse to blend the *Seven against Thebes* of Aeschylus with the *Antigone* of Sophocles; this play was overpraised as a counterblast to the Freudian defacement of ancient Greek plays by Hofmannsthal. *Das Spiel von den deutschen Ahnen* (1935), though the happy ending is still brought about by a miracle – the ancestors of a farmer return, after 180 years in the grave, to save a farmer whose wife hankers after the evil life of towns – is intermediary between the mystery plays proper and those in which there is a more classic conflict of human passions. Mell at last makes a bold bid for the laurels of the classic dramatist with *Der Nibelunge Not* (1942), in rough-hewn verse of four beats to the line. Of this the first part was produced during the war, and was proclaimed as a Teutonic epic drama worthy of the heroic spirit of the day. The second part, *Kriemhilds Rache* (1951), is generally admitted to fall off because the spirit of it has something of the preaching quality of the peasant moralities, which are, in sober truth, Mell's province by right of conquest. As a lyric poet he sings the revolving seasons of Styria in *Das bekränzte Jahr* (1911) and joy in earth in *Gedichte* (1919). *Gedichte* (1928) is a selection.

X

COSMIC IMPRESSIONISTS
AND EPIC INFINITIES

In the occult verse of Stefan George the mist is woven into the words; in that of ALFRED MOMBERT (1872-1942) it lies clinging over them, but shifting to reveal strange glimpses of the *Urwelt* or chaos, of planets rising half-formed from blind seas, with a spirit-being ('the sea-gull shoots freely through his body') ranging through the seething clouds: the poet-creator, or God, with *logos* nesting in his hair. At a cursory glance at this weltering vapour the wary reader may well say: *blauer Dunst* pure and simple, but with Mombert familiarity breeds a distant, if not effortless, comprehension. The terror is in the ideas, not in the language; this is of the simplest: it is even very often like the babbling of a child. Nor is there intricacy of rhythm or even the melody of rapt music: it is all rather prose poetry lifting here and there into ghost-like incantation. The early poems of *Tag und Nacht* (1894) have the lure of simplicity; the later verse (*Der Glühende*, 1896; *Die Schöpfung*, 1897; *Der Denker*, 1901; *Die Blüte des Chaos*, 1905; *Ataïr*, 1925; the two dramas *Aiglas Herabkunft*, 1929, and *Aiglas Tempel*, 1931) can only be (like Einstein) an acquired taste. *Der Held der Erde* (1919) is a mythically transfigured vision of the First Great War. 'Symphonic dramas' is the name he gives to the trilogy *Aeon, der Weltgesuchte* (1907), *Aeon, zwischen den Frauen* (1910), and *Aeon vor Syrakus* (1911); Aeon is the genius of humanity wedded at Syracuse, in the face of the teeming east and at the cradle of the seafaring nations, to Semiramis, the mother of peoples. Here all is symbol: thus Aeon is 'between two women' as in temporal dramas, but of these women one is Chaos and the other Form, or Gothic art (unformed and therefore to-be-shaped) and Greek art (formed and perfect). The poet's aim, at which he toiled for fifty years, was to present an entirely new mythical cosmology which should provide humanity, emancipated from the swathing folds of religions outworn, with a new doctrine in lyrically tensile sung rhythms. The salient feature is that 'the singer' with his ever changing names is always Mombert; thus the Aeon of the dramas is the Sfaira of the two final rhapsodies (or – since we have *Gesang* and *Gegensang* – symphonies): *Sfaira der Alte* (1936) is the last work published in Germany, while *Sfaira der Alte, Zweiter Teil* was published at Winterthur by the poet's Swiss friend who had ransomed him from a vile concentration camp in the south of France to care for him for the few months of life that remained to him. This second part had been partially written in the concentration camp and was completed at Winterthur. Into it he had woven, while still keeping the mood and music of his *'unnahbare Sage'*, the moving story of his arrest in 1940 in his Heidelberg home and of his *Abtransport*: into the hall of books steps *'Strammer, ein feister Fang-Dämon, | dröhnender Schritt – : er tritt heran, | aus der Gurgel vorstrudelt ihm blechern Gerassel, | flüstert's herab in Sfairas linkes Ohr: | "Wirst noch heute der Halle entschreiten – | werden den Sfaira geleiten | aus dem Bücher-Saal in Dämon-Weiten".'* The quintessence of Mombert is offered by himself in *Der himmlische Zecher* (1909; selections from four books) and the enlarged version published 1952, completed by the poet just before World War II from seven books. One should have the imagination with which Francis Thompson credits Shelley to run wild over the fields of ether with Alfred Mombert, to tumble about in the reek of chaos, with one's head between the lances of the lightning, and to see the butterfly moon, diamond-green, floating over the skies. But even the too wary reader might pick out broken fancies from the litter of Mombert's creation, and take a joy in their uncanny evocations. Today there is a new conception of Mombert as a man: the impression created by his verse had been that he was a monkish recluse. But in his early lyrics a sensual note now and then pierces through; and in a recent book, *Alfred Mombert. Briefe an Richard und Ida Dehmel* (1956) we find him as a successful barrister and later as a man of means travelling far and wide, and as a trenchant critic of the poetry of his day, including that of his best friend Dehmel. The letters to Frau Isi (p. 117), which reach from 1897 to 1942, ring with the ardour of a passionate love. With the help of this correspondence the personal (and one may say human) touches in Mombert's verse can be detected;

traces of his adoration of Isi run through even his cosmic myths; and it forms the pith and marrow of one book: *Die Schöpfung*.

To go from Mombert to CARL SPITTELER (1845-1924) is like an escape to mountain heights, particularly if we begin with his chief work, *Olympischer Frühling* (1900-10), an epic in bumping alexandrines, into which ancient mythology is thrown as into a melting-pot to be created anew both as a vision of ideal Switzerland, snowy Alps and radiant pastures, and as an expression of the endless struggle with evil of mind and morality lured to unscalable heights by beauty. For his first philosophical epic, *Epimethus und Prometheus* (1881), Spitteler had devised a startling Whitmanesque style (ostensibly prose but lyrically tensile) which had so much in common with that of Nietzsche's *Also sprach Zarathustra* that it was taken to be an imitation of it, especially as both works agree in their cult of the strong personality. As a matter of fact, it had been published two years before Nietzsche's string of charmed aphorisms, and it has been suggested that Nietzsche, who at all events referred to Spitteler as 'the finest aesthetic writer of his day', may have been the borrower, both as regards biblical style and ideas. Spitteler's *Literarische Gleichnisse* (1892) and *Balladen* (1896) are parables and allegories; his more specifically lyrical poems are in *Schmetterlinge* (1889) and *Glockenlieder* (1906); the quaintness of their symbolism (e.g. the Duke of Bells goes out to meet the King of Noon and spreads at his feet a carpet of undulating melody) fits the Swiss hardness of the verse. The Novelle *Conrad der Leutnant* (1898) embodies Spitteler's contribution to the problem of realism in fiction and belongs, though written in detachment from the school, to the history of naturalism. His other 'novel' (it is more in the nature of a running disquisition with the thread of a story) *Imago* (1906) is in the line of fantastic satire represented by F. T. Vischer's 'novel' *Auch Einer* (1878). The hero is Victor, a Swiss poet with no pecuniary present and with a future merged in mist. At a mountain resort he has met a Swiss girl, and when they part he, like an old Minnesinger, worships her image, which he christens 'Imago'. But she marries a prosperous scholar, and thenceforward she is for him not Theuda but Pseuda, an idol desecrated. She is damned to the stupidities of family life and the inanities of social intercourse (*'die Hölle der Gemütlichkeit'*). She is like precious china put to use at the breakfast-table. But Imago still remains, and Victor floats about the social orbit of the false one, 'like a harpooned whale'. In intent the tale satirizes (drastically!) Swiss polite society and cultural clubs (Pseuda is president of Idealia), and Spitteler romps over the remembered bitternesses of his early journalistic struggles when, after he had thrown off his parson's cassock and returned from a spell of tutoring in Russia, he wrote as Felix Tandem. This combative tone had already run riot in his volume of critical essays *Lachende Wahrheiten* (1898).

MAX(IMILIAN) DAUTHENDEY (1867-1918) as a boy at Würzburg reminds one of Ferdinand Freiligrath, Germany's classic of exotic poetry, who sat on a clerk's stool at Amsterdam dreaming of yellow African sands and lithe lions gliding to reeded lagoons to pounce on gazelle and giraffe; but before Dauthendey could begin to realize his dreams of the far away he had to serve seven years in the photographer's business of his father. His novel *Rauh-menschen* secured him his freedom, and the rest of his life was spent in travel the world over until he died at Java, where he had been interned, in 1918, shortly before the end of the War (his letters to his wife had been detained by the British censor but, when released, were published in 1930 as *Mich ruft dein Bild*). He contributed to the first *Folge* of *Blätter für die Kunst* poems which already have that reading of soul into colours (*Verseelung der Farben*) which is his special mark. He wrote the poems of his first volume of verse, *Ultra Violett*[1] (1893), on the Swedish coast, ignorant of the language of the country, in isolation which Rilke might have envied; and in this solitude, he says, '*Farben sangen und das Schweigen der schwarzen Wälder wurde tönende Wonnen.* . . . ' His intense sensitiveness to impressions of nature – in the 'stiff light' and 'steel-blue silence' of the landscape – explains the extravagant *mélange des genres* of his early verse: he makes perfumes and colours sing and sigh and lisp and winds burn. This experimental synaesthesia makes Dauthendey the most technically impressionist of his contemporaries: as a trick rider he may ride his horse to death but in the history of literature he does as a colourist make a record. There is sometimes a magic of mood in his grouping of '*satte Farben*':

> *Weinrot brennen Gewitterwinde,*
> *purpurblau der Seerand.*
> *Hyazinthentief die ferne Küste.*

[1] The title is a reminiscence of X-rays, which were discovered at his native Würzburg.

17

Ein Regenbogen, veilchenschwül,
schmilzt durch weihrauchblaue Abendwolken.

Im Taudunkel lacht
eine heisse Nachtigall.

This *'pointillierender Kolorismus'*, which is influenced by the paintings of the Munich Sezession as well as by the bright blue of sky
and sea by the Swedish *skjaers*, continues, though more discreetly
toned, in the verse of *Reliquien* (1899); and here to the play with
colour is added an intimate note of personal love experience.
Very sweet (as a lady might say) is:

Am süssen lila Kleefeld vorbei,
zu den Tannen, den zwei,
mit der Bank inmitten,
dort zieht wie ein weicher Flötenlaut
der sanfte Fjord,
blau im Schilfgrün ausgeschnitten.

Gib mir die Hand.
Die beiden Tannen stehen so still,
ich will dir sagen,
was die Stille rings verschweigen will.
Gib mir die Hand . . .
Gib mir in deiner Hand dein Herz.

Ausgewählte Gedichte aus neun Büchern contains the best of Dauthendey's lyric work (*Gesammelte Gedichte*, 1931); the separate volume
Die geflügelte Erde (1910), a description of his voyage round the
world, has metrical interest by reason of its Whitmanesque bulge
and billow of line, while *Bänkelsang vom Balzer auf der Balz* (1905)
gives us quite a different Dauthendey, a humorist in the black
woodcut manner of Hans Sachs and Wilhelm Busch. His verse
myths fail for lack of hardness and are readable only for their
pictorial qualities; the moors of the Isefjord in Iceland form the
background of *Die schwarze Sonne* (1897); *Phallus* (1897) fantastically symbolizes the erotic relations of man and woman – the last
daughters of men adorn themselves behind a glacier wall which
reveals barbarous sexual urges in the bogged deeps of modern
consciousness.

Dauthendey's first novel, *Josa Gerth* (1892), takes place apart in his work as being entirely psychological and having a German setting. The heroine, a highly gifted girl, comes in her growing years, unsatisfied and hysterically seeking, in the very exuberance of her girlish ripeness *manntoll*, to the gradual perception that the most ideal man is beast by impulse; she marries a clergyman, and, after her first night of physical disgust, is estranged by her conviction that atheism is a riper stage of religion; when her husband forbids her to publish the book she has written to prove this thesis, she leaves him, but returns to him when a consumptive botanist – a portrait of J. P. Jacobsen! – to whom she turns, unselfishly refuses to live with her. Having married the Swedish love of his lyrics Dauthendey took her to Mexico in 1897, intending to settle as a farmer; but what the experience brought him was his strange blend of novel and travel description, *Raubmenschen* (1911). The title relates to the ostensible theme: 'the world is all rapine (*eine Raubwelt*) and a man has to take from others even the woman he loves'. The real interest is in the poetic re-creation of Mexico: *tierra caliente*, Aztec ruins, and a curse over the land. Dauthendey's colour obsession appears even in such a casual observation as that of three red tomatoes, like red-hot coals, on a piece of blue linen print in front of a tawny Indian woman. The volcanic landscape broods over the hero's senses like a nightmare, and his timorous sympathy for the descendants of the Aztecs with their demonic ways puts the book in the front rank of the Mexican exotism of the period. The sensationalism which mars *Raubmenschen* fails to grip, too, in the poet's two collections of Oriental short stories, *Lingam* (1910) and *Die acht Gesichter am Biwasee* (1911). In *Lingam* the base of the narration is stark reality, fantastic only because it is literally Oriental, and (in intention) physiologically real because the strange happenings grouped as 'lingam' – the Indian symbol of sexual union – represent naïve Oriental phases of the truth that love is life. The tales range eastwards from India by way of Ceylon and Singapore to China and Japan, and the moods and colouring shift from country to country. What weakness there is – and it lies in a too naïve wonderment at exotic phases and a too physical interpretation of states of mind – can be best gathered by comparing the Chinese tale *Im Mandarinenklub* with Klabund's *Der letzte Kaiser*: in the background of both the boy Emperor dies in the sinister shadow of the Dowager Empress; but while Dauthendey's sketch is merely curious that of Klabund is both a fragile re-creation of the willow-pattern conception of China and at the same time a deeply suggestive symbolization of its effacement by Bolshevist ideas from the barbaric West, the dissipation of the delicate webs of dream by alien and brute thought. In *Die acht Gesichter am Biwasee* there is not the faint distortion or mockery of the typical *chinoiserie*; all is flower-like and *märchenhaft*, miniature but intense. One might be tempted to class the tales as *japoniaiseries*; for, after all, there must be crude reality even in Japan; and (e.g.) Dauthendey's idealization of the Yoshiwara or hive of geishas' love-booths bears the same relation to the night-life in Tokio as the barcarolle tune does to the green grease of Venetian canals. Nevertheless these dream-visions of Japanese life, with their sleepy incoherence and softly gliding rhythm, do at least give the delight that legend gives. The tale which closes the collection shows the author's hand; by exposing the conflict that must necessarily arise when a German woman marries a Japanese he makes it clear that the tales are studies of the physiological functions of love in Japan, set off against landscape and custom, with (apparently) the moral that the Japanese marriage, in which the woman loses herself in her lord, is the ideal marriage. The stories of *Geschichten aus den vier Winden* (1915) handle for the most part strange problems of European psychology in the conflicts of love, the relation of the soul to the shadow it casts, the illusory beauty of reflection set against the plain solidity of reality, the revelation by dream-vision of fleshly passions as unclean antediluvian beasts; the insistent main theme is that of the caged soul, tortured, dying, or escaping in fantastic dreams or music. Only one tale of this collection – *Himalayafinsternis* – is Oriental; it is notable for its ghostlike rendering of the district round Darjeeling, and for its symbolization of the sexual process by the doubling of a tiny Tibetan amulet – a female affixed in climbing posture to her man – with Everest and Kanchenjunga, gigantic figures draped in problematic mists which, as they shift, reveal snowy breast and clasping arm rose-hued in the first flush of dawn.

The most sky-wrapt and astronomical of the cosmic impressionists is THEODOR DÄUBLER (1876-1934). As a native of Trieste he was as familiar with Italian as with German; hence the Italian colouring in his work (according to Kasimir Edschmid it has the silvery shading of the Dalmatian coast). He has sketched his autobiography in *Wir wollen nicht verweilen* (1915). In the prose introduction to *Das Nordlicht* (1910; the second edition, 'die Genfer Ausgabe', 1921, is revised) he explains the genesis and meaning of his astral system. Sun is father, earth mother, moon hermaphrodite but tending to female. Sun and earth were once joined, and the earth is still striving to get back to the sun ('*Die Erde braust dem Sonnenlicht entgegen,* | *Als flöge sie in des Geliebten Arm*'). This is indeed the secret of life: everything that lives, plant and animal, has its flight to the sun (*Sonnenflug*), so that existence is synonymous with return to the sun. In other words sun is God. But all this, it transpires, is an inner process: and here we get to the roots of Däubler's mysticism; for literally he is in the line of the great mystics, although, since his medium of revelation is poetry, his system has no clear lines and is mingled with much of the dross of earth. Sun and earth, then, are within us. And just as at the pole the sun released by the earth and the sun of heaven embrace and produce the *aurora borealis*, so within us mystic irradiation meeting God brings a mystic play of glory. And thus the task of man is to achieve the future of the earth by means of the *aurora borealis*. Earth will again be luminous; but the nations must see to it that this star of ours shall one day be the brightest of all, and that will be when forth from man shines that sun which is Primeval Being (*Ursonne*). From this (more or less naïve) mysticism Däubler builds up his cosmogony, which is often an orgy of sensuous images: thus prolific and glowing India is the earth's tribute or sacrifice to the sun. And so Däubler storms across the face of the universe, weaving dream-pictures of clime and landscape. How many devoted dreamers will follow him through his vasty epic? Picking up the three volumes and 30,000 lines of the work one is apt to feel – as is the case with Klopstock's *Messias* and Spitteler's *Olympischer Frühling* – as a hen is said to feel when it is placed with its head facing a chalk line – hypnotized at the start of infinity. If, however, one frees oneself from the inhibitory spell and strides onward there will be sudden thrills: evening at Venice (*Auf des Tages Abendschleppe* | *Streut der Mond sein Lichtgeschmeid.* | *Über ferner Alpentreppe* | *Funkelt noch das Purpurkleid*); or some symbolic vision (*Florenz, am Himmel stehen weisse Lilien* | *Und strömen Pollengold zu Gott empor,* | *Auch schlingen Bäche sich wie Lichtreptilien* | *Durch manches burggekrönte Felsentor*); or that gruesome sonnet (known to anthologies) of tangled ivy climbing to the marble balcony of the

Gothic palace, shadowy as a spy intent on vengeance, growing as it gropes, and with a woman pale and rigid at the window-pane while the moon peeps round a high corner. In the prose visions of *Mit silberner Sichel* (1917) Däubler unfolds his moon-magic. In one section of this book – like Rilke in his 23rd Sonnet to Orpheus (Part I) – Däubler uses flying as the complicated symbol of his new mysticism: the goal of all dream and yearning is a star; this shimmers in the empyrean of our deepest being; and the bark of yearning, spun of moonbeams and with a magic haze for sail, wings aloft to it; and thus beauty itself can be quite simply defined as *Enterdung* (flight from the earth or reality), as *Sternung* (that reaching for a star with no return which in Rilke's poem makes the aviator the pattern of man self-perfected by selfless striving to enskied angel). Däubler's other works have the same concatenation of visions sprung from naïve equations dependent partly on the meaning of words: *Hymne an Italien* (1916), *Hesperion* (1918), *Treppe zum Nordlicht* (1920), *Päan und Dithyrambus* (1924). In *Der sternhelle Weg* (1915) and *Das Sternenkind* (1916) the best of his lyric work is gathered. His novel *L'Africana* (1928) is more attempt than achievement.

XI

NEO-CLASSICISM

At the beginning of the century a reversion from both the naturalistic and the neo-romantic drama to the clear-cut outlines of classical form was championed in theory and practice by Paul Ernst, Wilhelm von Scholz, and Samuel Lublinski. The theoretical writings concerned are Paul Ernst's *Der Weg zur Form* (1906), Wilhelm von Scholz's *Gedanken zum Drama* (1905), and Samuel Lublinski's *Die Bilanz der Moderne* (1904) and *Ausgang der Moderne* (1908). These writers demand a return to blank verse, the three unities, inevitability of the action; and, while they deny the relativity of morality which the naturalists had proclaimed, they define meticulously their own conception of the tragic hero. Restitution of the hero is common to both impressionism and neo-classicism; but whereas to the impressionists the hero is for the most part interesting by reason of his pathological and mental 'otherness' (*Anderssein*) to the neo-classicists he is the Aristotelian superman impelled to destruction by some fault which is an inevitable part of his own towering greatness. The neo-classicists for this reason find their themes mostly in history or legend; and each dramatist interprets his theme in the light of his own particular system of ethics. Hebbel, not Schiller, is the model; and therefore these neo-classic dramas have three main characteristic features: (1) the more closely the dramatists can apply the Aristotelian technique by contriving the strictest unity of action and the most drastic simplification of the plot, the more perfect they consider their tragedies to be; (2) their characters are philosophically aware of their doom and expound their *Weltanschauung*, probably in monologues, in uncompromising philosophic jargon; nor does it matter if the expression of this interpretation of life be grotesquely anachronistic, as, for instance, when in Paul Ernst's *Brunhild* and *Chriemhild* the protagonists and even the wakeman on the wall and even the serfs of the king discourse sententiously on the nature of man and existence, and on whether life is or is not a dream; (3) the photographic reality of present-day life is replaced by what is considered to be the logical reality of a theme in which all that happens is developed inevitably from what precedes. From Hebbel the neo-classicists take over the problem of the conflict of the individual (as the representative of 'higher being' the hero) and the universe (or the community). For the critic watching the outcome of these theories the trouble is that, whereas in Hebbel's plays there is consistent interpretation of the metaphysical idea which informs the dramatist's whole work, in the neo-classic tragedies – in Paul Ernst's particularly – there is neither consistency nor clarity, although the protagonists monotonously and undramatically express whatever metaphysical idea they may possibly represent in a given play.

The great difference between the conception of Paul Ernst and Wilhelm von Scholz is that while the former proceeds by mathematical or logical reasoning and in the plainest terms of versified prose, and regards 'fate' as the conflict between personal will or desire on the one hand and the moral law on the other, Scholz has the Maeterlinckian conception of fate as the mysterious unseen power or powers in whose guiding hand the human puppet is helpless. Paul Ernst is a rationalist, Scholz is a mystic. In both cases the conception of tragedy derives not so much from Aristotle through Lessing as from Aristotle as interpreted by Schelling and taken over by Hebbel; and the neo-classic tragedies will probably repel any reader familiar with Schiller's expansive style unless they read these plays (like a gourmet whose pleasure is in unusual tastes) as test-pieces of Schelling's illuminative interpretation of tragedy as the achieved harmony of the conflicting laws of necessity and liberty. These laws, Schelling says, conquer and are conquered: necessity conquers because it brings the catastrophe, liberty conquers by the hero's acceptance of the catastrophe. Hebbel, arguing from these premises, rejected 'tragic guilt' as interpreted by Lessing. Hebbel's Agnes Bernauer, for instance, is not guilty; neither is Paul Ernst's Brunhild; but their personal will being in conflict with the world-will they must perish; and they must attain the consecration of tragedy by recognizing that they must perish. Another tenet of Hebbel's which the neo-classicists take over is that the drama in its totality and in its elements must be symbolical –

thus in Paul Ernst's *Demetrios* Greek helot and tyrant symbolize the Socialist and the dictator of today, while in his *Chriemhild* Gunther is a symbol for Wilhelm II.

But if, demonstrably, the neo-classic tragedy is based on Hebbel in the case of Paul Ernst, and on Hebbel and Maeterlinck in the case of Wilhelm von Scholz, what is there actually 'new' or 'classical' in the movement? Hebbel is only classical in the sense that his most mature plays are in blank verse and in five acts; his handling of problems ranges him as the forerunner of Ibsen and G. B. Shaw. There is nothing new in this sense in the neo-classic dramas, and one is bound to say – and this amounts to condemnation perhaps – that their main interest is in their form; that is to say, in their attempt to show that the form actually of Racine is, by proof of logic and experience, the only proper form of modern tragedy, the only concession being that modern philosophy or modern social or political problems must be read into the ancient myth or the slice of history that is presented. Paul Ernst himself, in his preface to Scholz's *Meroë*, maintains that 'classicism' is a wrong term for the aims of the neo-classicists, and that they seek, in the form they consider most fit for contemporary drama, merely to reach the level of the classics: '*nicht Klassizismus erstreben wir, sondern Klassizität*'. Their justification is, they think, that they mark a return to the highest ideal of classic art: to represent life in its highest possible manifestations; they would bring tragedy back from the shallows into which naturalists and impressionists had dragged it down by their denial of the irrefragable laws of tragedy as established by Greek and academic criticism.

Wilhelm von Scholz in his *Gedanken zum Drama* (1914) bases his system on the idea that the action of a tragedy concentrates feelings in the mind of the spectator and that the catastrophe results in a violent discharge of these accumulated forces: the competence of the dramatist is in the measure of the skill with which he manipulates this gradual tension and happy release. The eyes of the spectator are thus fixed by the outer magic of the drama on the events which unroll the tragedy, and the inner magic of its suggestion gives him the illusion that he is himself the actor. Thus there are in the theatre two wills: the will of the tragedy to complete the action, and the will of the spectator to follow the action and to identify himself with it. Where Scholz seems to differ radically from the academically defined Aristotelian doctrine is that according to him the tragic action derives not from the character of the hero but from his fate; the tragic hero fights his fate which is contrary to his character; '*Schicksal ist alles.*' The necessary condition of the action is a situation which must inevitably have the development we see in the tragedy, with conflict of two wills, really the conflict between the will to self-assertion and the perception of what is right, both personal will and recognition of the moral law being equally justified. The Aristotelian canon, of course, states that the clash of characters creates the situation; or at least that, the characters being as they are, in the given situation the action must be as shown. To reveal the development of a character, Scholz argues, is the business of the *Erziehungsroman*, whereas tragedy is Fate, which provides the situation fraught with catastrophe for the characters. It might easily be shown that this idea of fate explains the failure of the neo-classic dramas generally, simply because it negates that clash of wills which Lessing established as the necessary condition of tragedy. In other words the failure of the neo-classic tragedies serves to prove once again the irrefutable logic of Aristotle and Lessing. Where there may be something acceptable is in the interpretation of the effect of tragedy: an electric discharge is at all events a cleaner image than the raw medical process of catharsis or purging; this, however, is a matter of theory, and appraisement of the value as literature of tragedies built up on these theories is another matter. One has throughout the feeling that here the proof of the pudding is more satisfying than the eating of it. Interesting in Scholz's system of dramaturgy is his conception of the dual nature of the tragic conflict: the great man – and this dual conflict of ethic forces is possible in great men only – is seen fighting his external battle to consummate his will; but within him there is another battle – that of the unseen powers which direct existence: 'the invisible life in the depth of us becomes in tragedy visible action'. Here we perceive the influence not only of Hebbel but of Maeterlinck; and indeed it is the idea which before long led Scholz away from neo-classicism to a species of irrational mysticism which interprets all external phenomena as symbols.

PAUL ERNST (1866-1933) has described his youth in his *Jugenderinnerungen* (1930) and *Jünglingsjahre* (1931). The son of a miner who had risen to be an overseer, he was born at Elbingerode in the Harz Mountains. He reminds one of another miner's son from the same district – Luther; both were stubborn champions of an idea, and both fought for German ideals and the heroic conception of morality against what each took to be alien predominance. But Luther crashed his way to recognition, while Paul Ernst fought on in the shadows. Till 1933: then he was raised to the pinnacle of fame as the grand old man of fighting literature. Gerhart Hauptmann might come forth from his castle in Silesian mountain solitudes and pay lip allegiance to the Führer; he remained '*volksfremd*', the creature of the Jew press, of Jew critics and Jew theatre directors, the exponent of polygamy, senile eroticism, and family dissension; while Paul Ernst, with his round face framed in its full beard and his defiant eyes, was the type of the Nordic hero facing a world of foes and fighting to the last. His time had come, not merely for national acknowledgment, which he got (with the full blast of propaganda), but for the production of his plays. Here, however, the Nordic theory came up against a blank wall – on the stage the neo-classic plays are . . . literature. As a matter of fact Ernst's popularity with the new régime was mostly due to his political writings: he had begun, when a theological student in Berlin and a member of *Durch*, as a convinced Marxist, but had progressed to a kind of non-Marxist Socialism, and had set down his creed in *Der Zusammenbruch des Marxismus* (1918; rechristened *Die Grundlagen der neuen Gesellschaft*, 1930).[1] He shows the breakdown of liberalism in *Der Zusammenbruch des Idealismus* (1919). His mature attitude to political problems and to the mystery of existence is set forth in the imaginary conversations of *Erdachte Gespräche* (1921): a king before his execution bandies arguments with the dictator who has encompassed his fall, Caesar converses with Antony, Goethe with Eckermann, Hebbel with a rich youth and a poor youth, Mesmer with Swedenborg, etc. The pithy maxims

---

[1] The political philosophy – derived from Machiavelli and Nietzsche – of this book served largely for Nazi propaganda. The brunt of the argument is: there are two classes of men, those born to serve (and they serve so that they may be happy) and those whose whole being strives for leadership. The latter class relinquish happiness for power; and therefore the leader is by necessity a tragic man. This is of course also a canon of Ernst's dramatic doctrine. The leader is by his very nature an aristocrat. The masses will only obey the leader so long as they see that his burden is heavier than their own. The state is the embodied will to power and the embodied morality of its group of leaders and therefore also of the people; for the leaders know that they can only serve the people so long as they stand within the people (*Volk*). The people is to its leaders what the poem is to the poet.

in short rhymed stanzas of his *Gedichte und Sprüche* have been ranked with the Germanic gnomic poetry of the Middle Ages; the core of his wisdom here is what constitutes the ethics of his neo-classic plays (*'Treue gegen sich selbst'*): *'Wer ist weise, wer ist gut? Wer nach seinem Wesen tut'*. His epic in three volumes, *Das Kaiserbuch* (1923-28), chronicles the achievements of the Frankish, Saxon, and Swabian emperors in plain verse, and in *Der Heiland* (1931) he has, like the Old Saxon scop of the ninth century, Germanized the Gospel story.

As a poet Paul Ernst began with *Polymeter* (1897), a collection of verse in the style of Arno Holz's *Phantasus*.[1] His first dramas, the two curtain-raisers *Lumpenbagasch* and *Im Chambre séparée* (both 1898) were in the strictest *Telegrammstil*. A visit to Italy in 1900 converted him to the belief that the ideal forms of art were to be found in ancient Greek tragedy and the medieval Italian *novella*. In 1902 appeared his *Altitalienische Novellen* (translations) and two collections of short stories: *Die Prinzessin des Ostens*, which closely imitate the technique of the old Italian *novella*: the narration is restricted to the bare bones of the action, which is presented as inevitable and due to fate and character, and is kept free from psychological and analytical interpretation. Paul Ernst's short stories rank prominently in the renaissance of the genre which now follows. Other collections of his Novellen are: *Die Hochzeit* (1913); *Der Tod des Cosimo* (1913); *Die Taufe* (1916); *Der Nobelpreis* (1919). In *Okkultische Novellen* (1921) there is something of the speculative mysticism in which Wilhelm von Scholz was now an adept. The *Geschichten von deutscher Art* (1928) cover a variety of social strata, and chronologically take in the period before, during and after the War. The *Komödianten- und Spitzbubengeschichten* (1920) revive the rogue tale such as we find it in the anecdote collections of the sixteenth century, and have that disquieting if ironical delight in wicked pranks which makes *Till Eulenspiegel* such a standard example of German humour; the Roman scene with the itinerant actors of the *commedia dell'arte* does not make the mood less German.

In height of achievement Paul Ernst, though a pioneer and theoretician of the regeneration of the short story, is left behind by his contemporaries, not because he is too faithful to his theory

---

[1] Holz had published poems of his *Phantasus* type in 1893 in Bierbaum's *Musenalmanach*.

of objectiveness and concentration, but because where he does infuse his personality the result is perfect form without magic of atmosphere. When he began his experimental renovation the accepted definition of a Novelle rested on the formulations of Paul Heyse and Friedrich Spielhagen, which stipulate that the character of the hero or the heroine, or both, should be revealed by a conflict which develops as the outcome of an unusual incident.[1] (See p. 474.) The narrator must be objective: that is, he tells the story without putting anything of himself into it. The salient modification of the technique of the Novelle now is that it is liberated from the criterion of absolute objectivity; the very best of the new Novellen tell a good story but are coloured by the author's personality and informed by his own outlook on life. Thus Ricarda Huch, though she continues the realistic method of Gottfried Keller, reads her own femininity and her anti-clerical bias into her short stories, while Jakob Wassermann inspires his with a sad sympathy for the very soul of the submerged classes (e.g. *Das Amulett*), whereas naturalistic *Armeleutepoesie* had merely recorded the conditions of poverty. There is a marvellous range and variety in the mass of these contemporary Novellen. Paul Ernst leads with his revival of the medieval anecdote, and is followed by Wilhelm Schäfer, who makes the *Anekdote* a definite modern genre. Wilhelm von Scholz reads his modern occultism into the picturesqueness of the Middle Ages. Novelists with a political message, like Bruno Frank and Stefan Zweig, make the Novelle poignant with the suffering and hopes of the post-War period. The greatest miracle, perhaps, is in the exotic Novelle (Dauthendey, Klabund): the strange reality of far-away lands and peoples is shown through a haze of dream. The *Künstlernovelle*, which we find Tieck elaborating at the very beginning of the modern Novelle (*Das Dichterleben, Der Tod des Dichters*), is now made more psychologically appealing; as for instance in the two pictures of Hölderlin in his madness: Klabund's *Hölderlin* and Hermann Hesse's *Im Presselschen Gartenhaus*.

Paul Ernst's technique in the Novelle may be gathered from one of his Romance tales: *Ein Familienbild von Goya*. The poet tells of his own visit to a Spanish count, the last scion of an ancient race of hidalgos, in his shell of a medieval castle. The count shows his visitor the family portraits, among which the narrator at once

[1] *novel a = Neuigkeit.*

detects a Goya: this leads the old count to tell the love story of the ancestor whose bold figure stands out from the canvas with wife and ten children. The 'strange happening' which the *Falkentheorie* requires is the marriage of this ancestor to a lady whose husband he had killed. Really we have here the medieval problem and the logical solution of it with which we are familiar from Hartmann von Aue's *Iwein* and Corneille's *Le Cid*; that *Iwein* may be the direct source of Paul Ernst's story is perhaps indicated by the fact that the lady's serving-maid pleads for the hidalgo, who, like Iwein, is a prisoner in the lady's castle. Other familiar medieval details are: the gentleman falls in love with the lady's picture (troubadour and Minnesinger motif); the detailed description of the lady's figure, with the omissions roguishly hinted at; the lady, dainty as she is, uses coarse sexual words. The medieval colouring is, however, nothing more than a graceful pretence: the handling of the theme is intellectual, and what impresses the reader – apart from the exciting story – is the count's regret for the effacement of the landed gentry or military caste by the cultured middle classes; Paul Ernst skilfully renders the melancholy of the theme familiar from so many Spanish works, and most of all as the very inspiration of *Don Quixote*, that poignant contrast of classes which the Socialist leader Friedrich Engels classified as the first literary expression of the idea of Socialism. This tale of Paul Ernst's, it will be clear, is not an objective narration of an event of the Heyse – Spielhagen type, for the author reads into it a personally coloured survey of social developments; and the characters, far from being *'fertig'*, undergo the same developments as do those of *Le Cid*.

In the novel Paul Ernst has academic interest of subject, but not greatness. *Der schmale Weg zum Glück* (1903) is historically one of the pioneer *Erziehungsromane*; it inculcates, with a too didactic insistence, a semi-religious seeking for happiness with the idea that this will be found in some narrow, insignificant retreat from the noise and bustle of the world. *Die selige Insel* (1908) is a notable contribution to the discussion of the *Ehe zu Dritt*. In *Saat auf Hoffnung* (1914) a selfless millionaire tries to save a people driven to distraction by the development of industry; but the Socialist world he builds up is destroyed in blind passion by the workers he would save. (There is the same theme and the same result in Georg Kaiser's *Gas*.) *Grün aus Trümmern* (1923) records the collapse of

Germany in the War and the effect at home. *Der Schatz im Morgen-brotsthal* (1926) and *Das Glück von Lautenthal* (1931) also depict Germany in the distress of a post-War period and hold out the hope of a miraculous recovery; the Thirty Years War is no doubt a symbol of contemporary conditions.

Paul Ernst's neo-classical tragedies have been criticized as being 'cold', 'stiff', 'anaemic', 'pseudo-classical'. He does, it is true, eliminate verbal magic; but it is part and parcel of his programme that greatness of dramatic style can only be achieved by austere restriction to the bare lines of the action: '*Es ist Grösse (Stilgrösse),*' he says, '*wenn ein Künstler es vermag, sich uf die Hauptlinien zu beschränken und alle Nebensachen, auch die blühendsten, duftigsten, auszuschliessen.*' This would seem to mean: let the dramatist stick to his plot and keep the poetry out. His first neo-classical tragedy in his own sense is *Demetrios* (1905), yet another attempt to master the problem of the pretender which Schiller planned in his *Warbeck* and both Schiller and Hebbel left uncompleted in the *Demetrius* of each. It is quite in keeping with the neo-classic manifestos that Ernst removes the problem from comparatively modern history to a mythical period; it is thus easier for the dramatist to eliminate *milieu* and *couleur locale* and confine himself to the stark ethical outlines. His Demetrios is a slave in Sparta in the second century before Christ; he establishes himself for a time as the son of the former king, who has been slain by a usurper. Demetrios has been brought up as a helot, and as King the problem for him is (in the terms of today) how to raise the standard of living among the masses; he finds, as other initially Socialist dictators have done, that he can only rule as a tyrant; and his tyranny leads to the proof that he is an impostor in so far as he is not the legitimate son of the tyrant of whom he is the very image, but merely this tyrant's bastard begotten on a slave girl. *Canossa* (1908) begins with a narration of the horrors of war which is lifted bodily from the beginning of *Simplizissimus*. The ethics are prophetic of Nazi doctrine: the 'higher life' lived by the hero covers the assumption that tyranny as the function of a hero's life is justified. *Ariadne auf Naxos* (1912) marks the transition to a more or less new type of Ernstian play: '*das Erlösungsdrama*'. The *Erlösungsdramen* – the others are *Manfred und Beatrice* (1912), *Preussengeist* (1914), *Kassandra* (1915), *York* (1917) – stress the idea that the hero is saved from suffering by overcoming it. In *Ninon de l'Enclos* (1910) – the heroine is the famous lady of many lovers whose own son has grown up without knowledge of her and, when he sees her, falls madly in love with her – it is not clear whether the mother is *erlöst* or the son when he stabs himself. But here we have practically the only approach to modern psychology in Paul Ernst's plays: Ninon has the cold, sexual, experimental curiosity of a man; hence her eternal youth, because she does not give herself, but takes, or rather tastes. Even she, however, is concerned with the metaphysical nature of life. Probably the most interesting of the neo-classical tragedies are Ernst's *Brunhild* (1909) and *Chriemhild* (1910). Ernst had dealt critically and suggestively with the dramatic possibilities of the *Nibelungenlied* in his *Die Nibelungen: Stoff, Epos und Drama* (1906), which he incorporated in *Der Weg zur Form*. The chorus-like dialogue between retainers with which the acts open projects in dignified language, in which Greek idiom is sporadically imitated, the dramatist's illumination of the ensuing action. In the actual drama the language, though for the most part programmatically plain, is nevertheless outrageously undramatic because it plays round the naïve philosophical ideas on which Ernst (imitating Hebbel's *Nibelungen*) bases the deeds of his protagonists. The *Weltanschauung* thus demonstrated is misty enough: the problem to the reader is whether in *Brunhild* guilt and responsibility for one's deeds are negated, because the individual does what his character makes him do,[1] or whether in great characters (like Siegfried) guilt is necessary to distinguish them from gods, but must be expiated in the Aristotelian way. The denial of right and wrong and the attribution of all happenings to fate are of course classical in the sense of the fate-drama; but in any case Paul Ernst has not made even fate seem inevitable; and his reduction of Gunther to a whining coward and of Chriemhild to a vicious termagant is hateful, while his final denunciation (in the mouth of Hagen) of the conception of *Treue* as the source of the two catastrophes comes as a surprise and is confusing. Ernst has, however, indicated that this is symbolical: Gunther stands for the ex-Kaiser, while Hagen and the other Nibelungen owe their sufferings to a ridiculous and cowardly conception of duty to their lord; that is, to slave morality. The trouble with Paul Ernst is that his dramas, for all

---

[1] Gunther: *Ja, ich bin feig. Doch weshalb bin ich feig?* | *Weshalb ward ich als Siegfried nicht geboren?* – Hagen: *Und jeder Mensch muss der sein, der er ist,* | *Drum ist verächtlich Reue; und die Schuld* | *Ist nur ein Wort, das wir im Traume sprechen.*

his theoretic insistence on the philosophic shaping of drama, show no consistency of views: thus in the Arthurian comedy *Ritter Lanval* (1905) there is clear teaching that determinism is a prison contrived by belief or fear, but a prison from which the individual may free himself as Merlin does, in the play, from the imaginary tower in which he is immured with Viviane. It might of course be urged that comedy does not need the heroic philosophy of tragedy.

WILHELM VON SCHOLZ (1874-) was born in Berlin as the only son of Adolf von Scholz, who later was Bismarck's Minister of Finance. In his memoirs, *Eine Jahrhundertwende*, he has related what he owes to Berlin, where he was brought up, and to the Lake of Constance, on the shores of which, at Schloss Seeheim, he lived. For six years he was the Director of the Court Theatre at Stuttgart, and for two years President of the *Dichterakademie* established by the Nazi régime. In drama he made a beginning with a one-act play, *Mein Fürst* (1898), a dialogue, naturalistic in its ideology but not in style, between a young ruling prince and his old tutor, who has been dismissed from his sinecure because of a speech he has made in a Socialist gathering; the tutor expounds the theory that either prince or people must sponsor revolutionary innovations. *Der Besiegte* (1898) belongs to that group of Maeterlinckian playlets of which Hofmannsthal's *Der Tod und der Tod* is the crown and glory. The central idea is the coming of Death: here he is a wandering knight who bears on his escutcheon a crimson rose on a sable ground – love and death. What enfeebles the play is that instead of concentration on one clear idea – as in Maeterlinck's *L'Intruse* – we get a complex of familiar motifs: in Palestine der Besiegte he has been defeated by the paramour of the châtelaine and is brought to her as prisoner – loved the Magdalene with her flaming hair, and cheated her of Christ; since then he wanders the world, winning the love of ladies with his lute-playing; they burn to his embraces but are chilled to the bone and die, while he escapes as a monk. In the picture of his riding through wood and wold with Walther von der Vogelweide we have no doubt a reminiscence of Dürer's *Knight, Death, and the Devil*, and perhaps, too, of Böcklin's *Selbstbildnis*, in which skeleton Death is playing the violin behind the painter's ear. *Der Gast* (1900) also uses a motley medieval setting for a dualistic picture of Death as a mysterious presence watching over life. The originality of the plot is dubious: in 1896

18

Hauptmann's *Die versunkene Glocke* had appeared; in Scholz's metrically similar play, four years after, we have again the mastercraftsman – this time a demonic architect building a cathedral – obsessed by his work and at the same time torn between his humdrum duty to a fanatically religious wife and his sensual love for a seductive harlot – like Tannhäuser between God and Venus. There is some prospect, as in Ibsen's *Master Builder*, of dizziness on the top of the tower when the work is completed; but the plague, the 'unbidden guest', comes to the city. There is a Maeterlinckian mood in the symbol of Death suddenly shadowing the revels of the vulgar and the star-ypointing dreams of the creative artist; life flares ere its extinction, and the austere artist yields to the seduction of his senses. Again the beauty of the conception is marred by melodramatic mystifications and a loose grip of character-drawing. *Der Jude von Konstanz* (1905) is yet another medieval picture, with the persecution of the Jews as the enfolding theme. The actual problem is that of the renegade Jew, as in Gutzkow's *Uriel Acosta*. Nasson, a Jew doctor in Constance, has embraced Christianity so that he can own his own house and have a hospital – that is, in order to do good; he is no more Christian than Jew, but quite emancipated from dogma. As a study of the Jewish question the play has topical interest today: 'blood pollution' is one of the motifs, the absurdities (to a freethinker) of both Christian and Jewish ritual quicken the plot, and the hopelessness of the Jews being assimilated by any nation is poignantly brought out – there can be no homeland, we are told, where death itself means sinking into alien soil. While *Der Jude von Konstanz* does not observe the unity of place *Meroë* (1906) observes neither the unity of place nor that of time, though it claims to be strictly of the neo-classical type, and is moreover intended to serve as the proof by practice of the neo-classic theories enunciated by Scholz in his *Gedanken zum Drama*. The time of the action is remote (*'ein grosses Drama spielt mit Vorteil in entlegener oder phantastischer Zeit'*), and there is tense concentration on the main conflict between two wills, each of which is dramatically equal to the other: monarchy and priesthood each claim absolute power. Paul Ernst's *Canossa* might be urged in relative disproof of the claim that a mythical period is best suited to drama: there is the same conflict as in *Meroë*, but Ernst's drama of Kaiser and Pope is rendered more vivid by the feeling that the conflict on the stage is the symbol of a conflict not yet ended. The lines of the conflict are actually more topical today than they were at the date of the appearance of Ernst's drama, and the conflict is practically between the same powers. In *Meroë* the conflict is equally topical, but the remoteness of the action veils the actuality; moreover the 'mythical' atmosphere is nullified by the fact that King Sarías is not only a dictator, he is a freethinker as well, who (in a mythical period!) tries to suppress the church. As in Ernst's *Canossa* there is a conflict between father and son: the son joins forces with the priests, defeats his father, but then asserts his rights as king against the claims of the church. Literary interest *Meroë* certainly has: for one thing Scholz varies the soporific regularity of the German *Iambendrama* by a free use of dactyls and trochees; for another thing, with its pseudo-mythical atmosphere and its barbarians who reason like Jesuits and with its melodramatic thrills, it comes near to being a revival of Baroque tragedy. One glaring fault is in its lack of originality: it has elements of the *Pflichtdrama* – like the Prince of Homburg the rebellious heir to the throne recognizes that he has been justly condemned to death; and there is no mistaking the borrowings from Hebbel's *Herodes und Mariamne* – in both the queen's brother is the High Priest and conspires against the king, and in both the king's nearest official is charged to slay the queen if the king dies before her.

In 1914 Scholz modified the framework of his dramatic system in the *Neue Folge* to his *Gedanken zum Drama*. His practical experience as Director (*Dramaturg und Spielleiter*) of the Court Theatre at Stuttgart (1914-23) may account for the more stage-like structure of the plays that follow, all of them mystical. In his treatise *Der Zufall, eine Vorform des Schicksals* (1923) he further expounded the dramatic doctrine of chance on which these plays are based; he attributes to chance or accident a power which may determine the fate of the individual, whereas of course Lessing postulated rigid necessity and excluded chance. Scholz's conception of chance is, however, mystical: chance, being ordained by Fate and obeying laws hidden to us, is 'organic', a complex, a connected process: that is to say, a causality in itself, in its own parts. This acceptance of chance does at least justify the construction of *Othello*, which Lessing had rejected because the catastrophe hinges on the chance falling and finding of a handkerchief.

The new series of plays begins with *Vertauschte Seelen* (1910), an adaptation of a comedy of errors by Tirso de Molina[1]: an old greybeard brings to an Oriental city a magic rhyme; he that speaks it falls into a trance and enters any corpse he wishes to. Thus a beggar at the city gates roams about the stage in the king's body, and the king in this beggar's body commits adultery with his own wife. The humour is very sad. In *Gefährliche Liebe* (1913), an adaptation of *Les liaisons dangereuses*, the unfolding of character is too nuanced for effective stage drama, but the psychological finesse makes it attractive reading. A boy just come from country to court is tragically contrasted with a hardened rake with his snake-like fascination, the 'hero' of endless and perilous amours; and there is all the glamour stung with pain of the Don Juan legend, of the Casanova legend, in the 'hero's' logic – the true heroism of great deeds, he tells the worshipping boy, is swallowed instantly by death, and all one has of life is what can be snatched of it as it flies past. *Gefährliche Liebe* is the most satisfying of Scholz's plays, probably because it is not written to the neo-classic pattern; it is not of course an impressionistic play – the intrigue is too calculated for that, and there is still that neo-classical elimination of imaged lyric beauty which gives hardness to the characters –, but there is an approach to impressionism in the shadowing of the glamour of scene and costumes by the gathering cloud of the Revolution, which ends the last act as the advent of a new period (this again a continuation of Hebbel's technique of prophetic symbolism). Judged by strict dramatical canons the play must fail; for instance, one of the heroines dies of a night of love, which is hardly likely. That the action is complex – there are five protagonists – removes the play from the uncompromising concentration of the neo-classic type to almost epic variety. *Die Feinde* (1917) is clearly inspired by events of the War: isolated attacks by villagers on German garrisons are transferred to somewhere in Germany just before Napoleon's retreat from Russia begins; and (as in Hebbel's *Judith*) a heroine who visits the enemy commander at night is overcome by her physical attraction to a strong man, enhanced by her revulsion from the feeble creature she was to marry. *Das Herzwunder* (1918) is a notable example of the miracle play, which now, in the progression from Hofmannsthal's *Jedermann* to Max Mell, and in the turn to religious mysticism due to post-War pessimism,

---

[1] *Über allen Zauber Liebe* (1931), *Der Richter von Zalamea* (1937), and *Das Leben ein Traum* are adaptations from Calderon.

becomes popular. The playlet begins with an intensely lyrical and theologically admirable exposition of mystical doctrine by the hero, Amandus, a monk who, long ago, as a soldier in Italy, had a love-night with a woman and felt the depths of his being stirred by some vague awakening of his better nature; thereafter he entered a monastery, but within him still burns (more or less a repetition of the central motif of *Der Besiegte*) love for the woman from whose black eyes the fire of pain had sent a kindling spark into his. This lovely harlot symbolizes the soul of man; she comes now, a penitent, to his confessional chair; and, by some spectacular hocus-pocus – which on the stage must thrill believers to the marrow! – she – the harlot! – is the Virgin Mary, whose image in the chapel speaks; and the heart Mary holds in her hand she exchanges for the heart of Amandus, who thereupon dies. In *Der Wettlauf mit dem Schatten* (1921), a glaring experiment in occultism which has had international success, a stranger visits a novelist and tells him that the fragment of a new novel he has read in public corresponds exactly with the events of his own life; he has thus a double existence, that of his real self and that of his shadow in the novel; and the race (*Wettlauf*) indicates the dramatic tension raised by the problem whether the further experiences of real self and shadow will coincide; the novelist goes away to the country to finish the tale, and in the meantime his wife comes near to being murdered by the stranger, whom she had deceived in his youth. Again life and novel, by telepathy or some subconscious chain of suggestion, correspond. The novelist returns, pierces the mystery, the stranger shoots himself (as foreseen in the novel), and the play ends with the words *Dirne!* from the husband and *Mörder!* from the wife.

Scholz's mystical creed is founded on the mystics he edits in *Deutsche Mystiker* (1908). His lyrical verse, too, is much preoccupied with ideas of fate and the beyond (*Der Spiegel*, 1902). His verse collections *Frühlingsfahrt* (1896) and *Hohenklingen* (1898) are more traditional in theme; *Hohenklingen* has a medieval background by the Lake of Constance. *Neue Gedichte* (1913) and *Die Balladen und Königsmärchen* contain his most mature verse. His free renderings of medieval lyrics (*Minnesang*, 1917) have interest to the Germanist, but Scholz's lyric note is too heavy and too thought-bound for the floating gossamer of his originals. As a writer of short stories – he began with *Die Beichte* (1919) – Scholz is to be classed with

Paul Ernst and Wilhelm Schäfer as a revivalist of the short, concise Novelle; but whereas these two writers keep to a plain psychology Scholz explores the world beyond the senses, somnambulism, second sight, subconscious impulses, particularly in *Das Zwischenreich* (1919), tales of the world between sense and infinity. His Novellen are collected in *Erzählungen* (2 vols., 1919) and *Die Gefährten* (1937). His two long novels, *Perpetua* (1926) and *Der Weg nach Ilok* (1929) also belong to literary occultism. The period of *Perpetua* is the sixteenth century, and the action turns round the life of two twin sisters, a witch and a nun whose souls interchange. *Der Weg nach Ilok* is a tale of Silesia in the fifteenth century; the hero is a fanatical Catholic, a papal legate who roots out heretics in Breslau, conquers Belgrade in the Turkish campaign, and dies in a monastery by the Danube. Scholz's miscellaneous writings are voluminous, and range from books of travel (*Städte und Schlösser*, 1918; *Der Bodensee*, 1920) to a collection of aphorisms (*Lebensdeutung*, 1924) and an edition of German ballads.

SAMUEL LUBLINSKI (1868-1910), a distinguished critic (*Literatur und Gesellschaft im 19ten Jahrhundert*, 1899, and the two volumes on *die Moderne* referred to above), began as a dramatist with naturalistic plays (*Hannibal*, 1902; *Peter von Russland*, 1906), and made his first experiment in neo-classicism with *Gunther und Brunhild* (1908). This play was written (before Ernst's own two Nibelungen plays) on the lines indicated in *Der Weg zur Form*: Gunther is a physically weak intellectual who prefers diplomacy to war (i.e. his weakness is his strength); Hagen is eliminated as unnecessary to the action, and Siegfried is stabbed in the back by Gunther. *Kaiser und Kanzler* (1910) has Frederick II and his chancellor Petrus von Vinea for protagonists.

While Paul Ernst and Lublinski are non-lyrical dramatists the other neo-classics are distinctly lyrical. HANS FRANCK (1879-), a Mecklenburger with the brooding nature of the northern German, has been brought to the fore as a racial and cultural influence. There can be no comprehension of his work without the realization that he is in the line of Hebbel, concerned mainly with the embodiment in art of ideas, and that these ideas continue Hegel. The very form of his sonnets (*Siderische Sonette*, 1920; *Tellurische Sonette*, 1931) is Hegelian, with *Satz* and *Gegensatz* in the octet and *Lösung* or *Überwindung* in the sextet; and this triple formula is indeed the key to all his work. All his thinking is dualistic, not of course the naïve contrast of qualities of Victor Hugo but an intensely philosophical and dramatic conflict of the physical and the spiritual; his 'siderial' and 'tellurian' cycle of sonnets typify this periodic occupation with sky-hung ideals followed by their realization on the satisfying earth, and his dramas and tales fall into siderial and tellurian groups. His aesthetics can be picked out of his two novels *Das dritte Reich* (1921; rechristened *Die Stadt des Elias Holl*, 1938) and *Meta Koggenpoord* (1926). In *Das dritte Reich* a seventeenth-century sculptor goes from his native Lübeck to Italy, is overcome by the art of the South and flees to the North, and in Augsburg works at a *Lucretia*. His first Lucretia is a hot Southern dame with the will to sex and death; his second a crabbed Nordic being laden with earthiness; his third an embodiment of North and South, form and beauty and will to truth as well, *Jenseitigkeit* and *Diesseitigkeit*. The dualism of naïveté and cerebralism in art Franck represents by contrasting his *Gedanken-Denker* from Augsburg with a *Dinge-Denker* – an artisan who tirelessly produces; perhaps, Franck asks, there is a 'Third Empire', in which Thought-Thinker and Thing-Thinker are one? This discussion is continued in *Meta Koggenpoord*, and we see that the handling of the problem in the two books is poignantly personal: he whose productivity has been hampered by meticulous thought has now, settled as he is by the shores of his Mecklenburg lake, found the synthesis he had longed for. His heroine Meta Koggenpoord is a portrait of the painter Paula Modersohn-Becker (p. 322, note), who painted simple things full of eternity, real things in which reality is transfigured. Here we have Hans Franck's rejection of naturalism as mere transcription of phenomena and of expressionism as mere preaching of ideas. The 'Third Realm' of artistic creation is this synthesis of soil and radiance, this irradiation of *Sein* and *Schein*, this radiance which is itself the meaning and the interpretation of the thing. Such syncretism, too, is the aim of a later novel, *Sebastian: Der Gottsucher* (1949), the hero of which, first a Catholic and then a Lutheran, renounces both these dogmas to dream of a Church in which all that is basically true in all religions shall meet and fuse. Franck's dramas are helped by his technical knowledge of the stage acquired as *Dramaturg* at the Düsseldorf Schauspielhaus – he threw up this post when the Rhineland was occupied by foreign troops, and settled in Mecklenburg. His first group of plays are siderial. *Herzog Heinrichs Heimkehr*

(1911) is a typical *Ideendrama* of Hebbel's type. His most interesting drama, *Godiva* (1919), one of a series of works on this English theme,[1] is distinguished by its skilful motivation of the ride: the conflict is that very modern one of the sensitive wife's resistance to the sexual aggressiveness of her husband and of his insistence on his legal rights: here the legend and the medieval atmosphere merely serve to give a discreet remoteness to the actuality of the problem (that of Soames and Irene in *The Forsyte Saga*). Franck's solution is in favour of the husband; which is good Nazi doctrine. The intention is to show that in the complicated dualism of male and female physical and spiritual forces repel and attract each other. *Opfernacht* (1921) more or less shadows Hebbel's *Gyges und sein Ring*: an Indian virgin in her wedding night passes through experiences which waken her to woman. In the comedy *Martha und Maria* (1922) the theme is again the rights of the flesh. Franck's tellurian dramas are deepened by his experiences of the War, his attitude to which he had defined in *Mein Kriegsbuch* (1916). In *Freie Knechte* (1919) the third and last son is called up on a little farm in Mecklenburg. There is a dualism of a mother – represented by a striking drawing by Ernst Barlach – calling on mothers to cry with her: 'Rather die than kill!' and the counter-cry of spirit which wills Fate and is ready for sacrifice. In *Klaus Michel* (1925) we have, in the last act, the birth of 'the new man'. The hero – a famous doctor whose concern is bodies and who mocks at 'souls' – is another version of 'der deutsche Michel', the eternal dreamer pursued by reality; his divine nature is released by sacrifice for others in the War: he perishes, but his two sons find salvation on the land. *Kanzler und König* (1926) is another Struensee play. *Kleist* (1933) puts the Prussian poet on the stage as a political agitator against Napoleon; he is made a mouthpiece for the specifically Nazi idea that poetry and Fatherland must be one. After the First Great War Franck was a prolific writer of fiction, particularly of short stories. In the nine tales of *Recht ist Unrecht* (1928) he once more uses love to bring home his doctrine of the union of opposites: true love, since it is blood and spirit, is the bridge by which physical experience passes to the spiritual; love is the pentagram which is the symbol of mystery; embodied spirit and spiritualized body. Dogmatic as the thesis may seem it is illustrated by *exempla*

---

[1] G. C. Lichtenberg: *Ein sittsamer Gebrauch zu Coventry in Warwickshire* (1779); Josef Lauff's novel *Regina Coeli* (1894).

varying in mood and scene: a European woman may dissect the love she takes, whereas in climes where human nature is lovely and strange as the landscape that moulds it (as in Java) the maid opens herself out to love which enters and possesses her; thus in these tales we have a further dualism of Nordic and exotic. Stories built up so elaborately on ideas are apt to prove wearisome, and it cannot be said that Hans Franck's long novels are an exception to the rule; in a short story on the other hand the significance given to the necessarily concentrated story may make it memorable (even *Märchen* – say *The Ugly Duckling* – may be better for a meaning); and if in Franck's *Der Regenbogen* (1928) the beauty of the idea rather spans the group than illuminates the series of seven times seven short anecdotes, it does stay in the memory as a colourful symbol of that idealism which binds earth and heaven over all the seven periods of German history and the panorama of German landscape. *Zeitprisma* (1932) is a collection of thirteen times thirteen anecdotes of a similar tendency – German fate and character are refracted in the evolutions of periods, but the prism is ever beautiful. The novel *Reise in die Ewigkeit* (1934) recounts, looking backward from the day of his death, the life of J. G. Hamann, the 'magus of the North'.

Several other dramatists stand between impressionism or expressionism and neo-classicism. They are too vigorous to be classed as neo-romantics but not too lyrical and romantic to be ranged with the neo-classicists. In the work of two Rhinelanders, Herbert Eulenberg (born Mühlheim a/Rh.) and Wilhelm Schmidtbonn (=Wilhelm Schmidt aus Bonn) there is a strong personal note: both are inspired by their own upwelling lust of life. Eulenberg's characters have a passionate greed of animal experience – they would live in the fire of their own wild hearts 'like a salamander', while Schmidtbonn's general theme is the grasping at happiness and brilliance of existence of characters who refuse to be thrust down into the shadows. The key-word of Eulenberg is *Leidenschaft*; of Schmidtbonn, *Glück*.

WILHELM SCHMIDTBONN (1876-1952) has certainly nothing of the cerebral planning of construction which is the hall-mark of the neo-classicists: he builds up, not to mathematical symmetry of a whole but to the thrill of lyrically heightened and startling situations. After naturalistic beginnings – the drama *Die goldene Tür* (1904) and the Rhineland stories *Uferleute* (1903) and *Raben* (1904)

– he broke through with *Mutter Landstrasse* (1904), which Max Reinhardt produced; it gives a new ending and the mood of the son-father conflict to the legend of the Prodigal Son – when the wanderer returns his iron-cast father turns him away from the door: there can be no reconciliation between the world of adventure and that of duty. In *Der Graf von Gleichen* (1908) Schmidtbonn questions the traditional morality of the legend of the man with two wives: his hero has love enough for the two, but the legal wife inevitably murders the Saracen woman, whereupon the Crusader leaves her to eat her heart out and rides away to the mystic East once more, with the squire who had been with him in all his campaigning – and this squire is Death. *Der Zorn des Achilles* (1909) aims at classic heights, and does certainly achieve occasional monumentality of expression. Achilles is very German – bluff and blond, angular and awkward; he has to learn that even a superman is hemmed in by other wills; his anger is like the raging sea, magnificent in its force but breaking itself against the hard rocks of fact. In his second handling of the Prodigal Son theme, *Der verlorene Sohn* (1915), a '*Legendenspiel*', Schmidtbonn keeps the Biblical ending; the father rejoices and forgives. *Die Stadt der Besessenen* (1917) stages the religious orgies of the Anabaptists at Münster. *Der Geschlagene* (1922) shows the marital misery of an aviator blinded in the War. *Die Fahrt nach Orplid* (1923) is a drama of emigrants bound for Peru.

It is customary to classify the work of HERBERT EULENBERG (1876-1949) as *Sturm und Drang* or *Affektdramatik*; that is, he obtains his dramatic effects by crass sensation. But this cult of sensation is due merely to the influence of the Elizabethan dramatists: the outrageous happenings are the necessary expression of abnormally passionate character. Not the poised conflict of two equally strong wills attracts him, but the conflict in the breast of his heroes of desire and dream with the grim hardness of reality. He probes 'the most tragic and uncanny problems of humanity', and magnifies bestial lusts to heroic grandeur. He depicts, in ever varying phases, the tragically lonely man, doomed to isolation by his own inhuman humanity; or the lonely of spirit, brooding on his own frustration and driven by the irreality of dream to lust for the most stinging bitternesses of reality, and for the bitterest sting of all – death. There is the Elizabethan pattern already in his *Dogenglück* (1898), with its glamour of Venice; and there is the impress of Webster at his wildest in *Anna Walewski* (1899). He calls *Anna Walewski* a *'Studentendrama'* – he was twenty-three when he wrote it; and certainly the style is sufficiently *burschikos* to remind one of Schiller's *Die Räuber*, particularly at the end, where the hero sets off to join the bandits. In the preface to the revised second edition Eulenberg states that the diction is stylized to reveal in every sentence 'horror' (it is significant that he uses the English word) at the flat language of common life; the hair-raising, however, comes not so much from the burning strangeness of language – in which the play is enwrapped as in the shirt of Nessus – as from the subject-matter: this is double incest, that is, incest which differs from the Cenci story with its violation of the female in that daughter-complex and father-complex meet with equal flame. There is dramatic power in the characterization of the father, the 'lonely lion' whose demonic power stands as a symbol for the suppressed heroism of the Polish nobles as well as for the revolt against the moral law; and the gloomy Polish castle hid in its wet woods where wolves prowl is a fit setting for the unnatural crime. *Münchhausen* (1900), with its glorification of the legendary liar, is a denial of naturalistic truth: there is the mood of Cyrano de Bergerac, of the poet who rises to beauty in the frantic fever of his dreams, in the lyric inventions of this Hanoverian junker. *Ritter Blaubart* (1905), a *'Märchenspiel'*, challenges comparison with Tieck's and with Maeterlinck's plays on the same theme. There is a Shakespearian blending of comic and tragic, particularly in the funeral scenes, but through all the play quivers the mental torture of Bluebeard because women remain a mystery to him: what were their dreams of love before he gave them the reality of love? In *Simson* (1910) the demonic character of the hero is a symbol for the artistic temperament enslaved by sex: Samson is a man of men, but his love for Delilah levels him to a beast thirsting for water in the desert. *Die Insel* (1919) is yet another attempt to re-create the mood and story of *The Tempest*.[1] Parallel with these lurid studies of demonic natures goes a series of obscenely witty or strangely romantic comedies or tragi-comedies. *Der natürliche Vater* (1907) delighted Wedekind. *Mückentanz* (1922), clearly influenced by Sternheim's anti-*Bürger* literature, has literally the construction of a *Sturm und Drang* play; it is full of the humour of the brothel. After *Alles um Geld* (1911) Eulenberg scored his first stage success

[1] See pp. 33, 38.

with *Belinde* (1912), a very original handling of the Enoch Arden theme. Belinde has married for love, but her husband is poor, and he loves her so much that he leaves her for ten years to make his fortune. It is in keeping with his character that he does not write; but he is sure of her fidelity. Her starved senses, however, yearn for love, and she gives her heart to a boy, who, moreover, is wealthy. But on the eve of the marriage the lost husband – he has officially been declared dead – returns. The lover agrees to an American duel; he loses, and shoots himself. The whole force of the drama is now put into the conflicting feelings of Belinde. She loves her returned husband and longs for him, but she shoots herself for very shame. The action might be sordid, but there is a transposed Elizabethan mood of mystery over it: the characters move like ordinary beings, but over volcanic passions. As a writer of short stories Eulenberg aims first of all at the '*unerhörte Begebenheit*' of the *Falkentheorie*. His *Sonderbare Geschichten* (1910) are in the line of E. T. A. Hoffmann, though the mystery is pathological rather than suprasensual: there is a duel between women; an old shepherd loves and fondles under the moon a beautiful female corpse he has found washed up naked by the river; a man of model behaviour must every three weeks or so have a Heliogabalic night; a good peasant lad defiles an image of the Virgin; an old scissors-grinder drinks the blood of all the cats he can catch. Very curious is *Das Geheimnis der Frauen*: it is a transposition to our own days of the Psyche and Amor or Melusine motif. Others of the tales belong to the genre of *Anekdoten* in Wilhelm Schäfer's sense, but without Schäfer's dull didacticism – there are such episodes (interpretative of the man, not of some moral implication) as *Schopenhauers Geliebte, Warum Gottfried Keller nicht heiratete, Gleim und die Karschin* (this tale is delightful Rococo!). *Platens letzte Liebe* comes close in theme to Thomas Mann's *Tod in Venedig*. The tale of Schiller's wooing of two sisters has the implications of the *Ehe zu Dritt*. The use of the Melusine motif – the inhibition to the husband of access at stated times – is used in another tale to symbolize monthly periods. The outrageous picture of Lesbian love in *Der Maler Rayski* adds another to the studies in the period of this pathological theme. The novel *Katinka, die Fliege* (1912) revives the satirical valuation of romantic love in Fischart's sixteenth century *Flöhhatz, Weibertratz*.

The dramas of EDUARD STUCKEN (1865-1936) are perhaps rather

completely romantic than neo-romantic, for he finds his themes
for the most part in the age of chivalry and keeps its romantic
trappings and sentiment; indeed, in his colouring and metrical
dexterity he is both a Tennysonian and a Pre-Raphaelite. Instead of
the congenital morbidity of the neo-romantics he has the morbid
sensationalism of the occultists; where he touches the neo-classicists
is in his elaboration of symbol. Between 1902 and 1916 he wrote
a cycle of plays which he loops together as *Der Gral*; for these he
devised a strange dramatic metre by adapting the Nibelungen
strophe. In their period these plays surprise by their ascetic note;
if Stucken were a greater poet one might call him a spiritualized
Tennyson; from Tennyson certainly he takes over the pretence of
heroic purity. The prelude to the cycle, though it did not appear
till 1913, is *Merlins Geburt*. The first in date was *Gawân* (1902), the
central idea of which is that the saintly hero is tempted, as Job
was, by the devil. The dramatic problem is loosely grasped: the
play is a confused blend of the medieval pacts with the devil, in
which the sinner is saved by the direct mediation of the Virgin,
and the modern *Pflichtdrama*; but the Virgin herself acts by arrangement with Death or the Devil as a decoy, not, however, as
in Wilhelm von Scholz's *Das Herzwunder* as love that yields, but
because she knows Gawân *cannot* succumb to the call of the flesh;
that is, logically she saves, not a repentant sinner, but one who
cannot sin; and, though Gawân first shrinks from death and then
faces it, it is 'purity' and not the idea of duty which is put forward
as the theme of the play. In the long-drawn-out temptation scene,
heightened by fleshly tints and fainting rhythms (Marie, bending
over Gawân as he lies in bed, clings to his lips with a vampire's
kiss and meshes him in the net of her golden hair) the dualistic
argument between chastity and sin rolls to and fro. Stucken's
source was Jessie Weston's version of the Middle English poem
The Green Knight. The Grail plays culminate in *Lanzelot* (1909), in
which the hero's love for Ginevra and Elaine symbolizes the dualism of self-expression and renunciation. *Astrid* (1913) handles the
Brunhild motif in an Icelandic setting; with *Die Gesellschaft des
Abbé Chateauneuf* we come to Ninon de l'Enclos again. Stucken is
known internationally by his historical novel *Die weissen Götter*
(1918), the first of a long series of such presentations of history
which rely for appeal as much on sensational sex episodes as on
the coloration of history. The novel shows Stucken's familiarity

with the medieval verse epics: the mass of it has the motley multifariousness of exotic adventure of the *Ritterepos* and is shot through with decadent crazes such as brother-and-sister incest, the sex appeal of a hermaphrodite, a black mass sadistically detailed (one of the most perversely elaborated episodes in the often lurid literature of the period). There is dovetailing with Gerhart Hauptmann's Mexican play; and indeed Hauptmann is credited with having delved into the novel rather than into Stucken's source, Prescott; and this should hold good of *Indipohdi* as well. The difference from Gerhart Hauptmann's picture is that the sympathy is altogether with the Spaniards: they are brutal, but they are Christians; indeed the chief interest of the book lies in the heaped horrors of the sadistically pictured heathen practices of the Aztecs: e.g. a prince is forced to eat his slaughtered wife's organs. As in Gerhart Hauptmann's *Der weisse Heiland* the coincidences of Messianic and Aztec legend are brought out. *Larion* (1926) depicts the turbid religious psychosis of old Russia; since Stucken was born in Moscow the data of the novel should have authenticity, but the interest, as in *Die weissen Götter*, is in religious sadism – here we have the Satanic cult of a sect who castrate themselves. *Im Schatten Shakespeares* (1930) describes the London of James I. *Giuliano* (1933) belongs to the Renaissance craze.

The neo-classic programmatic chastening of form does not appear more in the drama than in the Novelle, and here Wilhelm Schäfer and Rudolf Binding take equal rank with Ernst and Scholz. WILHELM SCHÄFER (1868-1952) has pleasantly told the story of his ancestors in *Meine Eltern* (1937) and his own story in *Lebensabriss* (1918) and *Mein Leben* (1934). As a delineator of his native Rhineland he belongs, though loosely, to *Heimatkunst*; while resident at Düsseldorf at the beginning of the century he edited the journal *Die Rheinlande*. He was, to begin with, an elementary school teacher, and his insistent didactic note derives perhaps from the peculiar saturation with the teaching microbe of this vocation.[1] His style shows the professional grammarian's command of sentence-building, but he eschews what he considers to be unessential graces such as mood-painting. He has the medieval conception of the story-writer's technique that not the mental life of the characters but the events they experience should hold the interest of the nar-

[1] Other elementary teachers of the period are Otto Ernst, Hermann Stehr, Heinrich Sohnrey, Friedrich Griese, Ilse Frapan, Hermann Claudius.

ration, and therefore it is not surprising that he should have made a speciality of what is a medieval genre, though he is no doubt justified in his claim that he schooled himself on Johann Peter Hebel's *Schatzkästlein*: his *Anekdoten*[1] are miniature stories much as are to be found in sixteenth-century collections of facetiae such as Kirchhoff's *Wendunmut*, to which Paul Ernst acknowledged his debt. The modern element Schäfer adds to the genre is that of patriotic selection: his aim is to show the heroic qualities of the German race in episodes from the lives of its famous men or from general types of German. This racial bias, of course, explains the tendency to over-estimate him in the Nazi period; an impartial judgment would deny him more than the rank of a popular story-teller but acknowledge the academic interest of his re-creation of the *Anekdote*. For this his mode of composition, as stated by himself, bears analogy to that of the neo-classic dramatists: he takes a known story, his '*Stoff*' (and therefore fertility of imagination is not to be expected), and restores the bare lines by stripping off all accretions till nothing remains but the decisive action ('*die Ent-scheidung*'), which corresponds to the catastrophe in a tragedy; and this he heads and tails with the shortest possible approach to it and a hint of what is to follow, morally spiced either by way of introduction or dismissal of the theme. What is needed in such a genre is the power of swift characterization, so that not the event so much as the victory over the event by the character should remain as pattern and example in the reader's mind. The schoolmaster's determined inculcation of virtue is yet more glaring In *Dreizehn Bucher der deutschen Seele* (1922), which (written in a period of national despondency) proclaimed a sturdy faith in racial excellence and proved this to exist in the great men and the great events that have shaped the destiny of the Germans from Nordic myth to the mistakes of the present. Schäfer was a pioneer too in the field of the *vie romancée*; but here his purpose is still educational. In *Lebenstag eines Menschenfreundes* (1915) he quietly tells the story of Pestalozzi, while in *Karl Stauffers Lebensgang* (1911; a fictitious autobiography of the Swiss painter Stauffer-Bern), *Winckel-*

---

[1] *Deutsches Anekdotenbuch*, edited by Paul Alverdes and Hermann Rinn (1938), is an anthology of short stories in the sense indicated. The first volume of Schäfer's *Anekdoten* appeared in 1908; this and the following volumes were collected in *Anekdoten* (1926); a further volume is *Wendekreis neuer Anekdoten* (1937). School edition, ed. Karl W. Maurer: *Die Anekdoten von Wilhelm Schäfer* (London, 1938).

manns Ende (1925), *Hölderlins Einkehr* (1925), and *Die Missgeschickten* (1909) he does his bit for the *Künstlernovelle*. There is still more of his own earnest self in his novel *Huldreich Zwingli* (1926), his tribute to the Swiss reformer. His genial Rhineland humour comes out in his novel *Der Hauptmann von Köpenick* (1930). The short stories *Die unterbrochene Rheinfahrt* (1913) and *Anckemanns Tristan* (1936) have more invention.

There is no reason to think that modernity of outlook or of vision is necessarily bound up with irregular form; there are indeed a group of poets – we may call them traditionalists or neo-classicists or neo-Hellenists – who express the moods of today in classically chiselled moulds (Rudolf Borchardt, Felix Braun, Josef Leitgeb, Hans Leifhelm). But there are likely to be subtle modulations of rhythm which reveal a new relation to nature (Wilhelm Lehmann) or to social problems (F. G. Jünger) or even to religion (R. G. Binding, R. A. Schröder, Josef Weinheber).

RUDOLF GEORG BINDING (1867-1938) was born in Basel as the son of a famous father, the professor of criminal law, Karl Binding. He read law at Leipzig, and turned from this to medicine, again a vain study; what made him, he says, was riding. He had been fond of horses from boyhood; and he sings their praises in his *Reitvorschrift für eine Geliebte* (1926): riding, he says in this prose poem, disciplined and steeled him, taught him patience, the love of all that is untamed. His love of sport comes out again and again in his fiction: riding and swimming in *Opfergang*, fencing in *Die Waffenbrüder*. At forty there was a psychic crisis in his life; residence in Italy saved him. A visit to Greece put the finishing touch to his transformation; here he realized that great art is timeless and ever near to men, '*wahrhafte Gegenwärtigkeit*'. The final phase of his mental growth was the War, through which he served as an officer of dragoons; his experiences he related in *Aus dem Kriege* (1925). Binding's lyric verse (*Tage*, 1924; *Ausgewählte und neue Gedichte*, 1930; *Die Gedichte. Gesamtausgabe*, 1937) is for the most part uncompromisingly traditional; it gives distinguished expression to a distinguished personality; but there is no marked note of originality, though imitation – particularly in the War poems – of contemporary experiments in rhythmic notation may give the illusion of hyper-modernity. His War poems – collected in *Stolz und Trauer* (1922) – have the sad resignation and the manly fortitude that broods in the bent gaze of his post-War portraits. For all their lack of spontaneity they have a certain effectiveness; there is for instance a leaden tone and the helpless horror of a nightmare in *Letzte Rekruten*: '*Sie nahen schon den andern Toten,* | *den stummen blassern grössern Toten*'; they come in wave on wave, with bent gaze, drawn by the dead who have gone, wave on wave, before. It is as a short story writer that Binding is likely to survive. His 'legends' and Novellen have the restraint and the objectiveness of the neo-classic pattern. The peculiarities of punctuation show some affinity with Stefan George, but the narrative style, though over-refined and perhaps even anaemic, is clear and smoothly insinuating; the too level rhythm glides along like a silk ribbon which fondles but does not grip. His *Legenden der Zeit* (1909) contrast life and religion, to the advantage of *Diesseitigkeit*; he thus shows himself the pupil of Gottfried Keller, and indeed these legends directly continue Keller's anti-religious *Sieben Legenden*. The literary purpose of both Keller and Binding is to show that the Christian conception of chastity is inhuman, and that life is only in love and marriage. These ironic stories are thus legends reversed, or (paradoxically) pagan legends, with the Christian paraphernalia humorously and almost lovingly tinged with comic effect (as they are, though unconsciously, in certain medieval *Marienlieder*). Binding achieves delightful effects by aping Baroque language in his description of the administrative routine of Heaven: he devises sentences like blown-out bags, and sumptuously paraphrases the vacuous verbosity of supreme authority. *Keuschheitslegende* plays gracefully with the medieval idea[1] that a maid's chastity is a shirt stronger than steel mail; and with the modern idea that it burns more fiercely than the flames of Hell. *Die Geige* (1911) is the first collection of Novellen proper. Of these *Die Waffenbrüder* is a supple combination of the Miles Standish–John Alden motif with that of the taming of the shrew and of the taming in the darkness of Brunhilde by Siegfried on behalf of Gunther; the period is that of the Franco-Prussian war. *Angelucia*, which shows the influence of Gerhart Hauptmann's *Hannele* and *Der arme Heinrich*, belongs to the literature of the eroticism of puberty (*Pubertätserotik*). In *Der Opfergang* we have again that contrast – an obsession with German writers – of the passionate southern woman with the cool, good German dame of the North. Really it is the same story as *Keuschheitslegende*: in both tales saintliness is equated with sexual coldness; a cold

[1] Gottfried's *Tristan*, ll. 12815 ff.; Hugo von Trimberg's *Der Renner*, l. 12766.

19

woman, however beautiful she may be, repels; she is safe, but abandoned.

With Binding as a neo-classic stands RUDOLF ALEXANDER SCHRÖ-DER (1878-), a Bremen man; or rather, since in his earlier years he uses Greek metres, he is a neo-Hellenist. Schröder has considerable historical importance; for instance, as co-founder of the journal *Die Insel*; and he has in recent years been loaded with honours from all quarters. He swept all before him when, as the greater poets of his generation passed away, he continued his mass production and established himself as a facile translator: *Homers Odyssee*, 1910; *Die Ilias*, 1943; Virgil's *Hirtengedichte*, 1924; Horace's poems, 1935; also translations of Shakespeare, Pope, Aubrey Beardsley, T. S. Eliot; translations of Molière and Racine and of Dutch and Flemish classics. Above all he is recognized, after his rebuilding of the hymnal lyric of Paul Gerhardt and Paul Fleming, as – literally – the laureate of the Protestant community. His more personal lyric work ranges from *Unmut* (1899), *Lieder an eine Geliebte* (1900), *Elysium* (1905), *Gesammelte Gedichte* (1912), *Deutsche Oden* (1914; patriotic verse, with a note of warning in the fear of war), *Heilig Vaterland* (1914; weak war verse) to the religious verse of *Widmungen und Opfer* (1925), with its turning to a Protestant mood, *Mitte des Lebens* (1930), *Die Ballade vom Wandersmann* (1937), *Der Mann und das Jahr* (1946), *Weihnachtslieder* (1947), *Alten Mannes Sommer* (1947). *Die weltlichen Gedichte* (1940) collects his secular poetry, *Die geistlichen Gedichte* (1950) his religious verse. The story of his youth is told in *Der Wanderer und die Heimat* (1931) and *Aus Kindheit und Jugend* (1934). His attitude to religion is enunciated in *Zur Naturgeschichte des Glaubens* (1936), while *Dichtung und Dichter der Kirche* (1936) has importance for hymnology. *Aufsätze und Reden* (1939) deal with translation problems and include essays on Hofmannsthal, Rilke, Binding, and other friends of his. As a neo-Hellenist and translator R. A. Schröder has a rival in THASSILO VON SCHEFFER (1873-1951): Aristophanes, 1924; *Hesiods sämtliche Werke*, 1940; Virgil's *Aeneis*, 1943; Homer's *Ilias*, 1947 and *Odyssee*, 1948; Ovid's *Metamorphosen*, 1948. There is a fund of Greek scholarship in his re-creations of Greek myth and legend: *Die Kyprien* (1934; in smooth hexameters) and the prose volumes *Hellenische Mysterien und Orakel* (1940), *Griechische Sagen* (1947). His lyric work (*Die Gedichte*, 1947; *Das lyrische Werk*, 4 vols., 1947) reaches post-war poignancy in *Wende und Wandlung* (1947).

XII

THE NOVEL
OF IMPRESSIONISM

There is no clear cut between the naturalistic novel and the impressionistic novel. The transition is gradual; with some writers there is no complete break, and with others what really happens is that they continue the poetic realism of the pre-naturalistic period, though with a more literal conception of reality. Taking the later phase of novels *en masse*, what remains in them of the naturalistic programme is that the *milieu* may still be presented in detail; this, however, is no longer wearisome. The *Milieuroman* merges into the *Charakterroman*, the difference being that while in the former the *milieu* swamps the characters in the latter the *milieu*, though still emphasized, serves as a background against which the characters stand out in vivid relief, and that these characters, instead of being the chemical product of the *milieu*, dominate it.

Typical of the change-over is the work of EMIL STRAUSS (1866-1956). A Swabian from Pforzheim, he gravitated to Berlin, and there moved in Gerhart Hauptmann's and Dehmel's circles; that is, in close touch with naturalism. Then he migrated to Brazil, but returned to Germany, and turned farmer in the Schwarzwald near Freiburg. He thus acquired a fund of experience which the doctrinaire naturalists – encysted in theories – cannot lay claim to. And experience shapes his heroes as it shaped him; they plunge into life, go wrong, make good, and so can face up to whatever fate may bring. This heroic conception of life is the direct opposite of the surrender to fate or rather to environment and mental state of the naturalists. Moreover, this development of character is altruistic: '*Du kannst die Welt nur vollenden,*' Strauss says, '*indem du dich vollendest.*' In addition Strauss as a Swabian brings to his fiction Swabian *Gemüt* and a certain leisureliness of narration. He repeatedly gives impressions of Brazil (in his drama *Don Pedro* as in the short stories of *Menschenwege* and *Hans und Grete*, and elsewhere), but quite simply – what exotic impressionism is can be seen at a glance by comparing his Brazilian pictures with Dauthendey's descriptions of Mexico. His novel *Der Engelwirt* (1901) is made up of old-fashioned irony: a Swabian landlord has no boy by his wife, and tries for one with the servant, Agathe; but she presents him with a daughter! He emigrates with Agathe and the girl to Brazil, where Agathe dies, and where he is cheated of all he has. A sadder and a wiser man, he returns to home and wife; and the point of the story is that this good woman, whose character is finely drawn, welcomes him. The next novel, *Freund Hein* (1902), created a sensation; not, however, because it was a literary masterpiece (it is far from that), but because it was an attack on the examinational tyranny of German secondary schools. As *Anklageliteratur* it should be naturalistic; but Strauss just tells the story, and lets the accusation emerge from the facts. There is rather impressionistic than naturalistic consistency in the psychogrammatic notation of a boy's mental torture. The hero is Heinrich Lindner; in local pronunciation he is Heinerich, Heiner for short; but 'Freund Hein' is a euphemism for Death. He is the grandson of a virtuoso on the violin, and the son of a lawyer who, in his own green youth, had been addicted to music, but had forced himself to relinquish this passion because it interfered with his legal studies. He expects his son, who has this hereditary gift for music, to practise the same self-control; but in Heiner the gift amounts to genius. He is already a composer, and do what he will he cannot tear himself away from the passion of his soul. He is physically incapable of reaching the required standard in mathematics, and is refused promotion to the 6th form. Desperately he shuts himself up, and grinds away at this detestable study – in vain; and when in the following year he is again refused promotion to the higher class he shoots himself. The discussion is twofold: the school motto, *non scholae sed vitae discimus*, is shown to be arrant humbug: the pupil is relentlessly sacrificed to the school, while individual bent and capacity are ignored. Actually Heiner is already a first-class musician, and the leaving certificate is not essential to him. The second theme is the tyranny of father over son; and this particular father, though he is as good as gold, is hopelessly incapable of seeing that his belief in the character-forming virtues of school discipline is sheer idiocy. Life, not school, forms character, is the moral of Strauss's work generally. As a contrast to Heiner – the German dreamer in the cruel grip of life – there is the figure of an active rebel, a boy poet who has read Darwin; he has been expelled from one school, and scamps the dull routine of the second simply because it is too slow and pedantic for his quick and practical mind. This boy will surmount his fate. In *Kreuzungen* (1904) the way to a true life is opened out; the hero throws up his post to live, without marrying her, with a girl who is pregnant by him. But passion fades; and when the girl realizes that merely a sense of duty is chaining the man to her she makes way, with cool determination, for another woman. Love is a hard test of character; what matters is not the wrong sort of experience, but the will to get over it. *Der nackte Mann* (1912) is a historical novel of Strauss's native town of Pforzheim; the theme is the struggle, at the beginning of the seventeenth century, between Calvinists and Lutherans. *Das Riesenspielzeug* (1935), with its anti-Socialist and anti-Marxist virus, belongs to Nazi *Blut- und Bodenliteratur*. The 'giant toy' is a farm in the Black Forest, and the hero turns from the culture of the schools to the nation-serving life of farm and field. Strauss's Novellen have readability (*Menschenwege*, 1898; *Hans und Grete*, 1910; *Der Schleier* – by common consent a masterpiece – 1931).

It is customary to pair Emil Strauss with HERMANN HESSE (1877-). Both are Swabians – Hesse from Calw in Württemberg, and both are vagabonds in sunny climes – Hesse is almost as Italianate as Paul Heyse or Isolde Kurz. He also to begin with shows the impress of pre-naturalistic models (e.g. of Gottfried Keller in the irony of *Peter Camenzind* and the first two collections of Novellen); here, however, the radical difference between Strauss and Hesse emerges – whereas Strauss hammers his characters out of hard dramatic experience Hesse, who has the morbidity of the true neo-romantics, dreams his characters into soft lyric moods and leads them gently through pain and pleasure to the peace of death. Moreover, Hesse develops – his later novels are finely philosophical and psycho-analytical; while Strauss remains the preacher of salvation by hard knocks. Strauss ends as a purveyor of Nazi doctrine; Hesse in later years was treated, somewhat gently, as a diseased and spineless Nordic who uses that Jewish infamy of psycho-analysis to undermine the sanity of his race.

Hermann Hesse began with an ironical analysis of the artistic temperament: *Hinterlassene Schriften und Gedichte Hermann Lauschers* (1901), and followed this up with a kind of inverted *Künstlerroman*: *Peter Camenzind* (1904); the artist divests himself of his artistry and levels himself to the humdrum existence of the ordinary mortal; here we have, not (as with Thomas Mann) the contrast with the tortured mentality of the artist of the happy normal being, but a sheer decadent surrender of personality. At least on the face of it: an ironical treatment of the glorification of the artist (*Künstlerverhimmelung*) may be the undertone; or, more likely, persiflage of the author's self. Hesse was the son of a missionary, and he was sent to the Protestant Theological College at Maulbronn[1] to be fitted for the same calling. Actually he earned his living for a time as a bookseller. Like Peter Camenzind he was a scholarship boy who failed in his calling and found himself again by lake and mountain as a child of nature. Peter Camenzind returns to his native Swiss village of Nimikon; Hesse too elected to live in Switzerland, though not till 1912; previously he had lived at Gaienhofen on the Lake of Constance. In *Unterm Rad* (1905) the autobiographical element is glaring: the hero goes from Calw to the Seminary at Maulbronn, breaks down under the strain of study, is sent home ill, and drowns himself. As in Strauss's *Freund Hein* – which may have influenced Hesse – the school system is blamed for the lad's martyrdom; in both novels there is a ring of reality in the gentle unfolding of the process of mental exhaustion. In the following novels the psychology deepens gradually. *Gertrud* (1910) has a musician for hero, and tells a tale of marital failure and of fading skill. *Rosshalde* (1914) is finely psycho-analytical. Veraguth, a famous painter, lives at Rosshalde, his country estate, but in an *atelier* in the grounds, while his estranged wife lives in the mansion. Man and wife meet for meals only. There are two sons: one, at the university, takes the mother's side (*Sohn-Vater-Kampf*); the other, Pierre, is a child. Veraguth would separate from his wife if she would let him have Pierre, all that remains to him in life except his work; but this she will not agree to. This state of affairs is revealed to an old friend, a rubber planter in the Far East, who spends a holiday at Rosshalde; he by cautious questioning probes the painter's state of mind, and shows him where healing might

---

[1] Where Hölderlin studied before proceeding to the higher Seminary at Tübingen.

lie – in separation, even at the price of relinquishing Pierre. The boy dies of meningitis, and the painter is free to go to the blazing tropics (where there are lovely native women to paint – and love . . .) with his sun-burnt and happy friend. The problem – whether love for a child should chain a man to a hard wife – is the same as that of Ricarda Huch's *Vita Somnium Breve*, but there is more verisimilitude in Hesse's picture of the suffering husband, who, immured in loneliness, lives doggedly on in the hypnosis of resignation, in illusory contact with a wife who has never had any feeling for his needs. Domiciled now in Switzerland, a hotbed of psycho-analysis, Hesse was himself treated by a pupil of Jung, when he fell ill as a result of mental stress during the War; he then wrote a series of typically psycho-analytical novels. *Knulp* (1915), the story of a vagabond lover, ranks with its description of *Wanderqual* as closely related to the substance of the great novels and reflects what may be interpreted as Hesse's own abandonment of the masculine principle of *bürgerlich* for the feminine principle of the nomadic life and Bohemian freedom (see also his poem *Auf der Reise*). In *Klein und Wagner* (1919) the schoolmaster Wagner murders his wife and children and Klein is conscious that in his heart of hearts he approves the deed; Klingsor in *Klingsors letzter Sommer* (1920) is similarly convinced, as he goes his way *zu den Müttern*, that all feelings, even cruelty, are good because they are stirrings that lead to a reversal of personality and a renewal of self. In *Demian* (1919) – as in Friedrich Huch's *Mao* (1907) – there is a minute delineation of states of adolescence as determined by the uprooting which school life means and by the chemical changes in the body before and after the shock of puberty; the psycho-analytic probing through a blanket of occultism reveals the two worlds of a boy's mind, the world of parents, home, and duty, and the luring forbidden world of mystery which begins with the servants in the kitchen and stretches out to drink and girls and bold ideas that frighten at the first impact and then grow familiar as friends; they who domineer in this other world are those with the mark of Cain – this, as it turns out, is merely the sign of superiority in strong faces which the inferior Abels fear. The (Byronic) fascination of Cain is in the face of Demian (? = demon), the school friend of the hero Sinclair[1]; rumour has it that Demian

---

[1] Hesse signed this novel with the name of Emil Sinclair. Sinclair is the name of Hölderlin's friend.

and his mother live as lovers. The kernel of the book is the conception of the mother: of her a boy has two images, one physical, the other ideal; in this novel the ideal image is transferred to Demian's mother, to 'Frau Eva', i.e. any mother, the mother of all; and the story ends with a promise that she will come to Sinclair when wanted – incest in symbol, since Sinclair and Demian are respectively the timid or angelic and the aggressive or demonic aspects of one character. The conception is a daring and delicate symbolization of the all-folding, cradling function of motherhood and motherliness: that creeping to breasts is one instinct in childhood and maturity, and in a woman's embrace man is always a child; any child's mother is his wife to be; any man's wife is his mother and ideal, whose brooding face has called him from the deeps to her bosom; 'mother' is alpha and omega, the far fountain spring and the vast safe harbour of love. The new morality in a world now breaking in pain through the shell must (as music does already) harmonize the two worlds, sundered at present by convention: love + sex, mother + vampire, man + beast, God + devil. *Siddhartha* (1922) is permeated with the Indian quietism with which Hesse had made himself familiar when, in 1911, he had fled from *'die Verrohung unserer Kultur'* to India. The novel is an attempt to weave what is on the face of it Indian philosophy, but is in the heart of it a considered Bolshevization of morality, stage by stage, into the story of a boy's relations to his father and the world. *Siddharta* is the completion of *Demian*: as in *Demian* one personality is split into halves (angel and demon), so it is in the later novel into the ever-seeking Siddharta and his friend Govinda, who is obedient to doctrine (heterodox and orthodox). In *Demian* boy moves ever nearer to mother as the centre of emotion; in *Siddharta* boy moves ever farther away from father, for a boy's experience of life is newer and therefore more true than the faded experience of a father; in mother boy surrenders self, for love absorbs all to create anew; he finds himself away from father (the son-father motive of expressionism explained by psycho-analysis). The hero of Hesse's novel *Der Steppenwolf* (1927), Harry Haller, an artist, calls himself 'the wolf of the steppes': the steppes are the wastes of existence in which the artistic temperament is shut out from the peace and comfort normal beings enjoy (the smell of furniture polish which he sniffs as he passes the first-floor flat on his way to his lonely attic rooms reminds him of the lost world, the world of mahogany, early rising, duty, mother). There can be no harmony when one is two, wolf and man, with the wolf snarling at the man. The man loves Mozart, poetry, ideals, peace; the wolf has wild urges, but in the higgledy-piggledy of society the wolf is penned with the sheep (the genius lives in contiguity with an alien crowd, and must adapt himself – or be slaughtered). Really one is more than two: personality is divided into chess-pieces: the individual has a multiple personality, he is wolf, tiger, monkey, bird of Paradise, and these are suppressed by wolf as wolf is suppressed by *Bürger*. Hermann, the friend of Haller's youth, is Hermine, who casts over him the spell of the hermaphrodite; she (he) is also the fresh and uncrumpled Pierrot with whom he dances. The mystic union of joy is the merging of personality in the mass: a fox-trot mingles us in a mass and makes us one. Haller is shown a mirror in which he sees himself as Haller and wolf of the steppes, each trying to devour the other: he is told that in order to extinguish the reflection he has only to laugh at it (humour begins when we learn not to take ourselves seriously). The novel ends in a medley of interfused symbolic craziness, like a film in which one picture is shot through another. There is a Magic Theatre, admission to which is by a trifling suicide; the doors of the closed boxes bear the legend: '*Alle Mädchen sind dein: Einwurf eine Mark*' (=all the girls I love are mine, for spirit pierces spirit). Mozart (a genius who – pigtail and girlish grace and Rococo – had harmonized the artist's and middle-class life) turns somersaults and plays trills with his heels; Haller pulls Mozart's pigtail, it lengthens, and carries Haller into icy space. Mozart appears again in evening dress, tinkers up a wireless set, and remarks that radio, though it projects music where it does not belong, does not destroy it: as radio cheapens the sublime, so does life in this Magic Theatre ('*nur für Verrückte*') of the world: the lesson is to laugh at it, not destroy it. With this consoling thought – 'the gallows humour of life' – suicide is not necessary. Hesse's next novel, *Narziss und Goldmund* (1930) is perhaps his masterpiece; it is at all events fascinating with its soft rhythm and its patient unravelling of psychic complications. Here again we have the old German progress from *tump* to *wîs*; the result is the proof, not that cloistered purity is the divine ideal, but that the life of the senses as much as the ascetic's flight from reality is service to the divine purpose – all ways lead to God. The dualism of existence is interpreted as a conflict of the paternal and maternal principles: paternal is the urge to abstract thought and the contemplative life; maternal is the tyranny of the senses. But only the maternal principle is creative; the paternal and therefore hard and masculine principle interprets – and should guide – its weak and pathetic contrary, the thinker 'obsessed with fine distinctions'. Thus Narziss is guide and mentor, and unselfish lover, of Goldmund, nature's darling, the doomed voluptuary and poet-dreamer; we first find them together as novices in a medieval monastery, and even then Narziss by patient questioning reveals to Goldmund his own inner nature. Narziss rises to be Abbot of the monastery; Goldmund, sent out to collect herbs on the moors, is initiated by a nut-brown gipsy; he disrobes her, and discovers beauty. Thereafter his life is that of the wandering scholar; woman after woman gives herself to him (*'die Weiber sind so gierig'*); characteristically the only one who turns contemptuously aside from his bloom and beauty is a Jewish girl whom he finds strewing her raven hair with the ashes of her father, whom the Nordic Christians of Germany have burnt by the wayside; he knows she will be seized and violated, for she too is a lone wanderer, but he takes leave of her 'as if she were a queen'. She teaches him that there is the will to die (*Sterbenwollen*) as well as the necessity of dying (*Sterbenmüssen*); and later he knows that life is ripe when the will to die is reached. This stage the belovèd vagabond attains when at long last women look at him as one spent and unseductive. The only thing worth living for, he had told Narziss, is copulation; and yet he has lived for more than woman. 'Your eyes are never merry,' says a girl who loves him, 'they seem to say that all this only lasts a minute.' He comes to realize that only creative art can save beauty and feeling for yet a little while from the Dance of Death; and he attaches himself to a great carver of wood, and creates as his first masterpiece the image of Narziss as the Apostle John – his expression of the worship of his contrary. He dreams of recapturing a fleeting mystery – the look in a woman's eyes in the spasm of copulation; and this distortion and contraction, this leap of fire and the fading of it, he has seen too in the eyes of a peasant woman over whom he held a candle when she was giving birth to a child; for rapture and pain, he realizes, are the same. His final masterpiece, he dreams, is to be his dead mother's face, which appears to him in dreams; but as age withers him it is no longer a personal face but that of all the women he has loved, the face of Eve, of the *Urmutter*, which lures to rapture, to birth, and, as the last grasp of her love, to death. But ere he has time to shape the mystery of her face she folds her hands round his heart and shapes him – to the will to death, to the fading of the fire she wakes. And before he dies Narziss, the lonely scholar with the fine face shaped by thinking, has bent over him and kissed him with the only kiss that life grants him. In *Der Kurgast* (1925) and *Die Nürnberger Reise* (1927) there is again the problem of nature's urges and the controlling function of the mind, and in the latter we read that nature is, as flowers are, lovely but fast fading, while reason, though it wearies, is durable as gold. *Morgenlandfahrt* (1923), with its secret league of sterling characters, comes still nearer to the synthesis of these opposites which is symbolically achieved in *Das Glasperlenspiel* (1943). This story of the bead-game, in the province of Kastalien round about the year 2400, shows mathematics and art in unison contriving control of the functions of existence. These bead-players live like monks, sundered from 'the forbidden and inferior world', devoting themselves to the works of the spirit, as happened in Goethe's *pädagogische Provinz* in the *Wanderjahre*. In days following the havoc of a great war, which has brought degradation to mankind, the bead-players in the peace of their Alpine valley practise this game of glass pearls which, '*der Inbegriff des Geistigen und Musischen*', synthetizes intellectual disciplines and in which all dissonance becomes unison. The purpose of their order is to rescue the world from that degradation of mind which had come from the 'warlike age', '*das feuilletonistische Zeitalter*', and to safeguard order, norm, reason, law, and measure. The protagonist is Josef Knecht, whose life is chronicled from his early orphan days till he rises to be Magister Ludi, the High Priest of this gameful religion. But he is initiated into historical studies by Pater Jacobus (what is quoted points to Jakob Burckhardt as model), and he learns that all historical phases are transitory. He realizes, too, that the bead-players preserve cultural values, but do not create them, and he observes that everything tends to change to its contrary. Thus he himself, Knecht by name, is Master of the Order. He discovers that he is not merely a Castalian, but a human being as well, and that as such his concern is with the world as a whole and not with a fraction of it. And so he sets out to find his earthly transformation, breaks way into the common life, and is drowned in a mountain lake.

Of Hermann Hesse's critical and essayistic work *Blick ins Chaos* (1920) has three essays on Dostoieffsky, whose influence on his fiction is clear, while *Dank an Goethe* (1946) details his debt to the sage of Weimar. The essays of *Krieg und Frieden* (1949), in particular *Der Europäer* and *Zarathustras Wiederkehr*, reflect Hesse's reactions to the World War II. His *Briefe* (1951), with date from 1927 to 1951, are addressed to correspondents who have sought his advice and to his contemporaries (Thomas Mann, Oskar Loerke, André Gide, C. G. Jung, Theodor Heuss, etc.) and are in essence self-interpretation.

As a lyric poet Hesse is traditional in form: *Gedichte* (1902), *Unterwegs* (1911), *Musik des Einsamen* (1915), *Trost der Nacht* (1928), *Stunden im Garten* (1936; an epic idyll), *Orgelspiel* (1940), and the complete edition *Die Gedichte* (1942 and 1947). His early verse draws from the common fund of romantic themes, moods, and imagery; for his mature poetry the key is the *Zweisinnigkeit* of his great novels, the saga of man passing '*im Zickzack zwischen Trieb und Geist durchs Leben*' – '*Bald Mönch, bald Wüstling, Denker bald, bald Tier*'. Often sensuous, vividly limned and coloured, but rarely subtle, they lack the compelling spontaneity of a poet proper; the verse is indeed *en marge* of the novels, in which, however, the ideological clash is consistently presented and defined, whereas in the poems it is scattered and fragmentary. They are pondered in patience, not poured forth in passion; that is, they are not *Rauschkunst*; and, moreover, there is a restricted range of theme and *ewige Wiederkehr* both in Nietzsche's sense and in the sense of iteration. One is tempted to say that, though in the novel Goldmund is clearly Hesse, the poems are thought out and morally contrived by Narziss, although of course this might mean that in them there is the synthesis the novels seek.

Gottfried Keller's ironic manner and Swiss sagacity come natural to JAKOB SCHAFFNER (1875-1944), who, born in Basel, began as a shoemaker's apprentice, and made use of his journeyman's experiences in his first novel, *Die Irrfahrten des Jonathan Bregger* (1905). Schaffner's ideal hero is a good European without religion except that of the solidarity of nations on the path of human brotherhood and progress. His ironic handling of customs and character sunders him from the *Heimatkünstler*, but in his descriptions of Swiss life, as in his village tale *Die Erlhöferin* (1908), he is vivid and close to reality. His great effort is *Konrad Pilater* (vol. I, 1910, vol. II,

1922), an autobiographical novel on the scale and pattern of Keller's *Der grüne Heinrich*. In *Der Bote Gottes* (1911) he goes back to the Thirty Years War. *Der Dechant von Gottesbüren* (1917) reflects his reactions to the First Great War. Religious problems provide the woof and weft of the trilogy *Johannes* (1922), *Die Jünglingszeit des Johannes Schattenbold* (1930), *Eine deutsche Wanderschaft* (1933). The great city is the background of *Der Mensch Krone* (1928). By the prominence he gives in his novels to the clash of Catholicism and Protestantism in Switzerland Schaffner ranges himself alongside Enrica von Handel-Mazzetti. He has attempted popular history in his *Geschichte der schweizerischen Eidgenossenschaften* (1915).

Ironic handling of life is the salient element in the novels of the two cousins, Friedrich Huch and Rudolf Huch; but since the literary clan of the Huchs – Ricarda Huch is Rudolf's sister – have their home centre at Brunswick it is natural that in their case the influence of Wilhelm Raabe should supplement that of Gottfried Keller. There is an implied didacticism in the novels of FRIEDRICH HUCH (1873-1913), but it is not conveyed with the breezy directness of Emil Strauss, it shines forth rather from a subtle quizzical treatment of human frailty and futility and would be scurrilous if it were not so sly. Born in Brunswick he studied philology, and was a tutor in various families. His first novel, *Peter Michel* (1901), has affinities with Hermann Hesse's *Peter Camenzind*: in both a dreamer of the feminine type – Peter Michel is obviously once again 'der deutsche Michel' – is disillusioned by life, and is shown in the closing pages as a smug, contented Philistine. In Hesse's novel, it is true, the hero is exceptional, a died-out artist, while Peter Michel is any German, or indeed any normal being anywhere who sees the dreams of his youth fade into the light of common day. That this common man we all know is represented in the novel by a teacher is part of the satire; and since Friedrich Huch was himself a teacher by trade he should know the depths of dullness of this profession; to a teacher reading the sad story the consolation must be that there *is* the spice of poetry in Peter – before he is ruined by routine and environment. Peter Michel is the usual scholarship boy who rises to be a secondary teacher; incidentally the description of school life is more life-like than in the other novels which show up the Philistinism of academic existence – the teachers are humdrum enough, but the headmaster here, though wrapped in routine and cramped by cant, displays tact in the exercise of his authority. Famous is the chapter in which one of the masters is accused by another of jeopardizing the morals of his boys by having a mistress: the headmaster is aware of the facts, but saves the school an excellent teacher by assuming that the delinquent (more or less) intends to regularize the situation by marrying the lady (he does not, but keeps his post). The novel stands out by its presentation of the son-mother motif: Peter is forced into opposition to his mother, particularly when she tries to keep him moral by getting him married. Marriage, the novel demonstrates, is the stamp of respectability, but it may brand deep. All the poetry of the tale (and there is a deeply probing psychology in the weft of it) is in the suppressed sexual emotion of Peter before his marriage, and that dulling of this vibrant emotion into the animal paternal functions which is the normal result of marriage. As a grammar school student Peter dreams himself into a sensitive love of Liesel, the daughter of the *Kantor* with whom he lodges; at the university, amid the bestial orgies of German student life (unsparingly pictured), his dreams of her keep him clean; however, as the course of events shows, what he loves is not Liesel but his dream-picture of her: when he sees his headmaster's wife he has an optical illusion that *she* is Liesel, and loves her even when it is clear that she is not; for *she* is now his dream-picture or his ideal woman. The situation is tensely dramatic, particularly in Chapter VII, which is masterly in every detail: the headmaster, sure of his wife, leaves her with Peter in a room where the red lamp-shade symbolizes what might be demonic danger – if the characters were not in the grip of respectability. The headmaster's wife talks it over with him, and sends him back to Liesel; but she – the only Bohemian in the book – refuses to marry into the teaching profession, though she does very energetically take him into the forest and seduces him (the only lapse of his exemplary career); finally she marries a Graf, and is a shining light of society – which is also life as it is. And thus we know that all a teacher (particularly) has to hope for is to grow mouldy, and to put up with his wife and children – and colleagues; and to talk grandiloquently of the contentment of home and duty. Marriage keeps Jean Paul's *Schulmeisterlein* in the clouds; Peter Michel it brings down to pipe and slippers and sloppy sentiment. In his next three tales Friedrich Huch specializes in the somewhat painfully detailed transcription, deduced by adult divination, of processes in the minds of children and growing youth, and of the relations of parents to these processes. If his children have attraction, it is that of constructed models. In *Geschwister* (1903) two girls represent the dualism – familiar in medieval literature as *Weltflucht* and *Welt freude* – of the brooding religious bent and the need of pleasure and company, with Hagen, the tutor of the girls' brother, as the man between the two. In *Wandlungen* (1905), the sequel to *Geschwister*, the boy of the previous tale and his relations to his father (*Sohn-Vater-Kampf*) move into the centre of interest, with the father's second wife (the woman with a past) estranging the two by her shallow character. In *Mao* (1907) the *Kinderpsychologie* is still more searching. A family who were poor but are now rich live in an old patrician house. The only son, Thomas, goes to the elementary school, and brings home the smell of the class, which is painful to him. He is exquisitely sensitive, and for that reason is bound to be tortured in the rough-and-tumble of school life. The book thus falls into line with the studies of school life in Emil Strauss's *Freund Hein* and Hesse's *Unterm Rad*. As a satirist of Philistinism Friedrich Huch pairs with Carl Sternheim; he has less glitter, but more depth. And he is more depressing; for while Sternheim makes the respectability look like a huge joke Friedrich Huch, quietly but pitilessly, pictures it as a sea of idiocy in which we are all submerged. A few dreamers, dangerously gifted, struggle to rise out of it; but either, like Peter Michel, they are sucked back or, like Pitt, the hero of *Pitt und Fox* (1908), they are isolated at the rim of decency. The title of the story was no doubt suggested by a remark of Goethe that he could not help picturing Pitt as a pug-nosed broomstick and Fox as a fat pig. The names stick from boyhood to two brothers who are elaborately contrasted, more or less as Wolfram von Eschenbach contrasts Parzival, as a dreamer swayed by moods, problematic and baffled, with Gawân, the shallow and insinuating masterful man who takes the women the other might have had if he had not been decent. For Pitt, who studies philosophy, the problem life presents is the conflict of will, feeling, and action; and, as the novel shows, the conflict is due to distance from 'primitivity', in which willing, feeling, and acting synchronize. Other problems of the day fill out the action: the son-father conflict, the right of the unmarried mother to refuse to marry her seducer. The most striking thing in the book is the delicate way in which the physical feelings of Elfriede – who falls in love with Pitt –, and the restraint imposed upon the two by good breeding are indicated: her longing for embraces is foiled by Pitt's gentlemanly aloofness, and the point made is that the female undergoes a sexual awakening in contact with a male whose attitude is one of intellectual interest and sympathy: for Pitt, Elfriede is a lady, not sex. Pitt is sexually awakened by a simple girl – the daughter of Fox's landlady – of whom by the accepted code of student (that is, Philistine) morality he has a right of possession: he is too decent to exercise this right and it is taken by his brother. The novel ranks as a penetrating study of sexual phases; the Dickensian element – an almost affectionate delineation of whimsicalities – fails by comparison with the English model. Friedrich Huch's last novel, *Enzio* (1910), is yet another in the long list of *Künstlerromane*: the hero has music and a sensuous response to beauty in his blood – his father is a conductor; and his musical career is ruined because he cannot control his sex impulses. He has a student's affair with a simple and very charming girl of the people; Enzio is condemned, not for this experience – to Friedrich Huch natural and beautiful – but for his disreputable drifting to worthless creatures. Admirable is the contrast of this restless genius with a cultured girl whose name, Irene, symbolizes her nature; when she hears the tale of his loose living she breaks off her engagement to him, and he skates down the river till the ice breaks and rids the world of one who has been spoilt, not shaped, by what should be the best life can offer. The lesson of the book is that life and work are parallels: Enzio loves music as he loves his women, but in both spheres he is tossed about on the waves of impulse; work and love should be *terra firma* for artist and lover to build his sanctuary on.

In the novels of RUDOLF HUCH (1862-1943) the fling-back to pre-naturalistic models is declared and decided. He fluttered the dove-cotes by his two pamphlets launched against naturalism, the over-estimation of Gerhart Hauptmann, Maeterlinck, Helene Böhlau, and against other crazes of a degenerate day (*Mehr Goethe*, 1899; *Eine Krisis*, 1904), and shaped his style on that of Goethe and Wilhelm Raabe. He satirizes the life of small towns in *Aus dem Tagebuche eines Höhlenmolches* (1895), *Der Frauen wunderlich Wesen* (1903), *Komödianten des Lebens* (1906), and *Die Rübenstedter* (1910). His best novels are *Die beiden Ritterhelm* (1907), *Familie Hellmann* (1908), and *Talion* (1913); and in these there is something of the

morbidity of subject he had scorched in his pamphlets. There is
delightful humour in *Wilhelm Brinkmeyers Abenteuer* (1911), *Alt-
männersommer* (1925), and *Humoristische Erzählungen* (1936). Generally speaking Rudolf Huch's aim was to educate the *Bürger* to a
realization of the vacuity of his existence; he is in this respect the
most academically minded of a group to which belong Friedrich
Huch, Heinrich Mann, Carl Sternheim, and Leonhard Frank.

EDUARD VON KEYSERLING (1855-1918) is an impressionist in the
true sense of the word: there is in all his work a nervous refinement of style, and the goal of his characters is not a moral mastery
of life but sensuous enjoyment of it. For him, when love ends,
life is over. His affinity is with that master of sensitive Danish
prose, Hermann Bang,[1] whose works, with their subtle delineation
of culture-worn aristocrats, had a great vogue in impressionist
Germany; but it is inevitable that he should be compared with
Friedrich Spielhagen, for both depict the junkers of north-east
Germany. The region of Spielhagen's predilection is Pomerania,
that of Keyserling is his native Courland, but the junker type is in
the characterization of both essentially similar. There is, however,
a difference which moves them worlds apart – while Spielhagen
describes these landed gentry as an outsider of radical and even
revolutionary views (though with a suppressed admiration for a
socially superior class) Keyserling takes it for granted that their
qualities are the prerogatives of their class. And these qualities –
the most questionable to us are the right to adultery and the
manorial right (exercised by all males of the family) to any girl on
the estate – to Graf von Keyserling represent vitality ('*Lebens-
kraft*'), adventure, 'the pleasurable sensation of the beast of prey'
('*angenehmes Raubtiergefühl*'). These junkers have no morality, but
they have *Herrenmoral*. However, – and this is the note of his work
– the characters he chooses to depict are not the bold bad Baltic

---

[1] Born in 1858, Hermann Bang lived in Berlin. His first novel – *Hoffnungs-
lose Geschlechter* in German – has for hero the last decadent scion of a noble
race. In his later works he has Maeterlinck's conception of fate as a secret
force which breathes around us. With the short stories of *Leben und Tod* his
attitude to life moves to a naïve hedonism: we can defy fate, and snatch what
fleeting joys we can: '*es gibt nichts als den Trieb; der allein ist Herr und Meister*';
'*Blut ist Blut; das will sieden, bis es matt ist oder kalt ist.*' Keyserling's *Herren-
menschen* have the frightful sensation of loneliness of Bang's characters, due
to the tragic intensity of their feeling that there is nothing in life but this
snatching at pleasure which *must* be shot with pain because it passes, and
because in the face of fate, which ironically permits it, it is so mean.

20

barons who live a full life, but the exceptional, thwarted dreamers of the stock, those whom their finer feelings force to stand by in the gnawing bitterness or helpless sadness of resignation, while their inferior but robust brethren seize life where it offers. '*Wir, an denen das Leben vorübergeht*', might be the motto of his works; and what happens in tale after tale is no happening at all, but just the melancholy inspection of what might have happened – '*Ereignis in der Ereignislosigkeit*'. In his novel *Dumala* (1907) the pastor of a parish is in love with the wife of the lame lord of the manor, but he knows she has a lover, and comes near to murdering him; all that he has of life is to gaze at a lighted window on which his lady's shadow is cast. In *Seine Lebenserfahrung*, one of the stories of *Bunte Herzen* (1908), a man who knows he is preferred puts off his courage to sin till the woman goes off for sheer boredom with an insignificant rival. In actual life Eduard von Keyserling was anything but a bold bad baron. The third son of the lord of the manor at Paddern in Courland (then in Russia), he was educated at Dorpat University; and, apart from a period when he managed the ancestral estate for his brother, he was exiled from the life which he sees in a mystic beauty of landscape through the haze of a dream. When, after the conclusion of his studies, he resided in Vienna, he appears to have been attracted to Socialism, and to have been disillusioned by contact with the movement; his experiences at this time are assumed to form the basis of his novel *Die dritte Stiege*. In Vienna began the disease which was to lay him low; from 1897 onwards he suffered (like Heine) from a spinal disease due to syphilis, and became blind in 1907. Of decisive importance was a stay in Italy: here – an almost traditional experience of German writers[1] – his mind opened out to the magic of his northern homeland; and, like him, his dreams came home – if only, as in *Schwüle Tage*, to die. In 1899 he settled in Munich. After 1914 he wrote no more.

Keyserling's naturalistic novels *Rosa Herz* (1883) and *Die dritte Stiege* (1890) have as little importance as his dramas (*Ein Frühlingsopfer*, 1899; *Der dumme Hans*, 1901; *Peter Hawel*, 1903); the dramatic sketch *Benignens Erlebnis* (1905) has the vain snatching at life and happiness of the Novellen. As a delineator of North German

---

[1] Typical is Heinrich Mann's confession: '*Ich ging, sobald ich konnte, heim nach Italien. Ja, eine Zeitlang glaubte ich zu Hause zu sein. Aber ich war es auch dort nicht; und seit ich dies deutlich spürte, begann ich etwas zu können.*'

aristocracy Keyserling is often ranged with Fontane; but the comparison is illusory – Fontane, with the sympathetic understanding of an outsider, gives his characters just as they are, as quite ordinary gentlemen, with their class prejudices and snobbishness, their tricks of conversation: in Keyserling's aristocrats there is decay – not so much the moral decay which Spielhagen sees, but the decay of blood quickened by experience (actual or in dream) of alien ways, of the mellow culture of the West or the hot passion of the South. Thus in *Schwüle Tage* (1906) Ellita, prisoned in her impoverished manor, excites her school-boy cousin, whose own blood is restlessly stirring in dream, by dancing the bolero under the forest trees. She has given a last spell of happiness to the lad's Casanova-like father, who has come home, stricken with disease, to die – but not before he has healed their secret sinning by arranging Ellita's marriage with an officer: she – '*eine Blüte der adligen Kultur*' – must sacrifice life to be true to her class; and the boy dreamer, by accident, sees her (a *Herrenweib*), in her last rendezvous with his father before her marriage, threaten the worn-out old rake with her riding-whip. Admirable in this masterly Novelle is the fitting of human moods to the tense atmosphere: plain and forest swelter in the late summer heat, and with the breaking of the gathered storm comes the catastrophe of marriage to Ellita, death by morphia to the exhausted lover, and disillusionment to the sensitive boy. The striking feature here as elsewhere is the delicacy of the characterization: we see vividly the suffering lines on the old rake's face, the physical exasperation of Ellita, the languid pose of an invalid and faded lady of her mother, the baffled wonderment and impatience of the boy, and the idiot-like receptivity of the barefoot girl who relieves the pressure of the boy's blood. Not less masterly is the contrast of the two types of women in *Beate und Mareile* (1903). 'Die weisse Beate' is once again the 'blossom of culture', ruling her manorial hall in a kind of silvery radiance; *Schlossherrin* rather than wife, not sensual because by the exigency of rank she may not be ('*Verlieben*', she says, '*fand ich lächerlich; Verlieben gehörte zur Kammerjungfer*'). Mareile is the daughter of the Inspector on the estate, earth-born and the full-blown flower not of culture but of passion; and when the gush of passion has spent itself and the manorial reveller returns to the cold decency of home he knows that henceforth for him life is to watch life go by: chastity is an essential of *tenue*, but stagnant. In this identification of vitality and sex Keyserling – he is utterly erotic – is of course not true to the junker type, in whom notoriously martial qualities come first; but the obsession is veiled by his association of it with the landscape, visionary in his notation – sweeping plains, brooding forests, park and pond by the manorial home, and with the extremes of the climate folding the mood of the moment. In sheer impressionism of landscape-colouring Keyserling is unsurpassed; for instance: '*Still und sandig lag das Land da, überall gelber Sand; Wiesen, Felder und Gärten lagen darauf, wie eine verblasste Stickerei auf einem blind gewordenen Goldgrund.*'

HERMANN STEHR (1864-1940), a Silesian and a saddler's son who began life as a village schoolmaster, is above all a visionary, a mystic seeking religious certainty. In youth he had his own mental crisis: brought up as a Catholic he studied Darwin and began to doubt; for his change of faith he was persecuted by his official superiors, and found relief from his suffering in writing stories. His Darwinian positivism gave way to a Maeterlinckian fatalism which, he says, is rooted in the Silesian character: '*Wir Menschen halten doch immer nur die Fäden in den Händen, das Schicksal aber webt, was es will . . .* '. Reason is, therefore, of no account in the government of life: the beginning of faith must be in a '*grundentstiegene Unsicherheit*'. Not reason decides the course of a man's life; and free will is like a doctor trying to cure a grievously sick man: man's fate is in his blood. Stehr, therefore, sets himself the task of piercing into those undiscovered regions of the soul where fate grows; that is, to plunge deep into subconsciousness and the urge of the senses; until he reaches his final conviction that '*das Denken ohne Bewusstsein erlebt die Bewegung des Weltalls, und das Gefühl, das sich nicht kennt, die Empfindungen Gottes*'. Stehr's own mental conflict is reflected in his first work, the short stories of *Auf Leben und Tod* (1898) and the novel *Der begrabene Gott* (1905). His conquest of mystic faith is symbolized in *Drei Nächte* (1909), in which Faber appears, a dismissed elementary teacher, the mouthpiece of Stehr himself. Faber reappears in *Der Heiligenhof* (1918), the scene of which is not, as is customary with Stehr, in his native Silesia but in Westphalia (as is also the case in the short story *Meister Cajetan*, 1931). *Der Heiligenhof* is one of the most alluring – though perhaps the most illogical – of those novels which have *Wandlung* for their theme. Here conversion is equivalent to a turning inward of thought in the person of the hero, a Berserker type of farmer, as the effect of his conviction that his blind daughter is holy, and that her holiness proves the spirituality behind reality of life. Now his reformed character earns for his farm the name which is the title of the book. The mystical idea is that which Gerhart Hauptmann weaves into *Und Pippa tanzt*: only the blind see; or, in other words the outer reality seen by the eyes of the body is corruption, while the inner reality visible to the soul is imperishable beauty. In the life behind life, and there alone, is the peace that passeth understanding, and clarification is a process that must come out of one's own deeps ('*Selbstheiligung*') – the idea of salvation by another was invented by priests, but the muddiest pool grows clear of itself when peace comes to it within itself. The girl's sight is restored, however, by the miracle of her love for Peter Brindeisener, the son of her father's inveterate enemy (the Romeo and Juliet motif in a rural setting once more), and the religious faith of the Heiligenbauer almost founders when this daughter, because marriage with her boy is impossible, drowns herself in a pond. He recovers his faith only in the conviction that what had come to him by the accident of the girl's blindness must be regained by his own soul stirred to its deeps and consciously piercing to the light of divine truth. *Der Heiligenhof* is in some sort a companion volume to Hauptmann's *Emanuel Quint* – both novels continue the seventeenth-century mysticism of Jakob Böhme, and in both hallucinations and fixed ideas constitute religion. Stehr, with his type of the new *Seelenmensch*, is already the *Gottsucher* of the expressionists; but in *Der Heiligenhof* the *Wandlung* of which the expressionists are so fond occurs with the impossible suddenness of the conversion in Masefield's *Everlasting Mercy*. At bottom Stehr's mysticism is not so much Silesian as Maeterlinckian: it is not the New Jerusalem beyond the horizon, but a mirage.

Stehr's next novel, *Peter Brindeisener* (1924), is a sequel to *Der Heiligenhof*. Peter Brindeisener, for the love of whom the blind girl had gone to her death, relates his own experiences in the form of a confession. The chief interest is in the exposition of Stehr's somewhat bloodless attitude to sex. In other novels of Stehr social problems are handled. *Leonore Griebel* (1900) has a *femme incomprise* for heroine; the pathological problem of a finely strung woman's decay by the side of a hopelessly prosaic husband and her indifference even to the child she bears him (she regards it as his and as another shackle of dull domesticity) is patiently interpreted.

Stehr's one drama, *Meta Konegen* (1905), is related in theme: the heroine is neglected by her husband, who is engrossed by his struggle to free schools from clerical interference. The two late novels *Nathaniel Maechler* (1929) and *Die Nachkommen* (1933) deal in chronological sequence with the evolution of political ideas. Nathaniel Maechler is a tanner's apprentice who is infected with the ideas of the 1848 revolution; gradually he learns to subordinate himself to the welfare of the community – which safeguards the family. His descendants, however, in the illusive outer splendour and inner poverty of imperialist Germany, are criticized for their selfish defection from this totalitarian self-effacement. Stehr's Novellen fail because of their lack either of concentration or clearness. His first collection, *Auf Leben und Tod* (1898), is drab naturalism. *Der Schindelmacher* (1899) is, for Stehr, violent and even melodramatic: the hero transfers his farm to his niece, who humiliates him to the dust; the ghost of his dead wife appears, and goads him to vengeance. He rages like King Lear, smashes the furniture, mows the corn, and hangs himself in the corner where his wife died. As a Silesian Stehr should have that knowledge of the gnomes of the mountains which goes to the making of so many *Märchen*. But a *Märchen* which a child cannot understand is, as a *Märchen*, damned; and *Wendelin Heinelt* (1909), Stehr's most famous *Märchen*, is merely a cryptic elaboration of the theme that happiness is not the golden gift of the sprites of the underworld. The short story *Der Geigenmacher* (1926) is the fanciful symbolic *Märchen* of a maker of violins who loves and by his passion loses a maid, Schönlein, and then in the passion of his grief carves a magic violin, as though out of his own heart, rounds and smooths it to the shape of Schönlein's body, and from its chords conjures forth the music of Heaven. He had made perfect violins before he found Schönlein; but their music was not divine. Only suffering and privation ripen a master's magic gift.

Any valuation of Stehr today can only be provisional. German critics maintain that only a German can appreciate him; apparently a down-weighted brain is needed, and a patience unconscious of length of time. To read *Der Heiligenhof* is a heroic task. Stehr has the plodding mind of an elementary teacher; he grinds on and on to the end. His style, laden as it is with laborious thinking, has a level and heavy rhythm; nor has it the flashes of flame of the mystics proper – the ultimate effect is that of an imposing mass of solidly constructed truth, not that of revelation fired with the sublime ecstasy of faith. The mysticism is that of a schoolmaster whose class has expanded to a nation; and probably only the German nation could be fascinated by novels so religiously formative.

Some at least of the tales of JAKOB WASSERMANN (1873-1934) may be ranked as *Heimatkunst*: born at Fürth, where he began life as a clerk, he describes Franconia, and with great intimacy Nuremberg: in *Die Juden von Zirndorf* and other tales he is the accredited interpreter of the spiritual and physical environment of the Franconian Jews. But, since Wassermann is a Jew, his native province is not so much Franconia as a world of ideas, unctuously Oriental to a great extent in substance and presentment, although, in his autobiographical sketch *Mein Weg als Deutscher und Jude* (1921), he has energetically asserted his claim to all the German heritage of soul and language. The declared aim of his laboured writing is to bring about the birth through tribulation of spirit of 'the new man', simple, humble, and good, who calls himself brother to the outcast, and will kneel (in *Christian Wahnschaffe*) even to a criminal who has raped and murdered a little girl. (A murderer is innocent, runs the argument in Stehr's *Der Heiligenhof*, in the depths of his soul, just as on the ocean bed there is peace while tempests rend its surface; we shall see that the expressionists proper will show that not the murderer but the murdered is guilty.) Wassermann's didactic tendency clearly runs parallel with that of Hermann Stehr, but there is a wide disparity in their technique: Stehr leads up to his *Seelenmensch* by inner experiences which illumine and purify the soul they awaken; Wassermann's characters are transformed in a welter of crass sensationalism which has elements of Eugène Sue or of the *Police Gazette*. If only by reason of this lurid excitement and concentration on physically criminal types one is forced to question the permanent value of Wassermann's writings. Of interest there is no lack; the obvious reason for his comparative failure is that the cerebrally evolved characters act, not dynamically, but to illustrate the theory (proclaimed in *Christian Wahnschaffe*) that to reveal humanity the novelist must 'sink himself into sick souls', and unveil what is secret and hidden by 'inquisition' into the causes of moral disease. Wassermann's creed as a novelist is set down in the treatise *Die Kunst der Erzählung* (1904). '*Ich will nicht die Verknüpfung äusserer Erlebnisse geben*', he says, '*sondern die Wirrnis der inneren; ich setze keinen Ehrgeiz darin, Fäden zu knüpfen und zu lösen.*' He means that he would not prune and shape his matter to a logical cohesion, but light up the inextricable confusion of human happenings by allusive symbol and give them the significance of a myth. Dream and myth are poetry; the psychologist's interpretation is a naturalistic negation of poetry; it is a shameless exposure, not an imaged illumination. The psychologist of present-day literature, Wassermann says in another treatise, *Der Literat als Psycholog* (1910), is the very contrary of poet, he is '*der Literat*', '*der vom Mythos losgelöste Mensch, der auch von der Gesellschaft losgelöste Mensch*'. The technician, probably, is not tied to his technique, or falls below it; but there is considerable originality in his method, though the influence of other writers is patent: e.g. of E. T. A. Hoffmann and Jean Paul in certain of his Novellen (*Der niegeküsste Mund*, 1903), of Balzac in his linking of novel to novel by the migration of characters, and of Dostoieffsky in his exhaustive illumination of the soul of outcasts.

Wassermann made his reputation with *Die Juden von Zirndorf* (1897), in substance a withering exposure of Jew mentality. In the prologue the Jews in Fürth and Nuremberg, who live in a close racial community, hear that at Smyrna a Messiah has arisen; and they would go out to him with caravans, but news comes that he has gone over to Islam. They found a village, Zionsdorf, which the Christians corrupt to Zirndorf. There remains the problem whether the Messiah was really a renegade and a cheat, or a typical Jew who goes where profit is. In the second part a new Saviour arises, Agathon Geyer, in Zirndorf itself; but he saves himself only by overcoming the narrow spirit of the law. *Die Geschichte der jungen Renate Fuchs* (1900) is built up on one of those typical theses of Wassermann which to sober sense must seem absurd. In this novel a character who is obviously a copy of Peter Altenberg utters the portentous aphorism: there is an indestructible asbestos soul, and every girl has it, even if she falls. Renate Fuchs is a Munich lady engaged to a duke; she leaves him to run away with a student. She wades through all the filth of the world – she falls to a demonic creature who is recognized as a study of Wedekind – before she is reborn as that which her name signifies, and as the new woman who has a night of love with Agathon Geyer, the Saviour of the previous novel, ere he dies, and she bears him the first child of a new era: Beatus. In *Der Moloch* (1902) Wassermann first handles the obsession which recurs in *Der Fall Maurizius:*

summum jus, summa injuria. Arnold Ansorge, an innocent country youth, is horrified by a legal crime committed against a Jew, goes to Vienna (*der Moloch = die Grossstadt*) to seek a righting of the wrong (the influence of Kleist's *Michael Kohlhaas* manifests itself here as also in *Caspar Hauser* and *Der Fall Maurizius*), but is himself contaminated by the miasmic life of the city, and in hopeless self-contempt shoots himself. *Alexander in Babylon* (1905) has something of the exotic splendour and the rich Oriental colouring and sensationalism of Flaubert's *Salammbô*, but the theme is essentially that of the medieval epic of *Alexander*: even the mightiest conqueror must depart from his conquests, and have his mouth stopped with dust. What is the use of life, the sulphur-faced young king asks, if I cannot keep it? Of all Wassermann's novels *Caspar Hauser oder die Trägheit des Herzens* (1908) is that into which he has put most clearly the perhaps naïve religious teaching which was so dear to his heart. The events narrated are historical; and, though Wassermann has interpreted them with obstinate wilfulness and obsessional bitterness, he has changed them but little in details. In the summer of 1828 a boy appeared in the streets of Nuremberg who could neither walk nor speak. His story, Wassermann says, has all the elements of an ancient myth: he is like an inhabitant of another planet straying into this world as if by miracle. A contemporary jurist wrote a treatise, *An Example of a Crime against a Human Being*, to prove that Caspar was a legitimate prince of the house of Baden. The key to the mystery, as provided by the novel, would be that the morganatic wife of the Grand Duke of Baden had done away with her husband's son by his consort, a stepdaughter of Napoleon; whether with her knowledge or not, the boy had been kept immured in a dark tower and suddenly released by his jailer; and as soon as opportunity offered the reigning dynasty caused him to be assassinated. This prince imprisoned from birth in a dark tower and thrust out into the light of day at maturity is a theme familiar in German literature from the translations of Calderon's *La vida es sueño*; it was to be used again by Hofmannsthal in *Der Turm*. Wassermann uses the story as a ready-made exemplification of his faith in pure humanity: Arnold Ansorge in *Der Moloch* had been such an innocent depraved by contact with wickedness, but he had had some conception of human depravity, whereas Caspar Hauser has the utter innocence of a new-born babe. The problem then is: is it possible for a grown-up person to be as morally white as the driven snow? The answer is in the affirmative; for Caspar Hauser is an angel, and would remain an angel if the world would let him. But his keepers torment him, and force him to lie. And inevitably – for he has a face of girlish gentleness, brown curls glossed like those of animals that live in the dark, the light brown eyes of a frightened fawn, flesh that smells like honey – the wife of his keeper attempts what Potiphar's wife attempted. What is wrong with the world is that we have got *Trägheit des Herzens*, sluggish hearts or hearts that won't wake up and glow in the worship of innocence and justice. This famous phrase was to be blazoned like a diamond in the forefront of their programme by the expressionists. But by Wassermann's showing no expressionist fervour would save humanity so long as there are dynasties of princes: their juridical system is an abomination, and innocence is a myth . . . In *Caspar Hauser* Wassermann tracks evidence with the relentless inquisitiveness of a criminologist and pronounces upon it with the apodictic certainty of a judge. In the novels which follow he plunges ever deeper into the investigation of strange crimes, and tends to interpret them as the effect of primitive urges, or, another adept in the occultism of the period, he hints at psychic transferences. In the short stories of *Die Schwestern* (1906) he presents a trio of women who are sisters in the morbidity and suffering of their souls: Joan of Castile, the mother of the Emperor Charles V, who takes about with her the painted corpse of her husband Philip the Fair, in which a watch takes the place of a heart; a washerwoman hanged for murder in Fleet Street in 1732; the daughter of the President of the French Republic in 1830 who opens her veins in a cell. *Das Gänsemännchen* (1915) is one of the most notorious handlings of a man's cohabitation with two wives. Wassermann's story is probably modelled literally on the life-story of the poet Bürger, who cohabited with his wife's sister as well as his wife. The hero of Wassermann's novel is a musician in Nuremberg, and the symbolic title is taken from the figure of a man with a goose under each arm on a fountain of one of the city market-places. The brunt of the story is the tragedy of the artist, the myth of the eternal enmity between the creative man-mind and the earthly woman-mind: '*Das Ewig-Weibliche zieht uns hinab*'. The main feature of *Christian Wahnschaffe* (1919) is that a rich man's son does what Buddha did: he turns his back on wealth and rank, and lives with outcasts. In the four volumes of the cycle *Der Wendekreis* (the first novel, 1920, has this title; then follow *Oberlins drei Stufen*, 1922; *Ulrike Woytich*, 1923; and *Faber oder die verlorenen Jahre*, 1924) the idea of psychic discontinuity comes into play – an individual is made up of various *I's* which come to the surface under the pressure of events; and this idea continues in *Laudin und die Seinen* (1925). Then in a trilogy of novels Wassermann probes his way to what he conceives as a new cerebralogically attested system of ethics and religion. *Der Fall Maurizius* (1928) is the most ambitious detective novel in German literature, but *qua* detective novel it is incredibly naïve and boring. Very irritating is Wassermann's technique, here relentlessly applied, of *Entschleierung* – strip-teasing should be the translation of the word: there is a mystery which is revealed shred by shred. Etzel Andergast, a boy of sixteen, sets out to unravel a murder mystery. His father, an attorney general, had procured the verdict; and he too, after Maurizius, the man condemned for the murder, has been doing penal servitude for eighteen years, renews the investigation by sitting with the prisoner day by day in his cell (!), listening to his interminable self-dissection. Etzel runs away to Berlin, where he ingratiates himself with the man who had been the chief witness at the trial, a homosexual Jew scholar, Waremme, who is clearly modelled on du Maurier's Svengali. Maurizius, married to Elli, had passionately loved Anna, Elli's sister, a strange creature compact of positive and negative qualities (with her *'ichlose Selbstischheit'* she is *'narzisshaft'*, *'Frau Holle im Schnee'*, *'eine seelenlose Lemure'*, *'eine Leiche, die man galvanisieren muss'*). Anna has been violated by Waremme, and she is hypnotically controlled by him as Trilby is by Svengali; and, though she fired the revolver and killed her sister, Waremme's diabolical will directed her aim. The real purpose of the novel, apart from the inquisition into problematical mental states, is the bitter Communistic accusation of German justice and of justice generally, continued from *Der Moloch* and *Caspar Hauser*. *Etzel Andergast* (1931) is the sequel to *Der Fall Maurizius*: the titular hero is now the pupil of a medical specialist, Joseph Kerkhoven, who pierces into the innermost mind of the crowd of characters. *Joseph Kerkhovens dritte Existenz* (1934) takes up the threads again. *Bula Matari* (1932) and *Christoph Columbus* (1929) mark the culmination of Wasserman's morbid skill in the delineation of strange characters. It had been said that the heroes of his tales were fantastically baroque, as unreal as (say) Lohenstein's Arminius: here he dissects historical characters, and lays bare what he considers to be their secret soul – together with its disease. In *Bula Matari* he illuminates the inner psychology of Stanley. To him Stanley is a type of *conquistador* – a *conquistador* not merely of vast new spaces of earth but of his own mysterious urges, and of 'the quagmire of life'. What makes the book alluring is the obvious influence of another adept in strange mentalities, Joseph Conrad: the whole book is indeed planned more or less as an interpretation of Conrad's *Heart of Darkness* by the light of Stanley's psychological experiences; perhaps, indeed, as an interpretation of the mysterious psychology of Conrad's tragic hero generally. Whether this interpretation is not too naïvely Freudian may be questioned: at all events Wassermann cannot understand Stanley's ostensibly clean sheet of erotic experience unless there is an assumption of paederasty; the explorer's bewilderment at the collapse of the subordinates he had left in charge of the rearguard in the Emin Pasha Relief Expedition is questioned as either naïveté or puritanical pretence, since it must be clear that these normal British men had succumbed to the erotic allurement of the African jungle. Only religious heroism of character (Livingstone, Stanley) can lead out of this poisonous inertia of the jungle, or symbolically the quagmire of life in general (*Trägheit des Herzens*), while those who have not this heroic strength of will (Emin Pasha, Stanley's subordinates) sink deeper and deeper into it. Wassermann's Columbus is a drastic case of *Entheroisierung*: he is a creature of impulse rather than discoverer, sailing the seas blindly, and 'buried in his own dark self, a joyless exile'. Wassermann is mainly concerned in denouncing the destruction by dynastic and religious greed of a symbiotic community.

Stehr's obstinate seeking for a new religion and Wassermann's programmatic Buddhism are symptomatic of the change that takes place in the novel after 1900 in the choice of hero: the great personality (Nietzsche's *Adelsmensch*), who has replaced the decadent *Nervenmensch*, tends to be a *Gottsucher*, or at all events he seeks some new moral way of escaping from the quagmire of life; the progression to the humanistic or communistic hero of the expressionists is typified by the sequence of Wassermann's social rebels. Many of these novels of the new century are, since they describe the development of the hero from youth to maturity through weal and woe, *Bildungsromane* or *Entwicklungsromane* more or less in the old sense; but the best of them are so intensely personal that they have been classified as *Bekenntnis- und Bildungsromane*: in their pages the author reveals himself.

The work of the two brothers Heinrich and Thomas Mann has from first to last this blending of confession and mental evolution, and at the same time criticism of society, gently ironic in the work of Thomas, corrosive in that of Heinrich, who has been called the German Juvenal. The two brothers are scions of an old patrician family of Lübeck. Their grandmother was a Brazilian creole, a skilled musician; she is the 'southern' mother, passionate and artistic, who in Thomas Mann's novels stands in stark contrast with the solid and practical German temperament of the men of the old stock. In Thomas the German temperament prevails and controls his slow, carefully considered and polished style with its sad rhythms; in Heinrich the romance blood is credited with the hectic rush of the sentences, with his gorgeous colouring, and with his Italianate rut of passion.

HEINRICH MANN (1871-1950) reveals his own personality, particularly in his Novellen, by those of his characters who are artists and poets. Mario Mavolto in *Pippo Spano* (one of the short tales of *Flöten und Dolche*, 1904-5) is self-portraiture; he is a poet who, forced to observe life, remains outside it; this disgust with art is again expressed in *Die Göttinnen* by the painter to whom it would be happiness if he could contemplate beauty without having to paint it. Art is reviled as 'a perverse debauch' that enervates its victim to such an extent that he is incapable of real feeling. Heinrich Mann's novels may be divided into two classes; the first class, the scenes of which are mostly in Germany, are caricature of the grotesque genre, in intent social criticism and culminating in a kind of political propaganda; the second class are as a rule localized in Italy, and, though they may be classed as *Bekenntnisromane*, since they reveal the author's orgiastic mind, are riotous paeans of life lived at fever heat in a world where common sense and goodness and pity do not count. *Im Schlaraffenland* (1901) caricatures and excoriates the stock-jobbers and literary hacks of Berlin; it is a picture of Sodom in which all the sinners are not worth a decent man's kick. The hero, obviously modelled on Maupassant's Bel Ami, is a *littérateur* who lives by love. *Die Jagd nach Liebe* (1904) transfers these literary orgies to Munich; its most lurid scene is when an actress who is to play Monna Vanna disrobes herself and finds the man before her dead. *Professor Unrat* (1905), well known as the film *The Blue Angel*, has for hero a grotesque schoolmaster who, tracking his pupils to a tavern where they wait on a light o' love, is himself drawn into her coils, marries her, loses his post, and avenges himself on his fellow-citizens, his former pupils, by luring them through his wife to debauch. The picture is repulsive; but Heinrich Mann is applying the method of Balzac: by exaggeration he aims at showing the terrific power of instincts and of passions latent in any respectable individual; a Philistine or an immaculate Methodist is a potential monster of vice, for, since virtue is vice reversed, intensity may be equal in a different direction, just as rising (according to the observer's standpoint) is falling upwards. In *Zwischen den Rassen* (1907) Heinrich Mann fights out the conflict in his own blood between north and south, spirituality and sensuality: the heroine, like the author, is half South American. The Romance lovers pounce on their women, while the Germanic hero timidly waits. *Die kleine Stadt* (1909) begins as an idyll in a little Italian town where the clerical party try to prevent an itinerant troupe of actors from producing their shows. But the action quickens to the passionate love-story of the young tenor and a beautiful girl he sees behind the door of the convent. In *Die Göttinnen oder die drei Romane der Herzogin von Assy* (1902-3), Heinrich Mann's most ambitious work, all this southern fever seethes into delirium. To blame his creole blood for the ravishing rut of it all is hardly scientific; much of it is due to his residence in Italy and still more to his cult of d'Annunzio, who, moreover, appears, thinly disguised, as one of the characters. 'I have discovered a new genre,' one of the characters proclaims, 'the hysterical Renaissance!' This term hits the nail on the head: the characters (*unbedenkliche Abenteurer, stolz und düster nach Grösse, blutbefleckt frei und unverwundbar*) are weaklings to whom their perversities are heroic strength; the keynote of the trilogy is the discord between desire and capacity. As in a German novel written a century before, J. J. W. Heinse's *Ardinghello*, the wickedness is a phantasmagoria, not a ruthless unfolding of strength as in the authentic history of the *cinquecento*. Conrad Ferdinand Meyer, himself a weakling worshipping the strong, had delineated Renaissance voluptuaries with the credibility of an historian; Heinrich Mann sees only one side of their mentality: worship of beauty unhampered by the moral law, and therefore lust, not love. The scene is set on a vast scale – the Duchess rules by right of beauty from Dalmatia to Venice,

Rome, Naples – but the inner meaning shrinks: she is in the first novel Diana achieving freedom, in the second Minerva ruling the realm of ideal beauty in art, in the third Venus seizing joy (*Freiheitssucht, Kunstfieber, Liebeswut*) – but in reality as the novel shapes we see her, in the first two novels empty and aching, and in the third Venus vulgivaga and nothing more. Nietzsche's doctrine of Dionysian joy is here like a cup drained to the dregs: a boy is loved to death at Capri; there are violations and sadism; there is a bout of Lesbian love by experts staged and watched like a boxing-match; a robust English dame, Lady Olympia, moves through the tale, coming from the ends of the earth and emerging at parties to whisper, with a velvet voice, to some stranger or other: '*Heute nacht sind Sie mein Geliebter – . . . Meine Gondel wartet.*' But the trilogy stands out in the history of literature both by reason of its extreme tendency and of its style. It stands on the threshold of expressionism, first because it is the *ne plus ultra* of Nietzschean *Schrecklichkeit*, and therefore nearest to the inevitable reaction from ideals of picturesque depravity dear to impressionism; and, secondly, because the style, so feverish that it rushes along in a succession of pictures, has passed beyond the coldly gemmed and chiselled style of impressionism, and is already *Rauschkunst*, the ecstatic style which presents life (*das rasende Leben*) in cinematographic flashes. It is strange to find so anti-religious a writer as Heinrich Mann among the *Gottsucher*, and no doubt *Mutter Marie* (1927) is rather a dispassionate study of religious conversion than a confession of personal belief in the efficacy of faith. Baroness Marie Hartmann recognizes in the heir of a general the son whom, twenty-five years before, when she was a servant girl, she had abandoned on the rim of a street fountain. And – horror of horrors! (but somewhat in the nature of the Ninon de l'Enclos motif) – she finds that her love for the boy is that of a woman for the male as well as that of a mother. She seeks a refuge in religion, and makes a hectic confession in the Hedwigskirche in Berlin. *Eugénie oder die Bürgerzeit* (1928), with its description of life in Lübeck in Geibel's days, is a side-piece to Thomas Mann's *Buddenbrooks* – but at a great remove. The historical novels *Die Jugend des Königs Henri Quatre* (1938) and *Die Vollendung des Königs Henri Quatre* (1938) represent a declension from the heights of literature to the level of Feuchtwanger and *hoc genus omne*. The first novel relates the king's career to his victory at Arques in 1589. There is a vivid picture of the Queen Mother,

Catherine dei Medici, whose sinister cunning is contrasted with the frank joyousness of the young king. Coligny too stands out, and the massacre of St. Bartholomew as the climax is descriptively fine. The construction is episodic, and the skein of the story is tangled. *Der Atem* (1949) is a hectic attempt to write in the ultra-expressionist style of the day.

The psychological and personal trend of Heinrich Mann's work develops, like that of his brother, in the direction of the regeneration of society by democracy; he ended as a declared friend of the Soviet Union. His political and social satire culminates in the trilogy *Das Kaiserreich* (*Der Untertan*, 1914 – the officials; *Die Armen*, 1917 – the proletariat; *Der Kopf*, 1925 – state policy), a scathing denunciation of the Wilhelminian state which is all the more daring as the first novel of the series was in course of publication when the War broke out. There was a question of prosecution for *lèse-majesté*, and presumably only the absorbing excitement of the War prevented it; the obvious portraiture of notabilities alive or dead may have been too illusive to ensure a conviction, but the mockery of the All-Highest was in plain terms. In *Der Untertan* the career is set forth of Diederich Hessling, the son of a factory-owner; he shows sadistic tendencies at school, is hardened by his experiences as a corps student, and has the usual affairs with women. He develops a fanatical admiration of the Hohenzollerns, and for that reason loathes the Socialists. In *Die Armen* Diederich is now Generaldirektor Geheimer Kommerzienrat Hessling. As a political move he introduces profit-sharing, a system under which the workers are worse off than they were before. The troubles and struggles of the proletariat are depressing reading, and are not helped by the melodramatic intrigue: Balrich, a young worker, has a trump card in his hand, for he can prove financial villainy in his employer's family; he learns Latin and Greek, and turns agitator. The struggles against capitalists helped by dynasty and State proves hopeless; Balrich gives up his books and returns to the life of a suppressed worker; and the novel ends with the picture of him and his fellow-workers marching away to the War along beflagged streets. In *Der Kopf* public life is described by one character as a private affair – the personal struggle of Wilhelm II with Social Democracy. As a *roman à clefs* the novel has historical interest. Secretary of State Lannas is understood to represent Bülow. There is no need to give the key to Knack, the iron and steel magnate, with his daughter Bellona. Tolleben is stated in the novel to be 'like Bismarck'. The agitation of the industrialists, supported by Admiral von Fischer, to make the fleet strong enough to annihilate the British fleet is a vital element of the intrigue: England and France are under the thumb of the Jews, and hence are the deadly foes of Germany. Round these pillars of the State flit and flash two glittering scamps, Terra and Mangold. Mangold marries Bellona, becomes secretary to Graf Lannas, and rises to be Chancellor. Terra personally advises the Kaiser to abolish the death penalty: then it will not be possible to charge him with lusting for mass murder by means of war. The Kaiser is at first impressed, but then replies in very vulgar German. When the War is lost Terra and Mangold, in 1918, die a picturesque death: linking arms, they shoot each other and fall in the shape of a cross, to the music of a military band playing outside. In spite of the political filth the novel would be comparatively clean if it were not for the women – of the key characters as stated. The verdict must be that as a cross-word puzzle the cycle is exhausting, while as fiction it is too dirty even for real life. In his preface to *Die grosse Sache* (1931), which continues the political and social novels, Heinrich Mann expatiates on his conception of the *Bekenntnisroman*: a novel, he says, should always be a sort of confession made by the author to himself but also to his contemporaries. The action is compressed into a period of three days.

Nothing could be more different from the whipped haste and the darting radiance of Heinrich Mann's style than the quiet flow and the guarded flame of THOMAS MANN'S (1875-1955) writings. The ever-recurring theme in his tales (short and long) is the glaring contrast between the normal man (*der Bürger*), who is fit to live (*lebenstüchtig*), and the artist or poet (*der Künstler*), who is not fit to live (*lebensuntüchtig*, '*unheilbar unbürgerlich*'). Thomas Mann's artist is another version of Schnitzler's over-ripe decadent; but whereas Schnitzler's creature dies under kisses as under a gradual anaesthetic, Thomas Mann's artist is tortured by the inescapable contemplation of his normal fellow-men with blue eyes and the rosy glow of health and no self-consciousness. The 'citizen' is cased in his insensitive skin as in thick armour; he lives a charmed life, while the artist, to whom beauty is full of arrows, is assailed and driven despairing into the lonely corners of self-contempt. The artist is shut out inexorably from life; he is an outcast, a

21

cripple, often an attitudinizing fraud. Something of this strange conception of the artist may be due to the vogue about 1900 of Lombroso's *Man of Genius*; but it is also by way of reaction from the old romantic *Verhimmelung* of the poet as one born in a golden clime, dowered with heaven knows what, ambrosial-locked, adulated, in short Tennyson or Paul Heyse or Wedekind's *Kammersänger*, or Hofmannsthal's *Tizian*. There is only one previous author with whose interpretation of the tragedy of the artist Mann's can be compared. But in Gottfried Keller's *Der grüne Heinrich* the lesson that life lies away from dream and mental effort is rather to be gathered by the wise than thrust to the front of all eyes; Keller's significance here is rather in the example of his own life – he, a great and sensitive artist, turned his back on art and letters and did his tedious duty for years as *Staatsschreiber* of the canton of Zurich. To go farther back, Goethe was lost for years in the common round of duties useful to his fellow-men: was he then a traitor to his genius or, for a period, sane?

Thomas Mann wrote *Buddenbrooks* (1901) when he was twenty-five; it made him a reputation which he progressively consolidated. It is a story of the parallel decay in the fortunes of a merchant's family in Lübeck and in the capacity for life of the members of it as succeeding generations take on more and more of the polish of culture. Through all Thomas Mann's work winds the grey thread of this idea that degeneration is the fruit of culture, that with culture goes physical decay. One ghastly detail recurs with unpleasant frequency: the carious teeth of the cultured; the last of the Buddenbrook dynasty suffers agonies and in the end dies from diseased teeth. Two of Mann's characters (the author Spinell in the short story *Tristan* and the fat, degenerate husband in *Luischen*) are beardless in manhood (like Conrad Ferdinand Meyer before his Indian summer). It is in this conception of catastrophe springing, not from the classic conception of 'tragic guilt' or the romantic conception of uncontrollable passion, but from a natural and inevitable process like that of seeding after flowering, that Thomas Mann is an innovator; to have proved with a slow, painstaking logic supported by all the evidence of science that culture is death (and with this idea he interweaves the still more tragic conception that love is death) is to have earned a secure seat with the immortals who have struck out into new paths in literature. The lesson is, in *Buddenbrooks* as in the following stories, enforced by

THOMAS MANN

an intricate use of symbol; e.g. though the Buddenbrooks die guiltless and in utter decency the last head of the firm, the immaculate senator Thomas, falls into a puddle in the streets and is brought home stained and bleeding to die; or, in plain terms, physical decay brings back the flower of gentility to the gutter. The technique of the novel is on the whole masterly, with its slow contrasts of character and its minute rendering of the *milieu* of an ancient Hanseatic city; faulty, perhaps, is the Dickens-like caricature of the eccentrics and villains; and very dubious is the use of leit-motifs, i.e. the wearisome repetition of facial and personal peculiarities and tricks of diction and gesture. This not only tends to bore if not to irritate the reader, it limits the characters; that is, at a certain moment they *must* say a certain thing or make a certain gesture – they are bound up in the piffling trammels of their personal habits instead of having unrestricted freedom of movement and self-revelation. To this practice, however, Thomas Mann keeps; thus in *Königliche Hoheit* Imma always speaks 'with pouted lips', and the Grand Duke always sucks his upper lip.

The most poignant expression of the artist's tragedy, perhaps, is in *Tonio Kröger* (1903), the story of the Lübeck boy with a correct father and an exotic, passionate mother; he strays into art and longs to get back to decency, and is not surprised that when he returns as a famous author to his native city he is nearly arrested under suspicion of being a criminal. The three collections of short stories *Der kleine Herr Friedemann* (1898), *Tristan* (1903) and *Das Wunderkind* (1914) contain more than one acknowledged masterpiece. Asceticism and joy in life, or in other words dualism, are the theme of the short tale *Gladius Dei* and of the literary drama *Fiorenza* (1905). In *Gladius Dei* a religious fanatic declaims against the flaunting indecencies and the display of physical beauty in Munich, the typical art-city of our days; in *Fiorenza* Savonarola faces and defies Lorenzo dei Medici, while Florence, symbolized as the courtesan Fiore, has to choose between the two, between ascetic spirituality (*Geist*) and art that snares the senses. In *Königliche Hoheit* (1909) the individualism of the impressionists turns to the altruism which the expressionists were soon to proclaim: a prince (with a withered hand – bold symbolism before 1914!) stands for the artist or unusual character; he achieves salvation by sacrificing himself for the good of the community. The problem of the extraordinary personality here finds its solution, which is (in Mann's own words) that turning of the mind to democracy, common service, companionship, love, which had been proclaimed in the previous year in Heinrich Mann's novel *Die kleine Stadt*.

The problem of the artist is handled with painful incisiveness in *Der Tod in Venedig* (1913): a German author, ripe in years, with his work already in the schoolbooks, goes for a holiday to Venice; here, to his own horror, he falls in love with a beautiful boy, cannot tear himself away, dies. The negative solution is positive in scope: the romantic adulation of beauty is shameless (*'liederlich'*); the hero, if he had not been a romantic artist, might have controlled himself, might have left Venice and returned to duty.[1] The septentrional artist is softened and corrupted by the balmy south; but there is peril, too, in the indolent and consciousless east: the boy is a Pole, and smitten already with an incurable disease. The meaning of *Der Tod in Venedig* is clear enough in the hero's communings with himself: beauty, virtue, wisdom are, as Plato taught, divine; but of these only beauty is at once divine and visible to the senses; and since the artist works by the apperception of the senses, beauty is the artist's way to the spiritual. But how can he whose way to the spiritual goes through the senses attain wisdom and dignity? Is not this a devious way of sin that is bound to lead astray? The poet cannot take the way to beauty but Eros joins him as guide. . . . Poets are like women, passion is their exaltation, and their yearning must be for love. Mann's grim picture of the doomed artist is relieved by his interpretation of Schiller's character in the short tale *Schwere Stunde* (in *Das Wunderkind*): it is the physical incapacity caused by the overweight of mind that isolates the artist; the true artist, however, conscious of his frailty but also of the nobility of his task, develops the 'heroism of weakness' (*Heroismus der Schwäche*): Schiller, too, is doomed by disease, and realizes how terrible his fate is when he compares himself with Goethe; but he finds consolation in the thought that it is harder to be a hero than to be a god. Here, too, there is an acknowledgment by Mann that the artist may be god-like and raised above criticism: Goethe, *'der Göttlich-Unbewusste'*, creating by inspiration

---

[1] Dr D. M. Hall, in her dissertation *The Venice Legend in German Literature since 1880*, has made it seem likely that one of the sources of the book was the unabridged edition of Platen's diary (ed. Laubmann und von Scheffler, 1896-1900). In a speech on Platen (in *Leiden und Grösse der Meister*) Thomas Mann takes the poet's homosexuality for granted. Another possible source is *Ein Vermächtnis* (1911), the diary of the painter Anselm Feuerbach.

and not by knowledge, is worlds away from the man of letters to whom creation is a craft learned by rote and practised in tortured isolation.

This preoccupation with the problems of degeneration and disease culminates with Thomas Mann in his vast symbolic interpretation of life: *Der Zauberberg* (1924), perhaps the most deeply planned novel since *Wilhelm Meister*. Hans Castorp, the last scion of a patrician family in Hamburg, comes on a visit to his cousin, who is a patient at a sanatorium for consumptives at Davos; he comes for three weeks, he remains seven years, and leaves the place to fall in the Great War – rescued by a great cataclysm, returned from dream to duty. The Magic Mountain is a symbol of Europe before the First Great War; it is a questioning of all culture. The Magic Mountain is the world of the dead: the doctor in charge is Rhadamanthus, all reckoning of time is lost, the inmates eat greedily (it is a life from copious meal to meal), and fall in love, the diseased with the diseased. Hans Castorp is in love with a Russian lady (Madame Chauchat): that is, the cultured love beauty – but beauty is only the phosphorescence of a dead body. This, again, is the old medieval view of life which we call dualism. Life itself, Hans Castorp discovers, is the equivalent of death: for life is a process of decomposition just as takes place in the body after death; the only difference is that in life there is chemical renewal.[1] Disease quickens the greed for food and love: so does culture. Hans is X-rayed: he sees his skeleton. But he keeps consciousness of the world of duty; there is a contrast between the bright daylight of the world of duty without and the soft moonlight in which he lingers hallucinated; afar is manly dignity, on the Magic Mountain there is Claudia Chauchat (like *Vrou Werlt* of medieval days) '*schlaff, wurmstichig und kirgiesenäugig*'.

In *The Magic Mountain* all the resources of modern psychology, science, and criticism are massed and irresistibly brought into action in support of the thesis. There is an almost impossible delicacy in the use of psycho-analysis: e.g. sexual processes are suggested by the moving up and down of a pencil in a case unconsciously haunting the memory of a schoolboy, and there is some play, very effective in the diseased effulgence of *The Magic Mountain*, with the word *Liebe* as suggestive of two soft yielding

[1] *Der Trieb unserer Elemente geht auf Desoxydation. Das Leben ist erzwungene Oxydation.* Novalis.

lips with a fierce vowel like a red tongue shooting between them. Mann's most penetrating use of psycho-analysis is perhaps in the short tale *Unordnung und frühes Leid* (1926), in which a baby of a girl falls sick with erotic feelings for an adult: Prince Charming in a fairy-tale up to date. The self-irony of a criminal in *Bekenntnisse des Hochstaplers Felix Krull* (1938) serves as a variant of Mann's usual contrast of normality with artist morbidity, and expands the thesis hinted at in *Tonio Kröger* that there are affinities between artistry and criminality. A fragment of the Krull tale had been published in 1922; it was added to in the edition of 1954 (*Der Memoiren erster Teil*). As we have it now it is a picaresque novel in the sense of the English eighteenth century. Another story long known to exist was made available in 1931, but in French only, as *Sang réservé*. It is a translation, published in Paris, of *Wälsungenblut*, of which there had been a privately printed edition (1922) for the author's friends. This more or less suppressed tale served the Nazis as a stick to beat the author with: two Jews, they point out, twin brother and sister, commit incest on a bear-skin in the brother's bedroom after attending a performance of Wagner's *Walküre*.

In Hermann Hesse's *Narziss und Goldmund* the dualism of flesh and spirit is presented as two separate halves which are nevertheless one: for even abstract ideas, as Goldmund with his concrete vision points out, are sensuous images; the mind cannot reason save by sense; the immaterial is only an image of the material. In Thomas Mann's great series of four novels *Joseph und seine Brüder* (*Die Geschichten Jaakobs*, 1933; *Der junge Joseph*, 1934; *Joseph in Ægypten*, 1936; *Joseph der Ernährer*, 1942) Joseph is flesh and spirit in one; in him the flesh is sanctified by the divine law, but the spirit is in control of the flesh, and this by the consciousness of consecration to the higher life. Thomas Mann's purpose in this immense work is, therefore, as moral and 'cultural' (to use a Nazi word) as possible; and there is Nazi doctrine in the detailed account of the Nordic wandering of first culture, including the solar myth, from Atlantis. What is not Nazi doctrine is the demonstration that higher culture – the consciousness of mind (*Geist*) – is historically Jewish, and that culture really is the sublimation of the sense of duty as obedience to those instincts of refinement which sunder man from brute. Thomas Mann in these volumes interprets history – and therefore life – as an eternal recurrence (*ewige Wiederkehr*, p. 102) of myth, which is in origin a symbolization of nature processes; and culture, he shows, is the effort of man to extricate his mind from the swathing folds of these myths by piercing to the sense of the symbol. Knowledge unifies the myriad myths of history and religions as the multiple but identical imaginative shaping, ever repeated though varied, of processes mysterious and miraculous to the primitive mind, particularly the sexual act (=burial in the pit), birth (=resurrection from the pit), and death (=birth; for all that is buried – as: seed in slime – is reborn). The divine is split into male and female; but these are one, because they are one principle. The animal gods of Egypt are easily intelligible as deifications of the animal functions of man: the '*baumelnde Hoden*' of the god-bulls, the phallic spears of temples reared at the sun, and so much besides that Thomas Mann with gentle irony illuminates. The most daring interpretation is that of the Resurrection of Christ as *ewige Wiederkehr* and as a birth-myth: '*Bôr*' means so much – hole, prison, pit, underworld; and in Mann's story a stone is rolled away from the pit into which Joseph has been cast by his brethren. But though the elucidation of procreation myths is the crimson thread that binds the succession of tales, there is interwoven too in moving fashion a picture of the gradual creation of the idea of God by Abraham, Isaac, and Jacob: God as He evolves for them is that which consecrates to higher duties (that is, to humanity and culture); and if Jewish religion, created as it is by the spirit, still retains in veiled form the sexual symbols by which primitive man imaged his gods Joseph (and by implication Christ, as Joseph returning) marks the ultimate spiritualization of life. If there were only this far-cast net of thought in the work, it would be philosophy rather than literature; but to the general reader the lure of the tales will be in the superb characterization, particularly of Jaakob, a monumental and tragic figure; and in the vivid poetic realism of certain episodes – the birth of Reuben, Jaakob's marriage-night with Rachel and the nine times repeated frenzied union. Most curiously elaborated is the temptation of Joseph by Potiphar's wife; and if Philipp von Zesen in his seventeenth-century novel of *Assenat und Joseph* (1670) – a related experiment in the cramming of encyclopaedic knowledge into a tale showing the present in the past – makes this lady psychologically possible, Thomas Mann gives inevitability to her stung passion – not only is her 'husband' a eunuch priest, not only is she obsessed by the phallic ritual of Egyptian deities, but the poignancy of the situation is accentuated because Potiphar (a super-refined sybarite and gourmand) has been and is a second father to Joseph: as Joseph resists the woman he sees before him not only the face of his own father but that of his second father as well; it is indeed a composite face, with sterner features – those of God. Parental and divine inhibition therefore give the spirit strength to resist the flesh. And yet there is no defence of asceticism or even of chastity in the story: the chastity of priests and vestals is ruthlessly laid bare in all its futility; but Joseph is reserved – that is, sexual functions are for a purpose foreordained by God. The meaning of Mann's Joseph thus is that he simplifies the chaotic and fleshly symbols of the divine to what he himself is – spirit purified (more literally, superior and more cultured intellect). To spirit (*Geist*) the eternal peril is the flesh, the undying sphinx which, crouching, hides its sex, but which, male or female, is all sex and cruel clutching claws.

The action of *Lotte in Weimar* (1939) returns ostensibly to modernity – the date is 1816 –, but the foundation matter is still myth, the myth or legend of *The Sorrows of Werther*. The main theme, however, is that of the loss of a writer's productivity as the pitiless years take their toll. Lotte visits Goethe in Weimar and finds him, not so much aged as lost to life, as life is in female fancy. Goethe as we see him, stiffened and sterile, in *Lotte in Weimar*, exemplifies one of the main tenets stated in Mann's next novel, *Doktor Faustus* (1947): 'Choose good, you vegetate; choose evil, you attain knowledge and you create.' The narrator is Serenus Zeitblom, Ph.D., a grammar school teacher. In the two years from 1943 to 1945 he writes down the story of an old schoolfellow and lifelong friend, Adrian Leverkühn, who had died in 1940. They had studied together at Halle; Zeitblom philology, Leverkühn theology. Very clear in the story is the contrast of *Bürger*–Zeitblom, and *Künstler*–Leverkühn. Or, otherwise contrasted, they typify *Moralismus–Ästhetentum*. Leverkühn's study of theology at Halle is the first approach to the atmosphere of the Faust legend; however, he changes over to music. Zeitblom writes during the course of World War II; he is an anti-Nazi, but finds it prudent to keep quiet. The main idea of the book is that Dr Faustus is Germany, the collapse of which is symbolized in the last musical works of Leverkühn, *Apocalipsis cum figuris* and *Wehklag Dr. Fausti. Die vertauschten Köpfe* (1940) is an Indian legend ironically treated: an Indian woman attempts to produce a perfect husband by conjuring her friend's head on to her husband's body, and vice versa, only to find that the new heads adapt themselves to the bodies on which they are transposed. *Das Gesetz* (1944) continues in brief form the Joseph novels: it is the story of Moses and his passing of the Red Sea. In *Doktor Faustus* Mann had outlined the plot of a musical composition by Leverkühn: *The Birth of Pope Gregory*; this points forward to his next novel in chronological order, *Der Erwählte* (1951), the story of yet another nominal sinner. The source is the epic *Gregorius* by the Middle High German poet Hartmann von Aue, a medieval counterpart of the Greek legend of Oedipus; that is to say, it is a handling of the involuntary incest theme. The legend is ironically treated; indeed there are parodistic elements. *Die Betrogene* (1953) is a short novel – ironical once again: a widow of fifty falls in love with a young American whom she has engaged to teach English to her son; the explanation is that, after reaching the climacteric, she has a return of menstruation; this she identifies with a *Seelenfrühling*, a *Neuerblühen* (one is reminded of Goethe's *wiederholte Pubertät*). She has a renewed sensitiveness to scents; while out walking she gets a whiff of musk, follows it up, to find that it is the effluvium of a heap of rotting vegetable matter with excrements – the womb of nature. Therefore: *Moderduft und Liebeslust*. The explanation turns out to be that she is suffering from cancer of the womb.

One of the illuminative essays of *Leiden und Grösse der Meister* (1935) deals with Wagner; the others interpret Goethe, Platen, Storm, and Cervantes. Time itself has played ironically with this ironist; always (as a born patrician) a conservative – in spite of his advanced thinking – he defended Germany during the First War (*Gedanken im Kriege*, September 1914) as the embodiment of '*Kultur*' against the mere '*Zivilisation*' of the allies; and in a further 1914 essay, *Friedrich der Grosse und die grosse Koalition* (published 1915), he found 'the urge of destiny, the spirit of history' in Frederick's defiance of Europe. Other collections of essays and speeches are *Betrachtungen eines Unpolitischen* (1918); *Rede und Antwort* (1922); *Bemühungen* (1925); *Die Forderungen des Tages* (1930); *Goethe und Tolstoi* (1923); *Freud und die Zukunft* (1936); *Achtung, Europa!* (1938).

GEORG HERMANN (1871-1943) was ranged among the disciples of Thomas Mann when, in 1906, his novel *Jettchen Gebert* won him lasting fame. The outline of the story does indeed suggest *Buddenbrooks*: the Geberts are Berlin patricians and merchants, and there is something of an implication that culture brings incapacity for business in the person of Uncle Jason, who has a distant resemblance to Christian Buddenbrook, not however as the fool of the family but as one by the bent of his character forced apart from the family, an *enfant terrible*, a man about town and a wit, a collector of rare books as well as of costly porcelain; he speaks himself (in distinctly Mannsian terms) of his *'seelische Empfindung des Ausgeschlossenseins von der Familie, dem Bürgertum, dem Staat'*. The spirit of the story is, however, different from that of *Buddenbrooks*; and where in details of technique, such as the ticketing of individual characters by recurrent phrases and long passages in which season and weather move in lyric unison with the story, both authors, no doubt, are directly imitating Dickens. Decay by culture is certainly not the theme: the revered ancestor, the Court Jeweller of his day, had culture (of the Voltairean sort) to his finger-tips, and he combined a robust capacity for life with fine feelings (*Lebensstärke und Sinnenfeinheit*), while his brother, Uncle Eli (the patriarch among the Geberts, a blunt old fellow whose culture runs to carriages and horses) and two of his children, Salomon and Ferdinand, have less fineness of nerves but undiminished capacity for business. The decay is in the reverse direction to that of *Buddenbrooks*, except, of course, in the case of Uncle Jason. The main reason for Uncle Salomon's and Uncle Ferdinand's lack of intellectual interest is family environment: they have both married Jacobys, Polish Jewesses from the Posen district, squat little women with 'eyes like two black currants in a fat bun'. And here we have the obvious theme of the story: the stark contrast and the unending conflict between two types of Jew represented by the Geberts and the Jacobys – and the Berlin patricians, being honest and restrained, must be outmanœuvred by the unscrupulous, bumptious immigrants from the dirty East. The Berlin Jews have the indifference to ritual of men of the world; the Posen Jews put all their narrow pride of race into the observance of every racial rite. The pride of race of the Berlin Jews springs from quite a different source – they consort with Christians, but they are true to their tribe because of age-old memories of unjust persecution. And when the heroine of the tale, Jettchen Gebert, falls passionately in love with a handsome young Christian, Dr Kössling, an author at the beginning of whatever career the future may have in store for him but therefore to sound business men for the present a social outcast, the family with a good conscience are adamant. Uncle Eli and Uncle Jason would indeed not withhold consent, but as members of the family they must uphold its tribal authority. And so by cruel moral pressure Jettchen is forced into marriage with a loathsome cousin, Julius Jacoby, just arrived with all his green pushfulness from Posen. His two aunts arrange the affair. The reader, well informed of Jettchen's strong will and intellectual leanings and her physical revulsion (her fine nerves shiver at his approach as if her two hands touched a toad in the dark) would expect her to elope rather than yield; but – and it comes as a dramatic surprise – she *cannot* resist, because she is a good Jewess as well as a passionate lover: she is an orphan – her father had been killed fighting for Prussia against Napoleon, a volunteer with Jason, who came off with a lame leg; and she has been brought up, with all a father's care and affection, for twenty years by Uncle Salomon, who now is entitled to present the bill which Jettchen must pay. Like one hypnotized she goes through all the agony of the marriage festival, but at its close steals out into the starry night. The sequel, *Henriette Jakoby* (1908), falls below the level of *Jettchen Gebert*: there is too little in the way of action and the painting of moods is too extensive. The marriage, of course, is a failure from the first, and Henriette takes refuge with Uncle Jason. Gradually the truth dawns on her that Uncle Jason loves her. The relations with Kössling are renewed, and in a weak moment she gives herself to him. Then she realizes that Uncle Jason's love is more to her, and she commits suicide. Jettchen is one of the most charming ladies in recent German literature. We see her, a perfect little housewife, preparing the immense family banquets; and we admire her with Dr Kössling's eyes when in the first chapter we find her going to market (like a dainty Doulton lady) in her silver grey taffeta gown, coal-scuttle bonnet tied by pink buds, lavender gloves and long-fringed Cashmere shawl and velvet bodice. The presentation of the *Biedermeierzeit*, the period of 1840 with its crinolines and daintily figured stuffs, its stately *intérieurs* with massive furniture and costly porcelain, is generally praised as scholarly, accurate, and for all its gentle irony appreciative. How delightful it is to go with Jettchen and her aunt for a summer holiday in sylvan Charlottenburg, and to hear why Uncle Ferdinand's family prefer the more open solitudes of Schöneberg! Algettoher *Jettchen Gebert* must be given high rank as more or less (in spite of an occasional false note due to Dickens worship, to which German novelists are prone[1]) a Jewish classic, and certainly the one Berliner Roman of the period which is likely to live. The Berlin novels of the naturalists failed because, as *Milieuromane*, they subordinated character to *milieu*; *Jettchen Gebert* succeeds because, over and above its masterly and detailed presentation of the *milieu* of a given period, it creates vividly individualized characters and handles racial and social problems with inner knowledge and keen insight. Georg Hermann's other works show him still a master of irony, but he does not again find a theme of so simple an appeal as *Jettchen Gebert*. In *Heinrich Schön junior* (1915) he again shows his knowledge of art matters; the theme – that of Don Carlos – is a young man's love for his stepmother in the Potsdam of 1844. *Kubinke* (1911) is yet another Berlin novel, but of our own days: Emil Kubinke is a barber's assistant who, meshed in the toils of three calculating females, hangs himself to avoid marriage with his *fiancée* while faced with two affiliation orders.

Animal symbolism as an interpretation of human character by implied comparison reaches its high-water mark in Kipling's *Jungle Book*. In German literature there is nothing nearly so good. Bölsche's *Das Liebesleben in der Natur* is, as a start, too scientific for pure literature, while Hermann Löns's *Mümmelmann* and Waldemar Bonsels' *Die Biene Maja und ihre Abenteuer* (1912), *Himmelsvolk* (1915), and *Mario und die Tiere* (1927) play about the surface. WALDEMAR BONSELS (1881-1952) is a Holstein man and has that love of sea-faring and far lands that Holstein men often have. His *Indienfahrt* (1916) is too peacefully dream-like for exotic thrills, the radiant vagabond of his numerous stories is never more than a hero for happy people, and the theosophical doctrine he propounds has no tangibility.

[1] The influence is most marked in the novels of Wilhelm Raabe (1831-1910) and Max Kretzer. Stefan Zweig deals with Dickens in *Drei Meister*.

XIII

THE WOMEN WRITERS

It has been traditional in German literature from the days of
Gräfin Ida Hahn-Hahn's (1805-80) notorious novels and the
more calmly reasoned ones of Fanny Lewald (1811-89) that
women writers should face up to the menfolk and claim equality
– particularly of passion. After 1880 there are so many of these
Amazons that only the leaders can be dealt with here. Not all
women writers, of course, are rebels; and perhaps as good an
arrangement as any is to divide them into two armies of naughty
girls and good girls, with Else Lasker-Schüler – she is not flagrantly naughty but she would have been terribly shocked if she
had been classed as one of the good girls – as a dividing pinnacle.

The feministic campaign moves in two directions: one continues that movement for social, political, and physical equality
which can be traced back to Friedrich Schlegel's *Lucinde* and the
cry of *Jung Deutschland* for the 'emancipation of the flesh'; the
other, essentially modern because based on medical hygiene, concentrates on the depiction of the peculiar nervous and physiological system of woman, of her need of sexual activity for the
completion of her personality, and of her right to unrestricted
liberty in her sexual functions, even if perverse. In the first direction Helene Böhlau and Gabriele Reuter may be taken as the most
aggressive iconoclasts in the novel; in the second (which leads to
sensational and not infrequently disgusting revelation of inner
urges) Clara Viebig may be taken as the type.

In education equal rights for women were fought for as defiantly as British women fought for the vote. The German universities were not opened to women till 1896, and even then some
professors refused to lecture to them; it is notorious that one
famous Berlin professor tried to frighten them away by spicing
his lectures on German literature with the most obscene terms in

the language. In the novel this movement finds its voice in ILSE FRAPAN'S (1855-1909) *Wir Frauen haben kein Vaterland* (1899): a German girl, unable to obtain a scholarship in her native Hamburg, studies under stress at Zurich. HELENE BÖHLAU (1859-1919) had her own fight with German social custom. The daughter of a publisher, she went to Turkey with a married man, and was married to him by Turkish law; her novel *Isebies* (1911) is based on this experience. She began with Novellen in which she turned her upbringing to account – her youth was passed in Weimar, and the old folks she knew could tell tales of the spacious days of Goethe and Schiller, the stars of the social circles she describes in her jolly *Ratsmädelgeschichten* (1888) and *Altweimarische Liebes- und Ehegeschichten* (1897). Her *Rangierbahnhof* (1896) is feministic in so far as it is a study of Grillparzer's poignant Sappho theme under modern conditions (the 'shunting station' symbolizes the ceaseless din of the modern city in which an artist may have to work) – the right of the woman of genius to wedded happiness. The conclusion is that the activity of a woman's intellect is subject to her physical functions, and that married life makes demands which may prove fatal to an artist.[1] The result is not anti-feminist; for what the feminists claim is equal liberty *either* as artist *or* in the functions of love. *Das Recht der Mutter* (1896) is the first outspoken defence of the unmarried mother. As a polemic it does, it is true, lose directness of impact by virtue of the *Märchen*-like atmosphere in which it is bathed: where it is uncompromising is in the comparison of the care lavished on the married mother with the brutal treatment of the girl who has given her body in a moment of natural passion: here the contrast is heightened by the parallel pregnancy of two sisters, one the wife of a smug professor in Jena. (The contrast is not so poignant in Clara Viebig's *Das tägliche Brot*, where the pregnant mistress of the house draws her skirt around her lest the hem of it should touch her pregnant maid.) Helene Böhlau gives all the social dignity and ultimately real happiness to the girl who whistles the world away and lives for her child. In *Halbtier* (1899) the interest is mainly physiological: woman and wife exist, in man's estimation, 'to fulfil animal functions' ('*sind Nützlichkeitstiere*'),

[1] The theme of *Rangierbahnhof* is, so to speak, in the germ in Adalbert Stifter's *Der Kondor* (1840, his first novel). Rilke's painter friend Paula Becker married the Worpswede painter Otto Modersohn and died in childbirth: Rilke comments on this in his *Tagebuch* that God had punished her for trying to be woman and artist at the same time.

THE WOMEN WRITERS 323

such as, for instance, the suckling of children, so offensive a spectacle to men of artistic temperament; and in the novel the horror reaches its height in the picture of hospital childbirth, where the woman's head is covered while students watch. The total impression is climaxed as: '*das rechtlose, zum Halbtier herabgedrückte, geistberaubte, schmerzbeladene Weibtum dieser Welt*'. The solution suggested is that women should have the right both to children and independent work. *Muttersehnsucht*, one of the short stories of *Sommerbuch* (1902), defends a wife's claim to a child; here the husband is an old scholar, and his young wife gets her child from a single and unregretted union with a man of her own age. *Das Haus zur Flamm* (1908) is a plea for warmness of heart in human relations: '*das einzige, was auf Erden das Herz ruhig und glücklich macht, ist: gut miteinander zu sein*'.

GABRIELE REUTER (1859-1941) made a sensation with her novel *Aus guter Familie* (1895), in which quite discreetly she shows the devastating results of sex suppression in a girl who, because of her good family, must uphold the pretence of decent ignorance of what in the dark is stirring her senses; she ends, as some old maids do, by using disgusting sex words in a nervous breakdown. In her later novels Gabriele Reuter's heroines act as emancipated characters; she is certainly miles removed from the traditional point of view of Georg von Ompteda, who, in *Cäcilie von Sarryn*, sees no comfort for unmarried daughters except in ungrudging service to the family they belong to. In *Frau Bürgelin und ihre Söhne* (1899) Gabriele Reuter takes up the cudgels for the suppressed husband, and this time too for the son, who resists the formative efforts of his mother. The heroine of *Ellen von der Weiden* (1900) marries in all decency – but the wrong man. Brought up in the Harz Mountains, she is a creature of fell and forest, a '*Waldnixe*' scrambling about on the rocks, a '*Brockenhexe*' untamed and full of fun. Her husband is a Berlin doctor, a typical German husband, who, moreover, has learnt from his patients that women's nervous diseases are due to the desuetude of the husband's ancient right to corporeal castigation. ('*Vergiss die Peitsche nicht!*') But Ellen meets the poets and artists of *die Moderne* – monstrosities to her husband; and falls in love with a painter of wild new things splashed with blinding colour (Böcklin?). While on holiday at her father's home in the Harz Mountains her husband threatens to lock her in her room; she jumps through the window, and allows herself, sprite-like, to be caught and taken in a cave by her colourful painter. The child she bears is, however, her husband's – though he is not sure of it; she is divorced by arrangement; and, since she will have nothing more to do with the painter (she has told him that he must live for his work, and this requires freedom), she resigns herself to living without connubial bliss: she has her child to live for. Such determined resignation (and consideration for the male) is typical of Gabriele Reuter: for her – so long as her heroines have had experience of life – such an ending is a happy one. The heroine of *Liselotte von Reckling* (1903) takes an active part, as the wife of its apostle (Moritz von Egidy is said to be meant), in a new ethical movement for the regeneration of society. In *Das Recht der Mutter* Helene Böhlau merely pleaded for the girl who has had a moment of weakness; in *Das Tränenhaus* (1909) Gabriele Reuter sees no weakness in such a moment, but demands the experience for all women. The heroine is an unmarried mother, a woman writer deserted by an author, an aesthete who has the attitude to marriage of Schnitzler's *Künstler* in *Der einsame Weg* and *Der Weg ins Freie*. 'The house of tears' is the maternity home where she is awaiting her confinement; and here she comes to the conclusion that marriage – whether legal or free – is equivalent to the tyranny of the woman over the man. The terrible thing is not that men desert the women they have had, but that these women should be so cruelly treated by those who should be their sisters, and who, as women, should realize that motherhood, even out of marriage, is sacred. The height of the argument is this: '*Die Frauen sind keiner Rechte wert – keiner bürgerlichen und keiner ideellen – so lange sie dieses ihr heiligstes Recht – ihre gewaltigste Pflicht und Macht nicht erfassen wollen.*'

CLARA VIEBIG (1860–1952) is not so much a feminist as a naturalist: that is, her uncompromising sexualism is based on her conception of the forces of nature (*Naturgewalten*) as, together with geographical *milieu*, conditioning fate: the urge is double, from the blood and from the landscape. (The '*Blut- und Bodenliteratur*' (p. 429) has the same starting-point.) Her conception of *Heimat* as a driving force makes her psychology as much that of masses as of individuals; and her mass psychology may be sexual, religious, or patriotic. The regional influence is in the main that of the Eifel (she was born at Treves), of the Rhineland, or that of the Polish frontier, where she lived for some time. Geographically her novels thus fall into three groups: (1) *Kinder der Eifel*, 1897; *Das Weiberdorf*, 1900; *Einer Mutter Sohn*, 1906; *Das Kreuz im Venn*, 1908; (2) *Die Wacht am Rhein*, 1902; *Rheinlandstöchter*, 1896; (3) *Das schlafende Heer*, 1904; *Absolvo te*, 1907. *Das tägliche Brot* (1902) describes the life of a servant-girl in Berlin. The influence of Gabriele Reuter's campaign of social regeneration shows itself, though hysterically, in such novels as *Rheinlandstöchter*, the heroine of which fights the traditional belief that woman is a chattel. The theme of *Das Weiberdorf* is, frankly, sex starvation in women. Gerhart Hauptmann's *Die Insel der grossen Mutter* is a more discreet parallel, and a curious English parallel is J. D. Beresford's *A World of Women*: a new plague has killed off all the males except a butcher at High Wycombe, and he is to women what Hauptmann's island god is. The butcher's role is in *Das Weiberdorf* filled by the only man who remains behind in the lonely upland village in the Eifel, while the men are away at work in the Ruhr district. The men only come home periodically, and then the starved women, so to speak, devour them. *Das Kreuz im Venn* combines a vivid rendering of the uncanny scenery – perilous swamps, deer-infested pine-forests, piled winter snow, rugged crosses marking the scene of accidents – of the Eifel uplands with a hectic description of the orgies of pilgrims to the shrine of St. Willibrord at Echternach and the mental torture of a convict who by his very nature *must* violate women. There is religious hysteria, too, in *Absolvo te*, this time on the Polish frontier: the story varies the Mark-Isolde motif of old husband and young wife. *Das schlafende Heer*, with its picture of the enslaved masses of Polish peasants, brings out the never-resting racial conflicts in the vast melancholy of the Polish plains. The War novel *Töchter der Hekuba* (1917) is poignant with its revelation of starvation and suffering on the home front.

It is usual to classify two women writers, ISOLDE KURZ (1853-1944) and RICARDA HUCH (1864-1947), as disciples, in style and choice of theme, of Conrad Ferdinand Meyer. Both have his dignity of attitude, his apparent detachment from the characters of the story, his cult of flawless form, his symbolization of history, and above all his predilection for Italy and the Italian Renaissance. But Isolde Kurz strenuously maintained that she had not read Conrad Ferdinand Meyer when she wrote her first stories of Renaissance Italy; she credited her father, the poet and novelist Her-

22

mann Kurz[1] (1813-73), with the shaping of her literary tastes and style. Moreover, in the case of both these women writers the influence of Paul Heyse cannot be missed; for instance, Ricarda Huch's doctrine *Schönheit ist vollkommenes Leben* is pure Paul Heyse. It is also pure romanticism; and nothing is more certain than that in the period of naturalism and impressionism these two ladies are out-and-out romanticists. They have the finer nerves and the more complicated psychology of our own day, but they have the romantic rejection of reality, though they may in odd places be sufficiently infected by the spirit of their time to see reality and to romanticize it: the obvious instances are Ricarda Huch's fantastic vision of the cholera epidemic in Hamburg in 1892 (by common consent it is like a scar on the smooth lyricism of *Erinnerungen von Ludolf Ursleu dem Jüngeren*) and her approach to *Armeleutepoesie* in *Aus der Triumphgasse*, where the pity seems pasted on to the delight in picturesque violence and even the sufferings of a cripple have the glinting lights of dream. Both writers lived in Italy: Isolde Kurz had long made her home in Florence, and Ricarda Huch, when she married her first half-Italian husband, Dr Ceconi, lived with him in Trieste, where she wrote her tales of that city, *Aus der Triumphgasse*. Isolde Kurz is actually less Italianate than Ricarda Huch, though the latter is North German (she belongs to a Brunswick merchant family); there is, it is true, a Swabian softness in Isolde Kurz's love of beautiful people and landscapes as in her easily flowing style, but she has a certain masculine ruggedness – this is indeed the mark of her thoughtful lyric verse (*Gedichte*, 1899; *Neue Gedichte*, 1905) and of her book of aphorisms, *Im Zeichen des Steinbocks* (1905). According to her own statement Isolde Kurz preferred to depict Italians because they are less sicklied o'er than the Germans; she loved their '*ungeschminkte und ungezierte Menschheit*'; that is, like Paul Heyse, she craved warm flesh tones and passion on the boil. She is at her best in *Florentiner Novellen* (1890); and one of the tales in this collection, *Die Humanisten*, is fit to compare both for subject (Renaissance hunting in German monasteries for classical manuscripts) and quality with Conrad Ferdinand Meyer's *Plautus im Nonnenkloster* (1882). The short stories of her *Phantasien und Märchen* (1890), of her *Italienische Erzählungen* (1895; these have their scenes in the Italy of our own day), of *Lebensfluten*

---

[1] His *Schillers Heimatjahre* (1849) compares favourably with Walter von Molo's *Der Schillerroman* (1912-14).

HEINRICH MANN

RICARDA HUCH

(1907), *Genesung* (1912), *Nächte von Fondi* (1923) have traditionally romantic moods.

It is by sheer distinction of style that Ricarda Huch takes rank as the foremost woman writer of her day. She took her doctor's degree at Zurich, taught in a Girls' High School there and was secretary in the town library; it is thus natural that Swiss localities and characters should find a place in her work generally; she records her recollections in *Frühling in der Schweiz* (1938). In her case the influence of Conrad Ferdinand Meyer and Gottfried Keller is flagrant, though Goethe's rhythms and syntax may also be distinguished in her nevertheless markedly individualized prose style, which, moreover, extraordinarily supple, adapts itself to the subject and atmosphere of her successive works. Her first novel on a large scale, *Erinnerungen von Ludolf Ursleu dem Jüngeren* (1893), lives by reason of its lyrical style with its sad, sated rhythms; it set the model for neo-romantic prose as Hofmannsthal's *Der Tod des Tizian* and *Der Tor und der Tod* set it for verse drama. The story itself is irritatingly decadent; it runs its hectic course in that Dionysian cult of beauty the peril of which was to be shown forth by Thomas Mann's *Tod in Venedig*; there is the familiar ostentation of illicit love as the right of personality ('*Mein Glück, das ich haben könnte, ist mein Recht. Ich darf es erkämpfen*'). But subconscious forces and the problematic nature of passion are (to the author and the period) the justification; and, since love is fate, there is the same inevitability of seizure as in the tale of Tristan and Isolde. No modern writer handles the mystery of existence more elusively and more poignantly than Ricarda Huch; in this first novel life is fate; in the following novel *Vita Somnium Breve* a strong man's will deflects fate by the rejection of the love that fate wills – but to what purpose? As in Thomas Mann's *Buddenbrooks* the main tenor of the Ursleu story is the decay of a Hanseatic patrician family, here in Hamburg, but (since the style is in pointed hostility to the naturalistic formula) without that weaving in of business affairs which makes *Buddenbrooks* as good a commercial novel as Freytag's *Soll und Haben*. *Buddenbrooks*, by the way, comes eight years later; and it has been suggested that Thomas Mann owes his theme of cultural development inducing incapacity for the boredom of business to this novel of Ricarda Huch's. The story is related by Ludolf Ursleu, who has escaped from the world of such tragic happenings to the peace of the Swiss monastery of Einsiedeln (the framework may have been suggested by E. T. A. Hoffmann's *Die Elixiere des Teufels*): the events he relates, as they pass before him in procession, are thus softened by distance. He is at peace, he muses; but therefore he is dead – for life is the stormy ocean; and where there are no storms of passion, no conflicts of personality, there is no life. The decay of a business firm – Hamburg (*'die kalte Handelsstadt des Nordens'*) is again indicated, though Ricarda Huch, true to the romantic formula, does not specify localities – is once again in the background of *Vita Somnium Breve* (1902; later rechristened *Michael Unger*); actually the hero, though as the eldest son of patrician parents he should carry on the firm, throws up his business career to win distinction as a zoologist, and makes frantic efforts to leave his wife for the sake of a woman painter who has physical and mental qualities which his uncongenial wife has not. The wife turns Catholic, and therefore cannot divorce him; but what chains him to her – and here is the grip of the story – is his love for his one child, a son who, as the close of the novel hints, will repay his father's sacrifice of love by being a charming and lively but socially worthless fellow in whom the vigorous old stock will dishonourably die out. To save the boy's fortune the father has returned to business and rescued the firm, brought to the verge of bankruptcy by the brother next in age – artist and poet in an amateur way – who had taken his place at the deserted office desk. The conflict as thus outlined must be common in everyday life; but Ricarda Huch gives it something of the tragic intensity of Racine's *Andromaque*, in which too the theme is the tyranny of child over parent. What gives the novel its value – it must be admitted that many reject it as too hazy, and certainly it is hard to read through – is the slow and careful unfolding of the hero's mental suffering, and the tragic implication of the tale that though duty to family is the paramount consideration it may mean absolute sacrifice of what is best in a man's personality. Certainly what accrues from the sacrifice is treated with a suggestion of irony – and irony (sly, pathetic, or extravagant) is almost half of Ricarda Huch's technique after the Ursleu book; but the main brunt of the theme is surely that a man grows strong by self-mastery. One suspects, too, that a current idea of the time, the doctrine of the Danish philosopher Søren Kierkegaard that a man's character as genius, poet, hero, or saint is made by his *not* getting his girl, may be in the weft of the tale; Ibsen's *Love's Comedy* and

Brand had familiarized the idea. Michael Unger is man as Ricarda Huch fondly imagines him: the tortured angel, lured by beauty but fettered by duty, to whose problematic lips woman would, if she could, bring the balm of bliss: an utterly romantic and feminine estimation of the male. The woman Michael loves is unconvincing: nothing she says or does has the flash of magic personality; all that is clear is that she is capable and solid and that she is ready to mother her man when he comes to her with his plea – sufficiently hackneyed – of loneliness of spirit. There is attraction for the literary reader in the description of student life in Zurich, that home of *die Internationale*, and still more in two portraits – one obviously of Ernst Haeckel in his conflict with established religion and in his senile eroticism: dismissed from his professorship he takes over Michael's discarded mistress; and the other – quite delightful! – of Stefan George as Aristos, the latest sensation in poetical fashion: '*sein Gesicht war hager und knochig und so farblos, dass er mit geschlossenen Augen einem Totenkopf glich*' . . . '*ungeheuer wie ein ewiger Gletscher*'. From Conrad Ferdinand Meyer Ricarda Huch takes over the device of the *Rahmenerzählung*: Ludolf Ursleu unfolds the saga of the past much as Dante does in the Swiss novelist's *Die Hochzeit des Mönchs*; and in *Aus der Triumphgasse* (1902) the patrician owner of a medieval mansion (the home of his ancestors), now decayed to a hive of flats, little by little reveals the tangled lives of his tenants and their neighbours in this ancient street of Trieste through which the dark narrow road climbs through a Roman Arch of Triumph – an ironical erection! More fitting were Dante's *Lasciate ogni speranza, voi ch'entrate*; and indeed the Arch and what lies before and behind it is a symbol of life itself: through such a gateway youth climbs, but to the defeat of all hope and to the endless strain and struggle by which all that is human lives. In this street with the illusory name is crowded, like vermin, the scum of the city – cripples, murderers, thieves, and girls who give themselves for bread or passion. At their worst these creatures, as Ricarda Huch shows, with her detached, fondling touch, are intensely human; at their best they may be heroic. Starvation cannot blunt their avid hold on life and may, when the heart is good, give them a ripe humour that lights up even this sordid existence. They are ministered to by a mysterious young priest with a beautiful, sad face: the foster-brother of a murderer and a prostitute who are still close to his heart. In so sad a book humour might not be expected; but it is there – a naughty humour which comes natural to Ricarda Huch as a disciple of Gottfried Keller, as in the story of how the Civic Prize for Virtue is awarded to a girl who is virtuous because her lover is a stoker mostly at sea but who entertains him in bed while her mother and most of the street are on a holy pilgrimage. Ricarda Huch's other novels, except those with themes from history, have hardly more than academic interest. The problem of royalty outworn in a hustling world of business is dreamily approached in *Von den Königen und der Krone* (1904): the son of a Slav king, while doctor at a hospital for children, marries the daughter of a German oil magnate. Here, if anywhere, the realism of Thomas Mann's *Königliche Hoheit* was needed; but Ricarda Huch, refining her Romantic fancifulness, lifts earth to the clouds, which will not bear it. *Der Fall Deruga* (1918), an experiment in the criminal novel, is painful in the ir-reality of its realism: a doctor has given his dying wife, at her own request, a sleeping draught, and the court proceedings which the story reports try to bring home the crime to the culprit. Close scrutiny may find a loving care in the characterization of this doc-tor with an Italian name, but one cannot credit that anywhere a murder could be investigated in so strange a way.

Both the close-packed style of Gottfried Keller and his ironical treatment of religion are closely imitated by Ricarda Huch in a series of short stories[1] whose content varies from tragic or pathetic to quaint or grotesque. Keller had made his game of religion in the Gottmacher's tales in *Der Grüne Heinrich*, and in *Sieben Legenden* (1872) he had transmuted the old Catholic legends of chastity into proof that nothing is closer to the heart of God than the joys of wedlock[2] – His means to His purpose. In *Der arme Heinrich*, one of the tales of *Fra Celeste und andere Erzählungen*, Ricarda Huch reads the consummation of sexual desire into this physically most absurd of medieval legends. The anti-religious satire, though with-out coarseness, misses its mark by overstraining probability in *Der Hahn von Quakenbrück* (1910): Catholics and Calvinists dispute as to the punishment that should be meted out to the Mayor's cock for laying eggs with scarlet yokes; and in *Lebenslauf des heiligen*

---

[1] *Der Mondreigen von Schlaraffis* (1896), *Teufeleien* (1897), *Hadewig im Kreuz-gang* (1897), *Fra Celeste und andere Erzählungen* (1899), *Seifenblasen* (1905). Col-lected in two volumes as *Erzählungen* (1919). Followed by *Der neue Heilige* (1920), *Der wiederkehrende Christus* (1926), *Die Hugenottin* (1930).
[2] Rudolf G. Binding does the same in his *Legenden* (p. 277).

Wonnebald Pück (in *Seifenblasen*): an utter fool, a scoundrel and an oozy voluptuary, rises by virtue of his very vices and idiocy to be abbot and bishop, and on his death is canonized because his story is believed that the image of the Virgin in his church has given him Her own jewelled crown – which in sober fact he had stolen to pay for his loose living.

Ricarda Huch breaks new ground as much by her regeneration of the historical novel or *vie romancée* as by her elaboration of a lyrical prose style: she frees it from restrictions of locality and raises it to epic grandeur and timeless significance in *Die Geschichten von Garibaldi* (*Die Verteidigung Roms*, 1906; *Der Kampf um Rom*, 1907), *Menschen und Schicksale aus dem Risorgimento* (1908), and *Das Leben des Grafen Federigo Confalonieri* (1910). Typical of the psychological method of her historical tales is the Confalonieri volume: the ripening of a mind in twelve years of imprisonment and the analysis of patriotic idealism provides the interest. Ricarda Huch makes Garibaldi a symbol of genius, isolated (in Thomas Mann's sense) by his own 'difference from the others' (*Anderssein*), prone to excess, and inevitably the tool (as an engineer controls elemental forces) of inferior but calculating minds (Cavour). In her prose epic of the Thirty Years War, *Der grosse Krieg in Deutschland* (1912-14), we have her new conception of historical fiction brought to fruition: in her vision of these vast events – since her aim is to portray not individuals but a whole period with its inner impulses, its mass psychology, its cumulative devastation – she does not bring the great leaders out in stark relief, but lets them take their place (even Gustavus Adolphus and Wallenstein) as actors controlled by the drama rather than controlling it, as scene billows after scene in the ocean of happenings with no ordered beginning and no clear-cut ending.

Her lyric verse (*Gedichte*, 1894; *Neue Gedichte*, 1907), modelled as it may be on that of Conrad Ferdinand Meyer, is marked by a somewhat hectic speculative cast rather than by plastic presentation of image and substance. The philosophical staple is that of the prose work: the most insistent idea is that personality should struggle with and wrest from existence the utmost it can bestow – *Alles oder nichts*,[1] for instance, concentrates the doctrine (essentially that of *Vita Somnium Breve* as of other works) in a sonnet. Certain

---

[1] The title of the poem was familiar as the programme of Ibsen and of Ibsen's hero Brand ('*Intet eller alt!*').

of her poems with a more sentimental appeal have won permanent place in the anthologies, but one doubts whether the bulk of the verse is not superficially imitative or a metrically skilful play with current fancies, though she may give them the ring of intense feeling, as in *Sehnsucht*, which owes its poignancy to its Swiss[1] setting:

> *Um bei dir zu sein,*
> *Trüg' ich Not und Fährde,*
> *Liess' ich Freund und Haus*
> *Und die Fülle der Erde.*
>
> *Mich verlangt nach dir,*
> *Wie die Flut nach dem Strande,*
> *Wie die Schwalbe im Herbst*
> *Nach dem südlichen Lande.*
>
> *Wie den Alpsohn heim,*
> *Wenn er denkt, nachts alleine,*
> *An die Berge voll Schnee*
> *Im Mondenscheine.*

She gets farthest away from traditional moods – and metrically at least her poetry is for the most part wearily traditional – in impressionistic freaks of fancy such as *Erinnerung*:

> *Einmal vor manchem Jahre*
> *War ich ein Baum am Bergesrand,*
> *Und meine Birkenhaare*
> *Kämmte der Mond mit weisser Hand.*
>
> *Hoch überm Abgrund hing ich*
> *Windbewegt auf schroffem Stein,*
> *Tänzende Wolken fing ich*
> *Mir als vergänglich Spielzeug ein.*
>
> *Fühlte nichts im Gemüte*
> *Weder von Wonne noch von Leid,*
> *Rauschte, verwelkte, blühte,*
> *In meinem Schatten schlief die Zeit.*

A close examination of Ricarda Huch's work would very likely prove that the scholarly elaboration of current ideas which shows

---

[1] *Heimweh* itself is a Swiss word which has naturalized itself in German.

in her verse is, rather than original fire of genius, what by the nature of her imitative talent she is best qualified to do. Even the general view of critics that she has a very masculine mind – she certainly has a strong man's capacity for taking infinite pains – needs qualifying by the admission that she has to the full those feminine weaknesses – e.g. worship of man – which make women so delightful to men. At all events any male scholar might be proud of her great mass of critical work. Her literary criticism (*Die Blütezeit der Romantik*, 1899; *Ausbreitung und Verfall der Romantik*, 1902; *Gottfried Keller*, 1904) is academically accepted, though rather brilliant than academic; and she even manages to make theology interesting in *Luthers Glaube* (1916). To her historical work she brings the sound academic training of her Zurich days; it is nevertheless poet's history. Her *Römisches Reich deutscher Nation* (1934), in which she traces the cultural and political development of the Empire, did not find favour with Nazi critics because she does not definitely reject the fascination for the German emperors of Rome and all Rome implied. Where she does, perhaps, prepare Nazi ideology is in her philosophical disquisition *Entpersönlichung* (1921): she compares the medieval ideal '(*heidnisch-christlich-germanisch*') with the contemporary aim to be as comfortable as possible; in the Middle Ages man strove to complete his personality and to be god-like, but progress has been '*von der Persönlichkeit zur Entpersönlichung*'. The Germans are less able to resist this rotting of personality because they are no longer racially pure.

LOU ANDREAS-SALOMÉ (1861-1937) in her novels (*Ruth*, 1895; *Fenitschka*, 1898; *Ma*, 1901) marks the transition from naturalism to impressionism. Born in St. Petersburg as the daughter of a Russian general, she was fond of German Russians for her characters, and the scene of her tales is often in Russia. One of her best bits of work is the description of the steppes in *Wolga* (one of the short stories of *Im Zwischenland*, 1902), in which, too, there are studies of puberty considered daring at the time they were written. She is intellectualized through and through (*durchgeistigt*), and the realism of her keenly psychological depiction is both tormentedly Russian and ruthlessly Nietzschean. She is best known as the friend of Nietzsche and Rilke; her *Friedrich Nietzsche in seinen Werken* (1894) and *Rainer Maria Rilke* (1929) are important because of the first-hand knowledge they convey.

VICKI BAUM (1888-), a Viennese actress who turned to writing, has in her feverish style something of the expressionist manner. In her early novels critics detected the influence of Hermann Bang and Thomas Mann; in her later work she has developed her own manner. She has the light touch of a born story-teller; she does not build sentences, but lets her quick, lively periods fall into a natural sequence and caps them, often, with a sad illuminative climax; and if she has any poetry it is in the feeling she glosses over with her cynically realistic conversational tone rather than in any literary phrasing. She has her own technique, too; for instance, in *Das grosse Einmaleins* (1935) she will show the man's state of mind during a crisis of the action, and then literally repeat it to show the woman's far more intense feeling from moment to moment. In *Menschen im Hotel* (1929) she came near to devising a new film-like way of narration: she presents a metropolitan hotel, with the swing doors and the great hall as a kind of *open sesame*, as an atom-like conglomeration: a miniature but complete replica of the world as a totality, pulsing with pain and passion in its interrelated types. She had written considerably before, but with this burst of talent she conquered her world, helped by the insight of critics who at once detected in the pathetic figure of the dancer on the threshold of her decline a picture of that darling of capitals, Pavlova. The excellent thing in *Menschen im Hotel* is the intimate rendering of the irradiation of life from a nucleus; in *Zwischenfall in Lohwinckel* (1930) the gathering-point is a small German town, whose detached intimacies are set fluttering by the old romantic device of an accident to travellers. It is this intimate rendering of German life, seen with a Jewish keenness of eye, which makes Vicki Baum's American tales, by contrast, so artificial, though allowance must be made for expressionistic distortion. The pity is that so German a writer should have been transplanted by the exigencies of 1933 to the United States, where she was naturalized. *Leben ohne Geheimnis* (1933) attempts an unravelling of the mysteries of Hollywood, but actually pictures only what is known. To film-goers of course there must be a thrill in detecting the originals of these waxworky characters. From the view-point of literary continuity Vicki Baum's most interesting tale may well be *Stud. Chem. Helene Willfüer* (1929); academic readers it will attract or repel by its description of alleged student life in Heidelberg and Munich. It carries the theme of Helene Böhlau's *Das Recht der Mutter* a stage further: the heroine gives herself to her boy, not because she has a thrill of desire, but

because he is suffering, and generally there is much of Gabriele
Reuter's consideration for suffering males in this story. (On the
other hand Vicki Baum may be hard on her own sex: 'she was
female almost to the pitch of obscenity', she writes of one of her
characters.) A friend of the heroine sends her boy away after a
night of excitement – to a looser woman; and syphilis is the result.
Is the continence that propriety requires of engaged couples a
social prejudice, a hygienic evil, or a stern necessity? Is not the
vital consideration for a university girl student the fact that she
cannot be pregnant and study for her examination or write a
thesis? Helene, as a student of chemistry, can follow the chemico-
biological process of pregnancy in her own body, and there is the
problem of the expediency or otherwise of abortion. This is still
forbidden by German law; but, as the novel stresses, contempt
for the unmarried mother is now forbidden – she has helped the
Fatherland, and is entitled to be addressed as 'Frau'. (The right to
provide cannon-fodder for a grateful country was not exactly what
Vicki Baum's predecessors had fought for.) Having borne her
baby, Helene isolates a hormone which stimulates the sexual functions and has a rejuvenating effect; this is successfully marketed
under the name of 'vitalin', and thus the novel has a happy ending
– of a new sort.

ELSE LASKER-SCHÜLER (1876-1945) was claimed as one of themselves by the expressionists; she was at all events in the very centre
of their Berlin circle, and as the wife of Herwarth Walden, the
editor of Der Sturm, she chaperoned the movement so to speak.
But in her origins she is a naturalist: her drama Die Wupper (1908)
is, though fantastically coloured, a sordid depiction of low life in
the Ruhr district. The drama, however, was tentative: she is her
own strange self in her poems. She has no ethics of any sort, and
for that reason cannot be an expressionist proper; but her verse
and prose have an expressionist appearance in the sense that they
do seem to be expressing something that only those who are poetically gifted can make head or tail of. What does emerge is that she
is an Oriental princess – Prinzessin Tino von Bagdad – who has
the tales of Scheherezade to tell; and we should see her sunk in
harem silks and cushions, or in a moonlight halt among the sheiks
of the desert. Or: she is on pilgrimage to the New Jerusalem, and
is in some strange way herself the angel before the gates of Paradise, with his star glittering on her brow and his broken pinion

on her shoulder. Her *Hebräische Balladen* (1913) have some Hebrew melodies, but for the most part are pathologically modern. *Die Kuppel* (1925) is a collection of lyrics in the same vein: apparently artless notations of intensely personal fancies, with broken rhythms and fainting falls. Altogether delightful – to the initiated – is *Das Peter Hille-Buch* (1906), in which she wreathes a halo round the shaggy head of the disreputable vagabond poet, her great friend; the whole thing is as close to reality as Eichendorff's *Taugenichts*. 'The Black Swan of Israel' ended her days as a kind of national Jewish poet in Jerusalem. Her most poignant book is her last, *Das Hebräerland* (1937): travel impressions of the Holy Land and at the same time a vision of the poetry and tragedy of Jewish history in the homeland. Very pathetic are her own illustrations. Her own quaint drawings indeed adorn all her books, and this alone makes them prizes for collectors – one would not even deface them by having them bound: they are things to keep clean in the original paper binding with the incredible and luring picture on the cover. *Dichtungen und Dokumente* (1951) contains a good cross-section of her ever-varied work with its strange moods and fancies.

There can be no questioning of the womanish element in the novels of ENRICA VON HANDEL-MAZZETTI (1871-1955). Born in Vienna, she lived at Steyr in Upper Austria, and she belongs to *Heimatkunst* because her best work is narrowed down to delineation of this her homeland. Strictly speaking, however, she is not a *Heimatkünstlerin*, because the theme she has made her own is not so much the regional aspects of life and landscape as the fierce strife of religious sects, which would be the same without as within her homeland. Her first novel, *Meinrad Helmpergers denkwürdiges Jahr* (1900), is located at the beginning of the eighteenth century, when Lutheranism had ossified into a dogma as intolerant as ever Catholicism was. The son of Baron Mac Endall, a British atheist who has been tortured to death by the Berlin parsons, is won over in a monastery to the Catholic faith; the abbot, a man of hard nature, has failed to influence the lad, but he is moulded by the loving gentleness of a simple monk, Meinrad Helmperger. The decisive factor in the conversion, however, is the picturing – sadistically detailed – of the torture to which the defiant atheist has been put; and here for once the author is unfair to the contrary faith, for the Catholics would hardly have been more lenient to an atheist; she does, however, credit nobility of character as well as unflinching

sincerity of conviction to this friend of Leibniz whom the Protestants have martyred. Enrica von Handel-Mazzetti's best novel is no
doubt *Jesse und Maria* (1906). Jesse, a Protestant iconoclast, has
designs against the miracle-working image of the Virgin at Steyr
(where it is still the bourne of pilgrims), and Maria, for the sake
of the Catholic faith, betrays him; she is then torn by remorse,
and the story shows that in her heart she loves the man whose
death she has compassed. What the story brings out is that there
is as much sincerity and true goodness in one religion as in the
other; what matters is the essential humanity of characters who
are estranged by the intensity of their own convictions. So fair to
Protestants is this writer that she has been accused of upholding
or condoning Protestant doctrine; and certainly any Protestant
might swear that her next novel, *Die arme Margaret* (1910), gives
the palm of victory to the Protestant heroine. The intention probably is, however, to show that salvation rests with the Virgin and
even with her carven image, and perhaps by reason of this argument and because of the general womanishness (in a good sense)
of the story *Die arme Margaret* gives a better idea of the author's
essential qualities than does *Jesse und Maria*. The tale has breathless
interest and a faultless heightening of the tension to the final too
sensational but compelling scenes; and yet, if reduced to its bare
outlines, it is in the nature of an old saint's legend (*Heiligenlegende*),
with the devil nearly triumphing over a woman's chastity and
balked only in the moment of seizure by the intervention of the
Virgin. Poor Margaret is the young widow – very lovely with her
lily-white skin and golden locks – of a Protestant in Steyr who
has been executed for heresy. Since she remains obstinately Protestant a company of twenty-five Pappenheim dragoons under the
command of a strapping and perfectly handsome lieutenant is sent
to force her to recant. The lieutenant, a mere boy, still a virgin in
spite of his campaigning, has *carte blanche*; he billets himself and
his men in her little cottage, leaving Margaret only the windy
attic for herself and suckling child, and proceeds – fanatically convinced that he is thus serving God – to put the poor woman to
torture; and the author dwells on the pressure of his devilish
devices with that love (sadistic or otherwise) of the description of
suffering which is a marked feature of her work. The climax of
the piled-up agony comes when the lieutenant, in a terrific thunderstorm, attempts to rape his prisoner; her desperate resistance

is described – *con amore* – as, step by step, he forces her to the edge of the bed from which he has displaced her; and she is on the very verge of collapse when she snatches from his breast the scapulary with an image of the Virgin – which, as he has told her, is all that remains to him of the mother he has never known – and holds it before his face. He reels back; her purity – or the Virgin? – has saved her. In the drenching rain she runs out into the town, and is rescued by a patrician of the district, a strict Catholic who is given the picturesque attributes of the Moses of the Bible and of Michelangelo. He rouses the burghers, jealous of their chartered liberties, to a fever-heat of indignation, and the army authorities are forced to bring the delinquent to trial. They might save him if he would swear that the woman tempted him; but he is too simple and true to lie – and he loves the fair body he has touched. And to everybody's surprise Margaret refuses to accuse him; '*es ist nicht beschehen*', she says (he did *not* do it). But she bears the imprint of his five fingers on her arm; and in any case attempted rape is according to army regulations as heinous a crime as rape committed; so the boy is condemned and stabbed to death with lances. But he dies in the arms of Margaret, who holds before his dying eyes his mother's scapulary, which had been taken from his neck. Margaret weeps over her perfect brute as Kriemhild wept over hers ('*si huop sîn schœne houbet in ir vil wîzen hant*'); and it may be taken as praise or blame to say that in this modern story there is the same elemental feeling as there is in the *Nibelungenlied*. The sentiment is not maudlin, because it is psychologically developed stage by stage; the characters, though touched up with religious colouring, have that simplicity and swift emotion which we find in the ancient masterpieces of literature. In a period which was priding itself on its psychological probing of complicated natures these novels of Enrica von Handel-Mazzetti are thus in the nature of throw-backs; nevertheless, the best critics may be right in giving to her the palm for the historical novel of recent years; she earns this precedence of place, in spite of her limited range, by her absolute sincerity of motive and by the consummate skill of her simple technique. Not the least of her qualities is her scholarly handling of the dialect of Lower Austria: chronicle style, *Volkslied*, *Kanzlei-sprache*, the *Alamode* language of seventeenth-century officials and soldiers, are skilfully imitated. Equally good is the rendering of those baroque features which make the seventeenth century in

Germany so fascinating a study: the violently strained rhetoric, the delight in glaring antitheses, the fiercely ethical conduct of life, the stern religious gloom which is the background against which flit and flash the dashing devilment and the picturesque uniforms of all the regiments of many-peopled Austria. Other novels in which she deserts the province and period she has made her own are mediocre (*Der deutsche Held*, 1920), but there is at least interest to the student of literature in her *Johann Christian Günther* (1927), in which she lays bare the contrition after much human sinning of that seventeenth-century lyric poet whose life, in Goethe's words, ran to waste because he had let go the reins. With Enrica von Handel-Mazzetti may be mentioned her disciple PAULA GROGGER (1892-), also a Styrian; her best tales are *Das Grimmingtor* (1927) and *Der Lobenstock* (1935).

The Catholic writer most in vogue today is FREIIN GERTRUD VON LE FORT (1876-). She was nearly fifty when she began to write the books that made her famous[1] - the reason being, she says, that 'all that is to ripen needs a long resting time and all that drives down deep must zealously guard the aloofness that is needed.' She has told her story in *Aufzeichnungen und Erinnerungen* (1951). The descendant of Huguenot immigrants, the great event in her life was her conversion to Catholicism in 1926. The main formative influence on her was her study of history and theology at Heidelberg as the pupil of the philosopher Ernst Troeltsch, whose posthumous works she edited. She made her reputation with the theological novel *Das Schweisstuch der Veronika* (1928); its sequel *Der Kranz der Engel* did not appear till 1946, but the two form one whole. In *Das Schweisstuch der Veronika* with its significant subtitle *Der römische Brunnen* we have the story of a sixteen year old girl in pre-1914 Rome who is so captivated by the history of the Imperium Sanctum, the grandeur of the Holy Roman Empire leagued with and leaning on the Church of Rome, that she turns Catholic, breaking away from the creed of her Protestant grandmother. In *Der Kranz der Engel* we find her as a student at Heidelberg; here there is a love match with a friend of her youth who, after his experiences in World War I, has come to hate Christianity (much as Ernst Wiechert did in his first phase). She seeks to redeem him by consenting to a civil marriage, but she falls danger-

[1] Her earlier works, verse and prose, are collected in *Die ersten Schritte* (1951).

ously ill and he returns to the fold. This theme of redemption by love is necessarily the main moving force in her work, for it is the integral concomitant of the Catholic faith. What constitutes the interest of the two novels is that sustained conflict between worldliness and unfettered thinking on the one hand and Catholicism with its rigidity of doctrine on the other which in our days marks the political history of Germany and Austria and in literature as in politics amounts to a Catholic revival. Of this Catholic revival she is a prop and stay. It is natural, therefore, that *Das Schweisstuch der Veronika* should have the stamp of all her subsequent fiction. Generally speaking her novels and short stories have to be classed as historical; but this is only chronologically so, for she is everywhere at grips with the problems of the present, and her solution of the conflicts round which she winds her intrigues points to the final goal where, as her shaping of the action shows, salvation lies. Critics deny that she preaches; and this holds good in the sense that truth is not something that can be taught, but is there, immutable, where the author sees it. The key to her striving – which is to save souls from the dark powers that threaten them – is that her works were composed during the onward rush and sweep of nationalistic and communistic doctrines. Both the great theological novels with their depiction of a girl's sacrifice of family tradition are written in the first person, and that has frequently been taken to indicate that they are autobiographical; this she emphatically denies – she uses the *Ichform*, she says, because it is particularly suggestive where the narrator's aim is to lay bare the inner nature of her chief character. Moreover, she affirms, her characters are not portraits painted from life, but types; that is, what happens in their minds is more important than what they are as persons. In other words they are evolved, as a mathematical proposition might be. But whether for this very reason they *live*, as do the characters of Enrica von Handel-Mazzetti, to whom the historical placing of her characters brings her close, is a moot question. *Der Papst aus dem Ghetto* (1930) brings the Jewish problem into the story of Anaclet II, the Jew pope who in 1130 was set up as antipope to Innocent II. *Die Letzte am Schafott* (1931) is a sort of *Heiligenlegende* written in letter form by a novice, the youngest of sixteen Carmelite nuns, who dies as the last of them during the French Revolution, with all the legendary heroism of a martyr. It is the base of Francis Poulenc's opera *Dialogues des Carmélites* (1956), with a

French text by Georges Bernanos. *Das Reich des Kindes* (1933) weaves the story in legend form round the last of the Carolingians and centres round the fate of Lewis the Child. *Die Magdeburgische Hochzeit* (1938) symbolizes the fall and destruction of Magdeburg during the Thirty Years War as such a marriage of temporal and eternal as will befall the world on the day of judgment. The Novelle *Die Abberufung der Jungfrau von Barby* (1940) with its orgies of image-breaking by fanatical iconoclasts has its sinister parallel in the mind of a nun who loses her faith and dies a violent death. There is a similarity of theme, the conflict between justice and pity, in the two short stories *Das Gericht des Meeres* (1943) and *Die Consolata* (1947). In the latter a papal legate besieges Padua and saves it from a ruthless dictator; the reference to Nazi ideology is transparent. These two Novellen are reprinted in *Die Tochter Farinatas* (1950), which adds two others, the title story and *Plus Ultra*; in the title story the heroine saves her native city Florence in the days of the Hohenstaufens, while in *Plus Ultra* a girl sacrifices her love for the Emperor Charles Quint because her love of the Holy Roman Empire is greater. The two stories of *Gelöschte Kerzen* (1953) again draw a parallel of trends and happenings in the Thirty Years War with those of today. The scene of *Die Frau des Pilatus* (1955) begins in Judea at the time of Christ's trial and moves to Rome, where Pilate's wife Claudia is threatened by the fate of Christians who are thrown to lions in the circus, for she is a convert to Christianity. Her dilemma is that, though she is a bride of Christ, she is still the loving wife of a husband who sanctioned the crucifixion of her Heavenly Bridegroom. The letter form of *Die Letzte am Schafott* is again effectively used: the writer is Claudia's maidservant, who records the story from close experience and without partiality. The first book of Gertrud von le Fort's verse which counts is *Hymnen an die Kirche* (1924), a dialogue between the Creator and the soul. This was followed by *Hymnen an Deutschland* (1932), the burden of which is that Germany can find salvation only if the State is wedded to the Holy See. *Gedichte* (1949) gathers in poems written between 1933 and 1945; it reflects the moods and misery and the hope springing eternal of these years. The ode *Vergessenes Vaterland* is a terrible picture of war's ruin, and this is heightened by such poems as *Die Kathedrale nach der Schlacht*, *Den zerstörten Domen*, *Die Heimatlosen*. The lovely poem *Deutsches Leid* is a moving protestation of the poet's love for a Germany laid in

23

ruins. *Die Stimme des Heilands* brands the horror of war – the Saviour speaks His pity for all His peoples. Of Gertrud von le Fort's essayistic work the most widely read is *Die ewige Frau* (1934); the interpretation of '*die Frau in der Zeit*' is doubled by that of '*die zeitlose Frau*'. *Die Krone der Frau* (1952), consisting of selections from the author's works, is in the nature of a companion volume. There are mystical currents philosophically reasoned in *Die Opfer-flamme* (1938), which pays tribute to death as a form of love, while *Unser Weg durch die Nacht* (1949), addressed to '*meine Schweizer Freunde*', proclaims her love, *quand même*, of Germany.

AGNES MIEGEL (1879-), who was born in Königsberg, is essentially a lyric poetess (*Gedichte*, 1901 – title changed to *Frühe Gedichte*, 1939; *Balladen und Lieder*, 1907; *Gedichte und Spiele*, 1920; *Gesammelte Gedichte*, 1927, 1931, 1952; *Herbstgesang*, 1932). Her verse is traditional in form, but there is a vigorous feminine note in the themes, and even sexual disclosure, though decent and discreet, and marked with patient suffering or expectation rather than revolt, in such poems as *Mädchenlied, Das letzte Mal, Wie Ischtar, Ungeborenes Leben, Schöne Agnete*; and her ballads are differentiated from the merely narrative species by a vibrant assertion of feminine psychology (*Agnes Bernauerin, Griseldis, Mary Stuart, Abisag von Sunem, Magdalena*, etc.). The plenitude of British ballad themes is due to early residence in England, though also, perhaps, to the influence of Fontane. In her Novellen (*Geschichten aus Altpreussen*, 1926; *Gang in die Dämmerung*, 1934) she keeps to her native province of East Prussia, and relates historical episodes with the bias of the *Heimatkünstler. Audhumla* (1938) is dedicated to the cows of East Prussia, and tells their story from the mythical *Urkuh* of the Eddas to the flight from the Russians in August 1914.

What Agnes Miegel is to East Prussia LULU VON STRAUSS UND TORNEY (1873-1956) is to Westphalia. One of the best-known collections of verse in our period is *Reif steht die Saat* (1926), her collected poems and ballads. Her long ballads (*Libussa, Das Gericht von Calais, Geusenbotschaft*, etc.) have great variety both of form and theme, and are dramatic rather than lyrical; their exultant tone and sonorous rhythm mark her delight in the vigorous life and self-assertion of her vividly individualized characters. Her manly love of adventure and the open life comes out in her tales of peasant life in the lands around the Weser: *Bauernstolz* (1901), *Judas* (1911; title changed to *Der Judashof*, 1937) and in her historical tales: *Der Hof am Brink* (1906; the period is that of the Thirty Years War), *Lucifer* (1907; describes the resistance of peasants to the tyranny of the Church), *Sieger und Besiegte* (1907). There is the visionary fever of the expressionists in her tale of the Anabaptists, *Der jüngste Tag* (1921): a consumptive weaver preaches, in 1535, the coming of the Last Day, and when it does not come sets the village on fire with his own hand.

HELENE VOIGT-DIEDERICHS (1875-1952) belongs to *Heimatkunst*; but, though she lovingly describes the life of the landed gentry and farmers in her native Schleswig-Holstein (as in her short stories: *Schleswig-Holsteiner Landleute*, 1898) she is a feminist too, and in the best sense of the term, in her novels, which reveal keen insight into the minds of growing girls, and throw light on the interrelationship of mothers and daughters. She has a sense of humour to relieve the strain of the tragic conflicts she evolves. Into *Auf Marienhoff* (1925) she weaves memories of the estate of the same name where she grew up. The awakening life of maiden-hood is her theme in *Regine Vosgerau* (1901) and *Dreiviertel Stund vor Tag* (1905). She deals honestly but decently with the problem of the *Ehe zu dritt* in *Ring um Roderich* (1929). *Aus Kinderland* (1907) gathers in her tales told to children.

In present-day criticism INA SEIDEL (1885-) is given very high rank. She is a member of a literary dynasty: her uncle was Heinrich Seidel of *Leberecht Hühnchen* fame; her brother is Willy Seidel, who has been called 'a German Kipling' for the sake of his exotic tales; she married her parson cousin, who writes too; and Georg Ebers was her mother's stepfather. As a writer of verse (*Gedichte*, 1914; *Neben der Trommel her*, 1915 – war poems; *Weltinnigkeit*, 1918; *Neue Gedichte*, 1927) she has good technique, but is imitative. Her earlier novels (*Das Haus zum Monde*, 1917, with its sequel *Sterne der Heim-kehr*, 1923) stand out by their careful and insistent handling of woman's importance in family life; her speciality is the relation-ship of brothers and sisters (*Brömseshof*, 1928; *Renée und Rainer*, 1928). More interesting is *Das Labyrinth* (1922), a painfully Freud-ian study of Georg Forster – who first translated the Sanscrit drama *Sakuntala* – as the scholarly German dreamer helpless in a world of schemers. His youth in Warrington is described, where his father was a teacher – dismissed in due course for freethinking – before sailing round the world with Cook, taking his boy with him. On their return the father was appointed professor of natural science at Halle, while Georg taught in a school at Kassel. He is attracted by Karoline Michaelis – later the wife of August Wilhelm Schlegel and then of Schelling, and Schiller's 'Dame Lucifer' – but marries Therese Heyne, the daughter of the famous Göttingen professor of Latin. She is unfaithful to him, but he forgives her, and they go to live at Mainz, where the plot thickens and history, with the French occupation, leads the characters deeper into the labyrinthine tangle. The effect is somewhat televisionary: there is too much grouping of figures familiar to us all as Germanists: these figures are vividly portrayed, but too much in the ideal light of literary history – even such figures as Schiller's friend Huber. The sting of the criticism should be that, interesting as the grouping of these familiar figures is, it is only so in a sense extraneous to the sense of the novel as such: certainly they rob the story of concentration on the protagonists: Georg Forster is not so much the hero around whom the groups revolve as one of a crowd. Moreover, he is depicted as a pathological figure, so that the novel has naturalistic *Heldenlosigkeit*. However, the depressing tale does give a psychological interpretation of the marital promiscuousness of the period – particularly of the tendency of the literary ladies to sample poet after poet. Forster himself is of the type of Schiller when he wrote *Freigeisterei der Leidenschaft* – and for the same reason: he is so intellectually excited that his sexual activity is dormant or spasmodic. The tale ends with Therese living under Huber's protection while Georg goes to Paris as a deputy of the Mainz Convention. Here he dies in misery; and ere he dies he realizes that life is a labyrinth, through which we grope, with hope vanishing, to that terrible mystery the Minotaur – that is, death. Ina Seidel's masterpiece is *Das Wunschkind* (1930). The hero's mother is the daughter of a patrician family in Mainz; she is married to a Prussian officer, whose child – *das Wunschkind* – she conceives in the night before his departure to fight the French revolutionaries. He is killed. As the boy grows up the situation is that of Parzival's mother: the boy belongs to a Prussian family of officers; he *must* fight; he is dedicated to death as his father was. The mother's sister marries a French officer who has risen from the ranks; and in time the child of this union, a daughter, is brought up with the old grandfather, a man of heroic mould, on the Prussian estate. The boy falls in love with his cousin, though the French blood in her veins makes her flighty and unfit for a

Prussian hero. He is, in the novel's showing, more than Prussian: the great collective ideal for thé future is the fusing, say by a kind of State chemistry, of German provincial characteristics into a perfect character who will stand for ideal and supreme Germany; and thus in this boy the artistic qualities of the Rhineland are blended with the hard metal of military Prussia. Perhaps a more insistent burden of the tale is the absolute and the statesmanlike necessity of the Prussian military machine, and its essential humanity – in the sense that the man is served by the machine, which must no more be questioned than the machines in a factory. This doctrine of the categorical imperative is developed at immense length and with insinuating simplicity. *Der Weg ohne Wahl* (1933) is a *Künstlerroman* which develops the theme that the conquest of fate can only come by wishing one's fate. *Lennacker* (1938) is a *Heimkehrerroman*: an officer welded to the ways of the War has to adapt himself to the life of peace. But the chief problem is that of the mental peace of parsons.

XIV

THE REGIONAL NOVEL

Round about 1900 an attack was launched on the literature of town life (*Grossstadtroman*), and a demand was made that writers should turn their backs on the cities – to which for the most part they had migrated from the provinces of the countryside – and confine themselves to the description of their native province: *Asphaltkunst* should give way to *Heimatkunst*. Experience was to show that this amounted to a return to the *Bauernroman* or the *Dorfnovelle*; and as a matter of fact this rural literature formed part even of naturalism – certainly in the Lusatian novels of Wilhelm von Polenz. The attack was led by three writers – Heinrich Sohnrey (a Hanoverian), Fritz Lienhard (an Alsatian), and Adolf Bartels (from Dithmarschen). *Heimatkunst*, they urged, would make the novel *deutschnational* or *heimisch*: born of the soil and redolent of the soil (*Schollendichtung*), national in its ideals as in its traditions, whereas the *Grossstadtroman* was for a great part the purlieu of international Jews who would have no literary life off the asphalt whose stink they loved. (Actually it was a philosophical Jew, Berthold Auerbach, who had given the village tale a classical habitation in the Black Forest.) The movement, which in England produced the regional novels (Hardy for Wessex, etc.), was, however, not merely literary but also a spontaneous development due to a heightened love of locality; and in Germany, too, the development would have been inevitable without the fanatical propaganda which merely made it conscious of its tendencies. Even the first requisite, the change of scene from urban to rural, was illusory: for, strictly speaking, a town is just as much *Heimat* as a village, so that the main difference in the new orientation is that whereas the naturalistic novel devotes itself to the proletariat and the brain-workers, *Heimatkunst* prefers for hero the horny-handed tiller of the soil, stolid and grimly determined, throwing himself on manual

346

labour (as the hero of Ebner-Eschenbach's *Das Gemeindekind* does) 'like a lion on his prey'. We may surely reckon *Heimatkunst* as an integral part of naturalistic and impressionistic literature, for it is governed by the same cult of externals – the essential thing is the rendering of *milieu*, and character is more than ever shaped by surroundings. Definite criteria, by which one might at once class a novel as *Heimatkunst* or not, are impossible; generally speaking the main thing in the genre is that peasants are idealized. This rules out Ludwig Thoma and Josef Ruederer, to whom the peasants of their native hills are more or less dirty louts and the more so the merrier (for their artistic purpose).

One thing is clear: masterpieces must not be expected in regional literature. No Thomas Hardy appeared in Germany. The most tangible result is the new picturesqueness won for given localities, the bringing into relief of racial characteristics, and the stressing of the lesson – to be exploited by the Nazis – that the soil is a shaping as well as a nourishing force. The trumpet-blowers of the movement worked out this doctrine in journalistic polemics and in their journal *Die Heimat* (1900-). As creative writers they themselves are mediocre. ADOLF BARTELS (1862-1945), a peasant's son born, like Hebbel, in Wesselburen, wrote a historical novel, *Die Dithmarscher* (1898), in glorification of his native heath; but he is best known for the absurd anti-Semitic virus of his various histories of German literature. FRITZ LIENHARD (1865-1929) expounded his ideas in *Neue Ideale* (1901), wrote the regional and historical novel *Oberlin* (1910), *Lieder eines Elsässers* (1895), and *Lesedramen* (some Arthurian), which have thematic interest. HEIN-RICH SOHNREY (1859-1943), an elementary teacher to begin with, has the lovable nature of the genuinely popular writers. He is one of those authors, formerly suppressed by supercilious critics, who have moved up since 1933. He himself put all his pride in being a *Volksschriftsteller* – a writer not indeed for the masses but for the simple in heart, whether rich or poor. Not that he is naïve: he writes naïvely because the readers he desires are good in the parson's sense, and therefore naïve. He plainly regards it as the stern duty of a *Volksschriftsteller* to sacrifice his artistic ideal to his social ideal. The didactic note is as insistent as in Jeremias Gotthelf's writings, but without the Swiss parson's black vigour of outline: it really amounts to a gospel of salvation by unquestioning labour, of slavery to the soil that feeds us, and to the masters set over us by a wise providence. The reward of goodness is a contented mind, and sin is punished. What is attractive in Sohnrey's tales is the delineation of Hanoverian peasant life and of folk customs ('*Brauchtum*'). He was born near Göttingen, in the district which is the scene of his best-known sketches, *Die Leute aus der Lindenhütte* (2 vols.: *Friedesinchens Lebenslauf* and *Hütte und Schloss*, 1886-7); Socialist agitator and the introduction of machinery are shown as destructive elements of squire-ridden country life. His peasant novels are *Philipp Dubenkropps Heimkehr* (1888) and *Der Bruderhof* (1897).

Of the regional writers with a reputation when the war-cry *Los von Berlin!* was raised PETER ROSEGGER (1843-1918) was *facile princeps*. Born in a lonely hamlet in Upper Styria, he had tended his father's sheep in the upland fields between the forests, had gathered his education piecemeal, and – too frail for farm work – had been for four years a journeyman tailor, roving from farm to farm and squatting on farm tables to do his stitching and with eager ears taking in a vast store of rural lore and stories. As if by instinct he began to write dialect verse and to fashion his simple tales, which soon (1864) began to appear in the pages of the local newspaper, *Die Grazer Tagespost*. From now on, he says: *Das Fabeln ging alleweil besser als das Nadeln*. His first book was a collection of his dialect verse, *Zither und Hackbrett* (1869), but as a poet he has not more than calendar merit. He is at his best in his short stories (*Allerhand Leute*, 1888) and in his autobiographical meanderings (*Waldheimat*, 1897, *Als ich jung noch war*, 1895; *Mein Weltleben*, 1898). His novels have the inevitable didacticism of the rural popular writer. *Die Schriften des Waldschulmeisters* (1875), in diary form, has something of the *Simplizissimus* development: a soldier returning, morally damaged, from the Napoleonic wars finds recovery and comfort in unselfish service in a forest valley. *Der Gottsucher* (1883) takes us to a medieval village which is under a ban of excommunication because a priest has been murdered: religion having perished the community perishes, and the villagers are shown groping their way to religious security. *Jakob der Letzte* (1888) ventilates a grievance of the Styrian farmers: the hero fights against the tyranny of the hunting landlords. In *Peter Mayr, der Wirt an der Mahr* (1893) Rosegger blends village tale and historical novel – the subject is the revolt of the Tyrolese peasants against the French. *Erdsegen* (1900), *Martin der Mann* (1891), and *Weltgift* (1903) are *Tendenzromane*. In three books Rosegger is a forerunner of the expressionist *Gottsucher*: the intrusion of the 'modern spirit' into the idyll of the rural world is discussed in *Das ewige Licht* (1897), while *Mein Himmelreich* (1901) and *INRI* (1905) define Rosegger's personal attitude to the dogmas of Christianity. INRI (the initials represent *In Not Ruft Ihn*) is really a Life of Christ presented as an insertion (Frenssen repeats the device in *Hilligenlei*): the manuscript has been written by a condemned criminal on the eve of his execution. In *Mein Himmelreich* Rosegger had stated that any faith is good so long as it comforts a potential doubter; but his interpretation of Christianity follows the lead of the new criticism – e.g. 'Virgin' to him means a girl without lust but not necessarily intact. The view that any religion will serve we find again in *INRI*: Jesus is for any man just what this man needs; a Jesus we can love is the right Jesus.

Graz, the capital of Styria, looms large in regional literature. Here was born RUDOLF HANS BARTSCH (1873-1952), who glorifies his native town in his novel *Zwölf aus der Steiermark* (1908). Regional too is *Die Haindlkinder* (1908). *Elisabeth Kött* (1909) is the story of an Austrian actress. The short stories of *Bittersüsse Liebesgeschichten* (1910) and *Vom sterbenden Rokoko* (1909) are popular, but tend to be frivolous. [The excellent *Grazer Novellen* (1898) of WILHELM FISCHER IN GRAZ (1846-1932; the regional location mark is to distinguish him from all the other writing Fischers) are archaic rather than regional, though they have regional characters such as the Styrian Minnesinger Ulrich von Lichtenstein.] The regional writer of Vienna is EMIL ERTL (1860-1935), who wrote a cultural cycle: *Ein Volk an der Arbeit* (1906-26).

Passing from Austria to Bavaria we find *Heimatkunst* of Anzengruber's type in full bloom in the works of LUDWIG GANGHOFER (1855-1920). His intimate knowledge of forest life and hunting is due to the circumstance that his father was an official in the State Forestry Department. He wrote several *Volksschauspiele* (the most popular is *Der Herrgottschnitzer von Ammergau*, 1880; also popular as a short story) and a long series of tales of the Bavarian Highlands (*Jäger vom Fall*, 1883; *Der Klosterjäger*, 1892; *Das Schweigen im Walde*, 1899; *Der hohe Schein*, 1904). Ludwig Thoma's (1867-1921) Bavarian peasant tales (*Der Wittiber*, 1911) we must allot to naturalism because to him a peasant is a lousy peasant (see p. 65).

Switzerland and the Black Forest are the natural home of the peasant tale. ALFRED HUGGENBERGER (1876-) follows in the wake of Keller; e.g. in *Die Frauen von Siebenacker* (1925), in which a strong woman rescues a farm which her weak husband would otherwise have lost. *Die Bauern von Steig* (1912) is the novel of a whole Swiss village; short peasant tales are *Dorfgenossen* (1914), *Die heimliche Macht* (1919), and *Der Kampf mit dem Leben* (1926). Huggenberger, who, though famous as an author, still worked his farm, related the story of his youth in *Der Brunnen der Heimat* (1927). JAKOB CHRISTOPH HEER (1859-1925) is best known for his novels *Der König der Bernina* (1900), the scene of which is the Engadine, and *Joggeli* (1923), one of the novels of youth psychology which are a feature of the period. *An heiligen Wassern* (1898) has the mountains of Valais for scene. ERNST ZAHN (1867-1952), who kept the railway restaurant at Göschenen on the St. Gotthard railway, builds more on mountain scandal than on regional idealism (*Albin Indergand*, 1901; *Die Clari-Marie*, 1904; *Lukas Hochstrassers Haus*, 1907). *Gewalt über ihnen* (1929) is a somewhat limp study of senile eroticism in an Alpine setting. HEINRICH FEDERER (1866-1927), a Brienz man, reaches a higher literary level than Ernst Zahn. He was a Catholic priest till ill health forced him to resign, and this explains the religious mood of his stories (*Lachweiler Geschichten*, 1911; *Berge und Menschen*, 1911; *Pilatus*, 1912). The Black Forest is represented by the sturdy figure of HEINRICH HANSJAKOB (1837-1916), the Stadtpfarrer of Freiburg. The son of an innkeeper and baker at Haslach in the Kinzigtal, he was a classical master in schools, but made himself impossible in this capacity by his fighting propensities as a politician; relegated to a parish on the shore of the Lake of Constance, he emerged as one of the fieriest Ultramontane fighters in the Baden Landtag, and as such fought Bismarck tooth and nail in the *Kulturkampf*. In 1878, politically disillusioned, he turned to literature, and wrote his charming *Aus meiner Jugendzeit* (1880), which he followed up with *Aus meiner Studienzeit* (1885). His racy peasant tales are garnered in *Wilde Kirschen* (1888); *Schneeballen* (1892); *Bauernblut* (1896); *Erzbauern* (1899).

The new aspects of the regional tale shape themselves in the north. In Schleswig-Holstein there was a model in Theodor Storm; his tales are not of the peasant type, but he does describe his homeland. Particularly he gives us – as Hermann Allmers does in his *Marschenbuch* (1858), the first fine description of this region – the poetry of dikes and dunes, of *Marsch* and *Geest*; and this is more or less the hall-mark of regional literature in '*Schleswig-Holstein meerumschlungen*'. The poetry of the dikes we get farther inland, too, where the great rivers run low; e.g. in Max Halbe's Vistula plays and in JOSEPH LAUFF's (1855-1933) novel *Frau Aleit*, in which the dike-law is expounded and the mysteries unfolded of the *Deichrolle* which lies on the table when the *Deichgeschworenen* are convened in committee by the *Deichgraf* or *Deichhauptmann*. The grim and silent mould of man is the typical hero of TIMM KRÖGER's (1844-1918) short stories: *Eine stille Welt* (1891); *Hein Wieck und andere Geschichten* (1900); *Um den Wegzoll* (1905); *Aus alter Truhe* (1908).

World-famous as the novelist of Schleswig-Holstein is GUSTAV FRENSSEN (1863-1945). More specifically his region is Dithmarschen. Born at Barlt, on the North Sea coast, as a carpenter's son, he was for ten years a parson in his native province. His first novels, *Die Sandgräfin* (1896) – which already unrolls its pageant of dikes and dunes – and *Die drei Getreuen* (1898) fell flat; his third novel, *Jörn Uhl* (1901), provided the regionalists with the pattern that justified their theories and its author with a princely income – for it sold in hundreds of thousands. We follow the fate of Jörn Uhl from early boyhood at *die Uhl*, the extensive farm in the alluvial *Marsch* which has been in the possession of his family for generations. Both his father and his three elder brothers are lazy drunkards; and Jörn, whose bent is to study, has to work like a slave in a vain effort to save the farm from being seized by creditors with keen eyes on a rich prize. His mother, who had died young giving birth to his sister Elsbe, had come from a farm on the sandy *Geest*, where the land rises above the fat loam of the *Marsch*, and *Marschbauern* and *Geestbauern* are contrasted as racially different: the gipsy-like, red-haired stock who till the heathery *Geest* are of Wendish origin, while the farmers of the *Marsch* are pure Nordics, with rye-coloured hair and broad faces. Frenssen provides a racial surprise by elevating one of the farm-hands who had come from a *Geest* family to possession of the Uhls' ancestral farm; but his theme is that the superior stock is prone to sloth begotten by inherited wealth, while the *Geest* people are hard and canny. Jörn's desperate struggle to save the farm, the corruption of his family, and his own final salvation by his engineering bent – freed from the nightmare of the farm he goes to the Technical College at Hanover, and ends by helping to build the Kiel Canal – follow pretty closely the model of Sudermann's *Frau Sorge*; and *David Copperfield* obviously provides the story of Jörn's sister, who goes astray like little Emily, and is sought for in strange places by her weird uncle from the *Geest*. The construction is very poor: the characters have the habit of telling stories which are mostly irrelevant to the main theme and nullify characterization by being in the author's language, not in that of the character; what results is a farrago of folklore embedded in a story which might be enthralling but for this anecdotal discursiveness. There are pages and pages of parson's preaching – already sporadically anti-Christian. What delighted readers in the first onslaught of the regional craze was the boisterous face-to-face style of the narration, and this certainly is often excellent, particularly where it reveals the mentality of children; but this style is taken over from Björnson's peasant tales. (This style of *Jörn Uhl* is later seized and distorted by H. F. Blunck, who obviously claims it as the native saga style of Schleswig-Holstein.) There is of course a healthful tone in the book, and the showing up of race-proud wastrels is in the best sense moral; as is too, in the author's intention, the repeated stressing of the sexual needs of robust women. If Frenssen is at all original it is here, in his bold denial that nature is the devil. In his next novel, *Hilligenlei* (1906), Frenssen unfrocks himself for the sake of nature and natural religion. He unfolds with epic ease of movement a picture of life in a *hallig*, but the action leads up to a *Life of Christ*, modernized in accordance with the higher criticism of the gospel story and written by the hero Kai Jans, a freethinking Protestant parson whose life of religious speculation and self-sacrifice has close affinities to that of the Saviour. The Low German name Hilligenlei is rendered as 'Holy Land', and the story wistfully belies the local legend that some day this grey township by the sea – a kind of Bethlehem whose Jerusalem is Hamburg – should bring forth a saviour of mankind. At thirty Kai goes into the wilderness – of Berlin – to ruminate; and here, in the sight of suffering in tenement houses swarming with criminals and paupers, his faith is formed. From the point of view of Church doctrine there is marked anti-Christian feeling in the novel (in particular the Virgin birth is ridiculed), but the simple ethical teaching of Jesus is accepted as spiritualized Socialism, which accepts extra-marital cohabitation as human and therefore 'holy'; thus the inevitable robustious woman of the story does not reveal to the man she marries that she has for a period taken the place of an invalid wife. The construction is again poor: the main theme (the regeneration of society by a modernized and secular Christianity) fits awkwardly into a multiplicity of loosely connected incidents extraneous to the plot of the story. As literature this best-seller can only be placed low: it is ruined by its rank preaching. The demand for sexual experience as healthful belongs of course to the hygienic doctrine of the period; but the way in which it is here defended tempts one to call *Hilligenlei* a dirty book. There is again a lack of originality: apart from the coincidence of an inserted *Life of Christ* here and in Rosegger's *INRI*, which is dated 1905 – this may of course be accidental in either case – the superimposing of the religious element on the delineation of the Hilligenlei people as pretentious provincial fools, ludicrously credulous and easily swindled, seems grafted from Gottfried Keller's Seldwyla tales. *Peter Moors Fahrt nach Südwest* (1907) has interest as a description of the campaign against the Herreros. The technique is again specifically that of Dickens: secondary characters are actually given more prominence than the tortured mystic who is the hero of the tale, and Dickens's device of characterization by the reiteration of idiosyncrasies is naïvely practised. The hero of *Klaus Hinrich Baas* (1909) is a modern Dick Whittington. His surname 'Baas' (our English 'boss') has come to him, with his hereditary qualities (for this is a novel of eugenics), as a mark of his domineering nature. It is from a village in Dithmarschen, where his father is a farm-labourer, that he sets out to make his fortune; and the first scenes paint the life of peasants and the glamour of Hamburg, that flaming octopus on the horizon. Then Hamburg itself, with Klaus Baas climbing the commercial ladder; the Dutch Indies, a vivid episode; routine in a sleepy market town of Dithmarschen again, at the side of a wife constitutionally unfit to be a wife; separation from her, Hamburg again, and a masterful struggle for victories in trade. Klaus Baas is an idealized democrat; in patrician society he is like a fish out of water; he is a merchant pure and simple. It is only when his health begins to fail that he returns to the books he dreamt of in his boyhood; but for twenty years he has been a monster of concentration. He could not have been that if he had not been 'full-blooded' – only the blue-blooded patricians waste their time over art, at Florence, and such things; but his full blood had other needs than those of a merchant's conquests; and these needs, as well as those of the other full-blooded beings with whom he comes into contact, are fully and frankly described by an author to whom sexual enlightenment is a doctrine vital to the future of his race. *Otto Babendiek* (1926) is in outline autobiographical. With *Jörn Uhl* Frenssen shot like a meteor into the sky of fame; and like a meteor he fell. Not so much the humanization of Christ in *Hilligenlei* – though this shocked many – as the doctrine that healthy girls are entitled to sexual experience, in or out of marriage, diminished his glory, though not yet his phenomenal sales. He was fair game to the critics: they relentlessly detailed how much he took from Raabe, or Dickens, or Sudermann, or others. The tendency was to give guarded praise to *Jörn Uhl* as the best of the regional novels, while rejecting the rest of his work as mannered and tendentious. His impressionistic rendering of landscape, however, is admittedly fine. His colonial novel *Peter Moors Fahrt nach Südwest* was appreciated as at least a stirring account of German heroism in strange places; and it is indeed a good forerunner to Hans Grimm's South African fiction. With the advent of the Nazis to power this critical evaluation rushed to the other extreme: Frenssen, the Germans were told, is one of the prophets of the racial doctrine, and one who cast away the Jewish leaven of religion and sought for the free Christianity he interpreted in his *Dorfpredigten* (1899), in *Hilligenlei*, and in the tractate *Der Glaube der Nordmark* (1936). A final verdict must be left to time.

The Battle of Jutland, in German credence the first great naval victory of the Reich, is bound to be legendary. Here fell GORCH FOCK (1880-1916), the accredited writer of tales of North Sea fishermen and sailors (*Seefahrt ist Not*, 1912; *Hein Godenwind*, 1912; *Fahrensleute*, 1915). Not a native of Hamburg, but one who wrote the famous novel of Hamburg life *Die Hanseaten*, is RUDOLF HERZOG (1869-1943). (The first two novels of business life in Hamburg, Ernst Willkomm's *Reeder und Matrose* and *Banco*, both 1857, followed close on Freytag's pioneer Breslau tale, *Soll und Haben*, 1855). As a regionalist this writer's habitat is rather his native Rhineland (he was born at Barmen), and this district is the background of his *Die vom Niederrhein* (1903), *Die Wiskottens* (1905; the Ruhr industries), and *Die Stoltenkamps und ihre Frauen* (1918: the epic of the Krupp dynasty).

The writer who aimed at representing Hamburg and all its outlying lands with its history back to mythical man is HANS FRIEDRICH

BLUNCK (1888-). He had a meteoric rise, but is now a faded star. As a novelist Blunck began by garnering the impressions of his travels in South America: *Die Weibsmühle* (1927) and *Land der Vulkane* (1929) describe the life of German colonists and their descendants in Brazil and Central America respectively. He aimed at cloudy heights of literature with two novel trilogies, *Werdendes Volk* (1933) and *Die Urvätersaga* (1934); the first pictures the evolution of the German people by showing the inception and the successive phases of their religious and cultural convictions; the second shows three successive phases of the search for the national God. *Stelling Rotkinnsohn* (1923), the first volume of *Werdendes Volk*, has its scene in the marshes round Hamburg and on the North Sea with the encircling lands. The second member of this trilogy, *Hein Hoyer* (1919), is wearisome: it shows Hamburg at the height of its power as a Hanse city, and there is a stirring description of the Battle in the Hamme (the theme of one of Liliencron's ballads), in which the peasants of Dithmarschen slaughtered the knights of the Dukes of Holstein. The girl who, in male attire, follows the hero, is less convincing than her prototype in Kleist's *Käthchen von Heilbronn* or Conrad Ferdinand Meyer's *Gustav Adolfs Page*. *Berend Fock* (1921), the third of the series, is a blend of three legends: *The Flying Dutchman*, *The Wandering Jew*, and *Doctor Faust*. The hero, Berend Ohnerast, rebels against God, but, since he is a God-seeker, he yearns to find and question Him. The cultural enclaves in this mass of matter have interest for students: the revolt of the *Sprachgesellschaften* against *Alamode*, the beginnings of the opera in Hamburg, etc. Hebbel's drama *Moloch* was intended to show the birth of religion and culture in the mythical period; Blunck attempts the same desperate task in the trilogy *Die Urvätersaga*. In this type of novel he had been directly preceded by the Danish novelist Johannes V. Jensen. But while Jensen's myths have the simplicity of tales told to children those of Blunck are tangled and self-contradictory, and too burdened with that solar myth nonsense which is the shaking foundation of Nazi philosophy. *Gewalt über das Feuer* (1928), the novel of the Glacial Period, relates the myth of a German Prometheus, Börr, who captures fire to guard by night the mouth of the caves where his people dwell, after which come the first blessings of civilization, damp clay hardened by the hearth, the first bow and arrow, the taming of the wolf to be a dog. In *Kampf der Gestirne* (1926), the novel of

356 MODERN GERMAN LITERATURE

the Stone Age, the hero gives his people sun-worship in place of their old moon-worship; the events symbolize the age-old urge to the South and the sun of the Germanic race. In the tale the worshipper follows the red sun-shield[1] till he sees it rest on icy mountains; he cannot capture it; and so the change between day and night, life and death, must endure. *Streit mit den Göttern* (1925), the novel of the Bronze Age, defaces the clean-cut legend of Wayland the Smith by contaminating it with motifs from other legends.

HERMANN LÖNS (1866-1914) is honoured as one of the heroes of the War – he fell before Reims in September 1914. He had proclaimed that Nazi doctrine which we see foreshadowed in Blunck's weltering trilogies: 'We Germans', he writes, 'make out that we are Christians, but we are nothing of the sort, and never can be. For Christianity and race-consciousness are as incompatible as Socialism and culture are.' Since the War Hermann Löns has been idolized in Germany much as Rupert Brooke has been in England; and the culmination of the cult was his re-burial, twenty years after his death, on the Lüneburg Heath, the region he so lovingly described. As a lyric poet (*Der kleine Rosengarten*, 1911) he wrote songs which have the freshness and sometimes the vogue of *Volkslieder*, but he is best known for his descriptions of the heathlands he loved (*Mein grünes Buch*, 1901; *Mein braunes Buch*, 1907), for his descriptions of animal life (*Mümmelmann*, 1909), and for his peasant novels: *Der letzte Hansbur* (1909); *Da hinten in der Heide* (1910); *Die Häuser von Ohlendorf* (1917). His most famous novel is *Der Wehrwolf* (1910), which combines regionalism and history in the way of Lulu von Strauss und Torney, another Westphalian regionalist. Actually *Der Wehrwolf* is more regional than historical; for, though it gives a vivid picture of the whole course of the Thirty Years War, it limits the scene of action to the Lüneburg Heath with Celle, the old capital of the Dukes of Brunswick; and the intention is obviously to show the sterling qualities of the heath-dwellers ('*Haidjer*') through the ages: we see these blond Nordics, 'tough as eel-leather', displacing the scattered aborigines, helping their neighbours of the Teutoburger Wald to defeat Arminius, helping Weking (=Widukind) to make mincemeat of the Franks, and finally turning Christian, though the horse's head sacred to Wodan still stands out on the gables of their farm-houses. The

[1] Represented by the swastika; see p. 366.

title is a homonym which serves to enforce the idea of these German tribesmen: the law is with those who defend hearth and home from those who nominally are in the service of the law; when their farms are plundered, when their womenfolk are violated by successive waves of marauders from both sides and all armies, all equally ferocious, they entrench themselves in the peat-moss and destroy the straggling bands as they come for spoil. They are, it is true, men turned to wolves; but they are wolves defending the law, not outside it; indeed they pronounce and execute judgment in the old tribal way in open court on the heath ('*Ding auf offner Heide*'). The interest never flags – it is essentially a boy's book like *Hereward the Wake*; if there must be criticism it might be that it consists of endless repetition of the opening scene of *Simplizissimus*, and that, justified as the endless killing is, there is a feeling that it is, if not a natural taste, at least an acquired one.

The best-known regional novelist of the Rhineland is JOSEF PONTEN (1883-1940), who hails from the Eupen district. In his novel *Siebenquellen* (1908) he describes that part of the district which was ceded to Belgium after the War. In his novels and tales (particularly in the novel *Der babylonische Turm*, 1918) he contrasts the man of feeling with the man who strives for financial and social success; he has thus a cultural message, which comes out best in his monumental work *Volk auf dem Wege*. The first volume, *Die Vater zogen aus* (1934) begins with the destruction of Speyer by the French in 1689; those rendered homeless go to Russia and settle on the Volga. The second volume, *Im Wolgaland* (1933), one of the great *Auslandsromane* of recent years, is the chronicle, reaching to the time before the beginning of the War, of their colonist work and of their fighting with marauding hordes from Asia, against whom they serve as a bulwark. The third volume, *Rheinisches Zwischenspiel* (1937), describes the visit to Germany of a teacher in the Volga colony. Ponten is one of the best writers of more or less expressionist or fanciful short stories: *Die Bockreiter* (1919); *Der Meister* (1919); *Der Knabe Vielnam* (1921); *Der Jüngling in Masken* (1922); *Der Gletscher* (1923); *Die letzte Reise* (1923); *Der Urwald* (1924).

Silesia is represented in *Heimatkunst* principally by Hermann Stehr, though in his work it is a secondary element. PAUL KELLER (1873-1932), who lived in Breslau, is first and foremost a popular writer, but there is a leaning to Silesian *Märchen* and saga in his

24

work, together with naturalistic environment (*Waldwinter*, 1902; *Die Heimat*, 1904; *Der Sohn der Hagar*, 1904).

The emigration of the original Swabians who founded the German colonies in Hungary and their struggle to keep their German speech and culture is described by ADAM MÜLLER-GUTTENBRUNN (1852-1923) in his novels *Die Glocken der Heimat* (1910) and in his trilogy of historical novels *Der grosse Schwabenzug, Barmherziger Kaiser, Josef der Deutsche* (1913-16). He launches out in the accepted German fashion against the oppression of these long-suffering colonists by the Hungarians in *Götzendämmerung* (1908). In *Sein Vaterhaus* (1928) he describes his youth in Hungary. His *Meister Jakob und seine Kinder* (3 vols., 1919-21) spins its story round the tragic figure of Lenau, the German-Hungarian poet.

XV

THE NOVEL
OF EXPRESSIONISM

Politically the First Great War marks the end of a period, 'the Age of Imperialism', which began with the accession of Kaiser Wilhelm II in 1888. In literature the War is a disturbing force, but it does not mark a break in development; it accelerated and intensified expressionism, which had begun before 1914.[1] The War literature itself is either naturalistic or expressionistic, or both at once. Expressionism is only the naturalism of writers who again select their reality as the poetic realists had done, and who flood their reality with their own passion. There is the same reversal of fashion in literature as in abstract thought and painting: just as Ibsen is eclipsed by Strindberg and Wedekind, Manet and Renoir yield pride of place to Van Gogh, while the ideas of intuition as certainty, of life as movement, of the *élan vital*, of creative development, come in with the acceptation of Bergson, and are reinforced by the phenomenology or *reine Wesensschau* of Edmund Husserl.[2]

The naturalists had aimed at photographic reproduction of nature; the cry of the expressionists is: *Los von der Natur!* The naturalists had been, in intention, outside what they described (though, of course, their sympathies appeared in their choice of matter); and their matter might be in its presentation as dull as life; in other words, the matter was not animated (theoretically) by mind (*Geist*). The expressionists demand both feeling and mind: in other words they are both passionate and brilliant. They put

---

[1] The term *Expressionismus* was first used in 1911 by Otto zur Linde as a label for the *Charon* group of poets in their opposition to impressionism. *Ausdruckskunst* (as against *Eindruckskunst* for 'impressionism') is a synonym.

[2] See p. 442.

their own passionate heart into their matter and flood it with light; that at least is their intention. 'Be ecstatic!' they cry; and the result is *Rauschkunst*,[1] which expresses *das rasende Leben*, life in fevered haste to exhaust existence. Since, as Bergson teaches, only time that has lived has permanence, and since there is no life with sluggishness of heart,[2] the expressionists live their life with a fiery heart full to overflowing; and their expression of this life is '*ein geballter Schrei*', a clenched cry of ecstasy, a spate of ideas too fierce and young for dignity, so rushing and rapid that they would be profaned by beauty of form – there can be no calm and patient shaping in the white heat of ecstasy. In short, the idea is to give the palpable essence of things, their qualities sharply intensified, not their appearance in reality.

The expressionists cry for a more real reality; but to them reality is not the outer world, it is the inner world of thought and vision. Thought is real, for it exists. The momentary semblances of naturalism are not real; what is real is not the image of time, but the very essence of it. The outer world presents itself through the eyes of the mind; but what the expressionists render is not reality as seen by eyes, but as seen, with the eyes as a gateway, by the mind. The expressionist creates his vision just as the composer creates his music: neither need be anything like anything ever heard or seen in nature; but they exist, for they are seen and heard. Art reproduces things seen, i.e. art is vision fixed on paper or in marble or in colours. But what is vision? The eye is an intermediary between the outer world and the mind: the eye *passively* receives the vision of reality, but conveys this vision to the mind, which *actively* receives, i.e. transforms this reality – differently according to individuality. There is an apparent distortion (the eye of the body cannot see all four sides of a cube at the same time, the eye of the mind can), but the image attempted – all representation in space of inner vision can only be approximate – is that of an instantaneous conception inwardly visualized. In literature much of this expressionistic distortion might be traced back to the *unanisme* of Jules Romains, who (e.g.) visualized the morning debouchement at a city railway station 'as poured out of a bent full bottle's neck', or said of a man and wife in bed (Parisian *gourmands* no doubt) that their bellies 'swell out towards each other like two clouds'. It is not far from this to Hanns Johst's description in *Der König*,

[1] See pp. 94, 104, 307.   [2] See p. 301.

one of the typical expressionistic plays, of streets filled like bowels with dysentery.

The ethics of expressionism can be stated in a few catchwords. '*Nicht ich, sondern du*', or '*Wirbewusstsein*', means altruism or love of others. Freethinkers, but thrusting forward a fanatical pretence of religion, the expressionists are 'seekers of God'. They claim to have the ecstatic belief in God of Klopstock, the ecstatic faith in humanity of Schiller in his green youth; in their cry for the brother-hood of races and the reconciliation of races they repeat Schiller's *Millionen, seid umschlungen!* They accuse the pre-War Germans of having gone to sleep on *Trägheit des Herzens*; this state they replace by *bewegte Fülle des Herzens*. That man is an intermediary form be-tween two kingdoms (*ein Zwischenwesen zweier Reiche*) is expressed by the idea of *das dritte Reich* explored by Johannes Schlaf in the trilogy of novels thus called, but discussed, too, by Ibsen in *Emperor and Galilean*, and logically involved in Lessing's *Die Er-ziehung des Menschengeschlechts*. *Wandlung*, or moral transformation, may be explained as psychic discontinuity, and no doubt owed something to Freud: there is in all of us a series of 'I's' any one of which may come to the surface as another is submerged. The enthusiasm for freedom takes intense symbolic form in the fre-quent use of the son-father conflict.[1] Post-War youth held their fathers responsible for the War, but the revolt against parental authority had long been brewing – it went with the swift growth of the *Jugendbewegung*, which sent the youth of the country hiking in gay bands.

There is plenty of expressionistic ethics and form in the later work of the impressionists: psychic discontinuity, for instance, in Wassermann's cycle *Wendekreis*. God-seeking takes the direction of Wodan-finding in the novels of racialists such as Blunck and Hans Grimm. But the expressionists proper are those who begin as such and practise, in varying degrees, that discontinuity of form which reflects the leaps and flashes of life.

The programme of the expressionists was proclaimed by KASIMIR EDSCHMID[2] (1890-) in *Über den dichterischen Expressionismus* (1919); he demands, not 'rockets', but (in harmony with Bergson's theory

---

[1] This conflict begins earlier and with a more reasoned sociological import in Samuel Butler's *The Way of All Flesh*; here the father represents 'the con-scious' (acquired qualities, tradition), and the son 'the unconscious'.

[2] =Eduard Schmidt (born Darmstadt).

of emotion as permanent) *dauernde Erregung*; i.e. a work of art must be one whole ferment of ecstasy; and this fever of excitement is in his tales; his aim, expressed in a passionate image, is: '*das Leben furchtbar packen wie eine unendliche Geliebte*'. These words occur in his collection of short tales *Das rasende Leben* (1916). There is the same ferment of ecstatic feeling and style in another collection of tales, *Die sechs Mündungen* (1915) – actually the pioneer work of expressionistic prose –, and in the novels *Die achatenen Kugeln* (1920), with their scabrous eroticism, and *Die gespenstischen Abenteuer des Hofrats Brüstlein* (1926; title later *Pourtalès Abenteuer*, 1947), while *Lord Byron; Roman einer Leidenschaft* (1929) probes into the poet's passion for his half-sister. Edschmid began to free himself from expressionism in *Die Engel mit dem Spleen* (1923), a novel in E. T. A. Hoffmann's manner. The reversal is complete in the novel *Sport um Gagaly* (1927), a glorification of the sportsman's life, and in Edschmid's numerous travel books from *Das grosse Reisebuch* (1926) and *Basken, Stiere, Araber* (1926) to *Bunte Erde* (1948). The tales of *Hallo Welt* (1930) and the novels *Deutsches Schicksal* (1932) and *Das Südreich* (1933) have this multi-racial texture, while *Feine Leute oder die Grossen dieser Erde* (1930) with its pitiless exposure of international high finance on the Lido, interweaves geographical enlightenment with its portraiture of scamps and their loosely living women of the *haute élite*. In his later work this *gesundeter Expressionist* stands out as an inveterate globe-trotter, and his matured philosophy of existence is a sane and practical internationalism. He is at his best in his books of Italy: *Italien – Lorbeer, Land und Ruhm* (1935), *Gärten, Männer und Geschichte* (1939), and in his description of tropical lands: *Afrika – nackt und angezogen* (1930), *Glanz und Elend Südamerikas* (1931). Some of the best of his work is his latest: the four short stories of *Im Diamantental* (1940); his biography of *Albert Schweitzer* (1949); his novels *Das gute Recht* (1946), which has an autobiographical substratum, *Der Zauberfaden* (1949), a chronicle of the Rhineland silk industry, and *Wenn es Rosen sind, werden sie blühn* (1950), the hero of which is Georg Büchner, whose works he edited.

KLABUND (1891-1928), a native of Crossen on the borders of Silesia and the March of Brandenburg, devised his exotic-looking pen-name – his real name was Alfred Henschke – by a shortening of *Kla(bautermann)* and *(Vaga)bund*. He was the type of vagrom, never-satisfied poet sketched in Rilke's poem *Der Fremde*, collecting impressions of towns and women to weave into ever-changing moods of verse or prose. He died young – of consumption – at Davos; and his expectation of death lends pathetic interest to such a nostalgic prose reverie as *Herbstliche Wanderung*, which reveals, too, the passionate love for him of a young actress who sought from him that enrichment by suffering which d'Annunzio had given to Eleonora Duse. Generally speaking Klabund's lyric poetry is derivative and often forced, but he is a skilled translator and adapter, particularly of Oriental poetry (*Dumpfe Trommel und berauschtes Gong*, 1915; *Li-Tai-Pe*, 1916; *Das Sinngedicht des persischen Zeltmachers*, 1917, etc.). It is as a weaver of Oriental visions that he is likely to keep his place in literature. His Chinese drama *Der Kreidekreis*, produced by Reinhardt, was the literary success of 1925; Elisabeth Bergner played the heroine and after the first performance Klabund kissed her hand on the stage. The very pearl of his Oriental dreaming is, however, *Der letzte Kaiser* (1923), a short story which, with the colouring and delicate tracery of Chinese painting, tells how the last Emperor immolated himself at the first shock of revolution on the altar of the goddess of chastity. This dainty *chinoiserie* is recent history and yet *märchenhaft* with its willow-pattern scenery, its camel-back bridges, its kites and eunuchs and mandarins. And – the dragon snatching the fairy – there is at the end the blatant blast of Communism in the raw raving of a common soldier guarding the filigree palace. There is Communism in other work of Klabund's: the short story *Störtebecker*, for instance, the hero of which, a North Sea pirate familiar from ancient ballads, is presented as one whose aim is the welfare of the people; and though his 'red flag' goes down it will return to regenerate the world. *Störtebecker* is remarkable for its style – short paragraphed dialogue and the rush of a film scenario – and also for its preaching of the Wodan cult and its idealization of the Frisians round Hamburg as the perfect type of German fighter and rebel. The Novellen appeared in *Klabunds Karussell* (1913), *Der Marketenderwagen* (1916 – mostly War experiences), *Die Krankheit* (1916 – stories of Davos).

One of the leaders of the expressionists was RENÉ SCHICKELE (1883-1940). An Alsatian with a French mother, it was natural that he should have that comprehension of French mentality which is the mark of the Alsatians. He probes the problem of Alsace in his drama *Hans im Schnakenloch* (1916) and in the sequence of novels

Das Erbe am Rhein: Maria Capponi (1925), *Blick auf die Vogesen* (1927), and *Der Wolf in der Hürde* (1931). Before World War I broke out he was editing the expressionist review *Die weissen Blätter* in Berlin; and during the War he edited it as a refugee in Switzerland. Here, on the Swiss side of the Lake of Constance, he was the centre of that group of writers who were launching anti-war literature: here Leonhard Frank's *Der Mensch ist gut* was evolved. Schickele's *Benkal der Frauentröster* (1914), a prophetic picture of the War written just before it began, would alone have made him an outlaw in Germany: it shows the idiocies of war by the experiences of the hero, who is called 'comforter of women' because he reveals their sufferings. For English taste there is too much harping on women's physical need of husbands: actually an army of wives in the capital go on the street by way of protest; and when the Central Power is beaten by the Kremmen (=Russians) they lead the revolt of the proletariat against the military caste. Benkal himself miraculously blossoms out from a drunken loafer into a sculptor whose speciality is the female figure; and women feel strangely comforted and saint-like when they gaze on the religious ugliness of these shapes which compel reverence for the deformity of mother. His mistress is a famous dancer, who disappears when she realizes that she is dying; the motif is that of Vicki Baum's *Menschen im Hotel*. With *Aïssé* (1916) Schickele provided his type of expressionist Novelle: its style apes the chaste distinction of the French eighteenth-century erotic *conte*, and already shows Schickele's peculiar weaving of suddenly strange vision and symbol into a prose pattern. The tale appeared in the series *Der jüngste Tag*, in which Edschmid's *Das rasende Leben* and other pioneer expressionist work first saw the light.

With René Schickele as the interpreter of Alsace and the apostle of cultural blending should be paired OTTO FLAKE (1882-) as the representative of Lorraine (he is a native of Metz). He is, however, not so much an expressionist as one of those (Albrecht Schaeffer, Josef Ponten, Frank Thiess and others), who, while influenced by expressionism, are in the main impressionists and naturalists. In the preface to his novel *Die Stadt des Hirns* (1919) he proclaims the manifesto for the new novel; everything that is not intellectual is to be eliminated, that is, narration of consecutive action, discussion of middle-class problems, description of *milieu* and landscape, sentiment of any kind. This programme points forward to the Proustian pattern of Musil's *Der Mann ohne Eigenschaften*. Flake's most personal novel is *Montijo oder die Suche nach der Nation* (1931), the tale of a German Spaniard who opts for German culture. Flake himself is a cosmopolitan who roams the wide world over for scene and characters: his novels *Ruland* (1922), *Villa USA* (1926), etc., range from Alsace to Petersburg. He had begun with a denunciation of the tyranny of the school: *Freitagskind* (1913; in later editions *Eine Kindheit*), but passed over to a strikingly masculine handling of erotic problems in (particularly) *Der gute Weg* (1924): the men, coldly calculating, dominate the women. *Nein und Ja* (1920), with its scene in Zurich, has a curious interest for its portrait of the dadaist Hans Arp.

LEONHARD FRANK (1882-), a Würzburg man, has been classed as a 'vulgarisator of expressionism', and he is at all events an easy approach to the expressionist style, but only because he tells a story which is plain and often exciting in spite of the tricks of discontinuity of the new manner. The son of a journeyman carpenter, he began as a factory worker, and in all his work he is on the side of the proletariat, to him the salt of the earth. His first success was *Die Räuberbande* (1914); it describes with uproarious humour the escapades of a band of youths whose heads have been turned by the Wild West stories of Karl May; sexual awakening and Red Indian pranks make a brand of natural filth and Romantic idiocy. In *Die Ursache* (1915), an attack on capital punishment, a teacher is murdered by a former pupil in revenge for the damage done to his character at school, which unfitted him for life. *Der Mensch ist gut* (1917) constitutes in substance an anti-war tract, ghastly in its exhibition of suffering, which was credited with having very seriously weakened German *morale* on the home front; it was one of the miracles of the war that, in spite of its message, it found its way all over Germany. In *Der Bürger* (1924) a human soul is damaged by existing society ('*die bestehende Seelenmord-Gesellschaftsordnung*'): a man is paralysed in youth by his father, his teachers, and finally by the social community, for which he has been unfitted by his training; he may, by conforming, accept the conventional moulding, but he is then merely a standardized product of the social machine, not a shaping spirit with the daring zest of his own native originality. In *Das Ochsenfurter Männerquartett* (1927) we meet the old *Räuberbande* once again in Würzburg, middle-aged men now, impoverished by the war, and with the spirit of adventure knocked out of them. *Karl und Anna* (1928) is one of the most original of the *Heimkehrerromane*: two soldiers, Karl and Richard, are inseparable companions on the eastern front; and in the lone watches Richard describes his wife and their married life so intimately that Karl has every detail imprinted on his mind. Karl gets home first, and his resemblance to Richard enables him to impersonate his comrade. Anna suspects; but – and here is the real theme of the tale – Karl has the very soul of a lover, and as a woman she is won: she yields to love, not to a husband. Richard returns; and Karl and Anna leave him to his misery and set out to find a new home. Karl has seen a star in the east and followed it and found it; Richard has longed for his bed-mate, and lost her. *Bruder und Schwester* (1929) once again proves the uncanny fascination of incest for German authors – from the *Gregorius* of Hartmann von Aue onwards. Flagrantly communistic is *Die Jünger Jesu* (1950): once more as in *Die Räuberbande* a band of youths turn robbers to serve the ends of justice; what they steal from the rich they give to the poor. In *Die deutsche Novelle* (1951) a baroness falls into the power of her servant; she shoots him and herself. *Links wo das Herz ist* (1952) rolls out the saga of Leonhard Frank's own life in the form of a novel with, in places, scant regard for elementary decency.

Leonhard Frank's favourite theme of the ruin of man by society is feverishly and in dithyrambic Nietzschean prose demonstrated by HERMANN BURTE (1879-) in his famous novel *Wiltfeber der ewige Deutsche* (1912): the hero, a *Herrenmensch*, perishes because he cannot adapt himself to the pettiness and disgrace of life. Wiltfeber is a symbolic distortion of Weltfieber, the disease of Germans, who roam away from dying villages to the wastes of the outer world and to the stone wildernesses of cities. This picture of the city as a ferment of decay (*Verwesungsstätte*), infected with the virus of Marxism, is Nazi doctrine before the War, and the strange thing is that already in this tale of a lost German in quest of his homeland the swastika is proclaimed as the symbol of regeneration. The German nation, we read, is '*entrasst und entgottet, von einer fremden Rasse unterworfen einem fremden Gotte*'. Christ is described as one who conquered Judaism in Himself; '*ja, der Widerjuden Grösster ist der Christ*'. The first task of the German is to recover his racial purity, to return to primitive Germanity, and to escape from the heritage of Rousseau, who from his filthy mouth blew the breath of pestilence over the world. In Burte's dramas there is the fanatical cult of the German conception of duty as sacrifice of self to the state. The hero of *Katte* (1914) is the friend who tried to arrange the escape from prison of the Crown Prince of Prussia, later Frederick the Great. Frederick is forced to watch Katte's execution. The play is a *Pflichtdrama*, and so too is *Herzog Utz* (1915). The hero is that Duke Ulrich or Utz of Württemberg who, as we know from Hauff's *Lichtenstein*, slew Hans Hutten. He has disgraced himself as a man and as a prince by going down on his knees to crave from Hutten the body of his wife. This lady denies herself as Hutten's wife, but is willing as Hutten's widow; Ulrich, however, ripened by the events, sacrifices love to princely duty. It might be interesting to compare Burte's third play, *Simson* (1917), with that of Herbert Eulenberg on the same subject: in the latter Samson is a grandiose symbol of the degradation of man to beast by woman, while from the mass of detail of Burte's play only the strong man's sacrifice of himself to his race emerges. If Schiller had completed his *Warbeck* tragedy, he would have adhered to the historical concept of the hero as a pretender; for Burte in his *Warbeck* (1935) his hero is the genuine heir to the throne and the last scion of the house of Plantagenet; he abandons his rightful claim because to achieve it would mean war. As a lyric poet Burte made his mark as a sonneteer (*Patricia*, 1910; *Die Flügelspielerin*, 1913). Though a native of Baden, Burte is classed as an Alemannic poet, and as such he has emulated Johann Peter Hebel in his books of dialect verse (*Madlee*, 1923; *Ursula*, 1930).

The ground-work in the novels of ALFRED DÖBLIN (1878-1957), a physician in Berlin, is science and philosophy. He came to the fore during the War with his Chinese novel *Die drei Sprünge des Wang-Lun* (1915); the son of a Chinese fisherman founds a sect of the poor in spirit and teaches that 'to be weak, to endure is the pure way'; the hero 'jumps' from passivity, which is holiness, to action, and back again to holiness. Döblin's long historical novel *Wallenstein* (1920) is still actuated by Chinese philosophy; but here the problem of to do or not to do is represented by the contrasted characters of Wallenstein as the principle of action and the pathologically conceived passive Emperor Ferdinand. *Wadzeks Kampf mit der Dampfturbine* (1918) comes to epic grips with machinery; *Berge, Meere und Giganten* (1924) in a nightmare of activity raging mad gives us the age of the superman with machinery supreme

A.D. 2700-3000. The technological novel had scored its most popular success with BERNHARD KELLERMANN'S (1879-1951) *Der Tunnel* (1913), in which the building of a tunnel under the Atlantic is described. But while *Der Tunnel* uses engineering in Jules Verne's way to provide the elements of an exciting story, *Berge, Meere und Giganten* subordinates the story to the problem of the mechanization of the cosmos; it is the idea of Samuel Butler's *Erewhon* that machinery is destined to become master of man. As the slave of machinery, man goes to battle with nature; with the fire of Iceland's volcanoes he frees Greenland from ice; but nature turns on him and puts him in his proper place – down with the beasts of the earth; the *Wandlung* to a new humanity is not to be achieved by an ascent of man to God over an enslaved nature but by a humble return of man to nature. *Berlin Alexanderplatz* (1929) is notable as the first thorough-going German imitation – after Jahnn's *Perrudja* (see p. 404) – of James Joyce's *Ulysses*. The hero serves a sentence for murder, lives as a bully, is arrested unjustly for the murder of a prostitute, and after a period in a lunatic asylum ends as a porter. As a detailed picture of the lowest Berlin life the novel has interest; as a continuous recording of the waves of thought and sensation in this typical brute it fails, because even a practising physician cannot guarantee the authenticity of such streaming consciousness in a person of such limited mentality. When in 1933 Döblin's books were banned and burned, he found refuge in Paris; during the German occupation he found his way to California, but returned to Germany after the war and joined the Roman Catholic Church. His Catholic outlook on world problems appears at once in his mystery novel *Der Oberst und der Dichter oder das menschliche Herz* (1946) and in his autobiographical *Schicksalsreise. Bericht und Bekenntnisse* (1949). In *Die Babylonische Wanderung oder Hochmut kommt vor dem Fall* (1934) a Babylonian god experiences the comicality and the misery of existence here below. *Pardon wird nicht gegeben* (1935) pictures post-war conditions and the perils of proletarian and Nazi ideology; a middle-class profiteer is induced by his dominating mother to give up the revolutionary convictions of his youth for safety's sake; problematically considered his natural development is thwarted by family interference. There is complex symbolic inference and a destructive analysis of cultural and political tendencies in our own days, as well as of religious pretence through the ages, in Döblin's next work, the

vast South American trilogy which in its moods and pitiless probing of racial domination is largely the fruit of the author's suffering
in exile. In the historical sense the trilogy is an epilogue to Eduard
Stucken's *Die weissen Götter* (p. 273) and Gerhart Hauptmann's
Der weisse Heiland (p. 33); these describe the conquest of Mexico,
while *Das Land ohne Tod* (1936), the first volume of Döblin's trilogy, is a panorama of the conquest of Peru. Just as the Aztecs in
Mexico welcome Cortès as the 'White Saviour', so the Incas see
in the Spaniards the fulfilment of age-old prophecies of the coming
of strange gods: this they see realized in the pale skins and the
bearded faces of the invaders, in their horses, and their fire-spitting
tubes laden with death. There is a stark contrast of these happy
and innocent 'pagans' with the 'religion' of the Christians; actually
there is only one true Christian among them – Las Casas (p. 496).
In the second volume, *Der blaue Tiger* (1936) – the blue tiger is the
beast of destruction of Indian saga – the Jesuits make their historic
attempt to institute humane colonization, but are thwarted by
secular policy. The third volume, *Der neue Urwald* (1936), applies
a parallel to the conditions of today, and drives home the lesson
that the barbarians are the whites. The tetralogy *November 1918*
(1939 ff.) chronicles happenings in Berlin from 22 November to
7 December 1918; the series runs: *Der Zusammenbruch; Verratenes
Volk; Heimkehr der Fronttruppen; Karl und Rosa*. The revolution is
a failure; inevitably so, for individual action is motivated by illusion and self-deception.

The chiliastic dream of the New Jerusalem or *das dritte Reich* in
the ideal sense is another obsession. In JOSEF WINCKLER's (1881-)
Der chiliastische Pilgerzug (1922) it is shown up as mania. A rich
Indian king leads those who are weary and heavy laden on a pilgrimage to Paradise; on the way the poor wretches lose what
shreds of humanity they had on starting out. They discover the
utter avarice and selfishness of the Christian kingdoms. Their
numbers are much reduced by an experiment at the North Pole,
but at last they found the city of Paradise in the centre of Asia,
the cradle of the human race, which finds itself again, stripped of
the illusions of the ages, where it began. The essence of the novel
is the satiric handling of expressionistic Communism and the dream
of the common brotherhood of man. Winckler then in *Trilogie der
Zeit* (1924) girds at the mechanization of the cosmos; this too is
a true expressionist theme (Döblin's novel of the giants, Toller's

Die Maschinenstürmer, etc.), the revolt against the reduction of man to a cog in a machine; his last stage is reached in Winckler's tale as '*der physiologische Mensch*' or living robot who can be pulped down when exhausted. Winckler, a dentist by profession, had founded a futurist community, *Band der Werkleute auf Haus Nyland*, so called because they met at his ancestral home Haus Nyland; they aimed at a 'new nobility of labour' and a synthesis of imperialism, culture, industry, art, modern economic life, and freedom. Disciples of Dehmel, they had their own organ in *Quadriga*. Winckler achieved popularity with *Der tolle Bomberg* (1923), a weltering collection of anecdotes which are alleged to have gathered round the person of Baron von Bomberg, 'the Westphalian Eulenspiegel'; if there is a purpose in the book it must be to snatch the mask from everything that is ideal to expose the dirt beneath it; it is the filthy humour which has delighted the German public. *Pumpernickel* (1926) manages to be popular without wallowing in filth. The *Werkleute auf Haus Nyland* made a splash in poetry; Winckler's *Eiserne Sonette* (1912 in *Quadriga*, 1914 in book form) have a vigorous but brutal ring.

The most noted of the poets of expressionism is FRANZ WERFEL (1890-1945), a Jew from Prague. The very titles of his collections of poems indicate their tendency: *Der Weltfreund* (1911), *Wir sind* (1913), *Einander* (1915); *Der Gerichtstag* (1919). There is anti-war feeling in this lyric verse; *Troerinnen* (1914), his adaptation of the *Trojan Women* of Euripides, shows by implication the utter senselessness of the First Great War; all the post-War disillusionment is here, but also the lesson that duty bids us cling to life when all seems lost, and that to be good is better than to be happy. *Der Spiegelmensch* (1920) is a trilogy of rhymed dramas, the action of which portrays the conflict between man's two souls: the *Seins-Ich* and the *Schein-Ich* or *Spiegel-Ich*. The latter steps out of the mirror and confronts the hero, Thamal. While Seins-Ich is consumed by yearning for absolute reality, Schein-Ich lures to the enjoyment of mirror-reality, i.e. that unreality which is the vain self-enjoyment of man; harmony can only be attained by the persistent fighting down into annihilation of the *Spiegelmensch*, that is, of one's own selfish self. The drama is planned on a grandiose scale as a modern *Faust* (Schein-Ich is another version of Mephistopheles), but there is rather an acrobatic leaping over abysses than a descent into dark deeps. Werfel's tale *Nicht der Mörder, der Ermordete ist schuldig*

(1920) deals with the son-father motif. [Georg Kaiser, too, in *Hölle, Weg, Erde* (1919) had shown that the victim of a would-be murderer was guilty of the crime.] The drama *Paulus unter den Juden* (1926) deals with the problem of Jesus and the Jews. The doctrine of 'love thine enemy' is the theme of the tragedy *Juarez und Maximilian* (1924), a contrast of monarchical and republican ideas in Mexico, and of the 'novel of the opera' *Verdi* (1924), in which Verdi and Wagner are contrasted. For Thomas Mann Wagner is an inspiration breathing through '*die wissende Wehmut der Sterbensreife*'; to Werfel he is decadent over-ripeness. Wagner in this novel is the she-man from whom erotic effulgence emanates, the impersonation of the picturesquely abnormal, while Verdi is the embodiment of self-sacrificing goodness and duty, the artist turned citizen in Thomas Mann's sense. The novel reads like a counter-blast to the romantic idea of a musical genius in Wassermann's *Das Gänsemännchen*; both novels deal with the history and technique of music. Verdi has not found peace of mind, for in his rural retirement he is mentally sterile, and his fame has been eclipsed by that of Wagner; he has with him the score of *Tristan*, but in his instinctive fear of its alien genius he keeps it locked up. He goes to Venice, where Wagner is staying, but when at last he nerves himself to visit his rival he finds at the door that he has just died. His jealousy fades into love, and he composes *Otello*. Apart from the main theme, the *Wandlung* of the hero, there is much that is fine in the novel, particularly the symbolization of Venice cradled in age-rotted mud and dying to the rhythm of lapping waves; Venice, moreover – 'the terrible temptress, tired from too many loves' – identified with a *Halbweib*, a *prima donna* who moves through the tale with nothing more than a *baiser colombin* and hysterical quiverings for her lover, decadent Venice answering the baton of decadent Wagner. Some of the foundation work of the tale may be from d'Annunzio's *Il Fuoco*, in which Wagner dies in fevered, autumnal Venice, and in which the experiences of Duse and her lover are only lightly veiled. The Novellen *Der Tod des Kleinbürgers* (1926) and *Geheimnis eines Menschen* (1927) were followed by the novels *Der Abituriententag* (1928) and *Barbara oder die Frömmigkeit* (1929). *Barbara* is mainly interesting for its dramatic psychic problem: during the War the hero, an Austrian lieutenant, is in charge of a firing party who are to shoot three men for treason; one of them is the son of the old nurse (Barbara) who has brought him up; and he refuses. After the War he is swept into the revolution but arrives at respectability as a doctor. There is a good description of conditions in post-War Vienna. *Die Geschwister von Neapel* (1931) is a searching study of the effects of Fascism on the individual. Domenico Pascarelli is a small banker in Naples; as the widowed father of six children, three sons and three daughters, he is shown as a dictator to them; one of the old school, he is rigid, austere, scrupulously honest, a stickler for old forms of decorum and decency; and Werfel's novel shows the decay of all independent spirit under his well-meant domination. Domenico himself risks destruction by the Fascist régime when he upholds his independence of outlook and action, and he is saved from ruin only by the intervention of an Englishman who marries one of his daughters. The two volumes of *Die vierzig Tage des Musa Dagh* (1933) have for theme the persecution and mass slaughtering of Armenian Christians in Turkey during World War I. *Höret die Stimme* (1937) takes us back to ancient Palestine to picture the oncoming doom of the gloomed present in the remote past; we hear the voice of Jeremiah crying unheeded in the wilderness; his denunciations foreshadow the doom of today. *Der gestohlene Himmel* (1939) – the title was changed in the 1948 edition to *Der veruntreute Himmel* – is the tale of a Moravian servant who, to make sure of getting to Heaven herself, pays for her nephew to be trained as a priest; but, as he tells her when she finds him again as a disreputable renegade, she has trained him to be an intellectual. *Das Lied von Bernadette* (1941) was written in America to fulfil a vow made by Werfel when, in 1940, he found sanctuary in Lourdes. Apart from this pathetic biographical interest the book has polemical substance. Against a grim background of mean humanity, hypocrisy and self-seeking stands the pathetic figure of Bernadette Soubirous, moving in her absolute *naïveté* and naturalness and unselfishness; she has visions, as Shakespeare and Michelangelo had; she shapes them differently; and the beauty of her vision defies representation in verse or prose or marble. She denies every vestige of resemblance in her beautiful lady with golden roses on her feet to the statue of the Virgin chiselled from her description by a famous sculptor; she sees the beautiful, and she loves it: *j'aime* (her last words) is her religious doctrine. Pitiful is the frantic exploitation of the girl's visions by the Church; but the unfolding of the story is concerned with the progress of dogma to Bernadette's consecration as a saint. It would be unfair to credit Werfel with denigration of the Catholic Church; indeed a Catholic may well read the tale with edification and approval, for the main impression conveyed is that of the rock-like sincerity of the high prelates whose portraits are drawn with practised skill. Very vivid is the character sketch of the Bishop of Tarbes, a great prelate sprung from the people, but with the strong man's contempt for the mass of humanity. As to the miracles, they are narrated soberly and without bias in either direction; we have a picture of cures which baffle the science of doctors; and in one terrible chapter at the end of the book, gruesomely headed 'The Hell of the Flesh', we have a Dantesque panorama of disease with no hope of relief save by miracle – if miracle there be. And Bernadette herself is afflicted; we see her sicken and die of tuberculosis. But she is transfigured, not disfigured, by her suffering, because by her very nature she loves the divine mystery which is before us all. Werfel's last novel, *Stern der Ungeborenen* (1946), completed two days before he died in America, is a species of *Divina Commedia* up to date: F.W. is guided by a new Virgil over an 'astromental' world of aeons to be, a world in which all that has afflicted mankind – nations, labour, disease, even death – exists no more; man has conquered all – except himself. There is the 'dwelling wilderness' (*Wohnwüste*) of culture in final conflict with the joyfully coloured oases (*farbenfrohe Oasen*) of the jungles; and the working men from the jungles conquer the intellectuals: in their waste world working men can subsist without intellectuals, but not the reverse.

In Franz Werfel expressionism culminates. But his later work, clinging as it does to clear facts (e.g. *Verdi* is impeccable musical history and criticism), moves in the direction of the phase which (nominally at least) displaces expressionism – *die Neue Sachlichkeit*. The aim of the writers of this group is atomistic exactitude, but not merely in the painting of externals; they seek to penetrate into the last recesses of psychic reality, and to show a 'more real reality', illuminated, and serviceable because made intelligible. The final phase of this new sense of reality is the *Tatsachenroman*: things that have actually occurred are related in the form of a novel, as in Carl Haensel's (1889-) *Der Kampf ums Matterhorn* (1928), or in the autobiographical tales of the workmen poets.

The transition is discernible in the short stories of ARNOLD ZWEIG (1887-): he moves away from psychological probing and aesthetic

25

refinements to a plain narration of sensations, physical and mental. His *Novellen um Claudia* (1912) mark an experimental innovation: a series of short tales are fitted together to form a novel. There is the same striving for *Sachlichkeit* in his collections of Novellen *Frühe Fährten* (1925) and *Regenbogen* (1926). *Der Streit um den Sergeanten Grischa* (1926-7) is one of the most notable of the War novels: a recaptured Russian prisoner is sentenced to death as a spy because he has assumed the name of a Russian soldier making for home in an opposite direction: his identity is proved, but Headquarters say the original sentence must be carried out, and the Divisional Commander resists in vain. Sergeant Grischa is just a simple soldier; he is the victim of Prussian bureaucracy – who shall count how many others? Here lies the poignancy of the story: any soldier is a man, with senses that cling to love and life – to the war machine he is not a man, but a number. *Sergeant Grischa* was planned as the first of eight novels which were to epitomize and analyse the years following World War I. The second novel, *Junge Frau von 1914* (1931), is, however, the chronological start; it is the love story of a Berlin banker's daughter and an author without means who is called up; the background is the upheaval of the war, the moving spirit is vicious criticism of the conditions which led to it and of those (particularly Jews) who profit by it. The title of *Einsetzung eines Königs* (1937) refers to the candidature of the Duke of Teck for the throne of Lithuania; the incompetence and arrogance of German officers is exposed; the intelligentsia tends to be the Jewish non-commissioned officers, who have mostly soft administrative jobs away from the fighting. The hero ends as a Communist. The paltry intrigue of *Erziehung vor Verdun* (1935) involves a like accusation of military justice. *De Vriendt kehrt heim* (1933) is a *vie romancée*, though the name of the real hero, a Dutch poet, is changed to De Vriendt, who is shot by an orthodox Jew in Palestine; the interest is not so much in the hero's conflict with the Zionists and his literary avocations as in the complication of his psyche by homosexuality. In *Das Beil von Wandsbeck* (1947) a man of examplary character, a master-butcher, feeling the competition of the chain-stores in 1937, takes the chance of restoring his finances by secretly acting as executioner to the Nazis, a function for which he sharpens 'the axe of Wandsbeck', a family heirloom.

ERICH KÄSTNER'S (1899-) *Lyrische Haus-Apotheke* (1938), an anthology of his own verse, rings with the real reality of the new school; the poems are from his collections *Ein Mann gibt Auskunft*, *Herz auf Taille* (1928), *Lärm im Spiegel* (1929), *Zwischen zwei Stühlen*. His novel *Fabian, die Geschichte eines Moralisten* (1932) is utterly sceptical and cynical: the hero is a Nihilist who, while Communists and Nazis are shooting one another in Berlin, cannot wait for the inevitable revolution; Fabian, with nerves quivering to the sense of reality, afraid of life, is a true type of the generation he represents. Kästner's later work has won world-wide popularity, particularly his *Emil und die Detektive* and *Emil und die drei Zwillinge* (1936); *Das fliegende Klassenzimmer* (1933), with its picture of life in a German secondary school and *Drei Männer im Schnee* (1934), a tale of simple people who win prizes entitling them to spend a period at a Grand Hotel in the Alps, have that boisterous humour which wins the quick reader.

HANS FALLADA (1893-1947), too, has this surprisingly juvenile bent of mind; he reproduces the atmosphere of the traditional *Märchen* in *Altes Herz geht auf die Reise* (1936): there is a group of village boys led by a girl in conspiracy against a tyrannous foster-father (who in this realistic setting of an old *Märchen* stands for the ogre). Stories for children are *Hoppelpoppel – wo bist du?* (1936) and *Geschichten aus der Murkelei* (1938). But the majority of Fallada's novels are very seriously purposed; in the main they concentrate on the difficulties of earning a living in the days he lived in. In *Kleiner Mann, was nun?* (1932) we have the post-war problem of what the morrow will bring. *Wolf unter Wölfen* (1937) has for theme the inflation before the war. In *Der eiserne Gustav* (1938) the difficulty of earning a living is due in the first place to social changes; a Berlin cab-driver is forced out of business by the advent of taxis and in the end follows his son into the Nazi camp. This struggle for life plays a great part in Fallada's own life and is reflected in his novels. *Wir hatten mal ein Kind* (1934) gives a picture of peasant life, and Fallada himself during the Hitler period withdrew to his farm in Mecklenburg, and here he wrote *Heute bei uns zu Haus* (1943), his autobiographical tale of the life of an author turned farmer; this had been preceded by his book of memories of childhood and youth, *Damals bei uns daheim* (1942). *Der Alpdruck* (1947) has also an autobiographical element in so far as the author who is the hero lays bare his own share in the guilt which led to the *débâcle* of 1945. There is the same laying bare of moral weakness in *Der Trinker* (1950), published after his early death. Through all of Fallada's serious fiction runs the problem of character with its strength (*Der eiserne Gustav*) or weakness; the hero breaks his fate or is broken by it, as he is in *Wer einmal aus dem Blechnapf frisst* (1934); here a released prisoner fights hard to recover a place in the social scale, but finds himself at last back in prison.

If in Fallada's tales there is a return to the *Märchen* in those of ERNST PENZOLDT (1892-) there is a new phase of the idyll. He began with poems (*Der Gefährte*) and turned to silver-pencilled prose in *Idyllen* (1923). His Novelle *Der arme Chatterton* (1928) probes the secret of the very nature of poetry: the boy-poet dreams himself into his tragic illusion. In *Der Zwerg* (1927) Penzoldt dreams his idyllic moods into the days of rococo in his own Franconia.

XVI

EXOTIC LITERATURE
AND THE COLONIAL NOVEL

The fog of pessimism during and after the First War is no doubt one of the explanations of the vogue of literature which describes far-away climes: it represents a flight from reality. Exotic literature, of course, goes back to the end of the eighteenth century[1] (Georg Forster's *A Voyage towards the South Pole and round the World*, 1777, and J. G. Seume's verse tale *Der Wilde*[2]) and continues with Chamisso's *Reise um die Welt in den Jahren 1815-18* and Alexander von Humboldt's *Kosmos* (1845-58). Exotic fiction shapes itself on such writers as Fennimore Cooper in the American and Wild West novels (*'Wildwest-Romantik'*) of Charles Sealsfield (1793-1864) and Friedrich Gerstäcker (1816-72). There is still an English undertone in the exotic writings of Paul Lindau's brother RUDOLF LINDAU (1829-1910: *Erzählungen eines Effendi*, 1896): he was a far-travelled diplomat, as much international as German (his first work, on Japan, was in French, and as Swiss consul at Yokohama he founded the *Japan Times*, the best English newspaper in Japan). The new exotic style blooms with tropic splendour in the impressionistic prose (*Gedankengut aus meinen Wanderjahren*, 2 vols., 1913; *Erlebnisse auf Java*, 1924) of Max Dauthendey (pp. 245 ff.), and he has a good second in the Luxemburger NORBERT JACQUES (1880-). We get the Far East in

[1] Gabriel Rollenhagen's *Vier Bücher wunderbarlicher indianischer Reisen* (1603) repeat ancient fables, and the exotic novels of the seventeenth century are also fabulous.

[2] Seume's knowledge of America was first-hand: he was kidnapped in Hesse, and sold to England to fight the American rebels. His prose travel descriptions are good forerunners of those by *die Europamüden* of today. The craze for America was held up to ridicule by Ferdinand Kürnberger in his novel *Der Amerika-Müde* (1855); he had never been in America, but used Lenau's American experiences (1832).

377

Jacques's novel *Der Kaufherr von Schanghai* (1925), in his *Reisetage-buch*, in his travel descriptions *Die heissen Städte* (1911, 1921) and *Auf dem chinesischen Fluss*; and in Max Brod's *Abenteuer in Japan* (1938). WILLY SEIDEL (1887-1934) gets to Egypt with his frivolous humour in *Der Sang der Sakije* (1914), to the Bedouin desert with *Der Garten des Schuchan* (1912) and to Samoa with *Der Buschhahn* (1921). Waldemar Bonsels as a theosophist wanders about India (p. 320). Dauthendey's successor as impressionist globe-trotter is ALFONS PAQUET (1881-1944), who began as a good lyric poet: *Lieder und Gesänge* (1902); *Auf Erden* (1906); *Held Namenlos* (1912), and captured his public with brilliant books of travel: *Li oder im neuen Osten* (1912), *Erzählungen an Bord* (1914). His expressionistic style makes even Paris exotic in his novel *Kamerad Fleming* (1912); in his utopia of the new humanity, *Die Prophezeiungen* (1922), he takes us to Siberia. Africa is the scene of Ernst Jünger's *Afrika-nische Spiele*; and, of course, Jakob Wassermann's *Bula Matari*, with its symbolic illumination of the fermenting African jungle, is exotic literature in the extreme sense. French colonial life gives interest to Friedrich Schnack's travel pictures *Auf ferner Insel: Glückliche Zeit in Madagaskar* (1931). Asia comes (with Turkey) into the work of Armin T. Wegner (*Im Hause der Glückseligkeit*, 1920; *Der Knabe Hussein*, 1917), while Kasimir Edschmid finds scope for his pic-torial extravagances in South America and the Wild West (*Der Lazo* in *Die sechs Mündungen*). The more sensational phase of exotic literature is represented by Hanns Heinz Ewers in his travel books (*Indien und ich*, 1911; *Mit meinen Augen*, 1914) and in his Novellen, and by Eduard Stucken's *Die weissen Götter* (p. 273) with the Mexican matter that follows it: Gerhart Hauptmann's two Aztec plays, Klabund's ballad *Montezuma* (1919), Jakob Wassermann's *Das Gold von Caxamalka* (in *Der Geist des Pilgers*, 1923), and Bruno Brehm's *Die schrecklichen Pferde* (1934).

The *Kolonialroman* is obviously exotic, but it forms a distinct genre, though not an extensive one unless we include literature descriptive of colonies in the wider sense of lands colonized by Germans wherever they may lie, so long as the colonists preserve the German language and German culture. This would bring in such works as Josef Ponten's *Im Wolgaland*, not to speak of *Aus-landsromane* from Transylvania and all the other German enclaves or colonies. To the German mind, of course, every land where German is spoken is *Heimat*; and for this reason every *Kolonial-*

roman belongs to *Heimatkunst*. In the narrower sense of literature descriptive of life in colonies which belong to or did belong to Germany Frenssen's *Peter Moors Fahrt nach Südwest* points the way to the South African tales of Hans Grimm, which are probably more important politically than in the sense of literature.

HANS GRIMM (1875-), born in Wiesbaden as the son of a professor of law, but by extraction belonging to the district of the Middle Weser, worked in London as an unpaid clerk (*Volontär*) and then as a clerk in Cape Colony (Port Elizabeth); in 1901 he established himself as an independent merchant in East London and spent his week-ends on his farm by the Nahoon river. He now lives in the *Heimat* of his ancestors, in an old cloister-house by the Middle Weser near Kassel. He returned to Germany before the First Great War, and during and after his military service – he did not serve at the front as he had only one eye – he wrote tales embodying his colonial experiences (*Der Gang durch den Sand*, 1916). He had begun with *Südafrikanische Novellen* (1913), but ripened his brusque style – face-to face like that of Blunck but much more natural, and like Blunck's style modelled on the straightforward story-telling of the Old Norse sagas – in *Die Olewagen-Saga* (1918) and *Der Ölsucher von Duala* (1918). The latter tale is aimed at the French: the hero, a German colonist, is taken prisoner in the Cameroons and sent, with 250 other Germans, to the fever swamps of Dahomey, where they are tortured to death. Hans Grimm's great effort is *Volk ohne Raum* (1926), an interminable novel written between 1920 and 1926 after he had visited what had been German South-West Africa. The events are vouched for as essentially true, as are the names of the seven typical colonists whose experiences are described. The first part of the story is strict *Heimatkunst*: life in a hamlet in the Middle Weser district is meticulously described, and the hopelessness of outlook stressed: even this handful of people in the heart of the woods is 'without space', and those who cannot find work locally must move on to factory work at Bochum, or emigrate. How to save the German race from this '*Sklavennot der Enge*' is the theme of the book; for this little village is a symbol of all Germany, now robbed by England of its place in the sun. 'The whole world belongs to England', the novel points out; but 'the Germans must be the allies of every nation that chooses freedom and defies England'; 'new countries must be divided according to population and colonizing capacity.' Grimm's remaining South African tales are in the same vein: *Das deutsche Südwester-Buch*, 1929; *Der Richter in der Karu*, 1930; *Lüderitzland*, 1934.

XVII

THE HISTORICAL NOVEL

In the new historical novel we get a symbolic interpretation of history. Whether – except, perhaps, in the scholarly handling of Ricarda Huch – there is always the advance which is claimed on the archaic *Professorenroman* of Dahn and Ebers is open to question: MAX BROD'S (1884-) *Tycho Brahes Weg zu Gott* (1916) for instance – probably the most morally satisfying and philosophical of them all – is in style hardly less naïve than that of Ebers. A difference in the problem there certainly is: whereas the archaeological novel made a show of erudition, the new historical novel illuminates, in intention, the state of mind or the character of people famous in history. Moreover, whereas the archaeological novel portrayed the hero and his period as chronologically isolated, the new historical novel interprets the present by shifting its problems to past times. In *Tycho Brahes Weg zu Gott* there is a contrast of two types of intellect: the onrushing Danish astronomer and the cool and patient Kepler; it is a history, not of stirring events, but of Tycho's brain-storms ending in a moral victory by complete abnegation of self (*Wandlung*); it is the seeking of God that matters, not the scientist's seeking of truth. This is the aim and purpose, too, of *Reübini, Fürst der Juden* (1925) and *Galilei in Gefangenschaft* (1948), two novels which the author groups with the Tycho Brahe novel as a trilogy. In 1939 Max Brod emigrated to Palestine as a Zionist and was appointed director of the Hebrew theatre in Tel Aviv. Here he devoted himself to editing the great edition of Kafka (pp. 452-3). The background of his novel *Unambo* (1949) is the recent Arab-Jewish war. There is symbolical interpretation of biblical history in *Der Meister* (1952); the hero of the novel, Jeschua (that is, Jesus), rebels against Roman rule and, betrayed by Jehuda (Judas), dies for love of his native land. In *Armer Cicero* (1955) the Roman orator, after his divorce from his first wife, marries his seventeen-year-old Publilia and is thereafter a slave to senile eroticism. After the Ides of March he proclaims war against Antony, but is forced to flee from Rome, and is overtaken by assassins outside his villa at Formiae. Max Brod has written one drama: *Lord Byron kommt aus der Mode* (1929; see p. 33). Not the least readable of his works is *Heinrich Heine* (1934).

Mysticism read into history appears in the novels of ERWIN GUIDO KOLBENHEYER (1878-), a German of Sudeten descent born in Budapest. In *Amor Dei* (1908) he interprets Spinoza, and shows him in stark contrast with Rembrandt; the novel has merit if only for its patient mastery of historical detail and its skilful creation of an archaic language suitable to the period. The best thing is the technically excellent though simple explanation of the growth and exposition of Spinoza's pantheism; this alone makes the novel valuable for students of German literature. Silesian mysticism is expounded in. *Meister Joachim Pausewang* (1910). Pausewang is a cobbler of Breslau who tells his own story; behind him looms the fascinating figure of another cobbler, Jakob Böhme, against the dark background of the Thirty Years War. Kolbenheyer's greatest effort – possibly his masterpiece – is his Paracelsus trilogy: *Die Kindheit des Paracelsus*, 1917; *Das Gestirn des Paracelsus*, 1921; *Das dritte Reich des Paracelsus*, 1925. Here it is not so much the philosophical ideas of the hero that matter as the author's conception – common to all his work – of the Germanic hero: the last volume closes with the device, in great letters, *Ecce ingenium teutonicum*. Kolbenheyer's tales consistently show sacrifice of self in characters perfected by the mental torments of experience in a hostile world. This self-sacrifice or philosophic *Wandlung*, we are to understand, is a typically Germanic process: Paracelsus, the first modern physician, frees himself in toil and travail of mind from the bondage of Mediterranean thought, from the cobwebs of Galen and Hippocrates. This is the theme, too, of Kolbenheyer's 'prentice work, *Giordano Bruno* (1893), a kind of tragedy, revised and rechristened *Heroische Leidenschaften* (1929). The Italian philosopher has to evolve his pantheistic concept (*die Göttlichkeit des Alls*), but he can only do this by working himself free from the trammels of Mediterranean scholasticism; and he can do it because his mother was a German; he too is an *ingenium teutonicum*. Two novels of Kolbenheyer – *Montsalvatsch* (1912) and *Das Lächeln der Penaten* (1926) – deal with social and moral problems of today; in the former a

Viennese student (self-portraiture is assumed) struggles with forces that might drag him down; in the latter an artist's family life helps him to resist the debasing influences of *milieu*. A later novel, *Reps, die Persönlichkeit* (1932), shows the German *Bildungsphilister* on shaky ground in a small town.

The historical novels of WALTER VON MOLO (1880-1958) have Kolbenheyer's heroic conception of German character as exemplified in the great men of the race. He drew energetic pictures of Schiller in *Der Schiller-Roman* (4 vols.; 1912-16) and of Frederick the Great in *Der Roman meines Volkes* (*Fridericus*, 1918; *Luise*, 1919; *Ein Volk wacht auf*, 1921), of the Protestant Reformer in *Mensch Luther* (1928), of the famous economist in *Ein Deutscher ohne Deutschland: der Friedrich List-Roman* (1931), of Prince Eugene in *Eugenio von Savoy* (1936), and of Heinrich von Kleist in *Geschichte einer Seele* (1938).

An Austrian historical novel with the old romantic hero worship is *Radetzkymarsch* (1932) by JOSEPH ROTH (1894-1939), who in *Die Flucht ohne Ende* (1927) had written the most terribly hopeless and cynical of the *Heimkehrerromane*. *Radetzkymarsch* glorifies Austria in the person of the Emperor Franz Joseph with his officers and executives; a Lieutenant Trotta saves the Emperor's life at Solferino by throwing himself on him and forcing him to the ground when bullets begin to whizz in his direction. Trotta is given the rank of Baron and the picture is filled out by the experiences of his son and grandson. In spite of the patriotic heroifications of Franz Joseph in white uniform and red sash – with a drip at the end of his nose – the general tone is anti-royalist, if only because the officers are of poor intelligence. The Trotta saga is continued in *Die Kapuzinergruft* (1939), which ends with the coming of Hitler and the *Anschluss*; there is the note of utter hopelessness as the tale fades out with the march of the Germans into Vienna, while Trotta walks away from the sordid pub he was sitting in – and goes through empty streets, alone, except for an ownerless dog that follows him.

The reverse of hero worship is the rule in those German historical novels and *vies romancées* which have an international market. It is perhaps because they are written mostly by Jews that they have this tendency to de-bunk (to use the Yankee rendering of *entheroisieren*); and this fact is one of the reasons why a public holocaust was made of such stories in 1933. Psycho-analytical inquisitiveness is of course the chief means of revealing reality by stripping biography of romance; *vie romancée* thus means, not the romance of a life, but a fictional rendering of it. The historical novels of LION FEUCHTWANGER (1884-1958) show little originality. *Jud Süss* (1925) follows a novel of the same title by Wilhelm Hauff, and the daughter hidden away in a rural bower and discovered by the sovereign is the heart of Conrad Ferdinand Meyer's tale of Thomas à Becket (*Der Heilige*), while the two queens in *Die hässliche Herzogin* (1926) are obviously the traditional German conceptions of Elizabeth of England and Mary of Scotland. *Erfolg* (1931) is a *roman à clefs* picturing the fall of the Communist government in Bavaria. The originals of the characters in *Der falsche Nero* (1936) are easy to guess; a potter who strikes dramatic poses is discovered and made an emperor by a capitalist – till he is cast down and crucified by his own gang, a gigantic soldier and a sly secretary. Feuchtwanger had some success as a dramatist with expressionist leanings; of special interest are the '*Drei angelsächsische Stücke*' (1927): *Die Petroleuminseln*; *Kalkutta, 4 Mai* (with Bert Brecht as collaborator); *Wird Hill amnestiert?*

STEFAN ZWEIG (1881-1942), a Viennese Jew with international culture, is on a higher plane. He began at twenty with a mannered book of verse (*Die Silbernen Saiten*) and reached his maturity as a lyric poet as much in his masterly translations of Verhaeren, Verlaine, and Baudelaire as in the refined but somewhat imitative descriptiveness of *Die frühen Kränze* (1907); his collected verse appeared in 1924 (*Die Gesammelten Gedichte*). He is a *Formkünstler*, too, in his essays, intuitive rather than academic, but often, because of their psycho-analytical method, more illuminating than the documented interpretations of university specialists; *Drei Meister* (1919) analyses Balzac, Dickens, and Dostoieffski; *Der Kampf mit dem Dämon* (1925) uncovers the pathological ferments which inspired Hölderlin, Kleist, and Nietzsche; *Drei Dichter ihres Lebens* (1928) interprets Casanova, Stendhal, and Tolstoy. His books on *Verhaeren* (1910) and *Romain Rolland* (1920) revealed with brilliant insight the ultra-modernity of these writers. *Marceline Desbordes-Valmore* (1928) is informed by the most intimate appreciation of this poetess. *Triumph und Tragik des Erasmus von Rotterdam* (1935) fails by the fact alone that there is no adequate estimation of the Latinity of this great stylist, but it grips by its obvious bringing into relation of its subject with the conditions of today – it is in some sort an idealized approximation of the essayist's self as one hating the clash of conflicts of today and yet drawn at least to their orbit by intellectual rank and race. His denunciation of war rang out at the very height of the War from his drama *Jeremias* (1917); here again there is obvious identification of author and hero. Other dramas of his are *Tersites* (1907) and an adaptation of Ben Jonson's *Volpone* (1927). His short stories have again mastery of form, but they sometimes glide over feeling rather than probe into it. In *Erstes Erlebnis* (1911) there are distressing studies of the awakening of sexual knowledge in a delicate boy and in girls. Sordid sexual experience gives the note of *Amok* (1923); in *Verwirrung der Gefühle* (1926) there is more of the complicated mental shock of passion. *Sternstunden der Menschheit* (1928) are five historical miniatures; they condense episodes vital to the progress of culture and are by their nature at the rim of the work by which Stefan Zweig has won his public all over the world – his historical novels or rather romanced history. *Joseph Fouché* (1929) and *Marie Antoinette* (1932; a great success as a film) indicate his formula: against a swiftly moving and vivid historical background thrilling episodes of personal feeling. For British readers this formula achieves its best – and worst – in *Maria Stuart* (1935): there is the traditional German contrast of the two queens – Mary is the passionate lover, while Elizabeth is the erotically malformed half-woman, 'mutilated in spirit because abnormal in body', whose relations with her lovers are torture because she cannot give herself wholly. In 1935 Stefan Zweig emigrated to England, where he was naturalized; in 1942 he committed suicide together with his second wife in Rio de Janeiro. He tells the story of his life in *Die Welt von gestern* (1944); this is not a consecutive and consistent autobiography; it is more a book of memories with Zweig (to use his own term in the preface) as the pivot. His private and intimate life is actually cut out; there is nothing of the love affair which led to his second marriage or of his matrimonial affairs; these come out in the book published after his death by his first wife, Friderike Zweig: *Stefan Zweig wie ich ihn erlebte* (1947) and in *Stefan Zweig – Friderike Zweig* (1952), his correspondence stretching from 1912 to 1942. His posthumously published *Balzac* (1948) had been planned as a *magnum opus*; he had been working at it for ten years, and it was not finished when he died. Balzac's life is treated as a tragedy with comic relief; and the comic elements in the sordid story detract from Balzac's stature as a novelist. The failure of the book is due to the psychologically interesting but generally speaking repulsive features of the 'case'.

There is a hectic tempo and a heaping up of lurid horror touched up by expressionistic psychology in the historical novels of ALFRED NEUMANN (1895-1952). He made his reputation with *Der Teufel* (1926), a melodramatic handling of Olivier le Daim in his relationships with Louis XI and his court. The background of *Rebellen* (1927) and its sequel *Guerra* (1928) is formed by the Carbonari risings in Italy. History is detailed in *Königin Christine von Schweden* (1935), but the thrill is in the erotic peculiarity of the queen, her early Lesbian experiment, her love for the Marquis de la Gardie (who presented the silver codex of Ulfilas to the University of Upsala) and, in Rome, for Cardinal Azzolino. 'The tragedy of the nineteenth century' is unrolled in a trilogy of novels which chronicle the life and times of the Emperor Napoleon III: *Neuer Cäsar* (1934), *Kaiserreich* (1936), *Die Volksfreunde* (1941). *Es waren ihrer sechs* (1944) deals with a rebellion of students against Hitler during World War II.

The sexual extravagance is horrific in ROBERT NEUMANN'S (1897-) *Struensee* (1935); this fascinating doctor is a disciple of Rousseau, whose ideas he tries to put into practice when he rises to power in Denmark; the novel presents him as a political and social reformer, a Socialist or even Communist of the Jew type, while the Danish aristocrats are represented as decadent sexual brutes. *Sir Basil Zaharoff* (1934) romanticizes the career of the 'armaments king', who came from the slums of Constantinople to be the richest man in Europe. *Sintflut* (1929) plays round the antics of financiers in the Vienna of our day, while the satire of *Die Macht* (1932) is aimed at the Nazis. In 1932 Robert Neumann emigrated to England and wrote in English (*Blind Man's Buff*, 1949); several of his novels (*Die Kinder von Wien*, 1948; *Die Puppen von Poschansk*, 1952) have been translated from English into German. His anecdotal *Erinnerungen an Menschen und Gespenster* (1957) is a book of memoirs, while *Mein altes Haus in Kent* (1957) tells the story of the cottage in which he settled in Kent and of what has happened to him there; the two books together commemorate his sixtieth birthday.

BRUNO FRANK (1887-1945) has expressionistic humanity and a fine Jewish culture, but in style and outlook he is a solid, sensible Liberal, almost old-fashioned (by comparison) in his directness of expression. His historical novel *Die Tage des Königs* (1924) is a scholarly well-documented study of Frederick the Great, who also dominates the scene in *Trenck, Roman eines Günstlings* (1926), a lively picture of Prussian rococo. Bruno Frank's enlightened Liberalism shines out from *Politische Novelle* (1928), a discussion rather than a story, which rejects the plea that antagonism between France and Germany is a necessary evil and in its vivid pen-pictures of Briand (as Dorval) and of Stresemann (as Carmer) shows how elementary the idea of permanent peace really is. His *vie romancée* of *Cervantes* (1935) is a thorough de-bunking; there is topical interest in the satirical account of the decrees for the prevention of blood-pollution at a time when there was not a grandee's family in Spain but Jewish blood flowed in his veins. *Don Quixote* is shown to be the product of utter disillusionment, not so much of sex (though Dulcinea is depicted as a literal portrait of the country girl Cervantes marries) as of the hopeless misgovernment of Spain. *Chamfort erzählt seinen Tod* (1937) is the *vie romancée* of this French aphorist. *Der Reisepass* (1937) is yet another denunciation of the Nazi régime by an emigré (to the United States). Several of Bruno Frank's dramas were successful on the English stage; of these *Zwölftausend* (1927) throws a lurid light on the sale by a German princeling of 12,000 of his subjects to England as cannon fodder. *Sturm im Wasserglas* (1930) – James Bridie's *Storm in a Teacup* (1937) – is uproarious in its picture of a platitudinous dictator engrossed in self and dead to human pity. *Nina* (1931) is a study of a guttersnipe transformed to a film-star; for love of her husband she sacrifices her glamorous career, which is taken over by a double. *Die Tochter* (1943) is based on the life of the mother of the author's wife, a cabaret artiste who is half Jew and half Pole, and of her father, an Austrian officer; the ground theme is anti-Semitism. Bruno Frank is most effective where his allusions are transparent – e.g. the theatre director in his Novelle *Der Magier* (1929) resembles Max Reinhardt; where he handles merely pathological problems he has no incisiveness – e.g. in his drama *Die Schwestern und der Fremde* (1918), in which a physically cold intellectual humanitarian satisfies the desires of a girl doomed by consumption, but, when she dies, tells her robust sister, who wishes to fill the gap, that he is an icy monster.

XVIII

THE DRAMA
OF EXPRESSIONISM

In the expressionistic drama there is a continuation of Haupt-mann's innovation in *Die Weber* and *Florian Geyer*: the charac-ters are not extraordinary individuals but types representing groups and masses; and since they are symbols they are given no names, but appear as 'the father' (that is, any father), 'the son', 'first sailor', 'second sailor', 'the clerk', etc. The characterization is not by stage directions but by what is said and done on the stage. The language, following the theory that expression must be *'geballt'*, i.e. frantically concentrated like strength in a clenched fist, is grotesquely ungrammatical – conjunctions and articles fall out, sentences are syncopated, separable verbs obstinately cling together – and the clause is reduced to rudimentary forms, differing, how-ever, from the *Telegrammstil* of the naturalists in that whereas the latter indicated the conversational carelessness of mental apathy, a scattering of small shot, the expressionistic shortening comes from the swiftness of ecstasy or frenzy, the whizzing of a bullet straight at the mark. In dramatic construction there is a return to antiquated technique: monologues reappear, verse and prose alter-nate, rhyme heads off a climax. For the looseness of construction and stylistic grotesqueness of these plays the models were found, not only in Strindberg[1] and Wedekind, but in the *Sturm und Drang* dramas of Lenz and Klinger, and particularly in Georg Büchner's (1813-37) *Woyzeck* (published 1879). The new technique appears

[1] Technique is influenced by Strindberg's *Nach Damaskus* (1898); here there is no plot, and the construction is merely a juxtaposition ('*Nebenein-ander*') of 'stations'. All the strength of such plays is in the passion and despair of their monologues. These 'ecstatic' explosions are derided as '*Schreidramen*' (particularly those of August Stramm and Oskar Kokoschka) and '*O Mensch Dramen*'.

in REINHARD JOHANNES SORGE'S (1892-1916) *Der Bettler* (1912); on a stage illuminated by searchlights the walls of a café recede and the hero recites his lines against the purple night-sky; or he turns to the spectators and harangues them. Son and father fight out their quarrel with the lyric logic loaded against the parent in WALTER HASENCLEVER'S (1890-1940) drama *Der Sohn* (1914); only a convenient fit of apoplexy saves the father from being shot by his son. 'It is the old song against injustice and cruelty,' cries the son; father is to son as King Philip was to Don Carlos. This literary spirit of revolution had its share in the smashing of the old régime; but it quickly degenerated into political Communism.

It is in the drama that the grotesque suggestiveness of expressionism forces its claim to at least historical significance. Disciples of Wedekind are Paul Kornfeld, Carl Sternheim, and Georg Kaiser. PAUL KORNFELD (1889-) turns away not merely from reality but from psychology, which, he says, tells us as little as anatomy does of the nature of man, who is 'the mirror and shadow of the eternal and God's mouth'; reality is a mistake, the truth is raptness of soul (*Beseeltheit*). Kornfeld would, therefore, banish character from the stage and replace it by soul, i.e. the divine, or the non-human and non-temporal; 'let us leave it to the working day', he cries, 'to have character, and let us be nothing but soul.' In harmony with this conception, actors are not to be afraid of waving their arms about; intensity of expression is beyond the means of traditional acting; exaltation is to be achieved, not by physical illusion such as the cothurnus gave the Greeks, but by illumination from within; the soul is to shine forth in the dimness of reality like a luminous dial in the night. Therefore, in Kornfeld's dramas (*Die Verführung*, 1913; *Himmel und Hölle*, 1918) there are no characters, only souls 'making mighty speeches with mighty gestures'. CARL STERNHEIM (1878-1942) in his comedies shows up the respectable middle classes, to which by birth he belonged (he was a banker's son); to him the *Bürger* is not Monsieur Homais, slippered and sleek and harmless, but a loathsome blend of venomous toad, braying ass, and scarecrow. In his prose treatise *Tasso oder Kunst des Juste Milieu* (1921) he pillories Goethe himself as a petty Philistine! His most characteristic work is to be found in a series of eleven comedies, written 1908-22, and grouped under the ironic title *Aus dem bürgerlichen Heldenleben*. Typical of his comedies 'of manners' – they are as cold and sharp as a surgeon's knife – is *Bürger Schippel* (1913),

26

the story of a bastard who happens to be so good a singer that he is indispensable for a concert which is to be given at the local Court: he is admitted to the quartet which traditionally carries off the honours, but not to the society to which the other members of the quartet belong; he has, however, the rapture of seeing the inside of their houses and of marrying his forms to a cushioned arm-chair; and when the maiden sister of his host passes through the room he can sniff the air and murmur in Wagnerian alliterations: *Weisse Wäsche weht vorüber!* The dizzy height of happiness would be to marry this unapproachable lady; and she is actually thrust at him when she is compromised by the local prince – but Schippel turns forth a lofty pride and refuses her as tainted goods; upon which he is challenged to a duel by one of the quartet, who is in a state of collapse before pistols are raised, but not more so than Schippel, who, however, discharges his weapon, perhaps by the shaking of his nerves, and is then canonized as a member of the middle classes. Islanded in the play like a green refuge is the love scene of prince and maiden, with the shreds of ragged romance and echoes of ancient verse still clinging to the stripped sentences gaunt with disillusionment. *Oskar Wilde: sein Drama* (1925) has no more than symptomatic interest. In Sternheim's short stories – the best are collected as *Chronik von des zwanzigsten Jahrhunderts Beginn* (1918) – there is the same pitiless dissection of the middle classes; but here he has more scope for uncovering the hidden springs of impulse and action: the powers that decide lie '*wo wie ein geschwellter Kessel der Leib zwischen Schenkel und Hüfte eingelassen ist*'; and perhaps the pencil sketch of Sternheim given by Soergel, which shows him lying immaculately dressed but with his abdomen bared and simmering, sufficiently pictures his conception of the genesis of art as of vital energy. In the tales there is something of a Nietzschean approval of characters who see through their fellow-men and exploit them: thus the hero of *Schuhlin* (1913) is a pianist and composer who lives on the wealth of a rich pupil and the labour of his wife; the grim humour lies in the efforts of each worshipper to outdo the other in sacrifice, and the end of the comedy is that the pupil, his last penny gone, stabs the wife, who would still, if she remained over, have the comfort of her body to offer the sybarite. As to Schuhlin: '*Sanfte Trauer hindert ihn nicht, unverzüglich neue Verbindungen zu suchen, die die Mittel zu jenem Leben sichern sollen, das er als ihm gemäss und seiner Bedeutung zukommend, ein für allemal erkannt hatte.*' The titular hero of *Napoleon* (1915) is a chef in Paris who, a master of his art, is entitled to look down with withering scorn on the creatures he feeds. *Meta* (1916) records the triumphs of a servant girl who resists her lover but, after his death in the War, exhausts her virgin body with his dream-shape, and, inured by pain and observation to the demoniac nature of love, enslaves master and mistress. Sternheim's style in his tales is wilfully experimental and typically expressionistic: articles and prepositions are cast away, Saxon genitives prevail, the limbs of the sentence are closely compressed, and there is a metallic harshness in the denotation of the rushed action. In the long novel *Europa* (1919), an ambitious attempt to show West European society ripening for its ruin in the War, this 'precious' style ossifies.

GEORG KAISER (1867-1945) was certainly a gifted dramatist: he was steeped in the routine of the theatre, and did not stand above sensational effects, but he had the daring of the pioneer and a skill in the symmetrical handling of symbol which made even his failures interesting. His first plays were studies, influenced by Freud, of sexual states and problems. The first to be published was *Rektor Kleist* (1905); this play – a *Tragikomödie* he calls it – ends with the suicide of a grammar-school boy owing to the tyranny of his teachers. In spite of the not inadequately motivated catastrophe it is mainly farcical satire and belongs to the contemporary revolt against the school system (see pp. 17, 280). Much of the fun is provided by the writhings of the headmaster under the stinging irritation of his gluteal callosities (*Gesässgetriebe*). What value the play has lies in the corrosive analysis of this diseased headmaster too feeble to have children – and of the blustering gymnastics master as the opposite extreme of robustious health (he is the father of twins) and naïve boy-scout morality. *Die jüdische Witwe* (1911) shows a Judith unwillingly chaste; her marriage with an old man has not been consummated, and her people reward her for slaying Holofernes by making her a Virgin of the Temple, privileged to tread the Holy of Holies with the High Priest; in him she at last finds her man. There is much that is loathsome in this recklessly Jewish drama: above all, the bath scene with its detailed unfolding of sexual obsession in the doddering old scholar into whose limp arms the girl has been thrust by her decent family, and the maid's awakened body calling even for the crazed and impotent old fool, like a child for its toy; but the intention, to concentrate in a symbol expanding and bursting like a gorgeous tropical flower the physical need which is the source of existence, is realized in the final scene where the virgin widow, who has saved herself by a swing of Holofernes' curved sword from the trampling lust of the Assyrian army, is again brought by her decent family to the sacrifice, this time to be thrust for religion's sake into a loathsome virginity. She writhes and recoils, as she had done at the first sacrifice of her body; but as, while she is held, the priest from Jerusalem is stripped shred by shred of his ceremonial vestments and his manly beauty of thews and sinews lights the black gloom of the Temple, her struggles cease: '*leise tasten ihre Finger, denen die Hände mit grösseren Flächen langsam nachgehen, an den eigenen Gliedern herab. Ihr Leib spannt sich – und aus aller Verfolgung, Vorwurf und Bestimmung baut er sich neu und voller auf. Ihre Finger zittern um den Saum ihres kurzen Kleides, als höben sie daran. Die Säule ihres zur Erde stehenden Haares trägt die Stirn ihrer schönen Mädchenkraft, wie die Krone heiligsten Gebietens.*' Such a picture, electric and sated with symbol – the self-sacrifice and consummation of love in the Holy of Holies, where priest is husband and husband is priest – is the measure of Georg Kaiser's exploring spirit. Through *König Hahnrei* (1913) Tristan and Isolde move almost as hallucinated automatons, while the interest is concentrated on the senile erotic impotence of King Mark. In hiding he has heard Isolde tell Tristan how in Ireland her boy brother embraced her with his feet pressed on her lap; the picture becomes a fixed idea, which drives the old man crazy. The end is vivid: Mark hurls a spear, Isolde covers Tristan's back with her breast, the spear pierces both, and unites them in death. The 'new man' of expressionist ethics stands four-square to the blasts of fate in *Die Bürger von Calais* (1914): when six volunteers are called for to be delivered up to King Edward, seven come forward; one too many means that one may hope to survive; the sacrifice for the city would thus be a gamble; but one of the seven slays himself to end the conflict. He is the new man who is born: he who readily sacrifices himself for others. The play is notable for the chiselled majesty of its language; it is as monumental and rugged in words as Rodin's group is in bronze. *Europa: Spiel und Tanz* (1915) is a skit on the aesthetic effeminacy of modern times. In *Von Morgens bis Mitternachts* (1916) Kaiser pursues his idea that industrial man is an automaton: a bank-clerk turned by routine into a calculating machine runs out into life – with 60,000 marks from the till; only to find, between morn and midnight, that money buys nothing worth having. *Der Zentaur* (1916) shows the influence on Kaiser of Sternheim's satirical comedies. A grammar-school master is engaged, and his *fiancée* is, by the terms of grand-mamma's will, to forfeit the fortune bequeathed to her unless within the space of one year there is a child. But the schoolmaster has always lived a model life, and has no idea whether he will be able to; so he tries himself out on a loose woman, gets the reputation of being a centaur, and loses *fiancée* and post. *Koralle* (1917) is a striking presentation of life as a flight from starvation; and millionaires are simply those who flee farthest; hence they are the most abject cowards. That they trample under foot those who cannot or do not flee does not stay their feet. Poverty is contrasted with wealth in the very effective second act, the scene of which is on the deck of the millionaire's luxurious yacht: below the tourists lolling in the tropic heat are the stokers in the hold: and the two worlds are separated only by thin planks. (We find this *motif* in Freiligrath's poem *Von unten auf.*) The son and the daughter of the millionaire – himself the son of a worker cast off when too old to slave – turn Socialist; and the millionaire's heartless theories beat helplessly against the armoured convictions of their new humanitarianism. In his despair the millionaire listens to his secretary, who, a clergyman's son, comparing the paradise of his own childhood with the pampered upbringing of the millionaire's son, states the law that experience proves: '*Vater und Sohn streben von-einander weg. Es ist immer ein Kampf um Leben und Tod.*' The millionaire has worked for another law: that the son is the inner double (*Doppelgänger*) of the father. But to the son the paradise prepared for him is hell, because he has looked below himself, and the only double the father has is an outer double: his secretary. For secretary and millionaire are each the living image of the other, and the secretary's identity has to be marked by a coral on his watch-chain. As the secretary unfolds the happiness of his youth (though he, too, had followed the law and rebelled, to strike out a career for himself) the millionaire realizes that wealth is stored within, in recollections that the experiences of manhood may ruffle but only as the wind stirs the sea, and he takes up the revolver with which his son had intended to kill him, shoots the secretary, puts the coral on his own watch-chain, is condemned for the murder of himself, but is happy: 'I have got back to the paradise behind us,'

MGL N *

he says; 'I have smashed the gate open, and now I stand in the softest meadow green. Over me streams the blue of heaven.' Here again *Glück* rhymes with *zurück* as in the village idylls of Voss and his followers. In the two parts of *Gas* (*Gas I*, 1918; *Gas II*, 1920) Kaiser deals with the problem of the mechanization of humanity by factory labour; the son of the millionaire who in *Koralle* is executed for murder tries to liberate these mechanized slaves, and fails lamentably: they will not relinquish, for healthy natural labour amid the fruit and flowers of the field, the quick gain that machines bring them. They are not even frightened by an explosion that wrecks the factory, although they are aware that it may be repeated. The factory hand is not to be turned into the 'new man'; in his case it is too late for *Wandlung*. Faultlessly symmetrical and gruesome in its Wellsian glare of futuristic science is *Gas II*, which ends with the extinction of all and everything by a pellet of poison gas. Kaiser managed to remain in Germany during the Nazi period – but silenced and almost starving – until just before the outbreak of the war he found a refuge in Switzerland. Here he wrote thirteen plays, the most successful of which was *Der Soldat Tanaka* (1940); the hero is a Japanese private soldier who suddenly realizes what a horrible business soldiering is. Thereafter Kaiser turned, like Gerhart Hauptmann in his final stage, to Greek themes; his Hellenic trilogy (1948) *Zweimal Amphitryon, Pygmalion,* and *Bellerophon* is in iambic verse. It might be shown that the 'classical' form in these Greek dramas is negatived by an absolutely modern and brutal form of realism which is, or is not, compensated for by Kaiser's specific symbolism or playing with ideas ('*Denkspielerei*'), whereas Hauptmann comes nearer to the traditional form of Greek drama on (more or less) the Greek pattern. The trilogy might actually be classed as anti-myth; for not only is a great part of the action reduced to crass reality by the reflection that provides the modern symbol, but the gods and goddesses themselves are, in greater or less degree, comic. The other dramas of Kaiser show the same flair for piquant plots (*Der Brand im Opernhaus*, 1919; *Hölle, Weg, Erde,* 1919 – one of the great successes of expressionist staging; *Der gerettete Alkibiades,* 1920; *Die Flucht nach Venedig,* 1923 – de Musset and George Sand). Kaiser tried his hand at a novel with *Es ist genug* (1932): the theme is a father's prepared plan of incest with his own daughter.

ERNST TOLLER (1893-1939) pairs with Kaiser as a Communistic

dramatist; but while Kaiser would lift up the proletariat and liberate them from the deformation of routine labour, Toller descends to them wholeheartedly and identifies himself with their aims and hatreds; where Kaiser uses politics for the drama, Toller uses the drama for politics. In *Die Wandlung* (1919) a soldier, who by patriotism has earned the respect of his fellow-countrymen, casts off all outward honour to be born again as pure man calling, in love, his brothers to revolution. *Masse Mensch* (1920) discusses the question whether murder in the cause of progress is to be tolerated or not; the State that murdered by means of generals was Moloch, and so are the masses if they murder for the sake of a cause. In *Die Maschinenstürmer* (1922) the mass of the workers are the collectivist hero. The revolutionary propaganda is taken back to the Luddite riots in England; it proclaims Kaiser's doctrine that machinery makes men automatons and destroys the soul. *Der deutsche Hinkemann* (1923) is bitter with disillusionment; a war veteran returns, with his virility shot away, to his wife. *Feuer aus den Kesseln* (1930) dramatizes the revolt of the sailors at Kiel which was the beginning of the end of the War. In 1919 Toller was imprisoned for his share in Kurt Eisner's *coup d'état* in Munich, and during his incarceration he wrote his poem *Das Schwalbenbuch* (1923): a pair of swallows make their nest in his cell, and he describes their summer life. In *I was a German* (1934), written as a political exile in English, and in *Eine Jugend in Deutschland* (1934), Toller tells his own story. He hanged himself, as a refugee, in New York in 1939.

The Communism in the plays of Toller and other *Aktivisten* is interesting in its revelation of the mentality produced by the collapse of the militaristic system in 1918. The war at sea found its dramatist in REINHARD GOERING (1887-1936); the action of his *Seeschlacht* (1917) takes place in the turret of a cruiser before and after the Battle of Jutland; the conflict is between duty and revolution; the seven sailors fire the guns rather than rebel, because it is easier to obey, but the ideas of mutiny are not so much political as bound up with the question of intense individual life calling away from an impersonal fate that rolls its slaves round and round as cogs in a grinding wheel. The action of *Scapa Flow* (1919) is before and after the sinking of the surrendered German fleet.

The war on land finds its most lyrical expression in the verse plays of FRITZ VON UNRUH (1885-). He had begun, while serving as a Prussian officer, with two tragedies, *Offiziere* (1912) and *Louis*

Ferdinand, Prinz von Preussen (1913), both influenced by Heinrich von Kleist; both have actually the same problem as Kleist's *Der Prinz von Homburg* – whether an officer is entitled to act contrary to his instructions, even when success is achieved by insubordination. The experience of the War turned von Unruh into a pacifist. The revulsion from war which was to become a general feature of German literature began as early as 1914 with his dramatic poem, written in the field, *Vor der Entscheidung* (published 1919). The prose epic *Opfergang*, written during the fight for Verdun in 1916, was published in 1918. *Ein Geschlecht* (1917), a verse drama, is a phantasmagoria of orgiastic passions let loose by war: there is a tragic mother two of whose sons have been condemned to death, one for cowardice and the other for violating women (he cannot conceive why the individual in war should not have the same right to cut through law that the State has); he even rages with incestuous desire for his sister, who feels the same flame. Sister and brother curse their mother, in whom they see merely a tool of the State producing sacrifices for the State. In the sequel, *Platz* (1920), the restoration of order is shown to depend on the victory of expressionistic ethics: humanity must turn away from mechanized civilization and find salvation in the love of all for all. *Stürme* (1923) continues Unruh's fight for his concepts of a new ethical doctrine which grants freedom of the will, while *Heinrich von Andernach* (1925), a *Festspiel* written for the celebration of the millennium of the Rhineland, calls for peace among the nations. In *Bonaparte* (1927) the proclamation of Napoleon as Emperor is stultified by his judicial murder of the Duc d'Enghien. In Unruh's Renaissance novel *Die Heilige* (1951) Catherine of Siena, determined to save the soul of an atheist, feels an inrush of earthly love in his presence; 'this is the grave', he tells her in her cell; 'the bride of Christ must choose between two bridegrooms, between the call of the senses and that of mystic devotion to an idea.' The novel is starred with a motto from Balzac: 'Facts are nothing. They do not exist. Nothing remains to us but ideas.' Thus in Unruh's work generally, crude and violent as it may seem, the driving force is the mysticism of ideas mightier than law and custom. This is the tenor too of the somewhat grotesquely handled novel *Fürchtet nichts* (1952), which plays round the *accouchement* of the court goat at St Petersburg.

The dramas of the Viennese writer ANTON WILDGANS (1881-1932), who for a time, after experience as a judge, was director of the Burgtheater, evolve from the hectic naturalism of his first two plays, *In Ewigkeit, Amen* (1913), in which his knowledge of law-court procedure comes to the fore, and *Armut* (1915) – an official is stricken with illness, his wife is embittered, the daughter talks of selling herself to the lodger, while the lyrically exalted son mouths a hymn to humanity – to what has been called *Halb-expressionismus* in *Dies Irae* (1919), another notorious handling of the eternal son-father conflict: the son shoots himself with a toy pistol because the father will not understand him. *Liebe* (1919) treats the pathetic dying down of the erotic urge in the married life of ageing couples. Wildgans had planned a trilogy of Biblical plays: *Kain* (1920), *Moses*, and *Jesus*, but only the first was com-pleted. More lasting probably will be his lyrical work: *Herbst-frühling* (1909), *Und hättet der Liebe nicht* (1911), *Die Sonette an Ead* (1913), *Österreichische Gedichte* (1915), *Mittag* (1917). There is a venturesome modernity of thought in some of the poems, often rawly expressed as in *Klimakterium, Dirnen*. He analyses his own sexuality in his *Sonette an Ead*. Ead is his name for the lover of his dreams: a poet, the argument runs, cannot be chained to hearth and wife (*Ihm ziemt zu rasen, | Wenn aus seinem Leib | Schwelende Schwüle nebelt zum Gehirne*), and so for him was created *die Dirne*, but not she who prowls for prey under the lamplight of towns, but the woman to whom God has given beauty and passion; and so she queens it over creative spirits. The Queen of all is she who comforted Christ on the Cross (*Hure und eines Heilands Trost*); and she is Lilith, Astaroth, Omphale, and Salome who, denied her desire, asked for the head of the prophet on a charger. Dreaming of the lover of his fevered dreams the poet asks: 'Am I faun or Pan?' As the cycle closes he knows that he has dreamt of her as a faun, but that now, purified by vision, he is Pan – and Poet. There is a light lift in the rhythm of the sonnets and a wealth of allusion and imagery. His *Dorfidylle* in somewhat clumsy, often flatly pro-saic hexameters, *Kirbisch oder der Gendarm, die Schande und das Glück* (1927) is generally rated higher than Gerhart Hauptmann's *Anna*. It is a village idyll which is the reverse of idyllic, as the full title indicates; actually it is not so much a negative counterpart of Goethe's *Hermann und Dorothea* as a symbol of Austria in the last decaying days of the old Austrian Empire; the gendarme who is the titular hero is typical of the self-indulgent guzzling Austrian who took things easy. *Musik der Kindheit* (1928) is a sketch of his boyhood and youth. It is completed by *Autobiographische Skizzen und Fragmente* in the sixth volume of his *Sämtliche Werke* (5 vols., 1930; 6 vols., 1948 ff.) and by *Ein Leben in Briefen* (1947).

To the group of activists centred round *Die Aktion* belonged Bert Brecht and Arnolt Bronnen. BERT(OLT) BRECHT (1898-1956), an Augsburg man, began with *Baal* (1922), the drama of a Wedekindian *Frauenverwüster*, and won his way through with *Trommeln in der Nacht* (1922): a returned soldier finds his wife living with another man. *Im Dickicht der Städte* (1924) is a cinematographic picture of Chicago with the glare of contrasts that is usual in films: a proletarian faces a yellow plutocrat, dingy attic alternates with Chinese hotel, Chinese bars, and all the thicket of Chicago. *Leben Eduards II. von England* (1924) is an adaptation, in collaboration with Lion Feuchtwanger, of Marlowe's tragedy. *Mann ist Mann* (1927) is a khaki comedy: an Irish packer goes out to buy a fish for his wife and reappears as a machine gunner of Kulkoa. *Die Dreigroschenoper* (1928) – a great success as drama, opera (set to music by Kurt Weill), and film – is basically an adaptation of Gay's *The Beggar's Opera* (1728), but is drastically reshaped to a Marxist exposure of the capitalistic society of today, and, with its songs distilled from Villon and Kipling, parodies heroic opera. *Dreigroschenroman* (1934) is a variation by way of a novel. This genre of *epische Oper*, as Brecht terms his innovation, is continued in *Aufstieg und Fall der Stadt Mahagonny* (1929), which satirizes the barbarism and decked up culture of our great cities; it was also set to music by Kurt Weill. Today Brecht is known as a poet committed heart and soul to Communist propaganda; typical of this is the very title of his play *Badener Lehrstück* (1929). The plays which directly follow are classified as *Lehrstücke*. In *Die Massnahme* (1931) we have what is now the stereotyped 'confession' of a Communist 'comrade' before he is executed. *Der Flug der Lindberghs* (1930) is a paean to man and the elements he conquers. *Die heilige Johanna der Schlachthöfe* (1932) in a final tableau parodies Schiller's *Die Jungfrau von Orleans*: a Salvation Army lassie perishes because she fails to convert the capitalists of Chicago. In 1933 Brecht exiled himself and in 1941 reached the United States by way of Vladivostok, where he joined company with other Communist *émigrés*. In 1948 he was back in Berlin. Several of the plays which follow are world-famous because they exemplify his principle of epic realism and what is considered his revolutionary stagecraft. This epic or narrative drama differs from the traditional *'Illusionstheater'* in the sense that there are pauses in the action, while the actor explains who he is and what he is doing; or an announcer addresses the audience through a loud speaker; that is, the action is accompanied by its interpretation to an audience who are thus freed from the illusion that it is the purpose of the traditional theatre to induce in minds too sleepy to pierce to the hard core of the reality that life everywhere and always is. Added to this is Brecht's doctrine of alienation: one incident is counteracted by another. Thus in *Mutter Courage* a Lutheran hymn is sung while a girl tries on a whore's hat; and thus religious solemnity is alienated by the actuality of life. Masks may be worn to counteract the illusion of the dialogue, and there are interludes of songs and music which symbolize the inner sense of the action. Brecht has interpreted his technique in essays labelled *Versuche*, issued as numbered *Hefte*. Much of his sensational success he owed to his inventiveness as a play-producer; his company *Berliner Ensemble* are recognized as first-rate even by critics who are not swept off their feet. His great help was his wife Helene Weigel, who as a rule plays the leading character. The first of the post-exile plays is *Der gute Mensch von Sezuan* (1942). Three gods set out in quest of one good human being; unless they find one the world is to be destroyed; at last they find a Chinese prostitute, Shen Te, who is good and kind; they set her up in a little tobacco shop, where she is cheated by her customers until she develops a second self in the person of a hard-hearted wicked cousin whom she impersonates; he makes short work of the spongers, but he is brought to trial for murdering Shen Te, who has disappeared; the gods return to judge this *alter ego*, but give it up as hopeless and return to Heaven, leaving the world to its wickedness. Brecht's best known work is *Mutter Courage und ihre Kinder* (1941), set to music by Paul Dessau. The period is the Thirty Years War. The twelve *'Bilder'*, which owe something to Grimmelshausen's *Simplizissimus*, show an old woman, a camp follower, trudging with her mobile canteen in the wake of the armies to snatch a bare living, the result being that in the end she loses her sons one by one and her daughter; but still she carries on courageously and still sings her ribald songs, for she has to live on the profits of the filth and foulness of war. Mother Courage has good things to say: battles are won by good generals, not by brave soldiers; a defeat does not mean destruction

– the dog may die, but the fleas live on. There is no intention of glorifying Mother Courage as 'heroic'; she is just as she is seen, greedy of the gain she can snatch, foul-mouthed, fighting to the last – for this is the Hell we know life is. In *Galileo Galilei* (1942) the astronomer formally abjures his discoveries at the bidding of Church and Inquisition as a price to be paid for being allowed to prolong his life with its creature comforts; he is guilty of that passive acceptance of tyranny which enables tyrants to keep their power. But the play ends on a note of confidence – *eppur si muove.* *Der kaukasische Kreidekreis* (1947), also set to music by Paul Dessau, is based on an old Chinese play[1]: a rich, heartless mother abandons her baby, which is rescued by a servant girl, to whom it is adjudged by the Chinese test of the chalk circle which reminds one of the judgment of Solomon. *Herr Puntila und sein Knecht* (1948) has a fine setting in the lakes and woods of Finland; it shows the unbridgable gap between a servant and his master, who is only human when he is drunk. As a lyric poet Brecht, influenced to begin with by Rimbaud and Villon, gave new life to the old ribald *Bänkellied* in his *Hauspostille* (1927) and *Lieder, Gedichte, Chöre* (1934). *Hundert Gedichte* (1950; poems 1918-50) and *Gedichte und Lieder* (1956) are selections.

ARNOLT BRONNEN (1895-1944; born in Vienna) wrote the most *awful* son-father tragedy, *Vatermord* (1920): the son stabs his father when the latter breaks into the bedroom where his mother, naked, is trying to seduce him. In *Anarchie in Sillian* (1924) there is an industrial strike and the nightmare of machinery. *Katalaunische Schlacht* (1924) has one terrific scene in the (comparatively speaking) concrete comfort of a trench in the deafening din of drum-fire: the brother of the commanding officer comes with his batman – a woman dressed as a soldier; the commanding officer sends his brother to certain death, and takes the woman himself; after the war the soldiers who have known of this act pursue the officer through the hell of the inflation, hound him to death, and fight for the woman themselves. There is in Bronnen's plays a wild haste and scurry and the sensationalism of the cinema: his aim is to quicken drama to the rushed pace of contemporary life; and he is more cinematographic in his plays than in his novel of film life, *Film und Leben Barbara la Marr* (1928).

'Explosive diction' or frantic expressionism runs through the

[1] See p. 363.

poems and plays of OSKAR KOKOSCHKA (1886- ; a Czech by descent);
in his plays (*Mörder, Hoffnung der Frauen*, 1907; *Die träumenden
Knaben*, 1908; *Der brennende Dornbusch*, 1911; *Hiob*, 1917; *Vier
Dramen*, 1919; *Der weisse Tiertöter*, 1920; *Der gefesselte Kolumbus*,
1921) the problem is that of 'senseless desire from horror to horror,
insatiable circling in empty space' caused by the splitting of humanity into sexes. Kokoschka belongs to that group of 'Bolshevized
painters' (including Otto Dix and Franz Marc) whose works were
in August, 1937, by official decree ignominiously cast forth from
all German art galleries, and who were forbidden to exercise their
craft; and the qualities of his painting – distortion used to reveal
the innermost psychological instincts, writhing lines glinting in
splashed colour – warp and obscure his literary work in still
greater measure. He is now a naturalized Briton.

ERNST BARLACH (1870-1938) was a famous sculptor (mostly in
wood), and the characters of his dramas (*Der tote Tag*, 1912; *Der
arme Vetter*, 1918; *Die echten Sedemunds*, 1920; *Der Findling*, 1922;
Die Sündflut, 1924) are like figures massively sculptured, awkward
and hampered because left in the rough, but lifted as though by
the wind or the breath of God in their folds; they belong to two
worlds, earth-bound as 'creatures of this side' but as 'creatures of
the other side' hearing 'the rustling of the blood of a higher life
behind the ship's planks of everyday custom'; they are thus ghosts,
but in the flesh. Barlach attempts to interweave – with the delicacy,
the cruelty, and the intricacy of a spider's web – the unseen with
the seen in a new creation of myth. In *Der tote Tag* the problem of
a mother's relations to her son is viewed from a totally different
angle from that of Hesse in *Demian*: a very physical mother and a
son in whom spirituality stirs live in the great hall of a house with
a cellar attached; the son's father is a god ('all sons have their best
blood from an invisible father'); the mother wishes to keep her
son tied to her apron-strings, by cellar and kitchen and broom;
she would fain have him 'a suckling grown up' (Herzeloyde in
the same way would have prisoned Parzival to the warmth of her
breast, if angels from afar had not lured him forth); '*Sohneszukunft*',
says the mother in Barlach's play, '*ist Muttervergangenheit*'; and
when the invisible father sends a magic steed (*Sonnenross*) to spirit
the lad into radiance she stabs it to death in the night; for, she
says, 'the son who rides forth on a steed comes back hobbling on
a beggar's staff' – as her long-vanished husband does during the

action of the play, blind with gazing on misery and with, for sole possession, a stone which symbolizes sorrow; 'a man', he says, 'is he who takes up the sorrow of others'. Sonnenross being slain, no dawn comes, but dense darkness swathes all – the 'dead day' of home and cradling mother love. Materialism has put out the light of idealism. In *Die Sündflut* Noah, a holy man, faces Calan, the embodiment of evil, who is drowned; but the two antagonists are equally near to God; with Barlach as with Kafka (p. 459) evil is part of good; evil is created by God, and itself creates; Jehovah himself is created by those he creates. The Nazis branded Barlach as degenerate ('*als Untermensch und minderrassig*'), as one '*besessen vom Dämon der ostisch-slawischen Menschheitsgruppe*', and his sculptures in public places were removed or destroyed. It is true that a two months' stay in Russia in 1907 had given him, as he says, his idea of limitless space in which human shapes – peasants, shepherds, beggars – stand out firmly chiselled and crystallized (he had the same experience as Rilke); hence in his work he tries to give a conception of '*das Menschliche*' firmly fixed in the sweeping vast of infinity. His bent to mystical configuration was strengthened by a visit to Italy in 1909, and by his intense study of Theodor Däubler's mythological poetry, by the radiance shining down from Däubler's land of stars on his own vale of tribulation here below. A revival and intensification of interest in Barlach's work, sculpture and drama, dates from 1945; it coincides with the vogue of existentialism and is partly to be explained by this. As a sculptor outward form was nothing to him; what he seeks to show forth is the soul beneath the surface; and man as a unity of body and soul lives, not in an environment of ideal beauty, but in a world mysteriously moved by the dark forces of fate. Hence, he says, the Russian, the Asiatic type, who can only be understood mystically, is more related to his own nature than his contemporaries covered by the folds of culture. '*Ich sah am Menschen das Verdammte, gleichsam Verhexte, aber auch das Ur-Wesenhafte*'. The purpose of life, he affirms, is to fight the battle of life against darkness; and in his dramas this battle of two forces is expressed, not so much in the clash of argument, reproof and retort, as in the character's communing with his inner self. But although his dramas matter for their meaning, he protests against their being acted too solemnly as mysteries; he wishes the humour that is an essential part of their build-up ('*es ist ein Berg Humor in der Sündflut*') to be given full scope, and he scoffs at the catchword '*barlachsche Plastik*'. Even the patriarch Noah in *Die Sündflut* is intended to be congenitally comic; his stage figure is to be in the nature of a landed proprietor walking heavily with a stick. Involved symbols of mysticism still wreathe the visionary shapes and the dream-like action of his later plays. *Der Graf von Ratzeburg* (1951) is the mystical story of a feudal lord who sets out to seek God; the lesson of it, '*ich habe keinen Gott, Gott hat mich*', comes close to Kafka's teaching. There is marked originality of tone and treatment in his autobiography, *Ein selbsterzähltes Leben* (1928), and there are autobiographical threads and snatches in the posthumously published novels *Seespeck* (1948) and *Der gestohlene Mond* (1948). His posthumous *Fragmente aus sehr früher Zeit* (1939) consist of sketches and miniature essays. Essential for comprehension of man and artist are his letters: *Aus meinen Briefen* (1947) and *Barlach: Leben und Werk in seinen Briefen* (1952).

Obviously these new dramatists make a desperate attempt to expand the scope of drama. The plays of HANS HENNY JAHNN (1894-) have to be considered because, revolting as they often are, they are symptomatic. Because of the sexual extravagances of his themes Jahnn has earned the title of *Prophet der Unzucht*. His first plays illustrate his declared conviction that 'man is capable of anything'. The hero of his *Pastor Ephraim Magnus* (1919) is a young clergyman whose nature as a modern man is made by brute instinct; he seeks God by way of torture and throttles his sister because of her incestuous love for him. Incest is again the theme of *Der gestohlene Gott* (1923), and abnormal sex relations are the subject of *Der Arzt, sein Weib, sein Sohn* (1922). In *Die Krönung Richards III* (1921) Richard murders in the exasperation of his rage at the decay of his own body, and the Dowager Queen Elizabeth murders the boys she has enjoyed. His *Medea* (1926) has the eyes torn out of a messenger who comes with bad news. Discussion of Jahnn flared up again when in 1948 *Armut, Reichtum, Mensch und Tier*, written in 1934, was performed: a Norwegian farmer is rent by his mystic love for a horse and is tragically caught between two women. In *Thomas Chatterton* (1955) he drives in the opposite direction from Ernst Penzoldt's pathetic Novelle *Der arme Chatterton*: in Jahnn's tragedy Chatterton fights for the prerogatives of his genius, and even if he resorts to cheating the cause of this is his inborn cleverness; he fights fate with the strength of his will; he is beaten, but that is the fate of genius. The defence of Jahnn, who is an ultra-respectable organ-builder in Hamburg, is that he is trying to pierce to the very roots of Freudian complexes; and if he is given credit for experimental psychiatry he at least deserves consideration by the side of Ernst Barlach. There is experimentation in his novel *Perrudja* (2 vols., 1929), a pioneer attempt in the manner of James Joyce's *Ulysses*, and still more in the trilogy of novels *Fluss ohne Ufer*, written in the Danish island of Bornholm, where Jahnn had found asylum during the Hitler terror; he had a farm there, and bred horses. The outward structure is that of grand opera: Part 1, *Das Holzschiff* (1937) is the overture; Part II, *Die Niederschrift des Gustav Anias Horn* (Vol. I, 1949; Vol. II, 1950) is the body of the work; Part III, *Epilog* (1952) is the finale.[1] The inner action runs on in themes, strophes, fugues, motifs, accords, rhythms. Music, Jahnn says, took its build-up from poetry; the novel is entitled to take back what music took. In *Das Holzschiff* a three-master sails away on a mysterious voyage; the captain's daughter, Ellena, disappears mysteriously. All on board are in danger, for Unseen Powers are at the helm; this is life on the shoreless river. The crew mutiny; the ship is wrecked, and sinks into the deeps taking its mystery with it. These mysteries are revealed in Part II. Ellena has been murdered by one of the sailors, Tutein, who for twenty years is swept about the world in close intimacy with the girl's betrothed, Anias Horn. The narration of their experiences in the ports of South America, in the coast lands of Africa, and in the lovely regions of Norway wallows in atrocious perversions and vices, which rise continuously like islands from this shoreless river of life. But the magic of art and music begin to weave into the tale and in the Epilogue (the finale, a *rondo, coro, minuetto*) the sense and texture of the complex weft is disentangled, while prospects open out which reflect Jahnn's central vision as it pierces through the overhanging gloom to primeval causes, which, being in the blood, make evil urges innocent. *Fluss ohne Ufer* with its wide sweep must be ranged with those monumental novel trilogies of recent years which have opened out new vistas (pp. 308, 355, 369). The difficulty for the reader is that Jahnn's trio is fitted not merely to musical technique but also to mathematical propositions. The physicist, Jahnn reminds us, proclaims that Time is an unknown dimension. What Time holds is Fate, and nothing is constant except Fate. And so Fate, being constant, cannot be changed by the Past into the

[1] Jahnn's scheme may be based on Wagner's *Ring*.

THE DRAMA OF EXPRESSIONISM 405

Future. The Present does not exist except as an integral of Time. What *Fluss ohne Ufer* describes is the inversion of Time.

The dramatic work of FERDINAND BRUCKNER (1891-1958) – like Wildgans and Arnolt Bronnen, Viennese by birth – marks the beginning of the new movement known as *die Neue Sachlichkeit* (p. 422)[1]; the term denotes an intention to get back to things as they are and to pathology that a physician might recognize as at least problematically possible. The writers of this 'New Factuality' or 'New Functionalism' do indeed aim at atomistic exactitude, but the reality which their psychic probing seeks may be trammelled in the inmost depths of consciousness. Sexual crises and perversions form the staple of Bruckner's *Krankheit der Jugend* (1926); in *Die Verbrecher* (1928) he lights up the misery of a block of flats which symbolize God's house of many chambers. His experimenting interested London audiences when his *Elisabeth von England* (1930) was produced at the Cambridge Theatre in 1931; the love element is weak (the Essex-Elizabeth motif discussed by Lessing still baffles all who attempt it), and the documentation is no doubt that of Strachey, but the doubling of the action – one side of a cathedral in London and the other in Spain, with the action alternating or synchronizing, Protestants and Catholics praying to one (? ironic) God – had at least the effect of novelty. Of Bruckner's later plays *Timon* (1932) is gloomed by the pessimism of Shakespeare's *Timon of Athens*; *Die Marquise von O.* dramatizes Kleist's Novelle; in *Napoleon I* (1936) the Emperor philanders with women who are intellectually his superiors; in *Heroische Komödie* (1938) Madame de Staël fights for freedom in love and elsewhere. His *Pyrrhus und Andromache* (1952) weds the matter of Euripides to the form of Racine; *Früchte des Nichts* (produced 1952), which shows forth the hopelessness of youth at the end of the Second World War, completes a series united in the volume *Jugend zweier Kriege* (1947); here *Krankheit der Jugend* and *Die Verbrecher* are followed by *Die Rassen* (1933), the theme of which is the mental conflict of a student who loves a Jewish girl. In *Der Kampf mit dem Engel* (1942) and *Der Tod einer Puppe* (1956) a chorus is introduced and there is some approach to T. S. Eliot's verse technique.

[1] The term was first used by Carl Sternheim as the sub-title of his comedy *Die Schule von Uznach oder Neue Sachlichkeit*, but whether in the sense of approval or satire is not clear.

27

CARL ZUCKMAYER (1896-) began with outrageous expressionist plays: *Kreuzweg* (1920) and *Pankraz erwacht oder die Hinterwäldler* (1925), the latter a play of the Wild West. In 1939 he found a refuge in the United States, where he ran a farm in Vermont Hill. In 1947 he returned to Germany. His comedy *Der fröhliche Weinberg* (1925) was awarded the Kleist prize because it was the first breakaway from the nebulosity of expressionism to life as it *might* be lived. From now on Zuckmayer ranks as a *gesundeter Expressionist*. The hero of *Schinderhannes* (1927) is a captain of robbers in the Rhineland in Napoleon's days; the left bank of the Rhine is occupied by the French, while on the right bank a German army is assembling. The doctrine is frankly soaked with the socialism of today; the real robbers are Church and State, while Schinderhannes takes nothing from the poor. In *Katharina Knie* (1928) we have a rope-dancer who is married by the landowner from whom she steals hay for her donkey. *Der Hauptmann von Köpenick* (1931) is a relentless exposure of Prussian militarism before the outbreak of the First World War; an out-of-work cobbler who has spent a good part of his life in prison steals a captain's uniform, walks into a town hall, arrests the mayor, and walks off with the civic cash-box. This breath-taking feat is only possible because the cobbler with miraculous ease drops dialect for the cultured German of the officer class. *Der Schelm von Bergen* (1934) varies a well known Rhineland legend; *Bellmann* (1938; in 1951 renamed *Ulla Winblad*) dramatizes the love-story of the Swedish poet. All these plays are put in the shade by *Des Teufels General* (1946), which throws a lurid light on conditions in Germany just before the United States came into the war. Zuckmayer had gone into exile in the belief that Hitler would be overthrown by the resistance movement in Germany, and in the play we see this resistance movement taking shape; aeroplanes are crashing because the workmen who produce them are using wrong alloys in the conviction that the only way to get rid of the Nazis is to lose the war; the ethical weakness of the idea is that good men who are not Nazis at heart are sacrificed. General Harras of the air force, who is not a member of the party, is under suspicion, and we see him coming to the conclusion that he has been the devil's general; to escape extinction in a concentration camp he takes the air in one of the new defective machines, crashes immediately, and is given a State funeral. *Der Gesang im Feuerofen* (1950) is in some sort a return to the ecstatic upsurge of expressionism. The furnace is occupied France; the song is the rising of the maquis against the occupying German troops. *Das kalte Licht* (1955) is up to date in the sense that the question raised is whether East or West should control atomic power, and there is a spy whose ideological convictions lead him to spy for Russia. The problem today is whether Zuckmayer is not rather a playwright with all the tricks of the trade at his fingers' ends than a dramatist proper. What cannot be missed is his abounding vitality, his verve and versatility. His wit is inexhaustible. He has a complete command of expression in all the dialects that are intelligible on the stage, and there is infinite fun in these dialects as he uses them. The action rarely flags, though in *Des Teufels General* the theme of Nazi devilment ('*Nationalität durch Bestialität*', as Grillparzer foresaw it in his epigram) is so exhaustively expounded that in the last act it is wearisome. Zuckmayer's immense reputation has been in a great measure won by his contemptuous disregard of restraint and decency. Most of what he has written has been filmed; in point of fact his best plays are more film-like than in the traditional sense dramatic; what we get is a loosely strung concatenation of scenes, and, it may be (as in *Des Teufels General*), a continuous debate or discussion. But the characterization is masterly. To say that Zuckmayer plays fast and loose with the established canons of drama would be merely captious criticism; for to a writer of Zuckmayer's type – and he represents a group – whatever was or is established is for that reason antiquated or obsolete. His qualities as a dramatist come out also in his fiction (*Der Bauer aus dem Taunus*, 1927; *Affenhochzeit*, 1932; *Liebesgeschichte*, 1934; *Salzware*, 1935; *Herr über Leben und Tod*, 1938; *Der Seelenbräu*, 1945). In *Herr über Leben und Tod*, for instance, nothing could be more finely concentrated and dramatically poised than the tension of the first part; but what follows the posing of the problem – whether a mentally and physically defective baby should be painlessly extinguished or allowed to live – is revoltingly sensational. As a lyric poet Zuckmayer is represented by *Der Baum* (1926), which is reprinted in *Die Gedichte* (1948). Autobiographical are *Pro Domo* (1938) and *Second Wind* (1940; in English only).

The revival of the historical drama begins with WOLFGANG GOETZ's (1885-) *Gneisenau* (1925); this was one of the great stage successes of the period. His *Kavaliere* (1930) handles the love story of Ludwig I, King of Bavaria, with the dancer Lola Montez.

Where Goetz attempts other than German history he falls off, as in *Robert Emmet* (1927) or *Kuckkuckseier* (1934), which pictures Shakespeare in country retirement in his old age. His great success after *Gneisenau* was *Der Ministerpräsident* (1936). The Prime Minister is apparently modelled on Bismarck. His son elopes, just as war is about to break out, with the Herzogin (there are no names, only titles), the daughter of the Prime Minister's most powerful enemy; the Herzogin admits that she throws herself at the man for political purposes. The play is essentially a *Pflichtdrama*; the son gives the woman up, because he cannot desert. The characterization is good; the dialogue is subtle, racy, and ultra-modern, and there is real wit, with effective contrast of characters. *Kampf ums Reich* (1939) portrays Fieldmarshal von Arnheimb as the pattern of a statesman during the Thirty Years War. Goetz has also written popular fiction. In *Reise ins Blaue* (1920) the British Government sends, at Napoleon's request, a bevy of girls to St. Helena to amuse the band of devotees still with him. *Das Gralswunder* (1926) is a comic story of the film world. He has also written critical work: *Du und die Literatur* (1951), and biographies: *Napoleon* (1926), *Goethe* (1938), *Mozart* (1941), *Schiller* (1944).

Though CURT GÖTZ (1888-), who lived for some time in Hollywood, is a namesake and almost of the same age as Wolfgang he is at the opposite end of dramatic creation. Curt's set purpose is to entertain, at whatever level, not to inculcate Prussian virtues. There is the lightest possible touch in the five grotesque sketches of *Nachtbeleuchtung* (1919) and in *Menagerie* (1920). There is a species of family relationship running from the comedy *Ingeborg* (1921) through the three one-act plays of *Die tote Tante* (1924) and the comedy *Das Haus in Montevideo* (1946). In *Dr. med. Hiob Prätorius* (1932) a doctor is on the track of the bacillus responsible for silliness. There is the same irresponsible sensationalism in the 'legend' *Tatjana* (1949) and his erotic novel *Die Tote von Beverly Hills* (1951).

No one in the Vienna of today would doubt for a moment that FRANZ THEODOR CSOKOR (1885-; pronounce Tschokor) is in the front rank of the writers of the present generation. It is more or less a *cliché* that as a dramatist he counts as equal with Zuckmayer and Bert Brecht, principally because his dramas are built up round the social and political problems of today. He described his war experiences in two books: *Als Zivilist im polnischen Krieg* (1939) and *Als Zivilist im Balkankrieg* (1947). As a narrative prose writer he is here at his best. Throughout the story the narrator is hemmed in by perils which have the excitement of romantic fiction; again and again he escapes by the skin of his teeth from Hitler's gangs, and in the last stage of the second book, when he is under the supervision of the kindlier or more careless Italians in his mountainous and densely wooded Dalmatian island he is in danger from the revolutionaries of the *macchia* (the Serbian maquis). The dramas by which he is best judged at the moment are the three collected as *Europäische Trilogie* (1952). The first play of the trilogy, *3. November, 1918* (1936) throws a glaring light on Austrian trends and moods at the end of the First World War. The characters are sharply individualized; they are symbols, but they are tangibly alive and real, and directly moved, each in his different way, by the tragic break-up of the Habsburg monarchy after defeat, but also under the shock of regionalist and socialistic ideology. In this clear and convincing exposition of revolutionary doctrines and of a new orientation of ideas *3. November, 1918* follows up Csokor's play *Gesellschaft der Menschenrechte* (1929), in which he portrays Georg Büchner as a revolutionary, for this too lights up the dying down of mouldy political beliefs and the onrush of a new humanitarian faith. Nothing could be more striking than this logical polarity in Csokor's thinking: he remains a Catholic, a conservative, and even a royalist, but in the clash of convictions from which he shapes his drama there is equal strength of argument on each side. It was inevitable that post-war drama should find themes in the resistance movements in occupied territory. Of these plays the most famous are Zuckmayer's *Der Gesang im Feuerofen* and the second play of *Europäische Trilogie*, Csokor's *Besetztes Gebiet* (1930), the scene of which is a town in the Ruhr. Here the polarity of parties is vividly rendered: the hero is the mayor, who is convinced that the wisest course for Germany is to submit and to atone for the injuries done in a war which must be recognized as brutal aggression. He is faced by a group of five partisans (*Freischärler*), whose aim is to inflict the greatest possible damage by clandestine attacks on the occupying French forces. *Der verlorene Sohn* (1946), the third play of the group, was originally written in blank verse, and for the best part this remains, though printed as prose; what results is a singsong dialogue which gives an air of unreality to the crass happenings, though it more or less fits the underlying approximation of part of it to the story of Bethlehem at Christmas. The action again passes in occupied territory; the prodigal son, Stipe, is away fighting with the insurgents in the maquis; he is the youngest of three brothers. The time is Christmas Eve and Christmas Day; and in the opening scene the Christmas candles are lit and the festive table laid, with a vacant seat for any guest who may come. Will it be Stipe? There is also religious symbolism which points forward to the mysticism of the following two plays; Marja (Mary), the wife of one of the brothers, gives birth to a son in the stable while the house is burning, and as the play ends she sets out, supported by Stipe, who has returned, to join the maquis (once again, by way of allusion, the flight into Egypt). The two following plays, *Pilatus* (1949) and *Caesars Witwe* (1953) together with *Kalypso* (1942) are published together under the title *Olymp und Golgotha. Trilogie einer Weltwende* (1954), to indicate that the motive which is common to all three, a crisis in the worship of gods or of a god, signifies a more revolutionary change in the seventy-seven years from the murder of Caesar to Golgotha than that between 1914 and 1945 which motivates the European trilogy. Of the other plays *Die Weibermühle* (1931) continues the old Viennese *Zauberstück*; *Gottes General* (1939) with its illumination of the religious experiences of Ignatius de Loyola lays bare also Csokor's own religious faith. The *Doppelbödigkeit* which is somewhat glaringly on the surface in the *Weltwende* plays makes up the action of the novel *Der Schlüssel zum Abgrund* (1955). It falls into twelve chapters with twelve interludes (*Intermezzi*) intervening; each interlude lights up something which is happening elsewhere at the same time as the apparently unrelated event narrated in the foregoing chapter, the idea being '*dass sich kein Geschehen der Welt ohne zeitverhaftete Beziehung zur gesamten geistesgeschichtlichen Lage vollzieht*'. Here we have an attempt to expand and deepen the range of the modern novel. The raw event is the symptom of mental or spiritual stirrings which occur elsewhere, which change the face of the world, and which recur through the space of time; thus, while the Anabaptists lash out in Münster, Henry VIII sends Anne Boleyn to the scaffold, because she does not bear him a son – but her daughter will be England's greatest monarch; Paracelsus discovers a new interpretation of illness as proceeding from the mind – a concept related ('*zeitverhaftet*') to what we now call psychoanalysis; the Anabaptists and the Lutherans have their fling, but Ignatius de Loyola allots the earth to his Society of Jesus. Csokor's lyric verse (*Die Gewalten*, 1912; *Der Dolch und die Wunde*, 1918; *Das schwarze Schiff*, 1944) is available in a collected edition, *Immer ist Anfang* (1951). The most important section is *Historische Balladen*; by their choice of theme and their illumination of character these ballads prove that Csokor is first and foremost a dramatist; *Kain* is the murderer who cannot be anything else, and there is a modern Freudian interpretation of old themes in such poems as *David und Abisag* (how different from Rilke's poem!), *König Salomon verfällt dem Weibe*, while *Karl Stuarts Todesgesang* reflects Csokor's determined devotion to the royal house of his own land. The exploration of sex feeling gives a morbid thrill to the lyrics generally; the loveliest is perhaps *Grabmal eines Poeten* with the lurid light it sheds on Baudelaire's inspiration.

HANS JOSÉ REHFISCH (1891-) was at one time dubbed '*der Sudermann der neuen Dramatiker*'. During the Second World War he was a lecturer in sociology in New York and edited the emigrants' journal *In Tirannos*. He began with the neo-romantic drama *Die goldenen Waffen* (1913), the theme of which is the fight of Ajax with Ulysses for the golden weapons of Achilles. Plays which followed were *Die Heimkehr* (1918); *Das Paradies* (1919); and *Deukalion* (1921), in which the hero with his wife survives the Deluge. A great success was *Chauffeur Martin* (1921), the hero of which revolts against God because in complete innocence he has run over a man. The comedy *Die Erziehung durch Kolibri* (1921) was in 1924 rechristened *Die Libelle*. The tragi-comedy *Wer weint um Juckenack?* (1924) had international success. Typical of Rehfisch's touch on the pulse of theatre-goers is *Hände weg von Helena* (1951); the heroine is highly tickled by attempts at artificial insemination. More solid than the ruck of these plays and based on historical study is the novel *Die Hexen von Paris* (1951), the story of the Marquise de Montespan.

BERNT VON HEISELER (1907-), the son of the Russian born dramatist and translator of Puschkin Henry von Heiseler (1875-1928), began with one-act plays which are collected in *Kleines Theater* (1940). His first full drama, *Schill* (1934), presents the Prussian patriot Ferdinand von Schill, who raised a rebellion against Napoleon. *Das laute Geheimnis* (1931) uses motifs of Calderon, while *Des Königs Schatten* (1939) is modelled on one of Goldoni's plays. Von Heiseler was forbidden to publish after his tragedy *Cäsar* (1941) had shown open conflict between dictatorship and democracy resulting from the murder of Caesar by Brutus. *Philok tet* (1947), modelled on the drama of Sophocles, calls for truth even in politics. The very titles of some of von Heiseler's plays indicate that thematically he has recourse to Renaissance and neo-romantic material, which he may bring into relation with problems of today. A great effort is his *Hohenstaufentrilogie* (1948); the prelude is *Die Stunde vor Konstanz* (1939), and the centre piece *Kaiser Friedrich II.* (staged in 1951 as *Botschaft an den Kaiser*) is completed by *Der Gefangene*, with the death of Enzio. *Semiramis* (1943) harks back to the draft of a play by Calderon. In *Das Neu-beurer Krippenspiel* (1945), produced in aid of the restoration of the Frauenkirche at Munich, religions which differ in doctrine collaborate for a good cause. *Das Haus der Angst* (1950) satirizes existentialism: the princess imprisoned in Bluebeard's castle undergoes all the stages from *Daseinsangst* onward of this doctrine of today. Von Heiseler's unquestioning Christianity, which gives tone and substance to the pith of his plays, emerges too in his lyric poetry: *Wanderndes Hoffen* (1935) and *Spiegel im dunklen Wort* (1949; a selection). He has written biographies: *Stefan George* (1936), *Kleist* (1939); and in *Ahnung und Aussage* (1939) he interprets Kleist, Hebbel, Mörike, and poets of today. In fiction he has to his credit the short stories *Die Unverständigen* (1936) and *Erzählungen* (1943) and a novel of Tyrolese peasant life, *Die gute Welt* (1938).

It is a commonplace of present-day criticism to class FRITZ HOCHWÄLDER (1911-) as the successor of Georg Kaiser and to group him with Ferdinand Bruckner, Zuckmayer and Csokor as a dramatist who breaks new ground. His plays have been successfully produced all over the world. Born in Vienna, he was, after an elementary school education, a decorator's apprentice. In 1938 he fled to Zurich, where he still lives. Friends who knew his first attempts at play-writing lent him a wooden hut, and here at Ascona on the shores of Lake Maggiore, in utter isolation and living on soup-cubes, he completed *Das heilige Experiment* (1942), a play which adheres to the classical principle of the unities of place, time, and action. A striking feature is that there is no female character. The scene is in the office of the Provincial in the South American headquarters of the Society of Jesus in Buenos Aires. We have here a subject which in recent years has been used by writers in revolt against tyrants and the whole concept of dictatorship (pp. 488, 496), most notably in Reinhold Schneider's *Las Casas vor Karl dem Fünften.* What emerges is that the Spanish colonists used the *indios* as slaves in their plantations and that they treated them as beasts, objecting even to their learning Spanish, whereas the Jesuits who colonized Paraguay established there a Christian state which had all the features of a Utopia such as we see featured as a dream and ideal in the spate of recent Utopian novels. But the Argentinian colonists agitate in Spain and even in Rome against this enlightened system, and the dramatic conflict begins with well reasoned argumentation on both sides when the Provincial forces his old university friend the Visitator, who has been sent by the Spanish Government to take over the realm the Jesuits have created, to acknowledge that this Christian state has been founded and is benevolently ruled by right and reason, whereas the colonists who are up in arms against it and the Spanish government to whom they appeal have no plan except confiscation for their own profit. There is one of the dramatic surprises of which Hochwälder is past master when an Italian, one of several people who seem to appear on the scene with no specific purpose, reveals himself to the Provincial as an emissary appointed by the General of the Order to supplant him and to hand over Paraguay to the Spanish king. The Provincial is wounded and dies during the fighting that ends the action, and the last words are spoken by the Visitator, who carries out his instructions but knows they are unjust: 'We have achieved our object. The kingdom of God is the devil's.' The whole argument is an exposure of political and Christian policy as it was then – and as it is now. Utopia is impossible, because the principles that rule it are justice and charity. *Hôtel du Commerce* (1944) is labelled 'Komödie in 5 Akten nach Maupassants Novelle *Boule de suif*'. There is unity of place, but not of time; the action lasts three days. The wit throughout the comedy is pungent and the general tenor is withering contempt of social 'respectability'. *Hôtel du Commerce* has its place apart in Hochwälder's work in that for once in a way there is a love interest, though it is shadowy; and as regards the 'burning actuality' which is claimed for Hochwälder's plays it does not touch contemporary phases of revolt except in so far as it is a scathing attack on caste feeling. In Zurich Hochwälder came into contact with Georg Kaiser, who passed on to him the idea and the plan of *Der Flüchtling* (1945). As in Georg Kaiser's *Von Morgens bis Mitternachts* there is expressionistic *Namenlosigkeit*; we know the three characters solely as

Der Flüchtling, Die Frau, Der Grenzwächter. *Meier Helmbrecht* (1946) is a dramatization of the late Middle High German satirical verse tale (written about 1250) of the farmer's son who, with his head turned by the epics of knightly derring-do, and spoilt by a doting mother and sister, dons armour and sets out as a marauding knight (*Raubritter*) to plunder and ravage the countryside. Essentially Hochwälder's theme remains constant to his general purpose: helpless peasants are plundered and murdered and there is no redress. Hochwälder modestly labels his *Der öffentliche Ankläger* (1949) as *Schauspiel*. It is much more than that. It is a tragedy in the classical sense, with the three unities observed. The time is 1793, the '*année terrible*'; the scene throughout is the Conciergerie, from the windows of which the guillotine is visible; the action lasts through the day into the early hours of the morning. There is no love interest. There is a dominating woman, Theresia Tallien, who is said to be, and as the action proves she is, the directive force of what is an apology for a government. It is a species of fate tragedy; for the terror grinds like an automatic machine – *la machine infernale* – , and there is no escape for those on whom the shadow of doom is cast. In an interview with Fouquier-Tinville, the Public Prosecutor, who sends victims to the guillotine in great batches, it emerges that Theresia has good grounds for getting her husband Tallien, the official head of the government, dispatched in the usual summary way. All that is needed is the pretence of a trial in which Fouquier-Tinville makes out some case or other. It is arranged that the name of the victim shall be in a closed envelope, which is to be opened in court as a stunning climax at the end of the trial. The spectator or reader is convinced from what is said that this is to be the last victim of the Terror, and that afterwards Fouquier-Tinville will retire and a reign of peace begin. The Public Prosecutor makes a long speech, and when the fatal envelope is opened the name is – Fouquier-Tinville. He has pleaded brilliantly for his own condemnation. These are ingeniously contrived stage effects, and there is marvellous skill in the manoeuvring of the dramatic tension. But the sum and substance of the tragedy is the programmatic depiction of all the horrors of the Terror, all the more vivid because the scene is the Conciergerie – just Fouquier-Tinville's office with, sitting there, his submissive clerk and, piled on the shelves, the dossiers of those who have gone and who are listed for the guillotine. It is an incisive study of tyrants and their technique; and, though the period is distanced from today, no one can miss the dramatist's intention – this is what automatically happens wherever there is government by a dictator or dictators. If there is a fault it is that the tying of the knot is too mathematically contrived (*ausgeklügelt* is the best term), but nevertheless the picture is basically true – both in those desperate days and in these. In *Donadieu* (1953), skilfully spun out of Conrad Ferdinand Meyer's poem *Die Füsse im Feuer*, the course of the action proves once again that right is helpless. But in this play the very heart of the argument is that vengeance is wrong, even if the means to it work into the avenger's hands; for, as Judith says to her father, '*Mein ist die Rache, spricht der Herr*'. This dénouement seems to run counter to Hochwälder's constant theme that, in the long run, right is might, and that tyrants perish because, as history proves, the will to destroy them springs eternal in the minds of the oppressed who, in the nature of the case, are in the majority. *Die Herberge* (1956) is labelled '*Dramatische Legende in 3 Akten*'. This is vague; there is nothing legendary in the story; it is literally a story of our own days, but *Legende* does suggest that the action takes place in a half mythical *Märchenwelt*. It is rather a species of modernized mystery play, but to call it that would give the idea of religious moralizing, of which there is none. The craftsmanship is first-class; the spectator is held in suspense. Generally speaking, if appreciation of Hochwälder is to be tempered by criticism it must be that his plays – with the exception of *Hôtel du Commerce*, which is, however, of a lighter texture – are all of a piece; his motto is that of Schiller's *Die Räuber*: *In tirannos!* In his Jesuit play only the idea of service to mankind remains; his Huguenot play ends with the comfort – for believers – that the Lord will repay. For a writer so obsessed – but logically, not morbidly – with the political and social aspects of the world of today, it should not be surprising that he eliminates love interest – there is a flicker of it in *Hôtel du Commerce* and *Herberge* only. This sums up to the conclusion that his range is limited. Where he excels is in his contrivances of sudden surprises. His dénouements are motived either by mathematical ingenuity (as in *Der öffentliche Ankläger*) or by *Wandlung*. But *Wandlung*, if normal, is a slow maturing by the fruits of experience, whereas in Hochwälder's plays it results from a crescendo of incontrovertible logic. Actually, as in *Der Flüchtling* and *Herberge*, the conversion may be that which we have at a

Salvation Army penitent form; and, though dramatically effective, it may come close to *Effekthascherei*. Moreover, in great drama what moves us is the clash of characters and of passion, not the chemical action of logic. To this objection the answer is: but here we have a new type of drama. New also is Hochwälder's reversion to the classical type of drama with the three unities, from which he swerves only in *Hôtel du Commerce* and *Meier Helmbrecht*.

XIX

PHASES OF LYRIC POETRY

There is no essential discontinuity between the lyric poetry of the naturalist and expressionist periods and that of the preceding period. Even the experiments in verse or stanza form of Arno Holz, Mombert, and others conform to the basic laws of German versification: the longest Whitmanesque line or Nietzschean dithyramb and the shortest expressionist ejaculation are still a matter of lift and dip handled for emphasis. All difference is one of mood and spirit due to the poet's personality, and the newness of the verse in this sense is in the measure of the poet's greatness. It would not even be safe to say that traditional form is a criterion of mediocrity: Stefan George's verse technique, for instance, is on close analysis traditional, the ballad writers of necessity keep to the old form of the ballad, and the expressionist hymn or ode is still as much a matter of variation of length of line as of rhetorical afflatus. The themes of poetry, too, are essentially the same: they are merely different in atmosphere and interpretation. Certain of the old themes may be neglected as outworn; but what is more likely is the rejuvenation of an outworn theme by fitting it to the need of the day or even (as is the case with Stefan George and his group) by conjuring new meaning into the abrased diction and phrasing of the theme. Thus sexual love is transformed from sentiment and glamour to Freudian realism; the poetry of the town takes on the form of *Grossstadtpoesie*; the eternal yearning for the regeneration of the world is renewed as chiliasm, or is variously transformed as salvation by sexuality, or by self-sacrifice to the common good or to the State; and the quest for God becomes an obsession. Themes that older poets rarely touched are freely interpreted: incest, paederasty, Lesbian love, the rotting of dead bodies. So intensified is the interpretation of such themes that merely to sort and classify them is a fascinating study (*Motiv-*

geschichte, Motivik). And all this thematic multiplicity can be ranged under the three headings of (1) *Ichgehalt*, that interest in self which necessarily inspires the Nietzschean or decadent cult of personality; (2) *Weltgehalt*, the cosmic feeling of those poets (Dehmel, Mombert, George, etc.) who would have the individual strive upward to a lofty ideal derived from contemplation of the divine; (3) *Zeitgehalt* or *Tendenz*, the lyric creed of those who would reform the institutions of temporal earth, and reverse traditional notions of morality, and either overthrow or glorify the State.

The social revolt goes back to naturalism and develops from the downright accusations of *Armeleutepoesie* (Dehmel, Karl Henckell, etc.) to a more philosophic consideration of the lot of the masses as conditioned by the help (Gerhart Hauptmann's *Im Nachtzug*, Winckler, etc.) or the tyranny (Paul Zech, etc.) of machinery. The most vigorous expression of these two phases is in the verse of the working-men poets (*Arbeiterdichter*). These poets are not necessarily free-thinking Socialists: Karl Bröger, Heinrich Lersch and Jakob Kneip were Catholics. The themes which dominate in their work are: (1) life in workshop and factory; (2) the problem of machinery and the revolt against the reduction by capitalism of man to a machine; (3) the relations of the working man to society (*die arbeiterliche Lebensgestaltung*). But the handling of these themes is not as a rule personal: the poet speaks for his fellow-workmen; and the political party has the relation to his poetry that the university has to the work of academically trained writers: it gives the lines of approach and attack.

The eldest of the working-men poets was KARL BRÖGER (1886-1944), a builder's labourer in Nuremberg. Before the War he had published one volume: *Die singende Stadt*. The patriotic poem he wrote when the War came, *Bekenntnis*, made him famous; this lyric then appeared in his book of War poems, *Kamerad, als wir marschiert* (1916). Later verse volumes are *Flamme* (1920); *Hymnen und Balladen* (1924), *Deutschland* (1924). In his cycle of verse legends *Die vierzehn Nothelfer* he describes the misery of the post-War years, and in his autobiographical novel *Der Held im Schatten* (1919) he pleads for the raising of the intellectual standard of the working man's life. His novel *Guldenschuh* (1934) attempts a picture of Nuremberg in the Middle Ages.

There is a higher poetic level in the lyric work of HEINRICH LERSCH (1889-1936), a boiler-maker of München-Gladbach on the

Rhine. His experiences as a workman and as a vagabond through Germany and Italy provide the substance of his first book: *Abglanz des Lebens* (1914). Here and in *Mensch im Eisen* (1925) he stresses the torment of mechanical soulless labour and the poisoning of the working man's soul by capitalism and class prejudice. He, too, wrote an autobiographical novel, or actually a typical *Tatsachenroman, Hammerschläge* (1930); his novel *Die Pioniere von Eilenburg* (1934), a story of the beginning of the co-operative movement in Germany about 1850, pleads for self-help among the workers. In *Mut und Übermut* (1934) Lersch humorously tells of his vagabondage; in the short stories of *Im Pulsschlag der Maschinen* (1935) he states his creed: the machine does not take a man's soul, on the contrary the workman gives his soul to the machine. His last book of verse, *Mit brüderlicher Stimme* (1933), is dedicated '*im Sinne des Führers*' to the community, and is typical of the general absorption of the *Arbeiterdichter* who survived to 1933 in the Nazi movement.

Quite a different set of working-men poets are the *Werkleute auf Haus Nyland* (p. 370), though Lersch and Bröger were loosely associated with them for a time. Like Lersch, they are at home by Rhine and Ruhr, and their theme is the glorification of labour in all its phases as they knew it in the Rhenish industrial districts. But they are disciples of Dehmel, and as such they fling themselves into vigorous praise of life as it is. The three founders of the group were Josef Winckler (p. 369), Jakob Kneip, and Wilhelm Vershofen, and the first book of the school was a common effort, *Wir Drei* (1904). In their journal *Quadriga* appeared Winckler's *Eiserne Sonette* (1912), in which he sings the new man of the Iron Age. Winckler's *Der Rheinbagger* marries ancient Rhine myths to the new myth of modern industry. The most gifted of the *Quadriga-leute* is JAKOB KNEIP (1881–1958). The son of a Hunsrück farmer, he was intended for the Catholic priesthood; his life in the seminary and his desertion of it at the call of life he has described in his novel *Porta Nigra* (1932). His native Hunsrück forms the background of his popular novel *Hampit der Jäger* (1927). As a lyrist he wrote one of the best War books, *Ein deutsches Testament* (1938); his other volumes of verse (*Bekenntnis*, 1917; *Der lebendige Gott*, 1919; *Bauernbrot*, 1934) bear the mark of his religious spirit and his love of the supernatural.

The revival of the ballad is as free from experiment in form as the *Arbeiterdichtung* is. Lulu von Strauss und Torney and Agnes

Miegel have been dealt with as women writers (pp. 342-3); both infuse into the ballad something of the new spirit of the revolt of woman. BÖRRIES FREIHERR VON MÜNCHHAUSEN (1874-1945) on the contrary merely carries on the ballad tradition of Graf Moritz von Strachwitz: the dashing bravery of the Germanic warrior, and, if the theme be modern, the ways of a junker with a lady, form the staple of *Die Balladen und ritterlichen Lieder* (1908) and *Das Balladenbuch* (1929; final edition 1950). The ballads handle motifs from Nordic myth (*Wodans Ritt, Weissagung der Wala, Wodans Lied vom Ymir-Kampf*), Danish history, the Middle Ages, the Thirty Years War, *Märchen* and legends. His poems of personal experience were collected in *Das Liederbuch* (1928) and *Idyllen* (1933).

The verse and stanza forms continue traditional, but with new melodic rhythms, in the work of certain poets who in this respect are transitional between impressionism and expressionism – Georg Heym, Georg Trakl, Ernst Stadler, Paul Zech, and Armin T. Wegner. As far as form is concerned Franz Werfel, too, may be ranged with this group, though actually he is the very apostle of expressionist ethics. The first two intensify certain morbid themes, and prepare for the expressionist doctrine of the regeneration of humanity by dwelling on the phases of decay, death, and decomposition, while Heym, Zech, and Wegner by their presentation of the city as a nightmare take their place by the side of Rilke.

GEORG HEYM (1887-1912) is with some fitness called 'the German Rimbaud', not because of any similarity of life – he was drowned at twenty-five when skating on the Havel – but because of his obvious imitation of the French decadent. His two volumes of verse (*Der ewige Tag*, 1911; *Umbra Vitae*, 1912; *Gesammelte Gedichte*, 1947) sing demonic gloom into pictures of Berlin. Typical of his manner is *Die Tote im Wasser*, the description of the corpse of a woman floating along a Berlin canal – a white ship manned by great rats[1] – '*Ihr dicker Bauch entragt | Dem Wasser gross, zerhöhlt und fast zernagt.*' This theme of the decomposition[2] of beauty we find again in Alfred Wolfenstein's (p. 425) brilliant translation of Rimbaud's *Ophélie*; it is ghastliest in Gottfried Benn's *Schöne Jugend* and again in Heym's *Ophelia* – here the dead girl floats along on a

[1] This recurs: Armin T. Wegner's *Die Ertrunkenen.*
[2] The ultimate inspiration is Baudelaire's poem *La Charogne*. See also Heym's *Schwarze Visionen, Der Schläfer im Walde* (obviously modelled on Rimbaud's *Le dormeur du val*), and *Bist du nun tot?* (the picture of a strangled woman's corpse).

river shadowed black by a primeval forest; a long white eel glides
over her breasts; she dreams of a crimson kiss; she floats on past
the din of cities and factories – through all eternity. Another theme
(probably from Maeterlinck's *Serres chaudes*) is that of the hospital
(*Das Fieberspital*). The general impression of Heym's poetry is that
of boyish elaboration of the macabre. But details – glimpses in
gloom – have the phosphorescence of fine poetry.

GEORG TRAKL (1887-1914) was a dispensing chemist in Salzburg
who went mad and poisoned himself after a battle on the eastern
front. He is a poet of country life, but as such glaringly impressionistic; e.g. *Herbstseele*:

> *Jägerruf und Blutgebell;*
> *Hinter Kreuz und braunem Hügel*
> *Blindet sacht der Wasserspiegel,*
> *Schreit der Habicht hart und hell.*

> *Über Stoppelfeld und Pfad*
> *Banget schon ein schwarzes Schweigen;*
> *Reiner Himmel in den Zweigen;*
> *Nur der Bach rinnt still und stad.*

The first general impression on reading Trakl's verse (*Gedichte*,
1913; *Die Dichtungen*, 1917; *Gesamtausgabe*, Vol. 1 1949, Vol. 2
1950; *Aus goldnem Kelch*, 1939) is that it is *schon dagewesen*: these
softly wreathed, faintly fading[1] rhythms with their sensuous variation of vowels (e.g. '*wenn verfallen der kalte Mond erscheint*') read like
a blending of Klopstock and Hölderlin, and the sense may be even
more nebulous. But there is a corpse-like mellowness in this verse
which is strange to the masculine melancholy of Klopstock and
the clean ephebe's vision of Hölderlin: Trakl is a decadent ten
years after his time, as Baudelairian – and to the verge of nausea –
as Heym is Rimbaud-like. It is only necessary to read a few poems
to fix the origins and the method. The main influence is that of
Maeterlinck's *Serres chaudes*: there is the same incongruous enumeration of details (the technique of seventeenth-century German
verse) which fuse to no composite picture but leave an impression
of the motley disorder of the world presenting itself as the reality
it is to the heightened poetic hearing and vision of a madman;
there is no sense in it save to the senseless; and how the magic

---

[1] '*verweht und matt*'.

28

beauty of it clashes with the filthy reality that belies it, even to a madman's vision! Trakl's range is very limited: really he has only one theme – the tints and odours of decay and decomposition, and the insistent idea that all existence is decay; nevertheless there is considerable variety in the wilful repetition – he returns like one obsessed to red splashes of fruit over fading autumn foliage, to the bleeding of sunset skies, to flies or ravens or crows gashing carrion, to the meeting of lovers in the rotting forest, to the green glint of decomposing flesh. He finds haunting images for the unity of life and death; in *Frauensegen* for instance:

> *Wie dein Leib so schön geschwellt*
> *Golden reift der Wein am Hügel.*
> *Ferne glänzt des Weihers Spiegel*
> *Und die Sense klirrt im Feld.*

He is at his best in the sick voluptuousness and the physiological evocation of certain lines: e.g. '*Resedenduft, der Weibliches umspült*'. There is a *nouveau frisson* in such of his poems as *Die Ratten*:

> *Im Hof scheint weiss der herbstliche Mond.*
> *Vom Dachrand fallen phantastische Schatten.*
> *Ein Schweigen in leeren Fenstern wohnt;*
> *Da tauchen leise herauf die Ratten*

> *Und huschen pfeifend hier und dort*
> *Und ein gräulicher Dunsthauch wittert*
> *Ihnen nach aus dem Abort,*
> *Den geisterhaft der Mondschein durchzittert.*

> *Und sie keifen vor Gier so toll*
> *Und erfüllen Haus und Scheunen,*
> *Die von Korn und Früchten voll.*
> *Eisige Winde im Dunkel greinen.*

Another early victim of the War was ERNST STADLER (1883-1914); he fell on the French front as a lieutenant of artillery. He had studied in Oxford, and was a Dozent in Strassburg. His one volume of verse is *Der Aufbruch* (1914), and here the form, though still heavily rhythmical, begins to break away from tradition, and his ploughing up of form (to use his own expression) is to him a symbol of his breaking away to his suffering brethren. He cries out like any expressionist:

Form ist Wollust, Friede, himmlisches Genügen,
Doch mich reisst es, Ackerschollen umzupflügen.
Form will mich verschnüren und verengen,
Doch ich will mein Sein in alle Weiten drängen . . .

Stadler uses by preference a long plunging line which is clearly an imitation of Whitman. *Der Aufbruch* has clear unity of theme: it is the story, once again, of the German youth as Parzival or Simplizissimus. There are four sections: *Die Flucht* pictures the flight of the youth from all that is base; *Stationen* relate episodes on the quest for the ideal; *Der Spiegel* is the revelation of truth and the relinquishment of self; *Die Rast* is appeasement. *Die Flucht* gives the sordid experiences of a boy; ideal beauty dies in the bed of prostitutes; the collapse of dream in the pollution of desire. The second poem states the goal of all the wildering quest; and it is notewrothy that *Der Aufbruch* leads up to the magic phrase found in *Der Cherubinische Wandersmann* of Angelus Silesius and which is to be one of the holy texts of the ethic expressionists: *Mensch, werde wesentlich!*

This call to man: to thine own self be true! is the very message of FRANZ WERFEL. It is not the general verdict that his novels (pp. 371-3) have more value than his lyric verse[1]; but the fact remains that he is a lyric poet in the sense that Schiller was – there is high moral or ethic fervour, but it is sonorously rhetorical. Through his series of verse volumes we have, not magic of line, but considered delivery of a doctrine, and even the ejaculatory hacking of the line is part of the plan to precipitate overpowering pathos. In *Der Weltfreund* (1911) Werfel makes his confession of faith in humanity; in *Wir sind* (1913) he proves that *we are* because we feel that we are one with our brother, and that the typical disharmony (at the period), that of father and son, is due to the splitting of the *Weltseele* or cosmic *Allseele* into reality – ideas which are fairly commonplace. In form Werfel has greater variety than Stadler but is much at the same stage: he too rhymes Whitmanesque lines of unequal length which sometimes overflow into the next. He has Whitman's ecstatic apostrophe, and like Whitman

[1] *Gedichte aus 30 Jahren* (1938).

he identifies himself with all sorts and conditions of men; very American sounds –

Ich lebte im Walde, hatte ein Bahnhofsamt,
Sass gebeugt über Kassabücher und bediente ungeduldige Gäste.
Als Heizer stand ich vor Kesseln, das Antlitz grell überflammt,
Und als Kuli ass ich Abfall und Küchenreste.

The tentacular city is the main theme of ARMIN T. WEGNER'S (1886-) *Das Antlitz der Städte* (1917). Wegner, a jack-of-all-trades ('farm labourer, dock labourer, tutor, editor, agitator, lover, idler' is his own enumeration) had published three other books of verse (*Im Strome verloren*, 1903; *Zwischen zwei Städten*, 1909; *Gedichte in Prosa*, 1910) before the War, which took him to Mesopotamia and inspired his anti-War book *Der Weg ohne Heimkehr; ein Martyrium in Briefen* (1919). The post-War work of this restless wanderer or, to use his own term, 'Poeta Ahasverus', is of the exotic variety: the lyrics of his *Die Strasse mit den tausend Zielen* (1924) carry the nightmare mood of *Das Antlitz der Städte* over the highroads of Europe and Asia; and two novels (see p. 378) have a Turkish scene.

The great city, '*die Megäre Stadt*', is a nightmare too in the robust and violent verse of PAUL ZECH (1881-1946), a disciple of Dehmel. He was the declared enemy of *die Werkleute auf Haus Nyland*, whom he accused of toadying to the industrialists; to their journal he opposed his own, *Das neue Pathos*, which counts in the early history of expressionism; his own visions of Rhenish industry find their place in the verse of *Das schwarze Revier* (1913) and in the short stories of *Der schwarze Baal* (1916). In the poems of *Der Wald* (1910) and *Die eiserne Brücke* (1914) there is a contrast of the fields and forests of the Vistula, from which he came, with the misery of mines (in which he had worked) and factories and factory towns. His reactions to the War are gathered in the poems of *Golgotha* (1920) and the prose of *Das Grab der Welt* (1919), with its description of the attack on Verdun; the sonnets of *Das Terzett der Sterne* (1920) escape to some hope of the future, while in the four tales of *Das törichte Herz* (1925) the slavery of labour again darkens the expressionist's vision of man's humanity to man.

All these early or 'half expressionists' have clear expression of humanitarian rather than revolutionary ideas, though Paul Zech sometimes wilfully buries his meaning. The shock troops of expressionism proper launched their attacks in journals and anthologies; e.g. in *Der Kondor* (1912), published by KURT HILLER (1885-), who couched the manifestos of the 'activists' (*die Aktivisten*). The first organ of the activist school had been *Die Aktion* (1910-), edited by FRANZ PFEMFERT (1879-1954); the 'action' demanded is a political acceptance of expressionistic ethics as a State programme. The poets of *Die Aktion* were all '*Chaotiker*' or '*Wortchaotiker*': to them the world was chaos, and their verse too is a chaos of words where sense may be as the needle is in the haystack. ALBERT EHRENSTEIN (1886-1950), who had attracted attention by his Novelle *Tubutsch* (1911), lashed at the War in *Barbaropa*. ALFRED WOLFENSTEIN (1888-1945) has pictorial intensity (*Die gottlosen Jahre*, 1914; *Die Freundschaft*, 1917; *Die Nackten*, 1917); his poem *Im Bestienhaus* has something of the symbolic significance of Rilke's *Der Panther*. JOHANNES R. BECHER (1891-1958) was terribly prolific as an activist; mercifully he anthologized his verse in *Das neue Gedicht* (1918). In his drama *Arbeiter, Bauern, Soldaten* (1919) the whole nation is transformed to goodness and sets out 'to God' with the spectators of the play; all march except the All-Highest. Critics praise the 'Bolshevist vision' of his *Maschinenrhythmen* (1924); these poems, one of them says, '*sind lange Maschinenhallen, in denen die Worte mechanisch wie geölte Kolben auf und nieder steigen.*' For the study of *Motivik* his verse is important; e.g. *Im Dunkel* is one of the most vivid handlings of the motif that in the misery of crowded cities people pass one another as utter strangers, dead to one another: city life is thus mechanical motion, a surging past, like cold sea waves, of lay figures, each passing to his or her illusive scrap of pleasure or to helpless misery; this is the purport too of Ernst Stadler's *Abendschluss*, Franz Werfel's *Menschenblick* and *Nur Flucht*, and Alfred Wolfenstein's *Begegnungen*. He lived in Russia from 1935 to 1945.

With the circle of *Der Sturm* we come to genuine atrocities of poetry. The journal – politically of the Red variety – lived twenty years (1910-30); the editor was Herwarth Walden (p. 335). The only poets of the circle who are worth mentioning are KURT HEYNICKE (1891- ; *Rings fallen Sterne*, 1917; *Ausgewählte Gedichte*, 1952) and AUGUST STRAMM (1874-1915). Stramm fell on the Russian front. *Du* (1914) is a book of love poems; *Tropfblut* (1919) of War verse; *Dichtungen* (1919), his collected work, includes his play *Sancta Susanna*, which, set to music by Hindemith, was produced in Berlin in 1918. The curiosity of Stramm's technique is that he loves lines of one syllable; thus some of his poems are stringed ejaculations. The reason for the monosyllabic lines is the expressionist conception of 'clenching' the feeling; such a line is *'geballt'*. This verbal idiocy is intensified in the 'verse' of the *Dadaisten*.

Die Neue Sachlichkeit or *Gebrauchslyrik* is theoretically at least a way out of this madness. The general idea of this 'functional poetry'[1] is that the poetic value of a thing is in the concrete use to which it can be put; the result of such a theory is *'Konkretisierung'* or *'Aktualisierung'* of poetry; or, shall we say, real reality transformed to novelty because things are shown not as glamorous visions or coloured impressions but as functions – that is, what is considered important is their purpose in life, not their significance or outward semblance in art.

It would be foolish to dismiss the Nazi lyrists as mere propagandists; after all Virgil was in the same boat. But there is no danger in saying that these poets who obey the lifted thumb of the new Augustus are less than any Roman poet. In those days they were a glittering galaxy; but the moment the tumult and the shouting dies they fade out like the stars at dawn. All the anthologies[2] of their racial fervour are practically unreadable out of Germany. A few poems have proved their singable qualities; for instance Dietrich Eckhart's *Deutschland erwache!* is an excellent onomatopoeic rendering of the tocsin – brazen clangour and clashed anger. Perhaps the best poems are those addressed to the Führer: here we have sometimes a striking personal note. The idealization may seem crazy; but for all we know Dietrich von Bern or Siegfried himself may have been, mentally, of the calibre of Hitler; to poetry legend is all.

[1] 'Functional architecture' = *Neue Sachlichkeit*; glass houses and factories have hygienic functions.

[2] *Rufe in das Reich* (1934), ed. Herbert Böhme, himself one of these bards (*Kampf und Bekenntnis, Des Blutes Gesänge*).

XX

THE LITERATURE
OF RACE AND SOIL

D*ie Neue Sachlichkeit* – essentially a return from the hectic
ideology of the expressionists to a raw reality (it is also
classed as *Der Überrealismus*) – was swept away in 1933 by
the fanatically political and politically purposeful creed of National
Socialism; this clamoured for the idealization of heroic figures or
'leaders' in past and present, for heroic self-sacrifice as a national
ideal, for a glorification of rural life, and for a painstaking exposition of the influence of landscape and local customs on the infinitely varied and yet uniformly 'Nordic' character of the *Stämme*.
In the Third Empire there was no place for ecstatic poet-apostle
or international dreamer: steeled body and alert mind, clean living,
joy in hardship, motherhood as family service to the State, now
dominated literature and made it a mere element in the worship
of race. It would be foolish to say outright that the new spirit is,
as a stimulus to literature, inferior to the old: at all events the
Nazi novel, though it may be on a lower level as literature, is at
least sane and healthy. The one thing that is quite clear is that
whereas the super-realism which gathered force in the twenties
hardened itself to feeling and made a vaunt of cynicism, so much
so that love itself was set forth as a physical function merely, the
literature of National Socialism revives the orgies of feeling of
Romanticism; indeed, this governmentally directed explosion of
feeling has so much in common with the philosophically directed
emotionalism of Romanticism that it might well be classed as
National Romanticism. Another glaring feature is the return to
plain traditional form; this leads to monotony, particularly in
lyric poetry, but the law was laid down by Hitler in a speech at
Nuremberg: '*Wer nur das Neue sucht um des Neuen willen, der verirrt*

427

sich (nur zu leicht) in das Gebiet der Narretei; unter der Parole neu sein um jeden Preis kann jeder Stümper etwas besonders leisten.'

One immediate result of the new standards was the drastic re-shuffling of reputations. All those writers who could be classified as '*volkhaft*' (racially minded) were whirled to the heights of Parnassus; those who could not were given back seats and ticketed '*undeutsch*' or '*volksfremd*'. All the Jews[1] without exception were branded as unfit for reading; non-Jews who had satirized Germany (e.g. Heinrich Mann) were outlawed ('*ausgebürgert*'); Liberals and 'good Europeans' (e.g. Thomas Mann) found it expedient to live in exile. Neo-romantics like Hermann Hesse, whose characters are too full of the sadness of life to be heroic except in the endurance of suffering, were damned with faint praise, or rejected as effeminate and 'aimless'. The places held in the eyes of Europe by these veteran writers were taken by a younger generation – Binding, Blunck, Kolbenheyer, Hans Grimm, Ina Seidel, Hanns Johst, Hermann Burte, Josef Ponten, Will Vesper; and of some of these '*Dichter des heimlichen Deutschlands*' (certainly of Ina Seidel and R. G. Binding) one might say that they were now given the rank due to them. One might also admit that the indignation of Germans over the fact that some of the best German writers remained unknown abroad while others never recognized as even third-rate in Germany (Feuchtwanger, Vicki Baum, Emil Ludwig for instance) had a vast foreign public had some justification, though it should be remembered that these mass purveyors would not circulate if they were not readable.

The first principle of Nazi literature is that it must express, not the feeling of the individual, but that of the race. This principle includes self-dedication of the writer to the communities within the race (*Hingabe an die Gemeinschaft*), so that poetry and drama tend to be *Gemeinschaftsdichtung*. Whereas the expressionists dreamt of regenerating all humanity the Nazis restrict their regenerative fervour to the German race. Moreover, while expressionism was violently individual (in spite of its *Wir-Bewusstsein*) National Socialism humbly accepts regulation from without. Expressionism followed the lines of Walther Rathenau's struggle against *Mechanisierung des*

---

[1] The problem of the Jews had been handled by Schnitzler in *Professor Bernhardi* and *Der Weg ins Freie* and by Hermann Bahr in *Die Rotte Korah* (1919). The works of the Jewish writers had to be published in foreign capitals where they found a refuge: Paris, Amsterdam, Stockholm, Zürich. Prague was a city of refuge till 1938.

Geistes; with the Nazis *Geist* is as mechanized as modern armies are. Expressionism stands for ethic ideals, National Socialism for State ideals; the ideal of the one is *Erneuerung der Menschheit*; that of the other *Erneuerung der Rasse*.

The second principle is that, since the health of the race springs from the soil of the country, the finest racial types will be found, not in the city, but on the land. The result of this doctrine is that approved literature is for the most part *Heimatkunst* or *Schollen-dichtung*; or, to use the term now preferred, *Blut- und Bodenliteratur*. The ideal German is the German *Bauer*; and the task of the poet or novelist is to show how this peasant's qualities derive from the land he tills. The difference between *Heimatkunst* and the new *Blut-und Bodenliteratur* is that the Nazi movement attaches more value to *Blut* than *Boden*; and *Blut* means race. Race in two senses; firstly it means the Nordic or Germanic race; and secondly the *Stämme* that make up this race in Germany. Idealization of the Nordic type occurs mainly with the *Kulturphilosophen*, while sub-racial idealization is the affair mainly of the new regional novelist. But the *Boden* or landscape, too, is differently glorified than it was by the *Heimatkünstler* of pre-War days, and takes on more mythical tints: what the Nazi novelists are set to evoke is not the surface but the very soul, the mystic and fateful soul, of the landscape. In H. F. Blunck's tales, for instance (even those which are in period historical), myth and symbol rather than description serve to evoke the landscape and to give it magical radiance. This splitting of literature into provinces had for result that Josef Nadler's *Literatur-geschichte der deutschen Stämme* was now the approved *History of Literature*.

The third principle is that, since the race is by its very blood heroic, literature, too, must be heroic and confident of the coming glory of the race; any other mood is treason to the race.

The ideals of the *Blut- und Bodenliteratur* were expounded by the Minister of Agriculture, Walther Darré, in his two books *Das Bauerntum als Lebensquell der nordischen Rasse* (1930) and *Neuadel aus Blut und Boden* (1930), which gave such currency to the term that it had its convenient abbreviation – *Blubo*. This to an outsider seems irresistibly hilarious; particularly in the light of Karl Kraus's ir-reverent witticism: '*Eine Verbindung von Blut und Boden ergibt immer nur Starrkrampf.*'

There were of course peasant tales still being written which in spirit differed radically from the *Blubo* tales; for instance, *Der Kopf-lohn* by Anna Seghers (p. 493). We must take it that a tale of country life cannot be ranged with the *Blubo* literature unless, before or after 1933, it rings true to Nazi ideals. After 1933 such totalitarian tales were stamped out of holy earth like the bristling German army. Only a few of those which project above the ruck can be dealt with here, and the very nature of *Blubo* literature exacts a geographical classification; the most convenient arrangement will be that of the three parallel belts of north, centre, and south which roughly coincide with the sub-racial division into Low Saxon, Franconian-Thuringian-Upper Saxon-Silesian, and Allemannic-Bavarian-Austrian, to which must be added the Germans without the Reich (*Auslandsdeutsche*).

The true home of the *Blubo* tale is the rich farmland of the North; if one can speak of classics of the movement they are Friedrich Griese in Mecklenburg and Ernst Wiechert in East Prussia.

FRIEDRICH GRIESE (1890-) was an elementary schoolmaster in East Mecklenburg and then in Kiel. Critics stress his early deafness: this gave him his close perceptions of the processes of nature – he heard the grass grow, as the saying goes. His conception of man's native soil as fate gathers intensity from tale to tale (*Feuer*, 1921; *Ur*, 1922; *Alte Glocken*, 1925) and reaches a climax in *Wintèr* (1927).

ERNST WIECHERT (1887-1950) is the novelist *par excellence* of East Prussia, the laureate of the vast forests and heathlands in which he grew up as the son of a forest ranger. The very best of him is in his evocation of the magic and mystery of these enchanted woodlands and the rough-hewn or moonstruck folk who are moulded to their environment. At the Oberrealschule and University of Königsberg he was disillusioned; here, he says, he renounced God, Christ, the Kaiser, State, parents, teachers, women. Formative influences which can be traced in his work are, above all, the Danish novelist Jens Peter Jacobsen, Wilhelm Raabe, the East Prussian Graf Eduard von Keyserling, and the Russian novelists. He was a secondary teacher for thirty years; he served in the First World War from start to finish, and then returned to his task as teacher at Königsberg and later in Berlin. Here the Board of Education were informed that 'every class that Wiechert takes is lost to National Socialism', and in 1933 he found it convenient to resign his post. He settled for a time on the Lake of Starnberg, but lectures he gave in 1934 at the University of Munich gave offence, and in 1938 he was sent to the concentration camp at Oranienberg, from which he was transferred to Buchenwald; five months later he was released, but kept under observation by the Gestapo and prevented from publishing anything; what he wrote he buried in his garden in a tin box. After the war he lectured in the United States, and then found a home in Uerikon near Zurich, where he died. Wiechert's autobiography is contained in *Wälder und Menschen* (1936), the story of his boyhood, and in *Jahre und Zeiten* (1949), which chronicles his life from his student days to the time of his settling in Switzerland and deals with the impact on him of the political turmoils of the day; *Der Totenwald* (1945-46) records his experiences at Buchenwald. His first novel, *Die Flucht* (1916), has also autobiographical elements; the hero, a teacher, flees from a loathsome world to the forests of Masuria and there commits suicide. In Wiechert's early work there is the reflex of his unhappy first marriage. There is the same conflict with the world of today in the novels which follow: *Der Wald* (1922), *Der Totenwolf* (1924), and in *Die blauen Schwingen* (1925), which was completed in the trenches of Champagne. In *Der Totenwolf* Christianity is specifically charged with life's misery, but this disgust with the world changed to a certain acceptance of Christian feeling. '*Ich war vierzig,*' he says, '*als der Durchbruch der Gnade über mich kam und die alte Form zerbrach. Er spülte den Hass hinweg, in dem ich aufgewachsen war.*' From now on there is a note of appeasement in his tales; his characters face up to death and devilry, and healing is found in shouldering the burdens life imposes; the lesson runs that not God, but man, decides. Wiechert's task as a writer is now to analyse the civilization of today and to find ethical principles which will make it bearable. In *Jahre und Zeiten* (1949) Wiechert dismisses the works of his first phase as self-centred and engendered by his *Kulturpessimismus* or nihilism of despair; he had written them to free his mind from the stifling sense of frustration that had overcome him in the satanized civilisation of the city. This finding of grace which heralds his '*zweite Geburt*' is not, however, a Christian conversion – he is still an agnostic, but he has found his way to a Christian conception which is all his own. It is in effect a return from the hectic and strident bustle and battle of the city to the peace of nature. There has been much discussion of Wiechert's attitude to Christianity. His intimate knowledge of the Bible shows throughout his work; his language is often markedly Biblical; but he often makes a mockery of Bible texts; e.g. such a text as 'whom the Lord loveth he chasteneth' serves him, with much else, for his angry rejection of the parson's cruel God. After Buchenwald the love of God is a mockery. The burden of his tales is still a weary renunciation; comfort is to be sought, not in God, but in nature with all her bounty and the unfathomable mystery that is within and behind her; man, emancipated from God and united with nature, finds himself. There is some show of a reasoned reconciliation with life in *Der Knecht Gottes Andreas Nyland* (1926), the story of a clergyman who throws up his living to walk the ways of Christ among stricken humanity in all stages of society, but comes to grief. The religious self-abasement, as it seems to some, of this first stage of Wiechert's mature period, has been branded as escapism; and indeed by comparison it marks a softening of the hard post-war doctrine of reclamation of the race and Fatherland such as we find it in the writings of Ernst Jünger. Wiechert's new idealization of nature and of nature-like man comes out in the Novellen of *Der silberne Wagen* (1928) and *Die Flöte des Pan* (1930), and his spiritual rebirth informs his novel *Die kleine Passion* (1929), the hero of which, Johannes, is told as a boy by his mentor, a freethinker who confirms him in his rebellion against hypocritical pedagogy and satanized standards of urban living, that what decides is 'blood', not in the sense of sex instinct, but with the meaning that any man acts potentially as his blood, or the imperative force of his physical nature, impels him. This is from now on Wiechert's deterministic doctrine; life is decided by blood (spiritual heredity or race-transmitted qualities). In Wiechert's concept blood with heredity as its corollary is one of the three saving forces of existence; the other two are loneliness (or concentration on one's chosen task in aloofness from distractions) and nature. It might be argued that if development of character is thus predetermined then the processes of the *Entwicklungsroman* must be ruled out. At all events, beautiful in some ways as *Die kleine Passion* is, it affords proof positive that Wiechert's gospel of the inherent rights of the strong personality is morally and socially impossible. On the side of technique the intrigue is inventively poor; if the novel is to be ranked high it can only be by reason of its mastery of language, its wealth of allusion, its undertones of poetry, its *Bilder, Düfte,*

Klänge (to use Wiechert's own way of putting it), the basic common sense of its rebellion against ingrained prejudice and biblical illogicality. *Jedermann* (1931) is a sequel; it recounts the experiences of Johannes in the war. The novel amounts to an uncompromising rejection of war as unnatural; there is, it is true, war in the processes of nature, but this is organic, never organized. In Wiechert's allusive symbolism, moreover, war is an outrage on the Motherland; for in his mystical mother-cult 'mother' embodies all that is good and creative; and therefore this more or less pacific war novel is in stark contrast to the general run of war novels with their cult of the Fatherland. But there is the reverse of defeatism in *Jedermann*; the good that comes from defeat is that it binds men together for common service and tolerance, to Jews as to all others. Wiechert's theme of escape from misery, which is the basic theme of *Jedermann*, is more mythically handled in *Die Magd des Jürgen Dostocil* (1932); the hero is an East Prussian ferryman on the Memel, a primitive gifted with second sight, and with age-old pagan beliefs piercing through his crust of Christianity. The ingrained heathen qualities surviving in these fastnesses of nature give the story with its inwoven undertones a luring charm. The hero of *Die Majorin* (1934) returns, after twenty years' service in the Foreign Legion, from a prisoners' camp in Africa and lives an outlaw's life in an East Prussian forest, till he is won back to faith in life by a great-hearted woman. *Die Hirtennovelle* (1935) is today classed as one of the finest short stories in German literature. Michael is a shepherd lad who guards the flocks of a lonely East Prussian hamlet near the frontier; there are cows, sheep, and goats, but the pride of the herd is Bismarck, the bull. One day the shepherd of the neighbouring hamlet, Laban – a name given in the district to chaps big in the bone but weak in the head – invades Michael's purlieus; there is a fight, and Michael hits Laban straight between the eyes with a stone from his sling. This Goliath recovers, but henceforth keeps his distance. The tale is marvellously fitted detail by detail to the Bible story of David, though the note is of halcyon peace till the war comes and the Russians and Michael is killed as he tries to save one of his lambs that has strayed from where he had hidden flock and village folk. *Das einfache Leben* (1939) introduces a third period of maturity: the gospel of the second period is still the staple, but it is reasoned more logically and with less acerbity of argument. Sex is clean cut out; the tone throughout is austere and noble. The manuscript, written after the Buchenwald experience, was recovered from the tin box buried in the garden. It is ostensibly a post-war novel, and the aim is rehabilitation after the First World War; but the war that is coming is foreshadowed, although Nazi activities are for discretionary reasons kept out of the picture, while Communists and Stahlhelm are episodically in the foreground. Very effective is the scorn poured on the cruel God of the Germans, who after murderous battles intone the hymn: *Nun danket alle Gott!* There is the same spirit of redemption by love and labour in *Die Jerominkinder* (2 vols., 1945 and 1947), in which there is again a delightful evocation of life in a lonely East Prussian village. Wiechert's last novel, *Missa sine nomine* (1950), yet another *Heimkehrerroman*, describes the fate of three brothers of the old nobility during and after the war. One of the three is obviously a self-portrait; on his release from a concentration camp he gradually, in the loneliness of nature, finds his Christian fate and realizes that God created good and evil for man to choose between them.

BENNO VON MECHOW (1897-), though born in Bonn, was brought up in Baden-Baden and Freiburg im Breisgau; he is, however, reckoned with the writers of the hard North. He began with *Das ländliche Jahr* (1930), a chronicle of bucolic life; the hero is a young *Gutsinspektor* who learns that he must face life on his own. *Vorsommer* (1933) is obviously modelled on Stifter's *Nachsommer*: it shows that subtle interweaving of nature and human life which is Stifter's theme. Von Mechow was associated with PAUL ALVERDES (1897-) as joint editor of *Das Innere Reich*, a journal which boomed the *Blubo* literature. Alverdes, an Alsatian, born in Strassburg, counts in Nazi literature for his War tales (*Reinhold oder die Verwandelten*, 1931; *Die Pfeiferstube*, 1934). Alverdes here coins one of the winged words of the day: all the heroism is for love of '*das unsichtbare Deutschland*'. WILL VESPER (1882-), a native of *das bergische Land*, was one of the Nazi *coryphaei*; he proclaimed their doctrines in his popular review *Die neue Literatur*. His most important original work is the novel *Das harte Geschlecht* (1931); it retells, from the Old Norse sagas of Greenland, the story of Lef the Cunning, who sails to Greenland, is converted to Christianity in Denmark, and dies on a pilgrimage to Rome.

FRIEDRICH SCHNACK (1888-) describes his native district, the land round the river Main; he hails from the Rhön. He served during World War I in Turkey, and was interned on the island of Prinkipo; in Asia were written some of the poems of *Das kommende Reich* (1920). This volume was followed by other verse: *Vogel Zeitvorbei* (1922), *Das blaue Geisterhaus* (1924), *Palisander: Gedichte aus den Tropen* (1933). In his trilogy of novels *Die brennende Liebe*, with its tale of three generations (*Beatus und Sabine*, 1927; *Sebastian im Wald*, 1926; *Die Orgel des Himmels*, 1927) there is an attempt at something new: the districts round Main and Neckar provide the setting, but the landscape, Schnack explains, is built up as a mirror of the spiritual (*Spiegel des Seelischen*), not as a coulisse. He eliminates the psychological method, because conceptions of psychology change from period to period, whereas the mirroring of landscape in the human mind (that is, the moulding of the mind by geographical *milieu*) is a permanent process. That literary psychology changes from school to school is more or less true, and probably Schnack's *volte-face* is to be explained as a reaction from the possibly depraved psychological experimentation of (e.g.) Jakob Wassermann's later novels or such a book as Edschmid's *Lord Byron*; Schnack's attitude, on the other hand, leads to the mentally depraved healthiness of *Blubo*. Man should serve as a literary object, Schnack continues, only in the measure that landscape passes into and moulds his life by the experience of it; landscape, therefore, *is* life, and breeding is of the soil and for the soil – which is *Blubo* metaphysics with a halo. Schnack, however, means more: his technique is a metaphysical elevation of plane above plane (*Überhöhung der Ebenen*): his novels stage plane above plane and thus show 'the manifold refraction of events and figures' – the finite landscape quivers into dream like unity with infinity, till Neckar and Nile are one and flow to the same crystal city. Schnack rejects, too, the term *Entwicklungsroman*, and classifies these later stories of his as *Entfaltungsromane*: his characters, though they change infinitely under the magic action of landscape, are unspoilt and whole, and the construction of the novels is a vertical elevation from stage to stage, not a growth by chance divagation. If landscape only constituted the stages of elevation Schnack's scope would be limited; but in *Die Orgel des Himmels* the fling of his theory takes in the construction of a railway, and in *Goldgräber in Franken* (1931) and *Das Zauberauto* (1928) we get the technical miracles of the present. He cultivates the symbolism of fauna and flora: *Das Leben der Schmetterlinge* (1928); *Der Lichtbogen* (1932);

Sibylle und die Feldblumen (1937). *Das neue Land* (1934) is one of the best of the back-to-the-land tales; in *Die wundersame Strasse* (1936) a hero with the musician's restless fancies in his brain goes back to the land but deserts it to follow his dream of a maid, only to find solid safety in the arms of a farmer's widow.

Swabian *Blubo* is represented by PETER DÖRFLER (1878-), a Catholic priest. He has written a trilogy: *Die Lampe der törichten Jungfrau* (1930), *Apollonias Sommer* (1931), and *Um das kommende Geschlecht* (1932); Apollonia is a multi-mother of her relatives to the third generation in the Allgäu. The life of peasants in the Allgäu who eke out their living by hand-weaving is the theme of *Die Notwender* (1934); once again the introduction of machinery threatens ruin, but here a young farmer shows how salvation lies in timely adaptation.

GEORG BRITTING (1891-), a Regensburg man by birth but resident in Munich, is the poet of the Lower Bavarian countryside. He began with expressionist plays (*Der Mann im Mond*, 1920; *Das Storchennest*, 1921; *Paula und Bianca*, 1922) and then went over to Novellen – *Valentin und Veronika* and *Der Eisläufer*, both 1948, reprint tales collected from previous volumes. There is a sensitive impressionism in these short stories, which are regional in the sense that the characters are Bavarian types of his *entourage* – villagers and small townsmen. In his loving depiction of children and adolescents he no doubt calls up reminiscences of his youth '*am Strom*', by the Danube. His experience of war service – he went straight from school into the army and had three years in the trenches – comes into the weft and woof of his one novel, *Lebenslauf eines dicken Mannes, der Hamlet hiess* (1932). Hamlet wages war in Norway on behalf of his stepfather, and the chronicle adumbrates the poet's own reactions as a soldier to the humbug which launches armies to torture and death; the mad brutality of modern warfare is ironically mirrored in the narrowed framework of a duodecimo campaign in the dim days of old. The outlines of the tale are as told by Shakespeare, but the feeling of utter helplessness of the paunchy Danish prince in the grip of fate is that of Britting himself in the trenches of Flanders. The style and language of the novel, expressionistically strange but sensuous and highly coloured, wends along wearily with the faint pulse and rhythm of dream. His books of verse are *Gedichte* (1930), *Der irdische Tag* (1935), *Rabe, Rose und Hahn* (1939), *Das Lob des Weines*

(1942), *Die Begegnung* (1947), *Unter hohen Bäumen* (1951). His earlier lyric manner, more or less rooted in expressionism, quickly develops to the solid shaping of his later verse, which varies in mood rather than in its general tenor. The structure of the verse is hard and firm, sometimes rough; traditional forms are broken up to give, not free rhythms, though these occur sporadically, but freedom to lengthen or shorten lines or to tail a stanza with an extra line. Already in *Der irdische Tag* we have the poet's full panoply. The forefront of what is presented is the exterior world as the year runs its changes of scene and feeling round the gardener's calendar. The procession of the seasons has been worked out by many poets since James Thomson; in Britting's sequence it is all new because the vision is regional: these are scenes centred on the Danube – always '*der Strom*' (*die Isar* is less lovingly given its name). Excursional jaunts to the Tyrol and Italy provide variety at the rim of the homeland landscape. *Die Begegnung* is a chain of seventy sonnets, which in substance renew and vary the medieval Dance of Death in language toned to the sharp-cut contours of the old woodcuts of the *danse macabre*. Significantly the sequence ends with a lovely finale: *Der schöne Tod*. Strange it seems that so robust a Bavarian gentleman, by friendly repute a lover of all good things, a Falstaffian, a *Zecher*, should write of Death; but is he indeed more himself, with his zest in life, in the congenial lyrics of *Lob des Weines*? Here, of course, the burden of the song is: Begone, dull care! *Unter hohen Bäumen* carries on the laud of nature of *Der irdische Tag*, but with less of *Ich* and more of *Du*; the poet, perhaps with some sense of social promiscuity, but more likely because of a ripening of his great, good heart, seeks approach to his fellow men – lover, vintager, thief, or whatever he or she may be.

RICHARD BILLINGER (1893-) was to have been a priest, but blossomed out into a writer of great versatility; he is the acknowledged poet and dramatist of Upper Austria. There is a strong religious element as well as pulsing melodrama in his peasant plays; *Das Spiel vom Knechte* (1926), *Das Perchtenspiel* (1928), *Rauhnacht* (1931), *Rosse* (1933), *Der Gigant* (1937) give the general note; the motive force is raw heathen passion under a thin crust of Christian discipline. Billinger deserts the peasant play in his comedies *Stille Gäste* (1933), *Lob des Landes* (1933), *Gabriele Dambrone* (1936), *Die Fuchsfalle* (1939), *Der Galgenvogel* (1946), *Das Haus* (1948).

29

Der Gigant was filmed as *Die goldene Stadt*, *Gabriele Dambrone* as *Am hohen Meer*. In his peasant tales too there is the same submission to Church doctrine offset by the animal urge away from it. In *Die Asche des Fegejeuers* (1931) he tells the story of his upbringing as a village *Heiligenbüblein*; murders abound. A farmer's obstinate clinging to his farm – as in Schönherr's *Erde* – and the relinquishment to his heir of farm and the girl he desired for himself is the theme of *Leben aus Gottes Hand* (1935). In *Das verschenkte Leben* (1936) the circus rider Pedro Klingsor[1] returns to the quiet village he left as Peter Klinger, and, to save his dying mother, sells his soul to the devil, who tempts him in the shape of a gipsy. His mother recovers, but Peter dies of consumption – after a last violent effort to recover for the sake of his passion for a woman. Billinger's early poetry (*Lob Gottes*, 1923; *Über die Äcker*, 1923; *Gedichte*, 1929) was collected in *Sichel am Himmel* (1931); then followed *Der Pfeil im Wappen* (1932), *Die Nachtwache* (1935), *Holder Morgen* (1942). The pith of this lyric outpouring is symbolization of Catholic ritual flanked by vignettes of farming life and age-old village custom, with here and there a flash of Communistic revolt, as in *Gebet der Knechte und Mägde*, and there is the crude criminal passion of the peasant plays in such a poem as *Knechtsballade*.

KARL HEINRICH WAGGERL (1879-), who was born in Bad Gastein as the son of a carpenter but has made his home at Wagrain in the Salzburg country, found his feet with his novel *Brot* (1930), which shows the influence of Knut Hamsun's *Segen der Erde*. Village life forms the staple of *Schweres Blut* (1931), *Das Wiesenbuch* (1932), and *Du und Angelika* (1933), while *Das Jahr des Herrn* (1934) has autobiographical elements – it was filmed with Waggerl himself as village schoolmaster (one of the half a dozen trades he has lived by, from lift-boy to Alpine guide). Unmarried mothers and a midwife – a finely drawn figure – come into the texture of *Mütter* (1935), and the two wars into *Und wenn du willst, vergiss* (1950). His Novellen have their scenes in the Salzburg localities of his homeland, which he describes in *Wagrainer Tagebuch* (1936). His legends – *Kalendergeschichten* (1937), etc. –, more or less in the manner of Gottfried Keller's *Sieben Legenden*, are naïve rather than subtle; for the most part they assume the possibility of miracles in the life of today and for this reason tend to be foolish to non-Catholics; but

---

[1] Klingsor is a magician in the M.H.G. poem *Der Wartburgkrieg*, Novalis in *Heinrich von Ofterdingen* changes the spelling to Klingsohr.

Die Schöpfung, with its quaint and humorous picture of the seven days of Creation, is delightful. Waggerl's racy humour is at its best in his for a great part anecdotal short stories; *Fröhliche Armut* (1948) tells the story of his boyhood in the Gasteiner Tal, and the tales of *Die Pfingstreise* (1946) and *Drei Erzählungen* (1952) are also autobiographical. His botanical avocation comes out in *Das Lob der Wiese* (1950), while *Heiteres Herbarium* (1950) is a book of flower aquarelles with a commentary in humorous verse. *Kleines Erdenrund* (1951) by Hanns Arens is an introduction to Waggerl's work in anthology form with commentary. Carinthia has its de-lineator in JOSEF FRIEDRICH PERKONIG (1890-), one of the few humorists of *Blubo*. The humour has a sad ending in *Der Schinder-hannes zieht übers Gebirg* (1935): a wretched tramp frightens the life out of the Almbäuerinnen (the women who tend the cattle in summer on the high mountain patches of pasture) by telling them he is the terrible robber Schinderhannes; the villagers lie in wait for the poor devil and shoot him. In *Nikolaus Tschinderle, Räuber-hauptmann* (1936) a tailor despised by his girl shows his prowess as a fantastic robber, an Eulenspiegel with the brain waves of Don Quixote. In *Honigraub* (1935) a wise old beekeeper at the edge of the village has a moral lapse – he starves his bees, so that they find their food in the hives of his neighbours; with dire local consequences – but all comes well in the end. In *Lopud, Insel der Helden* (1934) Perkonig descends from his bare mountains to a magic island on the Dalmatian coast.

The Sudetenland has quite a school of *Blubo*. The historian of tribal literature, Josef Nadler, is a Sudeten German; so too is the popular novelist KARL HANS STROBL (1877-1946), whose *Die Vaclavbude, Der Schipkapass* and *Das WirtshausZum KönigPrzemysl'* (1913) deal with the modern conflict of Czechs and Germans, while his *Die Fackel des Hus* (1929) is a historical novel of Bohemia.[1] The veterans of the Sudeten regional novel in the strict sense of the word are Gustav Leutelt, a teacher's son from Gablonz, and Hans Watzlik. In *Siebzig Jahre meines Lebens* GUSTAV LEUTELT (1860-1945) describes his life in a glass works, and the glass industry is the background of *Bilder aus dem Leben der Glasarbeiter, Hüttenheimat*, and *Der Glaswald*. His best novels are *Das zweite Gesicht* (1911) and *Die Königshäuser* (1906). HANS WATZLIK (1879-1948), 'der Dichter des

---

[1] Strobl's most characteristic fiction (*Eleagabal Kuperus*, 1908) belongs to the fantastic, supernatural tale (p. 72).

Böhmerwaldes', began with short stories, *Im Ring des Ossers* (1913). The magic of lonely mountain spaces and frowning forests fills all his tales. In his novel *Aus wilder Wurzel* (1920) he describes the settlement of the mountain wilderness of the Sudetenland by colonists escaping from the terrors of the Thirty Years War; *Der Pfarrer von Dornloh* (1932) is the chronicle of a Bohemian village during the same period. *Das Glück von Dürrnstauden* (1927) describes the decay of a village when ore is found: it is the theme (ruin by riches) of Gerhart Hauptmann's *Vor Sonnenaufgang*. Only in one tale does Watzlik desert his native province – in *Ums Herrgottswort* (1926); and even here he only just gets over the frontier into Austria. In the short stories of *Dämmervolk* (1928) and the novel *Der Teufel wildert* (1933) the supernatural beings who haunt all upland solitudes are interpreted as the demonic impulses of tempted and erring souls.

XXI

PHILOSOPHERS AND SOPHISTS

The influence of the philosophers on the successive schools has been indicated. The general line of development is that naturalism, while influenced mainly in its social creed by Marx and in its doctrine of *milieu* by Darwin, Taine, and Zola (whose conception of *milieu* corresponds to Herder's conception of *Klima*), is in agreement with the relative positivism (*relativer Positivismus*) of ERNST MACH (1838-1916) and RICHARD AVENARIUS (1843-96); the philosophers of this school reject metaphysics and 'the absolute' and accept only experience and the exact data of science. The most passionate of the positivists was the blind Berlin thinker EUGEN DÜHRING (p. 102): his teaching in certain respects – contempt of Christianity as Jewish slave morality – runs parallel with that of Nietzsche, who stands midway between the positivists and the philosophers acknowledged as guides by the expressionists. These recklessly take over Freud's psycho-analysis, which supplants the matter-of-fact psychology of WILHELM WUNDT (1832-1920) and probes '*das Jenseits der Seele*', '*das Parapsychische*', the subconscious and the irrational, and transforms biography and the most advanced phases of the novel. To Sigmund Freud poets themselves are bundles of complexes; the Zurich school of psycho-analysts, on the other hand, following their leader CARL GUSTAV JUNG (1875-) have some respect for poets and admit that in the unconscious impulses of action there is a spiritual *Urprinzip* as well as sexual urge. Another philosopher who based his universe on sexuality was OTTO WEININGER (1880-1903), a Viennese Jew who went over to Christianity; man, he teaches, can only win through to spiritual salvation by liberating himself from woman, 'the priestess of life', and the woman within himself. (He shot himself.) '*Der reine Mann*', he says, '*ist das Ebenbild Gottes, des absoluten Etwas, das Weib, auch das Weib im Manne, ist das Symbol des*

Nichts.' Weininger has glitter of style and dazzling paradoxes (*Geschlecht und Charakter*, 1903; *Über die letzten Dinge*, 1903).

The Freudian doctrine was countered by the philosophy of the vitalists (*die Vitalisten*; *Vitalismus = Lebensphilosophie*), whose system, with its stressing of intuition as against experimental science, arrives at much the same results as Bergson: their *Lebensschwung-kraft* and Bergson's *élan vital* come to much the same thing. With them there is a revival of metaphysics, although the leaders – HERMANN COHEN (1842-1918), PAUL NATORP (1854-1924), ERNST CASSIRER (1874-1945) – are keen mathematicians. GEORG SIMMEL (1858-1918) stands out among the *Geschichtsphilosophen*, and touches literature closely by his contacts with Stefan George and Rilke; his Berlin lectures on Stefan George in 1900 are historically important. Another bridge from philosophy to literature is provided by the *Gegenstandstheorie* of ALEXIUS VON MEINONG (1853-1921) and the *phänomenologische Methode* of Max Scheler and Edmund Husserl. MAX SCHELER (1875-1928) is notable for his revaluation of values: he puts these in stages, with religious values above intellectual values; for *Kultur* he substitutes *Bildung*, and for him this means character and 'integral humanism'. Very close to literature again is WILHELM DILTHEY (1833-1911), the apostle of *Geisteswissenschaften*: his *Das Erlebnis und die Dichtung* (1906), with its interpretation of poetry by the personal experience of the poet, has provided academic critics with a safe historical means of approach, while the Freudian method has been applied more by brilliant journalists as justification for their feats of intuition. Intuition is justified, too, by EDMUND HUSSERL'S (1859-1938) method of '*phänomenologische Reduktion*' by '*reine Schau*': what matters is not the '*hic et nunc Dasein der Gegenstände*' or their *existentia* but their *essentia*; that is, not *Dasein* but *Wesen* matters; this is the source of the '*wesenhafte Kunst*' of the expressionists and explains their iteration of the old mystic exhortation: *Mensch, werde wesentlich!* (p. 472). Expressionism and *Neue Sachlichkeit* are influenced by LEOPOLD ZIEGLER'S (1881-) *Florentinische Introduktion zu einer Philosophie der Architektur und der bildenden Künste*, in which the nature of space is interpreted, and by WILHELM WORRINGER'S (1881-) *Abstraktion und Einfühlung* (1908), in which spiritual reality supplants impressionistic reality. The modern conflict of spiritual values with the mechanization of life is the theme of WALTHER RATHENAU (1867-1922); he protests against the overlordship of machinery, but argues that the machine, though subordinated to mind, must keep its power; his doctrine is essentially one of mechanical production under the control of conscious mind.[1]

Man as the slave and ultimately the victim of machinery is the subject of *Der Mensch und die Technik* (1931) by OSWALD SPENGLER (1880-1936), who in his famous book *Der Untergang des Abendlandes* (1918-22) had argued that the victory of the city means the ultimate extinction of civilization; this, he says, is simply a cake of dead custom plastered over the vital urges of culture and stifling them. He – a mathematician – studies the morphology of cultures as Goethe studied the morphology of plants; he denies that one culture springs organically from another – Rome from Greece, etc. (though a new culture may finish off its façade with stones from the one it succeeds), but declares that it is an independent organism, which grows, unfolds its blossom of civilization, and must then by the very nature of a blossoming plant wither and die. The only remedy Spengler can find (*Preussentum und Sozialismus*, 1920) is in the fusion of Prussianism and Socialism; hence the saying that Spengler held Hitler over the baptismal font. In *Jahre der Entscheidung* (1933), however (written just after the accession to power of the Nazis), he rejects the worship of racial purity and argues that the Jews, by reason of their vitality, should be absorbed by and form part of the mighty Faustian race which some day must settle accounts with the black and yellow races. What is needed now is 'heroic pessimism', the first task of which is to crush the proletariat.

Post-War pessimism encouraged the vogue both of theosophy and mysticism. The head of the '*Anthroposophen*' was RUDOLF STEINER (1861-1925), who founded the Goetheanum. Christian Morgenstern ended his mystic meanderings in this shallow. Waldemar Bonsels weaves theosophy into his animal symbolism, and it provides GRAF HERMANN KEYSERLING (1880-1946), the cousin of Eduard von Keyserling, with an illusion of depth and an air of authority for the pretentious personal style of his *Das Reisetagebuch eines Philosophen* (1918) and *Schöpferische Erkenntnis* (1923). There is more depth and genuine brilliance of style in the mysticism of MARTIN BUBER (1878-): a Jew, he dreams a modern mysticism into the dogmatic clearness of Jewish religion; not medieval Ger-

---

[1] *Zur Kritik der Zeit* (1912); *Zur Mechanik des Geistes* (1913); *Von kommenden Dingen* (1917); *Wirtschaft, Staat und Gesellschaft* (7th ed. 1925).

many, but Asia is the mother of religion, and in prophetic Judaism is the vision of the religion to be. His *Drei Reden über das Judentum* (1911), with its contrast of *der sensorische Mensch* and *der motorische Mensch* (the first *'handelt in Bildern'*, the second *'empfindet in Bewegungen'*), gave a stimulus to the speculations of the expressionist theoreticians. Buber belongs to literature rather than to philosophy by his new translation of the Bible and the 'legendary anecdotes' of *Das verborgene Licht* (1924).

The *'Kulturphilosophen'* can hardly be set cheek by jowl with philosophers even of the calibre of Hermann von Keyserling; but they must have adequate treatment by reason of their immense influence on the National Socialist ideology and therefore on Nazi literature. The racialism of today goes back to PAUL DE LAGARDE (1827-91), one of the first to react against materialism and the Darwinistic interpretation of society (*Deutsche Schriften*, 1886). Another forerunner was JULIUS LANGBEHN (1851-1907), who created a sensation with an anonymous book, *Rembrandt als Erzieher. Von einem Deutschen* (1890). The author – 'der Rembrandtdeutsche', as he came to be called – was a disciple of Lagarde, and the very title of his book, which echoes Nietzsche's *Schopenhauer als Erzieher*, shows that he was a Nietzschean as well; certainly he continues Nietzsche in his thesis that Germany was in a process of decay, and that the only hope lay in its spiritual regeneration. This regeneration, he thought, would be effected by the Low German stock, to which he himself as a Holsteiner and his symbol Rembrandt as a Dutchman belonged. He held up Rembrandt as a great personality at the opposite pole of the tendencies of his own day: Rembrandt was a great creative soul, while today the world is run (to death) by the hair-splitting specialists of science. Regeneration would come from North-West Germany, he argued, because here is the cradle of the Aryans, and a nation is reborn from its birthplace. Racial fanatic as Langbehn is, he admits that assimilation of foreign cultures might improve the Nordic race: Rembrandt's close association with Jews (including Spinoza) no doubt led him to his conclusion that the aristocratic Jews of the West must be distinguished from the degenerated plebeian Jews of Poland and Russia. (Nietzsche had literally envisaged an improvement of the Nordic stock by assimilation of Jew culture.) There is a foretaste of the *Blut und Boden* theory in Langbehn's insistence that Rembrandt was an 'earth-born' artist with all the virtues of his native

Low German earth resplendent in his chiaroscuro. Langbehn, too, as a violent individualist, rejected Socialism as a reversion to primitive massing by herds. Salvation, he foretold, would come when the German masses and the separate States are welded together by a mighty Low German leader transfigured with the cultural radiance of his race ('*Zu einem Volk gehört notwendig ein Führer*'), and with this race-welding would go the incorporation of Holland and the Scandinavian lands.

Race worship is yet more extravagant in the notorious book of a renegade Englishman born at Portsmouth, HOUSTON STEWART CHAMBERLAIN (1855-1927): *Die Grundlagen des 19. Jahrhunderts* (1899-1904). The base of his philosophy is the idea of the self-willed regeneration of a nation ('*völkisch-seelische Erneuerung*'), possible in the creative Aryan race, which is contrasted with the inferior Semitic race. There was more of the substance of thought, perhaps, in ARTUR MOELLER VAN DEN BRUCK's (1876-1925) *Das Dritte Reich* (1923). His doctrine is based on his conception of '*das Primitive*'; in his studies of Italian art he stumbles on the discovery that Italian beauty was based on '*das Germanische*'. But Italian culture – and Romance culture generally – is exhausted; the Germans, on the other hand, are still 'primitive': therefore their future is to come. The Germans, too, with their eternally young idealism, are immune against the rationalism which has eaten up the vitality of other races. '*Wir sind heute*', he says, '*neue Deutsche, nach Geschichte und Bestimmung, nach Blut und Gesinnung, eine neue Nation auf der Erde.*' *Das Dritte Reich* was a best-seller, and more than anything else familiarized the term. The author committed suicide before his dream was realized. This 'Third Empire', according to the doctrines of Hitler's friend, the Russian-born ALFRED ROSENBERG (1893-1946), which he expounds in *Der Mythus des 20. Jahrhunderts* (1931) and *Blut und Ehre*, must be based on 'Nordic' culture, the only possible ideal of a German '*Volkstum*'. The attempt to displace Christianity is due mainly to Rosenberg's preaching; he explains as follows what his faith in the 'myth of blood' is: '*der Glaube, mit dem Blute auch das göttliche Wesen der Menschen überhaupt zu verteidigen, der mit hellstem Wissen verkörperte Glaube, dass das nordische Blut jenes Mysterium darstellt, das die alten Sakramente ersetzt und überwunden hat.*'

This is the philosophy approved by those in authority. But it may be that future historians of literature will give far greater prominence to that literature of revolt which no authority was able to repress, and will say that the finest eloquence of the Nazi period is in the protesting pamphlets of the Protestant and Catholic clergy. It is significant that religious scholars such as THEODOR HAECKER (1879-1945) found a market for books (*Satire und Polemik*, 1914-20; *Christentum und Kultur*, 1927) which have the traditional conception of culture. Haecker, a Protestant who turned Catholic, used Virgil (*Vergil, Vater des Abendlandes*, 1931), that *anima naturaliter christiana*, to show the very nature of culture. In *Was ist der Mensch?* (1933) he justified the Catholic faith and in *Schöpfer und Schöpfung* (1934) the ways of God to men. In *Schönheit: ein Versuch* (1939) he seeks the laws of beauty and love. His notes written down during the Nazi terror were published posthumously as *Tag- und Nachtbücher* (1947). His cultural philosophy is based on Kierkegaard, whom he translated and edited.

There are diverse currents in the Protestant existentialism of KARL BARTH (1886-), who, influenced by Kierkegaard, is very influential as a theologian; in England too he ranks with ALBERT SCHWEITZER (1875-) as an exponent of philosophical concepts as they touch Protestant or Unitarian religion (*Verfall und Wiederaufbau der Kultur*, 1923; *Kultur und Ethik*, 1923). His autobiographical works *Zwischen Wasser und Urwald* (36th thousand, 1926), in which he records his experiences as a Unitarian missionary in Africa, and *Aus meiner Kindheit und Jugend* (20th thousand, 1926), have been immensely popular. Existentialism or *Lebensphilosophie* (p. 448) as the literary movement that succeeds expressionism had its forerunner in RUDOLF KASSNER (1873-). He was born in Moravia, lived till 1938 in Vienna, and then settled in Switzerland. A facile label for him is *Dichter-Denker*; and his wide knowledge of languages and literatures is some justification for this: he has translated Plato's dialogues, Gogol, Puschkin, Tolstoy, Sterne (of whom he is very fond), Cardinal Newman, and André Gide. One of his first books was *Die Mystik, die Künstler und das Leben* (1900), now better known by its second title *Englische Dichter* (1920). Above all he is an iconoclast: he angrily topples over the cherished ideas and ideals of centuries, because, he asserts, they lead up to the nihilism of our own days, and he is so frightened by the rush to ruin of materialism that he sees safety only in being a Conservative ('*Aus meiner Erschrockenheit bin ich konservativ*'). What he fights for is the primacy of mind (*das Primat der Idee des Geistes*) and for '*Freiheit, die Idee der Ideen*'. He claims to be, not a philosopher (he detests the term), but a *Physiognomiker*, and he classes his system as *Physiognomik*. The meaning is that he takes into his vision all the things of the world, including man but with flora and fauna and all else equally graded as parts of a whole; in their outer appearances and in all he sees an inner and mystic meaning. Physiognomy in this sense replaces doctrine (*Lehre*). Like his contemporaries he sees German 'physiognomy' as distinctive and markedly different from that of other nations; it is '*ein Ausdruck der deutschen Einsamkeit oder, da dieser Einsamkeit nichts Romantisches mehr anhaftet, der deutschen All-Einheit*. Strange to say, though he is not a Christian, he accepts Christianity as a positive value, but the one philosophical system which he acknowledges as valid is existentialism, and this no doubt because he feels himself akin to Pascal and Kierkegaard. He has a vast variety of interests, enriched as much by his travels as his reading; although he was crippled and had to be wheeled about in a chair he saw much of England, travelled in North Africa and India, and in 1912 in Russia. His works which have most influenced his contemporaries are *Die Moral der Musik*, 1906 and 1922; *Melancholia. Eine Trilogie des Geistes*, 1908 and 1953; *Zahl und Gesicht*, 1919 and 1925; *Die Grundlagen der Physiognomik*, 1922 (second edition *Von der Signatur der Dinge*, 1951); *Die Verwandlung. Physiognomische Studien*, 1925; *Versuch einer Physiognomik der Ideen*, 1953; *Der Gottmensch. Gespräch und Gleichnis*, 1938. A good way of approach to this most difficult writer is by way of his autobiographical works: *Buch der Erinnerung*, 1938 and 1945; *Die zweite Fahrt*, 1946; and *Umgang der Jahre*, 1949, which includes his *Erinnerungen an England*.

XXII

EXISTENTIALISM AND
SURREALISM, POLITICAL AND
RELIGIOUS PHASES

One of the main ferments in the literature of recent years and of today is *der Existentialismus*. Though ostensibly a break-away from Expressionism it retains some of its main principles; cf. with what follows pp. 359 ff. Of programmatic Existentialism there are many aspects, simply because the writers classed on broad principles as existentialists interpret *existentia* (with its etymological roots in *ek-sistere*) each in his or her own way. The philosophical and religious tenets derive ultimately from the Danish thinker Søren Kierkegaard (1813-55). In Germany the concepts of existentialism have been defined and expounded by the philosophers KARL JASPERS (1883-) and MARTIN HEIDEGGER (1889-); both concern themselves with the real Being (*Sein*) of self and things, and they seek to eliminate whatever opposition there is between self and things. There is also the very extensive reflex action of foreign existentialists, particularly of the French writer Jean-Paul Sartre with his novel *La Nausée* (1938). Since Sartre derives his existentialism from Heidegger and Jaspers the term is obviously philosophical. The essence of its meaning is already woven into the later works of Thomas Mann, Hermann Hesse, and Jakob Wassermann with their mysticized expressionism, and in the Magic Realism (*der magische Realismus, die magische Wirklichkeit*) of Georg Heym, Ernst Stadler, Georg Trakl, Hans Carossa and Robert Musil it marks a new stage. The literary programme is best classed as *Surrealismus*, which is taken over from the term *surréalisme* coined by Sartre to blazon his decoction of Heidegger; literally interpreted it can only mean *Überwirklichkeits-*

448

kunst. This new trend first developed in France as *le mouvement Dada,* with Jean Cocteau as its irreverent iconoclast. Dadaism was a poets' revolt against the hegemony of reason; the creed of the Dadaists was that contraries are identical, that art is an absurdity, and that the crying need is the hilarious rending to shreds of everything in all the traditional forms of art; for real reality is not visioned by the eyes or reached by the processes of reason or analysis, but is apprehended intuitionally or even revealed in dreams. The aim must be to reach the spontaneous Unconscious, and for this we must sweep away the illusory cohesion of realism in its dictionary sense and impose what the French Dadaists dubbed *l'anti-poétique raison.* Der Dadaismus sobered gradually and passed over into *der Surrealismus,* which has glaring Freudian elements. The root concept is absolutely negative, for it springs from the (more or less conscious) feeling of the human creature that he is cast out (*Geworfensein* is the *cliché*) into a world on which he is helplessly dependent (*insecuritas humana*), and that if he seeks escape in art from the *Angst* which this *Gefährdetsein* brings it can only be by laughing it off derisively. For Jaspers, however, there are moments in which by the very intensity of this feeling we dimly feel the Transcendent, and the Surrealist may seize this perception to shape it in art. So that the final outcome of *Existenzphilosophie* may be either Nihilism or Mysticism. What we do get in the most representative Surrealists are glimpses of the Transcendent behind the raw reality of life. The protagonists of Surrealism were André Breton (*Manifeste du Surréalisme,* 1924), Louis Aragon, and Paul Eluard, and the study of these poets went to the shaping of German *Surrealismus.* The initiator of German Dadaism was the Alsatian Hans Arp (1887-), who in his verse (*Wortträume und schwarze Sterne,* selected poems, 1953) does succeed in freeing words from their hackneyed meanings. He has an international reputation as a sculptor and his volume of French verse *Le siège de l'air* (1946) counts in the history of Dadaism. Arp's last book, *Worte mit und ohne Anker* (1957), includes poems composed over a period of fifty years, and shows the poet still anchored to his ancient self. These new movements – we have much the same orientation here in the verse of T. S. Eliot and W. H. Auden – merge and fuse so intimately that they may be grouped together as *Transrealismus,* the sense of the term being that these *Neutöner* do not so much reduce realism to the absurd as that they follow *der Realismus* and (in intention) prove that the anti-poetical absurd pierces to Being in itself; 'things' are not merely sense-appearances but far more dream-appearances and mind-apperceptions; or in other words the poet's theme is the ultimate *chose*, not the evanescent *chose vue*.

One aspect or phase of Surrealism which is very much to the fore today, especially in the novel, is simultaneity (*Doppelbödigkeit*). Man is made up of two entities: (1) his visible body, which makes contact with the world in space through the medium of his senses, and (2) an invisible mind which has no contact with space but is conscious of time. Actually the pedigree of *Doppelbödigkeit* flings back to Joyce's *Ulysses*. It is really a question of creation on two planes of consciousness (*Gestaltung auf zwei Ebenen*). Man is conscious of time past, present, and future; and in this sense of time the novelists here concerned nestle in varying degrees of closeness to Proust.[1] But the lighter variants take over the technique of Virginia Woolf as well as of Thomas Wolfe, Thornton Wilder, and Ernest Hemingway. There may be an existential contradiction between what is said and what is thought, and thus we have the two phases of *Sagen und Meinen*. There may also be an existential contradiction between what one does and what one feels (*Tun und Empfinden*). What is essential is to reach the inner nature of the speaking character; the accepted term is *er-innern*. The gospel text is Kierkegaard's: '*Die Bewegung der Entwicklung geht nach innen, nicht nach aussen; die Szene ist innen, nicht aussen, ist eine Geisterszene.*' One essential feature of this *Doppelbödigkeit* is *das Diskontinuum*: the story or the poem is not built up systematically from A to Z, but leaps from phase to phase, as in Joyce's *Ulysses*, or follows Proust's principle of the flash-back to a previous phase (*Rückerinnerung*), so that there is no continuity but instead there are chunks of life, so to speak, which the reader must piece together. In the lyric this often leads to what reads like an enumeration of glimpses of something or other or a concatenation of jolted ejaculations (*Funkensprünge*) leaping from the thing to the idea of the thing. There is no middle and (may be) no ending; all is in flux – as life is.

We have Kierkegaard's *Geisterszene* in the writings of FRANZ KAFKA (1883-1924). Historically – that is, by period and contacts – he belongs to expressionism. But, judged by content, he is close to Sartre and closer still to Kierkegaard, and it is more fitting to

[1] 'I see the Past, Present and Future existing all at once before me.'— Thomas Blake.

classify him as an existentialist; in any case he is too remote from gush of sentiment and rush of rhetoric, too precise and thoughtfully sober in his style, too metaphysically introspective and self-probing, too clear and concrete to be put cheek by jowl with his friends Franz Werfel and Max Brod. Moreover he is monothematic, whereas the expressionists proper launch out all-embracing into worlds known and unknown. Today Kafka is classed both as a magic realist and as a surrealist; and certainly he is not shy of describing the lowest and even the filthiest aspects of life; but, as we shall see, his realism and obscenities are symbols. He is indeed a surrealist in the sense that his world is *überwirklich*; but this amounts rather to mysticism than to realism. In his division of existence into the two worlds of finite reality and metaphysical reality he is likely to have learned something from Dostoieffsky; e.g. Kafka's ultimate purpose is to reconcile these two worlds, which is the problem handled in *Crime and Punishment*. This reconciling of the two worlds of the sensuous and earthly and the irrational world of spirituality (*Geistigkeit*), the finite and the infinite, is the theme to which Kafka restricts his considerable fertility of invention – as it is, too, of Kierkegaard, in whose works Kafka was versed, particularly in *Furcht und Zittern*. What distinguishes Kafka from other religious thinkers is that he expresses the infinite in finite terms. In his writings the finiteness of reality does not exist; there are the outward chattels and furniture of reality, but the characters who move about in this nominally naturalistic environment and carry the sense of the story (the *Sinnfiguren*) are irrational, ghost-like.

No one who reads Kafka can miss the fact that there is no description of landscape; except, more or less, in the novel *Amerika*, where some idea of the outside scene is given; generally speaking, rooms and offices, courts of law, pubs, and all the rest are visionary. What presses in on the reader's consciousness is the sense of what is behind the scenes; what happens in actuality has often the appearance of rank nonsense. Neither is there psychology in the psychologist's sense; the probing into states of mind is religious, not medical. For this reason the cock-sure equivalences of the psychologists are beside the mark.

If we attach importance to the framework of the stories we must recognize that for the horrific happenings and the transmutations of animals to beasts, etc., there is a pedigree reaching from E. T. A. Hoffmann through Edgar Allen Poe to the neo-romantic *Grotesken* which were popular just as Kafka was trying his 'prentice hand. His contacts then were with the Prague Jews, whom he met in the cafés of the town; of these Gustav Meyrink in particular specialized in hair-raising nightmarish stories. In Kafka's stories, however, the horrors are not worked up to curdle the reader's blood; we read the most ghastly of them with nerves unthrilled and mind alert, realizing that they are intensified meta-physical symbols.

Kafka's life story is in great part the key to his work. Born in Prague as the son of well-to-do Jewish parents he was a pupil at the *Gymnasium* and thereafter was a student at Prague University, first of chemistry and German language and literature, from which he switched over to law. He made friends with a fellow student, Max Brod (p. 381), who, after Kafka's early death, published his friend's work. After taking his degree in 1906 Kafka was for a year a barrister without pay (*Referendar*) in attendance at the law courts; when, however, his father insisted on his earning money he worked for a year in the family business, then as an official in a workmen's insurance company. Since he finished work at 2.0 p.m. he had leisure to follow his literary leanings. In World War I he was granted exemption from military service on the grounds of poor physique and ill health. By 1917 he was known to be suffering from tuberculosis. He went to Berlin to devote himself to litera-ture; but the post-war privations aggravated his disease and he was removed to a sanatorium near Vienna, where he died in 1924 at the age of forty-one. In the last years of his life he lived happily with Dora Dymant, and wished to marry her, but her father for-bade the marriage because Kafka was not orthodox. Our know-ledge of Kafka's life comes mostly from Max Brod's *Franz Kafka: eine Biographie* (1936). The poet Richard Garta in Brod's novel *Das Zauberreich der Liebe* (1928) is more or less a pen-portrait of his friend. His love letters to Milena, a married lady who translated his early work into Czech, are revealing; there was love on both sides, but instead of consummation there was that helpless frus-tration which is one of the key-notes of his work. Dora Dymant has provided information concerning the last years of his life. One of the main facts is that of his relations with his father, who, a successful business man, had no understanding for the literary avocations of his son. In consequence there developed the son-father conflict and the persecution-conflict in the son. This is reflected throughout Kafka's work and is plainly stated in his famous letter of 1919 to his father: 'My writings,' he says, 'are all about you.' Of great importance are the *Tagebücher* in which he describes his work as *'Darstellung meines traumhaften inneren Lebens'*; they cover the period 1914-23 (Vols. 7 and 8 of the *Gesammelte Schriften*, 1935-7), and provide evidence of Kafka's continuous isolation and frustration. Wherever he turns, a 'black wave' surges against him. *'Ich kann nicht lieben,'* he writes, *'ich bin ausgewiesen.'* And again: 'one becomes aware of how every person is lost in himself beyond hope of rescue.' As a Jew in a town like Prague, contact with Christian officialdom made him feel that he was an outsider.

Kafka shrank from publishing his works. Max Brod persuaded him to publish a volume of short passages, *Betrachtung* (1913). It was coldly received. Other short stories and fragments published during his lifetime were: *Der Heizer* (1913, a fragment which was later the first chapter of his novel *Amerika*); *Die Verwandlung* (1915); *Das Urteil* (1916); *Ein Landarzt* (1919), made up of fourteen short stories or sketches; *In der Strafkolonie* (1919); *Ein Hungerkünstler* (1923). Max Brod, Kafka's executor, ignored testamentary directions to burn unpublished works; and the three novels *Der Prozess* (1925), *Das Schloss* (1926), and *Amerika* (1927), all unfinished, which he saw through the press, won world-wide fame and gave the dead author rank as one of the great innovators of the first half of the century.

The son-father conflict stands out in *Das Urteil*, in which a son drowns himself at his father's bidding, and in *Die Verwandlung*, later rechristened *Die Metamorphose*. In *Die Verwandlung* Gregor Samsa, a commercial traveller, wakes up one morning to find that in his sleep he has been transformed into a man-sized slimy insect (*ein ungeheures Ungeziefer*; the genus is not more clearly specified). He crawls about the room and hangs down, feet upwards, from the ceiling. When his father, mother, and sister find him thus transmogrified he understands what they say to him, but he cannot speak. To them he is an animal. He eats anything rotten, but turns away in disgust from anything fresh. At the same time this species of bug thinks himself entitled to be treated with all human consideration, and his faculty of thinking is unimpaired; he turns back in his mind to his old business life and the wretched-

30

ness of it and the abject subjection to tyranny that it was, especially since at home he was the victim of his family, who were unable to understand his yearning for higher things and creative activity. His sister at first shows pity, then gives him up. The furniture is removed; he covers with his slimy body the picture of a lady robed in furs; he still longs for the beautiful. In measure as his family's loathing for him grows, so does his feeling of isolation, until he dies of starvation. His family celebrate the occasion by going on a picnic. What is the meaning of this metamorphosis? There have been a variety of interpretations. But in the light of what we now know of Kafka's trend of thought in those days it seems clear that at all events one element in the story is Kafka's conflict with his father; in the 1919 letter to his father he refers to himself as '*Ungeziefer*'. Clear, too, is the reaction to Darwinism: not *Übermenschentum*, but *Übertier*, *Kreatürlichkeit*. Transmutations of human to beast and *vice versa* were elements of the neo-romantic *Märchen*; and in form *Die Verwandlung* has something of the *Märchen*; but these transmutations in the true *Märchen* are not symbols of intellectual processes; one might, therefore, class *Die Verwandlung* as, since it is the contrary of a *Märchen* proper, an *Antimärchen*. There is transformation, too, in *Ein Bericht für eine Akademie*, one of the sketches of *Ein Landarzt*: a monkey trained at Hagenbeck's Zoo is transformed to man. He has a wife, '*eine kleine halbdressierte Schimpansin*'; and, he says, '*ich lasse es mir nach Affenart bei ihr wohlgehen. Bei Tag will ich sie nicht sehen . . .*'. Here, too, there is a thinking process: *nach Affenart* is a sly dig at routine marriage. There is more of the later metaphysical Kafka in *Vor dem Gesetz*, another parable of *Ein Landarzt*: before the Law stands a doorkeeper. To him comes a man from the country and craves admittance. He is told that admittance cannot be granted. The man waits and waits close by the open door, but entrance is again and again refused. The door-keeper gives him a stool, and he sits on it days and years till at last he is on the point of death; the door-keeper then roars into his ears: 'Nobody could obtain admittance here; for this entrance was destined for you and none other. Now I will go and close it.' *In der Strafkolonie* tells of an explorer who inspects a machine which kills a man by engraving his sentence into his flesh with vibrating needles. The victim pinioned to the floor of the machine has no idea what his crime is, but 'he will feel it in his flesh'. Here we have one of Kafka's main concepts that by the very nature of the universe we are punished innocently: punishment as part of evil is in the nature of things. Can we change this torture? If so, it must be by destroying the machine which – incalculable and erratic but diabolically planned – brands us, prong by prong, with sins of which we are unconscious, or for natural impulses beyond our control but forbidden by the 'Law' which sets the machine in motion. The laws of society and religion are not ethical, but mechanical and out of date because transmitted from a time when, if they were even then absurd, they may have had more pictorial impressiveness because they were implicitly believed in, whereas now they are valid to none save the automatons who administer them.

In these sketches there are motifs of isolation (*Vereinzelung*) and frustration (*Vereitelung*). There is a haunting presentation of these themes and of the accompanying state of *Angst* in three tales of the posthumously published collection *Beim Bau der chinesischen Mauer* (1931). In *Der Bau* an animal bores deep down into the earth to escape contact with the outside world; but however deep it gets it never feels safe from attack; and its fear grows when it hears the least sound from afar. Man is in a state of fear, the meaning is, because he does not know *why* he fears and *what* he fears. Man's incomprehension of life as a whole and of the purpose of the Power behind life is vividly rendered in the titular story of the collection. Every individual working on this vast undertaking of the Chinese Wall sees only the stretch within the sweep of his vision. And yet a message is on the way to every worker from the Emperor in Peking; the perils of the journey are, however, such that the messengers never arrive. The meaning seems to be that we are not permitted to know the sense of existence in this world of ours; and we are in any case so preoccupied with our individual experiences that we have lost the chance of comprehending the binding together of all we see and have no consciousness of a composite whole. But the Power above knows and sends out his rays of hope; since, however, these do not reach us we blunder on in isolation, fear, and frustration. In *Forschungen eines Hundes* a dog engages in investigations into food and where it comes from; it can only do so in isolation from the rest of dog-kind. Since dog is to man as man is to God the problem is that of our relations to the Higher Power. As so often in Kafka's work the high seriousness is lit by flashes of humour: dogs by instinct water what is beneath them, and this dog ponders what the relation can be of this necessary habit with the origin of his necessary food. There is also, to the dog, the problem of music: this comes from another world than that of dog. But no proof is possible, to a dog, of a connection between the physical and the spiritual world. Thus we live in a world of mystery that it is futile to seek to fathom.

The three novels – 'a trilogy of loneliness', as Max Brod calls them – expand and intensify the processes of thought of the short stories. All three are unfinished; it was perhaps Kafka's idea that they were bound to be unfinished, for they each represent a quest for the infinite, and the infinite cannot be reached from the finite. We are in the position of the investigating dog.

In *Der Prozess* Josef K. (obviously self-identification of hero and author is indicated), a bank-clerk, is asleep in bed when he is roused by a warder and told that he is arrested. The routine of his life, he learns, may proceed as usual, but he is summoned to appear before an examining magistrate who holds court in the stuffy, slanting attic of a house in a slum. Josef K. is never told what the charge against him is, and there is no indication that he is not innocent. In his efforts to reach his judges he gropes like a grotesque automaton through the swiftly moving ghost-like happenings of a nightmare, impelled forwards but held back. No progress is made; that is, the trial is *zeitlos*, out of time. In the ante-room is a plump washerwoman, and the proceedings are interrupted when she is seized at the rear of the court by a legal acolyte in a sexual paroxysm; the code of the law which the presiding judge has before him opens with two cubist nudes of opposite sexes writhing towards each other but unable to unite because they are too stiffly drawn. Josef K. himself flirts with this washerwoman. After a year of such proceedings the end comes: two pale, fat men wearing frock coats and silk hats take him to a quarry and kill him, 'like a dog'. The situation has been interpreted as that of a Jew in a Christian bureaucracy; but against this we have what Kafka says: '*Es gibt nur eine geistige Welt; was wir die körperliche Welt nennen, ist das Böse in der geistigen.*' The meaning would thus be that the individual rebels against spiritual powers which he does not understand. Josef K., who was guiltless before his summons, incurs guilt because he does not acknowledge his judge. The parallel may be with Job, who disputes with God. Kafka is said to have stated that the lesson intended is that Everyman, instead of living heedlessly and comfortably, should take up his cross and bear it; he must realize that life has higher duties than those of routine existence, and that these are imposed by the Law, which must be accepted without contradiction, however unjust this divine justice may appear. Josef K.'s life has been that of any ordinary man who works dutifully and amuses himself normally; he pays a weekly visit to a barmaid, but that does not constitute guilt. His guilt is not that he has been immoral, but that he has lived without taking thought; now he awakens suddenly to the consciousness (his arrest is the symbol of this awakening) that he had lost, or never had, the sense of what is beyond life.

The next novel, *Das Schloss*, is a nightmare in which the dreamer's attempts to move forward are baffled at every step he tries to take. The hero, K., has been appointed to the post of surveyor at a castle; but when he arrives at the village at the foot of the Castle he is told that no surveyor is wanted; he makes endless but fruitless efforts to get in touch with those inside the Castle. He learns that the person of importance is 'divisional chief' Klamm; to get at this official he sleeps with Klamm's mistress Frieda; but this, too, leads to nothing. To keep going he accepts a job as janitor in the village school, while the love affair with Frieda goes on spasmodically. The sense of the tale is again the mystery of existence. Whereas Josef K. in *Der Prozess* was summoned because he did not seek the Law, K. in *Das Schloss* sets out in quest of the Law. Or: he is seeking Grace; and in this quest it is not a matter of whatever rights he may have as an individual, but of whether he is chosen (*Erwähltheit*) or cast out. *Das Schloss* is our existence between Here and Beyond. As events prove K. is not capable of finding what he seeks. He knocks and it is *not* opened unto him. As a surveyor in the Castle he would have been fulfilling his higher destiny; as a school janitor he is sundered from the higher life he seeks. He seeks what is out of reach for him. Very significant in *Das Schloss* is the role played by women. K. acts in the conviction that women are in direct touch with the Castle. That is why he seeks sexual intercourse with them; they are a means to his end. This was so, too, in *Der Prozess*. Women have a mediating function; they are a link with the irrational Powers who rule us. This is indicated by the fact that Frieda is the mistress of Klamm. Women give themselves unreservedly to the Castle officials; this is their privilege, their realization of self.

There is filthiness of detail – but life *is* filthy; thus K. and Frieda press face to face as they lie embracing in dregs of spilt beer on the floor of a pub. Thus the degradation of the function of sexual love is symbolized, the degradation of spirituality – which union in love should be – to animal sensuality. Thus in literature – the highest literature – as in life the nobility of man's mind is prostituted. In sex relations there is no need of the transformation to bugs or other unclean things: in the sex grip normal man and woman *are* unclean beasts. Both Josef K. and K. are intellectuals; they think, they seek; but by that very fact they plan success by means of sensual pleasure.

Amerika is generally considered the weakest novel of the trilogy because there is in it some lift of the spirit towards happiness. Karl Rossmann, a boy of seventeen, has been seduced by a servant at his home, a woman of thirty-five. She wishes to father on the boy the child she is to bear, and so he is packed off to America. The story of the seduction, transparently real in all its sexual details, cunningly framed but to the boy dream-like, makes it clear that Karl is not so much innocent as an innocent; in him we have once again *der reine Tor* of the medieval legends. At New York harbour, just as he is about to land, he notices that he has left his umbrella below and goes down to fetch it. He gets lost in a maze of corridors, and finally meets a stoker who complains to him of having been harshly treated by the chief engineer. They wander off together to the chief cashier's office, where the stoker makes his complaint to the captain, who happens to be present. The complaint meets deaf ears; all are against the plaintiff. When Karl himself pleads for him, he is asked for his name. He gives it, and a gentleman of prosperous appearance standing near the captain at once cries out that he is his nephew; he recognizes him from the description that has been sent him. The stoker is left with no hope of redress, and the senator takes the wondering boy to his luxurious home, where he is kept more or less in confinement; however he visits a friend of his uncle's, whereupon the latter casts him off. He works as a lift-boy in an hotel, but is dismissed. He has adventures in the glamorous panorama of a New York such as we know it from films. Karl remains ever innocent and good, ever *der reine Tor*, as he winds his way through these labyrinths of city life. The last chapter – found by Max Brod in his friend's posthumous papers – comes nearest in Kafka's work to joy and hope of happiness; there is a final refuge for Karl in the legendary nature theatre of Oklahoma, in which all waifs and strays and workless people find peace and occupation. But it must be noted that *Amerika* was begun first of the three novels (the first chapter, as pointed out, is *Der Heizer*) and Max Brod records that Kafka spoke of a tragic ending that he was planning.

Hochzeitsvorbereitungen auf dem Lande und andere Prosa aus dem Nachlass (1953), with notes by Max Brod, contains valuable autobiographical material; the long *Brief an den Vater* is at the same time an important document in the son-father conflict of expressionism.

From what has been said it will be clear that in Kafka's work the leading motifs of fear (*Angst*), isolation, frustration, the sense of being cast out (*das Ausgestossensein*), the feeling of being guilty somehow or other without knowing why, the premonition that judgment must be spoken, negative the doctrine of salvation by belief in God – Kafka's God is inscrutable. But 'God' is not a word used by Kafka; neither is Jehovah, but Jehovah, the old divinity of the Jews, who brings men to judgment and vengefully condemns them, comes to life anew as the Power behind these tales. In Kafka's fiction, however, as in the Hebrew scriptures He judges and casts out those who have cast themselves out. This is the Law, against which there is no appeal. Moreover the Law is indifferent to what we suffer in seeking it. It is no use praying; prayers are not heard. For the Divine ordinance acts immutably whatever we do; all we can hope to do is to act in accordance with the Divine ordinance. We must save ourselves. The door is open. The radiance beyond the door to the Law is reality, the only reality, the world of the spirit. We read: '*Die Tatsache, dass es nur eine geistige Welt gibt, beraubt uns der Hoffnung und – gibt uns Gewissheit.*' And again: '*Es gibt nichts anderes als eine geistige Welt; was wir eine sinnliche Welt nennen, ist nur eine Notwendigkeit eines Augenblicks unserer ewigen Entwicklung.*' What we need is humility and work for work's sake, not for reward. We can live a full life if we are innocent and humble, and if we do not question the inscrutable and possibly in appearance foolish ordering (but foolish only because we apply 'reason' to things that are divine) of whatsoever Power controls us. Reason is the foe of faith. Not reason but faith gives sense to life, and this faith we must seek as Parzival sought the Grail. Faith alone gives us power to endure the disharmony between the physical and the spiritual world. Finally: '*Wer sucht, findet nicht, aber wer nicht sucht, wird gefunden.*' This, Kafka might have said, is the theology of today – the theology of time-wearied men in great rotting cities.

Close to Kafka is HERMANN KASACK's (1896-) allegorical novel *Die Stadt hinter dem Strom* (1948), somewhat in the nature of Albert Camus' *La Peste* (1947). It is not so much the City of the Dead that is chronicled as an intermediary station (*Zwischenreich*) where those who have crossed the river from earth make a stay before their dissolution. The story is that an orientalist who has fallen in love with the wife of another man accepts a post as archivist in a town 'across the river', and that by his experiences here he acquires insight into the nature of life and death, above all the knowledge that life, washed round as it is with death, is a continuous process of clarification (*Klärung*) and purification (*Läuterung*). To this state the archivist attains in the embrace of the woman he had loved on earth and whom he finds here again – in her bare arm he notices a long scar from an incision and suddenly realizes that she is not flesh but spirit. She had committed suicide. Now his carnal passion for her fades into that human pity which we should all feel if we stripped ourselves of the trammels of self (*Entselbstung*). The doctor now recrosses the bridge earthwards, and crisscrosses the country in a series of linked railway trains which serve him in his mission as an itinerant preacher driving home the lessons he has learned. Life as it is on earth, he now comprehends, is at its best a transposition of matter to spirit; but all that is earthly must, because it is matter, be broken up after its term and returned to its origin for rebirth. This is symbolized by the two factories in the City across the River – in one of them artistic slabs are produced and these are then sent to the second factory to be ground into powder and afterwards returned to the first factory for re-making. His first impression of the City was that it had been laid waste by bombs, and when regiment after regiment of soldiers came marching over the bridge he had realized that a war was raging. This throws light on the origins of the novel: the first half was written 1942-44 and it was finished in 1946. It is thus one of the *Nachkriegsromane* of the late forties. The concept may owe something to Thornton Wilder's *Our Town* and *The Skin of our Teeth*.[1] The style

[1] The work is also highly reminiscent of Sutton Vane's play *Outward Bound*, produced at the Everyman Theatre, London, in 1923 and later made into a film.

of the symbolic state of being out of time and space is reminiscent of Ernst Jünger's *Auf den Marmorklippen* and *Heliopolis*. Equally close to Kafka is Kasack's *Der Webstuhl* (1949), again a visualization of the mechanized hell of the totalitarian State, which by the laws of its being necessarily disintegrates. What is described is the weaving of a carpet in which a country's life is centred. Originally the carpet was a symbol of ritual; but with the course of time the symbol has faded, and all that remains is mechanical repetition. Machines replace handlooms, production is intensified, and the carpet spreads and spreads until an explosion destroys all the looms and saves the threatened land from suffocation. The symbol in its total sense is that of the evolution of a State – or of religion – or of mankind. A third novel, *Das grosse Netz* (1952), is again a symbol of an Unseen Power; this shoots a film in which mankind, as the pictures turn, is shown as regimented, mechanized, and dehumanized by the planned economy gone mad of the world of today – we know the pattern from Aldous Huxley's more dynamic *Brave New World*. Kasack is also a dramatist: *Die tragische Sendung* (1920); *Vincent* (1924; the theme is – as in Johann Gunert's poem *Leben des Malers Vincent van Gogh* – the relation to world and time of Vincent van Gogh); *Die Schwester* (1926). His lyric verse is collected in *Das ewige Dasein* (1943).

There is again a ghostly and twilight atmosphere superimposed on realism in the work of ERNST KREUDER (1903-) in his short stories *Die Nacht der Gefangenen* (1939) as in his novels *Die Gesellschaft vom Dachboden* (1946) and *Die Unauffindbaren* (1948). But, as he has stated in his essays, his conception of reality is not that of the gloomiest of his contemporaries who are haunted by the inescapability of post-war chaos; on the contrary there is an ordered reality in the soul of man, and the cosmos is by its very nature an imposed order that winds its way out of chaos, wherefore the inwardness of romantic joy in life is justified now and ever. In agreement with this main concept the substance of Kreuder's novels is deliberately unrealistic, though they record in symbolic fashion the reality of experience; for Kreuder true reality has the pith and marrow of poetry. He is thus at the same time a surrealist and a neo-romanticist. *Die Gesellschaft vom Dachboden* was the first German work of fiction to be translated into English (as *The Attic Pretenders*) after the war. It may owe some prompting to G. K. Chesterton's *Manalive* (1912). A band of young folk found a secret society (*Geheimbund*) to fight the silliness which comes from starved imagination and in the grip of which men are crushed by the leaden load of day-to-day existence. *Die Unauffindbaren* records the doings of a band of anarchists who live in an America of imagination everywhere and nowhere in a land of dreams. There is again juggling with space and time and reality fused with dream in the poetry (*Gedichte*, 1947), dramas (the action of *Die Rotte Kain*, 1949, takes place '*mindestens zehntausend Jahre vor dem bekannten Bibelereignis*'), and in the fiction (*Nekya*, 1947) of ERNST NOSSACK (1901-). Something of Kafka's depiction of life as a nightmare occurs, too, in the fiction of HEINZ RISSE (1898-). His novel *Wenn die Erde bebt* (1950) has guilt and atonement for its basic problem; but there is a note of hope for a world rocked and shattered by wars in the motto of Novalis to which it is shaped: '*Unser Leben ist kein Traum, aber es soll und wird vielleicht einer werden.*' The theme is carried on in the Novellen *So frei von Schuld* (1951) and *Feldmäuse* (1951).

In the later work of ERNST JÜNGER (1895-) there is something of the mystic idealism of Ernst Kreuder's questing of the ideal city or of the ideal State, but the heart of his work is 'heroic realism'. And this holds good even of the dream imagery of his later mythological allegories. Indeed the whole of his work can be classed as heroic realism, but only in the sense that in his conception of it heroism is real; it is the age-old mark of the German character; it is cruel because it is real. And also: heroic leadership is the prerogative of the higher and the cultured classes; in other words Ernst Jünger is an aristocrat to his finger-tips; his sum and substance is the recovery of conservative supremacy and domination in the face of the democratic uplift of our days. At sixteen he ran away from school, made his way to Marseilles, and enlisted in the Foreign Legion, from which he was in due course released by family efforts; this escapade he describes from the mellow retrospect of maturity in his *Afrikanische Spiele* (1936). In 1914 he joined up as a volunteer, was frequently and seriously wounded in trench warfare, and was awarded the *Ordre pour le mérite* for his fearless leadership of his men. During the Nazi régime he was in contact with resistance circles, but escaped arrest. It is significant that after the Second World War he was forbidden to write; in public estimation he was still the fervent militarist who had made his reputation by his war diary *In Stahlgewittern* (1920; in 1942 the title was changed to *Ein Kriegstagebuch*). This was followed by *Der Kampf als inneres Erlebnis* (1920), *Das Wäldchen 125* (1925) and *Feuer und Blut* (1926), which together make up the epic of his war experiences. The title of *Die totale Mobilmachung* (1931) trumpets the sense of the text: the total mobilization of mankind is called for to build up totalitarian government. *Der Arbeiter* (1932) portrays the fashion and functioning of the totalitarian State, which by reason of its concern for totality can take no account of the individual soul and therefore must give no room to Christianity. The God of *Der Arbeiter* is Technique. We have here a determined and well reasoned reduction to absurdity of the tenets of Karl Marx; freedom, runs the argument, means stripping oneself of self, is labour not for self or personality, but as one merged in a mass, a 'type'. This Fascist doctrine – in essence the sanctified tradition of Prussian class supremacy – is further expounded in *Blätter und Steine* (1934). In *Das abenteuerliche Herz* (1929, revised version 1938) he comes to grips with post-war moods and tendencies; looking back to World War I he looks forward to the Second, which in *Der Arbeiter* he had declared to be inevitable and which is already casting its shadows before. The revised edition of the work issued in 1938 reveals a change of spirit and a full appreciation of western culture. This *Wandlung* comes out more clearly in the visionary speculations and the self-revelation of *Auf den Marmorklippen* (1939); he has had his fill of the totalitarian State and what he gives us here is a post-Fascist attack, veiled in dream-symbolism, on Nazi tyranny. It is an allegory of an ancient culture destroyed by a tyrant and his sub-human myrmidons. Now we hear of a trinity of Word, Might, and Spirit, which supplants the tyranny of War, Might, and Power of the earlier works. And the greatest power in the new trinity is the Word, which cannot exist without *Geist und Freiheit*. Moreover those who proclaim the Word are individuals, who have no place in the massed reality of *Der Arbeiter*. And the way to self-realization for the individual is the cultivation of the Beautiful. In form, *Auf den Marmorklippen* is one of the pioneer works on the principle of *Doppelbödigkeit*; the scene is contemporaneously in the region of the Lake of Constance, Dalmatia, and Burgundy, and the period is simultaneously that of classical antiquity, of German pre-history, the Middle Ages, the Renaissance, and the present. All this mirrors the development of Europe; and it is very noticeable that Ernst

Jünger now acknowledges the validity of religious faith; faith is a help in the pessimism that is inevitable in the face of perpetual evil, but the great comfort is that evil and catastrophe cannot quell the spirit of man: *'die Stunde der Vernichtung ist die Stunde des Lebens'*. Ernst Jünger served as an officer from start to finish of World War II, and part of his experience of it is covered by *Gärten und Strassen* (1942). Since the book betrayed sympathy with the sufferings of the French it was banned. It is made up of diary entries (1939-40) covering the preparations for war and the advance through France. Here Jünger faces up to the facts and fierceness of war, as he does courageously and clearly in *Der Friede* (1948), which circulated secretly in sheets; and here, too, he finds his way back to Christian concepts of love and charity. Clearly the ultimate aim of Jünger's 'heroic realism' is to get the best of the nation back from leftist extremes of democracy to the pith and marrow of a nationalist Conservatism. Another volume in diary form is *Strahlungen* (1949); the entries run from 1941 to 1945, and were written in Paris, Russia, and Germany. The works that follow World War II are intended to be a gospel of salvation for Germany; at a time when the only cathedrals that remain are 'those formed by the cupolas of folded hands' the only hope lies in spiritual regeneration. Jünger sets his face against the nihilism of the masses in *Über die Linie* (1950), which upholds the cultural ferment of Eros and the creative impulses of art and literature. In *Der Waldgang* (1950) we have a picture of the homeless individual of today, who resolutely crosses the meridian of nihilism (*Nullmeridian*) to reconquer freedom. The threads of *Auf den Marmorklippen* are taken up again in *Heliopolis* (1949), an allegorical novel more or less in the line of Kasack's *Die Stadt hinter dem Strom*; it is clearly influenced by Aldous Huxley's *Brave New World*. This 'city of the sun' is pictured as spiritually more real than the cities our earth has known. The action takes place between the overthrow of the first world empire and the foundation of the second. Actually the chronicle of our own time is interwoven in this vision of the future which – by the victory of truth, of freedom, of love – is bound to come. It is the world of Superman. In the world of fierce conflict between Landvogt and Proconsul (Hitler and Hindenburg), between Demos on the one hand and on the other *die Edeltrefflichen* – a class who through phases of change and levelling down have kept the qualities of their ancestors – the problems of Germany today are set out in clear lines. As a travel writer Ernst Jünger followed up *Atlantische Fahrt* (1947) with *Myrdun*. *Briefe aus Norwegen* (1948) and *Ein Inselfrühling*. *Ein Tagebuch aus Rhodos* (1949). In the essay *Sprache und Körperbau* (1947) we have the culmination of his musings on the mysteries of language, of the Word which, he says, is 'the sword-blade of meaning'; this interest in the symbolic magic of sound goes back to *Lob der Vokale*, one of the essays of *Blätter und Steine*, and recurs in other works. Jünger is indeed so conscious an artificer of language and style that he has been charged with a lack of spontaneity; his handling of words, it is suggested, is contrived to convey excogitated nuances of meaning. The more general view is that as a stylist he is ultra-refined and that, though he lacks the subtlety of (say) Hermann Hesse, he is one of the great craftsmen of recent years.

'Magic realism' as applied to the later novels of Hermann Hesse, in which, though the milieu is fantastic, the psychology is basically real, is a dubious term. It is a question whether it fits Ernst Jünger's mythical explorations of the present, if only because his conception of realism is ideal, not real; HANS CAROSSA (1878-1956) it fits exactly. For his symbolic interpretation of life is psychologically and literally true under the halo of dream; it is visionary, but what the vision bodies forth in a world of phantasy exists in everyday life. Carossa's own designation of himself is that he is a healer; he decided early that he would handle language as he handled *Heilgifte* (a favourite word of his) in his practice as a doctor; it is the poet-healer, he says, that a nation needs; and he is a *Lichtbringer*, a giver of light. His aim and purpose is to enlighten, and by means of enlightenment to regenerate humanity. The finest possible praise of him – it is common, and indeed often misapplied in detail – is that of all modern authors he is the nearest to Goethe. Where the two are most closely related is in their final outlook on life; and this will be clearer if Carossa is definitely classed as a 'life philosopher'. *Lebensphilosophie*, of course, proceeds directly from Goethe; but of all the *Lebensphilosophen* Carossa comes nearest to Goethe because both, as poet-scientists, interpret life biologically – thus in the boy and youth of Carossa's autobiography there are the stages of development by metamorphoses that there are in Goethe's plant. Carossa's anti-metaphysical trend of thought is therefore related to the practical philosophy of Bergson and to pragmatism, the base of which is that the aim of thought and knowledge must be directed to the betterment of life, and that the value of things is in their relation to their power of service to life. In the autobiography as a whole we have the same background as in *Dichtung und Wahrheit*, but the pattern of Goethe's tale is too fixed to literal fact to be Carossa's model; actually this is nearer to Goethe's *Wahlverwandtschaften* with its doctrine of 'elective affinities' or inner relationship (*Bezüge*) between person and person. Carossa himself indicates the influence in the earlier stages of the autobiography of the cosmic poet Alfred Mombert; this influence, so far as it can be traced, is one of atmosphere; this world of ours, in Carossa's term, is one of dream (*Phantasiewelt*), and what Carossa takes over from Mombert is the conception of walking, as sure as in a dream (*traumsicher*), through a spirit world, with cosmic forces mistily shifting but inexorably shaping. One element of cosmic philosophy that Carossa stresses is that organic changes come from light – that is, ultimately from the sun as a life-giving force. The opposite of light is darkness, which is Carossa's symbol for evil. If there is light, ᷁here must be darkness; evil is therefore a cosmic element which is as essential as what is good; good and evil, like light and darkness, are parts of one divinely ordained whole. In the moral sense, however, good must conquer evil as light must dispel darkness. We must, therefore, be strengthened by the faith that healing is hidden in the raging of destructive forces.

Chronologically and primarily Carossa must be classed as an expressionist, but as such he is essentially a symbolist; since the great mass of his work is his autobiography he himself in person is the great symbol for his message to the world; and throughout his writings he uses scientific phenomena – fauna, flora, etc. – as symbols. Prominent, too, in his fixed technique are recurrent symbolic happenings – *doppelte Zeichen*, as he calls them –, double recordings or double phenomena. These symbols are often recondite, but all converge in the one great lesson that from the chaos that follows wars a new world must be born, in which mind will rule – Carossa's *Königreich der Seele*, or (with a term that he takes over from Stefan George) the Third Realm (*das Dritte Reich*) of the spirit.

Carossa was born at Tölz in Lower Bavaria as the son of a practising doctor. The name is Italian; we know that his great-grandfather came from Piedmont and that, after serving as a sur-

HANS CAROSSA

FELIX BRAUN

geon in Napoleon's armies, he settled in a village on the Inn. Hans studied medicine at Munich and took his doctor's degree at Leipzig. He settled as a practitioner at and near Passau after periods in Munich and Nuremberg. It is characteristic of the man that he did not give up doctoring for writing till the end of the 1930s; he then lived in retirement at Rittsteig, near Passau. His first work – apart from the poem *Stella Mystica* (1907) and a thin volume of poems (*Gedichte*, 1910) – appeared when he was thirty-five; it was *Doktor Bürgers Ende* (1913; title changed to *Die Schicksale Doktor Bürgers*, 1930), a tragic tale which is glaringly modelled on Goethe's *Werther*; Dr. Bürger, having failed to save a patient who dies of consumption, commits suicide. Carossa corrects this pessimistic ending in a poem: *Die Flucht, Gedicht aus Dr. Bürgers Nachlass* (1916). From now onwards Carossa is hardened to the suffering he sees; for him now the destructive forces of nature are also constructive; for in the decomposition of matter are the germs of a new birth (*Untergang = Übergang*). In 1922 appeared the first volume of his autobiography, *Eine Kindheit*; this was followed in 1928 by *Verwandlung einer Jugend*; and the two sections were in 1933 published together as *Kindheit und Jugend*. Here with patient deliberation Carossa illuminates the stages of growth of a boy's mind; and it must be remembered that although outwardly the subject is Carossa it is inwardly a symbol of a process of shaping which is nature's way to maturity. In this sense the autobiography is an *Entwicklungsroman*. Development of mind, and of character as shaped by mind, is conditioned by successive shocks of experience which bring organic changes; for these Carossa's word is *Verwandlungen* (metamorphoses). And this chemical process is continuous – it is nature's magic, it is magically real. These shocks are often due to 'elective affinities'; that is, they come from human contacts and the clash of personalities, in which there is the fertilizing force of chemical combinations. The ultimate stage of *Verwandlung* is *Umwandlung*, which is the maturity of what is from the first embedded in our being. Carossa here and elsewhere writes with one plan and purpose: *Heilungen*; the healing of ferments that are bound to come, but which heal themselves if nature is helped by the exercise of will power. At the outbreak of war in 1914 he immediately volunteered, and his experiences as an army doctor are described in *Rumänisches Tagebuch* (1924; from 1938 title is *Tagebuch im Kriege*). *A Roumanian Diary* had in its day the same appreciation here and in America as Ernst Jünger's *Storm of Steel*; both equally do justice to the enemy as fighting men; but just because of this Carossa was denounced to the Nazis as a pacifist. The sense of this war diary, which eschews description of fighting, is that Carossa amid the crash of civilization resolutely and with quiet foresight sets about the work of reconstruction; in this sense *A Roumanian Diary* prepares the way for *Der Arzt Gion* (1931), in which the heroic way is shown to be the healing of the mental and moral degradation that comes in the wake of war. Three women are grouped round Dr. Gion: Cynthia and Emerenz as patients, Alruna as his dispenser; he has to tell Emerenz, a young country woman, who is pregnant, that to bear the child will cost her life; she chooses death, that the child may live. To Cynthia, a sculptress and painter, he makes it clear that marriage would cure her temperamental instability; he cures her by himself marrying her. *Führung und Geleit* (1933), the fourth volume of the autobiography proper, gives the story of Carossa's development as a writer and of his contacts with those who helped him; there are fascinating glimpses of Dehmel, Karl Wolfskehl, Stefan George, Rilke, and others. The autobiographical Case of *Geheimnisse des reifen Lebens* (1937) is obvious, but its contents are problematical. In an old cottage near Passau lives Angermann with his invalid wife Cordula. He is an author, and, though this is not stated, the presumption is that he is a retired doctor. As in *Der Arzt Gion* the symbolic theme is the problem of child-bearing; and, also as in *Der Arzt Gion*, round the central male figure there is a group of three women: Cordula, Angermann's sick wife; Barbara, the owner of a pottery in the woods near-by; and Sibylle, Barbara's companion. In *Rumänisches Tagebuch* there is a Freudian dream in which to the diarist are revealed the elective affinities of his wife, their servant, and a young Hungarian woman, in whose house he is sleeping, and the comment is: *Aber wie liebte ich die drei Frauen in der e i n e n Gestalt! Wie waren sie e i n Wesen, mächtig seiend eine in der anderen!*' We are apparently intended to feel that the three women are the three norns – Past, Present, and Future – of the Nornenbrunnen at Munich; man is enfolded by three elemental radiations of his female partner, these having their roots in the three phases of time. *Das Jahr der schönen Täuschungen* (1941) gives the autobiography from the beginning of Carossa's university studies in 1908 to the end of his first year as a medical student. There is some conflict with Carossa *père*, because, for one thing, the son neglected the *Ärztliche Rundschau* for the miasmic labyrinths of Goethe. There are erotic experiences; and the contrasting types of girls as they succeed each other have shaping significance. *Aufzeichnungen aus Italien* (1948) makes no show of multifarious information or guide-book enumeration, as Goethe's *Italienische Reise* does; the bulk of the book is made up of highly sensitive impressions, rather than notes, of travel. The *Aufzeichnungen* begin in Verona and end in Munich with the description of a day spent there after a bombing raid which had rocked the city just before Carossa arrived home. *Tag in München* is a terrible picture of devastation. This chapter is followed by *Abendländische Elegie*, which, written in 1943, was passed from hand to hand during the Nazi period. It is the poem of a seer; behind the shifting pictures we sense, though dimly, the outlines of the Völuspá, that old Eddic poem which foretold the darkness of the gods – and the fields growing green again when all the splendour that had been had sunk in ashes. *Ungleiche Welten* (1951) falls into two parts: the first, *Lebensbericht*, written 1945-48, deals with the whole period of Nazi rule and the three years after it; i.e. Nazi tyranny and its aftermath; and the book closes with *Ein Tag im Spätsommer 1947*. But the two sections are essentially one: they again exemplify Carossa's technique of double relation or double phenomena. The first part is the record of events, the 'story of my life literally reported', but illuminated by a commentary that pierces deep into the events of history and the mentality of the German people; and these are shown to be cause and effect. In *Ein Tag im Spätsommer 1947* we have a symbolic interpretation of the whole sense and purport of the first part of the book. The form is roughly that of the South German or Austrian *Dorfnovelle*; the figures are rough-shaped woodcuts; and they have the religious significance of the genre; the crass realities of the present are set against a mythical and a mystical background, and the tale is unfolded with the slow meditative precision which we expect from Carossa.

Der Tag des jungen Arztes (1956) is the closing volume of the autobiography proper; it comes between *Das Jahr der schönen Täuschungen* and *Der Arzt Gion*. It had been expected that it would deal in the main with the relations of son and father, but what conflict there is is dimly limned; actually what emerges is a reconciliation and on the son's part a feeling of filial affection for the

31

father with his amusing oddities and on the father's part a recognition that Hans will after all make a passable doctor; this shows when the 'angehender Arzt und unfertiger Dichter' acts as locum tenens at Passau while his father is away for the sake of his health. But poems are written which find their way into print, and for those who know the writers of the period – Dauthendey, Wedekind and the rest – there is a thrill when Carossa comes in contact with them during an excursion to Munich; and once more light is thrown on the influences which go to the making of him as a poet. It was Dehmel, he says, who stirred him to his depths, and it is strange to read that for two long years he was obsessed with the urge to write with Dehmel's ring and rhythm. Prose, he thought, was beyond his reach; but before his fancy hovered like a mirage the desire to write prose solidly built and yet lightly floating ('gediegen und doch schwebend'). Here in a few well coined words he gives the pith and essence of what was to make him the finest prose writer, perhaps, of his day. A pathetic interest attaches to his last book of all, Der alte Taschenspieler, Bruchstück aus einem weltlichen Mysterium (1956); a beautiful edition had been prepared by the Insel-Verlag as a birthday gift for the 15th December, but the poet had passed away in September. The first part of the poem is reprinted from the 1932 edition of Gedichte; the second part was completed in the spring of 1940. Since we are faced with a fragment pointing to an intended Faustian completion an elucidation is difficult. We can see that it has a close connection with the autobiography; we remember the old conjurer uncle whose tricks Hans tried to imitate in Eine Kindheit, and so, presumably, we have an old friend redivivus. Inwoven into the mystery play are Carossa's cosmic concepts, doubled by the idea that the heavenly powers, ever at work, must, by forceful enlightenment (or, prosaically stated, by the force of events), reclaim the rabid youths (Weltneuerer) who call for the destruction of all that is.

The definitive edition of Carossa's verse is Gesammelte Gedichte (1947). The first reading of the book as a whole is apt to leave the impression of opaqueness and metrical heaviness. But the mist lifts and the verse rings true if there is patient and expectant exploration. There are two keys to comprehension: familiarity with the life-story and an ever-present consciousness in the reader's mind of the essential factors of the poet's biological philosophy. The verse might be divided into poems of intense personal experience or of philosophical interpretation of things and phenomena. Thus we have poems which record remembered emotion and poems which interpret the doctrine of growth by organic change. There are a series of poems with exact though subtly imaged description of flora and fauna. Philosophically considered the most important poems are those in which we find the sun as life-giver (*Gesang zur Sonne*), the organic certainty of healing and renovation, and the call to a resolute acceptance of whatever ills may befall, in the faith that, if the demons of evil are fought with manly determination, nature herself will bring recovery (*An die Natur*).

FRANK THIESS (1890-), like Werner Bergengruen a Latvian, is one of those who, while influenced by expressionism and, in their later work, by existentialist tenets, are in the main impressionists and realists. As good a term as any is *transparenter Realismus*; this is used for writers, such as Hermann Hesse too, whose base of realism is in the main ideological and is illuminated by what Thiess calls '*die Scheinwerfer der Erkenntnis*'. Thiess – whose mother, an Eschenbach, is said to have been a descendant of Wolfram von Eschenbach – began with *Der Tod in Falern* (1921), the tale of a dying town, and won through to fame with *Die Verdammten* (1922), an epic unfolding of the decay of the Baltic aristocracy; the theme is incest of brother and sister. In *Angelika ten Swaart* (1923) we find the 'associative thinking' and word symbolism of existentialism; e.g. the name of the American research worker in medicine who marries Angelika, a Dutch aristocrat of aristocrats, is Morr; this by verbal suggestion verified by the course of the action is *mors*, *la mort*, or even *Mord*; and the pith of the meaning is: to the bride in the marriage night comes Death in the shape of the bridegroom; for he induces physical changes that bring the beginning of death. But the association of ideas is more complicated than this: to Angelika, Morr is a stranger; he is plebeian; and yet, as life fades, she realizes that she loves the father of her child. Death loves life, and in the end Life loves Death. In *Frauenraub* (1928) we have a daring exploration of sexual states: an architect marries a frail girl of nineteen; she is a disappointing bride: she can only give her husband excitement, not surrender –, for she has been physically spoilt by a Lesbian affair with an older woman. *Das Tor der Welt* (1926) explores the sexual awakening of a group of sixth form boys and girls in a small town in the Harz; here again we have word symbolism and the rest; e.g. *Gymnasiast* is related to γυμνός, 'naked'. In *Der Weg zu Isabelle* (1934) a German in the south of France has an affair, in 1914, with the daughter of a French officer who will not hear of their marriage. The lovers are torn asunder by the outbreak of war; the girl gives birth to a female child. Twenty years later the German learns that the mother had been killed by bombs, but he discovers a girl who in the light of evidence seems to be his daughter, and as such he adopts her and takes her to Germany. But she has led a loose life; sexual experience is in her blood; and she tells her presumed father that she would love him sexually even if she were sure he were her father. It turns out that he is not, and the presumption is that he marries her, though this is not stated. From a rapid indication of Thiess's field of fiction it might seem that he pounces on sensational best-seller themes; this is, however, far from the truth; he is a psychiatrist and he probes quietly and deep. The '*keusche Entblössungen*' of *Der Weg zu Isabelle* led to his rejection by Nazi critics on the score of morbidity, though *Tsushima, der Roman eines Seekrieges* (1936), which shows the heroic inception of the modern might of Japan, might have been expected to rehabilitate him.

WERNER BERGENGRUEN (1892-) was born, as the scion of a patrician house, at Riga, which at that time was in Russia. His name (-gruen is Swedish *gren*, 'branch') indicates the Swedish provenance of his family; it will be remembered that Latvia was once a province of Sweden. After completing his university course at Berlin he fought as a volunteer for the Germans in World War I and after the war against the Russians in the Baltische Landwehr in his homeland. He stresses that, though his themes cover the many lands he made himself at home in, the fundament of his work is his nostalgia for that heritage of the Baltic provinces – Livonia, Esthonia and Courland – which he felt to be the core of his being. Here in the great ports with their Hanseatic traditions the German-speaking upper strata, the great merchants and the landowners, were marked off from the working classes. During the Nazi period several of his works were banned; later he was placed under surveillance but allowed to write. He emigrated from Munich to Achenkirch in the Tyrol, from where, in 1945, friends managed to smuggle him into Switzerland. At Achenkirch he had written resistance poems which he recited at clandestine meetings. His first novel was *Das Gesetz des Atum* (1923), which has autobiographical elements. *Das grosse Alkahest* (1926), which followed, has its shifting scenes in the Russia of Catherine the Great. *Der goldene Griffel* (1931) is a novel of the inflation, with a criminal as central figure; here Bergengruen sketches out his main tenet, amplified in the work that follows, that evil can be overcome by spiritual means. His aim, he says, is: '*die ewigen Ordnungen sichtbar machen*'. There is deep religious faith in his work, and much of his apparent patience with wrong-doing is to be explained by his conversion in the late 1930s to Roman Catholicism; what we find is that contrast of evil and good which comforts converts; it is the dream-lore, the poetry of Catholic doctrine. If we are to believe Bergengruen, God reconciles conflicting forces, and evil must be accepted as belonging to God's ways with men. Bergengruen's great effort is in the batch of historical novels which follow *Das Kaiserreich in Trümmern* (1927); this goes back to the days of the Goths and describes the rush to glory of Odoacer and his downfall. In *Herzog Karl der Kühne* (1930) Charles the Bold, Duke of Burgundy, overreaches himself in his lust for power. Then came two novels which are considered to be Bergengruen's chief works. In *Der Grosstyrann und das Gericht* (1935) the problem of Nazi Germany is transposed to the Renaissance period in a small Italian State. Bergengruen's very personal technique is perhaps best exemplified in a novel which was banned by Goebbels, *Am Himmel wie auf Erden* (1940). The period is that of the Elector Joachim I of Brandenburg, who was fanatically opposed to Luther, and the twin towns of Berlin and Koelln are the scene. The tone is Catholic, and the theme is the disintegration of life through fear (as in Nazi days). A second deluge is prophesied by the State astrologer, who has read the coming event in the stars. He tells only the Elector, who also dabbles in astrology; arks are built, and there is general chaos. The young chamberlain sends his wife to a safe place; for this betrayal of the secret he is condemned to death by the Elector, and before his death he realizes that he who is afraid is not perfect in love. The Elector himself flees, but returns to stay with his people. And there is no deluge. The novel was begun in 1931 and finished in the summer of 1940, when a new catastrophe was impending. The pivotal idea is that events foretold by the Old Testament prophets recur through the ages. Bergengruen is a master of the Novelle, in which he is influenced by E. T. A. Hoffmann, and in his symbolization of history by Conrad Ferdinand Meyer. The starting-point mostly conforms to Goethe's definition of a Novelle

as *'eine sich ereignete unerhörte Begebenheit'*, but Bergengruen's unheard of event is a manifestation of eternal laws, the effect of which
tends to be, not so much a chance happening as a religious *Wandlung*, a moral regeneration which does not always carry conviction;
it is rather fixed up or *ausgeklügelt* than inevitable. There are sensational elements, as for instance in *Rosen am Galgenholz* (1923) and
Schimmelreuter hat mich gossen (1923). At all events these eminently
readable short stories, whether single (*Der spanische Rosenstock*,
1940; *Hornunger Heimweh*, 1942; *Schatzgräbergeschichte*, 1943; *Das
Tempelchen*, 1950) or grouped (*Die Sultansrose*, 1946; *Sternenstand*,
1947) have just the components which make translations saleable.
Typical is *Der letzte Rittmeister* (1952); here we have a *Rahmenerzählung*, tales strung together with the life story of the narrator
framing them in; we are made to realize that this last captain of
horse is such a 'shining fool' as Bayard or Bertrand du Guesclin.
He is the last of his class because he has done his last fighting
against the Red Army. Bergengruen meets him in his old age in
a village on a North Italian lake. Throughout the book we have
Bergengruen's characteristic note, that subtle blend of Baltic East
and Russia with Southern European moods and feeling. In this
respect Bergengruen pairs with HENRY VON HEISELER (1875-1928);
both have translated Russian classics, and both in their best work
have an undertone of love for the Russia of the good old days.
There is the same tone in the sequel to *Der letzte Rittmeister*; in
Die Rittmeisterin (1954) the captain is dead, but the narrator meets
a lady who was his friend and memories are revived in yet another
string of tales. Another collection of tales which cluster round the
Baltic coast and Riga is *Die Flamme im Säulenholz* (1955). In *Oster-
gruss, Sechs Erzählungen* (1955) there are tales from both the Russia
of the Czars and of the Communists. *Zwieselchen* (1951) is a delightful children's book written by Bergengruen for his own children.
As a lyric poet Bergengruen is best known for the 'resistance
poems' of his *Dies Irae* (1945), which were written in the Tyrol
and privately circulated. A few of these may survive, as historically
indicative, though all the resistance poems of the period tend to
fall into a common mould which palls with familiarity; the form
is as a rule so immaculately regular – sonnets are favoured – that
there can be no lasting popular appeal. There is something of a
declamatory effect in *An die Völker der Erde*, a call to the nations
of the world to repent for the guilt they incurred in the twelve

years (the holy number of fulfilment!) which cover World War II and what went before it: Germany, 'the heart-shield of the West', runs the argument, was seized by the Demon that drove her to war; but the nations round about her were passive in their *Trägheit des Herzens* and therefore equally guilty. The result is that Germany must suffer in their place (*stellvertretend*). All this may seem strange, but it is part and parcel of the obsessional Messianism of the Germans: Germany is chosen to save the world; and therefore: '*Völker, vernehmt mit uns allen das Göttliche; Metanoeite!*' But Bergengruen's lyrical work is mostly religious in tone and substance: *Die Rose von Jericho* (1946), *Der ewige Kaiser* (1937), *Die verborgene Frucht* (1938), *Die heile Welt* (1950). In *Lombardische Elegie* (1951) the poet recalls his Baltic origin, reflects on the fate of his ancestors and their possessions, and connects all this with his description of the great plain of Lombardy, which serves him as the starting-point of his excursions into the world of the past.

In the *Supranaturalismus* of the Rhineland novelist ELISABETH LANGGÄSSER (1899-1950) the fusion of past and present is extreme and extravagant. For her *Jetzt und Hier* are one with *Immer und Ewig*: '*Zeitlosigkeit und Zeit*', she says, '*fallen zusammen.*' Not only is the unity of all life her continuous theme but also the unity of the pagan antiquity of Greece and the Middle Ages with the world of today. She is a master of interior monologue. Her novel *Proserpina* (1932), a personal myth of childhood, was followed by *Triptichon des Teufels* (1932) and *Gang durch das Ried* (1936). The theme of *Die Rettung am Rhein* (1938) is Grace abounding, as it is declaredly of the masterpiece that made her famous, *Das unauslöschliche Siegel* (1946). The novel must have been written in the full consciousness that she was half a Jew, that she had been condemned to twelve years of silence, and that her elder daughter had been thrown into the concentration camp at Auschwitz. The chief character of the novel, Belfontaine, is a Jew complete, but he turns Catholic to marry into a Catholic family. He is in good circumstances and a *bon viveur*; and he accepts baptism cynically and keeps to his free-thinking. At the outbreak of the First World War he is on holiday on the Loire and is interned. Years after we find him at Senlis near Paris as a naturalized Frenchman married to a Frenchwoman. All seems to be going well with him, and he is still flaunting his Voltairean vice of enlightenment (*Vernunft*) when he hears a voice calling him in a thunderstorm: '*Lazarus, komm heraus!*' He disappears, to appear again in 1943 as an old Jew beggar who roams about between Russian concentration camps and Russian partisans, rich in the joy of prayer and in God's grace. This is the story that can be fished out of the ocean of monologues that wind on and on, insertions, and multifarious matter, and the leap-frog chronology between 1858 and 1945; the happenings range in scene from the Rhineland through France to the Pyrenees and eastwards to Russia. There is no psychology; for the fundament of all we read is that man is object, not subject; what is visioned and shown is the direct action of God on man. There are two opposing worlds: the world of saints – Thérèse of Lisieux, Bernadette Soubirous at Lourdes, and the rest – and the world of demons, and to these belong the marionettes of Satan, such as Belfontaine. The conflict is thus between God and the Devil; they fight for the souls of men. Belfontaine is saved in his sin; for he is baptized. His baptism was a fraud; but, being baptized, he bears a seal that cannot be effaced. A vile Voltairean might object that if the mere ceremony of baptism is miraculous, it is a heathen fetish; but symbol is heaped to prove that the baptismal font itself is a miracle; and in addition the grotto at Lourdes and even *die weibliche Scham* (and this is typical) are symbolized as fonts in which the miraculous process of salvation is carried out by God. The greatness of the novel is in description, in symbol; in short it is rather prose poetry than narrative. Marvellous is the use of classical mythology to image the common human conduct of all time; thus Leda with her swan serves to show forth by a callous spread of limbs the mechanical sexual receptivity of woman. The symbol is often raw, to mark the impulsion of brute desire; but it may have the loveliness and the rareness of a poet's vision. The artistic justification – if there can be one – of all this slow savouring of adultery, of Lesbian love, incest, brothels, is that it is necessary for the picture of 'purple Hell'. But the other-world contrast is the cloister with flagellation and fevered visions. Physically untrue as the presentation of mental states is, there is psychological interest in so far as the author's own obsessed psyche is revealed. She is the reverse of *anima naturaliter christiana*; she is a forced flower of fanaticism; and to many her aversion to Luther may be distressing. *Der Torso* (1947) and *Das Labyrinth* (1949) are collections of short stories. Of prime importance is her posthumously published novel on a vast scale *Märkische Argonautenfahrt* (1950), in which we find the same leap-frog chronology, the same insertions and divagations as in *Das unauslöschliche Siegel*; the multiple threads of the story, as of the argument, dangle loosely, and may escape the reader's grip. The reason for this may be the loosening grip of a dying woman's hand; there are signs that it was finished anyhow. The theme is once again the renovation of a ruined world by Grace abounding. Seven people, each oppressed by one of the seven great heresies, set out in the summer of 1945 from the ruins of Berlin on a pilgrimage to the monastery of Anastasiendorf ('the village of resurrection') in the south of the March of Brandenburg. They are on pilgrimage to themselves; for their Golden Fleece is to be their return home regenerated by Grace, saved from sluggishness of heart and nihilistic despair. Here again there is a daring use of sexual symbol, and the poetry and the sadness of it all is so lovely that the moral lesson floats away into limbo: the Golden Fleece and the soul's uplifting are in the magic and the haunting melody of the words, not in the austere cloister at the rim of Russia. The author's defence of herself would be that these pilgrims from the old to the new are not in history, but between two phases of civilization; and therefore they are in a state of nature (*Naturmenschen*) and free from all convention and sense of shame. Their sexual promiscuity as they roam through ruins is thus not immorality condoned, but is presented as inevitable, because they are as yet far from the joy of the spirit – that joy which is the purpose of God because it is *His* nature. There is high excellence in Elisabeth Langgässer's lyric verse, of which the main aspect is that Greek myth and fable are used for intricate symbolism woven into all the phases of nature; to her trees, plants, flowers, bees, animals are literally Demeter. Her cosmic conception is built laboriously into stiff rhymes and often into hard rhythms, though there may be a caressing melodiousness that makes the search for sense seem otiose. The main obsession is seminal reproduction, of plants and man. The worst that can be said – but if there were space for quotation the balance would be to the good – is that because of overweighting by learned allusions the verse sticks to the page. Chronologically listed her books of verse are as follows. *Der Wendekreis des Lammes. Ein Hymnus der Erlösung* (1924) marks her first appearance in print. *Tierkreisgedichte* (1935) is a subtle re-creation of classical mythology and legendary lore serving for the symbolization of modern life; the source is her conception of late

Hellenistic semi-mythical religion, in which Greek paganism blends with a primitive acceptance of Christian dogma. *Der Laubmann und die Rose. Ein Jahreskreis* (1947) probably derives from Brentano's *Romanzen vom Rosenkranz*; nature is christianized with (often) complicated and sometimes more or less obscene threads of relationship.

LUISE RINSER (1911-), an Upper Bavarian, was an elementary teacher near Salzburg; she now lives in Munich. From 1944 to the end of the war she was forbidden to write by the Nazis, imprisoned, and condemned to death; these experiences she describes in *Gefängnistagebuch* (1946). As a novelist she breaks with convention and ploughs her own furrow. In *Die Stärkeren* (1948) we have the collapse of the time-honoured middle-class and its displacement by the new type of race-conscious German. This clash of the old *Bürgertum* with its reverence for family life and the 'tween-wars generation, for whom marriage is more or less a mirage, provides the staple of *Mitte des Lebens* (1950). The novel is made up for the most part of a diary kept by a professor of medicine at Munich, Dr. Stein, and passed over to the heroine, Nina, after his demise. The diary entries record the old professor's love for one who in the first flush of her girlhood had been his pupil and is now a writer of repute with two novels to her credit. She is twenty years younger; the gap is, however, not so wide as that which yawned between Ruskin at sixty-eight and the art student of twenty he fell in love with. Ruskin, it is true, went mad when his correspondence with the girl was broken off, whereas Stein is faithful and devoted and quite sane till the day he dies. Nina yields to this male and that, '*aus Mitleid*' we are told; and this charitable readiness, we are to understand, is a feature of the psychology of new woman in an enlightened age. She has even married one of her promiscuous males, though she bears a child of which her husband is not the father. For once in a way she even sleeps with Professor Stein, *aus Mitleid* of course, but she still refuses to marry him. This more than anything else is the burden of Luise Rinser's tales: she brings it home that sex experience in a woman radically good does not tarnish; those who are morally despicable are the males – but only sometimes, for as a rule they just obey the pressure of nature, and are thus themselves innocent. There is really no ending, happy or otherwise; since Nina has not finished her work – she is busy as a writer – she has not finished living, and she faces whatever may be in store – as we all do 'in the middle of our life'. *Daniela* (1952) is the story of an elementary teacher from a comfortable home who at the beginning of her scholastic career, in a fit of reforming zeal, exiles herself to a remote moorland village. The beastliness of the peat-cutters here is incredible; they are sub-human. One hope Daniela has: the young priest, not long in the hamlet, robust, and fervent in faith. The name for him in the village is '*der Heilige*'; but it is a term of contempt. Daniela has some practical success with her de-lousing and general cleaning up of her pupils; but her efforts at moral cleansing are laughed at. She hears the priest sermonizing his flock, and in the sermon and in talk with Daniela there is much play with the idea that God has instituted sin *aus Mitleid* with humanity; He leaves us the choice between good and evil. The reasoning amounts to this: man is an animal, so made by God; the priest and Daniela are in an environment of animality; and they too, when the moment comes, fall. The problem of the book is the celibacy of the clergy; and this is a theme with a long pedigree from Zola's *La conquête de Plassans* and *La faute de l'abbé Mouret* onwards. The priest falls in Peter Rosegger's *Maria im Elend* (1852); and another Austrian woman, Emilie Mataja, who wrote under the name of Emil Marriot, made a speciality of such tales of priests; her novels *Der geistliche Tod* (1884) and *Mit der Tonsur* were famous. The finest handlings are George Moore's *The Lake* and Gerhart Hauptmann's *Der Ketzer von Soana*. There is a running chain of motifs in all these novels; and there is this and that in *Daniela* which has its parallel in what has preceded; thus Daniela, like George Moore's heroine, is not abashed by the expectation of an illegitimate child; in *The Lake* as in *Daniela* the woman is an elementary school teacher, and in both these novels the heroine refuses to allow her priest to join her when he has taken up a new vocation. This last detail, however, agrees with Luise Rinser's practice; she has stated in a *Selbstporträt* that she has no liking for happy endings; in *Daniela* as in *Mitte des Lebens* the reader is free to guess what the future will bring. Generally speaking, though in style and handling of the problem Luise Rinser is influenced by Georges Bernanos, *Daniela* is almost outrageously original. The title (one thinks of Daniel in the lions' den) suggests that to the author the woman is the principal character, not the priest, whom in any case she dominates (one might venture to say: whom she seduces – *aus Mitleid*), and this would conform to her line of attack in *Mitte des Lebens*, in which the men, even if they are intellectuals, are poor creatures who need women as God intended them to. This aspect, really, is what is new and daring in these novels of Luise Rinser, which are not to be judged superficially by their glaringly best-selling qualities.

Harrowing experiences of World War I come into the fiction of EDGAR MAAS (1896-); 'Verdun-Maas' as he is known to distinguish him from his brother Joachim. Both were born in Hamburg as sons of a merchant engaged in the export trade. Edgar, after serving on the west front during the war, emigrated to America, where he worked as manager of chemical factories in New York and elsewhere. He won fame with his novel *Verdun* (1936), which questions the time-worn ideology of God and Fatherland. *Im Nebel der Zeit* (1938), the theme of which is the after-war chaos, is a sequel. His brother JOACHIM MAAS (1901-) also emigrated in 1938 to America, where he was a university reader in German literature before returning to Germany in 1951. He followed up his dramatic poem *Johann Christian Günther* (1925) with his novel *Bohême ohne Mimi* (1930), which handles the life of Bohemian circles in Berlin. *Der Widersacher* (1932) is a novel of the after-the-war slump in quarters round the docks in a northern port – Hamburg is indicated. Two of his works are devoted to the experiences of childhood; in the short story *Borbe* (1934) a schoolboy is thrashed by his teacher, while the novel *Die unwiederbringliche Zeit* (1935) is built up from the story of the author's own childhood in Hamburg. *Ein Testament* (1939) is a novel of family life which in Dostoieffsky's way probes into the problems of good and evil. In *Das magische Jahr* (1945) too a lonely emigrant in America is filled with nostalgic recollections of his youth in Hamburg as it was in happier days; the reverse of the idyll is that once again there is a teacher who thrashes his pupils. *Stürmischer Morgen* (1937) chronicles the life of another Hamburg boy, Friedrich Ludwig Schröder (1744-1816), who rose to be one of the great actors of his time. *Der unermüdliche Rebell* (1948) is the life-story of Carl Schurz, one of the revolutionaries of 1848 who found asylum in America, rose to be a major-general in the Civil War, and helped his friend Abraham Lincoln to prepare his plans. *Der Fall Gouffé* (1955) is a first-class *Kriminalroman*. *Don Pedro und der Teufel* (1954) is a lightly written romance of a Spanish nobleman who flees from the Inquisition and fights with Pizarro in his campaign against the Incas.

Their experiences in World War II have been used by quite a

number of writers born after 1900 for work of sterling merit, which may range from crass realism to the symbolic waves-of-consciousness novel of Herbert Zand. WOLFGANG BORCHERT (1921-47), a Hamburg man, had a short life of intense suffering; he was condemned to death for defeatism, but released; in 1944 he was jailed in Moabit. He wrote a play, *Draussen vor der Tür* (1947); the leading character is a *Heimkehrer* from Siberia, one of those who return home to find no home – '*Ihr Zuhause ist draussen, nachts im Regen, auf der Strasse. Das ist ihr Deutschland*'. There is the same mood of hopelessness in his short stories: *Die Hundeblume* (1948), *An diesem Diensttag* (1948). His verse was published in *Laterne, Nacht und Sterne* (1946), with additions in his collected works, *Das Gesamtwerk* (1949).

There is something of Borchert's despairing mood in the work of HEINRICH BÖLL (1917-). Born in Cologne he served as an infantry man from 1938 to 1945, and was four times wounded. He made his reputation with the short stories of *Der Zug war pünktlich* (1949); the period covers three days and nights spent by men on leave from the front. There is a ghost-like atmosphere in the twenty-five ironic Novellen of *Wanderer, kommst du nach Spa* (1950); it is a grim picture of fevered life in a country at war and near to defeat – soldiers fighting in snow and ice on the Eastern front and snatching brief hours of love from the girls they meet, darkened stations with trains shunting at midnight, and then the aftermath of a lost war. His first novel *Wo warst du Adam?* (1951) covers the retreat from Rumania in 1943 and ends with the capitulation of Germany in 1945; it brands the sheer idiocy of war. The scene of his second novel *Und sagte kein einziges Wort* (1953) is a German town (Cologne is indicated) shattered by bombs, and the period is that directly following the reform of the currency. The novel probes into the conditions of post-war life and shows how much depends on the wife; there is no *Zuhause*; husband and wife have to live in a single room. The husband has returned from the front with disordered nerves; he takes to drink and lounges in *Groschenautomaten*. By contrast his wife endures in heroic patience, and in the end the husband finds his way back to her. There is a religious base – significant in the post-war Catholic Rhineland; the lesson is that faith gives restraint and courage to force a way out of illness and the direst poverty. *Haus ohne Hüter* (1954) is once again a novel of family life under strain and stress. The troubles which go with the aftermath of war are seen as they impress themselves on the minds of two schoolboys whose fathers were killed at the front. Martin's mother, a film fan, lives bemused by the make-believe of Hollywood, while Heinrich's mother depends on shifting relationships with men.

Of the novelists who made the Second World War their main theme none reaches the heights of Ernst Jünger. Of the influences discernible *L'homme révolté* of Camus and Hemingway's novels stand out; Ernst Jünger's *Strahlungen* also counts. The first of these novels to appear, often *Heimkehrerromane*, were by writers who for the most part had fought as privates and who, to begin with at least, were Communists – Theodor Plievier, Hans Werner Richter, Walter Kolbenhoff in particular. The representative novel of this *Anklageliteratur* is Plievier's *Stalingrad*. THEODOR PLIEVIER (1892-), born in Berlin, was a sailor and then a rancher in South America. From 1914 to 1915 he served in the German navy and was one of the leaders of the sailors' revolt at Wilhelmshaven. In 1933 he fled to Russia, and in World War II he was a member of the committee *Freies Deutschland*. In 1945 he returned to Germany with the Red Army. He had made his reputation with *Des Kaisers Kulis* (1929), the theme of which is a revolt of sailors after the surrender of the German fleet at Skagerrak and in which he gives vent to his personal resentment, as he does too in his *Der Kaiser ging, die Generale blieben* (1932). *Stalingrad* (1945) was written in Russia during the war; it was finished a year after the battle. Since his conviction then was that to be a prisoner of the Russians was to be saved the main tenor of the book is shot with illusion. *Stalingrad* relates the fate of an army and is made up of information collected on the battlefield, from diaries and letters, and from conversations with prisoners of war. It gives a credible description of the actual battle, but in intention and effect it is a symbol of the destruction of German military power. In form it is a series of pictures with the horror of happenings so heightened as to produce the maximum effect of shock on the reader's nerves. The language is sometimes ungrammatical – *Kolportagestil* is not an unfair term; and generally it is sensational – e.g. *Brüllen* is a favourite word. For the critic the problem is whether it is a novel or just journalese reporting ('*Reportage*'); the author dubs it both 'novel' and 'chronicle'. If it is to be judged by construction (*Aufbau*) and form it is hardly a novel, not so much so as Tolstoy's *War and Peace*. It is the raw material of history loosely shaped to a gigantic symbol; it has been classed as a 'monumental morality'. *Tatsachenroman* hits it off best perhaps. The *dramatis personae* are types, not characters; and therefore there is no psychology, but just man in the mass and massed effects which, as such, are sensational. The colonel of an armoured division and a gravedigger stand out from the rest. The gospel presented is that the individual does not exist; what does exist is *Massemensch* (to quote the title of Ernst Toller's play), the mass made up of men who count only as counters in the mass. There is the same mood and method in Plievier's following fiction: *Das gefrorene Herz* (1945) lashes out at the madness of war; *Im letzten Winkel der Erde* (1945) exposes the exploitation of labour in the saltpetre mines of Chile and brings in personal experience of Chile and its coast as Plievier had done in his earlier novel *Zwölf Mann und ein Kapitän* (1930) and as he does in *Haifische* (1949), a sequel to *Im letzten Winkel der Erde*. *Moskau* (1952) is on the grand scale of *Stalingrad*, but falls below it; even the language has lost brutality, and there is some attempt at balancing, for both sides of the front come into the picture. Of the other novels which denounce the war *Hinter Gottes Rücken* (1948) by BASTIAN MÜLLER (1912-) has its scene of action in Germany and the occupied countries in the period 1938-46; the author began as a goatherd and described his early struggle in *Die Eulen* (1939). HANS WERNER RICHTER (1908-), the son of a fisherman on the island of Usedom, had a hard struggle with privation in youth; notorious for anti-Nazi speeches, he had to flee to Paris in 1933, but was driven by hunger to return to Berlin in 1934. Forced into the army in 1940 he was taken prisoner in 1943 and was sent to a camp in the United States. On his return to Germany he founded *Gruppe 47*, a confraternity of writers to which these leftist writers belonged. His novel *Die Geschlagenen* (1949) begins in Italy; its highlight is the battle of Monte Casino. WALTER KOLBENHOFF (1908-), the son of a labourer, threw up his job as a factory worker when he was seventeen and tramped Europe as a street singer; afterwards he was a journalist in Berlin, fled to Denmark in 1933, was pitched into the German army in 1942, and went through the hells of Sebastopol, El Alamein and Monte Cassino; in 1944 he was captured by the Americans, and while a prisoner wrote his novel *Fleisch und Blut* (1947); his theme is the misery of those who hate the Nazis and are forced to fight; *Heimkehr in die Fremde* (1949)

lays bare the conditions in post-war Germany as a *Heimkehrer* finds
them in what should be home but is an alien land. RUDOLF KRÄMER-
BADONI (1913-) comes into the picture with his novel *In der grossen
Drift* (1949), a witheringly sarcastic picture of the average German
who takes things as they come and makes the best of them; he is
given a commission in the war and is actually decorated with the
Ritterkreuz by the Führer in person. He had begun with a novel
in Kafka's manner, *Jacobs Jahr* (1943) and made headway with his
cynical rogue's tale (*Schelmenroman*) *Mein Freund Hippolyt*, the hero
of which owes his Grecian name to the fact that his father was
half seas over at his baptism and would keep saying 'Hipp' and
addressing those present as '*Ihr Lütt*' ('you folks').

EMIL BELZNER (1901-) began with two verse epics: *Die Hörner
des Potiphar* (1924) and *Iwan der Pelzhändler* (1928), a story of life
in Moscow. His first novel was *Marschieren – nicht träumen* (1931);
this describes the experiences of a major in World War I. His
reputation was firmly fixed by *Kolumbus vor der Landung* (1933),
a waves-of-consciousness story in which the events of his past life
pass in dreamlike procession through the mind of the seafarer in
the moments before he lands in what he believes to be India.
Juanas grosser Seemann (1956) is a revised, expanded edition; Juana
is a playmate of his childhood, who already visioned the great
seaman to be in the boy Columbus. To English readers Belzner's
Ich bin der König (1948), with its motto *Inauditum nefas*, will be
problematical and to some repulsive: the 'unheard of crime' is the
beheading by James II of his nephew the Duke of Monmouth.
It is not so much a historical novel as an experiment in the most
recent literary phase, *Zweite Neuromantik*. Its relation to reality as
to history is remote; what the novelist drives at is the infamy of
governmental tyranny in the present as exemplified by events
centuries ago. In an epilogue Belzner explains that the work was
begun at the beginning of World War II with the object of fathom-
ing how far art can probe into the inner meaning of events (*zur
Ergründung des Späersinns der Kunst*), and it was continued during
the dictatorship at a time when the sense of what was printed had
to be reached by positing its contrary. But there are symbolic
depths in the novel, and, broadly speaking, the meaning would
seem to be that royalty or absolute power in any sense is *Puppen-
spielerei*. But the contrary of a puppet king is the producer who
keeps things going; here this king by character is Dudley Flint,

a farmer of gentry class who comes into close contact with both James II and Monmouth. His estate is by name Jewel; and the assumption may be that with his sterling qualities he represents 'this precious stone set in the silver sea . . . , this England'. A king must have his queen; and there is a wealth of poetry dreamt into the depiction of Jane, whom Flint, after an incredible opening with a display of *Fensterln* in the Bavarian style, marries with yet more ancient English ceremonial, which is entertaining because it is on the face of it apocryphal. But woman is congenitally prone to give way physically to the gilt and glamour of royalty; Jane remains faithful, but there is throughout the thrill of the sensation that no woman, however devoted to her husband she may be, can refuse a king. In the later stages of the novel the Mermaid Tavern fills the scene; it is the favourite haunt of James II, a brothel to which he brings Monmouth when the rebellion has failed. From a window Tower Hill is seen; and Kneller, who has his abode in the tavern, is ordered to paint for the delectation of the king a portrait of Monmouth after the severed head has been stitched on to the trunk. Here, too, Daniel Defoe functions dangerously as court fool, and represents an intrusion of sound sense and poetic pathos into the filth and folly of the closing scenes. In the epilogue there is a reference to the present Earl of Dalkeith as the direct descendant of Monmouth, with the assumption that he narrowly missed the royal rights to which Monmouth was legitimately entitled. There is still more of a welter of allegory in Belzner's last novel *Der Safranfresser* (1953); the background is the earthquake of Messina in December 1908.

Hermann Hesse's utopistic *Glasperlenspiel*, Josef Winckler's *Der chiliastische Pilgerzug*, Alfons Paquet's *Die Prophezeiungen*, and Franz Werfel's *Stern der Ungeborenen* are followed by Ernst Jünger's *Heliopolis*, the archtype of a series of novels which have for their purpose to interpret in symbol the events of our own time; they show as logically possible the existence of States which are the direct contrary of what we have experienced in the outcome of *Wilhelminismus* and the nightmare of Nazism. If instead of such an ideal State they give, still in symbol, a close depiction of what we have experienced (as Stefan Andres does in *Die Sintflut*) we may call them Utopias reversed. The Utopia proper generally follows the normal pattern of the genre by projecting its period into the far future (*Zukunfts- und Staatsroman*) while the Utopia reversed, in-

32

evitably more or less a *roman à clefs*, keeps to the recent past. In so far as these Wellsian tales of times to be build up their systems on the marvels of technical science their immediate progenitors are Bernhard Kellermann's *Der Tunnel* and Döblin's *Berge, Meere und Giganten*, though ultimately they derive from the British, French and American Utopias – William Morris's *News from Nowhere*, Blatchford's *Merry England*, Bellamy's *Looking Backwards*; in particular the influence of George Orwell's *1984* and of Aldous Huxley's *Brave New World* cannot be missed. And of course some of them are likely to be rooted on the solid ground of Oswald Spengler's *Der Untergang des Westens*.

The Rhinelander STEFAN ANDRES (1906-), born near Treves as the son of a miller, was destined for the priesthood, but deserted his convent school to study *Germanistik* at the universities and then turned to literature. He travelled extensively, and from 1937 to 1949 lived in Italy. His love of southern climes plays a great part in certain of his novels: Greece is the scene of *Der Mann von Asteri* (1940) and of his short story *Das Grab des Neides* (1940), Italy that of *Der gefrorene Dionysos* (1941; rechristened *Die Liebesschaukel* in the 1951 edition), of *Ritter der Gerechtigkeit* (1948) and of *Das goldene Gitter* (1951). But the continuously recurring theme of his best work is that of the conflict between devotional contemplation and the call to the rough and tumble of life outside the cloister. We have it in his first novel *Bruder Luzifer* (1932), which is clearly autobiographical; it is the tale of a novice in a Capuchin monastery who is lured away by the wiles of the world. In *Der Knabe im Brunnen* (1953) we have the same story as autobiography; it is one more *Eine Kindheit* in the wake of Carossa; the boy Steff dreams himself into a world in which he cannot reconcile the loving Creator with the angry God of the Old Testament. Other novels are *Entwicklungsromane* with heroes of peasant stock who make their way by study: *Eberhard im Kontrapunkt* (1934), *Die unsichtbare Mauer* (1934). The author's dominating theme shapes itself in *El Greco malt den Grossinquisitor* (1936), in which we have the contrast of an inquiring and independent mind with rigid orthodoxy, and is climaxed in *Wir sind Utopia* (1942). The scene of the latter is in Spain in a Carmelite monastery which is now used during the Civil War as a prison for captured soldiers. One of them is a renegade monk who by a miracle of chance finds himself lodged in the very cell which had been his twenty years before. As he lies on his plank bed he is hallucinated by the old familiar rust stains on the ceiling, and as he gazes at them he remembers that during his period of indoctrination he had fancied they mapped an island in a far-away southron sea; here was Utopia; in their separate regions Christians and pagans lived in harmony; for each religion was as good as the other. The pagans had their Temple of Dionysos and they still celebrated the mysteries of Demeter. The difference between them was that for the pagans nature was enwrapped in the Divine and therefore sinless, with the Divine accessible to the senses and with no need to be made perceptible by dogmatic formulas. What he tries to formulate by a process of logical reasoning is a synthesis of paganism and Christianity; in essence his musings lead him to the doctrine of Schiller's poem *Die Götter Griechenlands*. The youth confesses his journeys to Utopia to his professor of dogmatics, who tells him that no one has ever yet been able to create a Utopia on earth, not even He. The upshot is that Paco leaves the cloister and as a sailor and now a soldier has his full experience of life down to its dregs. And now in his cell he has a conversation with the lieutenant who is in command of the prisoners; this grubby soldier, it turns out, has murdered monks and raped nuns, and now he is in terror of dying unconfessed; and when he finds that this particular prisoner was once a monk he asks him to hear his confession. There are now dramatic possibilities; Paco with his knowledge of the monastery and its rust-frayed window-bars could escape; and, since he has managed to hide a knife in his pocket, he could ease escape for himself and his twenty fellow prisoners if, to begin with, he murders the man he is confessing; but the Christian teaching of his youth lays hold of him, and when he knows that the lieutenant has been ordered to murder the prisoners to ease retreat before the advancing enemy he prefers to be machine-gunned with the others. The dramatic tension is well contrived and held, but what gives the book its value is its frank and clear discussion of Catholic dogma and of the implications of the ceremony of confession; 'God loves the world,' his professor of dogmatics had taught him, 'because it is imperfect – *Wir sind Gottes Utopia, aber eines im Werden*'. It is verified Catholic dogma, this indoctrinated ex-monk tells his penitent, that: '*Die Beichte ist wie jedes Sakrament ein opus operatum und hängt nicht vom Glauben des Sprechenden ab.*' The trilogy *Die Sintflut* is reckoned with the great achievements of fiction in recent years. In the first of the three novels, *Das Tier aus der Tiefe* (1949), we have again a renegade priest who gives up his clerical vocation for political agitation and rises to be a dictator. The second novel, *Die Arche* (1951), covers the period from the dictator's accession to the outbreak of a Great War. The book describes the experiences of misguided and wicked individuals whose aim is to create a model type of man in a State that shapes them closely to fit its devices. The trilogy is completed by *Der Regenbogen* (1952). The Flood is that which has swept our own time and the Arc and the Rainbow have the same political significance. What the trilogy amounts to is an ambitious attempt to show the Hitlerian State in genesis and being. Since it depicts a State logically planned and ideologically welded together we may range it with the spate of Utopias of the period, but it has a contrast value as a Utopia reversed.

WALTER JENS (1923-), a Hamburg man, began with a pacifist Novelle, *Das weisse Taschentuch* (1948); a student called up for military service notices that only dark coloured handkerchiefs are permitted, because white ones might serve for deserting to the enemy. His novel *Nein – Die Welt der Angeklagten* (1950) is a political utopia reversed; it gives a horrific picture of a *Terrordiktatur*, in which personality is annihilated and all are merged in the egalitarianism of the brutalized masses, so that no '*Menschen*' remain alive except those who are accused, those who bear witness against them, and their judges. And therefore all the automatic functions of what remains of life converge round the central terror, the Palace of Justice. The hero accuses the woman he loves and for that is raised to the rank of witness; after this he qualifies for the highest rank of all, that of a judge; he declines the honour, and is shot. In this *Zukunfts- und Staatsroman* there would appear to be some influence of George Orwell's *1984*, to which, moreover, Ernst Jünger in *Heliopolis* refers as one of the *grauenhafte Utopien*. The hero of the short story *Der Blinde* (1951), a teacher who has fallen ill and been stricken with blindness, is a symbol of the individual whelmed by the horrors of darkness. The novel *Vergessene Gesichter* (1952) was followed by *Der Mann, der nicht alt werden wollte* (1955), a disturbingly academic novel: a university professor makes it his task to lay bare the development of an old student of his who at twenty-six committed suicide in Paris, leaving the fragment of a novel which the professor classes as a master-

EXISTENTIALISM AND SURREALISM 489

piece. There are the inevitable professorial analyses, with extracts from the dead writer's work which tempt the reader to criticize the critic.

One turns almost with relief from the symbolical *Terrordiktaturen* of Stefan Andres and Walter Jens to the raw reality of it all as history records it in the work of ERNST VON SALOMON (1902-). He made an international reputation by his *Fragebogen*, the geneses of which are his answers to the denazification questionnaire of the Americans who had arrested and interned him. His reputation and the books he had written gave them good cause for this. He had been imprisoned for six years for his complicity in the murder of Rathenau in 1922. He tells the story of this and of fighting in the Baltic provinces in his novel *Die Geächteten* (1950). His novel *Die Stadt* (1932) had already been autobiographical, as was also *Die Kadetten* (1933), which describes his life as a Prussian cadet between 1913 and 1919; these two books are valuable sources of information for our knowledge of life in Germany between the wars. But still more valuable are his *Boche in Frankreich* (1950) in which he seduces and brutally abandons a Basque girl; this episode is incorporated in the full autobiography, *Der Fragenbogen* (1951), which answers the American questionnaire seriatim with contempt and ironical cynicism; here von Salomon records his activities secret and open and throws light on the rise and ruin of Nazism. The upshot is that the author, who began as a typical Prussian ensign, was in the fatal years a Nazi, either by the force of circumstance or by conviction.

It will surprise many to find that BERNHARD VON BRENTANO (1901-), a member of the famous Catholic dynasty which springs from Clemens Brentano, writes his anti-Catholic literature from the extreme left (*Kapitalismus und schöne Literatur*, 1932). He is the exact contrary of Ernst von Salomon in that he has stripped himself of all Prussian ruthlessness to fight Hitlerism as a humanitarian pure and simple. He stands apart from his Utopian contemporaries in his clinging to traditional form; that is, he makes no pretence to originality of style. The hero of his novel *Theodor Chindler* (1936) has been elected from Rhenish Hessen to represent the Centre Party in the Reichstag and he is chosen as Minister of State in the revolutionary committee of his provincial government. The following novel, *Franziska Scheler* (1945), is a sort of sequel, with Chindler's son figuring as a famous author. *Prozess ohne Richter*

MGL Q *

(1937) is an attack on totalitarian tyranny; an innocent professor is sent to a concentration camp, where he commits suicide. *Die ewigen Gefühle* (1939) and *Die Schwestern Usedom* (1948) are fiction on hackneyed lines. Brentano counts also as a literary critic: *Tagebuch mit Büchern* (1943) and *Streifzüge* (1947) deal discursively with a wide range of authors, German and foreign; in the first book there are in particular excellent pen-pictures of Schopenhauer, Nietzsche, Mörike, Stefan George, Rilke, and Georg Heym. There is the same imaginative interpretation in his *August Wilhelm Schlegel* (1945) and his *Goethe und Marianne von Willemer* (1945). *Sophie Charlotte und Danckelmann* (1949) attempts history and centres round the relations with the queen of Danckelmann, the Chancellor of Frederick I of Prussia, who is admirably and sympathetically portrayed while literature and philosophy come in with Christian Thomasius and Leibniz.

Of the literary *émigrés* during the Hitler period quite a number established themselves in the United States and published works there; most of them eventually returned to the homeland, but HERMANN KESTEN (1900-) settled there and was naturalized. He began with the novel *Josef sucht die Freiheit* (1927) and the sequel *Ein ausschweifender Mensch* (1929); in both he is already, what he has been ever since, that fanatical fighter for morality in the good old sense and for unvarnished truth which gives him a place in his generation. The hero of *Der Scharlatan* (1932) is the type of what he hates. *Der Gerechte* (1934) with its version of the son-father conflict was the first of his books to be written in America. The first-fruits of his thorough-going studies of Spanish history were *Ferdinand und Isabella* (1936), which brings in the discovery of America, and *Ich, der König* (1950; first published 1937 as *Philip II*); the latter lays bare the roots of that lust for unlimited power which inevitably leads to pitiless tyranny. But the nearer purpose of the book is to show the identity of this Spanish *Staatsabsolutismus* with *Wilhelminismus* and Hitlerism and the utter contempt for humanity of both. Kesten shows too that the stirrings of revolt are likely to come to light in repressed youth; thus Philip comes into conflict with his son Don Carlos, whom he hates. This blend of history and fiction is one of quite a series of works which go to the great epoch of Spanish history to make clear how fatal to ruler and ruled this power craze is bound to be (pp. 496-7). These two novels together with *Um die Krone* (1952) make up a Spanish trilogy. The

Spanish scene shifts in *Die Kinder von Guernica* (1939) to the Basque country at the time of the Civil War. The political satire *Die Zwillinge von Nürnberg* (1946) serves for bringing out the light and the dark sides of life in the thirties. *Die fremden Götter* (1949) switches the study of tyrannical power from State to family, and here too youth rebels. A Jewish émigré in Nice, a merchant from Frankfurt, is sent by the Nazis to a concentration camp in France, while his two daughters are brought up as Catholics in an Italian convent; the elder daughter is cast off by her father because she refuses to return to the Jewish faith, but – *amor vincit omnia* – she falls in love with a freethinking Jew and listens to reason. The theme gives Kesten full scope for the qualities that mark him as a writer – he is satirical, cynical, cold-blooded, witty; his *romans à thèse* are stripped of sentiment; all his effort is, not to move the reader's feelings, but to show how wickedness callously twists the truth. But the main result is a display of verbal pyrotechnics, brilliant, but in the long run so much of the same sort that there is a risk of monotony. *Copernicus und seine Welt* (1948) is a biography which takes into its scope the other protagonists of truth – Savonarola, Luther, Giordano Bruno, Kepler, Newton – and lashes out at those in the opposite camp – the Church, the Inquisition, superstition. *Casanova* (1952) is also biographical.

Another refugee, ANNETTE KOLB (1875-), went to Paris in 1933, where she was congenitally at home; indeed she returned to live there after her return from New York, where she found asylum while the Germans were in France. This was natural, for she is bilingual and her culture is half French; she is the daughter of a French piano virtuoso and a Munich architect in the royal service. Heredity and upbringing are the deciding factors in her work with its fine distinction and gentle irony. Herself of royal descent, she moved in the circles of the high aristocracy which she so easefully describes, not only of Munich – in her autobiographically tinged novel *König Ludwig der Zweite und Richard Wagner* (1947), with its picture of the great composer sinking into loneliness with his coldly calculating wife Cosima to face – but also of London, where the heroine of her first novel *Das Exemplar* (1913), whose heart to all appearances is closed to love, goes to find the man, now married, whom she once loved. Rilke was fascinated by the story, and Thomas Mann's valuation of the authoress emerges from the fact that she is known to be the Jeannette Schierl of his *Doktor Faustus*.

Her second novel *Daphne Herbst* (1928) moves with nostalgic regret in a dying world, the Court circles of the Munich of 1914, while in *Die Schaukel* (1934) we have the Munich of her youth. In her monographs *Mozart* (1935) and *Franz Schubert* (1941) there is the same intimate infusion of her own feelings and experience that we have in her novel of King Ludwig and Wagner. Her inborn love of France balanced by devotion to Germany informs her essays: *Sieben Studien* (*L'âme aux deux patries*; 1906), *Wege und Umwege* (1914) and her *Dreizehn Briefe einer Deutsch-Französin* (1917), in which she avows her detestation of both Pan-Germanism and Pan-Romanism.

HANS LEIP (1893-) is a prolific and popular writer. The son of a Hamburg docker, he deserted teaching for literature. In the Hitler period he was suspect, but escaped because, as a soldier in Berlin in 1915, he had written *Lili Marleen*, an internationally known soldiers' marching song; even the British took it over. The title of his first novel, *Der Pfuhl* (1923), stands for the inflation slump in Hamburg. Hans Leip has that seaman's longing for far seas and shores which through the ages has fired the men of the Hanse towns to adventure and peril, and he has their love too of the *Wasserkante* at home. Thus it is natural that the major part of his fiction should be centred in Hamburg or radiate from the port, with tales of Hanse pirates (*Godekes Knecht*, 1925) relieved by idylls of the home front (*Jan Himp und die kleine Brise*, 1933) and excursions into rollicking humour (*Herz im Wind*, 1934). Outstanding in the motley mass of his work is his historical novel *Das Muschelhorn* (1940), which records four generations of a Hamburg family of Frisian extraction. It ends with the initial stages of the Reformation, which is foreshadowed as likely to reform the evils of the time, social as well as religious superstition, the despotism of secular as well as of spiritual overlords. End of the war stories are *Ein neues Leben* (1946), in which Hamburg is pelted with bombs, and *Abschied in Triest* (1949); a tale of just after the war is *Drachenkalb, singe* (1949), in which the author embodies memories of his years as a Hamburg choir-boy (*Drachenkalb*) at St. George's Church; a choir-boy makes up his mind to be a sailor, but, helped by the girl he loves, turns musician. As a poet Hans Leip is at his best in his breezy seaman's songs (*Die Hafenorgel*, 1948; *Das Schiff zu Paradeis*, 1938; *Die Laterne*, 1942). His song *Lili Marleen* was the core of two English films.

ANNA SEGHERS (1900-) is the chief exponent of the new socialist realism in the novel as Bert Brecht is in the drama. She fled from the Nazis, who banned and burned her works, to Paris, resided in Madrid during the Spanish Civil War, and in 1941 emigrated to Mexico. In 1947 she returned to Berlin. For the rest of her life she has been a link between East Germany and the Soviet. She made her reputation with her novel *Der Aufstand der Fischer von St. Barbara* (1928); it has marked originality of style and handling, but the depiction of the life of a small fishing port in Brittany is rather romancified than realistic; the village whore, for instance, plies her trade with too much femininity to be physically possible. In her later work she develops a hard masculinity which ruthlessly eliminates all traces of warmth of feeling. Her total task is a coldly critical examination of the rise and fall of Fascism. *Die Gefährten* (1932) describes the experiences of Communist emigrants after World War I. In *Der Kopflohn* (1935) the life of a village in the summer of 1932 is plastically described, and the climax of the action is the mishandling of the hero by SA ruffians. In *Weg durch den Februar* (1935) we have the rebellion of the workers in Vienna against the Dollfuss government. In *Die Rettung* (1937) there is a close depiction of the years 1929 to 1933, just before the accession to power of Hitler. It begins with a harrowing account of the entombment of a group of miners for eight days in a deep shaft; one of them, the good Catholic Bentsch, sustains the others by his example till they are rescued and is then acclaimed as a hero. But there is a second *Rettung* which is the real theme of the novel: the miners are still entombed – they have escaped from peril to limb and life to be sucked into the long-drawn-out starvation of body and mind in the slump. The details are inexorably charted – the queueing up, the marking of the day's ration on the loaf. The seven miners sink into the dumps of apathy; but there is a spokesman who rouses them to rebel, and the message to the masses is pressed home when Bentsch leaves them to form a cell of resistance against the Nazis. The MS. of *Das siebte Kreuz* (1941), written in exile in Russia, was saved from the Gestapo by a French teacher. The novel had a phenomenal success in America, where it was filmed. The nominal hero, Georg, is one of seven prisoners in the concentration camp at Westhofen in the Mainz district. He escapes, and his sufferings in his struggle to reach safety are described; finally he is helped by friends and anti-Nazis to get away by ship. What is new in the novel is that there is no concession to sentiment; what has happened to the other six internees, who did not escape, is episodically described and serves as a foil to the central figure, who gets away, not because he is the hero of the tale, but because he is the type of the tough average man who stands up to the buffeting of fate; he is not clearly defined as an exceptional individual, but is automatically impelled by the urge to save his skin, whereas the other six have the tragic weaknesses that lead to failure, while the subsidiary characters whom Georg meets as a fugitive – working men and middle class people, the representatives of the resistance movement – come into the picture one by one as the die-hards ready to risk all to help a comrade on the run. One may say that the collective hero of the book is the average man in his relationship to the Nazi creed before the war; the groups of characters coalesce to one firmly limned total type. *Transit* (1948) again describes the sufferings of people fleeing, in the years 1940 to 1941, from the Nazi terror. The harrowing story, a prose epic of hopelessness, is told with cold precision; it is in some sort one of Kafka's nightmares lived through in relentless daylight. In Marseilles, at a time when North France but not yet the South was occupied, a band of terrorized fugitives are waiting with flickering gleams of hope for their transit visas; they are sent away from shipping offices and consulates, and only a chance accident can open the way out. The narrator, Seidler, does actually get his visa, but only because he is supposed to be using a cover-name for the famous author Weidel. But Weidel, as Seidler knows, had committed suicide in Paris when the Nazis marched in. He falls in love with Weidel's wife, who haunts the cafés in search of her husband, although in the meantime she has escaped with a doctor whose mistress she now is. Seidler, realizing that she still loves the husband she had, lets his documents pass their due date. And by doing so he saves his life, for the ship in which Marie and the doctor sail, and for which he too had a ticket, is wrecked. He himself finds refuge with French friends as a labourer on their farm. *Die Toten bleiben jung* (1949) – outwardly a *Zeitroman* but once more a species of prose epic – covers the period from the revolution at the end of World War I to the collapse of Germany at the end of the second. All the political movements take their turn, with Rosa Luxemburg and Liebknecht, with *Börsenkrache*, inflation, the slump, and with Hitlerism to cap all. All classes of society play their part, from Wilhelminean officers to the great industrialists who throw in their lot with Hitler to the working men of Berlin with their families. There is no thrusting forward of the author's convictions; the narration is all plain statement; the facts speak; the indictment lies beneath the lines. Drastically realistic as these novels seem if the bare lines of the narration are followed, they are really deliberately unrealistic; they belong to existentialism because they render a tragic-heroic view of life based on insight into what is commonly conceived as 'reality'. That is, they are transrealistic; not the story moves us, but the sense of the story, the grip of the horror that life is as it is lived under the oppression of dictators. The Marxist-Leninist faith of Anna Seghers is still evidenced in her Novellen, with minutiae selected, sifted, and historically verified; in her *Hochzeit von Haiti* (1949), for instance, we see how the French revolution stirs the negro slaves in the French colonies, while the three short tales of *Die Linie* (1950) – dedicated to Stalin – show the workings of the Communist doctrine in China, France, and the Soviet Union.

If one is to be critically fair it would be impossible to say that the fanatical fighter in the opposite camp is more convincing than Anna Seghers. REINHOLD SCHNEIDER (1903-1958), son of a Protestant father and a Catholic mother but brought up as a Catholic, is not a religious propagandist, he is rather a voice calling all the peoples to repentance, an apostle of the universal brotherhood of men as decreed by God. In *Verhüllter Tag. Lebensbericht* (1956) he has stretched the story of his life from his boyhood at Baden-Baden. The university was banned to him, but in his daily ride in the bus to his business job he read voraciously, Spanish classical dramas by preference. From Schopenhauer he passed to Nietzsche; but the course of his life and thinking was changed, he says, by Unamuno, that 'tragic existentialist' whose philosophy had been changed by Kierkegaard and the Spanish mystics. An essay of Unamuno on Coimbra directed his attention to Portugal; he learned Portuguese, spent some time in the country, and wrote his books *Portugal. Ein Reisetagebuch* (1931) and *Das Leiden des Camoës oder Untergang und Vollendung der portugiesischen Macht* (1931); the latter is in substance an examination of the root causes of the downfall of Portugal in the sixteenth century. This was his first proof of competence in what he was to make his own special province in literature: to show that the disasters of the present have their parallels in those of past epochs, and that they are due to the same follies and moral failings. There is the same tenor in his essay *Philipp der Zweite oder Religion und Macht* (1931). He then turned to his own country and examined the grandeur and guilt of the Great Elector, of Frederick I and of Frederick the Great in his historical disquisition *Die Hohenzollern* (1933), and followed this up with *Auf Wegen deutscher Geschichte* (1934). Later he passed to this country with *Das Inselreich, Gesetz und Grösse der britischen Macht* (1936): '*Wie über Spanien, Portugal, Deutschland dämmerte über England der Untergang*', he says. During the composition of this book, which was suppressed when it appeared, his outlook on the world and the processes of history, he tells us, took on final and fixed form. In these works already he shows himself to be rather an interpreter of history than a historian proper, and in this field his most brilliant achievement is by common consent *Las Casas vor Karl V* (1938); here we have in the first place an epitome of the Spanish conquest of South America, with a horrifying account of the torturing and enslavement of the Indian natives together with a revelation of the political condition of Spain. For once in a way in Schneider's explorations of history we have some fictional interest, the love story of Las Casas for an Indian girl. But the chief interest is the life story of Las Casas, who to begin with was no better as a landowner than the rest of the Spanish colonists; but in the end he was moved by pity to change his ways. He joined the Dominicans and for the rest of his life carried on a campaign by writing and preaching in support of his passionate conviction that the Indios, simply because they were human beings, were entitled to be free. The culmination of this long contest was the Council held in 1550 at Valladolid to fight out the pros and cons of the argument: the disputation, as Schneider relates it, reduces itself to an attack on Las Casas by a learned doctor of law, who proves that by all the force of logic the Indios must first be rendered helpless and then by force converted, whereas Las Casas by an equal display of logic enforced by Gospel truth proves incontrovertibly that as men born free they cannot even be forced to accept the religion of the conquistadores. Charles V is present in person, but as the proceedings draw to a close he withdraws in high dudgeon, and it is thought that Las Casas has lost the battle. Charles goes to visit his mad mother Joan in the castle where she is immured; on his return he sends for Las Casas to visit him in the late evening and they have an all-night discussion, in which Charles agrees that Spanish policy has morally ruined state and nation. He shows Las Casas, whom he appoints Bishop of Chiapa, the new laws he has drawn up, in virtue of which the Indios are to be declared free. There is an indication that when the new laws are promulgated they will turn out to be impossible; for the system of slave labour is so firmly fixed that it cannot suddenly be overthrown, and history tells us that in fact Charles had to repeal them. The problem – and the interest – is here psychological: in the interview with Las Casas Charles is shown to be worn and weary. He is baffled; he sees that he has been unfaithful to Gospel teaching. He calls in his son Philip – later Philip II – who listens to the new laws and approves them. Charles has just been forced by the Moors to raise the siege of Algiers, which he had conducted in person. He is a beaten man, and every reader who knows Platen's sonnet sees him in the not distant future laying down his multiple crowns and immuring himself in the cloistered peace of San Yuste. The situation with the salient details is strikingly identical with that in Felix Braun's drama *Kaiser Karl der Fünfte*, which had appeared two years previously (see p. 519); in Schneider's essay we have the humiliation of defeat because Charles has withdrawn from the walls of Algiers, in the drama because he has been driven from Innsbruck; in the drama Charles is convinced by Luther's Articles as explained by Prince Max, the future Emperor Maximilian, and in the essay the future King Philip II is called in to the audience chamber to approve of the new laws; and in both plays there is a visit to the mad queen mother, Juana la loca. The two works of course coincide because they both keep close to history. But Felix Braun is, by comparison, a passive narrator, while Reinhold Schneider is himself in the thick of the clash and conflict of then as of today and lashed with indignation – he is himself Las Casas fighting his great fight for truth, freedom, and peace. He will be remembered, as Las Casas is remembered, for his fight against the tyranny of a dictator: in 1941 he was forbidden to publish anything, in 1943 he was accused of *Defaitismus* and in 1945 of *Vorbereitung zum Hochverrat*; in spite of all this his writings and poems were illegally printed, while his pamphlets were lithographed or printed and disseminated throughout Germany. He escaped to Switzerland, where he continued his activities. Schneider has also written short stories which, though attractively fictional, are historical in their placing and couched in the same vein. In *Elisabeth Tarakanow* (1939) the titular heroine – said to be the daughter of the Czarin Elisabeth – is involved in a conspiracy against Catherine the Great and has to choose between a great place in the world and renunciation. There is also a group of Novellen which centre round the lives of saints and in which the poignant lesson of *Entsagung* is by the nature of the theme to the fore. The same fight for his pacifist ideals stirs in Schneider's books of historical essays; of these the title of *Macht und Gnade* (1949) typifies his inrooted doctrine that the might of nations has its justification only by the grace of God. *Der Friede der Welt* (1956) again in its skilfully chosen instances from centuries of history revolves round the problems and possibilities of peace in the present as paralleled in the past. The solution is, he says (quoting Kant), to free ourselves from the wrappings of custom, from the abuse of power, and from lies which are the stock-in-trade of diplomatic technique. We today are living in a period of grace, which is anything but peace. But this *bittere Gnadenfrist* has existed throughout history: he enumerates the instances and interprets the plans for an 'eternal peace' which have been evolved by thinkers throughout the ages. The term *der ewige Friede* is said to have been first used by Kant in his momentous essay *Zum ewigen Frieden* (1795), but actually it was first used by Leibniz, who quotes it from an inscription on the gates of a cemetery. And this is tragically true: the dead have it, but all life is war. Even in our bodies there is war while life lasts; when this war of microbe with microbe ceases we are dead and therefore at peace. Kepler's cosmic harmony (*Weltharmonik*) is false: the stars, which look so peaceful from below, are at war. Great men have praised war; Moltke in particular – 'eternal peace', he says, 'is a dream, and not even a beautiful one; war saves us from sinking into lethargy and being degenerate'. Peace, then, is *'eine notwendige Unmöglichkeit'*, or, in the diction of today, *'eine unzugängliche Unumgänglichkeit'*. And yet: *'der Friede ist immer da – und nie'*. Peace *is*, because it is an incontrovertible idea, proved to be possible by thinkers and dreamers through the ages – Hugo Grotius, William Penn, Erasmus – and how many more? Peace, says Kant, is a static condition; if it can be changed it was not peace, but the end of hostilities. The very name then and the use of it is a lie; if there were truth war would indeed be impossible. The way to end wars for ever is, then, truth; and there can be no truth between nations unless there is trust and confidence between them. The nations, then, must give up their lust of aggrandisement: 'Give up all your colonies', says Jeremy Bentham, 'and give up colonizing.' The substance of the book is here and throughout seen to be pertinent to the problems of today. The last chapters, which sum up, are depressing; for Schneider shows that even religions have ever been at war and ever will be. The scene of his first novel, *Die silberne Ampel* (1956) is Portugal in the fifteenth century; the core of it is once again the conflict of power and faith. Schneider has also tried his hand at drama. *Der Kronprinz* (1948) is planned to continue the tradition of the political drama, but *'jenseits des Programms und der Tendenz'*. The forces moving between the two great wars are detached from the actual happenings and personified: the conflict is fought out between the hierarchic power of monarchy, leagued as it is by law and tradition with the divinely ordained world-order, and the grasping at power of the secularized masses. The Crown Prince is raised above the common herd when he turns priest and transforms the monarchy to a hierarchy. The protagonists can be identified at a glance: the action centres round the break-up of the Weimar Republic, with Hindenburg as an intermediary figure; 'the Party' with its leader Sass defects from the monarchy. (It must be remembered that Schneider is confessedly an upholder of monarchy as the ideal system of government.) The epilogue is an apotheosis: 'the Angel' appears and takes the crown into his keeping; the idea is that which runs through all Schneider's work – the kingdom of God (*das Gottesreich*) must supplant secularized government (*das Weltreich*). The whole drama – it is in verse – is a paean of praise and a prophecy of the coming of the New Kingdom when all else has failed. *Der grosse Verzicht* (1950) presents in dialogue form thirteenth century scenes which are medieval and well documented but in their inferences (as in the rest of his plays) are related to the present. The characters range from the hermit Petrus von Murrhone, who is elected Pope but lays down his triple crown, to King Adolf of Nassau and Pope Boniface III, who ends as a madman. *Der Traum des Eroberers* (1951) mirrors the tragedy of the modern world in the lust of conquest of William the Conqueror. *Zar Alexander* (1951) gives shape to the spiritual conflicts in Russia at the time of the mysterious death of this Czar in 1925. *Die Tarnkappe* (1951) is, in intention, an expansion of the *Nibelungensage* to a Christian epic by way of a new interpretation. Schneider's most exhaustive exposition of his politico-religious doctrine is in his panoramic drama *Innozenz und Franziskus* (1952); Pope Innocent III – the author of *De contemptu mundi!* – fights fiercely all his life to establish his complete dominion over all the world he can reach, but has to face the contrary claims of the Emperors of Germany, Otto IV and Frederick II; and the course of the argument and action leads up to the moral victory of St. Francis of Assisi, for whom there is only one power – the gospel. Inevitably there is the same ethical bias in Schneider's excursions in literary history: *Corneilles Ethos in der Ära Ludwigs XIV* (1939) for instance. *Der Pilger* (1940) analyses Eichendorff's conception of the world and existence in it, while *Der Katarakt* (1940) and *An den Engel in der Wüste* (1940) deal in turn with Lenau and Clemens Brentano. *Die Dichter vor der Geschichte* (1944) has for double theme Hölderlin and Novalis; *Im Anfang liegt das Ende* (1946) with Grillparzer in his relation to history pairs with *Kleists Ende* (1946). *Zur Zeit der Schneide zwischen Tag und Nacht* (1940) and *Erworbenes Erbe* (1948) both present Annette von Droste-Hülshoff in her struggles as woman and poet with the closing round her of life's relentless grip. In *Der Stein des Magiers und andere Erzählungen* (1949) we have short stories which throw a kindly light on the lives and temperament of Justinus Kerner, Kant, and Hebel. As a lyric poet Schneider is best known as a sonneteer. Thematically his lyric work is marked by the impact of the war, and sometimes the compressed picture of horror and devastation is overpowering: *Die letzten Tage* (1945); *Apokalypse: Sonette* (1946); *Die neuen Türme* (1946).

The high lights of Protestant literature are the poet Rudolf Alexander Schröder (p. 278) and the novelists ALBRECHT GOES (1908-) and Manfred Hausmann. Till 1953, when he retired, Goes was a Lutheran clergyman in Württemberg, and during World War II he served as a chaplain on the Russian front. If popularity were a reliable criterion he would have to be graded well up; he has been much translated. He is a lyric poet of the quiet self-satisfied Swabian type; he is credited with aiming at being a second Mörike, of whom he has written an excellent biography (*Mörike*, 1938), but he is too normal to be in that running. His poems from 1930 to 1950 are collected in *Gedichte* (1953). As a critic of literature he has taste and insight, as in his book of essays *Die guten Gefährten* (1942) and in his *Freude am Gedicht* (1951), an interpre-

EXISTENTIALISM AND SURREALISM 501

tation of twelve poems. He has found an audience for his heart-to-heart talks with a homilectic tendency (*Von Mensch zu Mensch*, 1949). As a novelist he is at his best in *Unruhige Nacht* (1950): a Lutheran chaplain serving in the Ukraine in 1942 has the duty of comforting the last hours of a young soldier condemned to be shot for desertion. There are telling vignettes of the brutal commanding officer and of the first lieutenant to whom duty is duty. What gives the Novelle distinction is that what passes in these night hours epitomizes the spiritual climate of the last years of the war.

MANFRED HAUSMANN (1898-) is an existentialist on the Protestant side; he was a freethinker converted to Christianity by the study of Kierkegaard and Karl Barth. He began with short stories (*Frühlingsfeier*, 1924; *Die Verirrten*, 1927; *Begegnung*, 1936); the Novellen of *Demeter* (1936) have autobiographical interest. He leapt into fame with his *Lampioon küsst Mädchen und kleine Birken* (1928), the tale of a tramp (*Stromer*) who, after committing a murder, roams the roads as a lover of lasses and landscapes. Very noticeable here and in the fiction that follows is the influence of Jens Peter Jacobsen and in particular of Knut Hamsun. There is a pensive mood, relieved by the ebullience of younger years as contrasted with Hamsun's age-worn weariness, in the next batch of his tales of the open road, *Salut gen Himmel* (1929); by now Hausmann's tramps rove the inner world of the spirit, but still with the open-heartedness of the earlier tales of an outer world of adventure. In 1929 he travelled in the United States and described his adventures in his travel book *Kleine Liebe zu Amerika* (1930), and after his return a new zest in life comes to the fore in his novel *Abel mit der Mundharmonika* (1932). The scene of *Abschied von der Jugend* (1937) unrolls experiences during a trip round Iceland; the theme is the problem of wedlock. Hausmann's religious *Wandlung* is the substance of his essay *Einer muss wachen* (1951), in the second volume of his *Gesammelte Schriften*; now he is at grips with the inner problems of existence and finds the only possible solution in absolute acceptance of Christianity. The shock of conversion had been conveyed in the short story *Der Überfall* (1947): a glass painter has suddenly lost his mind, it is thought; it turns out that the attack has been spiritual: '*er hat mich überfallen*', he whispers to a visitor; to the question 'Who?' the answer is 'God'.

33

XXIII

POST-WAR
AUSTRIAN WRITERS

Of the Austrian writers of our period Hofmannsthal, Rilke, Schnitzler, Hermann Bahr, Kafka, Franz Werfel, Weinheber are so markedly international and have had so profound an influence on German literature taken as a whole that they have been dealt with in their appropriate place as pioneers of new movements. Others have been fitted in with their fellow-craftsmen over the frontier; see Austrians and Viennese writers in the Index. The Austrians grouped in the present chapter have specifically Austrian qualities, but they are of course read outside of Austria.

ROBERT MUSIL (1880-1942), a native of Klagenfurt who lived in Vienna, ranks as the most systematic exponent of magic realism; in other words he is in the same category as Joyce and Proust. He began with a psychopathic novel, *Die Verirrungen des Zöglings Törless* (1906), of which the central theme is the ripening of a boy after the onset of puberty. The Novellen of *Vereinigung* (1911) and *Drei Frauen* (1924) foreshadow the coming influence of Freud: they explore the impact of remote atavism on the ultra-refined eroticism of our own day and show that morality rooted in custom is ever on the brink of primitive urges. He toiled for twenty years at his masterpiece, the waves-of-consciousness novel *Der Mann ohne Eigenschaften* (Vol. 1, 1931; Vol. 2, 1943; a fragment of the third volume was published in Switzerland after his death). This *magnum opus* was rewritten several times; and, though it runs to over 2000 pages, it was still unfinished when he died suddenly at Zurich, where he had found asylum after the *Anschluss*. Though by his technique of *Doppelbödigkeit* and his *existentieller Widerspruch* (there are two sides of everything and truth is only achieved when these two sides are contrasted and balanced) Musil ploughs the same furrow as Joyce, he angrily rejected the imputation that he was indebted to anybody; and indeed he was far too original to need discipleship. He was an exact scholar in philosophy; and so it is not surprising that throughout his immense work we have psychological two-dimensional probings into the inner consciousness and the sub-conscious currents of his characters. What action there is takes place in the year of destiny 1913-14; and it is concerned with the social contact of characters who have formed a committee in Vienna to prepare for the celebration there of the Emperor's jubilee. The honorary secretary of the committee is Ulrich, an ex-cavalry officer. Ulrich has shed his qualities; that is, he has cast off all the acquired prejudices which today make up the pattern of culture, the idea being that a man, if he is to be himself and not just the type convention requires, must do without qualities which represent no driving force of individuality. Having shed his qualities, Ulrich is in a state of existence out of time and space. Why should qualities which falsify the world exist? This and other such problems are posed, poised, dissected, and analysed with ruthless psychological insight into the inanity of all that by the laws of logic is not congenitally part of personality. A man who sheds his qualities, the lesson runs, is potentially in possession of all qualities. The world will be built up, not by types and patterns, but by men strong in the sense of power welling up from deep within them. Not man as he is, but as he will be is also the theme laboriously conveyed by Musil's drama *Die Schwärmer* (1921). His comedy *Vincenz und die Freundin bedeutender Männer* (1924) has a heavy sense of humour. *Nachlass zu Lebzeiten* (1936) is the curious title of his essays.

Another Viennese writer, HERMANN BROCH (1886-1951), wrote one of the best essays we have on Joyce: *James Joyce und die Gegenwart* (1936), and another equally good on Hofmannsthal, whose works he translated into English. After some trouble with the police he escaped to America, where, after naturalization, he was appointed professor of German at Yale University. He died in 1951 at New Haven. It is one of the curiosities of literature that Broch's fame as one of the principal innovators of metaphysical (or magic) realism was established in America – where he was awarded the Guggenheim prize and the Rockfeller prize – some years before his work was even obtainable in Germany. His first novel, *Die unbekannte Grösse* (1933), is conventional in plot and treatment; but he went over to the polyhistoric form of fiction as handled by Joyce, Proust, and Kafka in his trilogy *Die Schlafwandler*, a long drawn out chronicle which dissects middle-class German life from 1888 to 1918. The first volume, *Pasenow oder die Romantik 1888* (1931) shows a period dominated by the military class. The commercial magnate in this section is taken over into the second volume, *Esch oder die Anarchie 1903* (1931), to face his contrary, an anarchist book-keeper. The latter appears again in the third volume, *Huguenau oder die Sachlichkeit 1903* (1932), and is reduced to ruin by a deserter who has turned business man and is successful in all his dealings. From stage to stage of the triptych we see the decay of values and the disintegration of religious faith. Joyce's technique of inner monologue is effectively handled in Broch's masterpiece, *Der Tod des Vergil* (1945); this prose poem – for it is nothing less – is one of the most brilliant of those visionary existential tales in which past, present, and future are one dimension (*Zeitlosigkeit*). Virgil, on the point of dying, looks back wistfully on the stages of his development as man and poet, and in discussions with friends and the Emperor Augustus brands his *Aeneid* as a failure because it swerves from truth and falls short of perfection in what is humanly and poetically vital; for in these last hours the world, to which the true God is about to come, is revealed to the poet as a mystery rich beyond speaking, ruled by eternal love. Only the remonstrances of the Emperor prevent him from destroying the poem. The three-dimensional conception of time is again the groundwork of *Die Schuldlosen* (1950). The period chronicled, 1918 to 1933, directly continued that of *Die Schlafwandler*, and 'the guiltless' are average types who, with one war and the time before it to look back to and another projected, are callous and passive and not conscious that their ethical indifference creates the atmosphere for the totalitarian State which looms ahead. In *Der Versucher* (1954), published after Broch's death, we see the Nazi concepts working ruin symbolically in a mountain village; Hitler appears as Marius with his dwarf-like accomplice (Goebbels).

HEIMITO VON DODERER (1896-) may be classed as a neo-realist in the sense that he is fundamentally realistic, but his relationship to magic realism is patchy. One may rather say that he continues Musil and the magic realists but that he launches out in different directions. The result is that he has devised an entirely new type of novel and is therefore pre-eminently original. Critics in their interpretations of his aims and of the influences discernible in his work drive far apart, but they are generally agreed that in his treatment of contemporary society there is something of the wide sweep, the leisurely meandering and the allusive humour of Laurence Sterne and Jean Paul. He is commonly classed as post-baroque (*nachbarock*). In his representation of the life of one great city he is said to do for Vienna what James Joyce did for the Irish capital, but his intention is to typify European life generally (in each succeeding novel) at a given historical phase of a few years. A native of Lower Austria, von Doderer passed his youth in Vienna, served in World War I and for four years (from 1916) was a prisoner of war in Siberia. Here he gravitated to literature and noted down the lines of his novel *Das Geheimnis des Reichs* (published 1930), which deals with the disintegration of the Russian government. His first published work was a volume of verse, *Gassen und Landschaft* (1923); this was followed by a short novel, *Die Bresche* (1924). His verse is collected in *Ein Weg im Dunklen. Gedichte und epigrammatische Verse* (1957). He attracted attention in wider circles with his novel *Ein Mord, den jeder begeht* (1938); despite the title this is not a crime novel but the story of a man who finds himself by seeking for the undiscovered murderer of his wife's sister, whose portrait hallucinates him; this motif is recurrent in Doderer's later work. In 1940 came *Ein Umweg, ein Roman aus dem österreichischen Barock*; it is the story of Graf Manuel Cuendias and Corporal Paul Brandter; although their stations in the social fabric are at opposite extremes their fates are inextricably interwoven; thus *Ein Umweg* is once again a way to *Selbsterkenntnis*. Called up for military service in 1941 von Doderer served for six years as an officer in the air force. On his return to Vienna in 1946 he resumed work on his monumental novel *Die Dämonen*, which he had begun in 1931.

Die Menschwerdung des Amtsrates Julius Zihal, the sub-title of *Die erleuchteten Fenster* (1951), points to what is to be von Doderer's main theme: the ripening by experience from confusion of instincts and the trammels of habit to human feeling and the acceptance of whatever befalls. The fantastic humour and biting satire of this tale reminds one of Sir Tite Barnacle in the Circumlocution Office as Dickens saw it; Zihal has risen in the Office of Taxes in Vienna to the rank of Amtsrat and now on his retirement (in the kaiserlich-königlich period – the date is 1910) he rents a cheaper flat on the third story with windows which look down on to the flats opposite; since his new abode has been unoccupied for some time those who live in the flats below are unaware that they can be observed from above, and the very first night he sees full-bodied ladies preparing for bed in the nude or near it. The course of the story shows that he has lived as a troglodyte; his very language, as copious extracts show, illustrates the *Dienstpragmatik* of officialdom. But the close-wrapped folds of custom fall from him, and his marriage to a plump *Postoberoffizialin*, who, being full woman, has remained human, gives us a novellistic, though allusively ironical, happy ending. Though Doderer specifically rejects both *Zeitroman* and historical novel as illusory and therefore outworn, his historical studies (he graduated in *Geschichtswissenschaften*) peer out from the baroque ceremonial and depiction of custom in *Ein Umweg*; and they serve him too for the outlines of what to some readers will seem his most moving work, *Das letzte Abenteuer* (1953). It is a tale of troubadours and errant knights; a Spanish hidalgo has heard the story of a lovely lady in whose forests a dreadful dragon roams at will; he sets out with page and retinue to slay the monster; his sword is blunted on its scaly back; but the lady welcomes him, if not as a dragon-slayer, at least as a champion who has struck off the beast's horns. By all the laws of old romance he should marry the lady and be lord of her realm; but he is not drawn to her, and, ripe widow as she is, she prefers his page, now newly dubbed a knight. He sets out once more with a new page, and beyond the forest comes to villages where cottages are being burnt down and bodies of defenceless villagers lie on the roads; he finds a marauding gang, attacks them single-handed and forces them to flee; but in the moment of his victory he sinks from his horse and is stretched out dead, he too a victim of war as we know it today. The tale is dreamful and symbolic; the meaning lies embedded in what passes in the knight's mind. The dragon is Fate, and we are powerless to fight it; evil whelms us. We find the interpretation of this little story – and of much else in Doderer's work – in the *Autobiographisches Nachwort* which is appended; the author, quoting the saying of Mephistopheles: *Wer lange lebt, hat viel erfahren*, agrees but stresses that *lange* refers not to the chronicle of years but to the intensity of experiences; those whose experiences lay between 1871 and 1914 lived a short life, for there was no break in the continuity of their experience; 'those of my own generation', he continues, have lived long indeed, for they have lived through two wars, have seen the swamp of illusions dry up and the treasure of disillusions grow and grow. So too the knight errant of *The Last Adventure* felt his illusions fall away from him, but disillusion enriched him and ripened him to face the onslaughts of Fate. These great motifs of Doderer, *Desillusion, Selbsterkenntnis, Menschwerdung*, must be accepted as the staple of his work. He insists that he has no lesson to teach; psychology and the Freudian doctrine he rejects outright; he gives life as it is. Even the dreams and visions with which his work abounds, the sense of the identity of *Diesseits* and *Jenseits*, the unity of time, the dichotomy which he shares with Dostoieffsky, the biological fact that every being is double and that his ripening by experience is the stage to a new reality, his sense of the latency of goodness (*Latenz*) in all of us – all this is, so runs the argument, life as it is, and the field of the novelist.

Die erleuchteten Fenster points forward to *Die Strudelhofstiege oder Melzer und die Tiefe der Jahre* (1951) in so far as several of the characters appear in both novels; thus Zihal's story is fitted into the second novel and continued, with that of his wife. The period is roughly 1923-1925, but there are throw-backs to 1910-1911; that is, two levels of time are interwoven (*Doppelbödigkeit*). Thus the chronicle minutely records the mentality and atmosphere of Vienna between the two wars, but also, in nostalgic retrospect, there are glimpses of the kaiserlich-königlich days as they draw to their disastrous close. We thus see the characters at two stages of their lives. The idea is that the author has collected his information from the novelist Kajetan von Schlaggenberg, from Sektionsrat Geyrenhoff, who chronicles all that happens, and from Major Melzer, the central figure of the story. The build-up and style of *Die Strudelhofstiege* and of *Die Dämonen* are so closely related that both books must be taken as one; characters are introduced in *Die Strudelhofstiege* and their lives related in the period chosen, but the narration is taken up again in *Die Dämonen* and continued to its close. *Die Strudelhofstiege* is indeed described by Doderer as an ascending approach *Rampe* (an architectural term), and as a prelude (*Auftakt*, a musical term), or overture (see below), to *Die Dämonen*, which up to the present is the culmination of what was from the first planned as a monumental cycle of novels. The *Strudelhofstiege* is a flight of steps which links two streets, as in the story all is linked: present, past, and future and social grades of society; here and hereabouts the decisive events of the novel take place. As to the verbal style, a great feature (*nachbarock*) is Doderer's mastery of incapsulated sentences (*Schaltsätze*), which remain clear however long they may be. This in musical terminology is contrapuntal; indeed the whole structure is admittedly musical, built up as it is of four phases or movements, actually headed *Teile*, and the contrapuntal complexity of the style – wheels within wheels – pairs with the concept that the experiences, like the roads and alleys, wind and intersect but move finally to this controlling centre of the rising flight of steps. And this fitting of the structure to chamber music confirms Doderer's insistence that *Die Strudelhofstiege* and *Die Dämonen* are not intended by him to be a unity; for by comparison *Die Dämonen* has the construction of an opera on a great scale with overture and finale (*Das Feuer*). Very marked is the Austrian flavour of the vocabulary, and the apt use of racy dialect; this makes the picture of Vienna, with its description of hotels, cafés and eating-places and of its maze of streets (which matches the maze of the construction) and of localities central and suburban, delightful, though for full comprehension it entails reading with a map of the city by one's elbow. Another feature of Doderer's style is his allusive playing with the apparent and the latent meaning of words (*Latenz*): *Hingerissenheit* and *Gerissenheit; Ver-Zweiflung; Pro-menade; 'Ist nicht Zufall, das was einem Menschen zu-fällt?'; 'Liebe ist kein Bedingnis, sondern ein Bedingtes.'* In Doderer's type of novel there is another radical departure from traditional build-up. In a novel we have 'characters'; 'a man of character' succeeds because he is such; a man of weak character fails because that is what he is. But *does* a successful man owe his success to his character? There is no such thing as character in the accepted sense, Doderer seems to argue; some men get what they want or seek, but that is a matter of chance or situation; given the situation the event follows. It is not 'character' that matters in the shaping of life: character does not shape life and life does not shape character. On the contrary the course of events is shaped by οἱ τρόποι, or, more simply stated, turning points; all that happens is *situationsgemäss*. There are of course wide differences in persons; and it is the province of the novelist to pierce to the very essence of these differences, to the temperamental springs of impulse and therefore of 'action' – and 'action' itself is not governed by force of will but by temperamental instincts and urges, which are at the mercy of chance. For our 'hero', therefore, let us take a man with no character at all in the stereotyped novelist's (or historian's) sense: a man without qualities, *der Mann ohne Eigenschaften*, which is the very title of Musil's great novel, and this Doderer's cycle is perhaps intended to outstrip, if only because it is closer down to brute reality. The titular hero of *Die Strudelhofstiege*, Melzer – typically, his Christian name is not given – illustrates the argument. He is introduced as a lieutenant in the Austrian army, and in the final stages he is a retired major and a civil servant (*Amtsrat*). It is repeatedly stressed that he is considered to be a fool; this does not make him less fit to be the hero of a novel, for he is the perfect type of the majority of men, the type of man who, though opportunities are within his grasp, 'never gets there'; or, he always misses the bus. He is throughout an outsider on the rim of the happenings; he is sucked into the whirl, but not engulfed. That is, he is aware of the social cynicism which is the prerogative of the clever ones, but he remains decent; one may, therefore, if one is simple (or silly) enough, remain good, uncontaminated. Even as an Amtsrat, a minor official in the *Tabakregie*, he has, to begin with, no 'civil intelligence' (*Zivilverstand*); he is incapable of thinking, and it is only by learning to link the present with the past that he learns to think at all, or, as the sub-title indicates, to probe 'the depth of the years'. Surprisingly he marries a girl who to his knowledge has been the mistress of a former cavalry officer, a friend of his, the Rittmeister (facetiously: Zerrüttmeister) von Eulenfeld, who always gets there with women, because 'he is the major'. The ending is thus on the face of it happy; but judged by the course of other marriages in the book this seems to be ironical. More interesting than Melzer is René Stangeler; clearly he is a contrast figure; where Melzer fails to act René acts instantly and *situationsgemäss*; and therefore (throughout the cycle) women yield to him in animal fashion. René has intelligence and scholarship; he is, like Doderer, a history graduate and he has written a book on *Memoiren im Mittelalter*. He has qualities of a sort, but they have no importance; he remains vacuous. René is just the centre of a revolving crowd of more or less clearly defined characters. We see these characters clearly, with their physical traits and their ways of dressing and even the perfumes they diffuse – thus René has *schräge*

Augen, is always *ohne Hosenträger*, and attracts his women with his scent of lavender. But the core of people's characters is not to be gathered from their 'attitudes', but from the *Latenz* of these (i.e. what lies beneath their appearance or outward *Haltung*). The novellistic interest (in the accepted sense) centres in the female characters; in particular in René Stangeler's two sisters. A great part of the novel is taken up with revealing with great psychological detail how, why, and in what state of mind girls and married women of the higher classes give way to men. The result arrived at is that 'romance' as novelists depict it is – fiction; what decides is blood pressure, not 'love'. And the results do not imply continuance of the relationship; illegitimate children belong to nature's way. Thus girls who have given way have not been 'seduced'; what happened *had* to happen – at the given moment (p. 229, 235). The one really decent girl is Paula Schachl, in 1911 a shorthand-typist, seventeen years old when we first meet her. Stangeler accosts her in a street, and she responds with casual friendliness; they meet in cafés, they walk through the streets together, but the situation for the loss of the girl's virginity does not accrue. She fades out of the picture for a good stretch, and when she returns she is happily married to a working man; she and her husband do come into contact with the roystering ruck, but she remains bourgeoise and decent. She is an effective *Kontrastfigur*, but one feels that a walk in the woods with her boy might have ended *situationsgemäss*. The conclusion is that, morally considered, preservation lies not in a good upbringing or religious rectitude but in a chanceful escape from the situation. In other words there is no virtue in being virtuous, but just luck.

In 1956 appeared Doderer's *magnum opus*, at which he had been working for twenty-five years, *Die Dämonen*. It runs to 1345 pages. The title is admittedly borrowed from Dostoieffsky's *Die Dämonen*, of which the English title is *The Devils* or *The Possessed*. Thematically *The Possessed* is more close to the texture and intent of Doderer's novel; the leading motif is that we all tend to be obsessed by illusions which may go so far as madness but as a rule are a milder form of 'craze', 'fixation' may be or 'complex', or as the French say *lubie*. We are possessed of devils that cannot be driven into the Gadarene swine. Driven down to their root causes they are likely to derive from sexual urges. The nearest approach to demonology proper is the dubious idea of that medievalist René Stangeler that witches in the Middle Ages were not burnt for witchcraft, but because some *grand seigneur* or other was a sadist and fed his senses on the sight of torture; in the fifteenth century manuscript he discovers and makes his reputation by interpreting the feudal *châtelain* abducts two buxom and ultra-respectable middle-class women and deals with them as witches, feeding his eyes on their disrobing and whipping, because they obstinately reject his claim to seigneurial rights. Perversely enough they admit to their beds the two pages who keep guard on them by sleeping on their thresholds in the castle, and this satisfies the witch-hunter – he was possessed by the craving to prove that they were *not* virtuous, and, having found his pages in their beds, he releases them. The historical veracity of all this is obviously spurious; it serves merely as proof of the doctrine that we are pathologically possessed. And in this way, we must understand, a *Weltanschauung* logical on the face of it may degenerate by its very intensity of conviction into a morbid obsession; for it may take hold of one's original nature and transform it. These obsessions confront us as contraries, as in religion or politics; e.g. *Klasse oder Rasse*. Thus there is the contrast of the muscular sport-loving and studious girls of today ('*Denaturierte*'), who are dismissed by Schlaggenberg as vampyres because their only aim is to marry and be kept, with the ripe, experienced widows or wives whose natural function it is to mother young bloods who are thus saved the burden of marriage; he writes a *chronique scandaleuse*, which he hands over to von Geyrenhoff for his chronicle, on these *Dicke Damen*, for short D.D.'s. René von Stangeler adds to his *lubie* of lounging *ohne Hosenträger* the determined conviction that young men of the learned classes – in particular university hopefuls – should be excused marriage, but that they should be admitted to marital rights while postponing marriage or even, as he does, refusing it; professional scholars, he urges, should not be hampered by household obligations. And so in both novels of the cycle René is received as the unmarried husband of Grete Siebenschein; he works at his research in her room, and when her parents go out for the evening she is his. . . .

The period of *Die Dämonen* runs from the spring of 1926 to the burning down by incendiaries of the Justizpalast on the 15th of July, 1927; a conflagration which is symbolical of what is coming to all Europe and in Austria foreshadows the years after 1933 with the *Anschluss*. Vienna is once more intimately depicted. But, since the actual life of the period is the matter of the novel, the garden suburbs and health resorts in the wooded highlands come into the picture. The ideas which go to the making of the *Strudelhofstiege*, being permanent truths in the illumination of the social structure, are taken over; here one only needs to add several moral or metaphysical concepts which are stressed. Of these the unity of time gathers force by the continuous references to *das Diesseits* as identical with *das Jenseits* and vice versa; this doctrine blends with the lesson to which the action converges that every human being is double (dichotomy) and that if there is transformation (in the old sense of *Wandlung*) by experience it is because there is a ripening to a new reality. The manifestations of an individual's craze may run through the whole warp and woof of his life; and thus individuals can be classified and ticketed just like butterflies; but if experience serves its moral purpose then this outer casing of illusion may scale off and the inner man be revealed; what was within (*das Innere*, the inner man) is then without and in the light of day. The most striking instance of this finding of a new self (*Menschwerdung*) is the working man Leonhard Kakabsa; he is determined to remain a working man in his outlook and predilections, but he attains culture by studying Latin and Roman history and by social contacts, and in the end is appointed librarian to a nobleman and marries the Mary K. who is one of the few attractive characters of *Die Strudelhofstiege*; she has lost a leg by being run over in the street, but she fights her disability, gets accustomed to the wooden leg, and there is a 'happy ending' when she marries Leonhard Kakabsa, though she is a widow with two children, a *Gymnasiast* and a somewhat younger girl who has an eye on Leonhard herself. This is a problematic ending; but so too is the ingeniously contrived crowding of happy endings, almost in Dickensian fashion, to close the novel; the *Strudelhofstiege* has ended with a problematic marriage which disposed of Melzer; in the second novel there are engagements, as the Justizpalast burns, followed by marriages all round; even René Stangeler, now by a miracle of chance (*situationsgemäss*) fixed up in a remunerative post, marries his *ewige Braut*. To the reader who has familiarized himself with the mental make-up and the way of life of these people this glaringly novellistic contrivance is obviously part of the all-embracing satire. But there are characters who could not be so happily disposed of: in the plan of the novel the highest classes come into contact with the lowest strata of society, and indeed some of the most readable chapters (perhaps because they come close to 'what the public wants') are those which lay bare the lives of prostitutes who by reason of their haunts and calling come into contact with a murderer, the 'King of the Underworld'. Common to both novels is the financier Levielle, whose manipulations wind through the woof of the story and keep the reader's mind alert for the coming revelations; but these revelations – since money is recovered – conduce to the happy endings, and perhaps for this reason this wretch and rogue is permitted to 'retire' to Paris. The sum total of *Die Dämonen* would seem to be negative; the characters are one by one dissected, there is no condemnation of their mode of life – not even, in set terms, of the financial rogues; the reader condemns them or acknowledges that, constituted as they are, they cannot act otherwise. Certain people (aristocrats in particular) are congenitally empty-headed, we are told, and whatever experience they may have leaves them so. They may be attractive; they may, by luck or guile, be successful. Even René Stangeler is one of these people; he remains (for all his studies) unripened; there is no *Menschwerdung*, because there is no *Mensch*. All the same the total sense is positive. There is a cry for egalitarianism; this, however, means not *Gemeinschaft* but *Gemeinheit*, which can only be a passing phase; what lasts and shapes the world is that which is incommunicable, the sterling qualities of the gifted individual who has no 'demon'. Nothing in the whole cycle of novels is exaggerated or glaring. All is finely toned; but over all the epic panorama there is a mood of strangeness as if everything were seen through *erloschloto Fenster*. The intention is that the reader should be aloof (*distanziert*); feelings of sympathy or affection for the characters would be out of place; the reader observes – and comprehends. This is life – anywhere. . . .

Of MARTINA WIED (1882-), a Viennese born and bred, we can say that, though the main lines of her work are traditional in form and to some extent even sensational in theme, her technique is in intention existential. She prefaces one of her novels with Kierkegaard's *Geisterszene* motto; and she prides herself that her first novel, *Das Asyl zum obdachlosen Geist*, was the first in the existential mood and manner, for it was written in 1925-26, long before Sartre, and appeared serially in the *Wiener Zeitung* (in book form 1950 as *Kellingrath*). Her lyric poetry is collected in selected form in *Brücken ins Sichtbare* (1952). Two of her novels have a particular interest for this country – *Das Einhorn* and *Das Krähennest*, and this is due to the fact that during the war she was an exile, teaching in schools, in Scotland and England. *Das Einhorn* (1948), begun 1940 in Edinburgh and finished in Glasgow, is in the form of a diary, written by Sir James Graham, the 'unicorn' of the story, one of the famous painters of the day; nominally he is held back in Florence by a commission to paint the Duke of Albany, the Bonnie Prince Charlie of days long past, now a besotted drunkard. But the pivot of the action is the plot of certain Jacobites to have Sir James adopted as the son and heir of this last scion of the Stuarts; the plot was that he should land on the Scottish coast and march on Edinburgh. But Sir James is killed in a duel. Actually the interest centres to a great extent on the contrast of the rigid Scots nobleman, faithful to his shadow of a king, with the dramatist Alfieri, the lover of the wife of Charles Edward, as he is in 1777 and as he will be at the height of his powers; here we have the existential doctrine that 'what I shall be, I am'. The contrary picture is that of Charles Edward as a compound of sot in the present and of glamorous and dashing adventurer in the still unforgotten past; in the case of both we have the proof by contrast, by way of exemplifying the cardinal doctrine of the new technique, that time is permanent in change. In *Das Krähennest* (1951), finished in 1948 in Llandudno, the technique of magic realism is uncompromising. There is contrast of conscious and unconscious will; the happenings are on different levels (*Begebnisse auf verschiedenen Ebenen*); and regularly in the course of a dialogue the thoughts of a speaker are interpolated at length. (*Sagen und Meinen*) The story is that of unedifying happenings at a co-educational English secondary school with a very un-English assortment of teachers. *Die Geschichte des reichen Jünglings* (1952) is another experimental novel, and as such daringly extreme in mood and method. In the first place there is an obvious allusion to the story of the rich man's son in the Bible, for Adam Leontjew, the hero, is the son of a rich factory owner in the Polish town in Dymno, who is willing to cast away the privileges of his class to follow some leader or other and drifts away to Communism. He comes into contact with a Russian agent of Moscow, Iwanow, who has been a university teacher in Vienna, an intellectual who brilliantly expounds the new faith. But this Communism is just one of the multiple states of mind (*Seelen-*

zustände) which form the substance of the novel; actually it is induced, not so much by revulsion from wealth and luxurious living, as by Adam's own erotic experiences and those of his friends. In this sphere of conduct the prominent feature is that pre-marital experience is the rule; and it is relieved by the dictum that all experience, good or evil, is formative of character; what matters to a lover at a given moment, therefore, is what the lady *is*, not what she *has been*, and that indeed after sensual stages the new real love creates a new virginity. The inexorably drawn out tale, chronologically dated after World War I, ostensibly holds out a mirror to the state of Europe, but in the prologue – really an epilogue – there is a cinematographical dissolving picture of what the hero and all about him are in the chaos after World War II. In *Der Ehering* (1954) one of the characters of *Die Geschichte des reichen Jünglings* relates his love-experiences; the wedding ring of the title symbolizes the sanctity of marriage.

IMMA VON BODMERSHOF (1895-) pairs with Martina Wied as an exponent of the new technique, but she is more dreamful; she evokes rather than demonstrates. In her novel *Das verlorene Meer* (1952), a revised version of *Die Stadt in Flandern* (1939), magic realism is fitted to Bergson's philosophy as exemplified, above all, in Proust's *A la recherche du temps perdu*. In this evocative medley of myth and legend the ancient story of Flanders comes to life in the consciousness of the historical research worker Cornelius, who, between the two Great Wars, goes to Bruges to ransack the city archives. The urban picture throughout the tale is, as it is now, dominated by the Belfry, from which, above, the distant sea can be glimpsed. There is something of Georges Rodenbach's *Bruges la morte* in the atmosphere of the story, but the central idea is that of the city as a symbol, not only of the decay here below of all life, but also of eternal revival in religious faith. The legends and episodes of the past alternate with the happenings of today; for the past is the present; events wind onwards through the ages as the spiral staircase of the Belfry tower winds upwards to the outlook from its platform near the clouds. *Das verlorene Meer* is thus closely fashioned on what has been called the 'spiral principle' (*das Spiralenprinzip*) as it occurs in the contemporary novel; that is, phases of time and consciousness interlock and enlace as they wind upwards to a sweeping and comprehensive vision of what has been related and implied. The deeper meaning of this identi-

fication of past and present is that not only do we today live the
past history of our land, but that we expiate wrongs done by
our forefathers; thus the destruction of Ypres in World War I –
itself by now a myth in our memory – is the punishment after
centuries of deeds done by William of Ypres in the Middle Ages.
All destruction and havoc, then, and victories and defeats, are
links in an ever running chain; not the will of the living but the
guilt of the dead brings ruin. Deeper still is the symbol that Cornelius himself – and he in turn is a symbol of Man – is the dying
town; and so, when illness threatens his life, he awakens to the
consciousness that just as the sea has receded from the old city,
just as the canals have silted up, so, as age overtakes us, our veins
silt and harden; but, like the Belfry bells, the heart swings its call
to courage and will be the last within us that will die; and as we
rise to the utmost heights of faith, 'though inland far we be', we
see, as from the Belfry tower, the mighty waters of 'the lost sea'
rolling on the shore. *Die Rosse des Urban Roithner* (1950) is also
ranged with the novels of magic realism; but this classification is
illusory – actually the realism throughout is drastically real and
the magic of symbol is accidentally tacked on. The groundwork
of the tale is bucolic in the Virgilian sense, and farming life as
described is based on the practical experience of the author, who,
though she is the daughter of the famous professor of philosophy
Christian Freiherr von Ehrenfels and was, in days gone by, a friend
of Rilke and of Stefan George's Circle, has for over thirty years
managed her own estate in Lower Austria. What sunders *Die Rosse
des Urban Roithner* from the peasant novel proper is the deeper
meaning read into the common course of peasant life, and the
presentation of life in farm, forest and village in a lonely district
of Niederöstreich as the myth of a province. But what holds and
moves the reader is the unfolding of inevitable tragedy in the
hypertrophy of will power and elemental passion in a man who
stands out among the ruck of his peasant associates as an innovator who by sheer determination sweeps all before him till he is
himself swept by a superior force – the logic of events or the law
of retribution – into the abyss. Urban is a plain man of the people
and a man of today; but the consequences are the same for him
and those who depend on him as in a fate-tragedy, and the ethical
effect is indeed that of remote Greek tragedy. Moreover, while the
hero of Greek tragedy is beaten down by something impersonal

– 'fate' in the non-human sense – Urban is ruthlessly ruined by the devilish wickedness of his fellow-men; he makes a pact with *a* devil – the innkeeper who lends him the money to buy horses to start his business of transporting timber down the mountain-side –, but not with *the* Devil; he does indeed, in a moment of desperation, invoke any power above him, good or evil, either the Devil or the other power, and then all goes well for a time; but this is more by way of a fanciful addition of extraneous magic, motived by the memory of pacts with the Devil in local legend, than a set pact with this legendary Devil. Urban, as a man, has all the sterling qualities which should bring success; he is not brought to ruin by love of woman – patient, gentle Barbara, who has been disinherited for her love of him, bears his children on their lonely farm far from doctors and midwives, but his steady love for her is a saving factor; his fate is that deep down in his nature is a passionate love of horses; and this is vividly and consistently woven into the tale as the motive force of his grim tragedy. If there is indeed magic realism in the novel it is in the way these horses, in body and pulsing vigour as magnificent as he who drives them through the snow of hard winters, fill the landscape as the very heart of the action. Smuggled across the frontier by gipsies, they are bought and sold by Urban till he is arrested; technically innocent, for he has not crossed the frontier, he is guilty of cheating the revenue of entry dues, and is condemned to pay a large sum, which means that he must earn the money by this perilous transport work while his wife works herself to death on their farm. Barbara, too, is the victim of fate; she dies, in his absence, bearing their third child; he goes out then with his team of horses and drives over the ledge of the mountain into the abyss. His body is found; but in the forest above the villages the story persists that a turf-cutter on the mountain-top has seen him borne along at flying speed by his team of raven-black steeds, with his wife behind him – into the mystery of what lies behind this life of toil and trouble. The four short stories of *So lange es Tag ist* (1953), though each differs glaringly in tone and tenor, explore the same philosophic concept that all we do, however simple it may seem, wells up from the deep sources of being within us; our actions are inevitable, for they are our fate. In the centre tale, *Milch auf Gestein*, Sicily in its burning beauty and with its primitive peasants and their mode of life is described by one who knows the country from coast to

34

coast. A German author steeped in classical lore meets, as he climbs a mountain-side, a girl coming down with a pitcher poised on her head – water for her cottage from a distant well –, and as she paces spinning with both hands from a spindle; this is ancient Greece with amphora and the slender grace of perfect female form. Day by day he meets her at the same spot; she is married to a man who is nothing to her. She bears her lover from another world a boy; and when, some years later, he returns mother and child are lost to his quest. In the closing Novelle, a chronicle of two generations, there is double illegitimacy, of mother and daughter; 'they had only quite simply done what came in their way to do' – yielding to a lad on a summer night, doing nature's will, and dying worn and wasted by work without end. Sicily, 'the island under the eight winds', is again the scene of *Sieben Hand voll Salz* (1958), and there is again the contrast, in the character of a German who inherits a Sicilian farm, with the natives who are as hardened as the volcanic rocks that frame their soil.

Since 1920 there has been a striking revival of Roman Catholicism in Austria as a literary ferment, and it has gained momentum since the end of the Second World War. The most notable of the converts whose ardour of faith is the inspiration and almost the sum and substance of their new work is FELIX BRAUN (1885-), a Jew by race and in days gone by a close friend of the galaxy of writers, mostly free-thinking, who made the Austrian literature of their period world-famous – Rilke, Hofmannsthal, Stefan Zweig, Schnitzler, and the rest. From 1928 to 1937 he was *Privatdozent* in German literature at the University of Palermo and then at the University of Padua until, in 1939, he emigrated to England, where he lectured on art at evening Institutes. He distinguished himself by lyric verse in the taste of the day: *Gedichte* (1909), *Das neue Leben* (1913), *Das Haar der Berenike* (1919), *Das innere Leben* (1925). *Viola d'Amore* (1953) is the final selection of his verse. He is a determined traditionalist; his modernity lies rather in his sensitive linking of symbol, as, for instance, in *Der Fremde in kriegerischer Stadt*, in which the desperate pain of war-time in an exile's heart is conveyed by glimpses of harbour lights and the victorious tricolour fluttering in the wind that carries the newsvendor's raucous cry, but with, in the distance, the glimmer of the lighthouse (*der Fernschauer*), the spark of love burning like the star, far in the firmament over the roof yonder. Here, as in all that Felix writes, the lesson is that by divine ordinance love must unite those who are sundered by hate. There is a vast variety of theme, stretching from the familiar tales of the Old Testament and Greek myths, vignettes of Italy and poignantly personal notations to odes, most of which are in the grand manner. There is the same predominance of Biblical and Greek themes in the dramas, which in form are, like his verse, obstinately traditional; Felix is indeed, together with his friend Max Mell, the last German dramatist to remain faithful to the verse drama. Greek in theme are *Tantalos* (1917), *Aktaion* (1921) and *Der Tod des Aischylos* (1946); Biblical are *Esther* (1925) and *Die Tochter des Jairus* (1950), while *Ein indisches Märchenspiel* (1934) handles, in rhymed verse of varying length, an Indian fable. *Kaiser Karl der Fünfte* (1936) is a study of monarchical totalitarianism. Through the drama runs Karl's famous boast, effectively varied, that the sun never set on his dominions; and indeed as German Emperor, as the ruler of the Netherlands, Naples, Hungary, Spain with her great colonies in America, and as titular king of Jerusalem, he was speaking truth. But the leading idea is that as Holy Roman Emperor he had the divine right to rule the world; '*Nur e i n e Sonne leuchtet unsrer Welt*', he declares. He is of course merely voicing the proud device: A.E.I.O.U. (*Austriae est imperare orbi universo*). This doctrine runs parallel with Karl's conviction that in religion too only one sun can shine, and that, therefore, Papal rule of the world must be God's plan. (There is the same reasoning, in the same terms, in the drama *Irina und der Zar* – 1948 and 1956 –, a study of Russian totalitarianism.) But to a non-Catholic the action of the play proves the contrary; Karl admits, when Luther's articles are read to him, that there is substance in them, and there is also the slow disillusionment following defeat by the Protestants that leads to the Emperor's retirement to the monastery of San Yuste as we know it from Platen's famous poem. But the lesson intended by the dramatist is that Charles Quint failed tragically because he did not realize that not power, but love of one's fellow men, is the decree of God. One's first urge in turning to *Beatrice Cenci* (1937) is to compare it with Shelley's *The Cenci*. Both poets keep to the main lines of the story; the main difference is that whereas Shelley condones nothing in his picture of sixteenth century beastliness in Italy and brings out the venality of the Papal Curia, Felix Braun tends to tone down his motivation, psychologically convincing though it is, and to make his *dénoue-*

ment conform to the religious tenet that runs through his other dramas: *Leben ist Lieben*. Count Cenci's ravings in Act IV of Shelley's play have a Freudian modernity which is alien to Felix Braun's guiding of the action to Beatrice's confession, as she goes to execution, that she merits death because she has not loved her father, even after he had raped her. *Rudolf der Stifter* (1953) breaks new ground: decasyllabic iambic is thrown to the winds and there is effective use of Eliotic free rhythms. Here more than anywhere else – for we have Felix's earlier dramas to serve for comparison – we have proof positive that verse moulded to the dramatic mood of the speaker at a given moment and to the rise and fall of feeling rings more true because the stress falls on the vital word and that this can be marked by its place in the line. Rudolf der Stifter is that Archduke of Austria who, between 1358 and 1365, intrigued and fought to ensure that the Habsburgs should by right of birth be the Holy Roman Emperor in 'Felix Austria'. He dies at twenty-five, a beaten man; but he is the 'founder' of Austrian greatness to be because he has foreseen and planned it, and therefore it is fitting that in his last moments he should declaim an inspired prophetic vision of Austria through the ages, upwards to its apogee when the sun never sets on the dominions of Charles V and then its gradual decline till Vienna is laid waste by bombs and his cathedral of St. Stephen, as we see in an interpretative prose *Vorspiel*, lies in rubble and ashes. The dramatic conflict is double: between Rudolf and the Luxemburg Emperor in Prague, Albrecht II, and between Rudolf and his falcon-eyed wife Katharina, Albrecht's daughter, who fights for her father, not so much because dynastically she is in the opposite camp, but because the marriage is nominal and she is childless, while Rudolf has peasant girls brought to his bed. The ending is fanciful but impressive: in the palace of the Visconti in Milan, where Katharina finds Rudolf in the toils of the fiercely passionate daughter of the house, he confesses to and is absolved by a poet crowned already by the aureole of immortality – Petrarch, a priest ordained but living a worldly life, who confesses to his penitent that his own sin – to have desired, not loved – has been as futile as Rudolf's lust for power. Novellen and legends are gathered together in *Laterna magica* (1932); in the revised edition of 1957, which is fitted into the series of the *Ausgewählte Werke*, there are omissions of tales which could ill be spared. These Novellen are, whether for better or worse, distinctive, both for their softly gliding style which eliminates all rough notes, and for the Neo-Catholic reshaping of the myths and legends; certainly *Attila*, another ambitious attempt to epicize in prose the *Nibelungensage*, sacrifices all the dramatic vigour of the *Heldenlieder* as we know them in its remoulding as a myth. Attila is the son of a spirit demon and is himself a spirit with no flesh and blood, as are all the Huns he summons from the kingdom of the dead. And yet he marries Kriemhild and has a child! There may be some allusion to the ravaging hosts of today, especially since Attila is vanquished only, when at the end of the long-drawn-out slaughter of the Nibelungs, Dietrich von Bern holds before his eyes an iron cross and by relating the life of Christ teaches the heathen a word new to him: sacrifice. A much higher level is reached by those stories which, like *Die vergessene Mutter* (in its way a masterpiece), touch the heart by their simple pathos. Of the novels, *Die Taten des Herakles* (1921) swathes the myth of Hercules in a blanket of Christian mysticism; the deeds of the Greek demigod are ingeniously fitted to the formative experiences of a young Roman patrician, who in Greece meets St. Luke and his disciples, is converted, and perishes in his fight with a Numidian lion in Nero's circus. Austrian through and through is *Agnes Altkirchner* (1927; new edition 1957 as *Herbst des Reiches*), which unrolls the ruin of Austria between the years 1913 and 1919. The conviction that this national ruin, which threatens from without and within, can be remedied only by religion is obviously the driving force of Felix Braun's work of recent years. *Der Stachel in der Seele* (1950) is an endlessly winding interpretation of Catholic doctrine, a Dantesque vision of a Purgatory here below. The inspiration of the dream-like prose of *Briefe in das Jenseits* (1952) is that we all have communings with our dead loved ones; here the communings are shaped in epistolary form, which allows commemorative recordings, and has thus autobiographical interest. There had been an autobiographical fundament in *Der Schatten des Todes* (1910); there is at least the first part of the poet's autobiography, the story of his youth, in *Das Licht der Welt* (1949). The title is revealing: the dark night of the soul is dispersed by the Saviour, the Light of the World. We have the obsession of this image once again in *Die dunkle Nacht der Seele* (1952), possibly the loveliest translation in any language of the mystical lyrics of St. John of the Cross, which centuries before had inspired the *Trutz Nachtigall* of Friedrich von

MGL R *

Spee. As a critic and essayist Felix Braun is represented by *Ver-klärungen* (1916) and *Deutsche Geister* (1925); of particular interest are the essays of *Das musische Land* (1952), in which there is a discussion of the differences between the literature of 'the land of the Muses' – that is, Austria – and that of North Germany.

FRANZ NABL (1885-) is in the very first rank of the Austrian novelists of today. He stands apart from his fellow novelists in various ways: for one thing his narration moves more slowly and with a certain air of deliberation and solidity, and all is quietly evolved. It is not easy to define his pedigree; he is generally classed as in the line of Stifter; for this, however, there is too great an intensity of psychological probing. Critics indeed stress his *Tiefen-psychologie* – that is, he gets deeper into the mind of his character than is the common rule in the psycho-analytical novel; but in a letter to me he says he never heard the term *Tiefenpsychologie* until a few years ago a Viennese dissertation snowed in on him in which he was so ticketed; and he counters this by saying that his favourite author is Dickens. He is, it is true, miles apart from Dickens in that his endings in his first great novels at least are tragic rather than happy; but in his fiction we do get – as in *Die Ortliebschen Frauen* – the Dickensian device of assembling and grouping together of the characters for the finale. His humour, too, which critics point to as one of his main features, lies rather in his grimly ironical presentation of both character and situation. As regards foreign influences there is the consideration that he was never able to learn foreign languages; and he tells me that he has had to read Dickens in a frayed edition inherited from his grandfather. There is, too, a provincial stamp on his work, though Vienna comes in; and this is more due to his congenital feeling that he is at home and himself in the uplands of Styria. Born at Lautschin in the Böhmerwald, he was brought up in Vienna; but he has settled in Graz. After early experiments in the traditional vein he reached full maturity in *Ödhof* (1911), a novel which by its sweep of events and its concentrated delineation of one character driven to doom by his dominant passion is a veritable prose epic. The hero is Johannes Arlet, who by sheer ability wins his way to wealth as a townsman; he is a self-assertive, aggressive egoist (*Ichmensch, Kraft-mensch, Herrenmensch* – to group the critics' terms), who tyrannizes over his family. After the death of his first wife he moves from the city and buys an estate in the Voralpen, the Ödhof (the name is symbolic); and here in the elemental forces of the Alpine land-scape – raging torrents and forests bending in the wind – we have by symbol the outer expression of his forward-rushing strength of will. His son commits suicide, and in the end he is the victim of his own morbid determination to dominate all about him. *Ödhof* is thus a *Familienroman* in its outlines; but it marks a new genre by reason of its intensive study of the lust of possession (*Herrschsucht*) in a male; or, as the critics say, it is *männlich*, whereas the next novel, *Die Ortliebschen Frauen* (1917), may by way of contrast be classed as *weiblich*. The first and far better title (because symbolic of the inner meaning) was *Das Grab des Lebendigen*, but this was objected to in Nazi days as pessimistic, and had to be altered. This second novel is more complex; there is much more in it than possessive passion in the dominating character, the very demon of the story. This is Josefine, the elder daughter of a minor public official in Vienna, who has died leaving his wife in straitened cir-cumstances with two daughters who have left school, and a crip-pled son, Walter, who is still at school. Josefine with her iron will rules over the household from the time her father dies; what might be her saving quality is her overweening possessive love of her brother. She-devil as she is, she prevents her younger sister Anna from marrying, though the prospective bridegroom offers to take charge of the whole family. The boy is patronized by *die alte Dame* (her name is not given), whose gardener had been the Ortliebs' grandfather. Walter is allowed to play music with *die alte Dame*'s granddaughter, Olga; they have their little concerts in the man-sion; but Josefine, jealous of Olga, puts an end to what might have developed to a romance. And when Josefine finds that Walter is meeting a girl clerk at the bank where he is now working she locks him up in a cellar until a charwoman informs the bank manager, who sends the police. Josefine then, when the pistol she was carrying in her pocket has been taken away, hangs herself. The mother dies of heart failure. The cellar adumbrates the ori-ginal title, *Das Grab des Lebendigen*, but the symbol embraces the whole family. For the critic the problem is: is this melodrama, or is it *Tiefenpsychologie*? It is possible to argue that Josefine is a tragic character driven by one consuming passion, and, as such, as dra-matically convincing as, for instance, Phèdre. Before she hangs herself we find her crying: 'Walter! Mein Walter!' What motivates the tragedy is repressed sex feeling. There are elements in the novel that are experimentally new; thus the name of the family, the Ortliebs, is revealing: it means that in this novel there is *Ortlosigkeit* to convey that human frailties and passions do not need localizing. There is also to some extent *Namenlosigkeit*; the names of some of the characters are not given. If the novel is to be classed as a tragedy of intensified frustration then Nabl has been successful in his blend of genres. It is Dickensian in so far as the subsidiary characters tend to be grotesque, and in so far as at the end, after Josefine's suicide, the surviving characters are gathered together and that there is a prospect of a happy ending. *Die Galgenfrist* (1921) is the story of a rich *malade imaginaire*, 'der Glückliche', who, spoilt by his upbringing and with no courage to face life, turns himself into his own enemy. There is again the *Ichsucht* of Johannes Arlet, but here it burns inward and consumes this weak-willed Felix. The innovation here is the *Vorwort*, in which, ironically toned, the author introduces his characters (his '*Puppenkinder*') one by one to the reader and reveals the solution without detracting from the dramatic tension with which the book is read. There is a new turn in Nabl's handling of human fate in that after hard trials there is an acceptance of life (*Lebensbejahung*) when Felix learns that a human being must be a link in the chain of the community. *Ein Mann von gestern* (1935) once again handles the relationship of the individual to the community he lives among. The hero is again a man favoured by fortune, who voluntarily assumes burdens for the sake of others. It is everywhere admitted that Nabl is a master of the Novelle and the shorter story; the best of them are collected, with the exception of *Der Fund* (1937), in *Johannes Krantz* (1948). The finest of the tales is *Die Kindernovelle*, which probes the state of mind of a girl of thirteen and a boy of fifteen. Nabl tried his 'prentice hand at drama: *Weihe* (1905), *Requiescat* (1905). *Trieschübel* (1925) had its run of success on the German stage. The comedy *Schichtwechsel* (1928) plays with the idea of social changes which are incompatible with the God-given order of things. *Steirische Lebenswandlung* (1938) sketches Nabl's autobiography, but is filled in with loving descriptions of Styrian landscape and its people. There are autobiographical sketches, too, combined with the tales and essays of *Das Rasenstück* (1955), published on the occasion of the author's seventieth birthday. Valuable is the *Nachwort* which gives a short account by a friend of Nabl's life.

ALEXANDER LERNET-HOLENIA (1897-), Viennese born and bred, but of French extraction on his mother's side, is one of the most versatile and prolific writers of today. He belongs to existentialism in the sense that his work is prevailingly (but not ostentatiously) *doppelbödig*; that is, there are two levels, but the lower one is not bared. As a dramatist he has given the critic a handle by his own description of the mass of his work as *handfeste Theatralik*; that is, framed with malice prepense to entice the expectant public beyond the box-office. He began in expressionistic vein with yet another *Demetrius* venture on the grand scale, that Czar tragedy which Schiller and Hebbel had attempted but left unfinished. He aims at a high level, too, in his three one-act plays *Saul, Alkestis, Lepanto* (1946). He owes his great vogue, however, to a long range of light comedies sparkling with venturesome wit that glides over their biting irony; the titles of some of them are indicative – *Erotik* (1927), *Liebesnächte* (1932), *Die Frau des Potiphar* (1934). His fiction may be less sensational but more fanciful, or even far-fetched, as in *Mona Lisa* (1937), in which a nobleman falls in love with the famous face on the picture and goes to rack and ruin. Where he takes his themes from periods of history – and here as in his plays he ranges through the wide world – his ironical handling is apt to falsify verisimilitude, as in several of the Novellen of *Die Wege der Welt* (1952), or as when in the novel *Der Mann im Hut* (1937) the hero and his companion in their search for the grave of Attila come across the grave of the Nibelungs and the saga is re-told. In the best of his novels there is a metaphysical undercurrent, as in *Der Graf von Saint Germain* (1948), the story of a Viennese industrialist who, in 1935, falls into the hands of the Gestapo, or in *Die Abenteuer eines jungen Herrn in Polen*, which, with the muted notes of tragedy weaving through its staple of comedy, is probably better than his more famous novel *Die Standarte* (1934), a discreet variant of Rilke's *Cornet*. This latter novel was filmed as *Mein Leben für Maria Isabell*. The rogue tale *Der junge Moncada* (1950) with its picturesque Spanish colouring is a rendering of *Die spanische Komödie* (1948). There are fine qualities in Lernet-Holenia's lyric verse, in which the influence of Hölderlin and Rilke is clear at a glance. In *Die goldene Horde* (1933) his learnèd sock is on; he sings of Achilles and Priam, of the Crusades, of Dante, and, characteristically, relieves the heavy strophes of his classical themes by such a lightly lifting internationalized medley as *Neumexikanischer Schlager-*

komponist (with rhymes such as *Stolz – Colts, Fels – Hotels*); this poem and the soft-footed, low-voiced *Die Erzählung des Bedienten* show in masterly fashion how murder can be callously brought up to date. Indeed the most memorable of these new-toned poems are elegantly sensational, and this holds good of Biblical poems – *Der Bethlemitische Kindermord* for instance, which converts the Gospel text into the plain reporting of a newspaper correspondent. Indeed in all the lyric verse of this 'most Austrian of Austrian poets' there is this striving for a new poetic notation of ultra-modern concepts and conceits. In *Die Titanen* (1945) we once again find the long lines and heavy rhymeless rhythms of the neo-classical school; the sense of the titular poem is that we are returning, as our ultra-refinement decays and science takes the helm, to pre-civilization, to the life of the Titans; the world is to be re-created because all that was revered has crumbled. This mastery of moods playful or pseudo-solemn runs through the rest of Lernet-Holenia's lyric work: *Kanzonnair* (1923), *Das Geheimnis Sankt Michaels* (1927), *Neue Gedichte* (1945), *Die Trophäe* (1946), *Germanien* (1946), *Das Feuer* (1949). He is a fine craftsman, but he is contriving and constructive, not swept by feeling.

The most important work of BRUNO BREHM (1892-), an Austrian from Carniola, is a trilogy of novels which describe the break-up of the old Austrian Empire with the defection of the South Slav States: *Apis und Este*, 1931; *Das war das Ende*, 1932; *Weder Kaiser noch König*, 1932; these were published in 1952 in one volume with the title *Die Throne stürzen*. Of his lighter fiction *Der Lügner* (1949), the life story of a successful liar, reads like a preliminary study of his problematic *Schatten der Nacht* (1949), an anthological roping together of examples from world history over 3,000 years of the abuse of power; this is inevitable, runs the lesson; the whole range of history is a *chronique scandaleuse*. Apparently Brehm's purpose is to show that the atrocities of the Nazis pale by comparison with what has gone before.

OSCAR MAURUS FONTANA (1889-), born in Vienna as the son of a Dalmatian, ranks as one of the pioneers of expressionism in Austria. He came to the fore with his novel *Erweckung* (1918; in 1946 rechristened *Die Türme des Beg Begouja*), a novel which sympathetically describes the life of the lower classes in Serbia. The characters of his novel *Insel Elephantine* (1924; in 1947 rechristened *Katastrophe am Nil*) are a motley collection of international adventurers, and the action is climaxed with the bursting of the Nile dam and a revolt of the Nubians, but Europe is intended with the breaking through of a new epoch. There is the same clash of two periods in the sensational action of *Gefangene der Erde* (1928) before and after World War I. *Der Weg durch den Berg* (1936) centres round the breaking through of the St. Gotthard tunnel; thematically it belongs to the genre of novels which celebrate the triumphs of science (pp. 69, 368), as does also *Atem des Feuers: Roman der Gas-Energie* (1954). The heroine of *Der Engel der Barmherzigkeit* (1950) is Florence Nightingale; in his sufficiently authenticated chronicle of her life from childhood right to the end she is not so much an angel as a problematic figure with, in her mature stages, an emphasized leaning to Roman Catholicism. With the exception of Florence the characters of all grades suffer from a frustration which can hardly be classed as British. And common soldiers, who kiss her shadow as she passes along the wards, are grateful to her for restoring the afternoon tea of their civilian life.

CARL PIDOLL (1888-) – in full Carl Freiherr von Pidoll – is a typical Austrian of mixed race: his mother was a native of Luxemburg, while his father was the scion of an old military family in Austria. He is a composer and conductor as well as a novelist. There are autobiographical reminiscences in the family ramifications of the hero of his novel *Augustinus Duroc* (1948), a tale written in the first person (*Ichroman*) during the *débâcle* of 1945 and looking back over sixty years of a life spent as performing musician, composer, business man in the United States; it is Pidoll's own life of a far-travelled man, with intimate experiences of Chinese life and with a keen perception of whatever may be regarded as good in Chinese religion and philosophy. The novel has experimental interest: life on two planes is contrived by the simple device of interlarding chapters: the life-story from its beginnings runs through one series of chapters each of which is followed by one with the physical experiences and the mental reactions of the post-war years. But the narration of facts is not the main purpose of the book; this is to ventilate the problems of today, principally those of religion and politics. The book is thus rather a potpourri than a *Musikerroman*, which is the title claimed for it, as it is for the previous novel, *Boemo Divino* (1943). The narrator's religious faith has itself a reasoned acceptance of life ('*Ja-Sagen zum Leben*'), and this, in still greater measure, is the mood and meaning of

Pidoll's best-known work *Verklungenes Spiel* (1950), a *vie romancée* with more truth than romance and basically a masterly interpretation of Beethoven's character, music, thought, and religious feeling, flanked by a telling presentation of Austrian life during the period of the composer's heroic life and with side-lights on other contemporary musicians. Not the least interesting section of the book is that in which Beethoven's sturdy independence in the social sense is contrasted with Goethe's comparative subservience to ruling princes. Beethoven stands out from this book as one of the finest characters of history and as a freethinker – of a sort – with a deep religious faith in a God firmly fixed by elemental logic beyond the world of appearances. Another Austrian Beethoven novel is *Zehnte Symphonie* (1952) by the well-known Viennese music critic and dramatist OTTO FRITZ BEER (1910-); the interest lies mainly in the description of the composer's physical exhaustion and embittered state of mind after completion of the Ninth Symphony.

After Carossa's *Kindheit und Jugend* JOSEF LEITGEB's (1897-1952) *Das unversehrte Jahr* (1948) is the loveliest story of childhood and youth in recent literature. This *Chronik einer Kindheit* (as the subtitle reads) records, like so many German autobiographies, the thrill of first communion and the evolving experiences of school life, and runs on to the school-leaving age; the outbreak of the First World War is imminent. The district lies near Innsbruck, where Leitgeb lived, and Tyrolese life is described with intimate realism tempered with fine poetic feeling and relieved by a delightful humour that never descends to coarseness and brutality. The book is hardly to be classed with the South German *Bauernnovelle*: the boy's father is a railway official, and the contacts are rather with cultural avocations, the outlook being that of a lyrically attuned youth with feelings quivering forward to the most delicate expression of colouring and symbol. There are the same subtle rhythms and the same delicately toned response to the shifting moods of nature in Leitgeb's book of essays *Von Bäumen, Blumen und Musik* (1947) and in the prose of *Trinkt, O Augen* (1942). There is a considerable autobiographical fundament in the novel *Christian und Brigitte* (1938): a teacher who has served in the war (Leitgeb was a teacher after the war and rose to be *Stadtschulinspektor*) comes to an Alpine village and here finds love and his true self. *Kinderlegende* (1934) is the tale of another Tyrolese boy who, in the seventeenth century, is put to death as a 'Hexer'. Mastery of form is one's first impression from reading Leitgeb's verse: *Gedichte* (1922), *Musik der Landschaft* (1935), *Vita somnium breve* (1943), *Lebenszeichen* (1951), *Sämtliche Gedichte* (1953). Though he pays tribute to Walt Whitman and Trakl he is consciously traditional in theme as in form, and in his deepest musings he is always crystal clear. There is an uprush of tragic feeling in *Lebenszeichen*, his last book of verse, in which – in the pressure of his own experience (he served as an intelligence officer in the Ukraine) – he lashes out at the folly and fury of war. He records his impressions of the Ukraine in *Am Rande des Krieges* (1942); and his *Fünf Erzählungen* (1951) have the same factual fundament.

RUDOLF HENZ (1897-) is very prominent in the literary life of Vienna, both as a prolific writer and as the director of programmes in the Ravag (Radioverkehrs-Aktiengesellschaft). In his lyric verse (*Lieder eines Heimkehrers*, 1919; *Unter Brüdern und Bäumen*, 1929; *Döblinger Hymnen* (1935); and the selection *Wort in der Zeit*, 1945) he ranges from free rhythms – winged, to begin with, with expressionistic fervour – to formalist metres; the latter, however, particularly his distiches and terze rime, sometimes only read true to pattern if fixed accentuation is discarded in favour of phonetical emphasis and free syllabic division. *Der Turm der Welt* (1951) is a heroically laboured monumental epic which shows the present with its wars and the collectivization of the masses as a world ripening for judgment. In his novels art looms large; many of his chief characters are painters; and in particular the unnamed narrator of *Begegnung im September* (1939) is not merely a painter but is palpably a self-portrait of Henz. One term of Henz's which serves to inculcate the doctrine of *being something* is *Besonderheit* – – the quality of *besondere Menschen*; and what gives *Begegnung im September* its peculiar mark of distinction is the number of its characters with special qualities of mind and personality, and the range and variety of their *Besonderheiten*. The outer frame of this very complicated story is *Kunstgeschichte*; and there is also much play with *Volkskunde*, though here there is a touch of irony. Henz's historical novels (*Der Kurier des Kaisers*, 1941; *Der grosse Sturm: Lebensroman Walthers von der Vogelweide*, 1943; *Peter Anich, der Sternsucher*, 1946) are adequately documented, but tend to lose historical veracity because of the author's insistent didactic modernity. Of his dramas *Der Büsser* (1954) is on the Gregorius theme and follows

Hartmann von Aue. *Kaiser Joseph der Zweite* (1937) is the tragedy of that Austrian emperor who tried to introduce the forms of French enlightenment; this was the time when the Pope himself, aghast at the inroads of progress, went to Vienna to bring the Emperor to heel. The lesson conveyed is that God dictates – by the mouth of the Church.

SIEGFRIED FREIBERG (1901-) is another prolific writer who has a distinguished place in the literary life of Vienna today. It helps in the appreciation of his works if one remembers that he has risen from the ranks: his father was a railway employé, his grandmother a book-pedlàr who tramped from the German Böhmerwald. His first novel is *Salz und Brot* (1935), the most detailed and informative of those works of fiction which picture Austria in the war years 1914 to 1918. The hero is an awkward *Gymnasiast* who realizes, as the Empire falls to pieces, that the only hope for his countrymen is: *nicht dem Frieden erliegen, das Leben lieben und an den Kampf glauben*, and that redemption must come from great personalities and not from the collective grouping of demagogic masses. In two other novels, *Die harte Freude* (1938) and *Die Liebe, die nicht brennt* (1940) Freiberg continues the family chronicle begun in *Salz und Brot*, though only in so far as younger members – the Pilzers in particular – are protagonists. There are autobiographical elements in the trio of novels; for instance, Paul Pilzer is a railway employé. The three novels together thus – since they trace the evolution or the rise in the social scale of certain characters – sum up the social history of Austria – mainly of Vienna – from 1870 to 1945. It would, however, be incorrect to speak of *The Pilzer Saga*, for the Pilzers do not overshadow the rest of the characters: they are typical of a movement upwards as others typify a social descent. Whereas the first two novels of the Pilzer series concentrate on the life of working people and peasant folk and are for the most part built up of reminiscences of the author's hard youth, *Die Liebe, die nicht brennt* portrays the life of the better placed classes; it is thus an effective contrast to *Die harte Freude*. There is nothing of the relentlessly drab realism of the Pilzer trio in *Wo der Engel stehen sollte* (1948), which unfolds the ending of the Second World War. The atmosphere is necessarily differentiated, for here Freiberg attempts a kind of allegory: the Germans appear with their allies as *die Stämmigen*, the Americans as *Die Behelmten*, while *der Machtgewaltige* is Hitler. *Felice* (1948) is also a breakaway from realism to a delicately toned refinement of style; the whole thing is a dream, but through it as the end comes peers crass reality. Freiberg's verse is collected in *Sage des Herzens* (1951). It is throughout *Gedankenpoesie*, a garland of rhymed ideas. Inwoven in the hard-ringing stanzas is a wealth of imagery, apposite or (sometimes) ingeniously excogitated.

GEORGE SAIKO (1892-), a Viennese born in North Bohemia, had busied himself for a good part of his life as an essayist and art critic, but in fiction he had only short stories to his credit when, on the verge of sixty, he startled his contemporaries with two novels on the grand scale; these were considered so hostile to the best traditions of Austria that he could find no publisher there and had to find one in Hamburg. They have been attacked as anarchistic or communist, but they have also been praised as being in the direct succession of Musil and Hermann Broch. Saiko's own statement is that he has been influenced most of all by William Faulkner; and it is true that he has debunked Austria as Faulkner debunked the Mississippi regions. At all events Saiko must be ranged with the magic realists, and he comes last in the line as the most destructive of them all. In the case of Saiko's two novels, however, the term magic realism is somewhat illusive, if only because the unfolding of the 'animistic' doctrine is set off by sensational happenings which accrue from sex entanglements. The title of *Auf dem Floss* (1948) symbolizes the disintegration of what remains of the Austrian monarchy with its feudal fundament; the old order is envisaged as a rotten raft floating away to limbo. But in intention Saiko's novels are constructive, for their beacon light points to the new world of Communism. There are side-lights on the lightning-like smashing to pieces of the feudal system in Russia as compared with its sluggish crumbling in Central Europe. While political and social upheavals form the background the reality that is explored has, so Saiko says, a mythical sphere which is active within us all and which magically shapes the form and course of the individual's existence. This basic concept leads Saiko to lay bare the primitive urges of his characters and a great part of the narration consists in the detailing and analysis by suggestion of what the characters recall of their experiences in the past the world over. Their conflicts lie behind them, but they are ever-present because they return in memory; and they determine the rest of their existence, for they have formed and shaped their minds. *Auf dem Floss* is a '*Spiralroman*' that winds round a central story flanked by a welter of attached stories. The hero is a Fürst of the ancient régime who takes a gipsy girl, Marischka, as his mistress; when Gräfin Mary Tremblaye returns from abroad to visit a neighbouring estate he transfers his attentions to her and tries to hand Marischka over to a gigantic servant, Joschko, whom he attaches to himself as a factotum; Joschko, with his dog-like devotion, serves as a symbol of brute strength and of brainless obedience to a lord and master. Marischka, however, has a lover of her own choice, Imre; and to avenge herself on the Prince and to make sure of Imre she mixes poison in Joschko's food and he dies slowly. It now becomes a fixed idea with the Prince that when his *Prachtexemplar* of a servant is dead he will have him stuffed and exhibited in a glass case in the entrance to the castle as a hunting trophy. But Marischka stifles Joschko as he lies dying and with Imre's help sinks the corpse behind the reeds in the lake in the castle grounds. Marischka and Imre then find asylum with the gipsies, but Imre is by them branded as an outsider and a murderer, while Marischka, after her excursion into ordered ways of life, is restored to her former state of itinerant freedom. All this is to be read symbolically: gipsies represent robust primitivity, with its mystic call to the life of nature, while the Prince's castle and all connected with it represent the rottenness of European society (*das Europäertum*). The period of the second novel, *Der Mann im Schilf* (1955), is 1934, the time when Chancellor Dollfuss was murdered by the Austrian Nazis, and the scene is a provincial village on the Attersee. There is again the sensational central action with its related happenings which come into the woof to bind all together to a composite whole. But the story proper with its adjuncts is again not the main thing: the actual theme is the decadence of the representative supine Austrian, 'the man without qualities', and the proof that this is the root of fascism. The novel is indeed a study of fascism, and consequently the crowd of characters are corrupt. But there are two currents, the one political, the other erotic, which flow along together, with, of course, the sensational interest fettered to the love affairs. Two worlds face each other, the weak-willed strata of old Austria (and by inference of old Europe) and the new world of indoctrinated factionaries with a clear, fixed aim. In this novel once again Saiko brings in his wide knowledge of foreign countries, particularly of England – he has been dubbed a '*Wahl-engländer*'. The dominating figure is a fiercely sexed Englishwoman who can find no man fit to satisfy her.

HERBERT ZAND (1923-) is a new Austrian author who is striking out into new paths. *Letzte Ausfahrt* (1953) was hailed as the book of the year, and it has fairly correctly been described as the first German novel to give an epic description of the Second World War. It might be more correct to say that it attempts a merciless description of war as it is today with all its heaped horrors and its reduction of man to beast. But, though the handling is brutally realistic, this '*Roman der Eingekesselten*' aims at being an interpretation of life as it is bound to be, whether in war or out of it; war is just a symbol of cosmic plan and pressure. The range of fighting is narrowed down to some town or other on the German front hemmed in by encircling forces vaguely indicated by scraps of language as Russian. Life in the cauldron (*Kessel*) is whipped up to hectic incoherence till surrender can no longer be staved off. The concept is that we are all of us and always hemmed in within a narrow space of action, frantically seeking realization of self but with hostile forces pressing in on us. If finally there is escape it can only be into the mystery of infinity, into the Fourth Dimension. For to this battle of hostile forces corresponds the inner conflict of personality: *Jeder ist sein eigner Kessel*. We struggle on with all our faults and failings, which close in upon us until they grip us in a ring from which there is no break-out. Thus presented this vision of life as we are said to live it is not depressing – for it is heroic. But there is no idealization whatever of the characters; although collectively considered they are a molten mass of driven humanity we see them separately, vividly differentiated, and we follow their winding fate till it wraps them round. The epic of instinctive – indeed of forced – heroism is, however, not Homeric; it is raw but real. It may be that Zand has done for the last war what Henri Barbusse did for the 1914-18 war with his novel *Le Feu*; at all events both novels stand out by their sheer originality of conception and technique. But Zand's narration is so whipped and crowded and episodic that it lacks clarity. The love interest is merely physical; this, of course, fits in with the concept: what pleasures we snatch at random in this cauldron come only from the play of chance. Zand's next novel, *Der Weg nach Hassi el emel* (1956), might be classed as a Freudian thriller in plain language;

35

at all events it indicates a close reliance on Freud's discovery that in the lower layers of our brain there is a primitivity which shows through when in the crises of life we are thrown out of our orbit. One feature it shares with much of the Austrian novel of today is that localities are not defined, and that the ante-history of the two characters – the rest are mere accessories – is only revealed in snatches by what passes through their minds in strain and stress. Nevertheless we get a clear idea of the flying ace, Christopher Hall, who is a symbol but serves as a hero. He has been flying since he was a boy; he is married to his machine; and though, as we find out – but not till we are half way through the book – he has a wife, his relations with her are formal and casual; she is the daughter of his chief and as such keeps her distance, while he lives for his work ('repression'). As he stumbles along in the desert after baling out he has no memories of sex experience; he does remember Martine, a translation clerk, who smiled once as she was walking along by the office wall. We go along with Christopher as he follows the trace of two feet in the sand; close at his heels prowls a ravenous, dirty hyena, ready to spring. The footsteps lead to an amphitheatre of rocks, Hassi el emel, where, famished and fevered, he shelters in a cave from the spear-shafts of the sun. The sense emerges from the never-ending monologue that grows more and more hectic in the accretion of his fever and from his nightmares; we are not conscious of the bounties of nature, he realizes; we need to be lost in a desert or whelmed in war to savour the warm moisture of new-baked bread or (above all) to know what a boon and a need water is (there follows a highly poetical evocation of all the famed waters of the earth, from Memphis to the Alpine heights of Peru). As he lies in his desert cave these visions pass in procession through his fevered brain; they are ravings in an *Angsttraum*, but they are also Freudian truth. In the second half of the book we are with his wife, whose inner mind is likewise laid bare by what passes within it. She has been flown out to the desert and sets out in a motor-car to find her husband. As they approach the oasis where they find him she takes the wheel; as they bump over the rocks near the oasis the driver jolts against her repeatedly; this, in the then state of her brain, awakens her repressed sexuality, and she is so afraid of him that she gets out and walks the rest of the way. When she finds her man, and when he awakens from his torpor he whispers:

'Evelyne – Martine'. As they wind their way back over the desert, the urges of her awakened senses take shape: *'Lass mich ein Kind kriegen'* rises to her conscious mind. The end, therefore, foreshadows a happy married life. We realize, as we close the book, that the desert is life as we know it; but at the base of our consciousness is also the *Urheimat*, the life of Adam and Eve which Christopher has relived in his hallucinated dreams. We are for ever pursued by the hyenas of evil, but we struggle on to reach Hassi el emel (Arabic for 'well of hope'), the oasis of happiness.

XXIV

THE NEW VERSE

Formally considered neo-Hellenism (pp. 123, 278) finds its
most determined expression in the odes and elegies of JOSEF
WEINHEBER (1892-1945). Born in Vienna as the son of a
horse-butcher and innkeeper, he was, after the early death of his
parents, brought up in an orphanage; as a gifted pupil he had the
privilege of attending the Freies Lyzeum. The privations of his
boyhood and youth are the key to the almost savage anti-social
elements in his work. His first books of verse – *Der einsame Mensch*
(1920), *Von beiden Ufern* (1923), *Boot in der Bucht* (1923) – written
while he was a post-office clerk in Vienna (1911-32), fell flat,
possibly because they had, together with Baudelairean *nouveaux
frissons*, a fleshly admixture; or, to put it brutally, there was more
Tier than *Geist* in the poet's handling of his basic motifs – the
conflict of brute instincts and mental striving, of good and evil,
his neurotic hatred of those more favoured by fortune than the
poet doomed to loneliness by his nobler nature. After the publication in 1934 of *Adel und Untergang* he was the poet of the day;
here his solution for the conflict of contrasts is self-effacement at
the call of duty; this was interpreted as being in accord with the
ideals of the racial resurgence and therefore he was claimed as
theirs by the Nazis. He wrote birthday poems for the Führer, but
there is nothing specifically Nazi in *Adel und Untergang*; his much
quoted lines '*Uns ziemt | zu fallen; jedwedem auf seinem Schilde*' is and
ever was good British sentiment too. But it is rather form than
themes which gives *Adel und Untergang* its permanent place in the
history of lyric verse. In his *Gedanken zu meiner Disziplin* (in the
volume *Über die Dichtkunst*) Weinheber says that it was not because
of a longing for Hellas, not because of humanistic feeling, that he
turned to Greek forms, but because he had come to realize that in
rhymed verse the thought ends with the line (*Endstil*), whereas in

the verse measures of the Greek ode the sense can be carried over naturally (*Strophenverschlingung*) and without enjambment (*Hakenstil*); in other words the rhythm rolls along with the sentence. What results is that in *Adel und Untergang* and in the volume of verse which pairs with it, *Späte Krone* (1936), the antique measures of which Hölderlin is the great master are revitalized. We know that Weinheber found his way to Hölderlin too late for direct influence on his style to be possible; what influence there was is likely to have been that of Georg Trakl. It is a relief to turn from the architectural symmetry of *Adel und Untergang* to the gay garrulity of *Wien wörtlich* (1935). This is for the most part in the Viennese dialect, so real and redolent that it must be fascinating to the student of language difformation; here we have Wienerdeutsch as it is heard. *O Mensch, gib acht* (1937) is a species of calendar, dialectically coloured; the months with their appropriate poems, the legends of the zodiac and of the saints. *Zwischen Göttern und Dämonen* (1938) with its rhymeless verse and skilful *Hakenstil* forms a kind of trinity with *Adel und Untergang* and *Späte Krone*. The root meaning is veiled, but the brunt of the argument is that the demonic powers in one's breast must be tamed and tied down; in the conditions of 1938-39 this was interpreted to mean self-effacement for duty that calls; but basically it is just another phase of that conflict between flesh and mind which runs through all Weinheber's work, as it does through his (on the whole) ignoble life. In *Kammermusik* (1939) we have 'musical poems' adapted to the note of the instrument required for playing them; it is just another experiment in the reproduction of sound by words, the best examples of which are *Intarsia aus Vokalon* and *Ode an die Buchstaben* in *Adel und Untergang*; Weinheber was obsessed by 'phonetic' (his word) illusions, such as that the *o* in *Loch* and *hohl* represents the hole while R in *Rad* denotes whirring rotation. We may class *Wien wörtlich, O Mensch, gib acht*, and *Kammermusik*, since by contrast with the three 'classical' books they are popular and local in tone, as another trinity; all Weinheber's verse sounds *Von beiden Ufern*. Into *Hier ist das Wort* (1947), a posthumously published work, Weinheber's doctrine of prosody is inwoven; he sets forth his *modus operandi* for form and fashioning of the raw matter of language. There is the pith of his verse in the three books of selections *Vereinsamtes Herz* (1935), *Selbstbildnis* (1937), and *Dokumente des Herzens* (1944). Of Weinheber's essays, *Im Namen der Kunst* (1936) attempts an enunciation of the function and philosophy of poetry, while *Über die Dichtkunst* (1949) deals with his own development as man and poet. Of his novels he himself spoke contemptuously as '*korrumpierte Romandichtung*'. They are indeed poor as fiction; but they have autobiographical interest. *Das Waisenhaus* (1925) is just the story of a poor boy's education at an orphanage and of his trend to agnosticism and poetry and painting (the verse *Aquarelle* of his maturity have their canvas counterparts). *Nachwuchs* (1927) records the poet's struggle for a life fit for him. The title of *Gold ausser Kurs* (written 1933; first published 1953 in *Sämtliche Werke*) is a symbol for poetry; here we have a poet who has a volume of verse on his desk which publisher after publisher refuses; *Adel und Untergang* is meant. The final verdict will probably be that Weinheber was far from being a poet of the first rank. Generally speaking his intellect was coldly and architecturally constructive; his poetry was, as he himself said, by way of mathematical approximation. That is, as his biographer Josef Nadler neatly puts it: '*Fleissdichtung, nicht Inspirationsdichtung*'.

Several poets may be grouped as innovators in so far as they fall into line with the international tendencies of today. Of these HANS EGON HOLTHUSEN (1913-), the son of a Lutheran clergyman, began with the publication of his doctor's dissertation on Rilke's *Sonette an Orpheus. Versuch einer Interpretation* (1937) and, after serving for three years as a private in France and Russia, followed this up with the first collection of his poems, *Hier in der Zeit* (1949); the title indicates the stark actuality of the themes. The first poem of the volume, *Trilogie des Krieges*, in a loose hexametric form, is the first attempt – it was written in 1946 – to give poetic form to the mentality of the five years of war. There is Christian feeling in *Karsamstag*; this poem has the note of Baroque as it lives again in the religious verse of R. A. Schröder. The persistent note, however, is that of existentialism, of which there is a summing up in the final poem, *Das Unmögliche*; but here this doctrine of today combines with the lesson of Christian surrender to the Lord. Other poems take over, but with independent handling, favourite motifs of T. S. Eliot and W. H. Auden. Most insistent of these motifs – in the verse of the period it becomes a *cliché* – is T. S. Eliot's concept of time as he shapes it at the beginning of his *Four Quartets*. Thus youth and age are one; for youth will be age and age was youth. If the shadow of the war years lies over the earlier poems of *Hier in der Zeit* there is still the pang of it in some of the poems of *Labyrinthische Jahre* (1952). In the first of the poems, *Acht Variationen über Zeit und Tod*, the doctrine of the identity of past, present, and future is quickened by flash-lights on the Nazi régime: 'How great is Caesar: erect in his chariot, idol of the masses, receiving flowers and lies, his face threatening like a clenched fist; and others round him leather-clad, watchful and smiling, cocked revolvers under their cloaks. Caesar is great; four-motored bombers roar o'er his head. Fate speaks loud with the accents of dynamite. Truth is all in one: scenes in cheap marble and a shot in the mouth and poison; flags, parades, receptions, and the short, spongy body dragged out of the bunker of the Imperial Chancellery and two hundred litres of petrol poured on it.' Here history is epitomized in a way that instantly grips us. Only one poem, *Mit Rosen in Karon*, a tribute laid on Rilke's grave, has a true poet's tenderness. The pattern of Holthusen's verse is not repellent if it is realized that it is fitted to the sense and to the revelation of the sense by flashes. Stretches of apparently flat prose and crass realism are broken by a sudden rush of tensely phrased and lovely imagery. The poetry is in the totality of the poem; and even the totality of a single poem is merely a fragment of a great doctrine of mystic truth, a gospel which in these labyrinthine years of our wandering through the 'Waste Land' of existence brings comfort and intelligence of the way we go and whither. Holthusen's existentialism has the Protestant stamp of Kierke-gaard and Karl Barth; he has been at pains to stress his aversion to the French decoction of Heidegger represented chiefly by Sartre. The surest way to comprehension of Holthusen's verse is a careful study of his collection of eight essays *Der unbehauste Mensch* (1951); the implication of the title, 'Man without a Home', is that we men of today are wanderers in the 'Waste Land' (to use T. S. Eliot's term) of lost causes. The essay *Das Nichts und der Sinn* explores the theme which we know from Sartre's *L'Etre et le Néant*, shows the relation to it of Gottfried Benn's nihilism, and accepts T. S. Eliot's Christian solution of the problem. *Ja und Nein – Neue kritische Versuche* (1954) collects essays on Holthusen's contemporaries: Karl Krolow, Heinz Piontek, and others. Holthusen's first venture into fiction, *Das Schiff* (1956), is not happy; the action is on a ship sailing from America to Germany, and the hero acts as a catalysator on a clique of college girls, the chemical reactions in whose minds are disagreeably Americanized both with transliterated colloquialisms (a girl has *smarte Waden*) and slang. What is aimed at is an analysis, certainly smart, of the modern European. The influence of T. S. Eliot (*'Eliotismus'*), which is so marked in Holthusen, is evident too in other poets – Rudolf Hagelstange, Helmuth de Haas (*Lineaturen*, 1955), Hans Erich Nossack, Heinz Piontek; it is likely to result from study of the English texts as well as to the indirect influence of Holthusen. In the case of Marie Luise Kaschnitz the influence is direct; together with Dolf Sternberger she translated the *Four Quartets*, and this appeared in the journal *Wandlung* in 1945, which printed the first translation to make a lasting impression, Dolf Sternberger's version of *East Coker*. The influence is direct too in the later poems of Gottfried Benn. The impact is equally that of theme and form. The salient fact is that during the Nazi period practically no knowledge of the new trends in Anglo-American poetry reached Germany, so that when, after the war, there was access to the originals the effect was startling. Actually a translation by Ernst Robert Curtius of *The Waste Land* had appeared as early as 1927 in *Die neue Schweizer Rundschau*; but of this no influence is perceptible. After the war translations came in a rush, mostly published in periodicals, with Kurt Heinrich Hansen, Hans Hennecke and Ursula Clemen in the forefront. Nora Wydenbruck's translation of *The Dry Salvages* appeared in 1946 in the July number of *Atlantis*; her *Mord in der Kathedrale* followed in 1947 and her *Vier Quartette* in 1948. She also translated *The Cocktail Party*, while Rudolf Alexander Schröder (p. 278) published *Familienkonvent* (this together with Peter Suhrkamp) and *Der Mord im Dom* (1947). The translations of W. H. Auden did not begin till 1950, when Kurt Heinrich Hansen's rendering of *The Age of Anxiety* as *Das Zeitalter der Angst* appeared with a preface by Gottfried Benn. Holthusen's relation to Auden may be traced in *Labyrinthische Jahre*; e.g. in the poem *Himmel und Blut*, which is in the metre of Auden's ode *Spain*. Actually the poets who joined the new movement (*die Neutöner* as opposed to *die Traditionalisten*) were demonstrating the truth of Otto zur Linde's phonetic conception of stress (p. 155); what does result in *Eliotismus* is that the natural Germanic *freie Versfüllung* is established. There is also a more systematic use of *Strophenverschlingung* or strophic synaphe(i)a, which is a marked feature of Rilke's verse. Reversed accent too (*'Àn das kaukàsische Riff. Knébel des Schicksals'*

– Holthusen) occurs frequently; and here one might suspect the influence of Gerard Manley Hopkins ('*Hóme to his móther's hóuse private retúrned*'; but though he is discussed, and though the term *Sprungrhythmiker* is added to the apparatus of critics, there is no evidence that he influences the facture of verse. The 'inscaped diction' of Hopkins and his devices derived from Welsh poetry (*cynghanedd* or consonantal chime, which consists of a combination of alliteration and internal rhyme) defy imitation. His 'sprung rhythm' (*freie Versfüllung*) and 'counterpointed rhythm' – that is, the reversing of rhythm (– – in the middle of a line for –x–, etc.) – are not new either in German or English. Hopkins was introduced and interpreted by Irene Behn in her *G. M. Hopkins. Übertragung, Einführung und Erläuterung* (1948), and this was followed by the edition of Hopkins with the English text and translations by Ursula Clemen and Friedhelm Kemp (1954). There is no cult of Hopkins; but his practice and theories accentuate *Eliotismus*.

Among poets who have earned recognition in recent years RUDOLF HAGELSTANGE (1912-) stands out both for brilliantly imaged presentation of ethical ideas and as a daring innovator of form. He began with *Venezianisches Credo* (1946), a cycle of sonnets written in the north of Italy at the end of the war, when he was a soldier in the service of a Führer whom he loathed. The *Credo* of the title is to be taken in its full verbal significance; in the horror of the present he can still say: To me faith in a new day is indestructible. The frail vessel of God's truth is the young soldier-poet overwhelmed by the dream-like beauty of Venice: maidens barefoot and gliding like gazelles; and palaces like memories in stone, left on the lagoons, a glorious gift, by the receding sea. There is still the shadow of the war on *Strom der Zeit* (1948) and *Es spannt sich der Bogen* (1949). *Meersburger Elegie* (1950) has less of the decorative impressionistic pattern of the earlier verse, but is noticeably influenced by the line variation and free stressing of Rilke's *Duineser Elegien*. '*Die zarte Sibylle am steinernen Turme*', whose life is inwoven in the problematic arabesque of the poem, is Annette von Droste-Hülshoff; the elegy plaintively evokes her caged and cabined life, her patrician bondage in the Castle of Meersburg on the Lake of Constance; and Hagelstange, himself a North German (his youth was passed at Nordhausen in the Harz and afterwards he lived in Annette's Westphalia), identifies his own musings and memories of the lost homeland with hers. Hagelstange reaches full maturity in his *Ballade vom verschütteten Leben* (1952). The ballad dirges a new saga – the saga of Dust. The plain newspaper source is transcribed at the head of the poem: in June 1951 it was reported from Warsaw that an old bunker had been unearthed near Gdynia – Danzig of old, Gotenhafen in Hitler's trumped-up saga; into the light of day tottered two soldiers, whose outlet had been for six years barred by a bomb; they had been kept alive by a vast and varied store of food and drink. As there was no water they had washed themselves in cognac. They had lived in an inferno more torturing than Dante's hell, for it was merely the long drawn out fading of hope and the rotting of mind and body. The lyrics of his last collection, *Zwischen Stern und Staub* (1953), record impressions of travel and probe into the biological and scientific forces of existence (*Zeugung, Atom*), which even in the act of love and in the worship of what in nature is illusively lovely bind us to the dust of earth and drive us relentlessly on to what the stars have decreed. *Es steht in unserer Macht* (1955) is a collection of essays on a variety of themes; the chief interest lies in the light they throw on the life and trend of thought of the poet; the little sketch *Über die Schwierigkeit, am Bodensee zu dichten* must be ranged alongside *Meersburger Elegie* – Hagelstange himself lives on the shore of the Lake of Constance.

The classic of *die Neue Sachlichkeit* is GOTTFRIED BENN (1886-1956). One essential fact in Benn's poetic make-up is that by profession he was a surgeon – he began as an army doctor and after the war he was a specialist for skin and venereal diseases in Berlin. Certainly his method of treating reality is that of a surgeon. His first two volumes of verse, *Morgue* (1912) and *Fleisch* (1916) have been classified as dissectional lyric poetry (*Sektionslyrik*). Benn's primitive impulse is again *Sprachverzweiflung*: as a practical man he refuses to handle the pretty-pretty diction of poetry and turns naturally to his own profession for motif and image: a poet produces reality; to him the reality he knows from dissecting table and hospital bed is packed with symbol. Thus in one ghastly poem, *Mann und Frau gehn durch die Krebsbaracke*, a doctor conducts a lady visitor and describes the cancer cases:

> *Hier diese Reihe sind zerfressene Schösse*
> *und diese Reihe ist zerfallene Brust.*
> *Bett stinkt bei Bett. Die Schwestern wechseln täglich.*

. . . . .

Hier diese blutet wie aus dreissig Leibern.
Kein Mensch hat so viel Blut.
Hier dieser schnitt man
erst noch ein Kind aus dem verkrebsten Schoss.

. . . . .

Nahrung wird wenig noch verzehrt. Die Rücken
sind wund. Du siehst die Fliegen. Manchmal
wäscht sie die Schwester. Wie man Bänke wäscht.

Schöne Jugend handles the Ophelia motif (p. 420): a girl fished out
of the water is dissected, and a nest of young rats is found under
the diaphragm. *'Ein hirnzerfressenes Aas'* is Benn's lurid but honest
description of himself. (*Aas* is naturally a favourite theme in this
concretizing of sentimentality; Franz Werfel even makes carrion
odorous in his famous poem *Jesus und der Äserweg*.) In his *Probleme
der Lyrik* (1951) Benn discusses the origins of the lyric of today
and derives it from Verlaine, Rimbaud, Valéry, Apollinaire and
the surrealists with André Breton and Louis Aragon as pathfinders.
Benn's liking for modern French poetry may be congenital (his
mother was French Swiss), but it is more likely to be because by
temperament and vocational training he is a surrealist with a sharp
and cunning intellect that pierces straight to the core of phenomena. But as a surrealist he has outstripped all the rest in the
ruthless and raw cruelty of his interpretation; he has a very simple
idea that appearances are ectoplastic with *das Nichts* beneath them;
he is therefore classed as a nihilist, with nihilism in the philosophic
sense as his poetic creed, bound up with the corollary that pro
gressist concepts of development are mythical (Sartre's *L'Etre et
le Néant*). But *das Nichts*, he argues, is supplanted by art, which
creates from the very wilderness of chaos; nihilism is therefore
productive; the poet's or the artist's task is to keep his eyes fixed
to Being as it is, not to imagined idols; and his aim must be to
express, not the thing itself, but his contact with the thing. What
the poet has to see and figure is the Being (*das Sein*) of the thing.
Such figuring is by means of art, and for this *'Montagekunst'* or
'Artismus' of expression – which results from an adjustment (*Aus-
gleich*) of art and life, of mind and history – a *'Doppelleben'* is necessary. Benn's nihilism is thus in effect a disintegration which leads
to an integration, and the final result is a transcendence which

consists of the recognition of reality and the expressing of it in the new form. Benn's apparent pessimism – life is a matter of instinct and fate depends on chance – is extraneous to creative art. The best introduction to his work for those who dare to venture into it is his volume of selections *Trunkene Flut* (1949), together with his autobiographical and self-interpretative *Doppelleben* (1950). His early verse, collected in *Gesammelte Gedichte* (1927), is completed by *Ausgewählte Gedichte* (1936); *Statische Gedichte* (1948); *Fragmente* (1951); *Destillationen* (1953); *Aprèslude* (1955); and *Gesammelte Gedichte 1912-1926*. There is the same crass realism in Benn's Novellen (*Gehirne*, 1917), which (in intention) pierce and parcel the processes of an intricate mind in the way of X-rays detecting the lesions of a body. The cerebral elucubrations of a young surgeon crush all events from the book by treating experience as brain reflexes. One of the institutions the hero serves is an international brothel on the Red Sea; and throughout the book the relations of mind to copulation serve to show the hopelessness of transforming motion, mental or physical, to action without a purpose, as a third impulse between hunger and love, to restore unity of thought; this climax of speculation would apparently amount to panpsychism by way of a revival of Berkeley's ideas. What may be genuine philosophy in the disquisition is side-tracked by such things as syllogisms derived from the blue vein running from hip to pubic hair on the body of a prostitute. In his book of conversations *Drei alte Männer* (1949) Benn explores the existential situation of today, and in his descriptive sketches and critical or philosophic prose he diagnoses the symptoms of decay: *Fazit der Perspektive* (1930); *Nach dem Nihilismus* (1932); *Der Ptolomäer* (1949); *Ausdruckswelt* (1949); *Frühe Prose und Reden* (1950); *Essays* (1951). Benn's Introduction to *Das Zeitalter der Angst* (p. 540) throws light on his attitude to the new literary phases.

Perhaps the best introduction to WILHELM LEHMANN (1882-) is by way of *Bildnis der Eltern und erste Kindheit*, one of the essays of his *Bewegliche Ordnung* (1947), and the autobiographical matter in his *Mühe des Anfangs* (1952) and *Bukolisches Tagebuch aus den Jahren 1927-1932* (1948). Born in Venezuela as the son of a commercial employé from Lübeck he was brought back to Germany when three years old. He took his Ph.D. at Kiel and was then a teacher in various schools, for the best part of his life in the Gymnasium at Eckernförde. He served as an infantryman in World War I and was for two years a prisoner of war in England. Perhaps this is one reason why English literature forms so great a part of his culture, although, no doubt, he owes most to Jean Paul, Clemens Brentano, and the friend of his earlier years Oskar Loerke, whom he never tires of praising. It is a surprising fact that Lehmann's first lyric work did not appear until fifteen years after his beginnings as a prose writer. He began with novels: *Der Bilderstürmer* (1917), *Die Schmetterlingspuppe* (1918), *Weingott* (1921), *Ruhm des Daseins* (1953). The action is centred in Schleswig-Holstein, but the problems of the cosmos loom behind the parochial scene. As a lyric poet he was from the first appraised as *sui generis* and intrinsically of the first order. But it is only in recent years that this perception has pierced through. Lehmann's verse is difficult; he is specifically and intensively a *Naturdichter*, and in the strict sense that his continuous theme is nature both for itself and as symbol his verse may be so recondite that for full comprehension a knowledge of botany and of animal life is needed. Lehmann is a poets' poet, and as such he is appraised by most of those who write verse today. There is no doubt that his direct influence can be traced in much of contemporary verse; thus there is something of his chthonic concepts in the verse of Oda Schäfer (p. 552) and Martin Kessel (p. 553). It is now a matter of literary history that Lehmann's first volume of verse, *Antwort des Schweigens* (1935), resulted in the founding of a new school of poetry, '*die naturmagische Schule*'. (To critics in the opposite camp '*die Sumpf- und Moordichter*'.) Lehmann's own key to his lyric practice is, quite simply, '*Bestehen ist nur ein Sehen*'; that is: to live, we must look; the existential principle of lyric creation is to *see* what nature shows and to bring one's own personal observation into relation with what the great poets of all times have observed and dreamed into their verse. The real key to his creative power is that by the magic of his verbal rendering he transforms the world he sees. The outcome is a magic illumination of words: the word represents the thing, but the thing is transformed by the poet's representation of it. It is word magic rather than nature magic. He is a pioneer too in the cunningly conveyed modernity of his themes; one savours the nostalgic mood of a lovely poem (*Göttin und Diva*) with clear classic contours in which he dreams himself into the grove of Dodona, hailing Aphrodite and Diana and assuming that they have vacated their thrones to Marlene Dietrich and Claire Bloom.

The general note of despair in his verse of the bomber years is relieved by the upwelling thought: the mind still creates (*Ich bin genährt. Ich hör Gesang*). At first glance the facture of Lehmann's verse and stanzas is traditional, but the quickest reading brings home to the reader that there is everywhere the new handling of a radically new poet. Nor is there any change in form and texture as new volumes appear – *Der grüne Gott* (1942), *Entzückter Staub* (1946), *Noch nicht genug* (1950), *Überlebender Tag* (1954).

The most striking feature in the verse of KARL KROLOW (1915-) is the poignancy in his pathos. The verse is for the most part so smoothly fluent in its traditional cadences that at first contact he gives the impression of running on in the old grooves, but closer knowledge proves his ultra-modernity and – in some of his most drastic poems on post-war aspects of today – his rebellious rejection of time-consecrated lauds and soft emotional moods. He acknowledges the influence on his work of Droste-Hülshoff; this is less evident than that of Rilke, Trakl, and Wilhelm Lehmann. In the mass his verse is in the wake of Wilhelm Lehmann's cult of the interrelation of man and nature, but with surrealistic undertones and existential ideology. Thus *Stein* finely features *Dauer*. These existential ideas are by now commonplace, but in poetry the idea is merely the starting-point; what matters is the poem; and in Krolow's handling the notion is the soul of the poem, not its framework. *Gedichte* (1948) is a volume of selections with his volumes *Hochgelobtes gutes Leben* (1943) and *Auf Erden* (1949) as the staple. In *Heimsuchung* (1949) there is sometimes a poignant personal note; *Selbstbildnis* is Baudelairean – in the mesh of drunken dream the flask in the poet's hand swells out to a vessel that sails blessedly along under tropical heavens, on to Jamaica and the lips of negresses at the rim of the Paradise beyond this world. There is a ghostly thrill here and there; as in *Zerstörtes Haus* with its daring images and its poetization of the coarsest possible words. Such ultra-realism, however, is in stark contrast with the prevailing feminine refinement and delicacy of image (as in *Für mein Kind*). *Die Zeichen der Welt* (1951) is confessedly coloured by Krolow's contacts with Lorca, Supervielle, Eluard, and Auden.

FRITZ USINGER (1895-) began as a member of *Die Dachstuber* a group of young revolutionary poets and artists grouped around Joseph Würth, a master of handpress printing in Darmstadt; other members of the circle were Kasimir Edschmidt and ANTON

SCHNACK (1892-), the brother of Friedrich Schnack, who has been prolific both in verse and prose. Usinger's *Gedichte* (1940) is made up from selections from his previous work; this was followed by *Das Glück* (1947) and *Hesperische Hymnen* (1948). His important essays on the literature of today are collected in *Das Wirkliche* (1947) and *Geist und Gestalt* (1948).

Another poet who combines extreme modernity of theme with traditional form is FRIEDRICH GEORG JÜNGER (1898-). He makes great use of the trochaic four-line stanza, familiar to us from Goethe's *West-östlicher Divan*, and of the Klopstockian hexameter. He has discussed problems of form and syntax in his *Rhythmus und Sprache im deutschen Gedicht* (1952); he shows that the total effect aimed at is to cut out the monotonous singsong of the classical hexameter. What remains (as in free verse not in hexametric form) is a free blending of dactyls and trochees. Though F. G. Jünger, like Rudolf Hagelstange, has found a retreat in idyllic seclusion on the shores of the Lake of Constance, he is anything but remote from actual problems and the *Zeitgefühl* of today; indeed he is, like his elder brother Ernst Jünger, deeply immersed in them. He deserted the legal profession – he was a judge – for journalism, and made a splash with his poem *Der Mohn*, which branded National Socialism as '*das kindische Lied ruhmloser Trunkenheit*'. This poem, taken over into his first volume of verse, *Gedichte* (1934), was surreptitiously circulated, and to escape from the close watch by the Gestapo which was the result he settled, in 1937, at Überlingen in Switzerland. The verse of his first volume handles the moulds of Klopstock and Hölderlin; in *Der Taurus* (1937) he shows himself a master of the narrative elegy. *Der Missouri* (1940) and *Der Westwind* (1946) are flanked by the twin volumes *Die Silberdistelklause* (1946) and *Weinberghaus* (1947), both in four-foot trochees; they reflect the bucolic peace of his Swiss retreat. *Die Perlenschnur* (1948) was followed by *Gedichte* (1950), a collection from previous books of verse. In *Iris im Wind* (1952) there is a note of elementary cheerfulness. Taking him all in all the outstanding quality of his verse is energy; his main motifs are fire, fierceness, violence. With this goes his withering contempt for the masses. He is indeed an out-and-out aristocrat, to whom the great enemy today is Demos, whom he compares with rats: '*Was auch die Ratte tut,* | *Sie wird nichts mehren.* | *Und täte sie noch mehr* | *Sie wird nur zehren*'; or with grubs that gnaw at the root of life and whose aim is to draw everything down out of the light into the dark. In such poems as *Brautlied* and *Medea* (in *Der Westwind*) there is sexual symbolism identical with that of Elisabeth Langgässer: sex or the womb is Hades. As a writer of fiction F. G. Jünger began late with the short stories of *Dalmatinische Nacht* (1950) and *Die Pfauen* (1952). Of his essays, *Über das Komische* (1938) is audacious in its negative approach to all comic elements in literature – humour, wit, caricature, paradox – as compared with the beautiful; the line of argument, however, is not so incisive as that of George Meredith in *An Essay on Comedy and the Uses of the Comic Spirit.* The leading idea of the essay *Griechische Götter* (1943) is that the idea which the Greek gods represent – the ideal of beauty (Schiller in his poem *Die Götter Griechenlands* says the same) has been defaced by modern science and technology. This idealization of Greek concepts is followed up by *Titanen* (1944) and *Griechische Mythen* (1947), and in a more drastic sense by the attack on the '*Automatismus*' of today in the essay *Die Perfektion der Technik* (1946) and *Maschine und Eigentum* (1949). He brands this frenzied mechanization as 'demonic impulsion', and argues that it will lead to the anti-State and inevitably to the self-destruction of man. He sees in this perfection of technology a modernization of the Greek myth of Prometheus, who angered the gods by bringing down fire from heaven. *Orient und Okzident* (1948) is devoted to Klopstock and Martial together with Persian and other oriental poetry, while *Nietzsche* (1949) maintains that the philosopher can only be understood if the whole man and the whole mass of his work is grappled with.

PAULA VON PRERADOVIĆ (1887-1951) will be remembered as the author of the new national anthem of the Bundesrepublik of Austria: *Land der Berge, Land der Ströme.* As a lyric songster she began full-fledged with *Südlicher Sommer* (1929); this, with *Dalmatinische Sonette* (1933), is verse directly inspired by the racial and landscape poetry of Istria and Dalmatia, where, though she was Viennese born, her youth was passed. Her verse is collected in the three volumes of *Verlorene Heimat* (1949; the 'lost homeland' is the coast and the shimmering islands of Dalmatia), *Schicksalsland* (1952; mainly lyrics of Austria's *Leidenszeit* from 1934 to 1948, grim pictures of Vienna in the grip of war – air-raids, dug-outs and the rest), and *Gott und das Herz* (1952, poems laid on the altar of the Catholic faith as the saving power of her third, her spiritual homeland). Great originality and experimental daring – modernist innovation with outwardly an old technique – show in her novel *Pave und Pero* (1940); it is a *vie romancée* based on the correspondence (in the 1850s and thereabouts) of the author's grandfather Petar Preradovič, a general in the Austrian army and the national poet of Serbia (or perhaps, more narrowly, of Croatia), with his Italian-born wife Pave de Ponto. There is a strong academic interest, palpably for Slav scholars, but also for German specialists: there is a visit paid to Petar Preradovič in Vienna by the best-known collector of Serbian songs, Vuk Stefanovič, whose painstaking work Goethe praises in his essays. Jakob Grimm learnt Serbian from the grammar Vuk had written; and then Grimm, Vuk and his daughter, and Goethe translated these strange old poems into German verse. The short story *Königslegende* (1950) is in substance a Serbian ballad in prose; a tribal king is defeated by the Normans of Dalmatia and is taken to a small island where he lives in a fisherman's cottage and ends contented with the fisherman's calling. In *Die Versuchung des Columba* (1951), another short story, the Irish missionary is visited on the island of Iona by a girl from the heathen wilds of Donegal; she had been betrothed to him as a child, and now, pulsing with the vigour of her healthy life, she has found him out in his island fastness and tells him she has come to claim her man and her children. She comes near to sweeping the saint off his feet; not because he is a man in the flower of his youth, but because she has hung a bundle of aromatic herbs round his neck in memory of the old homeland; and these herbs are bewitched. They are removed and he is once again a saint; she too had been bewitched while she had the herbs on her breast; now they are removed she can repent, and she dies in lashing gales on a barren rock off Iona.

Existentialism is not glaringly prominent in the lyric verse of HEINZ PIONTEK (1925-); he rather represents a new type of drastic realism which is transformed to symbolic significance by the total import of the poem. He is by birth a Silesian, and the Silesian landscape with its Slav frontier comes into the staple of both his verse and his prose. His first verse volume was *Die Furt* (1952); the title is taken from one of the poems which is obviously based on the recollection of the poet as a soldier fording a shallow river just as, one assumes, he is still wading through the endless and perilous ford of daily existence. The main impression of his lyric

36

individuality is that of an impressionistically coloured idealization of landscape, wistfully lovely or perhaps ironically tinged as the component elements of the total picture pass before the reader's mind, and with the inwrapt meaning unfolding as a single truth as the parts merge into a visualized whole. Thus in *Der Bauarbeiter* we have a ruthless survey of the tricks and habits, when on duty, of a builder's labourer of today:

> *Am liebsten sitzt er still auf der Latrine*
> *und liest die Zeitung, knittriges Papier:*
> *inzwischen sucht ihn zornig der Polier –*
> *im Leerlauf knirscht der Stahl der Mischmaschine.*

And so forth. And then, as the poem ends, what passes through the rudimentary mind the fellow has:

> *Sei's drum! Er gibt den Pyramiden Dauer,*
> *die Towerquadern schmerzen ihn im Griff,*
> *früh hilft er einem Pantheonenbauer,*
> *in China sitzt er auf der Grossen Mauer*
> *und wartet auf den Feierabendpfiff.*

Here, as often in Piontek's verse, it is the last line that tells or bowls one over. Piontek's metrical technique varies: the earlier lyrics are strictly traditional in form, faultlessly rhymed and rhythmically smooth; then we have a stretch of unrhymed verse with lines of unequal length, this genre too as old as Goethe and differing only from the older pattern in the more pointedly impressionistic purpose and in the strict concentration; these poems are essentially thumb-nail sketches of *choses vues* and passing as on a television screen. The technique remains constant in *Rauchfahne* (1953). There is grim realism; thus in *Pferdejunge* Piontek builds up a picture of a stable-boy at his routined jobs and the effect of each one of them on him; the instances and the stable slang are so shockingly new that the total effect is that of an undiscovered world. One salient feature – as in Piontek's verse generally – is that the succeeding instances seem so distanced from one another in the far-fetched relativity of the linked concepts that the reader's mind leaps from impression to impression; this Piontek justifies learnedly by a saying of Heraclitus (placed as a motto at the head of one of the poems) that everywhere everything is linked and chained in floating impressions. In *Das Mahl der Strassenwärter* the chain of sensations is concentrated in the short time of a meal of road-menders by the wayside, but imaged in the four quatrains is the state of mind of the roughest class of workmen and their robust savouring of existence: *Die Kaffeekanne gluckst, die Krusten brechen, | dem Alten hängt im Bart das gelbe Ei, | der Ziegenkäse hindert sie beim Sprechen, | der Mittag zieht als Butterduft vorbei.* In the series *Vergängliche Psalmen*, with which the volume ends, the mood deepens, but the instances still leap, as in the psalm that answers the question *Was ist der Tod?* – it comes between love and riot, to a table in the Express Café, at 5.0 a.m. in a prison yard, under a roof of leaves shattered to shreds in Vietnam, and – '*ich finde ihn herbstlich im verwesenden Braun alter Bäume*' (the softly drifting sad rhythm of this last line aptly sums up the foregoing short-lined instances). In *Wassermarken* (1957) once again the far-fetched relativity of the linked ideas sums up to a symbol of existence. The titular poem visualizes the height of the tide or the depth at a given moment of the rolling river of time which sweeps us along. In several of the poems, if they are taken together, there is a poignant vision of soldiering through the centuries. There is a lighter lift of rhythm in the second section, *Östliche Romanzen*, in which the scene shifts to the Slav frontier and the rude pains and passions of low life, as in *Der besoffene Korschinsky*, the life-story of a besotted and bedraggled beggar. *Vor Augen* (1955) attempts a new technique of symbolic prose; in several of the *Proben* and *Versuche*, as the two sections are entitled, there may be the rough contours of a hinted short story, but in the generality of the 'probing experiments' we have characters and a situation but no ending – the narrative breaks off at a critical turn and the reader is left to think out for himself the inevitable ending. But, as in the sketches *Unterwegs* and *Versprengt*, Everyman is represented by a soldier on the Eastern front who has deserted or has lost his regiment – the endless Russian plains where he has campaigned stretch behind him and before him stretches an end as far beyond his reach as is the place where his cradle lay: Everyman is a displaced wanderer, or an Argonaut sailing to a mythical horizon. All the same there is in the more typical of these gloomily toned tales (*Proben*) a defiant ring of courage: the war is lost and all is lost, but *Überstehen* must be the watchword (*Ich werde den Kreig überstehen. . . . Ich will leben, ich habe den Mut dazu*). Thus we have before our eyes (*Vor Augen* is the title of the last *Versuch*) that heroic will to survive which is the secret of West Germany's place in the world today. And clearly *Vor Augen* must be ranged with the *Nachkriegsliteratur*. Stylistically – though in the three sketches grouped as *Oberschlesische Prosa* we have colourful vignettes of Piontek's Upper Silesian homeland – the prose is shorn and clipped to staccato sentences and dialogue, while the language is often that of the commonest speech, so that all this constitutes a challenge to established narrative style.

Apart from being a painter and a sculptor RUTH SCHAUMANN (1899-) is popular as poet and novelist. She is a convert to Catholicism, and thus it is natural that there should be a strong religious element in her work, as in the verse volumes *Der Knospengrund* (1924), *Das Passional* (1926), *Der Rebenhag* (1927), *Die Tenne* (1931), and *Der Siegelring* (1937). There are post-war moods of sadness in *Klage und Trost* (1947). Her prose fiction blends the ideals of home, the tasks of wife and mother, with her symbolization of Church legend and ritual, as in the nine stories of *Der blühende Stab* (1929). MARIE LUISE KASCHNITZ (1901-) collected her poems from a period of twenty years in *Gedichte* (1947). The feelings of the war and its aftermath come out strongly in her work, as in *Totentanz* (1946). She proves her mastery of free rhythms above all in *Zukunftsmusik* (1950). Of her novels *Liebe beginnt* tends to autobiography; *Gustave Courbet* (1950) is devoted to the life and times of the French painter who in 1871 was exiled for his participation in the revolution against the government of Thiers (*la Commune*). ODA SCHÄFER (1900-) is best known for her verse (p. 545), but she has also written fiction (*Die Kastanienknospe*, 1948; *Unvergleichliche Rose*, 1948; *Immortelle*, 1949). She is well known for her *Hörspiele*.

There is a hard note of personal experience – he was an American prisoner of war – in the verse of GÜNTER EICH (1907-); it begins with *Gedichte* (1930). In *Abgelegene Gehöfte* (1948) the poet's life in the prisoners' camp is described with unrelenting realism. It reeks of filth – as no doubt the camp did; but there are moments of relief as in the strange poem *Pfannkuchenrezept* which begins with '*Die Trockenmilch der Firma Harrison Brothers,* | *Chikago*', savours the eating of the succulent one eighth per prisoner, and then goes back in nostalgic memory to the smell of the kitchen in childhood's years and the clutching of mother's apron – '*Oh Ofenwärme, Mutterwärme . . .*' The limit is reached in *Latrine* with its third stanza that made case-hardened German critics squeal: *Irr mir im Ohre schallen | Verse von Hölderlin. | In schneeiger Reinheit spiegeln | Wolken sich im Urin.* But there is pure poetry in such a poem as *Abends am Zaun* – a masterpiece. Eich still fuses near and distant, present and future, in his other verse book, *Untergrundbahn* (1949). For the rest he is the writer of numerous radio plays (*Hörspiele*), which he has contrived to enliven with inventiveness.

Of the humorous poets of today one of the best known is ERICH KÄSTNER (see p. 374). Very popular, too, is the rollicking verse of EUGEN ROTH (1895-): *Ein Mensch* (1935), *Die Frau in der Weltgeschichte* (1936), *Der Wunderdoktor* (1939), *Mensch und Unmensch* (1948). He also writes serious verse, for the most part wistfully recording the season's moods: *Traum des Jahres* (1937), *Rose und Nessel* (1951); and Novellen: *Das Schweizerhäusl* (1950), tales and anecdotes from the years of his boyhood in Munich. Buffoonery runs riot in the rhyming of the itinerant cabaret mime JOACHIM RINGELNATZ (1883-1934), whose pet pose was that of a drunken sailor; his seafaring in early years provided him with the matter of his *Kuttel Daddeldu* (1933). His *Clownerien* are collected in *... und auf einmal steht es vor dir* (1950); a good approach is *Ausgewählte Gedichte* (1950). Another Brettl-Dichter was FRED ENDRIKAT (1890-1942); he began with *Die lustige Arche* (1935), a 'Tierfibel für Jung und Alt', and continued with *Höchst weltliche Sündenfibel* (1939), *Liederliches und Lyrisches* (1940), and *Der fröhliche Diogenes* (1942). *Verse und Lieder* (1949) is a selection.

Lack of space alone prevents an adequate appreciation of other lyric poets, some of them young but forging ahead. A good introduction is the Reclam anthology *Deutsche Lyrik der Gegenwart* (1955). KURT ERICH MEURER (1891-) is available in his *Cellokonzert. Ausgewählte Gedichte.* PAUL CELAN (1920-), a Slav by birth (born at Czernowitz in the Bukovina), made a good beginning with a volume of surrealist verse, *Mohn und Gedächtnis* (1952); his aim is to shadow forth the intimate interrelationship of things. A selection of PETER GAN's (1894-) poems (*Die Windrose*, 1935; *Die Holunderflöte*, 1941) is now available in an Inselbücherei number: *Preis der Dinge. Vom Dichter ausgewählt* (1956). There is something of Wilhelm Lehmann's chthonic concepts in MARTIN KESSEL's (1901-) *Erwachen und Wiedersehen* (1940) and *Gesammelte Gedichte* (1951). WALTER HÖLLERER's (1922-) expressed aim in *Der andere Gast* (1952) is to create '*Bilder für Bildloses*'.

Of the Austrian lyric poets, HANS NÜCHTERN (1896-) has written many volumes of verse, from *Wie mir's tönt von ungefähr* (1915) to *Zwischen den Zeiten* (1950). JOHANN GUNERT'S (1903-) form is throughout traditional, as in his first book of verse *Irdische Litanei* (1945). *Das Leben des Malers Vincent van Gogh: Eine Dichtung in 70 Ereignissen* (1945) points forward to that familiarity with the painters of all lands and all ages which is to be the mark of *Überall auf unserer Erde* (1951); typical is *Bauernhochzeit*, which drastically reproduces Breughel in the manner of Verhaeren's *Les flamandes* but also Flanders as Verhaeren knew it. Of the women poets of Austria KÄTHE BRAUN-PRAGER (1888-) is equally painter and poet, and therefore it is natural that the landscape moods of her native land should be visioned in her verse; this is true even of the section *England 1939-1949*, written while an exile, which we find in her volume of selected poems *Stern im Schnee* (1949); even in the poem *Köchin in der Fremde* she sees the snow-capped mountains when she spreads sugar on food. She has taken over the doctrine of her brother Felix Braun that 'living is loving', and this is the inspiration of her extensive anthology (verse and prose) *Liebe: Das Mass der Liebe ist Lieben ohne Mass* (1952) as it is of the companion anthology, compiled in collaboration with her brother, *Das Buch der Mütter* (1954). ERIKA MITTERER (1906-) began with *Dank des Lebens* (1930, which includes her world-famous correspondence in verse with Rilke. She is best known for her novels (*Höhensonne*, 1933; *Der Fürst der Welt*, 1940; *Wir sind allein*, 1945; *Die nackte Wahrheit*, 1951). HERMEN VON KLEEBORN (1908-) after her *Gedichte* (1947) established herself as an essayist and translator (Rimbaud, etc.). The inspiration of CHRISTINE LAVANT'S (1915-) *Die Bettlerschale* (1956) is strongly Catholic in its refined symbolism. Of the same age is CHRISTINE BUSTA (1915-), who has firmly fixed her reputation with *Jahr um Jahr* (1950); *Der Regenbaum* (1952); *Lampe und Delphin* (1955), as a still younger poetess, INGEBORG BACHMANN (1926-) has done with her *Die gestundete Zeit* (1953), *Anrufung des grossen Bären*, and *Die Scheune der Vögel* (1958).

BIBLIOGRAPHY

HISTORIES OF LITERATURE AND LEXICONS

Alker, Ernst: *Geschichte der deutschen Literatur von Goethes Tod bis zur Gegenwart.* Stuttgart, Vol. I, 1949; Vol. II, 1950

Bartels, Adolf: *Die deutsche Dichtung der Gegenwart.* Leipzig, 4th ed., 1901
—— *Geschichte der deutschen Literatur.* Vol. 3: *Die neueste Zeit.* Leipzig, 1928

Kindermann, Heinz, and Margarete Dietrich: *Taschenlexikon für deutsche Literatur.* Stuttgart and Vienna, 1953

Lennartz, Franz: *Die Dichter unserer Zeit. Einzeldarstellungen zur deutschen Literatur der Gegenwart.* 5th ed., Stuttgart, 1952

Rocca, Enrico: *Storia della letteratura tedesca, dal 1870 al 1933.* Florence, 1950

Salzer, Anselm: *Illustrierte Geschichte der deutschen Literatur.* (Vols. 4 and 5 deal with period 1880 to the present.)

Vogt, F., and M. Koch: *Geschichte der deutschen Literatur.* Vol. 3: *Neuere und neueste Zeit.* 5th ed., Leipzig, 1934

ESSAYS AND CRITICISM

Bertaux, F.: *Panorama de la littérature allemande contemporaine.* Paris, 1928

Betz, Louis P.: *Studien zur vergleichenden Literaturgeschichte der neueren Zeit.* Frankfurt a/M., 1902

Bieber, H.: *Der Kampf um die Tradition: die deutsche Dichtung von 1830 bis 1880*

Darge, E.: *Lebensbejahung in der deutschen Dichtung um 1900. Deutschkundl. Arb.* Breslau, 1934

Drake, William A.: *Contemporary European Writers.* London, 1928

Döblin, Alfred: *Die literarische Situation.* Baden-Baden, 1947

Eastlake, A. E.: *The Influence of English Literature on the German Novel and Drama in the Period 1880-1900.* London dissertation, 1937

Fechter, Paul: *Deutsche Dichtung der Gegenwart.* Reclam, Leipzig, 1929

Hall, D. M.: *The Venice Legend in German Literature since 1880.* London dissertation, 1936

Heller, Erich: *The Disinherited Mind. Essays on Modern German Literature and Thought.* Cambridge, 1952

Heller, O.: *Studies in Modern German Literature: Sudermann, Hauptmann, Women Writers of the 19th Century.* Boston, Mass., 1905

Hennecke, Hans: *Dichtung und Dasein*. Essays. Berlin, 1950
Holthusen, Hans Egon: *Der unbehauste Mensch. Motive und Probleme der modernen Literatur*. Munich, 1951
—— *Ja und Nein. Neue kritische Versuche*. Munich, 1954
Kindermann, Heinz: *Das literarische Antlitz der Gegenwart*. Halle, 1930
King, Adelaide H.: *The Influence of French Literature on German Prose and the Drama between 1880 and 1890*. London dissertation, 1933
Lange, Victor: *Modern German Literature 1870-1940*. New York, 1945
Law-Robertson, H.: *Walt Whitman in Deutschland*. Giessen, 1935
Leyen, Friedrich von der: *Deutsche Dichtung in neuer Zeit*. Jena, 1922; 2nd ed., Jena, 1927; with *Nachtrag*, 1925-30, Jena, 1931
Liptzin, Solomon: *Lyric Pioneers of Modern Germany. Studies in German Social Poetry*. New York, 1928
Mahrholz, Werner: *Deutsche Dichtung der Gegenwart*. Berlin, 1926
Maione, Italo: *Contemporanei di Germania*. (Dehmel, T. Mann, Rilke, Hofmannsthal, George.) Turin, 1931
Mumbauer, J.: *Die deutsche Dichtung der neuesten Zeit*. 2 vols., Freiburg, 1931-32
Muret, Maurice: *La littérature allemande d'aujourd'hui*. Paris, 1909
—— *La littérature allemande pendant la guerre*. Paris, 1920
Naumann, Hans: *Die deutsche Dichtung der Gegenwart 1885-1903, vom Naturalismus bis zur Neuen Sachlichkeit*. 6. Aufl., Stuttgart, 1933. (This 1933 edition is nazified.)
Necco, G.: *Realismo e idealismo nella letteratura tedesca moderna*. Bari, 1937
Pensa, M.: *La letteratura tedesca contemporanea (1910-1935)*. Bologna, 1936
Pollard, Perceval: *Masks and Minstrels of Modern Germany*. London, 1911
Roffler, Thomas: *Bildnisse aus der neueren deutschen Literatur*. Frauenfeld, 1933
Rose, William, and J. Isaacs: *Contemporary Movements in European Literature*. London, 1928
Rychner, Max: *Zeitgenössische Literatur. Charakteristiken und Kritiken*. Zurich, 1947
Soergel, Albert: *Dichtung und Dichter der Zeit*. 6th ed., Leipzig, 1922- ; *Neue Folge: Im Banne des Expressionismus*, 1925
Stammler, Wolfgang: *Deutsche Literatur vom Naturalismus bis zur Gegenwart*. Breslau, 1924; 2nd ed., 1927
Thomas, R. Hinton: *German Perspectives*. Cambridge, 1940
Usinger, Fritz: *Form und Wahrheit der zeitgenössischen Literatur*. Verlag der Akademie der Wissenschaften und der Literatur in Mainz, 1955
Walzel, Oscar: *Deutsche Dichtung der Gegenwart*. Leipzig, 1925

ANTHOLOGIES

Benn, Gottfried: *Lyrik des expressionistischen Jahrhunderts*. Wiesbaden, 1955

Benzmann, Hans: *Moderne deutsche Lyrik*. Reclam, 1904. Revised ed., 1907

Bethge, Hans: *Deutsche Lyrik seit Liliencron*. Leipzig, 1903. New ed., 1920

Bithell, Jethro: *An Anthology of German Poetry, 1800-1940*. London, 7th ed., 1955

Bochinger, R.: *Neue deutsche Gedichte. Deutsche Lyrik der Gegenwart.* Braunschweig, 1953

Busse, Carl: *Neuere deutsche Lyrik*. Halle, 1895

Fehse, Willi, and Klaus Mann: *Anthologie jüngster Lyrik. Geleitwort von Stefan Zweig*. Hamburg, 1927. *Neue Folge*, 1929. *Geleitwort von Rudolf G. Binding*

Fehse, Willi: *Deutsche Lyrik der Gegenwart*. Reclam, Stuttgart, 1955

Forster, Leonard: *German Poetry 1944-1948*. Cambridge, 1949

Grag, Hansjörg: *Ahnung und Gestalt. Salzburger Almanach der Georg-Trakl Preisträger*. Salzburg, 1955

Groll, Gunter: *De Profundis. Deutsche Lyrik in dieser Zeit. Eine Anthologie aus zwölf Jahren*. Munich, 1946

Heuschele, Otto: *Junge deutsche Lyrik*. Reclam, Leipzig, 6th ed., 1928; new ed., 1930

Höllerer, Walter: *Deutsche Lyrik 1900 bis 1950. Versuch einer Überschau und Forschungsbericht*. Stuttgart, 1953

Holthusen, Hans Egon, und Friedhelm Kemp: *Ergriffenes Dasein. Deutsche Lyrik 1900-1950*. Ebenhausen bei München, 1953

Jäckie, E.: *Zürcher Lyrik. Eine Anthologie*. Zurich, 1956

Jacob, H. E.: *Verse der Lebenden. Deutsche Gedichte seit 1920*. Berlin, 2nd ed., 1927

Michael, Friedrich: *Jahrhundertmitte. Deutsche Gedichte der Gegenwart.* Inselbücherei, Wiesbaden, 1955

Pinthus, K.: *Menschheitsdämmerung. Symphonie jüngster Dichter.* (Expressionistic verse.) Berlin, 1920

Röhl, Hans: *Deutsche Lyriker von Liliencron bis Werfel*. Leipzig, 5th ed., 1932

Rose, William: *Modern German Poetry*. (Augustan Books of Poetry.) London, 1931

Schulz, Otto: *Im Takte der Maschinen. Gedichte vom Rhythmus der Arbeit.* Hirts deutsche Sammlung, Breslau, no date

Sommerfeld, Martin: *Deutsche Lyrik (1880-1930) nach Motiven ausgewählt und geordnet*. Berlin, 1931

Urbanek, Walter: *Deutsche Lyrik aus zwölf Jahrhunderten*. Ullstein Bücher, Frankfurt, 1956

Virneburg, Kurt, and Helmut Hurst. *Junge deutsche Dichtung*. Berlin and Zurich, 1930

Weiner, A., and Fritz Gross: *Modern German Verse. An Anthology.* London, 1936

DRAMA

Arnold, R. F.: *Das moderne Drama des XIX. Jahrhunderts.* Strassburg, 2nd ed., 1918

Bab, Julius: *Das Theater der Gegenwart.* Leipzig, 1928

Benoist-Hanappier, L.: *Le drame naturaliste en Allemagne.* Paris, 1900

Besson, P.: *Le théâtre contemporain en Allemagne.* Paris, 1900

Blei, Franz: *Über Wedekind, Sternheim und das Theater.* Leipzig, 1915

Bulthaupt, Heinrich: *Dramaturgie des Schauspiels.* Vol. 4 (Wildenbruch, Hauptmann, Sudermann.) 6th ed., Oldenburg, 1909

Diebold, B.: *Anarchie im Drama.* 3rd ed., Frankfurt, 1925

Freyhan, M.: *Das Drama der Gegenwart.* Berlin, 1922

Kayser, R.: *Das junge deutsche Drama.* Berlin, 1924

Keller, M. V.: *Der deutsche Expressionismus im Drama seiner Hauptvertreter.* Weimar, 1936

Kerr, Alfred: *Das neue Drama.* Berlin, 1905

Lehmann, K.: *Deutsche Dramatiker unserer Zeit.* Düsseldorf, 1935

Schneider, Manfred: *Der Expressionismus im Drama.* Stuttgart, 1920

Stockius, Alfred: *Naturalism in the recent German Drama with special reference to Hauptmann.* New York, 1903

Willett, John: *The Theatre of Bertolt Brecht.* London, 1959

Witkowski, Georg: *Das deutsche Drama des 19. Jahrhunderts.* (*'Aus Natur und Geisteswelt'.*) Leipzig, 1923

THE NOVEL

Bennett, E. K.: *A History of the German Novelle from Goethe to Thomas Mann.* Cambridge, 1934

Bettex, A. W.: *The German Novel of Today.* Cambridge, 1939

Boeschenstein, H.: *The German Novel, 1939-1944.* University of Toronto Press, 1949

Bostock, J. K.: *Some well-known German War Novels, 1914-1930.* Oxford, 1931

Elster, Hanns Martin: *Die deutsche Novelle der Gegenwart.* Berlin, no date

Majut, Rudolf: *Geschichte des deutschen Romans vom Biedermeier bis zur Gegenwart.* Series *Deutsche Philologie im Aufriss.* Bielefeld and Berlin, 1954; 2nd ed., 1958

Mielke, H., and H. J. Homann: *Der deutsche Roman des 19. und 20. Jahrhunderts.* Dresden, 5th ed., 1920

Pongs, H.: *Im Umbruch der Zeit. Das Romanschaffen der Gegenwart.* Göttingen, 1952

LYRIC POETRY

Bender, Hans (editor): *Mein Gedicht ist mein Messer. Lyriker zu ihren Gedichten.* (Poets of today.) Heidelberg, 1955

Benn, Gottfried: *Probleme der Lyrik.* Wiesbaden, 1951

Closs, August: *Die neuere deutsche Lyrik vom Barock bis zur Gegenwart*. In series *Deutsche Philologie im Aufriss*. Bielefeld and Berlin, 1952; 2nd ed., enlarged, 1957

Ermatinger, E.: *Die deutsche Lyrik in ihrer geschichtlichen Entwicklung von Herder bis zur Gegenwart*. 3 vols., Leipzig and Berlin, 2nd ed., 1925

Jünger, F. G.: *Rhythmus und Sprache im deutschen Gedicht*. Stuttgart, 1952

Kommerell, Max: *Gedanken über Gedichte*. Frankfurt, 1948

Rasche, Friedrich: *Das Gedicht in unserer Zeit*. Hannover, 1946

NATURALISM

Bahr, Hermann: *Studien zur Kritik der Moderne*. Frankfurt a/M., 1894

Berg, Leo: *Geschichte des Naturalismus*. Berlin, 1889

— — *Der Naturalismus. Zur Psychologie der modernen Kunst*. Munich, 1892

— — *Der Übermensch in der modernen Literatur*. Paris, Leipzig and Munich, 1897

Bleibtreu, Carl: *Revolution der Literatur*. Leipzig, 1886

— — *Die Verrohung der Literatur*. Berlin, 1903

— — *Die Vertreter des Jahrhunderts*. Berlin, 1904

Conrad, M. G.: *Von Zola bis Hauptmann: Erinnerungen zur Geschichte der Moderne*. Leipzig, 1902

Dorner, August: *Pessimismus, Nietzsche und Naturalismus*. Leipzig, 1911

Hanstein, A. von: *Das jüngste Deutschland*. Leipzig, 1900; 3rd ed., 1905

Lessing, Otto E.: *Die neue Form. Ein Beitrag zum Verständnis des deutschen Naturalismus*. Dresden, 1910

Lublinski, Samuel: *Holz und Schlaf. Ein zweifelhaftes Kapitel Literaturgeschichte*. Stuttgart, 1905

Mauthner, Fritz: *Von Keller zu Zola*. Berlin, 1887

Steiger, E.: *Der Kampf um die neue Dichtung*. 2nd ed., Leipzig, 1889

Sydow, Eckart von: *Die Kultur der Dekadenz*. Dresden, 1921

Wolff, E.: *Die jüngste Literatur-Strömung und das Prinzip der Moderne*. Berlin, 1888

HEIMATKUNST

Bartels, A.: *Heimatkunst*. Strassburg, 1916

IMPRESSIONISM

Bahr, Hermann: *Die Überwindung des Naturalismus*. Dresden and Leipzig, 1891

— — *Renaissance. Neue Studien zur Kritik der Moderne*. Berlin, 1897

Breysig, H.: *Eindruckskunst und Ausdruckskunst*. Berlin, 1927

Duthie, E. Loury: *L'influence du symbolisme français dans le renouveau poétique de l'Allemagne*. Paris, 1934

Duwe, W.: *Deutsche Dichtung des 20. Jahrhunderts: die Geschichte der Ausdruckskunst*. Zurich, 1936

Hamann, R.: *Der Impressionismus in Leben und Kunst.* Cologne, 1907.
2nd ed., Marburg, 1923
Thon, Luise: *Die Sprache des deutschen Impressionismus.* Munich, 1928

EXPRESSIONISMUS AND NEUE SACHLICHKEIT

Bahr, H.: *Expressionismus.* Munich, 1918
Deri, M.: *Naturalismus, Idealismus, Expressionismus.* Leipzig, 1919
Edschmid, Kasimir: *Über Expressionismus in der Literatur.* Berlin, 1919
Friedmann, Hermann, und Otto Mann: *Expressionismus. Gestalten einer literarischen Bewegung.* Heidelberg, 1956
Knevels, W.: *Expressionismus und Religion.* Tübingen, 1927
Landsberger, F.: *Impressionismus und Expressionismus.* Leipzig, 1919
Martini, F.: *Was war Expressionismus? Deutung und Auswahl seiner Lyrik.* Urach, 1948
Roh, F.: *Nachexpressionismus.* Leipzig, 1926
Samuel, R., and R. H. Thomas: *Expressionism in German Life, Literature and the Theatre* (1910-24). Cambridge, 1934
Schneider, F. J.: *Der expressive Mensch und die deutsche Lyrik der Gegenwart.* Stuttgart, 1927
Utitz, T.: *Die Überwindung des Expressionismus.* Stuttgart, 1927
Worringer, Wilhelm: *Nach-Expressionismus.* Leipzig, 1926

EXISTENTIALISM AND SURREALISM

Berger, Charles: *Bilanz des Surrealismus.* Coburg, 1951
Gabriel, Leo: *Existenzphilosophie von Kierkegaard bis Sartre.* Vienna, 1951
Mounier, Emmanuel. *Existential Philosophy. An Introduction.* Translated by Eric Blow. London, 1948
Ruggiero, Guido de. *Existentialism.* Edited and introduced by Rayner Heppenstall. London, 1946

LITERATURE OF NATIONAL SOCIALISM

Bartels, Adolf: *Einführung in das deutsche Schrifttum für deutsche Menschen.* Leipzig, 1933
Helbing, Lothar: *Der dritte Humanismus.* Berlin, 1934
Jenssen, Christian: *Deutsche Dichtung der Gegenwart.* Leipzig, 1936
Langenbucher, Hellmuth: *Volkhafte Dichtung der Zeit.* 2nd ed., Berlin, 1935
— — *Dichtung der jungen Mannschaft.* Hamburg, 1935
— — *Nationalsozialistische Dichtung.* Berlin, 1935
Mulot, Arno: *Die deutsche Dichtung unserer Zeit. I. Das Bauerntum in der deutschen Dichtung unserer Zeit. II. Der Soldat in der deutschen Dichtung unserer Zeit.* Stuttgart, 1937 and 1938

MOTIVGESCHICHTE

Heuser, A.: *Die Erlösergestalt in der belletristischen Literatur seit 1890 als Deuterin der Zeit.* Bonn, 1936

Spiero, Heinrich: *Die Heilandsgeschichte in der neueren deutschen Dichtung.* Berlin, 1926

Rank, Otto: *Das Inzest-Motiv in Dichtung und Sage.* Vienna, 1912

Daffner, Hugo: *Salome. Ihre Gestalt in Geschichte und Kunst.* Munich, 1912

Hock, Stefan: *Die Vampyrsagen und ihre Verwertung in der deutschen Literatur.* Berlin, 1900

Liptzin, Solomon: *The Weavers in German Literature.* Göttingen, 1926

AUSTRIAN LITERATURE

Bianquis, Geneviève: *La poésie autrichienne de Hofmannsthal à Rilke.* Paris, 1926

Gunert, Johann: *Österreichischer P.E.N. Club. Bibliographie.* Vienna, 1952

Kindermann, Heinz: *Wegweiser durch die moderne Literatur in Österreich.* Innsbruck, 1954

Koch, F.: *Gegenwartsdichtung in Österreich.* Berlin, 1935

Langer, Norbert: *Dichter aus Österreich.* Vienna; vol. 1, 1956; vol. 2, 1957; vol. 3, 1958

Nadler, Josef: *Literaturgeschichte Österreichs.* Salzburg, 2nd ed., 1951

Schmidt, A.: *Deutsche Dichtung in Österreich.* Vienna, 1935

Teichl, Robert: *Österreicher der Gegenwart. Lexikon schöpferischer und schaffender Zeitgenossen.* Vienna, 1951

SWISS LITERATURE

Korrodi, E.: *Schweizer Erzähler der Gegenwart.* Leipzig, 1924

Nadler, Josef: *Literaturgeschichte der deutschen Schweiz.* Leipzig, 1932

INDIVIDUAL WRITERS

Bettelheim, Anton: *Ludwig Anzengruber.* Dresden, 1891

Kleinberg, L.: *L. Anzengruber.* Stuttgart, 1921

Kindermann, Heinz: *Hermann Bahr. Ein Leben für das europäische Theater. Mit einer Hermann Bahr-Bibliographie von Kurt Thomasberger.* Graz and Cologne, 1954

Liptzin, S.: *Richard Beer-Hofmann.* New York, 1936

Bänziger, Hans: *Werner Bergengruen. Weg und Werk.* Thal, St. Gall, 1950

Schuhmacher, E.: *Die dramatischen Versuche Bertolt Brechts, 1918-1933.* Berlin, 1955

CAROSSA

Gruss der Insel an Hans Carossa. Zum 70. Geburtstag des Dichters. Insel-Verlag, Wiesbaden, 1948

Clivio, Giuseppe: *Hans Carossa.* St. Gall, 1935

Haueis, Albert: *Hans Carossa. Persönlichkeit und Werk. Versuch einer Wesensdeutung.* Weimar, 1935
Klatt, Fritz: *Hans Carossa. Seine geistige Haltung und sein Glaubensgut.* Weimar, 1937
Langen, August: *Hans Carossa. Weltbild und Stil.* Berlin, 1955
Rohner, Ludwig: *Die Sprachkunst Hans Carossas. Der Stil als Spiegel des Weltbildes.* Munich, 1955
Schaeder, Grete: *Hans Carossa, der heilkundige Dichter.* Hameln, 1947

Ulbricht, H.: *Theodor Däubler. Eine Einführung in sein Werk und eine Auswahl.* (With bibliography.) Wiesbaden, 1951

DEHMEL

Bab, Julius: *Richard Dehmel.* Leipzig, 1926
Kunze, R.: *Die Dichtung Richard Dehmels als Ausdruck der Zeitseele.* Leipzig, 1914
Ludwig, Emil: *Richard Dehmel.* Berlin, 1913
Slochower, H.: R. *Dehmel, der Mensch und der Denker.* Dresden, 1928

Zerkaulen, Heinrich: *Max Dreyer. Sein Leben und sein Werk.* Leipzig, 1932
Bettelheim, A.: *Marie von Ebner-Eschenbach.* Berlin, 1900

STEFAN GEORGE

Bennett, E. K.: *Stefan George.* Cambridge, 1954
Bergenthal, Ferdinand: *Das Werk Georges.* Breslau, 1935
Bianchi, L.: *Dante und Stefan George.* Bologna, 1935
Boehringer, Robert: *Ewiger Augenblick.* (Privat-Druck der Az-Presse, Aarau.) 1945
— — *Mein Bild von Stefan George.* Düsseldorf, 1951
Broderson, Arvid: *Stefan George, Deutscher und Europäer.* Berlin, 1935
David, Claude: *Stefan George. Son œuvre poétique.* Bibliothèque de la Société des Etudes germaniques. Lyons and Paris, 1952
Drahn, H.: *Das Werk Stefan Georges, seine Religiosität und sein Ethos.* Breslau, 1925
Dulberg, Franz: *Stefan George. Ein Führer zu seinem Werke. (Germanische Studien.)* Munich, 1908
Farrell, R.: *Stefan Georges Beziehungen zur englischen Dichtung.* Berlin, 1937
Glur, Guido: *Kunstlehre und Kunstanschauung des Georgekreises und die Aesthetik Oscar Wildes.* Berne, 1957
Gundolf, Friedrich: *George.* Berlin, 1920
Kawerau, S.: *Stefan George und R. M. Rilke.* 2nd ed., Berlin, 1928
Koch, Willi: *Stefan George. Weltbild, Menschenbild, Naturbild.* Halle, 1933
Landmann, E.: *Georgika.* Heidelberg, 1924

Lepsius, Sabine: *Stefan George. Geschichte einer Freundschaft.* Berlin, 1939
Maier, H. A.: *George und Thomas Mann.* Zurich, 1946
Morwitz, Ernst: *Die Dichtung Stefan Georges.* Berlin and Godesberg, 1934 and 1948
Nohl, J.: *Stefan George und sein Kreis.* Berlin, 1924
Pensa, Mario: *Stefan Georg..* Bologna, 1935
Rosengarth, W.: *Nietzsche und Stefan George. Ihre Sendung und ihr Menschtum.* Leipzig, 1934
Salin, Edgar: *Um Stefan George.* Godesberg, 1948
—— *Hölderlin im George-Kreis.* Godesberg, 1950
Scott, Cyril: *My Years of Indiscretion.* London, 1924
Verwey, A.: *Mein Verhältnis zu Stefan George.* Strassburg, 1936. Translation of *Mijn verhouding tot Stefan George. Herinneringen uit de jaren 1895-1928.*)
Wolters, Friedrich: *Herrschaft und Dienst.* 3rd ed., Berlin, 1923
—— *Stefan George und die Blätter für die Kunst.* Berlin, 1930

Brecka, H.: *Die Handel-Mazzetti.* Vienna, 1923
Schnee, Heinrich: *Enrica Freiin von Handel-Mazzetti. Grossdeutschlands Dichterin.* Paderborn, 1935
Adler, F.: *Das Werk Ernst Hardts.* Greifswald, 1921
Schumann, H.: *Ernst Hardt und die Neuromantik.* Sötzen, 1913

GERHART HAUPTMANN

Bab, Julius: *Gerhart Hauptmann und seine besten Bühnenwerke.* Berlin, 1922
Behl, C. W. F., and Felix A. Voigt: *Gerhart Hauptmanns Leben. Chronik und Bild.* Berlin, 1942
Behl, C. W. F.: *Wege zu Gerhart Hauptmann.* Goslar, 1948
Fechter, Paul: *Gerhart Hauptmann.* Dresden, 1922
Fiedler, R.: *Die späten Dramen Gerhart Hauptmanns. Versuch einer Deutung.* Munich, 1956
Garten, Hugh F.: *Gerhart Hauptmann.* Cambridge, 1954
Gregor, Joseph: *Gerhart Hauptmann. Das Werk und unsere Zeit.* Vienna, 1952
Heise, Wilhelm: *Gerhart Hauptmann.* In the series 'Das Drama der Gegenwart'. Leipzig, no date
Mann, Thomas: *Gerhart Hauptmann.* Gütersloh, 1953
Schlenther, Paul: *Gerhart Hauptmann. Leben und Werke. Umgearbeitet und erweitert von Arthur Eloesser.* Berlin, 1922
Voigt, Felix A.: *Antike und antikes Lebensgefühl im Werke Gerhart Hauptmanns.* Breslau, 1935
Ziegenfuss, W.: *Gerhart Hauptmann. Dichtung und Gesellschaftsidee der bürgerlichen Humanität.* Berlin, 1948

HERMANN HESSE

Bode, H.: *Hermann Hesse.* Frankfurt, 1948
Engel, O.: *Hermann Hesse. Dichtung und Gedanke.* Stuttgart, 1947
Hafner, G.: *Hermann Hesse. Werk und Leben.* Reinbek, 1947

HOFMANNSTHAL

Hammelmann, H. A.: *Hugo von Hofmannsthal.* Heidelberg, 1956
Heuschele, Otto: *Hugo von Hofmannsthal. Dank und Gedächtnis.* Freiburg,
1949
Krüger, K. J.: *Hugo von Hofmannsthal und Richard Strauss.* Berlin, 1935
Metzeler, W.: *Ursprung und Krise von Hofmannsthals Mystik.* Munich, 1956
Naef, Carl J.: *Hugo von Hofmannsthals Wesen und Werk. Mit einer Hof-
mannsthal-Bibliographie von H. Steiner.* Zurich, 1938
Pulver, E.: *Hofmannsthals Schriften zur Literatur.* Berne, 1956

Döblin, A.: *Arno Holz. Die Revolution der Lyrik. Eine Einführung in sein
Werk und eine Auswahl.* Wiesbaden, 1951

RICARDA HUCH

Baum, H.: *Leuchtende Spur. Das Leben Ricarda Huchs.* Tübingen, 1950
Bäumer, G.: *Ricarda Huch.* Tübingen, 1949
Hoppe, Else: *Ricarda Huch. Weg, Persönlichkeit, Werk.* Stuttgart, 1951
Walzel, Oskar: *Ricarda Huch.* Leipzig, 1916

ERNST JÜNGER

Becher, H.: *Ernst Jünger. Mensch und Werk.* Warendorf, 1949
Müller-Schwefe, E.: *Ernst Jünger.* Wuppertal, 1951
Nebel, G.: *Ernst Jünger.* Wuppertal, 1949
Paetel, H.: *Ernst Jünger. Weg und Wirkung.* Stuttgart, 1948
Stern, J. P.: *Ernst Jünger.* Cambridge, 1953

FRANZ KAFKA

Anders, Günther: *Kafka.* Studies in Modern European Literature and
Thought. Cambridge, 1958
Beissner, F.: *Der Erzähler Franz Kafka.* Stuttgart, 1952
Brod, Max: *Franz Kafka. Eine Biographie.* Frankfurt, 1937; 3rd ed., 1954
—— *Franz Kafkas Glaube und Lehre.* Munich, 1947
Fronius, Hans: *Kafka-Mappe. Zeichnungen zu den Werken Franz Kafkas.
Mit einer Parabel von Franz Kafka und einem Vorwort von Otto Mauer.*
Vienna, 1946
Gray, R. D.: *Kafka's Castle.* Cambridge, 1956
Janouch, Gustav: *Gespräche mit Kafka.* Frankfurt, 1951

BIBLIOGRAPHY 565

Neider, Charles: *Kafka. His Mind and Art.* London, 1949
Reiss, H. S.: *Franz Kafka. Eine Betrachtung seines Werkes.* Heidelberg, 1952

GEORG KAISER

Diebold, B.: *Der Denkspieler Georg Kaiser.* Frankfurt a/M, 1924
Freyhan, M.: *Georg Kaisers Werk.* Berlin, 1926
Koenigsgarten, H. F.: *Georg Kaiser.* With bibliography. Potsdam, 1928
Linick, L. M.: *Der Subjektivismus im Werke Georg Kaisers.* Strassburg, 1938
Omanowski, W.: *Georg Kaiser und seine besten Bühnenwerke.* Berlin, 1922

Rudiger, Horst: *Der schwarze Schwan Israels* (=Else Lasker-Schüler). Meran, 1952
Jappe, H.: *Gertrud von le Fort.* Meran, 1950
Maync, H.: *Detlev von Liliencron.* Berlin, 1920
Spiero, H.: *Detlev von Liliencrons Leben und Werke.* Berlin, 1913
Kasack, H.: *O. Loerke. Charakterbild eines Dichters.* Wiesbaden, 1951
Ihering, Herbert: *Heinrich Mann.* Berlin, 1951
Schröder, Walter: *Heinrich Mann.* Vienna, 1932
Sinsheimer, H.: *Heinrich Manns Werk.* Munich, 1921

THOMAS MANN

Cleugh, J.: *Thomas Mann. A Study.* London, 1933
Eichner, H.: *Thomas Mann. Eine Einführung in sein Werk.* Berne, 1953
Eloesser, H.: *Thomas Mann, sein Leben und sein Werk.* Berlin, 1925
Hatfield, Henry: *Thomas Mann: an Introduction to his Fiction.* London, 1952
Heller, Erich: *The Ironic German.* London, 1957
Lesser, Jonas: *Thomas Mann in der Epoche seiner Vollendung.* Munich, 1952
Mayer, Hans: *Thomas Mann. Werk und Entwicklung.* Berlin, 1950
Peacock, Ronald: *Das Leitmotiv bei Thomas Mann.* Berne, 1934
Thomas, R. Hinton: *Thomas Mann. The Meditation of Art.* Oxford, 1956
Weigand, Hermann J.: *Thomas Mann's Novel 'Der Zauberberg'.* New York and London, 1953

ALFRED MOMBERT

Benz, R.: *Der Dichter Alfred Mombert.* Heidelberg, 1942
Hennecke, Hans: *Alfred Mombert. Eine Einführung in sein Werk und eine Auswahl.* Wiesbaden, 1952
Wolffheim, H. (editor): *Alfred Mombert. Briefe an Richard und Ida Dehmel. Abhandlungen der Akademie der Wissenschaften und Literatur.* Mainz, 1956

CHRISTIAN MORGENSTERN

Bauer, M.: *Christian Morgensterns Leben und Werk. Vollendet von Margarete Morgenstern unter Mitarbeit von* R. Meyer. 2nd ed., Munich, 1937
Geraths, F.: *Christian Morgenstern: sein Leben und sein Werk.* Munich, 1926
Hiebel, F.: *Christian Morgenstern. Wende und Aufbruch unseres Jahrhunderts.* Berne, 1957

NIETZSCHE

Andler, Charles: *Friedrich Nietzsche: sa vie et sa pensée.* Paris, 1920-28
Bertram, Ernst: *Nietzsche. Versuch einer Mythologie.* 9th ed., Berlin, 1929
Forster-Nietzsche, E.: *F. Nietzsche.* 3 vols., Leipzig, 1895-1904
Jaspers, K.: *Nietzsche.* Berlin, 1936
Klages, Ludwig: *Die psychologischen Errungenschaften Nietzsches.* Leipzig, 1926
Klein, J.: *Die Dichtung Nietzsches.* Munich, 1936
Knight, A. H. J.: *Some aspects of the Life and Work of Nietzsche and particularly of his connection with Greek Literature and Thought.* Cambridge, 1933
Knight, G. Wilson: *Christ and Nietzsche.* London, 1948
Köhler, F.: *Friedrich Nietzsche.* ('*Aus Natur und Geisteswelt*'.) Leipzig, 1926
Lea, F. A.: *The Tragic Philosopher.* London, 1948
Lichtenberger, Henri: *La philosophie de Nietzsche.* 2nd ed., Paris, 1948

RILKE

Andreas-Salomé, Lou: *Rainer Maria Rilke.* Leipzig, 1928
Bassermann, D.: *Der späte Rilke.* Munich, 1946
—— *Am Rande des Unsagbaren.* Buxtehude, 1948
Belmore, H. W.: *Rilke's Craftsmanship.* Oxford, 1953
Betz, Maurice: *Rilke vivant.* Paris, 1937
Buddeberg, Else: *Rainer Maria Rilke.* Stuttgart, 1954
Butler, E. M.: *Rainer Maria Rilke.* Cambridge, 1941; 2nd ed., 1946
Cammerer, Heinrich: *R. M. Rilkes Duineser Elegien.* Stuttgart, 1937
Cassirer-Solmitz, Eva: *Rainer Maria Rilke. Als Manuskript gedruckt.* Heidelberg, Gustav Koester Verlag Paul Obermüller, 1957
Dehn, Fritz: *Rainer Maria Rilke und sein Werk.* Leipzig, 1934
Demetz, Peter: *René Rilkes Prager Jahre.* Düsseldorf, 1953
Graff, W. L.: *Rainer Maria Rilke. Anguish of a Modern Poet.* Princeton, University Press; London, Cumberlege, 1956
Günther, Werner: *Weltinnenraum. Die Dichtung Rainer Maria Rilkes.* Berlin and Bielefeld, 1952

Holthusen, Hans Egon: *Rilkes Sonette an Orpheus. Versuch einer Interpretation*. Munich, 1937

—— *Der späte Rilke*. Zurich, 1949

—— *Rilke. A Study of his later Poetry*. Translated by J. P. Stern. Cambridge, 1952

Huppelsberg, Joachim: R. M. *Rilke. Biographie*. Munich, 1949

Kippenberg, Katharina: *Rainer Maria Rilkes Duineser Elegien und Sonette an Orpheus*. Wiesbaden, 1946

Klatt, F.: R. M. *Rilke*. Vienna, 1949

Kohlschmidt, Werner: *Rainer Maria Rilke*. Lübeck, 1948

Kreutz, H.: *Rilkes Duineser Elegien. Eine Interpretation* (with a bibliography). Munich, 1950

Mason, Eudo C.: *Rilke's Apotheosis. A Survey of recent representative publications on the Work and Life of R. M. Rilke*. Oxford, 1938

—— *Lebenshaltung und Symbolik bei Rainer Maria Rilke*. Weimar, 1939

—— *Der Zopf des Münchhausen*, Einsiedeln, 1949

—— *Rilke und Goethe*. Cologne, 1958

—— *Rilke, Europe and the English-speaking World*. Cambridge, 1959

Olivero, Federico: *Rainer Maria Rilke. A Study in Poetry and Mysticism*. Cambridge, 1931

Osann, Christian: R. M. *Rilke. Der Weg eines Dichters*. Zurich, 1941; 2nd ed., 1947

Ritzer, Walter: *Rainer Maria Rilke. Bibliographie*. Vienna, 1951

Rose, William, and Gertrude Craig Houston: *Rainer Maria Rilke. Aspects of his Mind and Poetry*. London, 1938

Schnack, Ingeborg: *Rilkes Leben im Werk und Bild*. With Introduction by J. R. von Salis. Insel-Verlag, Wiesbaden, 1957

Schröder, R.: *Rainer Maria Rilke*. Zurich, 1952

Sieber, Carl: *René Rilke. Die Jugend Rainer Maria Rilkes*. Leipzig, o.d. [1932]

Thurn und Taxis-Hohenlohe, Fürstin Marie von: *Erinnerungen an Rainer Maria Rilke*. Munich, 2nd ed., 1933

Wodtke, Friedrich Wilhelm: *Rilke und Klopstock. Als Manuskript gedruckt*. Kiel, 1948

Wydenbruck, Nora: *Rilke, Man and Poet. A biographical Study*. London, 1949

SCHNITZLER

Kapp, J.: *A. Schnitzler*. Leipzig, 1912

Körner, Josef: *Artur Schnitzlers Gestalten und Probleme*. Zurich, 1921

Liptzin, Solomon: *Artur Schnitzler*. New York, 1932

Droop, F.: *Wilhelm von Scholz und seine besten Bühnenwerke*. Berlin, 1922

Bettelheim, A.: *Karl Schönherr*. Leipzig, 1928

Sedlmaier, R.: *Karl Schönherr und das österreichische Volksstück.* Würzburg, 1920

Horst, K. A.: *Ina Seidel. Wesen und Werk.* Stuttgart, 1956

SPITTELER

Gottschalk, R.: *Carl Spitteler.* Zurich, 1928
Meszlény, R.: *Carl Spitteler und das neudeutsche Epos.* Halle, 1918
Schmidt, F.: *Die Erneuerung des Epos.* Leipzig, 1928
Stauffacher, W.: *Carl Spittelers Lyrik.* Zurich, 1947

HERMANN STEHR

Boeschenstein, Hermann: *Hermann Stehr.* Breslau, 1935
Köhler, W.: *Hermann Stehr: die Geschichte seines Lebens und seines Werkes in 5 Kapiteln.* Schweidnitz, 1927
Meridies, W.: *Hermann Stehr, sein Werk und seine Welt.* Habelschwerdt, 1924
Wocke, H.: *Hermann Stehr.* Berlin, 1922

Eisenlohr, F.: *Carl Sternheim.* Munich, 1926

ADALBERT STIFTER

Blackall, E. A.: *Adalbert Stifter.* Cambridge, 1948
Hohoff, C.: *Adalbert Stifter.* Düsseldorf, 1949
Lunding, Erik: *Adalbert Stifter.* Copenhagen, 1946
Michels, J.: *Adalbert Stifter. Leben, Werk und Wirken.* Leipzig, 3rd ed., 1943

Endres, Fritz: *Emil Strauss.* Munich, 1936
Harden, Maximilian: *Kampfgenosse Sudermann.* Berlin, 1903
Schoen, H.: *Sudermann, poète dramatique et romancier.* Paris, 1904
Droop, F.: *Ernst Toller und seine besten Bühnenwerke.* Berlin, 1922
Singer, P.: *Ernst Toller.* Berlin, 1924

GEORG TRAKL

Bayerthal, E.: *Georg Trakls Lyrik. Analytische Untersuchung.* Frankfurt, 1926
Ficker, L.: *Erinnerung an Georg Trakl.* Innsbruck, 1926
Goldmann, Heinrich: *Katabasis. Eine tiefenpsychologische Studie zur Symbolik der Dichtungen Georg Trakls.* Band IV der Trakl-Studien
Lachmann, Eduard: *Kreuz und Abend. Eine Interpretation Georg Trakls.* Salzburg, 1954
Riemerscheid, Werner: *Georg Trakl.* Vienna, 1947

JAKOB WASSERMANN

Bing, Siegmund: *Jakob Wassermann*. Berlin, 1929; *erweiterte Ausgabe*, 1933
Blankenagel, J. C.: *The Writings of Jakob Wassermann*. Boston, 1942
Goldstein, W.: *Wassermann: sein Kampf um die Wahrheit*. Leipzig, 1929
Voegeli, W.: *Jakob Wassermann und die Trägheit des Herzens*. Wintherthur, 1956

WEDEKIND

Dehnow, F.: *Frank Wedekind*. Leipzig, 1922
Elster, H. M.: *Frank Wedekind und seine besten Bühnenwerke*. Berlin, 1922
Fechter, Paul: *F. Wedekind*. Leipzig, 1920
Kerr, H.: *Frank Wedekind: eine Studie*. Leipzig, 1908
Kutscher, A.: *F. Wedekind*. 3 vols., Munich, 1924

Koch, F.: *Josef Weinheber*. Munich, 1942
Nadler, Josef: *Josef Weinheber. Die Geschichte seines Lebens und seiner Dichtung*. Salzburg, 1952
Stuhrmann, L.: *Josef Weinheber. Rausch und Mass*. Warendorf, 1951
Berendt, H.: *F. Werfel*. Bonn, 1920
Puttkammer, Annemarie von: *Franz Werfel. Wort und Antwort*. Würzburg, 1952
Specht, R.: *Franz Werfel*. Vienna, 1926
Ebeling, Hans: *Ernst Wiechert*. Wiesbaden, 1947
Ollesch, H.: *Ernst Wiechert*. Wuppertal, 1949
Klemperr, V.: *A. Wilbrandt*. Stuttgart, 1907
Scharter-Santen, Ed.: *Wilbrandt als Dramatiker*. Munich, 1902
Litzmann, B.: *Ernst von Wildenbruch*. 2 vols., Berlin, 1913-16
Pretorius, Emil: *Karl Wolfskehl. Privatdruck*, Passau, no date
Spiero, H.: *Ernst Zahn*. Stuttgart, 1927
Fülle der Zeit. Carl Zuckmayer und sein Werk. Frankfurt, 1956. (Appreciations by various authors.)
Arens, Hans: *Stefan Zweig. Sein Leben – sein Werk*. Esslingen, 1949. English edition: *A Tribute*, edited by Hans Arens, London, W. H. Allen, 1950
Rieger, E.: *Stefan Zweig. Der Mann und das Werk*. Berlin, 1928

INDEX

571